CPSIA information can be obtained
at www.ICGtesting.com
Printed in the USA
BVHW080350030721
611060BV00002B/292

# סִדּוּר מְשִׁיחִי פְּשִׁיטְתָה לְשַׁבָּת
# Messianic Peshitta Siddur For Shabbat

3rd Edition

Daniel Perek M.A.
to my beloved, Tzilah

Strategic Book Publishing and Rights Co.

Strategic Book Publishing and Rights Co., LLC
USA | Singapore
www.sbpra.net

For information about special discounts for bulk purchases, please
contact Strategic Book Publishing and Rights Co. Special Sales, at
bookorder@sbpra.net.

ISBN:   978-1-68235-457-5

Book Design: Suzanne Kelly

# Table of Contents

# � שלום! SHALOM!

Welcome the Tefilot! G-d said through the prophet Yesha-Yahu *"For My House shall be called a House of Prayer for ALL the people,"*

"כִּי בֵיתִי בֵּית תְּפִלָּה יִקָּרֵא לְכָל הָעַמִּים." (Yesha-Yahu 56:7)

The Shali'akh Shaul admonishes us, "Do you not know that your body is the "Heikhal" (Sanctuary) of the Ru'akh HaKodesh which abides in you?"

Prayer has always been an integral part of Biblical Jewish worship, even though the Torah itself does not explicitly command us to pray. The patriarchs all set the example of praying. According to Jewish tradition, Avraham is seen praying in the morning, Yitz'khak at noon, and Ya'akov at night. These times are not verifiable by scripture, but each of them did pray, creating pivotal moments in their lives. Moshe prayed. King David prayed, and established that he prayed three times daily: (Tehillim 55:18)

"עֶרֶב וָבֹקֶר וְצָהֳרַיִם, אָשִׂיחָה וְאֶהֱמֶה; וַיִּשְׁמַע קוֹלִי."

"Evening, and morning, and at noon will I pray and cry aloud, and He shall hear my voice".

The prophet Dani'El prayed three times daily, facing Yerushalayim (Dani'El 6:11), it is believed at these same times. Ezra restored the "Worship of David" (Ezra 3:10), which was the use of his "Tehillim" in the Temple services of Yisra'el. Our Master, יהוה Yeshua HaMashi'akh, prayed often, (Luka 5:16) the word used for prayer there being hitpallel, derived from the name of the word for prayer. Yeshua prayed at night (Luka 6:12), blessed children (Matai 19:13), and taught His Talmidim to pray, (Luka 11:1), and to pray a very specific prayer, saying, "When you pray, *say.. ."* And, He prayed for us! (Yokhanan 17) The Shali'akh Shaul encouraged the *gentile* congregations to *"pray without ceasing."* (I Thess 5:17)

For all these reasons, and for many more, the Messianic Peshitta Community has adopted a lifestyle of prayer, and it should not cease while we are assembled! There were many, many prayers recited in unison in the Beit HaMikdash: the book of "Tehillim" [Psalms] is a book of prayers, and from these, those who served in the Beit HaMikdash (Temple) and Beit K'nesset (Synagogue) in the time of Messiah prayed in unison.

Yeshua did not reject the Beit HaMikdash and its forms of worship; in fact, He was very zealous over it. (Tehillah 69, Yokhanan 2:17) He did correct the Pharisees for praying to be seen of men, but this kind of selfish prayer was done OUTSIDE of corporate prayer for the sake of getting personal recognition, not during the set times of prayer in the Beit HaMikdash or the Beit K'nesset among the congregants; so, Yeshua was not condemning all public prayer, and certainly not the

praying of scriptures together.

Just as Messiah did, we are supposed to pray alone, to pray for children, to pray with our brethren, and to pray in the assembly. Praying the very words of the Almighty Elohim in a congregational setting can be very powerful, if it is not done vainly, but *with faith, with fervor, with zeal, with passion.* The early believers in Messiah prayed or sang the Words of Elohim from the Tehillim in corporate settings, and many powerful things happened as a result! (*Ma'asei HaShlikhim 4:25-26, 16:25)* The words we utter together in this setting are all from scripture or derive directly from scripture, and as such were inspired by the power of the Ru'akh HaKodesh through Messiah Yeshua Himself, and they were established in the order of worship that was done in the Beit HaMikdash, and in the various assemblies.

Prayer is one of only a few services to Elohim that involves the whole human being, for the person who is self-disciplined to pray as did the patriarchs: "And you shall love יהוה your Elohim with all of your *heart,* with all of your *soul,* and with all of your *might."* Yeshua explains that the soul is synonymous with the *mind,* since He would never arbitrarily editorialize the Word of Elohim. (Yokhanan Markos 12:30) When the whole being is engaged by faith, accompanied by the Ru'akh HaKodesh and His Words written as prayers, then the supplicant(s) can *trust* that יהוה has heard, and will act. (Tehillim 55:18, Ya'akov 1:56, 5:16, Romim 8:26, Efisim 3:20). Prayer then becomes an act of obedience coupled with faith, and not a session of begging and pleading, or of wishing. Prayer is sacred, necessary, full of mystery and power, and is an emulation of a habitual custom of Messiah Yeshua Himself. He even prayed the Tehillim while hanging on the tree. The prayers that the prophets wrote were inspired, and they inspire us, and are the foundation of our "meditation" on Elohim and His Ways. Join us!

# *A Note On Transliteration*

Our transliteration is an effort to enable those who do not as yet read Hebrew, or who are still learning to read Hebrew, to participate in the Hebrew portions of our liturgical worship. There is not as yet one body of governance for transliteration, not even in Yisra'el. There is no standard set of rules in order to make transliteration the same when going from one document to another, one congregation to another, or one region or country to another. So, we have taken several different sets of rules, and chosen from them the phonetic representations we believe make the most sense, give us a sense of consistency, and simplify the transliteration as much as possible, consistent with Israeli pronunciation of the Hebrew syllables. We have tried to place here a summary of those simple rules.

There are five vowel sounds in Hebrew: We have represented these vowel sounds as simply and consistently as possible:

**Ah**   any transliterated syllable containing an "a" will be pronounced "ah".

> example: Barukḥ Atah

each syllable containing an "a" above is pronounced as "ah"; there are three. Each sharing the "ah" like the "a" in Bach or the "o" in "box".

Sometimes the "a" will be followed by an "h" for clarity.

**Eh**  any transliterated syllable with an "e" is pronounced as "eh".

> example: Melekḥ

each syllable containing an "e" above is pronounced as "eh"; there are two. Each sharing the "eh" like the "e" in red or the "ea" in "head".

**Ee**  any transliterated syllable with an "i" is pronounced as "ee".

> example: Shiviti

each syllable containing an "i" above is pronounced as "ee"; there are three. Each sharing the "ee" like the "ee" in beet or the "ea" in "mead".

**Oh**   any transliterated syllable with an "o" is pronounced as

"oh".

example: L'hodot

each syllable containing an "o" above is pronounced as "oh"; there are two. Each sharing the "oh" like the "oa" in boat or the "o" in "rope".

Sometimes the "o" will be followed by an "h" for clarity.

**Oo** any transliterated syllable with an "u" is pronounced as "oo".

example: Vayakḥulu

each syllable containing an "u" above is pronounced as "oo"; there are two. Each sharing the "oo" like the "oo" in boot or the "u" in "flute".

There are occasional "diphthongs" or vowel blends, which take two of the sounds above and blend them together to form other vowel sounds. We have distinguished these as well in the following manner:

**"Ai"** any transliterated syllable with an "ai" is pronounced as "i". It is a blend of the major vowel sounds "ah" and "ee".

example: Adonai

each syllable containing an "ai" above is pronounced as "i"; there is one. It is pronounced as the word "eye", or as the pronoun "I".

**"Ei"** any transliterated syllable with an "ei" is pronounced as "ay". It is a blend of the major vowel sounds "eh" and "ee".

example: Eloheihem

each syllable containing an "ei" above is pronounced as "ay"; there is one. It is pronounced as the "ai" in bait, or the a in cake.

Hebrew is a "gutteral" language, and has several letters that use a hard or soft gutteral rake in the back of the throat; some English speakers equate this to the "ch" in "Bach". Since there is no need to know the subtleties for transliterative reading, we have chosen to represent all gutterals with one phonetic representation of the

sound:

**kḥ** as in Barukḥ, or as in **Kḥakḥma**

This way, the kḥ is easily recognized as a distinct Hebrew sound, and there is no confusion as to whether or not it is a gutteral. Those who learn to speak Hebrew learn the subtle differences, but for transliteration, this is not necessary.

This is likely the most difficult transition for English speakers; but it is done simply by slightly closing the back of the throat with the back of the tongue briefly, and pushing air through, in similar fashion to clearing the throat, only softer.

Many prefixes in Hebrew have a very curt "eh" sound behind them. Also, adjoining two consonants can create this curt "eh" sound. We have represented this Hebrew characteristic with an apostrophe:

L'Olam "lay" "oh" lahm", where the L' is the curt "eh" sound.

Also, to make adjoining vowels distinct syllables, an apostrophe is used:

Va'ed "vah" "ed".

L'Olam Va'ed:  forever and ever.

In this revision, we have also added bold to the syllable in a multi-syllable word which bears the stress of that word:

**Barkḥi** naf**shi** et יהוה ; יהוה Elo**hai**, gada**l**ta me'**od**.  Hod v'ha**dar** lavash**ta**.

We have attempted to put the stress on the syllable according to current, Israeli pronunciation of the words, but confess there are likely subtleties in the lanuage that we have not mastered as yet, certainly not for every dialect; for any error, please forgive us! But we feel that this feature will assist one in becoming more authentic in their understanding and speaking of Hebrew.

# Preparing for Worship

## Blessing Upon Donning the Tallit/Tzitziyot

Preparing the heart, mind, and body for the hearing and
receiving of the Mitzvot
*Hebrew first, then English*

### Barkḥi Nafshi

Barkḥi nafshi et יהוה ; יהוה     בָּרְכִי נַפְשִׁי אֶת יהוה :
Elohai, gadalta me'od.     יהוה אֱלֹהַי גָּדַלְתָּ מְּאֹד;
Hod v'hadar lavashta.     הוֹד וְהָדָר לָבָשְׁתָּ.

Oteh or kasalma; noteh     עֹטֶה אוֹר כַּשַּׂלְמָה; נוֹטֶה
Shamayim kay'riah.     שָׁמַיִם כַּיְרִיעָה.

Bless יהוה, O my soul. O יהוה my Elohim, You are very great;
You are clothed with glory and majesty. Who covers Yourself
with light as with a garment, who stretches out the heavens like a
curtain. *(Tehillim 104:1-2)*

Barukḥ Atah, יהוה,     בָּרוּךְ אַתָּה יהוה , אֱלֹהֵינוּ,
Eloheinu, Melekḥ HaOlam,     מֶלֶךְ הָעוֹלָם, אֲשֶׁר קִדְּשָׁנוּ
asher kid'shanu     בְּמִצְוֹתָיו, וְצִוָּנוּ לְהִתְעַטֵּף
b'mitzvotav, v'tzivanu     בְּצִיצַת.
l'hitatef batzit-tzit.

Blessed are You, O יהוה our Elohim, King of the Universe, who
has consecrated us by His Mitzvot, and has commanded us
concerning the donning of the tzit-tzit. *(BaMidbar 15:38-41)*

Vayomer יהוה el Moshe     וַיֹּאמֶר יהוה אֶל מֹשֶׁה
l'mor.     לֵּאמֹר:

| | |
|---|---|
| Daber el b'nei Yisra'el, v'amarta aleihem, v'asu lahem tzit-tzit al kanfei vigdeihem l'dorotam; v'natnu al tzit-tzit hakanaf petil tekhelet. | דַּבֵּר אֶל בְּנֵי יִשְׂרָאֵל וְאָמַרְתָּ אֲלֵהֶם וְעָשׂוּ לָהֶם צִיצָת עַל כַּנְפֵי בִגְדֵיהֶם לְדֹרֹתָם; וְנָתְנוּ עַל צִיצָת הַכָּנָף פְּתִיל תְּכֵלֶת. |
| V'hayah lakhem l'tzit-tzit, ure'item oto uz'khartem et kal mitzvot יהוה, va'asitem otam; v'lo taturu akharei l'vaveikhem, v'akharei eineikhem, asher atem zonim akhareihem. | וְהָיָה לָכֶם לְצִיצָת וּרְאִיתֶם אֹתוֹ. וּזְכַרְתֶּם אֶת כָּל מִצְוֹת יהוה וַעֲשִׂיתֶם אֹתָם; וְלֹא תָתוּרוּ אַחֲרֵי לְבַבְכֶם וְאַחֲרֵי עֵינֵיכֶם אֲשֶׁר אַתֶּם זֹנִים אַחֲרֵיהֶם. |
| L'ma'an tizk'ru va'asitem et kol mitzvotai; vihitem k'doshim l'Eloheikhem. | לְמַעַן תִּזְכְּרוּ וַעֲשִׂיתֶם אֶת כָּל מִצְוֹתָי; וִהְיִיתֶם קְדֹשִׁים לֵאלֹהֵיכֶם. |
| Ani יהוה Eloheikhem, asher hotzeti etkhem m'eretz Mitzrayim, lihyot lakhem l'Elohim: Ani יהוה Eloheikhem. | אֲנִי יהוה אֱלֹהֵיכֶם אֲשֶׁר הוֹצֵאתִי אֶתְכֶם מֵאֶרֶץ מִצְרַיִם לִהְיוֹת לָכֶם לֵאלֹהִים: אֲנִי יהוה אֱלֹהֵיכֶם. |
| G'dilim ta'aseh lakh, al arbah kanfot k'sutekha asher t'khaseh bah. | גְּדִלִים תַּעֲשֶׂה לָּךְ עַל אַרְבַּע כַּנְפוֹת כְּסוּתְךָ אֲשֶׁר תְּכַסֶּה בָּהּ. |

And יהוה spoke unto Moshe, saying, "Speak unto B'nei Yisra'el, and bid them that they make them throughout their generations tzit-tzit in the kanfot (corners/hems/wings) of their garments, and that they put with the Tzit-tzit HaKanaf a thread of Tekhelet.

And it shall be unto you for a tzit-tzit, that you may look upon it, and remember all the Mitzvot of יהוה, and do them; and that you

go not about after your own heart and your own eyes after which you use to go astray; that you may remember and do all My Mitzvot, and be kadosh unto your Elohim. I am יהוה your Elohim, who brought you out of the land of Mitzrayim, to be your Elohim: I am יהוה your Elohim."

"You shall make yourself twisted cords upon the four corners of your covering, wherewith you cover yourself." *(BaMidbar 15:38-41, D'varim 22:12)*

## Tehillah 100
### Transitioning from the ordinary into the sacred, through thankfulness and through song.
*Hebrew first, then English*

Mizmor l'todah: Hariyu la יהוה, kol ha'aretz!

אֲמִזְמוֹר לְתוֹדָה: הָרִיעוּ לַיהוה כָּל הָאָרֶץ.

Ivdu et יהוה besimkhah; bo'u l'fanav birnanah.

בְּעִבְדוּ אֶת יהוה בְּשִׂמְחָה; בֹּאוּ לְפָנָיו בִּרְנָנָה.

De'u ki יהוה, hu Elohim. Hu asanu, v'lo anakhnu; amo, v'tzon maritoh.

גְּדְעוּ כִּי יהוה הוּא אֱלֹהִים: הוּא עָשָׂנוּ וְלֹא אֲנַחְנוּ עַמּוֹ וְצֹאן מַרְעִיתוֹ.

Bo'u sh'arav b'todah, khatzerotav bit'hilah; hodu lo, barkhu sh'mo

דְּבֹאוּ שְׁעָרָיו בְּתוֹדָה חֲצֵרֹתָיו בִּתְהִלָּה; הוֹדוּ לוֹ בָּרְכוּ שְׁמוֹ.

Ki tov יהוה, l'olam khasdo; v'ad dor vador emunatoh.

הְּכִּי טוֹב יהוה לְעוֹלָם חַסְדּוֹ; וְעַד דֹּר וָדֹר אֱמוּנָתוֹ.

A Mizmor [song/melody] of thanksgiving.

Shout unto יהוה, all the earth. Serve יהוה with gladness; come before His presence with singing. Know that יהוה, He is Elohim; it is He that has made us, and not we ourselves; we are

His people, and the flock of His pasture.

Enter into His gates with thanksgiving, and into His courts with praise; give thanks unto Him, and bless His Name. For יהוה is good; His compassion endures forever; and His faithfulness unto all generations.

## Justification – The Blood of Messiah

Recognizing the need of forgiveness and imparted innocence from יהוה , and our attainment of it through trust in Messiah Yeshua's shed blood.

*Hebrew first, then English*

| | |
|---|---|
| Reishit khokhma yirat יהוה , sekhel tov l'khol oseihem; tehilatoh omedet la'ad. | רֵאשִׁית חָכְמָה יִרְאַת יהוה שֵׂכֶל טוֹב לְכָל עֹשֵׂיהֶם; תְּהִלָּתוֹ עֹמֶדֶת לָעַד. |
| V'hu rakhum y'khaper avohn, v'lo yash'khit: V'hirbah l'hashiv apoh; v'lo ya'ir kol khamatoh. | לח וְהוּא רַחוּם יְכַפֵּר עָוֹן וְלֹא יַשְׁחִית: וְהִרְבָּה לְהָשִׁיב אַפּוֹ; וְלֹא יָעִיר כָּל חֲמָתוֹ. |
| Im nomar ki yesh lanu shutafut imo, u'mithal'khim Anu bakhoshekh, shakranim Anu v'lo ba'emet mitnahalim. Aval im mit'hal'khim Anu ba'or, k'asher hu va'or, yesh lanu shutafut zeh im zeh, v'dam Yeshua B'no y'tahareinu mi'kol khata'einu. | אִם נֹאמַר כִּי יֵשׁ לָנוּ שֻׁתָּפוּת עִמּוֹ וּמִתְהַלְּכִים אָנוּ בַּחֹשֶׁךְ, שַׁקְרָנִים אָנוּ וְלֹא בָּאֱמֶת מִתְנַהֲלִים. אֲבָל אִם מִתְהַלְּכִים אָנוּ בָּאוֹר כַּאֲשֶׁר הוּא בָאוֹר יֵשׁ לָנוּ שֻׁתָּפוּת זֶה עִם זֶה וְדַם יֵשׁוּעַ בְּנוֹ יְטַהֲרֵנוּ מִכָּל חֲטָאֵינוּ. |

V'im nomar sh'ein banu khet, mat'im anakhnu et atzmeinu v'ha'emet eineinah banu. Aval im nitvadeh et khata'einu, ne'eman hu v'tzadik lislo'akh et khata'einu, u'letareinu mi'kol avlateinu.

ח"וְאִם נֹאמַר שֶׁאֵין בָּנוּ חֵטְא מַתְעִים אֲנַחְנוּ אֶת עַצְמֵנוּ וְהָאֱמֶת אֵינֶנָּה בָּנוּ. ט"אֲבָל אִם נִתְוַדֶּה אֶת חֲטָאֵינוּ נֶאֱמָן הוּא וְצַדִּיק לִסְלֹחַ אֶת חֲטָאֵינוּ וּלְטַהֲרֵנוּ מִכָּל עַוְלָתֵנוּ.

The fear of יהוה is the beginning of wisdom; a good understanding have all they that do thereafter; His praise endures forever. *(Tehilah 111:10)* But He, being full of mercy, atones for iniquity and destroys not; often does He turn His anger away, and does not stir up all His wrath. *(Tehillah 78:38)* If we say that we have fellowship with Him and yet walk in darkness, we lie and do not follow the truth; but if we walk in the light as He is in the light, we have fellowship with one another, and the blood of Yeshua, His Son, cleanses us from all sin. If we say that we have no sin, we deceive ourselves and the truth is not in us. If we confess our sins, He is faithful and just to forgive us our sins, and to cleanse us from all our iniquity. *(Yokhanan Alef 1:6-9)*

## Sanctification – Obedience to His Commands

Setting ourselves apart from this world by His power, the power of His Word.
*Hebrew first, then English*

Aba, kadesh Otam ba'amit'kha, ki d'varekha shel'kha emet hu.

י"אַבָּא, קַדֵּשׁ אוֹתָם בַּאֲמִתְּךָ, כִּי דְּבָרְךָ שֶׁלְּךָ אֱמֶת הוּא.

B'khol libi d'rashtikha; al tashgeini mi'mitzvoteikha.

י"בְּכָל לִבִּי דְרַשְׁתִּיךָ; אַל תַּשְׁגֵּנִי מִמִּצְוֹתֶיךָ.

O Abba, consecrate them in Your truth, because Your Davar is truth. *(Yokhanan 17:17)* With my whole heart have I sought You; O let me not err from Your Mitzvot. *(Tehillim 119:10)*

# Attributes of Mercy

Leader and Congregation together

Known as the "Thirteen Attributes of Elohim," declared when He put Moshe in the cleft of the Rock. Each of us is placed in the cleft of the rock, Messiah's wounds.

*Hebrew first, then English*

יהוה , יהוה , El rakḥum v'khanun; erekḥ apayim, v'rav khesed v'emet.

יהוה יהוה אֵל רַחוּם וְחַנּוּן. אֶרֶךְ אַפַּיִם וְרַב חֶסֶד וֶאֱמֶת.

Notzer khesed la'alafim, noseh avohn vafesha v'khata'ah, v'nakeh.

נֹצֵר חֶסֶד לָאֲלָפִים נֹשֵׂא עָוֹן וָפֶשַׁע וְחַטָּאָה וְנַקֵּה.

יהוה , יהוה , El, merciful and gracious, longsuffering, and abundant in compassion and truth; guardian of compassion unto the thousandth generation; forgiving iniquity, and transgression, and sin, and pardoning. *(Shemot 34:6-7)*

# Unto Him Who Is Able

Leader and Congregation together

*Hebrew first, then English*

V'Lo hayakḥol lishmar'khem mimikḥ'shol ul'ha'amid etkḥem bli mum,

וְלוֹ הַיָּכוֹל לִשְׁמָרְכֶם מִמִּכְשׁוֹל וּלְהַעֲמִיד אֶתְכֶם בְּלִי מוּם

lifnei tifarto b'simkḥa, asher hu l'vado ha'Elohim haMoshiah otanu b'Yeshua HaMashi'akḥ Adoneinu. Lo hakavod, hashilton v'haikar v'hagdulah, lifnei khol olam, gam ata gam l'olamei olamim. Amein.

לִפְנֵי תִפְאַרְתּוֹ בְּשִׂמְחָה אֲשֶׁר הוּא לְבַדּוֹ הָאֱלֹהִים הַמּוֹשִׁיעַ אֹתָנוּ בְּיֵשׁוּעַ הַמָּשִׁיחַ אֲדֹנֵינוּ. לוֹ הַכָּבוֹד, הַשִּׁלְטוֹן וְהַיְקָר וְהַגְּדֻלָּה לִפְנֵי כָל עוֹלָם גַּם עַתָּה גַּם לְעוֹלְמֵי עוֹלָמִים. אָמֵן.

7

Now to Him who is able to keep you from falling and to present you faultless before the presence of His Majesty with exceeding joy, to the only Elohim our Saviour, through Yeshua HaMashi'akh Adoneinu, be glory, and majesty, dominion, and power, both now and in all the ages. Amein. *(Yehudah 1:24-25)*

# Vayakḥulu

Remembering why we observe the Sabbath, and its eternal decree
*Hebrew first, then English*

| | |
|---|---|
| Vayakḥulu hashamayim v'ha'aretz, v'kḥol tzeva'ahm. | אֲוַיְכֻלוּ הַשָּׁמַיִם וְהָאָרֶץ וְכָל צְבָאָם. |
| Va'y'kḥol Elohim ba'yom ha'shevi'i, malakḥtoh asher asah; va'yishbot ba'yom ha'shevi'i, mikol malakḥtoh asher asah. | בּוַיְכַל אֱלֹהִים בַּיּוֹם הַשְּׁבִיעִי מְלַאכְתּוֹ אֲשֶׁר עָשָׂה וַיִּשְׁבֹּת בַּיּוֹם הַשְּׁבִיעִי מִכָּל מְלַאכְתּוֹ אֲשֶׁר עָשָׂה. |
| va'yevarekḥ Elohim et yom ha'shevi'i, vayekadesh otoh; ki voh shavat mikol malakḥtoh asher barah Elohim la'asot. | גוַיְבָרֶךְ אֱלֹהִים אֶת יוֹם הַשְּׁבִיעִי וַיְקַדֵּשׁ אֹתוֹ כִּי בוֹ שָׁבַת מִכָּל מְלַאכְתּוֹ אֲשֶׁר בָּרָא אֱלֹהִים לַעֲשׂוֹת. |

And the heaven and the earth were finished, and all the hosts of them. And on the seventh day, Elohim finished His work which He had made; and He rested on the seventh day from all His work which He had made.

And Elohim blessed the seventh day, and hallowed it, because that in it He rested from all His work, which Elohim, in creating, had made. *(B'reshit 2:1-3)*

# V'Shamru (And They Shall Keep)
*Hebrew first, then English*

V'shamru v'nei Yisra'el et haShabbat, la'asot et haShabbat l'dorotam brit olam; beini u'vein b'nei Yisra'el, oht hee l'olam; ki sheshet yamim asah יהוה et ha shamayim v'et ha'aretz; u'vayom hashevi'i shavat vayinafash.

טזוְשָׁמְרוּ בְנֵי יִשְׂרָאֵל אֶת הַשַּׁבָּת לַעֲשׂוֹת אֶת הַשַּׁבָּת לְדֹרֹתָם בְּרִית עוֹלָם. יזבֵּינִי וּבֵין בְּנֵי יִשְׂרָאֵל אוֹת הִוא לְעֹלָם כִּי שֵׁשֶׁת יָמִים עָשָׂה יהוה אֶת הַשָּׁמַיִם וְאֶת הָאָרֶץ וּבַיּוֹם הַשְּׁבִיעִי שָׁבַת וַיִּנָּפַשׁ.

Therefore B'nei Yisra'el shall keep the Shabbat, to observe the Shabbat throughout their generations, for an eternal Brit. It is a sign between Me and B'nei Yisra'el forever; for in six days יהוה made the heavens and the earth, and on the seventh day He ceased from work, and rested. *(Shemot 31:16-17)*

# Ma Tovu (How Lovely)
Recognizing the oneness and beauty of the spiritual House of Elohim and Yisra'el, and the proper attitude in approaching our Elohim
*Hebrew first, then English*

Ma tovu ohaleikha, Ya'akov; mishkenoteikha, Yisra'el!

מַה טֹבוּ אֹהָלֶיךָ יַעֲקֹב; מִשְׁכְּנֹתֶיךָ יִשְׂרָאֵל.

Va'ani berov khasd'kha, avoh veiteikha; eshtakhaveh el heikhal kadsheikha, b'ir'ateikha.

וַאֲנִי בְּרֹב חַסְדְּךָ אָבוֹא בֵיתֶךָ; אֶשְׁתַּחֲוֶה אֶל הֵיכַל קָדְשְׁךָ בְּיִרְאָתֶךָ.

9

יהוה ahavti me'on beiteikha; um'kom, mishkan kevodeikha.

יהוה אָהַבְתִּי מְעוֹן בֵּיתֶךָ; וּמְקוֹם מִשְׁכַּן כְּבוֹדֶךָ.

Va'ani eshtakhaveh v'ekhra'a. Evr'kha lifnei יהוה osi.

וַאֲנִי אֶשְׁתַּחֲוֶה וְאֶכְרָעָה אֶבְרְכָה לִפְנֵי יהוה עֹשִׂי.

Va'ani tefilati lekha יהוה, et ratzon, Elohim b'rav khasdeikha, aneni b'emet Yisheikha.

וַאֲנִי תְפִלָּתִי לְךָ יהוה עֵת רָצוֹן אֱלֹהִים בְּרָב חַסְדֶּךָ עֲנֵנִי בֶּאֱמֶת יִשְׁעֶךָ.

How lovely are your tents, O Ya'akov, your dwelling places, O Yisra'el! But as for me, in the abundance of Your compassion will I come into Your house; I will bow down toward Your Heikhal Kadosh in the fear of You. *(BaMidbar 24:5, Tehillah 5:8)*

יהוה, I love the habitation of Your House, and the place where Your Kavod dwells. I will bow down and bend the knee; I will kneel before יהוה my maker. *(Tehillah 26:8, 95:6)*

But as for me, let my tefilah be unto You, O יהוה, in an acceptable time; O Elohim, in the abundance of Your compassion, answer me with the truth of Your Salvation. *( Tehillah 69:14 )*

## Kaddish: A Song of Praise
### Congregation and Mourners
*Hebrew first, then English*

Yitgadal v'yitkadash shemeh raba. Be'alma di vera khir'uteh v'yamlikh malkhuteh, b'khaiyeikhon uv'yomeikhon uvkhaiyei d'khol beit Yisra'el ba'agala uvizman kariv. V'imru, Amein.

יִתְגַּדַּל וְיִתְקַדַּשׁ שְׁמֵהּ רַבָּא. בְּעָלְמָא דִּי בְרָא כִרְעוּתֵהּ וְיַמְלִיךְ מַלְכוּתֵהּ, בְּחַיֵּיכוֹן וּבְיוֹמֵיכוֹן וּבְחַיֵּי דְכָל בֵּית יִשְׂרָאֵל בַּעֲגָלָא וּבִזְמַן קָרִיב. וְאִמְרוּ, אָמֵן.

Yeheh shemeh raba m'varakh l'olam ul'alemei alemaiya'. V'imru, Amein.

יְהֵא שְׁמֵהּ רַבָּא מְבָרַךְ לְעָלַם וּלְעָלְמֵי עָלְמַיָּא. וְאִמְרוּ, אָמֵן.

Yitbarakh v'yishtabakh v'yitpa'ar v'yitromam v'yitnaseh v'yithadar v'yit'aleh v'yit'halal shemeh d'kudsha', barikh hu l'ela min kol borkhata v'shirata, tushb'khatah, v'nekhemata, da'amiran b'alma. V'imru, Amein.

יִתְבָּרַךְ וְיִשְׁתַּבַּח וְיִתְפָּאַר וְיִתְרוֹמַם וְיִתְנַשֵּׂא וְיִתְהַדָּר וְיִתְעַלֶּה וְיִתְהַלָּל שְׁמֵהּ דְּקֻדְשָׁא בְּרִיךְ הוּא לְעֵלָּא מִן כָּל בִּרְכָתָא וְשִׁרָתָא תֻּשְׁבְּחָתָא וְנֶחֱמָתָא דַּאֲמִירָן בְּעָלְמָא. וְאִמְרוּ, אָמֵן.

Oseh shalom bimromav, hu ya'aseh shalom aleinu v'al kal Yisra'el. V'imru, Amein.

עֹשֶׂה שָׁלוֹם בִּמְרוֹמָיו, הוּא יַעֲשֶׂה שָׁלוֹם עָלֵינוּ וְעַל כָּל יִשְׂרָאֵל. וְאִמְרוּ, אָמֵן.

Magnified and sanctified be His great Name in the world which He has created according to His will. May He establish His kingdom during our lifetime, and during our days, and during the life of the whole house of Yisra'el, even swiftly and soon, And all say, "Amein." *(Divrei HaYamim 22:10)*

Let His great name be blessed forever and to all eternity, And all say, "Amein." *(Tehillah 113:2)*

Blessed, praised, glorified, exalted, extolled and honored, magnified and lauded be the name of the Holy One, blessed be He, though He is high above all blessings and songs, praise and consolations which are uttered in the world, And all say, "Amein." *(Neh 9:5)* He who makes peace in His heights, may He make peace upon us, and upon all Yisra'el. And all say, "Amein." *(Iyov 25:2)*

# Barkḥu (We Bless: A Call to Prayer)
## Leader sings

Barkḥu et יהוה בָּרְכוּ אֶת יהוה הַמְבֹרָךְ
hamevorakḥ.

Bless יהוה , the Blessed One. *(Tehillah 89:53)*

leader and congregation sing Hebrew together

Barukḥ יהוה hamevorakḥ בָּרוּךְ יהוה הַמְבֹרָךְ לְעוֹלָם
l'olam va'ed. וָעֶד

Blessed is יהוה , The blessed one, for all eternity. *(Tehillah 106:48)*

# Meditation
## Leader and Congregation together

Al tirah mipakḥad אַל תִּירָא מִפַּחַד פִּתְאֹם;
pitohm; umisho'aht וּמִשֹּׁאַת רְשָׁעִים כִּי תָבֹא;
resha'im, ki tavoh; utzu עֻצוּ עֵצָה וְתֻפָר; דַּבְּרוּ דָבָר
etzah, v'tufar; daberu וְלֹא יָקוּם כִּי עִמָּנוּ אֵל.
davar v'lo yakum; ki
imanu El.

V'ahd ziknah Ani hu, וְעַד זִקְנָה אֲנִי הוּא וְעַד
v'ahd seivah Ani esbol; שֵׂיבָה אֲנִי אֶסְבֹּל; אֲנִי
Ani asiti va'ani esah, va'ani עָשִׂיתִי וַאֲנִי אֶשָּׂא וַאֲנִי
esbol va'ahmalet. אֶסְבֹּל וַאֲמַלֵּט.

Be not afraid of sudden terror, neither of the destruction of the
wicked when it comes. Do your scheming, it shall not succeed;
make your plan, it shall not prevail; for Elohim is with us.
*(Mishlim 3:25, Yesha-Yahu 8:10)*

Even to old age, I am He; and even to gray hairs will I carry you;
I have made you, and I will bear you; yes, I will carry you, and I
will deliver you. *(Yesha-Yahu 46:4)*

# Kumu: Arise and Bless

Congregation Rises

Prayer for recognizing the new biblical month signified by a
renewed moon

*Hebrew first, then English*

Kumu, barkhu et יהוה קוֹמוּ בָּרְכוּ אֶת יהוה
Eloheikhem, min ha'olam אֱלֹהֵיכֶם מִן הָעוֹלָם עַד
ad ha'olam. Vivarkhu הָעוֹלָם; וִיבָרְכוּ שֵׁם כְּבֹדֶךָ,
shem k'vodeikha, וּמְרוֹמַם עַל כָּל בְּרָכָה
um'romam al kol b'rakha וּתְהִלָּה.
u'tehillah.

Atah hu, יהוה , l'vadeikha, אַתָּה הוּא יהוה לְבַדֶּךָ אֶת
Atah asitah et hashamayim, (אַתָּה) עָשִׂיתָ אֶת הַשָּׁמַיִם
shmei hashamayim v'khol שְׁמֵי הַשָּׁמַיִם וְכָל צְבָאָם
tzva'am, ha'aretz v'khol הָאָרֶץ וְכָל אֲשֶׁר עָלֶיהָ
asher aleiha, hayamim הַיַּמִּים וְכָל אֲשֶׁר בָּהֶם
v'khol asher bahem, וְאַתָּה מְחַיֶּה אֶת כֻּלָּם;
v'Atah mekhaiyeh et וּצְבָא הַשָּׁמַיִם לְךָ
kulam; u'tzevah מִשְׁתַּחֲוִים.
hashamayim, l'kha
mishtakhavim.

Hashamayim m'saperim הַשָּׁמַיִם מְסַפְּרִים כְּבוֹד
k'vod El; uma'aseh yadav אֵל; וּמַעֲשֵׂה יָדָיו מַגִּיד
magid harakiah. הָרָקִיעַ.

Stand up and bless יהוה your Elohim from everlasting to
everlasting; and let them say, 'Blessed is your glorious Name,
that is exalted above all blessing and praise'. *(Nekhem-Yah 9:5)*

You are יהוה , even You alone; You have made heaven, the
heaven of heavens, with all their hosts, the earth and all things
thereon, the seas and all that is in them, and You preserve them
all; and the host of Heaven worships You. *(Nekhem-Yah 9:6)*

The Heavens declare the K'vod of Elohim, and the firmament
shows His handiwork. *(Tehillah 19:2)*

13

## Ashrei: Happy Are They!
*Hebrew first, then English*

Ashrei yoshvei veiteikḥa, אַשְׁרֵי יוֹשְׁבֵי בֵיתֶךָ עוֹד
od yehalelukḥa, **Selah.** יְהַלְלוּךָ סֶּלָה.

Ashrei ha'**am** sh'kakḥah אַשְׁרֵי הָעָם שֶׁכָּכָה לֹו:
lo. Ashrei ha'**am** sheh יהוה אַשְׁרֵי הָעָם שֶׁיהוה אֱלֹהָיו.
Elo**hav.**

Happy are those who dwell in Your house, they are ever praising
You! Selah. *(Tehillah 84:5)*

Happy is the people that is in such a state. Yes, happy is the
people whose Elohim is יהוה . *(Tehillah 144:15)*

## Tehillah 92: A Psalm for Shabbat
*Hebrew first, then English*

Miz**mor** shir, l'yom מִזְמוֹר שִׁיר, לְיוֹם הַשַּׁבָּת.
hashab**bat.**

Tov l'ho**dot** la יהוה . טוֹב לְהֹדוֹת לַיהוה; וּלְזַמֵּר
Ul'**zamer** l'shimkḥa Ely**on.** לְשִׁמְךָ עֶלְיוֹן.

L'ha**gid** baboker לְהַגִּיד בַּבֹּקֶר חַסְדֶּךָ;
kḥas'**deikḥa,** v'emunateikḥa וֶאֱמוּנָתְךָ בַּלֵּילוֹת.
balei**lot.**

**Alei** asor, va'**alei** nah**vel;** עֲלֵי עָשׂוֹר וַעֲלֵי נָבֶל; עֲלֵי
alei higa**yon** bekḥi**nor.** הִגָּיוֹן בְּכִנּוֹר.

Ki simakḥtani יהוה כִּי שִׂמַּחְתַּנִי יהוה בְּפָעֳלֶךָ;
befo'aleikḥa; b'ma'asei בְּמַעֲשֵׂי יָדֶיךָ אֲרַנֵּן.
yadeikḥa ara**nen.**

Ma gad**lu** ma'aseikḥa יהוה ; מַה גָּדְלוּ מַעֲשֶׂיךָ יהוה;
me'**od** am**ku** מְאֹד עָמְקוּ מַחְשְׁבֹתֶיךָ.
makḥshevoteikḥa

Ish **ba**'ar lo yeda; ukḥsil lo yavin et zot,

אִישׁ בַּעַר לֹא יֵדָע; וּכְסִיל לֹא יָבִין אֶת זֹאת.

Bifroakḥ resha'**im** kemo esev, vayatzitzu kol po'alei aven. L'hishsham'**dam** adei ad.

בִּפְרֹחַ רְשָׁעִים כְּמוֹ עֵשֶׂב וַיָּצִיצוּ כָּל פֹּעֲלֵי אָוֶן: לְהִשָּׁמְדָם עֲדֵי עַד.

V'**atah** marom l'**olam**, יהוה .

וְאַתָּה מָרוֹם לְעֹלָם יהוה.

Ki hineh oyeveikḥa, יהוה , ki hineh oyeveikḥa yovedu. Yitparedu, kol po'alei aven.

כִּי הִנֵּה אֹיְבֶיךָ, יהוה , כִּי הִנֵּה אֹיְבֶיךָ יֹאבֵדוּ: יִתְפָּרְדוּ כָּל פֹּעֲלֵי אָוֶן.

Vatarem kire'eim kar**ni**; baloti b'she**men** ra'a**nan**.

וַתָּרֶם כִּרְאֵים קַרְנִי; בַּלֹּתִי בְּשֶׁמֶן רַעֲנָן.

Vatabet eini beshurai. Bakamim alai mere'im, tishmanah oznai.

וַתַּבֵּט עֵינִי בְּשׁוּרָי: בַּקָּמִים עָלַי מְרֵעִים תִּשְׁמַעְנָה אָזְנָי.

Tzadik katamar yifrakḥ; k'erez balevanon yisgeh.

צַדִּיק כַּתָּמָר יִפְרָח; כְּאֶרֶז בַּלְּבָנוֹן יִשְׂגֶּה.

Shetulim b'veit יהוה ; b'khatzrot Eloheinu yafrikḥu.

שְׁתוּלִים בְּבֵית יהוה; בְּחַצְרוֹת אֱלֹהֵינוּ יַפְרִיחוּ.

Od y'nuvun b'seivah; d'shenim v'ra'ananim yihyu.

עוֹד יְנוּבוּן בְּשֵׂיבָה; דְּשֵׁנִים וְרַעֲנַנִּים יִהְיוּ.

L'hagid, ki yashar יהוה ; tzuri, v'lo avlatah boh.

לְהַגִּיד כִּי יָשָׁר יהוה; צוּרִי, וְלֹא עַוְלָתָה בּוֹ.

A Mizmor, a Song. For Yom HaShabbat. It is good to give thanks unto יהוה , to sing praises unto Your Name, O Eliyon; to

15

declare Your compassion in the morning, and Your faithfulness in the night seasons, With an Asor, and with the Nevel; with a solemn sound upon the Kinor.

For You, יהוה , have made me glad through Your work; I will exult in the works of Your hands. How great are Your works, O יהוה ! Your thoughts are very deep. A brutish man knows not, neither does a fool understand this. When the wicked spring up as the grass, and when all the workers of iniquity do flourish; it is that they may be destroyed forever. But You, O יהוה , are on high for evermore.

For, lo, Your enemies, O יהוה , for, lo, Your enemies shall perish: all the workers of iniquity shall be scattered. But my horn have You exalted like the horn of the wild ox; I am anointed with rich oil.

My eye also has gazed on them that lie in wait for me, my ears have heard my desire for the evil-doers that rise up against me. A Tzadik shall flourish like the palm tree; he shall grow like a cedar in Levanon. Planted in Beit יהוה , they shall flourish in the courts of our Elohim.

They shall still bring forth fruit in old age; they shall be full of sap and richness; To declare that יהוה is upright, my Rock, in whom there is no unrighteousness.

# L'kḥa Dodi:  Come, My Beloved!
# (The Sabbath Bride)
*Hebrew first, then English*

Lekḥah dodi likrat kallah,     לְכָה דוֹדִי לִקְרָאת כַּלָה,
p'nei Shabbat nekabelah.     פְּנֵי שַׁבָּת נְקַבְּלָה.

Shamor v'zakḥor b'dibur ekḥad, hishmi'anu El ham'yukḥad; יהוה ekḥad ush'mo ekḥad; L'Shem ul'tiferet u'lit'hilah

שָׁמוֹר וְזָכוֹר בְּדִבּוּר אֶחָד, הִשְׁמִיעָנוּ אֵל הַמְיֻחָד; יהוה אֶחָד וּשְׁמוֹ אֶחָד, לְשֵׁם וּלְתִפְאֶרֶת וְלִתְהִלָּה.

Likrat Shabbat lekḥu v'nelekḥah, ki hi makor haberakḥah merosh mikedem nesukḥah sof ma'aseh b'makḥashavah tekḥilah.

לִקְרַאת שַׁבָּת לְכוּ וְנֵלְכָה, כִּי הִיא מָקוֹר הַבְּרָכָה מֵרֹאשׁ מִקֶּדֶם נְסוּכָה סוֹף מַעֲשֶׂה בְּמַחֲשָׁבַה תְחִלָּה.

Mikdash melekḥ ir melukḥah, kumi tze'i mitokḥ hahafeikḥah; Rav lakḥ shevet b'eimek habakḥa v'hu yakḥamol alayikḥ khemlah.

מִקְדָּשׁ מֶלֶךְ, עִיר מְלוּכָה, קוּמִי צְאִי מִתּוֹךְ הַהֲפֵכָה; רַב לָךְ שֶׁבֶת בְּעֵמֶק הַבָּכָא: וְהוּא יַחֲמוֹל עָלַיִךְ חֶמְלָה.

Hitna'ari me'afar, kumi, Livshi bigdei tifartekḥ ami, al yad ben Yishai beit halakḥmi korvah el nafshi g'alah.

הִתְנַעֲרִי מֵעָפָר, קוּמִי, לִבְשִׁי בִּגְדֵי תִפְאַרְתֵּךְ עַמִּי; עַל יַד בֶּן יִשַׁי בֵּית הַלַּחְמִי קָרְבָה אֶל נַפְשִׁי גְאָלָה.

Hit'oreri hit'oreri ki va oreikḥ; kumi ori, ori, ori, shir dabeiri k'vod יהוה alayikḥ niglah.

הִתְעוֹרְרִי הִתְעוֹרְרִי כִּי בָא אוֹרֵךְ; קוּמִי אוֹרִי, עוֹרִי עוֹרִי, שִׁיר דַּבֵּרִי כְּבוֹד יהוה עָלַיִךְ נִגְלָה.

Lo tivoshi! v'lo tikalmi! Mah tishtokḥai, umah tehemi? bakḥ yekḥesu aniyei ami, v'nivnetah ir al tilah.

לֹא תֵבוֹשִׁי! וְלֹא תִכָּלְמִי! מָה תִּשְׁתּוֹחֲחִי, וּמַה תֶּהֱמִי? בָּךְ יֶחֱסוּ עֲנִיֵי עַמִּי, וְנִבְנְתַה עִיר עַל תִּלָּה.

17

V'hayu limshisah shosayikh, V'rakhaku kol mevalayikh; Yasis alayikh Elohayikh, kimsos khatan al kalah.

וְהָיוּ לִמְשִׁסָה שֹׁאסָיִךְ, וְרָחֲקוּ כֹּל מְבַלְעָיִךְ; יָשִׂישׂ עָלַיִךְ אֱלֹהָיִךְ, כִּמְשׂוֹשׂ חָתָן עַל כַּלָּה.

Yamin ushmol tifrotzi, v'et יהוה ta'aritzi, al yad ish ben Partzi V'nismekhah v'nagilah.

יָמִין וּשְׂמֹאל תִּפְרוֹצִי, וְאֶת יהוה תַּעֲרִיצִי, עַל יַד אִישׁ בֶּן פָּרְצִי וְנִשְׂמְחָה וְנָגִילָה.

Bo'i v'shalom ateret ba'alah gam b'simkhah uvetzahalah Tokh emunei am segulah Bo'i kalah bo'i kalah.

בּוֹאִי בְשָׁלוֹם עֲטֶרֶת בַּעֲלָהּ גַּם בְּשִׂמְחָה וּבְצָהֳלָה תּוֹךְ אֱמוּנֵי עַם סְגֻלָּה בּוֹאִי כַלָּה בּוֹאִי כַלָּה.

P'nei Shabbat nekabelah; P'nei Shabbat nekabelah; Shabbat Shalom B'Yeshua, Shabbat Shalom, Shabbat Shalom; Shabbat Shalom B'Yeshua, Shabbat Shalom, Shabbat Shalom.

פְּנֵי שַׁבָּת נְקַבְּלָה; פְּנֵי שַׁבָּת נְקַבְּלָה שַׁבָּת שָׁלוֹם בְּיֵשׁוּעַ, שַׁבָּת שָׁלוֹם, שַׁבָּת שָׁלוֹם; שַׁבָּת שָׁלוֹם בְּיֵשׁוּעַ, שַׁבָּת שָׁלוֹם, שַׁבָּת שָׁלוֹם.

Come, my Beloved, to meet the Bride; the face of Sabbath we receive! "Observe" and "recall": in a single utterance, we were made to hear by the unified God. יהוה is one and His Name is one, in fame and splendor and praiseful song. *(Yo'el 2:16, D'varim 16:2)*

Let's go to greet the Shabbat, let's travel, for she is the wellspring of blessing from the beginning; from ancient times she was chosen. Though made last, conceived first. *(B'reshit 2:2-3)*

Sanctuary of the king, regal city, arise! Leave from the midst of the turmoil. Long enough have you sat in the valley of tears. Now He will take great pity upon you compassionately. *(Yesha-Yahu 40:9, Yirme-Yahu 49:31)*

Shake yourself free, rise from the dust! Dress in your garments of splendor, my people. The son of Yishai, the Bethlehemite, draws near, bringing the soul redemption. *(Yesha-Yahu 52:2)*

Rouse yourselves! Rouse yourselves! Your light is coming. Rise up and shine! Awaken! Awaken! Utter a song! The glory of יהוה is revealed upon you. *(Yesha-Yahu 26:19)*

Do not be embarrassed! Do not be ashamed! Why be downcast? Why groan? All my afflicted people will find refuge within you, and the city shall be rebuilt on her hill. *(Yesha-Yahu 54:4)*

Your despoilers will become your spoil. Far away shall be any who would devour you. Your Elohim will rejoice concerning you, as a groom rejoices over a bride. *(Yesha-Yahu 62:5)*

To your right and your left you will burst forth, and יהוה will you revere, because of the hand of a Man, the Son of Peretz, we will rejoice and sing happily. *(Shemot 34:24, Ruut 4:18-22, Matai 1:3)*

Come in peace, crown of her husband, both in happiness and in jubilation, amidst the faithful of the treasured nation. Come O Bride! Come O Bride! *(Shemot 19:5)*

The face of Sabbath we receive! The face of Sabbath we receive! Sabbath Peace in Yeshua, Sabbath Peace, Sabbath Peace; Sabbath Peace in Yeshua, Sabbath Peace, Sabbath Peace.

## Tehillah 145

*Hebrew first, then English*

| | | |
|---|---|---|
| Tehillah l'David. Aromimkha Elohai hamelekh; Va'avarekhah shimkha, l'olam va'ed. | אֲרוֹמִמְךָ לְדָוִד: תְּהִלָּהֿא וַאֲבָרְכָה הַמֶּלֶךְ; אֱלוֹהַי שִׁמְךָ לְעוֹלָם וָעֶד. | |
| B'khol yom avarekhekha; Va'ahalelah shimkha l'olam va'ed. | וַאֲהַלְלָה אֲבָרְכֶךָ; יוֹם בְּכָלֿב שִׁמְךָ לְעוֹלָם וָעֶד. | |

Gadol יהוה um'hullal
me'od;   V'ligdullato ein
kheker.

ᵍגָּדוֹל יהוה וּמְהֻלָּל מְאֹד;
וְלִגְדֻלָּתוֹ אֵין חֵקֶר.

Dor   l'dor,   yeshabakh
ma'aseikha; Ugvuroteikha
yagidu.

ᵈדּוֹר לְדוֹר יְשַׁבַּח מַעֲשֶׂיךָ;
וּגְבוּרֹתֶיךָ יַגִּידוּ.

Hadar   k'vod   hodekha,
v'divrei       nif'loteikha
asikhah.

ᵉהֲדַר כְּבוֹד הוֹדֶךָ וְדִבְרֵי
נִפְלְאֹתֶיךָ אָשִׂיחָה.

V'ezuz norotekha yomeru;
ugdulatekha asaprenah.

ᵛוֶעֱזוּז נוֹרְאֹתֶיךָ יֹאמֵרוּ;
וגדלותיך (וּגְדֻלָּתְךָ)
אֲסַפְּרֶנָּה.

Zekher rav tuv'kha yabi'u;
v'tzidkatekha yeranenu.

ᶻזֵכֶר רַב טוּבְךָ יַבִּיעוּ;
וְצִדְקָתְךָ יְרַנֵּנוּ.

Khanun v'rakhum יהוה ;
erekh   apaiyim   ugdal
khased.

ᶜʰחַנּוּן וְרַחוּם יהוה ; אֶרֶךְ
אַפַּיִם וּגְדָל חָסֶד.

Tov יהוה lakol;
V'rakhamav,   al   kal
ma'asav.

ᵗטוֹב יהוה לַכֹּל; וְרַחֲמָיו עַל
כָּל מַעֲשָׂיו.

Yodukha יהוה , kal
ma'aseikha; vakhasidekha
yevar'khukhah.

ʸיוֹדוּךָ יהוה כָּל מַעֲשֶׂיךָ;
וַחֲסִידֶיךָ יְבָרְכוּכָה.

K'vod   malkhutkha
yomeru;   Ugvuratekha
yedaberu.

ᵏכְּבוֹד מַלְכוּתְךָ יֹאמֵרוּ;
וּגְבוּרָתְךָ יְדַבֵּרוּ.

L'hodiya, liv'nei ha'adam g'vurotav; ukhvod, hadar malkhuto.

יֵּלְהוֹדִיעַ לִבְנֵי הָאָדָם גְּבוּרֹתָיו; וּכְבוֹד הֲדַר מַלְכוּתֹו.

Malkhutkha malkhut kal olamim; umemshal'tekha, bekhol dor vador.

יֵּמַלְכוּתְךָ מַלְכוּת כָּל עֹלָמִים; וּמֶמְשַׁלְתְּךָ בְּכָל דּוֹר וָדֹר.

Somekh יהוה , l'khol hanoflim; V'zokef l'khol hak'fufim.

יֵּסוֹמֵךְ יהוה לְכָל הַנֹּפְלִים; וְזוֹקֵף לְכָל הַכְּפוּפִים.

Einei khol eleikha y'saberu; v'atah noten lahem et okhlam b'itoh.

יֵּעֵינֵי כֹל אֵלֶיךָ יְשַׂבֵּרוּ; וְאַתָּה נוֹתֵן לָהֶם אֶת אָכְלָם בְּעִתֹּו.

Pote'akh et yadekha umasbi'a l'khol khai ratzon.

יֵּפוֹתֵחַ אֶת יָדֶךָ; וּמַשְׂבִּיעַ לְכָל חַי רָצֹון.

Tzadik יהוה , b'khol d'rakhav; v'khasid b'khol ma'asav.

יֵּצַדִּיק יהוה בְּכָל דְּרָכָיו; וְחָסִיד בְּכָל מַעֲשָׂיו.

Karov יהוה l'khol korav, l'khol asher yikra'uhu v'emet.

יֵּקָרוֹב יהוה לְכָל קֹרְאָיו לְכֹל אֲשֶׁר יִקְרָאֻהוּ בֶאֱמֶת.

Retzon yere'av ya'aseh; ve'et shavatam yishma, v'yoshi'em.

יֵּרְצוֹן יְרֵאָיו יַעֲשֶׂה; וְאֶת שַׁוְעָתָם יִשְׁמַע וְיוֹשִׁיעֵם.

Shomer יהוה , et kol ohavav; v'et kol haresha'im yashmid.

יֵּשׁוֹמֵר יהוה אֶת כָּל אֹהֲבָיו; וְאֵת כָּל הָרְשָׁעִים יַשְׁמִיד.

Tehillat יהוה yedaber pi: כא**תְּהִלַּת יהוה יְדַבֶּר פִּי׃**
Vivarekh kol basar, shem **וִיבָרֵךְ כָּל בָּשָׂר שֵׁם קָדְשׁוֹ**
kodshoh l'olam va'ed. **לְעוֹלָם וָעֶד׃**

A Tehillah of David. I will extol You, my Elohim, O Melekh; and I will
bless Your Name forever and ever.

Every day will I bless You; and I will praise Your Name forever and
ever. Great is יהוה , and highly to be praised; and His greatness is
unsearchable. One generation shall laud Your works to another, and
shall declare Your mighty acts.

The glorious splendor of Your majesty, and Your wondrous works, will
I rehearse. And men shall speak of the might of Your tremendous acts;
and I will tell of Your greatness.

They shall utter the fame of Your great goodness, and shall sing of Your
tzedaka. יהוה is gracious, and full of mercy; slow to anger, and of great
compassion. יהוה is good to all; and His tender mercies are over all
His works.

All Your works shall praise You, O יהוה ; and Your Khasidim shall
bless You. They shall speak of the Kavod of Your Malkhut, and talk of
Your might; to make known to the sons of men His mighty acts, and
the glory of the majesty of His kingdom.

Your Malkhut is a kingdom for all ages, and Your dominion endures
throughout all generations. יהוה upholds all that fall, and raises up all
those that are bowed down. The eyes of all wait for You, and You give
them their food in its time. O open Your hand, and satisfy every living
thing with favor. יהוה is righteous in all His ways, and gracious in all
His works.

יהוה is nigh unto all them that call upon Him, to all that call upon Him
in truth. He will fulfill the desire of them that fear Him; He also will
hear their cry, and will save them. יהוה preserves all them that love
Him; but all the wicked will He destroy. My mouth shall speak the
Tehillah of יהוה , and let all flesh bless His consecrated name forever
and ever.

# Tehillim for Shabbat

| Portion | Tehillah/ page | Portion | Tehillah/ page | Portion | Tehillah/ page |
|---------|----------------|---------|----------------|---------|----------------|
| B'reshit | 139/512 | Terumah | 26/253 | Sh'lakh L'kha | 64/335 |
| No'akh | 29/259 | Tetzaveh | 65/337 | Korakh | 5/211 |
| Lekh L'kha | 110/457 | Ki Tissa | 75/366 | Khukat | 95/416 |
| VaYera | 11/224 | VaYakekhel | 61/331 | Balak | 79/381 |
| Khayei Sara | 45/299 | Pekudei | 45/299 | Pin'khas | 50/308 |
| Toldot | 36/276 | VaYikra | 50/308 | Matot | 111/458 |
| VaYetzei | 3/208 | Tzav | 107/446 | Masei | 49/306 |
| VaYishlakh | 140/515 | Sh'mini | 127/496 | D'varim | 137/509 |
| VaYeshev | 112/460 | Tazria | 106/440 | Va'Etkhanan | 90/407 |
| Miketz | 40/287 | Metzorah | 120/490 | Ekev | 75/366 |
| VaYigash | 48/304 | Akharei Mot | 26/253 | Re'eh | 97/419 |
| VaYekhi | 41/290 | K'doshim | 15/228 | Shoftim | 17/230 |
| Shemot | 99/422 | Emor | 42/292 | Ki Tetzeh | 32/265 |
| Va'Eirah | 46/301 | B'har | 112/460 | Ki Tavo | 51/311 |
| Bo | 77/369 | B'khukotai | 105/436 | Nitzavim | 81/386 |
| B'Shalakh | 66/339 | BaMidbar | 122/492 | VaYelekh | 65/337 |
| Yitro | 19/239 | Naso | 67/341 | Ha'Azinu | 71/353 |
| Mishpatim | 72/357 | B'ha'alotkha | 68/342 | V'zot HaBerakha | 12/225 |

# Sh'monei Esrei: Amidah

*Hebrew first, then English*

**THE AMIDAH OPENING**

Ado**nai**, sefa**tai** tif**takh**; ufi ya**gid** tehilla**teik**ha.

אֲדֹנָי, שְׂפָתַי תִּפְתָּח; וּפִי יַגִּיד תְּהִלָּתֶךָ.

O Adonai, open my lips, and my mouth shall declare Your praise.

## 1. Avot (Fathers)

Barukh Atah, יהוה , Eloheinu v'Elohei avoteinu. Elohei Avraham. Elohei Yitz'khak. V'Elohei Ya'akov.

בָּרוּךְ אַתָּה יהוה , אֱלֹהֵינוּ, וֵאלֹהֵי אֲבוֹתֵינוּ. אֱלֹהֵי אַבְרָהָם. אֱלֹהֵי יִצְחָק. וֵאלֹהֵי יַעֲקֹב.

Ha'El hagadol hagibor v'hanora, El Elyon. Gomel khasadim tovim, V'koneh hakol.

הָאֵל הַגָּדוֹל הַגִּבּוֹר וְהַנּוֹרָא. אֵל עֶלְיוֹן. גּוֹמֵל חֲסָדִים טוֹבִים, וְקוֹנֵה הַכֹּל.

V'zokher khas'dei avot. Umevi go'el livnei v'neihem l'ma'an shemo b'ahavah.

וְזוֹכֵר חַסְדֵי אָבוֹת, וּמֵבִיא גּוֹאֵל לִבְנֵי בְנֵיהֶם לְמַעַן שְׁמוֹ בְּאַהֲבָה.

Melekh ozer umoshiya, umagen. Barukh Atah, יהוה , Magen Avraham.

מֶלֶךְ עוֹזֵר וּמוֹשִׁיעַ וּמָגֵן: בָּרוּךְ אַתָּה יהוה , מָגֵן אַבְרָהָם.

Blessed are You, O יהוה , our Elohim, and Elohim of our fathers, Elohim of Av'raham, Elohim of Yitz'khak and Elohim of Ya'akov, the great, mighty and awesome Elohim, the Most High God, who bestows compassion and creates all, and remembers the kindnesses of the fathers, and brings a redeemer to their children's children, for His name's sake with love. O King, helper, savior, and shield, blessed are You, יהוה , Shield of Av'raham.

## 2. Gibor (Might)

Atah gibor l'olam Adonai mekhaiyeh metim. Atah rav l'hoshia.

אַתָּה גִּבּוֹר לְעוֹלָם אֲדֹנָי, מְחַיֶּה מֵתִים. אַתָּה רַב לְהוֹשִׁיעַ.

Mekhal**kel** **khai**yim b'**khe**sed. Mekhai**yeh** me**tim** berak**ham**im ra**bim**. Somek**h** nof**lim** v'rofe**h** k**ho**lim uMatair asu**rim**. Um'kai**yem** emuna**to** lish**nei** a**far**.

מְכַלְכֵּל חַיִּים בְּחֶסֶד. מְחַיֵּה מֵתִים בְּרַחֲמִים רַבִּים. סוֹמֵךְ נוֹפְלִים וְרוֹפֵא חוֹלִים וּמַתִּיר אֲסוּרִים. וּמְקַיֵּם אֱמוּנָתוֹ לִישֵׁנֵי עָפָר.

Mi kamokh**a** ba'**al** gevu**rot**, u**mi** do**meh** lak**h**. Melek**h** me**mit** um'khai**yeh** umatz**mi**'ak**h** Yeshua**[h]**?

מִי כָמוֹךָ בַּעַל גְּבוּרוֹת, וּמִי דוֹמֶה לָךְ. מֶלֶךְ מֵמִית וּמְחַיֵּה וּמַצְמִיחַ יְשׁוּעָה?

V'ne'**eman** Atah l'hakhai**yot** me**tim**. Baruk**h** Atah, יהוה , mekhai**yeh** hame**tim**.

וְנֶאֱמָן אַתָּה לְהַחֲיוֹת מֵתִים: בָּרוּךְ אַתָּה יהוה , מְחַיֵּה הַמֵּתִים.

You are eternally mighty, Adonai, the Resurrector of the dead are You; great in salvation. Who sustains the living with kindness, resurrects the dead with great mercy, supports the fallen, heals the sick, releases the confined, and keeps His faith to those asleep in the dust.

Who is like You, O master of mighty deeds, and who is comparable to You, O King, who causes death and restores life and makes salvation sprout? And You are faithful to resurrect the dead. Blessed are You, O יהוה , who resurrects the dead.

### 3. Kadosh et Hashem יהוה (Holiness of the Name of יהוה)

Atah kadosh v'shimkh**a** kadosh uk'do**shim** v'k**hol** yom y'hallelukh**a**, Selah. Baruk**h** Atah, יהוה , Ha'**El** haka**dosh**.

אַתָּה קָדוֹשׁ וְשִׁמְךָ קָדוֹשׁ וּקְדוֹשִׁים בְּכָל יוֹם, יְהַלְלוּךְ סֶלָה. בָּרוּךְ אַתָּה יהוה , הָאֵל הַקָּדוֹשׁ:

You are holy and your Name is holy, and every day holy ones will praise You. Selah. Blessed are You, יהוה , the holy God.

### 4. Binah (Insight)

Atah khonen l'adam da'at. Um'lamed l'enosh binah. V'khanenu me'itkha khakhmah binah vada'at. Barukh Atah, יהוה, khonen hada'at.

אַתָּה חוֹנֵן לְאָדָם דַּעַת. וּמְלַמֵּד לֶאֱנוֹשׁ בִּינָה: וְחָנֵּנוּ מֵאִתְּךָ חָכְמָה בִּינָה וָדָעַת; בָּרוּךְ אַתָּה יהוה , חוֹנֵן הַדָּעַת.

You show favor to a man of knowledge and teach understanding to a mortal man. Be gracious to us; a mind of understanding and intellect is from You. Blessed are You, יהוה , who favors the knowledge.

### 5. Teshuvah (Repentance)

Hashivenu Avinu l'torateikha. V'karvenu Malkeinu la'avodateikha. V'hakhazirenu bitshuvah shelemah lefaneikha. Barukh Atah, יהוה , harotzeh bitshuvah.

הֲשִׁיבֵנוּ אָבִינוּ לְתוֹרָתֶךָ. וְקָרְבֵנוּ מַלְכֵּנוּ לַעֲבוֹדָתֶךָ. וְהַחֲזִירֵנוּ בִּתְשׁוּבָה שְׁלֵמָה לְפָנֶיךָ: בָּרוּךְ אַתָּה יהוה , הָרוֹצֶה בִּתְשׁוּבָה.

Bring us back, our Father, to Your Torah, and bring us closer, our King, to Your service, and make us return in complete repentance before You. Blessed are You, O יהוה , who desires repentance.

### 6. Selakh (Forgiveness)

Selakh lanu Avinu, ki khatanu. Makhol lanu malkeinu ki fashanu. Ki El tov v'salakh Atah. Barukh Atah יהוה , khanun hamarbeh lislo'akh.

סְלַח לָנוּ, אָבִינוּ, כִּי חָטָאנוּ. מְחַל לָנוּ מַלְכֵּנוּ, כִּי פָשָׁעְנוּ. כִּי אֵל טוֹב וְסַלָּח אָתָּה. בָּרוּךְ אַתָּה יהוה , חַנּוּן הַמַּרְבֶּה לִסְלֹחַ.

Forgive us, our Father, for we have erred; pardon us, our King, for we have intentionally sinned, for You pardon and forgive.

Blessed are You, יהוה , the Compassionate One, who pardons abundantly.

### 7. Ge'ulah (Redemption)

Re'**eh** na v'anyeinu. V'rivah rivenu. Ug'alenu ge'u**lah** sh'le**mah** mehe**rah** l'**ma**'an sh'**meikḥa**. Ki El go'**el** kḥazak Atah. Baru**kḥ** Atah, יהוה , go'**el** Yisra'el.

רְאֵה נָא בְעָנְיֵנוּ. וְרִיבָה רִיבֵנוּ. וּגְאָלֵנוּ גְאֻלָּה שְׁלֵמָה מְהֵרָה לְמַעַן שְׁמֶךָ. כִּי אֵל גּוֹאֵל חָזָק אָתָּה. בָּרוּךְ אַתָּה יהוה , גּוֹאֵל יִשְׂרָאֵל.

Behold our affliction, take up our grievance, and save us soon for the sake of Your Name, for You are a powerful redeemer. Blessed are You, O יהוה , the redeemer of Yisra'el.

### 8. Refu'ah (Healing and Health)

Refa'**enu** יהוה v'nera**feh**'. Hoshi'**einu** v'nivashe'ah. Ki tehilatenu Atah. V'ha'a**leh** arukḥah umar**peh** l'**kḥol** takḥalu'enu ul'**kḥol** makḥovenu ul'**kḥol** makotenu.

רְפָאֵנוּ יהוה וְנֵרָפֵא. הוֹשִׁיעֵנוּ וְנִוָּשֵׁעָה, כִּי תְהִלָּתֵנוּ אָתָּה. וְהַעֲלֵה אֲרוּכָה וּמַרְפֵּא לְכָל תַּחֲלוּאֵינוּ, וּלְכָל מַכְאוֹבֵינוּ, וּלְכָל מַכּוֹתֵינוּ.

Yehi ratzon milfaneikḥa, יהוה Elo**hai** v'Elo**hei** Avo**tai**. Sh'tishla**kḥ** mehe**rah** refu'**ah** shel'**mah** min hashamayim. Refu'**at** hanefesh urefu'**at** haguf l'**kḥoleh** b'**tokḥ** she'**ar** kḥolei Yisra'el.

יְהִי רָצוֹן מִלְּפָנֶיךָ יהוה אֱלֹהַי וֵאלֹהֵי אֲבוֹתַי, שֶׁתִּשְׁלַח מְהֵרָה רְפוּאָה שְׁלֵמָה מִן הַשָּׁמַיִם. רְפוּאַת הַנֶּפֶשׁ, וּרְפוּאַת הַגּוּף, לְחוֹלֶה בְּתוֹךְ שְׁאָר חוֹלֵי יִשְׂרָאֵל.

Ki El Melekh rofeh ne'eman v'rakhaman Atah. Barukh Atah, יהוה , rofeh kholei amo Yisra'el.

כִּי אֵל מֶלֶךְ רוֹפֵא נֶאֱמָן וְרַחֲמָן אָתָּה. בָּרוּךְ אַתָּה. יהוה , רוֹפֵא חוֹלֵי עַמּוֹ יִשְׂרָאֵל.

Heal us יהי , and we shall be healed, save us, and we shall be saved, for You are our praise. And bring complete recovery for all our sicknesses, our diseases, and all our wounds. May it be Your will, יהי , my Elohim, and the Elohim of my forefathers, that You quickly send a complete recovery from heaven, spiritual healing and physical healing to the patient (son or daughter) of (mother or father's name) among the other patients of Yisra'el, for You are Elohim, Melekh, the faithful and merciful healer. Blessed are You, O יהי , who heals the sick of His people Yisra'el.

### 9. Birkat HaShanim (Blessings of the Years)

Barekh aleinu, יהוה Eloheinu, et hashanah hazot v'et kol minei tevu'atah l'tovah v'et berakhah al p'nei ha'adamah, v'sabeinu mituvah. Uvarekh shenatenu kashanim hatovot. Barukh Atah, יהוה , mevarekh hashanim.

בָּרֵךְ עָלֵינוּ, יהוה אֱלֹהֵינוּ, אֶת הַשָּׁנָה הַזֹּאת וְאֶת כָּל מִינֵי תְבוּאָתָהּ לְטוֹבָה וְאֶת בְּרָכָה עַל פְּנֵי הָאֲדָמָה, וְשַׂבְּעֵנוּ מִטּוּבָהּ. וּבָרֵךְ שְׁנָתֵנוּ כַּשָּׁנִים הַטּוֹבוֹת. בָּרוּךְ אַתָּה יהוה , מְבָרֵךְ הַשָּׁנִים.

Bless for us, יהי , our Elohim, this year and its crops. Give us a blessing, and give dew and rain for blessing on the face of the earth, and satisfy us from Your goodness, and bless our year like the other good years. Blessed are You, O יהי , who blesses the years.

## 10. Kibbutz Galuyot (Ingathering of Exiles)

Teka b'shofar gadol lekḥerutenu. V'sheh nes lekabetz galuyotenu. V'kobetzenu yakḥad meherah me'arbah kan'fot ha'aretz l'artzeinu. Barukh Atah, יהוה , mekabetz nidkḥei ahmo Yisra'el.

תְּקַע בְּשׁוֹפָר גָּדוֹל לְחֵרוּתֵנוּ. וְשָׂא נֵס לְקַבֵּץ גָּלֻיּוֹתֵינוּ. וְקַבְּצֵנוּ יַחַד מְהֵרָה מֵאַרְבַּע כַּנְפוֹת הָאָרֶץ לְאַרְצֵנוּ: בָּרוּךְ אַתָּה יהוה , מְקַבֵּץ נִדְחֵי עַמּוֹ יִשְׂרָאֵל.

Sound the great shofar for our freedom, and raise a standard to gather our exiles, and gather us from the four corners of the earth. Blessed are You, O יהוה , who gathers the dispersed of His people Yisra'el.

## 11. Birkat HaDin (Restoration of Justice)

Hashivah shofteinu k'varishonah. V'yoatzeinu kevat'khilah. V'haser mimeinu yagon va'anakḥah. U'melekḥ aleinu meherah. Atah יהוה le'vad'kha b'khesed uvrakḥamim. V'tzadkenu b'tzedek uv'mishpat. Barukh Atah, יהוה , Melekḥ ohev tzedakah umishpat.

הָשִׁיבָה שׁוֹפְטֵינוּ כְּבָרִאשׁוֹנָה. וְיוֹעֲצֵינוּ כְּבַתְּחִלָּה. וְהָסֵר מִמֶּנּוּ יָגוֹן וַאֲנָחָה. וּמְלֹךְ עָלֵינוּ מְהֵרָה. אַתָּה יהוה לְבַדְּךָ בְּחֶסֶד וּבְרַחֲמִים. וְצַדְּקֵנוּ בְּצֶדֶק וּבְמִשְׁפָּט. בָּרוּךְ אַתָּה יהוה , מֶלֶךְ אוֹהֵב צְדָקָה וּמִשְׁפָּט.

Restore our judges as in early times, and our counselors as at first; remove from us our sorrows and troubles; we want you, יהוה , alone, to rule over us with kindness and compassion and to justify us in justice. Blessed are You, O יהוה , King who loves righteousness and justice.

29

## 12. Tzadikim (The Righteous)

Al hatzadi**kim** v'**al** hakhasi**dim**. V'**al** zik**nei** she'**erit** ahm'**kha** Beit Yisra'el. V'**al** peleitat sofre**hem**. V'**al** ge**rei** hatze**dek**. V'**aleinu**, yehemu nah rakhameikha, יהוה Eloheinu. V'**ten** shekhar tov lekhol habot'**khim** b'shimkha b'emet.

עַל הַצַּדִּיקִים וְעַל הַחֲסִידִים. וְעַל זִקְנֵי שְׁאֵרִית עַמְּךָ בֵּית יִשְׂרָאֵל. וְעַל פְּלֵיטַת סוֹפְרֵיהֶם. וְעַל גֵּרֵי הַצֶּדֶק. וְעָלֵינוּ, יֶהֱמוּ נָא רַחֲמֶיךָ יהוה אֱלֹהֵינוּ. וְתֵן שְׂכָר טוֹב לְכָל הַבּוֹטְחִים בְּשִׁמְךָ בֶּאֱמֶת.

V'**sim** khelkeinu imahem. Ul'**olam** lo nevosh ki v'**kha** vatakhnu. V'**al** khasd'**kha** hagadol b'emet (uv'tamim) nish'anenu. Barukh **Atah**, יהוה , mishan umivtakh latzadi**kim**.

וְשִׂים חֶלְקֵנוּ עִמָּהֶם. וּלְעוֹלָם לֹא נֵבוֹשׁ כִּי בְךָ בָטָחְנוּ. וְעַל חַסְדְּךָ הַגָּדוֹל בֶּאֱמֶת (וּבְתָמִים) נִשְׁעָנְנוּ: בָּרוּךְ אַתָּה יהוה , מִשְׁעָן וּמִבְטָח לַצַּדִּיקִים.

On the righteous, on the devout, on the elders of Your people, the house of Yisra'el, on the remnant of their scribes, on the righteous converts and on us. May Your compassion be aroused, יהוה , our Elohim, and give good reward to all those who truly trust Your Name. May You put our share among them, and we shall not be ashamed forever, for You we trust. And upon your compassion we rely. Blessed are You, O יהוה , who supports and safeguards the righteous.

### 13. Binyan Yerushulayim (Rebuilding Yerushalayim)

V'liyrushalayim irkha b'rakhamim tashuv. V'tishkon b'tokhah ka'asher dibarta. Uvneh otah b'karov b'yameinu binyan olam. V'khiseh David avdekha meherah l'tokhah takhin. Barukh Atah, יהוה , boneh Yerushalayim.

וְלִירוּשָׁלַיִם עִירְךָ בְּרַחֲמִים תָּשׁוּב. וְתִשְׁכֹּן בְּתוֹכָהּ כַּאֲשֶׁר דִּבַּרְתָּ. וּבְנֵה אוֹתָהּ בְּקָרוֹב בְּיָמֵינוּ בִּנְיַן עוֹלָם. וְכִסֵּא דָוִד עַבְדְּךָ מְהֵרָה לְתוֹכָהּ תָּכִין. בָּרוּךְ אַתָּה יהוה , בּוֹנֵה יְרוּשָׁלָיִם.

And to Yerushalayim Your city You shall return with mercy, and You shall dwell in it, as You have spoken. May You rebuild it soon in our days for eternity, and may You establish the throne of David within it. Blessed are You, O יהוה , the Builder of Yerushalayim.

### 14. Malkhut Beit David (Davidic Reign)

Et tzemakh David avdekha m'herah tatzmiakh. V'karno tarum bishuatekha. Ki lishuatekha kivinu kal hayom. Barukh Atah, יהוה , matzimiakh keren yeshuah.

אֶת צֶמַח דָּוִד עַבְדְּךָ מְהֵרָה תַצְמִיחַ. וְקַרְנוֹ תָּרוּם בִּישׁוּעָתֶךָ. כִּי לִישׁוּעָתְךָ קִוִּינוּ כָּל הַיּוֹם: בָּרוּךְ אַתָּה יהוה , מַצְמִיחַ קֶרֶן יְשׁוּעָה.

May the offspring of David, Your servant, flourish speedily and exalt his honor with Your salvation. For Your salvation (Yeshua) we hope all day long. Blessed are You, O יהוה , who makes the horn of salvation to flourish.

### 15. Tefillah (Acceptance of Prayer)

Shema kolenu, יהוה Eloheinu. Khus v'rakhem aleinu. V'kabel b'rakhamim uv'ratzon et tefilatenu. Ki El shome'a tefilot v'takhanunim Atah. U'milfaneikha malkeinu reikam al teshivenu, ki Atah shome'a tefilat ahm'kha Yisra'el berakhamim. Barukh Atah, יהוה shome'a tefilah.

שְׁמַע קוֹלֵנוּ, יהוה אֱלֹהֵינוּ. חוּס וְרַחֵם עָלֵינוּ. וְקַבֵּל בְּרַחֲמִים וּבְרָצוֹן אֶת תְּפִלָּתֵנוּ. כִּי אֵל שׁוֹמֵעַ תְּפִלּוֹת וְתַחֲנוּנִים אָתָּה. וּמִלְּפָנֶיךָ מַלְכֵּנוּ, רֵיקָם אַל תְּשִׁיבֵנוּ. כִּי אַתָּה שׁוֹמֵעַ תְּפִלַּת עַמְּךָ יִשְׂרָאֵל בְּרַחֲמִים. בָּרוּךְ אַתָּה יהוה , שׁוֹמֵעַ תְּפִלָּה.

Hear our voice, יהוה , our Elohim. Have mercy and compassion for us, and accept our prayers mercifully and willingly, for You are Elohim who listens to prayers and supplications. From before Yourself, our King, turn us not away empty handed, for You hear the prayer of Your people Yisra'el mercifully. Blessed are You, O יהוה , who hears prayers.

### 16. Avodah (Restoration of Temple Service)

Retzeh יהוה Eloheinu b'ahm'kha Yisra'el v'litfilatam. V'hashev et ha'avodah lidvir beitekha.

רְצֵה יהוה אֱלֹהֵינוּ בְּעַמְּךָ יִשְׂרָאֵל וְלִתְפִלָּתָם. וְהָשֵׁב אֶת הָעֲבוֹדָה לִדְבִיר בֵּיתֶךָ.

V'ishei Yisra'el ut'filatam meherah b'ahavah tekabel b'ratzon. Utehi l'ratzon tamid avodat Yisra'el ahmei'kha. V'tekhezeinah eineinu b'shuvkha l'Tzion b'rakhamim. Barukh Atah, יהוה , hamakhazir shekhinato l'Tzion.

וְאִשֵּׁי יִשְׂרָאֵל וּתְפִלָּתָם מְהֵרָה בְּאַהֲבָה תְּקַבֵּל בְּרָצוֹן. וּתְהִי לְרָצוֹן תָּמִיד עֲבוֹדַת יִשְׂרָאֵל עַמֶּךָ: וְתֶחֱזֶינָה עֵינֵינוּ בְּשׁוּבְךָ לְצִיּוֹן בְּרַחֲמִים. בָּרוּךְ אַתָּה יהוה , הַמַּחֲזִיר שְׁכִינָתוֹ לְצִיּוֹן.

Be favorable, יהוה our Elohim, toward Your people Yisra'el and their prayer, and restore the most holy service of Your house. Accept in love the offerings and prayers of Yisra'el, and may the service of Your people, Yisra'el, always be favorable to You. May our eyes behold Your return to Tzion in mercy. Blessed are You, O יהוה , who restores His presence to Tzion.

### 17. Modim (Thanksgiving)

Modim anakḥnu lakḥ. Sha'atah Hu יהוה Eloheinu v'Elohei Avoteinu l'olam va'ed, tzur khaiyeinu, magen yisheinu atah Hu ledor vador. Nodeh l'kha un'saper tehilatekha al khaiyeinu hamesurim b'yadekha. V'al nishmoteinu hap'kudot lakḥ. V'al niseikha sh'bekḥol yom imanu. V'al nifloteikha v'tovoteikha sh'bekḥol et. Erev vavoker v'tzohorayim.

Hatov ki lo kḥalu rakḥameikḥa v'hamerakḥem. ki lo tamu kḥasadeikḥa. Ki me'olam kivinu lakḥ.

מוֹדִים אֲנַחְנוּ לָךְ. שָׁאַתָּה הוּא יהוה אֱלֹהֵינוּ וֵאלֹהֵי אֲבוֹתֵינוּ לְעוֹלָם וָעֶד, צוּר חַיֵּינוּ, מָגֵן יִשְׁעֵנוּ אַתָּה הוּא לְדוֹר וָדוֹר. נוֹדֶה לְךָ וּנְסַפֵּר תְּהִלָּתֶךָ עַל חַיֵּינוּ הַמְּסוּרִים בְּיָדֶךָ. וְעַל נִשְׁמוֹתֵינוּ הַפְּקוּדוֹת לָךְ. וְעַל נִסֶּיךָ שֶׁבְּכָל יוֹם עִמָּנוּ. וְעַל נִפְלְאוֹתֶיךָ וְטוֹבוֹתֶיךָ שֶׁבְּכָל עֵת. עֶרֶב וָבֹקֶר וְצָהֳרָיִם.

הַטּוֹב כִּי לֹא כָלוּ רַחֲמֶיךָ. וְהַמְרַחֵם כִּי לֹא תַמּוּ חֲסָדֶיךָ. כִּי מֵעוֹלָם קִוִּינוּ לָךְ.

V'al kulam yitbarekh v'yitromem shimkha, malkenu, tamid l'olam va'ed. V'khol hakhaiyim yodukha selah. Vihalelu vivarkhu et shimkha hagadol b'emet l'olam, ki tov. Ha'el yeshuateinu v'ezrateinu, selah.

וְעַל כֻּלָּם יִתְבָּרַךְ וְיִתְרוֹמֵם שִׁמְךָ מַלְכֵּנוּ תָּמִיד לְעוֹלָם וָעֶד: וְכֹל הַחַיִּים יוֹדוּךָ סֶּלָה. וִיהַלְלוּ וִיבָרְכוּ אֶת שִׁמְךָ הַגָּדוֹל בֶּאֱמֶת לְעוֹלָם כִּי טוֹב. הָאֵל יְשׁוּעָתֵנוּ וְעֶזְרָתֵנוּ, סֶלָה.

Barukh Atah יהוה hatov shimkha ulekha na'eh lehodot.

בָּרוּךְ אַתָּה יהוה , הַטּוֹב שִׁמְךָ וּלְךָ נָאֶה לְהוֹדוֹת.

We thank You, for You are יהוה , our Elohim and the Elohim of our forefathers forever and ever. The rock of our lives, the shield of our salvation, You are in every generation. We shall thank You and tell Your glory for our lives which are in Your hands, and for our souls that are entrusted to You, and for Your miracles that are with us every day, and for Your wonders and favors that happen all the time, evening and morning and noon.

The Good One, for Your compassion was not exhausted, and the Compassionate One, for Your merciful deeds have not ended; always have we put our hope in You. For all these, may Your Name be blessed and exalted, our King, always, forever and ever; and all the living will thank You – Selah – and praise Your Name truly, O Elohim, our salvation and help – Selah! Blessed are You, O יהוה , the Good One is Your Name, and You are proper to thank.

### 18. Sim Shalom (Establish Peace)

Sim shalom tovah uv'rakhah. Khen vakhesed verakhamim aleinu v'al kal Yisra'el ahmeikha. Barkheinu, Avinu, kulanu k'ekhad b'or paneikha. Ki v'or paneikha natata lanu, יהוה Eloheinu, torat khaiyim v'ahavat khesed. Utzdakah v'rakhamim v'khaiyim v'shalom.

שִׂים שָׁלוֹם טוֹבָה וּבְרָכָה. חֵן וָחֶסֶד וְרַחֲמִים עָלֵינוּ וְעַל כָּל יִשְׂרָאֵל עַמֶּךָ. בָּרְכֵנוּ אָבִינוּ כֻּלָּנוּ כְּאֶחָד בְּאוֹר פָּנֶיךָ. כִּי בְאוֹר פָּנֶיךָ נָתַתָּ לָנוּ יהוה אֱלֹהֵינוּ תּוֹרַת חַיִּים וְאַהֲבַת חֶסֶד. וּצְדָקָה וְרַחֲמִים וְחַיִּים וְשָׁלוֹם.

V'tov b'eineikha l'varekh et kol ahm'kha Yisra'el b'khol et uv'khol sha'ah bishlomekha. Barukh Atah, יהוה , hamevarekh et amo Yisra'el bashalom.

וְטוֹב בְּעֵינֶיךָ לְבָרֵךְ אֶת כָּל עַמְּךָ יִשְׂרָאֵל בְּכָל עֵת וּבְכָל שָׁעָה בִּשְׁלוֹמֶךָ: בָּרוּךְ אַתָּה יהוה , הַמְבָרֵךְ אֶת עַמּוֹ יִשְׂרָאֵל בַּשָּׁלוֹם.

Oseh shalom bimromav, hu ya'aseh shalom aleinu v'al kol Yisra'el.

עֹשֶׂה שָׁלוֹם בִּמְרוֹמָיו, הוּא יַעֲשֶׂה שָׁלוֹם עָלֵינוּ וְעַל כָּל יִשְׂרָאֵל

Establish shalom, goodness, and blessing, graciousness, kindness, and compassion upon us, and upon all Yisra'el Your people. Bless us our Father, all of us as one, with the light of Your countenance; for with the light of Your countenance You gave us, יהוה our Elohim, the Torah of Life, and a love of kindness, righteousness, blessing, compassion, life and peace.

May it be good in Your eyes to bless Your people Yisra'el, in every season and in every hour with Your peace. Blessed are You, O יהוה , who blesses His people Yisra'el with peace. He who makes shalom in His heights, may He make shalom upon us, and upon all Yisra'el.

## CONCLUDING PRAYER

| | |
|---|---|
| Netzor leshonkha merah, us'fateikha, midaber mirmah. | נְצֹר לְשׁוֹנְךָ מֵרָע; וּשְׂפָתֶיךָ, מִדַּבֵּר מִרְמָה. |
| Yihyu l'ratzon imrei fi, v'hegyon libi l'faneikha. יהוה , tzuri v'goeli. | יִהְיוּ לְרָצוֹן אִמְרֵי פִי, וְהֶגְיוֹן לִבִּי לְפָנֶיךָ. יהוה , צוּרִי וְגֹאֲלִי. |

Guard your tongue from evil, and your lips from speaking deceitfully. May the expressions of my mouth and the thoughts of my heart find favor before You, יהוה , my Rock and my Redeemer.

## Adon Olam: Master of the Universe
### *Hebrew first, then English*

| | |
|---|---|
| Adon Olam asher malakh, b'terem kol yetzir nivra, le'et na'asah v'kheftzo kol, azai melekh shemoh nikra; v'akharei kikhlot hakol, l'vado yimlokh nora. V'hu hayah v'hu hoveh v'hu yihyeh b'tifarah. | אֲדוֹן עוֹלָם אֲשֶׁר מָלַךְ, בְּטֶרֶם כָּל יְצִיר נִבְרָא. לְעֵת נַעֲשָׂה בְחֶפְצוֹ כֹּל, אֲזַי מֶלֶךְ שְׁמוֹ נִקְרָא. וְאַחֲרֵי כִּכְלוֹת הַכֹּל, לְבַדּוֹ יִמְלוֹךְ נוֹרָא. וְהוּא הָיָה, וְהוּא הֹוֶה, וְהוּא יִהְיֶה בְּתִפְאָרָה |
| V'hu ekhad v'ein sheni, l'hamshil lo l'hakhbirah; bli reshit, bli takhlit v'lo ha'oz v'hamisrah; v'hu Eli v'khai goeli, v'tzur khevli b'yom tzarah. | וְהוּא אֶחָד וְאֵין שֵׁנִי, לְהַמְשִׁיל לוֹ לְהַחְבִּירָה. בְּלִי רֵאשִׁית בְּלִי תַכְלִית וְלֹא הָעֹז וְהַמִּשְׂרָה. וְהוּא אֵלִי וְחַי גּוֹאֲלִי, וְצוּר חֶבְלִי בְּיוֹם צָרָה. |

V'**hu** nissi umanos li, menat kosi b'**yom** ek**rah**; b'yado af**kid** ruk**ḥi**, b'**et** ishan v'a'i**rah**; v'**im** ruk**ḥi** geviya**ti**, Ado**nai** li v'**lo ira**.

וְהוּא נִסִּי וּמָנוֹס לִי, מְנָת כּוֹסִי בְּיוֹם אֶקְרָא. בְּיָדוֹ אַפְקִיד רוּחִי, בְּעֵת אִישָׁן וְאָעִירָה. וְעִם רוּחִי גְוִיָּתִי, אֲדֹנָי לִי וְלֹא אִירָא.

Master of the Universe who has reigned before anything was created, at the time that everything was created at His will, then "King" was His Name proclaimed.

After all has ceased to exist, He, the Awesome One, will reign alone. And He was and He is, and He shall be in Glory! And He is One, and there is no second to compare to Him, to declare as His equal.

Without beginning, without end, He has the might and dominion. And He is my Elohim and my living Redeemer, and the Rock of my Salvation in time of trouble.

And He is my standard and a refuge for me, the portion of my cup on the day I call. In His hand I will deposit my spirit, when I am asleep, and I shall awaken, and with my spirit shall my body remain. Adonai is with me and I shall not fear.

## Kadosh: Consecrated
### Hebrew first, then English

V'**kara** zeh el zeh v'**amar**, Ka**dosh** ka**dosh** kadosh יהוה Tzeva'**ot**. Melo kḥol ha'**aretz** k'vo**doh**.

וְקָרָא זֶה אֶל זֶה וְאָמַר, קָדוֹשׁ קָדוֹשׁ קָדוֹשׁ יהוה צְבָאוֹת; מְלֹא כָל הָאָרֶץ כְּבוֹדוֹ.

Va'yikre'**u** b'**kol** gadol b'ahm**rahm**: haYeshu'**ah** l'Elo**hei**nu, hayo**shev** al hakis**eh**, v'laSeh.

וַיִּקְרְאוּ בְּקוֹל גָּדוֹל בְּאָמְרָם: הַיְשׁוּעָה לֵאלֹהֵנוּ, הַיּוֹשֵׁב עַל הַכִּסֵּא וְלַשֶּׂה.

Ra'**uy** Ha**Seh** hatavu'akḥ
l'kabel **ko**'akḥ v'**osher**
v'kḥakḥmah v'**oz** vi**kar**
v'ti**feret** u'v'**rakḥa**.

רָאוּי הַשֶׂה הַטָּבוּחַ לְקַבֵּל
כֹּחַ וְעֹשֶׁר וְחָכְמָה וְעֹז וִיקָר
וְתִפְאֶרֶת וּבְרָכָה.

Layo**shev** al haki**seh**
v'la**Seh** hab'**rakḥa**
v'haye**kar** v'hati**feret**
v'hashil**ton** l'ol'**mei**
ola**mim**.

לַיּוֹשֵׁב עַל הַכִּסֵּא וְלַשֶׂה
הַבְּרָכָה וְהַיְקָר וְהַתִּפְאֶרֶת
וְהַשִּׁלְטוֹן לְעוֹלְמֵי עוֹלָמִים.

And they called to each other, and said, "Kadosh, Kadosh, Kadosh, is יהוה Tzeva'ot; the whole earth is full of His Kavod" *(Yesha-Yahu 6:3)* Yeshua[h] belongs to our Elohim, who sits upon the throne, and to HaSeh. *(Hitgalut 7:10)*

"Worthy is HaSeh that was slain, to receive power, and riches, and wisdom, and might, and honor, and glory and blessing." *(Hitgalut 5:12)* "To Him who sits on the throne, and to HaSeh, be blessing, and honor, and glory, and dominion, forever and ever." *(Hitgalut 5:13)*

## Ein Ka'EL

*Hebrew first, then English*

Ein ka'**El** Yeshu**run**.
Rokḥev shama**yim**
be'ez'rekḥa, uv'ga'ava**toh**
shekḥa**kim**.

אֵין כָּאֵל יְשֻׁרוּן: רֹכֵב שָׁמַיִם
בְּעֶזְרֶךָ, וּבְגַאֲוָתוֹ שְׁחָקִים.

M'**onah** Elo**hei** ke**dem**,
u'mitakḥat zero'ot olam.
Vayega**resh** mipaneikḥa o**yev**,
vaiyo**mer** hash**med**.

מְעֹנָה אֱלֹהֵי קֶדֶם, וּמִתַּחַת
זְרֹעֹת עוֹלָם; וַיְגָרֶשׁ מִפָּנֶיךָ
אוֹיֵב, וַיֹּאמֶר הַשְׁמֵד.

Vayish**kon** Yisra'**el** b'ta**kḥ**
ba**dad** ein Ya'a**kov**, el eretz
da**gan** v'ti**rosh**. Af sha**mav**,
ya'ar**fu** tal.

וַיִּשְׁכֹּן יִשְׂרָאֵל בֶּטַח בָּדָד
עֵין יַעֲקֹב, אֶל אֶרֶץ דָּגָן
וְתִירוֹשׁ; אַף שָׁמָיו, יַעַרְפוּ
טָל.

Ashreikḥa Yisra'el! Mi kamokḥa? Am nosha ba יהוה , magen ez'rekḥa, va'asher kḥerev ga'avatekḥa, v'yikakḥashu oyveikḥa lakḥ, v'atah al bamoteimo tidrokḥ.

אַשְׁרֶיךָ יִשְׂרָאֵל מִי כָמוֹךָ, עַם נוֹשַׁע בַּיהוה, מָגֵן עֶזְרֶךָ, וַאֲשֶׁר חֶרֶב גַּאֲוָתֶךָ; וְיִכָּחֲשׁוּ אֹיְבֶיךָ לָךְ, וְאַתָּה עַל בָּמוֹתֵימוֹ תִדְרֹךְ.

"There is none like unto Elohim, O Yeshurun, who rides upon the heavens as your help, and in His excellency on the skies. *(D'varim 33:26)*

The eternal Elohim is a dwelling-place, and underneath are the everlasting arms; and He thrust out the enemy from before you, and said, 'Destroy!' *(33:27)*

And Yisra'el dwells in safety, the fountain of Ya'akov alone, in a land of grain and choice wine; yes, his heavens drop down dew. *(33:28)*

Happy are you, O Yisra'el! Who is like unto you? A people saved by יהוה , the shield of your help, and He who is the sword of your excellency! And your enemies shall dwindle away before you, and you shall tread upon their high places." *(33:29)*

## Shir Moshe: The Song of Moses
*Hebrew first, then English*

Ashira la יהוה , ki ga'oh ga'ah, sus v'rokḥ'voh, ra'mah va'yam.

אָשִׁירָה לַיהוה כִּי גָאֹה גָּאָה, סוּס וְרֹכְבוֹ רָמָה בַיָּם.

Ozi v'zimraht Yah, vayehi li' lishu'ah; zeh Eli v'anvehu, Elohei Avi va'ahrom'meinu.

עָזִי וְזִמְרָת יָה, וַיְהִי לִי לִישׁוּעָה; זֶה אֵלִי וְאַנְוֵהוּ, אֱלֹהֵי אָבִי וַאֲרֹמְמֶנְהוּ.

יהוה Ish milkḥamah, יהוה sh'moh.

יהוה אִישׁ מִלְחָמָה; יהוה שְׁמוֹ.

39

Mark'vot Paroh v'kheiloh, yarah va'yam; umivkhar shalishav, tub'u vaYam Suf.

מַרְכְּבֹת פַּרְעֹה וְחֵילוֹ, יָרָה בַיָּם; וּמִבְחַר שָׁלִשָׁיו, טֻבְּעוּ בְיַם סוּף.

T'homot y'khasyumu; yardu bimtzolot, k'mo aven.

תְּהֹמֹת, יְכַסְיֻמוּ; יָרְדוּ בִמְצוֹלֹת, כְּמוֹ אָבֶן.

Y'mineikha יהוה , ne'ehdari bako'akh; yemineikha יהוה tiratz oyev.

יְמִינְךָ יהוה , נֶאְדָּרִי בַּכֹּחַ; יְמִינְךָ יהוה , תִּרְעַץ אוֹיֵב.

Uvehrov ge'oneikha, taharos kameikha; t'shalakh kharoneikha yokhleimo kakash.

וּבְרֹב גְּאוֹנְךָ, תַּהֲרֹס קָמֶיךָ; תְּשַׁלַּח, חֲרֹנְךָ יֹאכְלֵמוֹ, כַּקַּשׁ.

U've'ru'akh apeikha ne'ermu mayim, nitz'vu khmo ned noz'lim; kafu t'homot b'lev yam.

וּבְרוּחַ אַפֶּיךָ נֶעֶרְמוּ מַיִם, נִצְּבוּ כְמוֹ נֵד נֹזְלִים; קָפְאוּ תְהֹמֹת, בְּלֶב יָם.

Amar oyev er'dof asig, akhalek shalal; timla'eimo nafshi arik kharbi, torisheimo yadi.

אָמַר אוֹיֵב אֶרְדֹּף אַשִּׂיג, אֲחַלֵּק שָׁלָל; תִּמְלָאֵמוֹ נַפְשִׁי אָרִיק חַרְבִּי, תּוֹרִישֵׁמוֹ יָדִי.

Nashaf'tah v'rukhakha, kisamo yam; tzal'lu ka'oferet, b'mayim, adirim.

נָשַׁפְתָּ בְרוּחֲךָ, כִּסָּמוֹ יָם; צָלְלוּ, כַּעוֹפֶרֶת, בְּמַיִם, אַדִּירִים.

Mi khamokha ba'elim יהוה? Mi kamokha? Ne'edar bakodesh, norah tehilot, oseh feleh?

מִי כָמֹכָה בָּאֵלִם יהוה , מִי כָּמֹכָה נֶאְדָּר בַּקֹּדֶשׁ; נוֹרָא תְהִלֹּת, עֹשֵׂה פֶלֶא.

Natitah y'mineikḥa tivla'eimo, aretz.

נָטִיתָ, יְמִינְךָ תִּבְלָעֵמוֹ, אָרֶץ.

Nakḥitah v'kḥasd'kḥa, am zu ga'altah; nehaltah v'azekḥa, el neveh kadsheikḥa.

נָחִיתָ בְחַסְדְּךָ, עַם זוּ גָּאָלְתָּ; נֵהַלְתָּ בְעָזְּךָ, אֶל נְוֵה קָדְשֶׁךָ.

Sham'u ahmim, yirgazun; khil akḥaz, yoshvei p'lashet.

שָׁמְעוּ עַמִּים, יִרְגָּזוּן; חִיל אָחַז, יֹשְׁבֵי פְּלָשֶׁת.

Az nivhalu, alufei Edom elei Mo'av, yokḥazemoh ra'ad; namogu, kal yoshvei Kḥ'na'an.

אָז נִבְהֲלוּ, אַלּוּפֵי אֱדוֹם אֵילֵי מוֹאָב, יֹאחֲזֵמוֹ רָעַד; נָמֹגוּ, כֹּל יֹשְׁבֵי כְנָעַן.

Tipol aleihem eimatah vafakḥad, big'dol zero'akḥa yidmu ka'aven: ahd ya'avor ahm'kḥa יהוה , ad ya'avor ahm zu kanita.

תִּפֹּל עֲלֵיהֶם אֵימָתָה וָפַחַד, בִּגְדֹל זְרוֹעֲךָ יִדְּמוּ כָּאָבֶן: עַד יַעֲבֹר עַמְּךָ יהוה , עַד יַעֲבֹר עַם זוּ קָנִיתָ.

T'vi'emo, v'tita'emo b'har nakḥalateikḥa makḥon l'shivtekḥa pa'altah, יהוה; mikdash, Adonai kon'nu yadeikḥa.

תְּבִאֵמוֹ, וְתִטָּעֵמוֹ בְּהַר נַחֲלָתְךָ מָכוֹן לְשִׁבְתְּךָ פָּעַלְתָּ, יהוה; מִקְּדָשׁ, אֲדֹנָי כּוֹנְנוּ יָדֶיךָ.

יהוה yimlokḥ l'olam va'ed.

יהוה יִמְלֹךְ, לְעֹלָם וָעֶד.

Ki va sus Paroh birkḥ'bo uv'farashav, b'yam, vayashav יהוה aleihem et mei hayam; uv'nei Yisra'el hal'kḥu vayabasha, b'tokḥ hayam.

כִּי בָא סוּס פַּרְעֹה בְּרִכְבּוֹ וּבְפָרָשָׁיו, בַּיָּם, וַיָּשֶׁב יהוה עֲלֵהֶם, אֶת מֵי הַיָּם; וּבְנֵי יִשְׂרָאֵל הָלְכוּ בַיַּבָּשָׁה, בְּתוֹךְ הַיָּם.

41

"I will sing unto יהוה , for He is highly exalted; the horse and his rider has He thrown into the sea. Yah is my strength and my song, and He is become my Yeshu'a[h]; this is my Elohim, and I will glorify Him; my father's Elohim, and I will exalt Him.

יהוה is a man of war, יהוה is His Name. Paroh's chariots and his army has He cast into the sea, and his chosen captains are sunk in Yam Suf. The deeps cover them, they went down into the depths like a stone.

Your right hand, O יהוה , is glorious in power, Your right hand, O יהוה , dashes in pieces the enemy. And in the greatness of Your excellency You overthrow them that rise up against You; You send forth Your wrath, it consumes them as stubble.

And with the blast of Your nostrils the waters were piled up, the floods stood upright as a heap; the deeps were congealed in the heart of the sea. The enemy said, 'I will pursue, I will overtake, I will divide the spoil; my lust shall be satisfied upon them; I will draw my sword, my hand shall destroy them."

You did blow with Your wind, the sea covered them; they sank as lead in the mighty waters. Who is like unto You, O יהוה , among the gods? Who is like unto You, glorious in kodesh, awesome in praises, doing wonders? You stretched out Your right hand, the earth swallowed them. You in Your love have led the people that You have redeemed; You have guided them in Your strength to Your kadosh habitation.

The peoples have heard, they tremble; pangs have taken hold on the inhabitants of Pelashet. Then were the chiefs of Edom affrighted; the mighty men of Mo'av, trembling takes hold upon them; all the inhabitants of Kena'an are melted away. Terror and dread falls upon them; by the greatness of Your arm they are as still as a stone; till Your people pass over, O יהוה , till the people pass over that You have gotten. You bring them in, and plant them in the mountain of Your inheritance, the place, O יהוה , which You have made for You to dwell in, the Mikdash, O יהוה , which Your hands have established. יהוה shall reign forever and ever. For the horses of Paroh went in with his chariots and with

his horsemen into the sea, and יהוה brought back the waters of the sea upon them; but B'nei Yisra'el walked on dry land in the midst of the sea." *(Shemot 15:1-19)*

## Shir Khanah: The Song of Hannah
### *Hebrew first, then English*

**Alatz** libi ba יהוה , **ramah** kar**ni** ba יהוה; Rakh**av** pi al oy**vai**, ki sa**makh**ti bishua**teikh**a.

עָלַץ לִבִּי בַּיהוה, רָמָה קַרְנִי בַּיהוה; רָחַב פִּי עַל אוֹיְבַי, כִּי שָׂמַחְתִּי בִּישׁוּעָתֶךָ.

**Ein** ka**dosh** ka יהוה , ki ein bil**teikh**a; v'**ein** tzur k'Elo**hei**nu.

אֵין קָדוֹשׁ בַּיהוה, כִּי אֵין בִּלְתֶּךָ; וְאֵין צוּר, כֵּאלֹהֵינוּ.

**Al** tar**bu** t'dab'**ru** g'vo**ha** g'vo**ha,** yetzeh atak mipikh**em**: Ki El De'ot יהוה , v'**lo** nit'keinu ali**lot.**

אַל תַּרְבּוּ תְדַבְּרוּ גְּבֹהָה גְּבֹהָה, יֵצֵא עָתָק מִפִּיכֶם: כִּי אֵל דֵּעוֹת יהוה , וְלוֹ נִתְכְּנוּ עֲלִלוֹת.

**Ke**shet gibo**rim,** kha**tim;** v'nikh**shalim,** az**ru** kha**yil.**

קֶשֶׁת גִּבֹּרִים, חַתִּים; וְנִכְשָׁלִים, אָזְרוּ חָיִל.

S've'**im** balekh**em** niskaru, ur'ei**vim** kha'delu, ad aka**rah** yal**dah** shi**vah,** v'ra**bat** ba**nim** um'lala.

שְׂבֵעִים בַּלֶּחֶם נִשְׂכָּרוּ, וּרְעֵבִים חָדֵלּוּ, עַד עֲקָרָה יָלְדָה שִׁבְעָה, וְרַבַּת בָּנִים אֻמְלָלָה.

יהוה , m'**mit** um'kha**yeh;** mo**rid** she'**ol,** vaya'**al.**

יהוה , מֵמִית וּמְחַיֶּה; מוֹרִיד שְׁאוֹל, וַיָּעַל.

יהוה , mo**rish** uma'ah**shir;** mash**pil,** af m'ro**mem.**

יהוה , מוֹרִישׁ וּמַעֲשִׁיר; מַשְׁפִּיל, אַף מְרוֹמֵם.

Me'**kim** me'afar dal, me'ash**pot** yarim ev**yon**, l'ho**shiv** im n'di**vim**, v'k**hiseh** k**havod** yan'k**hilem**: ki la יהוה m'tzu**den** eretz, vaya**shet** a**lei**hem te**vel**.

מֵקִים מֵעָפָר דָּל, מֵאַשְׁפֹּת יָרִים אֶבְיוֹן, לְהוֹשִׁיב עִם נְדִיבִים, וְכִסֵּא כָבוֹד יַנְחִלֵם: כִּי לַיהוה מְצֻקֵי אֶרֶץ, וַיָּשֶׁת עֲלֵיהֶם תֵּבֵל.

Ra**glei** k**hasi**dav yish**mor**, u'resha**yim** bak**hoshek**h yida**mu**: ki lo v'k**ho**'ak**h** yig**bar** ish.

רַגְלֵי חֲסִידָו יִשְׁמֹר, וּרְשָׁעִים בַּחֹשֶׁךְ יִדָּמּוּ: כִּילֹא בְכֹחַ, יִגְבַּר אִישׁ.

יהוה yek**hatu** m'rivav, **alav** bashama**yim** yarem יהוה; Ya**din** af**sei** aretz; v'yiten ohz l'mal**ko**, v'ya**rem** k**eren** Meshi**kho**.

יהוה יֵחַתּוּ מְרִיבָו, עָלָו בַּשָּׁמַיִם יַרְעֵם יהוה, יָדִין אַפְסֵי אָרֶץ; וְיִתֶּן עֹז לְמַלְכּוֹ, וְיָרֵם קֶרֶן מְשִׁיחוֹ.

"My heart exults in יהוה, my horn is exalted in יהוה; my mouth is enlarged over my enemies; because I rejoice in Your Salvation. There is none as kadosh as יהוה, for there is none beside You; neither is there any rock like our Elohim.

Multiply not exceedingly proud talk; let not arrogance come out of your mouth; for יהוה is El De'ut, and by Him actions are weighed.

The bows of the mighty men are broken, and they that stumbled are girded with strength. They that were full have hired out themselves for bread; and they that were hungry have ceased; while the barren has borne seven, she that had many children has languished.

יהוה kills, and makes alive; He brings down to the grave, and brings up. יהוה makes poor, and makes rich; He brings low, He also lifts up. He raises up the poor out of the dust, He lifts up the needy from the dung-hill, to make them sit with princes, and inherit the throne of glory; for the pillars of the earth belong to

יהוה , and He has set the world upon them.

He will keep the feet of His K'doshim, but the wicked shall be put to silence in darkness; for not by strength shall man prevail. They that strive with יהוה shall be broken to pieces; against them will He thunder in heaven;

יהוה will judge the ends of the earth; and He will give strength unto His **Me**lekh, and exalt the horn of His Mashi'akh." ( *Sh'muel Alef 2:1-10)*

## HaElohim Asher
*Hebrew first, then English*

B'k**ḥol** minei afanim u'vk**ḥol** minei tzu**rot**, di**ber** haElo**him** mike**dem** el Avote**inu** banevi'**im**; uv'ak**ḥarit** hayamim ha'eleh di**ber** aleinu biv'**no**, asher sam Oto l'yoresh kol u'**vo** asah et ha'ola**mim**;

בְּכָל מִינֵי אֲפָנִים וּבְכָל מִינֵי צוּרוֹת דִּבֶּר הָאֱלֹהִים מִקֶּדֶם אֶל אֲבוֹתֵינוּ בַּנְּבִיאִים; וּבְאַחֲרִית הַיָּמִים הָאֵלֶּה דִּבֶּר אֵלֵינוּ בִּבְנוֹ, אֲשֶׁר שָׂם אוֹתוֹ לְיוֹרֵשׁ כֹּל וּבוֹ עָשָׂה אֶת הָעוֹלָמִים;

asher hu zohar k'vodo v'tzel**em** yeshuto v'ok**ḥez** ha**kol** b'k**ḥo'akḥ** d'va**ro**; v'Hu b'atz**mo** asah et tihur k**ḥata'einu** v'yashav li**min** hag'dul**ah** bamro**mim**.

אֲשֶׁר הוּא זֹהַר כְּבוֹדוֹ וְצֶלֶם יְשׁוּתוֹ וְאוֹחֵז הַכֹּל בְּכֹחַ דְּבָרוֹ; וְהוּא בְּעַצְמוֹ עָשָׂה אֶת טְהוּר חֲטָאֵינוּ וַיֵּשַׁב לִימִין הַגְּדֻלָּה בַּמְּרוֹמִים.

From of old Elohim spoke to our fathers by the Nevi'im in many forms and in many ways; and in these Akharit HaYamim He has spoken to us by His Son, whom He has appointed as heir of all things, and by whom also He made the worlds; for He is the brightness of His Kavod, and the express image of His Nature, upholding all things by the power of His D'var; and when He had Himself cleansed our sins, then He sat down on the right hand of the Majesty on high. *(Ivrim 1:1-3)*

45

# Tehromem Nafshi

*Hebrew first, then English*

| | |
|---|---|
| Tehromem nafshi et יהוה | תְּרוֹמֵם נַפְשִׁי אֶת יהוה |
| Vatagel rukḥi b'Elohim moshi'i | וַתָּגֵל רוּחִי בֵּאלֹהִים מוֹשִׁיעִי |
| Asher ra'ah b'shefel amatoh, ki hineh me'atah b'rukḥa yikra'uni kol hadorot: | אֲשֶׁר רָאָה בְּשֵׁפֶל אֲמָתוֹ, כִּי הִנֵּה מֵעַתָּה בְּרוּכָה יִקְרָאוּנִי כָּל הַדֹּרוֹת: |
| ki g'dolot asah li, Shadai Hu, v'kadosh sh'moh: | כִּי גְדוֹלוֹת עָשָׂה לִי, שַׁדַּי הוּא, וְקָדוֹשׁ שְׁמוֹ: |
| v'rakḥamav l'dor dorim al yereh'av: | וְרַחֲמָיו לְדוֹר דּוֹרִים עַל יְרֵאָיו: |
| pa'al nitzakḥon bizro'oh ufizer ge'im bimzimot libam: | פָּעַל נִצָּחוֹן בִּזְרוֹעוֹ וּפִזַּר גֵּאִים בִּמְזִמּוֹת לִבָּם: |
| miger takifim mikisotam vayarem sh'falim: | מִגֵּר תַּקִּיפִים מִכִּסְאוֹתָם וַיָּרֵם שְׁפָלִים: |
| r'evim hisbiah tov va'ashirim shilakḥ rekam: | רְעֵבִים הִשְׂבִּיעַ טוֹב וַעֲשִׁירִים שִׁלַּח רֵיקָם: |
| azar l'Yisra'el avdoh lizkor et rakḥamav: | עָזַר לְיִשְׂרָאֵל עַבְדּוֹ לִזְכֹּר אֶת רַחֲמָיו: |
| ka'asher diber im avoteinu, l'Avraham v'im zeroh ad olam. | כַּאֲשֶׁר דִּבֶּר עִם אֲבוֹתֵינוּ לְאַבְרָהָם וְעִם זֶרְעוֹ עַד עוֹלָם: |

"My soul magnifies יהוה , and my spirit rejoices in Elohim my Savior; for He has regarded the meekness of his handmaid; for

behold, from henceforth, He will bless me in all generations. For He who is mighty has done great things for me; Kadosh is His Name.

And His mercy is for ages and generations, upon those who reverence Him. He has brought victory with His arm; He has scattered the proud in the imagination of their heart.

He has put down the mighty from their thrones, and he has lifted up the meek. He has filled the hungry with good things; and dismissed the rich empty. He has helped His servant Yisra'el, and has remembered His mercy, just as He spoke with our forefathers, with Avraham and with his descendants, forever." *(Luka 1:46-55)*

## Pakad et Amo

*Hebrew first, then English*

Barukh יהוה Elohei Yisra'el, ki pakad et amoh ufa'al lo Yeshu'ah

בָּרוּךְ יהוה אֱלֹהֵי יִשְׂרָאֵל כִּי פָּקַד אֶת עַמּוֹ וּפָעַל לוֹ יְשׁוּעָה

V'hekim lanu keren Yeshu'ah b'veit David Avdoh:

וְהֵקִים לָנוּ קֶרֶן יְשׁוּעָה בְּבֵית דָּוִד עַבְדּוֹ:

ka'asher diber b'fi nevi'av hak'doshim asher m'olam:

כַּאֲשֶׁר דִּבֶּר בְּפִי נְבִיאָיו הַקְּדוֹשִׁים אֲשֶׁר מֵעוֹלָם:

Yeshu'ah m'oyveinu u'miyad kol soneinu:

יְשׁוּעָה מֵאֹיְבֵינוּ וּמִיַּד כָּל שׂוֹנְאֵינוּ:

la'asot khasdo im avoteinu v'zakhar et britotav hakod'shot;

לַעֲשׂוֹת חֶסְדּוֹ עִם אֲבוֹתֵינוּ וְזָכַר אֶת בְּרִיתוֹתָיו הַקְּדֹשׁוֹת:

47

| | | |
|---|---|---|
| et hashevu'ot asher nishbah l'Avraham Avinu: | אֶת הַשְּׁבוּעוֹת אֲשֶׁר נִשְׁבַּע לְאַבְרָהָם אָבִינוּ: | |

L'hatzileinu miyad oyveinu ul'avdoh bli pakhad — לְהַצִּילֵנוּ מִיַּד אֹיְבֵינוּ וּלְעָבְדוֹ בְּלִי פַחַד

kol yemei khayeinu bitz'dakah uvik'dusha. — כָּל יְמֵי חַיֵּינוּ בִּצְדָקָה וּבִקְדֻשָׁה.

Blessed is יהוה the Elohim of Yisra'el, for He has visited His people and wrought Salvation for him. And He has raised up a horn of Salvation for us in the house of His servant David;

just as He spoke by the mouth of His Nevi'im K'doshim, who have been for ages, that he would save us from our enemies and from the hand of all who hate us. He has shown mercy to our fathers, and He has remembered His consecrated covenants,

and the oaths which he swore to Avraham our father, to grant to us that we may be saved from the hand of our enemies, and serve before Him without fear, in justice and tzedaka all our days. *(Luka 1:68-75)*

## B'khol Birkhot

*Hebrew first, then English*

Barukh HaElohim Avi Adoneinu Yeshua HaMashi'akh, asher ber'khanu b'khol birkhot haRu'akh bashamayim baMashi'akh. — בָּרוּךְ הָאֱלֹהִים אֲבִי אֲדֹנֵינוּ יֵשׁוּעַ הַמָּשִׁיחַ אֲשֶׁר בֵּרְכָנוּ בְּכָל בִּרְכוֹת הָרוּחַ בַּשָּׁמַיִם בַּמָּשִׁיחַ.

K'fi shehikdim uv'kharanu bo lifnei mos'dot olam liyot k'doshim uv'li mum l'fanav, — כְּפִי שֶׁהִקְדִּים וּבְחָרָנוּ בּוֹ לִפְנֵי מוֹסְדוֹת עוֹלָם לִהְיוֹת קְדוֹשִׁים וּבְלִי מוּם לְפָנָיו,

48

Uv'ahavah hik**dim** v'tzi**yen**
otanu lo v'**sam** otanu
l'va**nim** b'Yeshua
HaMashi'ak**ẖ** katov b'e**nei**
r'tzo**noh,**

וּבְאַהֲבָה הִקְדִּים וְצִיֵּן אוֹתָנוּ
לוֹ וְשָׂם אוֹתָנוּ לְבָנִים בְּיֵשׁוּעַ
הַמָּשִׁיחַ כַּטּוֹב בְּעֵינֵי רְצוֹנוֹ,

L'**ma**'an yishtabak**ẖ** k'vod
k**ẖ**as**do** asher hishpiah
aleinu al ye**dei** ahu**voh.**

לְמַעַן יִשְׁתַּבַּח כְּבוֹד חַסְדּוֹ
אֲשֶׁר הִשְׁפִּיעַ עָלֵינוּ עַל יְדֵי
אֲהוּבוֹ:

**asher** bo yesh **lanu** pe**dut,**
uv'da**moh** slik**ẖat**
hak**ẖ**ata'**im** k'o**sher**
k**ẖ**as**doh:**

אֲשֶׁר בּוֹ יֵשׁ לָנוּ פְּדוּת,
וּבְדָמוֹ סְלִיחַת הַחֲטָאִים
כְּעֹשֶׁר חַסְדּוֹ:

**asher** shafah banu b'k**ẖol**
k**ẖ**ok**ẖmah** uv'**k**ẖol** binah
ruk**ẖ**anit

אֲשֶׁר שָׁפַע בָּנוּ בְּכָל חָכְמָה
וּבְכָל בִּינָה רוּחָנִית

v'hodianu et sod r'tzo**noh**
asher m'**rosh** kavah l'**hotzi**
lapo'**al** bo:

וְהוֹדִיעָנוּ אֶת סוֹד רְצוֹנוֹ
אֲשֶׁר מֵרֹאשׁ קָבַע לְהוֹצִיא
לַפֹּעַל בּוֹ:

l'hes**der** m'**loht** ha'i**tim,**
sh'**kol** mah sh'bashama**yim**
uva'**aretz** shuv yit'k**ẖadash**
baMashi'ak**ẖ,**

לְהֶסְדֵּר מְלֹאת הָעִתִּים,
שֶׁכָּל מַה שֶׁבַּשָּׁמַיִם וּבָאָרֶץ
שׁוּב יִתְחַדֵּשׁ בַּמָּשִׁיחַ,

Lo hayak**ẖol** bigvurah
la'**asoht** l'ma'aneinu yoter
mi**kol,** v'yoter mimah
she'anu m'vak**shim**
v'k**ẖ**osh**vim,** k'**fi** kok**ẖo**
hapo'**el** b'kir**beinu,**

לוֹ הַיָּכוֹל בִּגְבוּרָה לַעֲשׂוֹת
לְמַעֲנֵנוּ יוֹתֵר מִכֹּל, וְיוֹתֵר
מִמַּה שֶׁאָנוּ מְבַקְשִׁים
וְחוֹשְׁבִים, כְּפִי כֹּחוֹ הַפּוֹעֵל
בְּקִרְבֵּנוּ,

Lo hakavod b'kerev adato b'Yeshua HaMashi'akh, l'dor vador olamei haolamim, Amein.

לוֹ הַכָּבוֹד בְּקֶרֶב עֲדָתוֹ בִּישׁוּעַ הַמָּשִׁיחַ, לְדֹר וָדֹר עוֹלְמֵי הָעוֹלָמִים, אָמֵן.

Barukh Elohim, HaAv of Adoneinu Yeshua HaMashi'akh, who has blessed us with all spiritual blessings in heaven through Mashi'akh. Since, as from the beginning, He has chosen us through Him before the foundation of the world, that we may become consecrated and without blemish before Him, in love, as at the first, for Himself. And He marked us for Him, and appointed us to be sons through Yeshua HaMashi'akh, as was the pleasure of His will, to the praise of the glory of His compassion that He has poured upon us by His beloved one. In Him we have redemption, and in His blood, forgiveness of sins, according to the richness of His compassion which has abounded in us in all wisdom and spiritual understanding. And He has made known to us the Sod of His will, that He has ordained from the very beginning, to work through it. He did so in the stewardship of the fullness of times, that all things might be made new in heaven and on earth through Mashi'akh.

Now to Him who is able by power to do for us more than anyone else, and to do for us more than we ask or think, according to His mighty power that works in us, unto Him be glory in His assembly by Yeshua HaMashi'akh throughout all ages, forever and ever. Amein.*(Efisim 1:3-10, 3:20-21)*

50

# BiD'mut Ha'Elohim
*Hebrew first, then English*

Asher af ki hayah bid'mut HaElohim lo l'shalal khashav et zot sh'hu shaveh l'Elohim,

אֲשֶׁר אַף כִּי הָיָה בִּדְמוּת הָאֱלֹהִים לֹא לְשָׁלָל חָשַׁב אֶת זֹאת שֶׁהוּא שָׁוֶה לֵאלֹהִים

elah herik et atzmoh valibash d'mut eved, v'hayah dumah shel b'nei adam v'nimtzah b'tzurah k'ven adam.

אֶלָּא הֵרִיק אֶת עַצְמוֹ וַיִּלְבַּשׁ דְּמוּת עֶבֶד, וְהָיָה דְּמָה שֶׁל בְּנֵי אָדָם וְנִמְצָא בְּצוּרָה כְּבֶן אָדָם,

Vayashpel et atzmoh v'tziyet ad mavet, mitaht hatz'lav.

וַיַּשְׁפֵּל אֶת עַצְמוֹ וְצִיֵּת עַד מָוֶת, מִיתַת הַצְּלָב.

Al ken gam higbiyoh haElohim me'od v'natan lo shem na'aleh mikol hashemot,

עַל כֵּן גַּם הִגְבִּיהוּ הָאֱלֹהִים מְאֹד וְנָתַן לוֹ שֵׁם נַעֲלֶה מִכָּל הַשֵּׁמוֹת,

k'dei she'b'shem Yeshua tikhrah kol berekh asher bashamayim u'va'aretz v'asher mitakhat la'aretz,

כְּדֵי שֶׁבְּשֵׁם יֵשׁוּעַ תִּכְרַע כָּל בֶּרֶךְ אֲשֶׁר בַּשָּׁמַיִם וּבָאָרֶץ וַאֲשֶׁר מִתַּחַת לָאָרֶץ,

v'khol lashon todeh ki יהוה Hu, Yeshua HaMashi'akh, la'shevakh HaElohim Aviv.

וְכָל לָשׁוֹן תּוֹדֶה כִּי יהוה הוּא יֵשׁוּעַ הַמָּשִׁיחַ לְשֶׁבַח הָאֱלֹהִים אָבִיו.

Who, being in the likeness of Elohim, did not consider it robbery to be equal with Elohim; but made Himself of no reputation, and took upon Himself the likeness of a servant, and was in the likeness of the sons of men; and, being found in the form of Ben Adam, He humbled himself and became obedient to death, even the death of the stake;

Therefore, Elohim also has highly exalted Him and given Him a Name which is above every name, that at the Name of Yeshua every knee should bow, of those in heaven, of those on earth, and those under the earth, and every tongue shall confess that He, Yeshua HaMashi'akh, is יהוה , to the glory of Elohim His Father. *(Filipim 2:6-11)*

## Hu D'mut

*Hebrew first, then English*

**V'hu** d'mut haElo**him** ha**bil**ti ni**reh** uv'**khor** kol habri**yot**

וְהוּא דְּמוּד הָאֱלֹהִים הַבִּלְתִּי נִרְאֶה וּבְכוֹר כָּל הַבְּרִיּוֹת;

**uvoh** niv**rah** kol ma sh'basha**may**im uva'**aretz**, kol hani**reh** v'khol **asher** ei**nei**nu ni**reh**, im ki**sot** v'im maru**yot**, **v'im** rashu**yot**, **v'im** shilto**not**, v'**kol** b'ya**doh** ulema'**anei**hu nivra'u:

וּבוֹ נִבְרָא כָּל מַה שֶׁבַּשָּׁמַיִם וּבָאָרֶץ, כָּל הַנִּרְאֶה וְכָל אֲשֶׁר אֵינֶנּוּ נִרְאֶה, אִם כִּסְאוֹת וְאִם מָרֻיוֹת, וְאִם רָשֻׁיוֹת וְאִם שִׁלְטוֹנוֹת, וְכֹל בְּיָדוֹ וּלְמַעֲנֵהוּ נִבְרָאוּ;

**V'hu** b'**terem** hakol v'hakol ka**yam** boh.

וְהוּא בְּטֶרֶם הַכֹּל, וְהַכֹּל קַיָּם בּוֹ.

**V'hu** rosh guf ha'edah **asher** hu harosh hab'**khor** mi**bein** hame**tim**, l'**ma'**an yi**yeh** ri**shon** ba**kol**:

וְהוּא רֹאשׁ גּוּף הָעֵדָה, אֲשֶׁר הוּא הָרֹאשׁ וְהַבְּכוֹר מִבֵּין הַמֵּתִים לְמַעַן יִהְיֶה רִאשׁוֹן בַּכֹּל;

ki khen ha**yah** harat**zon** lish**kon** boh et kol ham'**loh**.

כִּי כֵן הָיָה הָרָצוֹן לִשְׁכֹּן בּוֹ אֶת כָּל הַמְּלוֹא;

ul'ratzot l'atzmo et hakol; v'ritzah b'dam tz'lavoh al yadoh im et asher ba'aretz v'im et asher bashamayim.

וּלְרַצּוֹת לְעַצְמוֹ אֶת הַכֹּל; וְרִצָּה בְּדַם צְלָבוֹ עַל יָדוֹ אִם אֶת אֲשֶׁר בָּאָרֶץ וְאִם אֶת אֲשֶׁר בַּשָּׁמַיִם.

He is the image of the invisible Elohim, and the first-born of every creature: and through Him were created all things that are in heaven and on earth, visible and invisible; whether imperial thrones, or dominions, or principalities, or powers, all things were in His hand and were created by Him;

and He is before all things, and by Him all things are sustained. And He is the Head of the body, the assembly; for He is the beginning, the firstborn of the resurrection from the dead, that in all things He might be the first;

for it pleased Elohim that in Him all fullness should dwell; and by His hand to reconcile everything to Himself; and through His blood, shed on the stake, to make shalom both for those who dwell on earth and for those who dwell in heaven. *(Kolossim 1:15-20)*

## Mashi'akh Eved HaY'hudim
*Hebrew first, then English*

Va'Ani omer sh'Yeshua HaMashi'akh sheret et hamilah l'ma'an emet haElohim, k'dei l'kayem et hahav'takha asher la'avot:

וַאֲנִי אֹמֵר שֶׁיֵּשׁוּעַ הַמָּשִׁיחַ שֵׁרֵת אֶת הַמִּילָה לְמַעַן אֱמֶת הָאֱלֹהִים, כְּדֵי לְקַיֵּם אֶת הַהַבְטָחָה אֲשֶׁר לָאָבוֹת.

V'hagoyim y'shab'khu et haElohim l'ma'an rakhamav aleihem, kakatuv: Odekha bagoyim u'leshimkha azam'rah.

וְהַגּוֹיִים יְשַׁבְּחוּ אֶת הָאֱלֹהִים לְמַעַן רַחֲמָיו עֲלֵיהֶם כַּכָּתוּב: אוֹדְךָ בַגּוֹיִם וּלְשִׁמְךָ אֲזַמֵּרָה.

V'od amar, gilu goyim im amoh.

וְעוֹד אָמַר: גִּילוּ גוֹיִם עִם עַמּוֹ.

V'od amar, Hallelu et יהוה kol goyim shabekḥuhu kol ha'umim:

וְעוֹד אָמַר: הַלְלוּ אֶת יהוה כָּל גּוֹיִם, שַׁבְּחוּהוּ כָּל הָאֻמִּים.

V'od Yesha-Yahu amar, v'yihyeh shoresh Yishai asher omed l'nes amim, elaiv goyim lidrosh:

וְעוֹד יְשַׁעְיָהוּ אָמַר: וְיִהְיֶה שֹׁרֶשׁ יְשַׁי אֲשֶׁר עֹמֵד לְנֵס עַמִּים, אֵלָיו גּוֹיִם יִדְרֹשׁוּ.

V'Elohei hatikvah hu y'maleh etkhem kol simkḥa v'shalom ba'emunah, l'ma'an tishpe'u b'tikvato big'vurat Ru'akḥ HaKodesh.

וֵאלֹהֵי הַתִּקְוָה הוּא יְמַלֵּא אֶתְכֶם כָּל שִׂמְחָה וְשָׁלוֹם בָּאֱמוּנָה, לְמַעַן תִּשְׁפְּעוּ בְּתִקְוָתוֹ בִּגְבוּרַת רוּחַ הַקֹּדֶשׁ.

Now I say that Yeshua HaMashi'akh was a minister of the circumcision, for the truth of Elohim, to confirm the promises made to the fathers, and that the Goyim might glorify Elohim for His mercies which were poured upon them; as it is written, "Therefore I will praise you among the Goyim and sing to your name." And again He says, "Rejoice, Goyim, with His people." And again, He says, "Praise יהוה, all Goyim; and praise Him, all nations." And again Yesha-Yahu said, "There shall be a root of Yishai, and He that shall rise will be a prince to the Goyim; unto him shall the nations seek."

Now may the Elohim of hope fill you with all joy and shalom, so that by absolute trust you may abound in hope, through the power of The Ru'akh HaKodesh. *(Romim 15:8-13)*

## Tefillat HaTalmidim: The Disciples' Prayer
*Hebrew first, then English*

Avinu sh'bashamayim, yitkadesh shimkha. Tavoh malkhutekha, y'aseh retzonkha k'vahshamayim gam ba'aretz.

אָבִנוּ שֶׁבַּשָּׁמַיִם, יִתְקַדֵּשׁ שְׁמְךָ, תָּבוֹא מַלְכוּתֶךָ, יֵעָשֶׂה רְצוֹנְךָ כְּבַשָּׁמַיִם גַּם בָּאָרֶץ.

Ten lanu et lekhem tzarkenu hayom, Um'khol lanu et khovoteinu kemo shegam anakhnu makholnu l'khayaveinu.

תֵּן לָנוּ אֶת לֶחֶם צָרְכֵּנוּ הַיּוֹם, וּמְחַל לָנוּ אֶת חוֹבוֹתֵינוּ כְּמוֹ שֶׁגַּם אֲנַחְנוּ מָחַלְנוּ לְחַיָּבֵינוּ.

V'al tevi'enu lidei nisayon, elah hatzileinu min hara, ki shelkha hi hamalkhut v'hagevurah v'hatifarah l'olemei olamim.

וְאַל תְּבִיאֵנוּ לִידֵי נִסָּיוֹן, אֶלָּא הַצִּילֵנוּ מִן הָרָע, כִּי שֶׁלְּךָ הִיא הַמַּלְכוּת וְהַגְּבוּרָה וְהַתִּפְאָרָה לְעוֹלְמֵי עוֹלָמִים.

'Avinu Sh'bah Shamayim, may Your Name be made kadosh. May Your Kingdom come. May Your will be done, as in Heaven, so on earth.

Give us the bread we need today. And forgive us our offenses, as we have forgiven our offenders;

And do not lead us into the power of testing, but deliver us from the Evil One. Because Yours is HaMalkhut, and the power, and the glory, for ever and ever. Amein.' ( *Matai 6:9-13* )

## Na'eh LaSeh
*Hebrew first, then English*

Kadosh Kadosh Kadosh יהוה Elohim Okhez HaKol, Hayah V'Hoveh, V'Yihyeh.

קָדוֹשׁ קָדוֹשׁ קָדוֹשׁ יהוה אֱלֹהִים אוֹחֵז הַכֹּל, הָיָה וְהֹוֶה וְיִהְיֶה.

L'kha na'eh, יהוה Eloheinu, HaKadosh, laset kevod, vikar, ug'vurah, ki Atah baratah hakol v'hakol bir'tzon'kha hayu v'nivra'u.

לְךָ נָאֶה יהוה אֱלֹהֵינוּ הַקָּדוֹשׁ לָשֵׂאת כָּבוֹד וִיקָר וּגְבוּרָה כִּי אַתָּה בָּרָאתָ הַכֹּל וְהַכֹּל בִּרְצוֹנְךָ הָיוּ וְנִבְרָאוּ.

Na'eh LaSeh HaTavu'akh, l'kabel ko'akh v'osher v'khokhma v'oz vikar v'tiferet uv'rakha

נָאֶה לַשֶּׂה הַטָּבוּחַ לְקַבֵּל כֹּחַ וְעֹשֶׁר וְחָכְמָה וְעֹז וִיקָר וְתִפְאֶרֶת וּבְרָכָה.

V'khol briyah asher bashamayim v'al ha'aretz umitakhat la'aretz va'asher al hayam, v'khol asher bahem, et kulam shamati omrim: Layoshev al hakiseh v'laseh, hab'rakha v'haikar v'hatiferet v'hashilton l'olamei olamim.

וְכָל בְּרִיָּה אֲשֶׁר בַּשָּׁמַיִם וְעַל הָאָרֶץ וּמִתַּחַת לָאָרֶץ וַאֲשֶׁר עַל הַיָּם, וְכָל אֲשֶׁר בָּהֶם, אֶת כֻּלָּם שָׁמַעְתִּי אוֹמְרִים: לַיּוֹשֵׁב עַל הַכִּסֵּא וְלַשֶּׂה הַבְּרָכָה וְהַיְקָר וְהַתִּפְאֶרֶת וְהַשִּׁלְטוֹן לְעוֹלְמֵי עוֹלָמִים.

Shabekhu et Eloheinu kol avadav vire'av, hak'tanim im hag'dolim!

שַׁבְּחוּ אֶת אֱלֹהֵינוּ כָּל עֲבָדָיו וִירֵאָיו, הַקְּטַנִּים עִם הַגְּדוֹלִים!

Kadosh, Kadosh, Kadosh, יהוה Elohim Okhez HaKol, who was, and is, and will be. You are worthy, Adoneinu and Elohim, to receive glory and honor and power, for You have created all things, and by You they are, and by Your will they exist, and were created. *(Hitgalut 4:8, 11)* Worthy is HaSeh that was slain, to receive power, and riches, and wisdom, and might, and honor, and glory and blessing." And every creature which is in heaven and on the earth and under the earth, and all that are in the sea and all that are in them, I heard saying, "To Him who sits on the throne, and to HaSeh, be blessing, and honor, and glory, and dominion, forever and ever. *(Hitgalut 5:12-13)* Praise our Elohim, all you His servants

56

and you who worship Him, both small and great! *(Hitgalut 19:5)*

# MESSIAH

| | | | |
|---|---|---|---|
| Barukh | Atah | יהוה | בָּרוּךְ אַתָּה יהוה , אֱלֹהֵינוּ, |
| Eloheinu, | | Melekh | מֶלֶךְ הָעוֹלָם, אֲשֶׁר נָתַן לָנוּ |
| ha'olam, asher natan lanu | | | אֶת דֶּרֶךְ הַיְשׁוּעָה בְּמָשִׁיחַ |
| et derekh hayeshu'ah | | | יֵשׁוּעַ. |
| baMashi'akh | | Yeshua. | |
| Amein. | | | |

Blessed are You, O יהוה our Elohim, King of the Universe, Who has given us the way of Salvation in Messiah Yeshua.

And HaDavar became a Body and dwelt among us, and we saw His glory, a glory like that of the first-born of Ha'Av, full of compassion and truth. For He who did not know sin, for our sakes He became a Khatat, that we may through Him be made the tzedaka of Elohim. *(Yokhanan 1:14, Korinti'im Bet 5:21)*

And you also are familiar with the news which was published throughout Y'hudah, which sprang from the Galil, after the immersion declared by Yokhanan, concerning Yeshua from Natzrat, whom Elohim anointed with The Ru'akh HaKodesh and with power, and who, because Elohim was with Him, went about doing good and healing all who were oppressed by evil. *(Ma'asei HaShlikhim 10:37-38)*

They found Him in the Heikhal, sitting in the midst of the teachers, listening to them and asking them questions. And all those who heard Him were amazed at His wisdom and His answers. *(Luka 2:46-47)*

He taught on Shabbat in their Beit K'nessets. And they were amazed at His teaching; for He taught them as one with authority. And Yeshua travelled in all the cities and villages, teaching in their Beit K'nessets, and declaring B'sorat HaMalkhut, and healing every kind of sickness and disease. Yeshua said to them, "Allow the little children to come to Me, and do not stop them, for Malkhut HaShamayim is for such as

these." When Yeshua saw the multitudes, He had mercy on them, because they were tired out and scattered, like sheep which have no shepherd. *(Yokhanan Markos 1:21-22, Matai 9:36)*

He had no form nor comeliness that we should look upon Him, nor beauty that we should delight in Him. He was despised, and forsaken of men, a man of pains, and acquainted with sorrows, and as one from whom men hide their faces: He was despised, and we esteemed Him not. Surely our sickness He did bear, and our pains he carried; whereas we did esteem Him stricken, smitten of Elohim, and afflicted. But He was wounded because of our transgressions, He was broken because of our iniquities: the chastisement of our shalom was upon Him, and with His stripes we were healed. All we like sheep did go astray, we turned every one to his own way; and יהוה has made to light on Him the iniquity of us all. *(Yesha-Yahu 53:2-6)*

And you, who once were dead in your sins and the uncircumcision of your flesh, He has granted to live with Him, and He has forgiven you all your sins; and by His mitzvot He cancelled the written record of our sins, which stood against us; and He took it out of the way, nailing it to His stake; and by putting off His mortal body, He exposed the powers of evil, and through His nature put them openly to shame. *(Kolosim 2:13-15)*

Mashi'akh died for our sins according to the scriptures; and He was buried, and He rose again on the third day according to the scriptures. And now we know Mashi'akh is risen from the dead, and has become the firstfruits of those who have died. And thanks be to Elohim, who has given us the victory through Adoneinu Yeshua HaMashi'akh! *(Korinti'im Alef 15:3,20,57)*

Blessed are You, O יהוה our Elohim, King of the Universe, Who has given us Messiah Yeshua, our KING!

Barukh Atah יהוה בָּרוּךְ אַתָּה יהוה , אֱלֹהֵינוּ,
Eloheinu, Melekh ha'olam, מֶלֶךְ הָעוֹלָם, אֲשֶׁר נָתַן לָנוּ
asher natan lanu Mashi'akh מָשִׁיחַ יֵשׁוּעַ, מַלְכֵּנוּ.
Yeshua, Malkeinu! Amein.

# Ț̣oₐₐₕ ᴘ̣ₒₒₑₛₛₒₙ אמ

## Honoring the Torah as the likeness of Messiah

Yeshua is the "D'var," the "Word," The Torah, (Yesha-Yahu 2:3) or the living expression of the heart of Elohim in flesh. The written word, rooted in the Torah, from which all the rest of His Word derives its authority and truth, has been sufficiently preserved through the Jewish people for 4000 years. To honor the written word as a "Shadow" of Messiah and His perfect obedience is not to worship the Torah itself, but to worship the one who gave it to us: on the tablets of Moshe, on the scrolls, and ultimately, in the body of Messiah Yeshua Himself. The scroll comes out of the "ark," descends, is honored [not worshipped] by the congregants with a touch. It ascends again to the Bimah, and is declared. This hearkens to the fact that Messiah came out of His Father, to earth, was honored, was seen, touched, held, and heard, and ascended again, clearly declaring His Father's will to us by the Ru'akh, through the written word.

## Ein Kamokḥa: There Is NONE Like You

### Congregation rises as the Ark is Opened
#### Leader and Congregation together
*Hebrew first, then English*

Ein kamokḥa va'elo**him**, Adonai , v'**ein** k'ma'aseikḥa. Malkḥuteikḥa Malkḥut kol ola**mim**, u'memshalteikḥa b'**khol** dor va dor. יהוה me**lekh**. יהוה ma**lakh**. יהוה yim**lokh** l'olam va'**ed**. יהוה oz l'a**mo**, yiten y'varekḥ et a**mo** va'sha**lom**.

אֵין כָּמוֹךָ בָאֱלֹהִים, אֲדֹנָי , וְאֵין כְּמַעֲשֶׂיךָ. מַלְכוּתְךָ מַלְכוּת כָּל עֹלָמִים, וּמֶמְשַׁלְתְּךָ בְּכָל דֹּר וָדֹר. יהוה מֶלֶךְ, יהוה מָלָךְ, יהוה יִמְלֹךְ לְעֹלָם וָעֶד. יהוה עֹז לְעַמּוֹ יִתֵּן, יהוה יְבָרֵךְ אֶת עַמּוֹ בַשָּׁלוֹם

There is none like unto You among the gods, O Adonai , and there are no works like Yours. *(Tehillah 86:8)* Your Malkhut is a kingdom for all ages, and Your dominion endures throughout all generations: *(Tehillah 145:13)*

יהוה reigns, יהוה has reigned, יהוה will reign forever. יהוה will give strength unto His people; יהוה will bless His people with shalom. *(Tehillah 146:10, 29:11)*

## Av Harakḥamim: Father of Compassion

Leader and Congregation together:
*Hebrew first, then English*

Av HaRakḥamim, hetivah virtzonkḥah et Tzion, tivneh khomot Yerushalayim. Ki v'kḥa l'vad batakḥnu, Melekh El ram v'nisah, Adon olamim.

אַב הָרַחֲמִים, הֵיטִיבָה בִרְצוֹנְךְ אֶת צִיּוֹן, תִּבְנֶה חוֹמוֹת יְרוּשָׁלָיִם. כִּי בְךְ לְבַד בָּטָחְנוּ, מֶלֶךְ אֵל רָם וְנִשָּׂא, אֲדוֹן עוֹלָמִים

Father of compassion, deal kindly with Tzion according to your will. Rebuild the walls of Yerushalayim, for we trust You alone, O King, revered and honored Elohim, Master over the entire universe. *(Tehillah 51:20)*

## Vayehi Binsoah Ha'Aron

### When the Ark Went Forward
### The Torah rises to 'go forth'

Va'yehi binsoah haAron, vayomer Moshe, "Kumah, יהוה , v'yefutzu oyeveikḥa, v'yanusu me'saneikḥa mi paneikḥa; Ki mi Tzion tetze Torah, ud'var יהוה miYerushalayim; Barukḥ sh'natan Torah l'amo Yisra'el bik'dushatoh."

וַיְהִי בִּנְסֹעַ הָאָרֹן וַיֹּאמֶר מֹשֶׁה, קוּמָה, יהוה , וְיָפֻצוּ אֹיְבֶיךָ, וְיָנֻסוּ מְשַׂנְאֶיךָ מִפָּנֶיךָ. כִּי מִצִיּוֹן תֵּצֵא תוֹרָה, וּדְבַר יהוה מִירוּשָׁלָיִם; בָּרוּךְ שֶׁנָּתַן תּוֹרָה לְעַמּוֹ יִשְׂרָאֵל בִּקְדֻשָׁתוֹ

And it came to pass, when the Aron set forward, that Moshe would say, "**Arise**, O יהוה , and let Your enemies be **scattered**; and let those who hate You **flee** from before You." For from Tzion shall go forth the Torah, and the word of יהוה from Yerushalayim. Blessed is He who in holiness gave the Torah to His People, Yisra'el." *(BaMidbar 10:35, Yesha-Yahu 2:3)*

The Torah is escorted through the congregation and honored, as if Messiah Himself were in our presence. We do not worship the Torah, except that we worship Messiah Yeshua, the LIVING TORAH. The Torah scroll then, is a 'picture' of the Messiah leaving the heart of His Father, descending, touching and being touched and honored, and then ascending again. It is honored by the congregation, reminding us that any who 'honored' Him while He was here were healed, comforted, loved, and even raised from the dead. The Torah then ascends to the Bimah, from where it will be read. Messiah Yeshua ascended, and from heaven He declares His Truth to us.

## Shemah!: The Greatest of Commandments
*sing all together*

**Shema, Yisra'el:** יהוה יהוה  שְׁמַע, יִשְׂרָאֵל:
**Eloheinu,** יהוה **Ekḥad.**  אֱלֹהֵינוּ, יהוה אֶחָד.

**Barukḥ Shem K'vod,** מַלְכוּתוֹ כְּבוֹד שֵׁם בָּרוּךְ
**Malkḥuto, L'Olam Va'ed.**  לְעֹלָם וָעֶד

Hear, O Yisra'el: יהוה is our Elohim, יהוה is ONE. Blessed is the name of His Glorious Kingdom forever and ever. *(D'varim 6:4)*

## Ekḥad Eloheinu: Our Elohim is ONE

**Ekḥad** Eloheinu, **Gadol** אֲדוֹנֵנוּ, גָּדוֹל אֱלֹהֵינוּ, אֶחָד
Adoneinu, **Kadosh** קָדוֹשׁ שְׁמוֹ.
Shemoh.

Gad'lu la יהוה iti; וּנְרוֹמְמָה אִתִּי; לַיהוה גַּדְּלוּ
uneromeima sh'moh שְׁמוֹ יַחְדָּו.
yakhdav.

Our Elohim is One; Great is our Adon; Holy is His Name. O magnify יהוה with me, let us exalt His Name together! *(Tehillah 34:4)*

## Mi Kamokḥa: Who is Like You

Mi kamokḥa ba'elim יהוה? , מִי כָמֹכָה בָּאֵלָם יהוה
Mi kamokḥa, ne'edar מִי כָמֹכָה נֶאְדָּר בַּקֹּדֶשׁ;
bakodesh; nora tehilot, נוֹרָא תְהִלֹּת, עֹשֵׂה פֶלֶא.
oseh feleh.

Who is like unto You, O יהוה , among the gods? Who is like unto
You, glorious in kodesh, awesome in praises, doing wonders?
*(Shemot 15:11)*

# TORAH CEREMONY

## Blessing the Oleh/Olah

To honor our members, an "Oleh," or "The one who ascends," is called to the Bimah to read from the weekly parasha schedule, usually on the anniversary of that person's Hebrew birth date. This blessing is recited in order to recognize the honored person and send blessings upon him and his family. Yeshua was called to the Bimah to read from Isaiah 61, at "his turn." He was the "Oleh" that day (Luke 4:16-20).

Leader and Congregation together
*Hebrew then English*

Mi Sheberakḥ Avoteinu: Avraham, Yitz'kḥak, v'Ya'akov, Hu yevarekḥ et: {State the name of the Oleh/Olah}

מִי שֶׁבֵּרַךְ אֲבוֹתֵינוּ: אַבְרָהָם יִצְחָק וְיַעֲקֹב, הוּא יְבָרֵךְ אֶת

Sheh alah likhvod ha makom, v'likhvod haTorah. HaKadosh, Barukh hu, yishmarehu, v'yagtzileihu mikol tzara v'tzuka, u'mikol negah u'makhalah; v'yishlakh b'rakha v'hatzlakha b'kḥol ma'aseh yadav. Amein.

שֶׁעָלָה לִכְבוֹד הַמָּקוֹם וְלִכְבוֹד הַתּוֹרָה. הַקָּדוֹשׁ, בָּרוּךְ הוּא, יִשְׁמְרֵהוּ, וְיַגְצִילֵהוּ מִכָּל צָרָה וְצוּקָה, וּמִכָּל נֶגַע וּמַחֲלָה; וְיִשְׁלַח בְּרָכָה וְהַצְלָחָה בְּכָל מַעֲשֵׂה יָדָיו: אָמֵן.

May He who blessed our Fathers: Abraham, Isaac and Jacob, may He bless:

{State the name of the Oleh/Olah}

Who has come up to honor this place, and to honor the Torah. May the Holy One bless him, protect him, and deliver him from all tribulation and oppression, and from every plague and illness; and may He send blessing and prosperity on all the work of his hands. Amein.

## Barkḥu: We bless: A Call to Prayer
### Leader sings

Barkḥu et יהוה haMevorakḥ.

בָּרְכוּ אֶת יהוה הַמְבֹרָךְ

Bless יהוה , the Blessed One. *(Tehillah 89:52)*

*leader and congregation sing Hebrew together*

Barukḥ יהוה haMevorakḥ le'olam va'ed.

בָּרוּךְ יהוה הַמְבֹרָךְ לְעוֹלָם וָעֶד

Blessed is יהוה , The Blessed One for all eternity. *(Tehillah 106:48)*

*leader and congregation sing Hebrew together*

Barukḥ Atah, יהוה , Eloheinu, Melekḥ ha'olam, asher bakḥar banu mikol ha'amim v'natan lanu et torato. Barukḥ Atah יהוה , noten haTorah.

בָּרוּךְ אַתָּה יהוה , אֱלֹהֵינוּ , מֶלֶךְ הָעוֹלָם, אֲשֶׁר בָּחַר בָּנוּ מִכָּל הָעַמִּים וְנָתַן לָנוּ אֶת תּוֹרָתוֹ. בָּרוּךְ אַתָּה יהוה , נוֹתֵן הַתּוֹרָה.

Blessed are You, O יהוה our Elohim, King of the Universe, Who has chosen us from all peoples, and has given us Your Torah. Blessed are You O יהוה , giver of the Torah.

## Torah Portion is Read by the Oleh/Olah

## Blessing After Reading Torah

*leader and congregation sing Hebrew together*

Barukh Atah יהוה , Eloheinu, Melekh HaOlam, asher natan lanu Torat emet, v'khayei olam nata b'tokheinu; Barukh Atah יהוה , noten haTorah.

בָּרוּךְ אַתָּה יהוה אֱלֹהֵינוּ מֶלֶךְ הָעוֹלָם, אֲשֶׁר נָתַן לָנוּ תּוֹרַת אֱמֶת, וְחַיֵּי עוֹלָם נָטַע בְּתוֹכֵנוּ. בָּרוּךְ אַתָּה יהוה , נוֹתֵן הַתּוֹרָה.

Blessed are You, O יהוה our Elohim, King of the Universe, who gave us the Torah of truth and planted among us life eternal. Blessed are You, O יהוה , giver of the Torah.

## Blessing of the Haftarah

Barukh Atah, יהוה , Eloheinu, Melekh HaOlam, asher bakhar b'nevi'im tovim, v'ratzah v'divreihem, ha'ne'emarim b'emet; Barukh Atah יהוה , habokher baTorah u'v'Moshe avdoh, uv'Yisra'el amo, u'vinehvi'ei ha'emet v'tzedek.

בָּרוּךְ אַתָּה יהוה אֱלֹהֵינוּ מֶלֶךְ הָעוֹלָם, אֲשֶׁר בָּחַר בִּנְבִיאִים טוֹבִים, וְרָצָה בְדִבְרֵיהֶם הַנֶּאֱמָרִים בֶּאֱמֶת, בָּרוּךְ אַתָּה יהוה , הַבּוֹחֵר בַּתּוֹרָה וּבְמֹשֶׁה עַבְדּוֹ, וּבְיִשְׂרָאֵל עַמּוֹ, וּבִנְבִיאֵי הָאֱמֶת וָצֶדֶק.

Blessed are You, O יהוה our Elohim, King of the Universe, who selected good Nevi'im, delighting in their words, which were spoken truthfully. Blessed are You, O יהוה , who chose the Torah, your servant Moshe, your people Yisra'el, and the Nevi'im of truth and righteousness.

## Haftarah Portion is Read by the Oleh/Olah

# Blessing After Reading the Haftarah
### Leader and Congregation together
*Hebrew then English*

בָּרוּךְ אַתָּה יהוה אֱלֹהֵינוּ
מֶלֶךְ הָעוֹלָם, צוּר כָּל
הָעוֹלָמִים, צַדִּיק בְּכָל
הַדּוֹרוֹת, הָאֵל הַנֶּאֱמָן
הָאוֹמֵר וְעֹשֶׂה, הַמְדַבֵּר
וּמְקַיֵּם, שֶׁכָּל דְּבָרָיו אֱמֶת
וָצֶדֶק. נֶאֱמָן אַתָּה; הוּא
יהוה אֱלֹהֵינוּ, וְנֶאֱמָנִים
דְּבָרֶיךָ, וְדָבָר אֶחָד
מִדְּבָרֶיךָ אָחוֹר לֹא יָשׁוּב
רֵיקָם, כִּי אֵל מֶלֶךְ נֶאֱמָן
וְרַחֲמָן אָתָּה. בָּרוּךְ אַתָּה
יהוה הָאֵל הַנֶּאֱמָן בְּכָל
דְּבָרָיו.

Barukḥ Atah יהוה, Eloheinu, Melekḥ HaOlam, tzur kol haOlamim, tzadik b'kḥol hadoroht; Ha El HaNe'ehman, ha'omer v'oseh, ha'medaber u'mekayem. Sh'kol d'varav emet vatzedek. Ne'eman Atah; Hu יהוה Eloheinu, v'ne'emanim d'vareikḥa, v'davar ekḥad mid'vareikḥa akḥor lo yashuv reikam, ki El Melekḥ ne'eman v'rakḥaman Atah. Barukḥ Atah יהוה, Ha El ha'ne'eman b'kḥol d'varav.

Rakhem al Tziyon, ki hi beit khayeinu, v'la'aluvaht nefesh toshia bimherah v'yameinu. Barukh Atah יהוה , mesame'akh Tziyon b'vanei'ha. Sahmkheinu, יהוה Eloheinu b'Eliyahu HaNavi av'deikha, uv'malkhut beit David Meshikheikha, bimherah yahvoh v'yagel libeinu, al kisoh lo yeshev zar, v'lo yin'khalu od akherim et k'vodoh, ki v'shem kadsheikha nishba'etah lo sh'lo yikhbeh gero l'olam va'ed. Barukh Atah יהוה , Magen David.

רַחֵם עַל צִיּוֹן כִּי הִיא בֵּית חַיֵּינוּ, וְלַעֲלוּבַת נֶפֶשׁ תּוֹשִׁיעַ בִּמְהֵרָה בְיָמֵינוּ. בָּרוּךְ אַתָּה יהוה , מְשַׂמֵּחַ צִיּוֹן בְּבָנֶיהָ. שַׂמְּחֵנוּ יהוה אֱלֹהֵינוּ בְּאֵלִיָּהוּ הַנָּבִיא עַבְדֶּךָ, וּבְמַלְכוּת בֵּית דָּוִד מְשִׁיחֶךָ, בִּמְהֵרָה יָבֹא וְיָגֵל לִבֵּנוּ, עַל כִּסְאוֹ לֹא יֵשֶׁב זָר, וְלֹא יִנְחֲלוּ עוֹד אֲחֵרִים אֶת כְּבוֹדוֹ, כִּי בְשֵׁם קָדְשְׁךָ נִשְׁבַּעְתָּ לוֹ שֶׁלֹּא יִכְבֶּה גֵרוֹ לְעוֹלָם וָעֶד. בָּרוּךְ אַתָּה יהוה , מָגֵן דָּוִד

Blessed are You, O יהוה our Elohim, King of the Universe, Rock of all ages, righteous throughout all generations. You are the faithful God, promising and then performing, first speaking and then fulfilling, for all your words are true and righteous. Faithful are you, O יהוה our Elohim, and faithful are your words, for no word of yours shall remain unfulfilled. You are a faithful and merciful Elohim and King.

Blessed are You, O יהוה our Elohim, who are faithful in fulfilling all your words. Have mercy on Tzion, it is the fountain of our life, and very soon deliver her who grieves deeply. Blessed are You, O יהוה , who makes Tzion rejoice with her children. Make us joyful, O יהוה our Elohim, with the Navi, Eli-Yahu your servant, and with the kingdom of the House of David your anointed. May Eli-Yahu come soon, and bring joy to our hearts. Allow no stranger to sit on David's throne or inherit his glory. For by your Holy Name You swore to him that his light would not be quenched forever. Blessed are You, O יהוה , the Shield of David.

# Blessing of the Brit Khadasha
Leader and Congregation together
*Hebrew then English*

Barukh Atah יהוה ,
Eloheinu, **Melekh** HaOlam,
**asher** natan lanu
Mashi'akh Yeshua
v'had'va**rim** shel Brit
HaKhada**shah**; Baru**kh**
Atah יהוה , no**ten** Brit
HaKhada**shah**.

בָּרוּךְ אַתָּה יהוה אֱלֹהֵינוּ
מֶלֶךְ הָעוֹלָם, אֲשֶׁר נָתַן לָנוּ
מָשִׁיחַ יֵשׁוּעַ וְהַדְּבָרִים שֶׁל
בְּרִית הַחֲדָשָׁה. בָּרוּךְ
אַתָּה יהוה , נוֹתֵן בְּרִית
הַחֲדָשָׁה.

Blessed are You, O יהוה our Elohim, King of the Universe, who
has given us Messiah Yeshua and the words of the Brit
Khadashah. Blessed are You, O יהוה , giver of the Brit
Khadashah.

## Brit Khadashah Portion is Read by the Oleh/Olah

# Blessing After Reading the Brit Khadasha
Leader and Congregation together
*Hebrew then English*

Barukh Atah יהוה ,
Eloheinu, Melekh
HaOlam, **asher** natan lanu
D'var Emet, V'kh**ayei**
Olam natah betokh**einu.**
Baru**kh** Atah יהוה , no**ten**
Brit HaKhada**shah**.

בָּרוּךְ אַתָּה יהוה אֱלֹהֵינוּ
מֶלֶךְ הָעוֹלָם, אֲשֶׁר נָתַן לָנוּ
דְּבַר אֱמֶת וְחַיֵּי עוֹלָם נָטַע
בְּתוֹכֵנוּ. בָּרוּךְ אַתָּה יהוה ,
נוֹתֵן בְּרִית הַחֲדָשָׁה.

Blessed are You, O יהוה our Elohim, King of the Universe, who
has given us the Word of Truth, and planted among us life
eternal. Blessed are You, O יהוה , giver of the Brit Khadashah.

# Congregational Response After Reading the Torah

V'**zot** haTorah asher sam Moshe lif**nei** b'**nei** Yisra'el al pi יהוה b'**yad Mo**she; Etz kḫayim hi, lamakḫazi**kim** bah; v'tom'**khei**'ah m'u**shar**; d'rakḫeiha darkḫei no'**am**. V'**kḫol** n'tivotei'ha shalom; orekḫ ya**mim** biminah; Bismolah osher v'khavod; יהוה khafetz l'ma'an tzidko, yag**dil** Torah v'ya'**dir**.

וְזֹאת, הַתּוֹרָה, אֲשֶׁר שָׂם מֹשֶׁה, לִפְנֵי בְּנֵי יִשְׂרָאֵל עַל פִּי יהוה בְּיַד מֹשֶׁה: עֵץ חַיִּים הִיא, לַמַּחֲזִיקִים בָּהּ; וְתֹמְכֶיהָ מְאֻשָּׁר; דְּרָכֶיהָ דַרְכֵי נֹעַם; וְכָל נְתִיבוֹתֶיהָ שָׁלוֹם; אֹרֶךְ יָמִים, בִּימִינָהּ; בִּשְׂמֹאולָהּ, עֹשֶׁר וְכָבוֹד; יהוה חָפֵץ, לְמַעַן צִדְקוֹ; יַגְדִּיל תּוֹרָה, וְיַאְדִּיר.

And this is The Torah which Moshe set before B'nei Yisra'el. *(D'varim 4:44)* It is in accord with the direction of יהוה by the hand of Moshe. *(BaMidbar 9:23)* It is an Etz Khayim to them that lay hold upon it, and happy is every one that cleaves unto it. Its ways are ways of pleasantness, and all its paths are shalom; Length of days is in its right hand; in its left hand are riches and honor. *(Mishlim 3:16-18)* יהוה was pleased, for the sake of His tzedaka, to make The Torah **great** and **glorious**. *(Yesha-Yahu 42:21)*

*Traditional melody's lyrics*

Etz Kḫayim hi, la'makḫazikim bah, v'tomkḫe'ah me'ushar. D'rakḫeiha darkḫei no'am, v'kḫol netivotei'ha shalom.

Hashiveinu יהוה , eleikḫa v'nashuvah. Kḫadesh, kḫadesh yameinu; kḫadesh yameinu k'kedem. *(Eikha 5:21)*

*On Yom Teruah, go to page 160*

*On Yom Kippur go to page 180*

# D'rash

# Aleinu: It is Our Duty

Congregation Rises :: Leader and Congregation together
*Hebrew then English*

Aleinu l'shabeakh la'adon hakol. Latet gedulah l'yotzer b'reshiit. Sh'lo asanu k'goyei ha'aratzot. V'lo samanu k'mishpekhot ha'adamah. Sh'lo sam khelkenu kahem v'goralenu k'khol hamonam.

עָלֵינוּ לְשַׁבֵּחַ לַאֲדוֹן הַכֹּל. לָתֵת גְּדֻלָּה לְיוֹצֵר בְּרֵאשִׁית. שֶׁלֹּא עָשָׂנוּ כְּגוֹיֵי הָאֲרָצוֹת. וְלֹא שָׂמָנוּ כְּמִשְׁפְּחוֹת הָאֲדָמָה. שֶׁלֹּא שָׂם חֶלְקֵנוּ כָּהֶם וְגוֹרָלֵנוּ כְּכָל הֲמוֹנָם:

Sh'hem mishtakhavim l'hevel varik umitpalelim el el lo moshei'a. Va'anakhnu kore'im umishtakhavim umodim lifnei Melekh Malkhei hammelakhim, hakodosh barukh Hu'.

שֶׁהֵם מִשְׁתַּחֲוִים לְהֶבֶל וָרִיק וּמִתְפַּלְלִים אֶל אֵל לֹא מוֹשִׁיעַ: וַאֲנַחְנוּ כּוֹרְעִים וּמִשְׁתַּחֲוִים וּמוֹדִים לִפְנֵי מֶלֶךְ מַלְכֵי הַמְּלָכִים הַקָּדוֹשׁ בָּרוּךְ הוּא:

Sh'Hu noteh shamayim v'yosed aretz umoshav. Y'karo bashamayim mima'al ush'khinat uzzo b'gav'hei m'romim Hu Eloheinu ein od.

שֶׁהוּא נוֹטֶה שָׁמַיִם וְיוֹסֵד אָרֶץ וּמוֹשָׁב. יְקָרוֹ בַּשָּׁמַיִם מִמַּעַל. וּשְׁכִינַת עֻזּוֹ בְּגָבְהֵי מְרוֹמִים: הוּא אֱלֹהֵינוּ אֵין עוֹד:

Emet malkenu. Efes zulato kakatuv betoratoh. V'yadatah hayom v'hashevota el levavekha ki יהוה Hu ha'elohim bashamayim mim'al v'al ha'aretz mitakhat ein od.

אֱמֶת מַלְכֵּנוּ. אֶפֶס זוּלָתוֹ. כַּכָּתוּב בְּתוֹרָתוֹ. וְיָדַעְתָּ הַיּוֹם וַהֲשֵׁבֹתָ אֶל לְבָבֶךָ. כִּי יהוה הוּא הָאֱלֹהִים בַּשָּׁמַיִם מִמַּעַל וְעַל הָאָרֶץ מִתָּחַת. אֵין עוֹד:

71

Vehayah יהוה l'melekh al kol ha'aretz bayom hahu, yiyeh יהוה ekhad, ushmo ekhad.

וְהָיָה יהוה לְמֶלֶךְ, עַל כָּל הָאָרֶץ; בַּיּוֹם הַהוּא, יִהְיֶה יהוה אֶחָדוּשְׁמוֹ אֶחָד.

It is our duty to praise the Master of all, to ascribe greatness to the Molder of Creation, for He has not made us like the nations of the lands, and has not placed us like families of the earth. For He has not assigned our portion like theirs, nor our fate like all their crowds. For they bow down to vanity and emptiness and pray to a god who does not save. But we kneel, and bow and acknowledge our thanks, before the King who reigns over kings, the Holy One. He stretches out heaven and establishes earth (Isaiah 51:13); the seat of His glory is in the heavens above, and His powerful presence is in the loftiest heights. He is our Elohim and there is none other.

True is our King, there is nothing beside Him, as it is written in His Torah: "Know this day, and lay it to your heart, that יהוה , He is Elohim in heaven above and upon the earth beneath; there is none else." And it is said: "And יהוה shall be Melekh over all the earth; in that day shall יהוה be Ekhad, and His Name Ekhad."

## Returning the Torah to the Ark
### Leader

Y'halelu et shem יהוה , ki nisgav sh'mo l'vado.

יְהַלְלוּ אֶת שֵׁם יהוה כִּי נִשְׂגָּב שְׁמוֹ לְבַדּוֹ;

Let them praise the Name of יהוה , for His Name alone is exalted.

Leader and Congregation

Hodo al eretz v'shamayim,
vayarem keren l'amo;
t'hilah l'khol khasidav,
livnei Yisra'el, ahm k'rovo;
Hallelu Yah!

הוֹדוֹ עַל אֶרֶץ וְשָׁמָיִם; וַיָּרֶם
קֶרֶן לְעַמּוֹ; תְּהִלָּה לְכָל
חֲסִידָיו; לִבְנֵי יִשְׂרָאֵל, עַם
קְרֹבוֹ: הַלְלוּ יָהּ.

His splendor is above the earth and heaven. And He has lifted up a horn for His people, a Tehillah for all His Khasidim, even for the children of Yisra'el, a people near unto Him. Hallelu Yah!

Leader and Congregation

U'v'nukho yomar, 'Shuva,
יהוה, rivevot al'fei Yisra'el.
Kumah, יהוה,
lim'nukhatekha, Atah
v'aron uzekha; Kohaneikha
yilb'shu tzedek,
vakhasideikha yeranenu.
Ba'avur David avdeikha, al
tashev p'nei Meshikhekha.
Ki lekakh tov natati
lakhem, Torati al ta'azovu.

וּבְנֻחֹה, יֹאמַר: שׁוּבָה יהוה
רִבְבוֹת אַלְפֵי יִשְׂרָאֵל.
קוּמָה יהוה לִמְנוּחָתֶךָ;
אַתָּה וַאֲרוֹן עֻזֶּךָ. כֹּהֲנֶיךָ
יִלְבְּשׁוּ צֶדֶק; וַחֲסִידֶיךָ
יְרַנֵּנוּ. בַּעֲבוּר דָּוִד עַבְדֶּךָ
אַל תָּשֵׁב פְּנֵי מְשִׁיחֶךָ. כִּי
לֶקַח טוֹב נָתַתִּי לָכֶם תּוֹרָתִי
אַל תַּעֲזֹבוּ.

And when [the Ark] rested [Moshe] would say, "Return, O יהוה, unto the myriads of Yisra'el." Arise, O יהוה, unto Your resting-place; You, and the Aron of Your strength. Let Your Kohanim be clothed with righteousness; and let Your Khasidim **shout** for **joy**! For Your servant David's sake, turn not away the face of Your Mashi'akh. For I give you good doctrine; do not forsake my Torah.

73

After the Ark is closed, Leader and Congregation:

Barukh Atah יהוה , בָּרוּךְ אַתָּה יהוה , אֱלֹהֵינוּ,
Eloheinu, Melekh מֶלֶךְ הָעוֹלָם, אֲשֶׁר נָתַן לָנוּ
HaOlam, asher natan lanu
haDavar haKhai הַדָּבָר הַחַי בַּמָּשִׁיחַ יֵשׁוּעַ.
baMashi'akh Yeshua.

Blessed are You, O יהוה our Elohim, King of the Universe, who has given us the Living Word in Messiah Yeshua.

## Aharon's Blessing

*Families gather under the tallit of the head of the household,*
*symbolic of Messiah gathering us "under His wing."*
Leader sings the blessing over the congregation

Y'varekhekha יהוה , יְבָרֶכְךָ יהוה , וְיִשְׁמְרֶךָ.
v'yishmerekha.

Ya'er יהוה panav eleikha יָאֵר יהוה פָּנָיו אֵלֶיךָ, וִיחֻנֶּךָ.
vikhunekha.

Yisah יהוה panav eleikha יִשָּׂא יהוה פָּנָיו אֵלֶיךָ, וְיָשֵׂם
v'yasem lekha shalom. לְךָ שָׁלוֹם.

יהוה bless you, and keep you; יהוה make His face to shine upon you, and be gracious unto you; יהוה lift up His countenance upon you, and give you shalom.

# SHABBAT IN THE HOME

## Blessing for Consecrating Shabbat

The woman of the house lights the candles, then says this blessing

Barukh Atah יהוה , Eloheinu, Melekh HaOlam, asher kid'shanu b'mitzvotav v'tzivanu l'kadesh et yom HaShabbat, u'liyoht or l'amim b'Mashi'akh Yeshua.

בָּרוּךְ אַתָּה יהוה , אֱלֹהֵינוּ, מֶלֶךְ הָעוֹלָם, אֲשֶׁר קִדְּשָׁנוּ בְּמִצְוֹתָיו, וְצִוָּנוּ לְקַדֵּשׁ אֶת יוֹם הַשַּׁבָּת, וְלִהְיוֹת אוֹר לְעַמִים בַּמָשִׁיחַ יֵשׁוּעַ.

Blessed are You, O יהוה our Elohim, King of the Universe, who has consecrated us by His Mitzvot, and commanded us to sanctify the Sabbath Day, and to be a light to the nations in Messiah Yeshua.

Those present say, "Amein," and Shabbat has begun

(When a High Sabbath falls on the weekly Shabbat, add this blessing after lighting the lights)

Barukh Atah יהוה , Eloheinu, Melekh HaOlam, sh'hekheyanu v'kimanu v'higi'anu lazman hazeh. Amein.

בָּרוּךְ אַתָּה, יהוה , אֱלֹהֵינוּ, מֶלֶךְ הָעוֹלָם, שֶׁהֶחֱיָנוּ וְקִימָנוּ, וְהִגִיעָנוּ לַזְמָן הַזֶה.

Blessed are You, O יהוה our Elohim, King of the Universe, who has kept us in life and has preserved us, and has enabled us to reach this season. Amein.

# Kiddush
## VaYakhulu

All standing, the head of the house lifts the cup while the following prayers are
sung (or recited)

Acknowledging the Blessings of Shabbat and the Creator's Example

Vayakhulu hashamayim v'ha'aretz, v'khol tzeva'am.

וַיְכֻלּוּ הַשָּׁמַיִם וְהָאָרֶץ, וְכָל צְבָאָם

Vah'y'khol Elohim bayom ha'shevi'i malakhto asher asah; va'yishbot bayom ha'shevi'i mikol m'lakhto asher asah.

וַיְכַל אֱלֹהִים בַּיּוֹם הַשְּׁבִיעִי, מְלַאכְתּוֹ אֲשֶׁר עָשָׂה; וַיִּשְׁבֹּת בַּיּוֹם הַשְּׁבִיעִי, מִכָּל מְלַאכְתּוֹ אֲשֶׁר עָשָׂה.

Vayevarekh Elohim et yom hashevi'i va'yekadesh otoh; ki voh shavaht mikol m'lakhto, asher barah Elohim la'asot.

וַיְבָרֶךְ אֱלֹהִים אֶת יוֹם הַשְּׁבִיעִי, וַיְקַדֵּשׁ אֹתוֹ: כִּי בוֹ שָׁבַת מִכָּל מְלַאכְתּוֹ, אֲשֶׁר בָּרָא אֱלֹהִים לַעֲשׂוֹת.

Thus the heavens and the earth were finished, and all the hosts of
them. And on the seventh day Elohim finished His work which
He had made; and He rested on the seventh day from all His
work which He had made. And Elohim blessed the seventh day,
and hallowed it; because that in it He rested from all His work
which Elohim in creating had made.

# Pri HaGafen

Lifting a full cup of wine high, the blessing is sung (or recited)

Barukh Atah יהוה , Eloheinu, Melekh HaOlam, boreh pri hagafen: Barukh Atah יהוה , Eloheinu, Melekh HaOlam, asher natan lanu et hadahm shel Yeshua HaMashi'akh.

בָּרוּךְ אַתָּה יהוה , אֱלֹהֵינוּ, מֶלֶךְ הָעוֹלָם, בּוֹרֵא פְּרִי הַגָּפֶן: בָּרוּךְ אַתָּה יהוה , אֱלֹהֵינוּ, מֶלֶךְ הָעוֹלָם אֲשֶׁר נָתַן לָנוּ אֶת הַדָּם שֶׁל יֵשׁוּעַ הַמָּשִׁיחַ.

Blessed are You, O יהוה our Elohim, King of the Universe, who creates the fruit of the vine: Blessed are You, O יהוה our Elohim, King of the Universe, who has given us the blood of Yeshua the Messiah.

Everyone present partakes of the wine at this point

# HaMotzi

The head of the house lifts the bread high while the prayer is sung (or recited)

Barukh Atah יהוה , Eloheinu, Melekh HaOlam, hamotzi lekhem min ha'aretz, v'hotzi Yeshua HaMashi'akh min ha'she'ol.

בָּרוּךְ אַתָּה יהוה , אֱלֹהֵינוּ, מֶלֶךְ הָעוֹלָם, הַמּוֹצִיא לֶחֶם מִן הָאָרֶץ, וְהוֹצִיא יֵשׁוּעַ הַמָּשִׁיחַ מִן הַשְּׁאוֹל.

Blessed are You, O יהוה our Elohim, King of the Universe, who brings forth bread from the earth, and who brought forth Messiah Yeshua from the grave.

Everyone present partakes of the bread at this point

# L'khu Neranenah

L'khu, Neraneinah la יהוה; nariah l'tzur yisheinu.

לְכוּ, נְרַנְּנָה לַיהוה; נָרִיעָה, לְצוּר יִשְׁעֵנוּ.

O Come, let us sing to יהוה! Let us shout for joy to the Rock of

our Salvation!
It is fitting to sing a song about the Sabbath here, Shabbat Shalom, Yom Zeh
L'Yisra'el, etc

# Blessing for Boys

Perform "smikḥah," placing the hand on the head of the eldest
boy first

Y'simkḥa Elohim יִשְׂמְךָ אֱלֹהִים כְּאֶפְרַיִם
k'Efrayim, ukḥi וְכִמְנַשֶּׁה.
Menasheh.

May Elohim make you like Efrayim and like Menassah.

# Blessing for Girls

Perform "smikḥah," placing the hand on the head of the eldest
girl first

Y'simeikḥ Elohim יִשְׂמֵךְ אֱלֹהִים כְּשָׂרָה,
k'Sarah, Rivkah, Rakḥel רִבְקָה, רָחֵל וְלֵאָה.
v'Le'ah.

May Elohim make you like Sarah, Rebekkah, Rachel, and
Leah.

# Aharon's Blessing for All Children

The Father says the blessing; wrapping his children in his tallit is
customary for some

Yevarekḥekḥa יהוה , יְבָרֶכְךָ יהוה , וְיִשְׁמְרֶךָ.
v'yishmerekḥa.

Ya'er יהוה panav eleikḥa יָאֵר יהוה פָּנָיו אֵלֶיךָ,
vikḥunekḥa. וִיחֻנֶּךָ.

Yisa יהוה panav eleikḥa יִשָּׂא יהוה פָּנָיו אֵלֶיךָ, וְיָשֵׂם
v'yasem l'kḥa shalom. לְךָ שָׁלוֹם.

' יהוה bless you, and keep you; יהוה make His face to shine upon
you, and be gracious unto you; יהוה lift up His countenance upon
you, and give you shalom.'

79

# Eshet Khayil

Blessing over the wife from the husband *(Prov 31:10-31)*
Customarily sung.

Eshet khayil mi yim**tzah**?
V'ra**khok** mip'ni**nim**
mikh**rah**.

אֵשֶׁת חַיִל, מִי יִמְצָא; וְרָחֹק
מִפְּנִינִים מִכְרָהּ.

Bata**kh** bah lev ba'e**lah**;
v'sha**lal**, lo yekh'**sar**.

בָּטַח בָּהּ, לֵב בַּעְלָהּ; וְשָׁלָל,
לֹא יֶחְסָר.

G'malaht**hu** tov v'**lo** rah;
kol y'**mei** khayei**ha**.

גְּמָלַתְהוּ טוֹב וְלֹא רָע כֹּל,
יְמֵי חַיֶּיהָ.

Dar**shah** tze**mer** ufish**tim**;
vata'**as** b'**kha**fetz kapei**ha**.

דָּרְשָׁה, צֶמֶר וּפִשְׁתִּים;
וַתַּעַשׂ, בְּחֵפֶץ כַּפֶּיהָ.

Ha'i'**tah** ka'ani**yot** so**kher**;
mimer'**khak** ta**vih**
lakh**mah**.

הָיְתָה, כָּאֳנִיּוֹת סוֹחֵר;
מִמֶּרְחָק, תָּבִיא לַחְמָהּ.

Va'**ta**kam b'od lai**lah**;
vati**ten** te**ref** l'vei**tah**;
v'**khok** l'na'arotei**hah**.

וַתָּקָם, בְּעוֹד לַיְלָה וַתִּתֵּן
טֶרֶף לְבֵיתָהּ; וְחֹק,
לְנַעֲרֹתֶיהָ.

Zam'**mah** sa**deh**,
va'tika**khei**hu; mi'**pri**
khapei**ha** natah **ka**rem.

זָמְמָה שָׂדֶה, וַתִּקָּחֵהוּ;
מִפְּרִי כַפֶּיהָ, נָטַע כָּרֶם.

khag'**rah** v'**oz** motnei**ha**;
va't'**ametz** zero'otei**ha**.

חָגְרָה בְעוֹז מָתְנֶיהָ;
וַתְּאַמֵּץ, זְרוֹעֹתֶיהָ.

Ta'a**mah** ki tov sakh**rah**; lo
yikh**beh** balai**lah** ne**rah**.

טָעֲמָה, כִּי טוֹב סַחְרָהּ; לֹא
יִכְבֶּה בַלַּיְלָה נֵרָהּ.

Yadeiha shilkḥa va'kishor; v'kḥapeiha tam'kḥu falekḥ.

יָדֶיהָ, שִׁלְּחָה בַכִּישׁוֹר; וְכַפֶּיהָ, תָּמְכוּ פָלֶךְ.

Kapah par'sa l'ani; v'yadeiha shilkḥah, la'evyon.

כַּפָּהּ, פָּרְשָׂה לֶעָנִי; וְיָדֶיהָ, שִׁלְּחָה לָאֶבְיוֹן.

Lo tirah l'veitah mi'shaleg; ki khol beitah lavush shanim.

לֹא תִירָא לְבֵיתָהּ מִשָּׁלֶג: כִּי כָל בֵּיתָהּ, לָבֻשׁ שָׁנִים.

Marvadim as'tah lah; shesh v'argaman l'vushah.

מַרְבַדִּים עָשְׂתָה לָּהּ; שֵׁשׁ וְאַרְגָּמָן לְבוּשָׁהּ.

Nodah bashe'arim ba'elah; b'shivtoh im ziknei aretz.

נוֹדָע בַּשְּׁעָרִים בַּעְלָהּ; בְּשִׁבְתּוֹ, עִם זִקְנֵי אָרֶץ.

Sadin as'tah v'timkor; va'kḥagor nat'nah l'k'na'ani.

סָדִין עָשְׂתָה, וַתִּמְכֹּר; וַחֲגוֹר, נָתְנָה לַכְּנַעֲנִי.

Ohz v'hadar l'vushah; va'tis'kḥak l'yom akḥaron.

עֹז וְהָדָר לְבוּשָׁהּ; וַתִּשְׂחַק, לְיוֹם אַחֲרוֹן.

Pihah paht'kḥa v'khokḥmah; v'toraht kḥesed al l'shonah.

פִּיהָ, פָּתְחָה בְחָכְמָה; וְתוֹרַת חֶסֶד, עַל לְשׁוֹנָהּ.

Tzofiah halikḥot beitah; v'lekḥem atzlut lo tokḥel.

צוֹפִיָּה, הֲלִיכוֹת בֵּיתָהּ; וְלֶחֶם עַצְלוּת, לֹא תֹאכֵל.

Kamuh vaneiha vayahshruhah; ba'elah va'y'haleilah.

קָמוּ בָנֶיהָ, וַיְאַשְּׁרוּהָ; בַּעְלָהּ, וַיְהַלְלָהּ.

Raboht banoht asu kḥayil, רַבּוֹת בָּנוֹת, עָשׂוּ חָיִל;
v'et alit al kulanah! וְאַתְּ, עָלִית עַל כֻּלָּנָה.

Sheker ha'kḥen, v'hevel שֶׁקֶר הַחֵן, וְהֶבֶל הַיֹּפִי:
hayofi: Isha yiraht יהוה , hi אִשָּׁה יִרְאַת יהוה , הִיא
tithalal. תִתְהַלָּל.

T'nu lah mi'pri yadeiha; תְּנוּ לָהּ, מִפְּרִי יָדֶיהָ;
vihaleluha va'she'arim וִיהַלְלוּהָ בַשְּׁעָרִים מַעֲשֶׂיהָ.
ma'aseiha.

A woman of valor who can find? For her price is far above rubies. The heart of her husband does safely trust in her, and he has no lack of gain. She does him good and not evil all the days of her life.

She seeks wool and flax, and works willingly with her hands. She is like the merchant-ships; she brings her food from afar. She rises also while it is yet night, and gives food to her household, and a portion to her maidens.

She considers a field, and buys it; with the fruit of her hands she plants a vineyard. She girds her loins with strength, and makes strong her arms. She perceives that her merchandise is good; her lamp goes not out by night. She lays her hands to the distaff, and her hands hold the spindle.

She stretches out her hand to the poor; yes, she reaches forth her hands to the needy. She is not afraid of the snow for her household; for all her household are clothed with scarlet. She makes for herself coverings; her clothing is fine linen and purple.

Her husband is known in the gates, when he sits among the elders of the land. She makes linen garments and sells them; and delivers girdles unto the merchant. Strength and dignity are her clothing; and she laughs at the last day.

She opens her mouth with wisdom; and the Torah of compassion is on her tongue. She looks well to the ways of her household,

and eats not the bread of idleness. Her children rise up and call her blessed; her husband also, and he praises her: "Many daughters have done valiantly, but you exceed them all."

Grace is deceitful, and beauty is vain; but a woman that fears יהוה , she shall be praised. Give her of the fruit of her hands; and let her works praise her in the gates.

## Ashrei Ish

Blessing over the man of the house from the wife  (Tehillah 112)

| | |
|---|---|
| Halle**lu** Yah!    Ash**rei** ish ya**reh** et יהוה , b'mitzvo**tav** kha**fetz** me'ohd. | הַלְלוּיָהּ אַשְׁרֵי אִישׁ, יָרֵא אֶת יהוה;    בְּמִצְוֹתָיו, חָפֵץ מְאֹד. |
| Gi**bor** ba'aretz yih**yeh** zar'**oh**;    dor yesha**rim** y'vo**rakh**. | גִּבּוֹר בָּאָרֶץ, יִהְיֶה זַרְעוֹ; דּוֹר יְשָׁרִים יְבֹרָךְ. |
| Hon va'**o**sher b'vei**to**; v'tzidka**to** o**me**det la'**ad**. | הוֹן וָעֹשֶׁר בְּבֵיתוֹ; וְצִדְקָתוֹ, עֹמֶדֶת לָעַד. |
| Za**rakh** bakho**shekh** or layesha**rim**;    kha**nun** v'ra**khum** v'tza**dik**. | זָרַח בַּחֹשֶׁךְ אוֹר, לַיְשָׁרִים; חַנּוּן וְרַחוּם וְצַדִּיק. |
| Tov ish kho**nen** u'mal**veh**; y'khal**kel** d'va**rav** b'mish**pat**. | טוֹב אִישׁ, חוֹנֵן וּמַלְוֶה; יְכַלְכֵּל דְּבָרָיו בְּמִשְׁפָּט. |
| Ki l'o**lam** lo yi**mot**; l'**zekher** o**lam** yih**yeh** tza**dik**. | כִּי לְעוֹלָם לֹא יִמּוֹט; לְזֵכֶר עוֹלָם, יִהְיֶה צַדִּיק. |
| Mishmo**ah** ra'**ah** lo yi**rah**; na**khon** li**bo**, batu'**akh** ba יהוה . | מִשְּׁמוּעָה רָעָה, לֹא יִירָא; נָכוֹן לִבּוֹ, בָּטֻחַ בַּיהוה. |

83

**Samukḥ liboh**, lo **yirah**; ad **asher** yireh v'tzarav.

סָמוּךְ לִבּוֹ, לֹא יִירָא; עַד אֲשֶׁר יִרְאֶה בְצָרָיו.

**Pizar** natan la'evyo**nim**; tzidka**toh** ome**det** la'**ad**; kar**no** ta**rum** b'khavod.

פִּזַּר, נָתַן לָאֶבְיוֹנִים, צִדְקָתוֹ, עֹמֶדֶת לָעַד; קַרְנוֹ, תָּרוּם בְּכָבוֹד.

**Rashah** yireh v'kha'**as**; shi**nav** ya'**kharok** v'**namas**; ta'**avat** r'sha**yim** to**ved**.

רָשָׁע יִרְאֶה, וְכָעָס שִׁנָּיו יַחֲרֹק וְנָמָס; תַּאֲוַת רְשָׁעִים תֹּאבֵד.

Hallelu Yah! Happy is the man that fears יהוה, that delights greatly in His Mitzvot. His seed shall be mighty upon the earth; the generation of the upright shall be blessed.

Wealth and riches are in his house, and his merit endures forever. Unto the upright He shines as a light in the darkness, gracious, and full of mercy, and a Tzadik.

Well is it with the man that deals graciously and lends, that orders his affairs rightfully. For he shall never be moved; a Tzadik shall be had in everlasting remembrance. He shall not be afraid of evil tidings; his heart is steadfast, trusting in יהוה. His heart is established, he shall not be afraid, until he gazes upon his adversaries. He has scattered abroad, he has given to the needy. His tzedaka endures forever; his horn shall be exalted in honor.

The wicked shall see it, and be vexed; he shall gnash with his teeth, and melt away; the desire of the wicked shall perish.

## Kol Yereh יהוה

*Blessing over others, over guests; if the guest is a woman, only say verses 1-2, 5 & 6. (Tehillah 128)*

**Shir** Hama'**alot**; ash**rei** kol **yereh** יהוה ; haho**lekḥ** bid'rak**ḥav**.

שִׁיר הַמַּעֲלוֹת; אַשְׁרֵי כָּל יְרֵא יהוה הַהֹלֵךְ בִּדְרָכָיו

84

Yegiyah kapeikḥa ki tokḥel, ashreikḥa, v'tov lakh. יְגִיעַ כַּפֶּיךָ כִּי תֹאכֵל; אַשְׁרֶיךָ וְטוֹב לָךְ.

Esht'kḥa k'gefen poriyah; b'yark'tei v'teikḥa; baneikḥa kishtilei zeitim; saviv l'shulkḥaneikḥa. אֶשְׁתְּךָ כְּגֶפֶן פֹּרִיָּה בְּיַרְכְּתֵי בֵיתֶךָ: בָּנֶיךָ כִּשְׁתִלֵי זֵיתִים סָבִיב לְשֻׁלְחָנֶךָ.

Hineh, khi khen y'vorakḥ gaver; yereh יהוה הִנֵּה כִי כֵן יְבֹרַךְ גָּבֶר יְרֵא יהוה.

Y'varekḥ'kḥa יהוה mi'Tzion; u're'eh b'tuv Yerushalayim, kol yemei khaiyekḥa. יְבָרֶכְךָ יהוה מִצִּיּוֹן: וּרְאֵה בְּטוּב יְרוּשָׁלָם כֹּל יְמֵי חַיֶּיךָ.

U're'eh vanim l'vaneikḥa: Shalom al Yisra'el! וּרְאֵה בָנִים לְבָנֶיךָ: שָׁלוֹם עַל יִשְׂרָאֵל.

A Song of Ascents. Happy is every one that fears יהוה , that walks in His ways. When you eat the labor of your hands, happy shall you be, and it shall be well with you. Your wife shall be as a fruitful vine, in the innermost parts of your house, your children like olive plants, round about your table. Behold, surely thus shall the man be blessed that fears יהוה. יהוה bless you out of Tzion; and may you see the good of Yerushalayim all the days of your life, and may you see your children's children. Shalom be upon Yisra'el!

# V'Shamru

Acknowledging the commandment to protect the Sabbath from defilement.

Sing!

V'shamru v'nei Yisra'el et HaShabbat; la'asot et HaShabbat l'dorotam, brit olam.

וְשָׁמְרוּ בְנֵי יִשְׂרָאֵל אֶת הַשַּׁבָּת לַעֲשׂוֹת אֶת הַשַּׁבָּת לְדֹרֹתָם בְּרִית עוֹלָם

Beini u'vein b'nei Yisra'el, oht hi l'olam. Ki sheshet yamim asah יהוה et HaShamayim v'et HaAretz, u'vayom ha'shevi'i shavat vayinafash.

בֵּינִי וּבֵין בְּנֵי יִשְׂרָאֵל אוֹת הוּא לְעֹלָם: כִּי שֵׁשֶׁת יָמִים עָשָׂה יהוה אֶת הַשָּׁמַיִם וְאֶת הָאָרֶץ וּבַיּוֹם הַשְּׁבִיעִי, שָׁבַת וַיִּנָּפַשׁ.

Wherefore the children of Yisra'el shall keep the Sabbath, to observe the Sabbath throughout their generations, for a perpetual covenant.

It is a sign between Me and the children of Yisra'el forever; for in six days יהוה made the heavens and the earth, and on the seventh day He ceased from work and rested.

### Partake of the Sabbath Meal

# Birkat HaMazon

Thanking the one who feeds us [grace after the meal]

Barukh Atah יהוה , Eloheinu, Melekh HaOlam, hazan et ha'olam kulo. B'tuvo, b'khen, b'khesed, uv'rakhamim, hu noten lekhem l'khol basar, ki l'olam khasdo.

בָּרוּךְ אַתָּה יהוה אֱלֹהֵינוּ, מֶלֶךְ הָעוֹלָם, הַזָּן אֶת הָעוֹלָם, כֻּלּוֹ בְּטוּבוֹ בְּחֵן בְּחֶסֶד וּבְרַחֲמִים הוּא נוֹתֵן לֶחֶם לְכָל בָּשָׂר כִּי לְעוֹלָם חַסְדּוֹ .

Blessed are you, O יהוה our Elohim, King of the Universe, who feeds all His world. In His goodness, in grace, and in

compassion and mercy he gives bread to all bodies, for His mercy is endless.

# L'KḥA Dodi: Come, My Beloved!
## (The Sabbath Bride)
*Hebrew first, then English*

Lekḥah dodi likrat kallah p'**nei** Shabbat nekabel**ah**

לְכָה דוֹדִי לִקְרַאת כַּלָה, פְּנֵי שַׁבָּת נְקַבְּלָה.

Sha**mor** v'zakḥor b'di**bur** ekḥad hishmi'anu El ham'yukḥad; יהוה ekḥad ush'**mo** ekḥad; L'**Shem** ul'tiferet u'lit'hi**lah**

שָׁמוֹר וְזָכוֹר בְּדִבּוּר אֶחָד, הִשְׁמִיעָנוּ אֵל הָמְיֻחָד; יהוה אֶחָד וּשְׁמוֹ אֶחָד, לְשֵׁם וּלְתִפְאֶרֶת וּלְתִהְלָה.

Li**krat** Shabbat lekḥu v'nelekḥah ki hi ma**kor** haberakḥah me**rosh** mike**dem** nesukḥah sof ma'aseh b'makḥasha**vah** tekḥilah

לִקְרַאת שַׁבָּת לְכוּ וְנֵלְכָה, כִּי הִיא מָקוֹר הַבְּרָכָה מֵרֹאשׁ מִקֶּדֶם נְסוּכָה סוֹף מַעֲשֶׂה בְּמַחֲשָׁבָה תְחִלָּה.

Mik**dash** me**lekḥ** ir melukḥah kumi **tze**'i mi**tokḥ** hahafeikḥah Rav lakḥ **shevet** b'eimek habakḥa v'hu yakḥa**mol** alayikḥ khem**lah**

מִקְדַּשׁ מֶלֶךְ, עִיר מְלוּכָה, קוּמִי צְאִי מִתּוֹךְ הָהְפֵכָה; רַב לָךְ שֶׁבֶת בְּעֵמֶק הַבָּכָא: וְהוּא יַחֲמוֹל עָלַיִךְ חֶמְלָה.

Hitna'ari me'afar ku**mi** Liv**shi** big**dei** tifar**tekḥ** ami al yad ben Yishai beit halakḥ**mi** korv**ah** el nafshi g'al**ah**

הִתְנַעֲרִי מֵעָפָר, קוּמִי, לִבְשִׁי בִּגְדֵי תִפְאַרְתֵּךְ עַמִּי; עַל יַד בֶּן יִשַׁי בֵּית הַלַחְמִי קָרְבָה אֶל נַפְשִׁי גְאָלָה

Hit'oreri hit'oreri ki va oreikḥ kumi ori, ori, ori shir dabeiri K'vod יהוה alayikḥ niglah

הִתְעוֹרְרִי הִתְעוֹרְרִי כִּי בָא אוֹרֵךְ; קוּמִי אוֹרִי, עוֹרִי עוֹרִי, שִׁיר דַּבְּרִי כְּבוֹד יהוה עָלַיִךְ נִגְלָה.

Lo tivoshi v'lo tikalmi mah tishtokḥai umah tehemi bakḥ yekḥesu aniyei ami v'nivnetah ir al tilah

לֹא תֵבוֹשִׁי! וְלֹא תִכָּלְמִי! מָה תִשְׁתּוֹחֲחִי, וּמָה תֶהֱמִי? בָּךְ יֶחֱסוּ עֲנִיֵּי עַמִּי, וְנִבְנְתָה עִיר עַל תִּלָּה.

V'hayu limshisah shosayikḥ V'rakḥaku kol mevalayikḥ yasis alayikḥ Elohayikḥ kimsos kḥatan al kalah

וְהָיוּ לִמְשִׁסָּה שֹׁאסָיִךְ, וְרָחֲקוּ כֹּל מְבַלְּעָיִךְ; יָשִׂישׂ עָלַיִךְ אֱלֹהָיִךְ, כִּמְשׂוֹשׂ חָתָן עַל כַּלָּה.

Yamin ushmol tifrotzi v'et יהוה ta'aritzi al yad ish ben Partzi V'nismekḥah v'nagilah

יָמִין וּשְׂמֹאל תִּפְרוֹצִי, וְאֶת יהוה תַּעֲרִיצִי, עַל יַד אִישׁ בֶּן פַּרְצִי וְנִשְׂמְחָה וְנָגִילָה.

Bo'i v'shalom ateret ba'alah gam b'simkḥah uvetzahalah tokḥ emunei am segulah Bo'i kalah bo'i kalah

בּוֹאִי בְשָׁלוֹם עֲטֶרֶת בַּעְלָהּ גַּם בְּשִׂמְחָה וּבְצָהֳלָה תּוֹךְ אֱמוּנֵי עַם סְגֻלָּה בּוֹאִי כַלָּה בּוֹאִי כַלָּה.

P'nei Shabbat nekabelah;
**P'nei Shabbat nekabelah;**
Shabbat Shalom B'Yeshua, Shabbat Shalom, Shabbat Shalom; Shabbat Shalom B'Yeshua, Shabbat Shalom, Shabbat Shalom.

פְּנֵי שַׁבָּת נְקַבְּלָה; פְּנֵי שַׁבָּת נְקַבְּלָה שַׁבָּת שָׁלוֹם בְּיֵשׁוּעַ, שַׁבָּת שָׁלוֹם, שַׁבָּת שָׁלוֹם; שַׁבָּת שָׁלוֹם בְּיֵשׁוּעַ, שַׁבָּת שָׁלוֹם, שַׁבָּת שָׁלוֹם.

Come, my Beloved, to meet the Bride; the face of Sabbath we receive! "Observe" and "recall": in a single utterance, we were made to hear by the unified God. יהוה is one and His Name is one, in fame and splendor and praiseful song. *(Yoel 2:16, D'varim 16:2)*

Let's go to greet the Shabbat, let's travel, for she is the wellspring of blessing from the beginning; from ancient times she was chosen. Though made last, conceived first. *(B'reshit 2:2-3)*

Sanctuary of the king, regal city, Arise! Leave from the midst of the turmoil. Long enough have you sat in the valley of tears. Now He will take great pity upon you compassionately. *(Yesha-Yahu 40:9, Yirme-Yahu 49:31)*

Shake yourself free, rise from the dust! Dress in your garments of splendor, my people. The son of Yishai, the Bethlehemite, draws near, bringing the soul redemption. *(Yeshua-Yahu 52:2)*

Rouse yourselves! Rouse yourselves! Your light is coming. Rise up and shine! Awaken! Awaken! Utter a song! The glory of יהוה is revealed upon you. *(Yesha-Yahu 26:19)*

Do not be embarrassed! Do not be ashamed! Why be downcast? Why groan? All my afflicted people will find refuge within you, and the city shall be rebuilt on her hill. *(Yesha-Yahu 54:4)*

Your despoilers will become your spoil. Far away shall be any who would devour you. Your Elohim will rejoice concerning you, as a groom rejoices over a bride. *(Yesha-Yahu 62:5)*

To your right and your left you will burst forth, and יהוה will you revere, because of the hand of a Man, the Son of Peretz, we will rejoice and sing happily. *(Shemot 34:24, Ruth 4:18-22, Matt 1:3)*

Come in peace, crown of her husband, both in happiness and in jubilation, amidst the faithful of the treasured nation. Come O Bride! Come O Bride! *(Shemot 19:5)*

The face of Sabbath we receive! The face of Sabbath we receive! Sabbath Peace in Yeshua, Sabbath Peace, Sabbath Peace;

Sabbath Peace in Yeshua, Sabbath Peace, Sabbath Peace.

# Tehillim for Shabbat

There are certain Tehillim that are customarily read on the Sabbath; from this list, choose one or more of the Tehillim to be read with Tehillah 92, the Tehillah for the Sabbath Day:

Tehillah 92, the Tehillah for the Sabbath Day

Tehillah 93
Tehillah 29
Tehillah 95
Tehillah 96
Tehillah 97
Tehillah 98
Tehillah 99
*The Tehillim begin on page 206*

# HAVDALAH

Havdalah closes out the Sabbath (late on the 7th night). The word means "separation." It is rooted in the ability to make a clear distinction between two opposites, especially "light" and "dark." We are to recognize the brilliance of Shabbat compared to all the other "ordinary" days. We may remember that the first thing Elohim did in creating the world was to create "light", and this was done on the 1st day of creating, the demarkation of the first week of the history of the world. Havdalah begins the first day. Shabbat, the seventh day, ends, and the first day begins. The first use of the word "havdil," from where we get "havdalah," is in Genesis 1:3 וַיַּבְדֵּל אֱלֹהִים, בֵּין הָאוֹר וּבֵין הַחֹשֶׁךְ, "and Elohim 'separated' the light from the darkness."

The custom of Havdalah goes back thousands of years, and is actually seen in the Brit Khadasha in two "distinct" places. Acts chapter 20 shows us a Havdalah service, and 1 Corinthians 9 anticipates upcoming Havdalah services. This ceremony starts the first day of the week, closing out the Sabbath, and resuming ordinary work. The desire is to carry the blessing of Shabbat with us into the week, and the first thing we are to do is take care of the needs of the Body, providing for those within the congregation who have any lack first, before we do any other mundane task. This comes from the Prophet Yesha'Yahu's instructions on Shabbat in chapters 56-58, and is clearly seen in the Messianic Congregations of scripture. We are making a distinction between His Consecrated Day, and the six working days. This ceremony releases us to our work, but helps us continue in the blessings we have received by observing the Sabbath of Elohim, and gives us an opporunity to bless anyone in need, spiritually or physically. There is a picture of Creation and Resurrection in the Havdalah ceremony.

For this service, we use a candle with more than one wick. A full glass of wine and a box of spices are also used to invoke the mindset of Havdalah. First, we light the candle before the rest of the ceremony is observed. The rest of the ceremony then starts an hour after sundown (looking for three stars is a good benchmark, or waiting atleast an hour after sundown). The

candle is therefore actually lit on Shabbat, since the sabbath ends when the ceremony finishes. This carries the light of Shabbat into the following week. After the Havdalah candle has burned for a while, and everyone is ready, then the other blessings are said.

## Blessing the Light of the Fire

the candle has already been lit, holding up the havdalah candle, recite the blessing

*Hebrew first, then English*

Barukh Atah יהוה , Eloheinu, **Me**lekh Ha**Olam**, boreh m'orei ha'esh.

בָּרוּךְ אַתָּה יהוה , אֱלֹהֵינוּ , מֶלֶךְ הָעוֹלָם, בּוֹרֵא מְאוֹרֵי הָאֵשׁ.

Blessed are You, O יהוה our Elohim, King of the Universe, who creates the light of the fire.

## Blessing Yah for Salvation

Next, we lifting the cup of Eli-Yahu and the spices reciting the blessing:

Hi**nei** El Yeshu**ati**, evtakh v'**lo** efkhad, ki ozi v'zimrat Yah, יהוה , vaye**hi** li lishuah. Ushavtem mayim b'sason mima'anei haYeshuah. La יהוה haYeshuah, al am'kha virkhatekha, selah.

הִנֵּה אֵל יְשׁוּעָתִי, אֶבְטַח וְלֹא אֶפְחָד, כִּי עָזִּי וְזִמְרָת יָהּ , יהוה , וַיְהִי לִי לִישׁוּעָה. וּשְׁאַבְתֶּם מַיִם בְּשָׂשׂוֹן, מִמַּעַיְנֵי הַיְשׁוּעָה. לַיהוה הַיְשׁוּעָה, עַל עַמְּךָ בִרְכָתֶךָ סֶּלָה.

93

יהוה Tzeva'ot imanu, misgav lanu, Elohei Ya'akov, selah. יהוה Tzeva'ot, ashrei adam bote'akh bakh. יהוה hoshi'ah, hamelekh ya'aneinu v'yom koreinu. LaYehudim hayetah orah v'simkha v'sason vikar. Ken tiyeh lanu. Kos Yeshuot esa uv'shem יהוה ekrah.

יהוה צְבָאוֹת עִמָּנוּ, מִשְׂגָּב לָנוּ אֱלֹהֵי יַעֲקֹב סֶלָה. יהוה צְבָאוֹת, אַשְׁרֵי אָדָם בֹּטֵחַ בָּךְ. יהוה הוֹשִׁיעָה, הַמֶּלֶךְ יַעֲנֵנוּ בְיוֹם קָרְאֵנוּ. לַיְהוּדִים הָיְתָה אוֹרָה וְשִׂמְחָה וְשָׂשׂוֹן וִיקָר. כֵּן תִּהְיֶה לָנוּ. כּוֹס יְשׁוּעוֹת אֶשָּׂא, וּבְשֵׁם יהוה אֶקְרָא.

Behold, El Yeshua'ti; I will trust, and will not be afraid; for Yah, יהוה , is my strength and song; and He is become my Salvation'. Therefore with joy you will draw water out of the wells of Yeshua[h]. Salvation is from יהוה ; may Your blessing rest upon Your people. יהוה Tzeva'ot is with us; the Elohim of Ya'akov is our high tower. Selah. O יהוה Tzeva'ot, happy is the man that trusts in You. Save, O יהוה ! Let HaMelekh answer us in the day that we call. The Yehudim had light and gladness, and joy and honor; may we have the same. I will lift up the cup of Salvations [yeshu'ot], and call upon the Name of יהוה .

Next, we recite the following blessings as we hold up the full cup of wine and the spices:

## Blessing Over the Wine

Barukh Atah יהוה , Eloheinu, Melekh HaOlam, boreh pri hagafen.

בָּרוּךְ אַתָּה יהוה , אֱלֹהֵינוּ מֶלֶךְ הָעוֹלָם, בּוֹרֵא פְּרִי הַגָּפֶן.

Blessed are You, O יהוה our Elohim, King of the Universe, who creates the fruit of the vine.

# Blessing Over the Spices

Barukh Atah יהוה , אֱלֹהֵינוּ , בָּרוּךְ אַתָּה יהוה
Eloheinu, **Melekh HaOlam**, מֶלֶךְ הָעוֹלָם, בּוֹרֵא מִינֵי
**bo**reh mi**nei** v'sa**mim**. בְשָׂמִים.

Blessed are You, O יהוה our Elohim, King of the Universe, who creates the various spices.

> The spices are passed around and everyone enjoys the aroma of the spices, reminding us that יהוה has called everyone to Himself, and that He takes joy in the many different peoples who come to serve Him. *(II Kor 2:15)*

> Now, we are ready to recite the Havdalah blessing. Holding the glass of wine again,    we recite the following blessing:

## *Making Distinction*

Barukh Atah יהוה , בָּרוּךְ אַתָּה יהוה , אֱלֹהֵינוּ
Eloheinu, **Melekh HaOlam**, מֶלֶךְ הָעוֹלָם, הַמַּבְדִּיל בֵּין
hamav**dil** bein **ko**desh קֹדֶשׁ לְחוֹל, בֵּין אוֹר לְחֹשֶׁךְ,
le**khol** bein or le**kho**shekh בֵּין יִשְׂרָאֵל לָעַמִּים, בֵּין יוֹם
bein Yisra**'el** la'a**mim** bein הַשְּׁבִיעִי לְשֵׁשֶׁת יְמֵי
yom hashevi'i l'**she**shet הַמַּעֲשֶׂה. בָּרוּךְ אַתָּה יהוה
**ye**mei hama'a**seh**. Ba**rukh** , הַמַּבְדִּיל בֵּין קֹדֶשׁ לְחוֹל.
Atah יהוה , hamav**dil** bein
**ko**desh le**khol**.

Blessed are You, O יהוה our Elohim, King of the Universe, who separates between the consecrated and the profane; between the light and dark; between Yisra'el and the other nations; between the seventh day and the six days for working. Blessed are You, O יהוה , who separates between the consecrated and the ordinary.

> We extinguish the Havdalah candle with the wine; after the light is extingished, we drink the rest of the wine, taking the last taste of Shabbat.

> Next, we look forward to the coming of Eli-Yahu by singing "Eli-Yahu HaNavi." There is a promise that Eli-Yahu

restores Yisra'el to יהוה , by first restoring the hearts of the fathers and their children to one another.

## Eli-Yahu HaNavi

Eli-**Ya**hu HaNavi Eli-**Ya**hu HaTish**bi** Eli-**Ya**hu, Eli-**Ya**hu, Eli-**Ya**hu HaGila**di** Bim'he**ra** v'ya**me**inu Yavoh e**le**inu im Mashiakḥ ben David im Mashiakḥ ben David Eli-**Ya**hu HaNavi Eli-**Ya**hu HaTish**bi** Eli-**Ya**hu, Eli-**Ya**hu, Eli-**Ya**hu HaGila**di.**

אֵלִיָהוּ הַנָבִיא, אֵלִיָהוּ הַתִּשְׁבִּי אֵלִיָהוּ, אֵלִיָהוּ, אֵלִיָהוּ הַגִלְעָדִי. בִּמְהֵרָה בְיָמֵינוּ יָבוֹא אֵלֵינוּ עִם מָשִׁיחַ בֶּן דָוִד, עִם מָשִׁיחַ בֶּן דָוִד. אֵלִיָהוּ הַנָבִיא, אֵלִיָהוּ הַתִּשְׁבִּי, אֵלִיָהוּ, אֵלִיָהוּ, אֵלִיָהוּ הַגִלְעָדִי.

Elijah the Prophet, Elijah the Tishbite, Elijah the Gileadite: speedily in our day please come to us, with Messiah Son of David.

# THE DAILY PRAYERS

## Blessing Upon Arising

Khasdei יהוה ki lo tamnu, ki lo khalu rakhamav.

חַסְדֵי יהוה כִּי לֹא תָמְנוּ כִּי לֹא כָלוּ רַחֲמָיו.

Khadashim labekarim, rabah emunatekha.

חֲדָשִׁים לַבְּקָרִים רַבָּה אֱמוּנָתֶךָ.

Surely the compassions of יהוה are not consumed, surely His mercies do not fail. They are new every morning; great is your faithfulness.

## Awakening to יהוה

Reshit khokhmah, yir'at יהוה Sekhel tov lekhol oseihem; tehilato omedet la'ad.

רֵאשִׁית חָכְמָה יִרְאַת יהוה. שֵׂכֶל טוֹב לְכָל עֹשֵׂיהֶם; תְּהִלָּתוֹ עֹמֶדֶת לָעַד.

Barukh Shem K'vod, Malkhuto, L'Olam Va'ed.

בָּרוּךְ שֵׁם כְּבוֹד מַלְכוּתוֹ לְעֹלָם וָעֶד.

The fear of יהוה is the beginning of wisdom; a good understanding have all they that do thereafter; His praise endures forever. Blessed is the Name of His glorious kingdom, forever and ever.

## Blessing of Purity

La יהוה ha'aretz umlo'ah, tevel, v'yoshvei vah.

לַיהוה הָאָרֶץ וּמְלוֹאָהּ; תֵּבֵל וְיֹשְׁבֵי בָהּ.

Ki hu al yamim yesadah, v'al neharot y'khoneneha.

כִּי הוּא עַל יַמִּים יְסָדָהּ; וְעַל נְהָרוֹת יְכוֹנְנֶהָ.

Mi ya'aleh v'**har** יהוה; u**mi** yakum bim**kom** kod**sho**?

מִי יַעֲלֶה בְהַר יהוה; וּמִי יָקוּם בִּמְקוֹם קָדְשׁוֹ.

Ne**ki** kḫapaiyim, uvar levav. A**sher** lo nasa la**shav** naf**shi**; v'**lo** nishba lemir**mah**.

נְקִי כַפַּיִם וּבַר לֵבָב: אֲשֶׁר לֹא נָשָׂא לַשָּׁוְא נַפְשִׁי; וְלֹא נִשְׁבַּע לְמִרְמָה.

The earth belongs to יהוה , and the fullness thereof; the world, and they that dwell therein; For He has founded it upon the seas, and established it upon the floods. Who shall ascend into Har יהוה ? And who shall stand in His consecrated place? He that has clean hands, and a pure heart; who has not taken My Name in vain, and has not sworn deceitfully.

## Blessing Upon Donning Tallit/Tzitziyot
Preparing the heart, mind, and body for the hearing and receiving of the Mitzvot
*Hebrew first, then English*

## Barkḥi Nafshi

Barkḥi naf**shi** et יהוה ; יהוה Elo**hai**, gada**lta** me'**od**. Hod v'ha**dar** lavash**ta**.

בָּרְכִי נַפְשִׁי אֶת יהוה: יהוה אֱלֹהַי גָּדַלְתָּ מְּאֹד; הוֹד וְהָדָר לָבָשְׁתָּ.

O**teh** or kasal**ma**; no**teh** Shama**yim** kay'**riah**.

עֹטֶה אוֹר כַּשַּׂלְמָה; נוֹטֶה שָׁמַיִם כַּיְרִיעָה.

Bless יהוה , O my soul. O יהוה my Elohim, You are very great; You are clothed with glory and majesty. Who covers Yourself with light as with a garment, who stretches out the heavens like a curtain.

Barukḥ Atah, יהוה , Eloheinu, Melekḥ HaOlam, asher kid'shanu b'mitzvotav, v'tzivanu l'hitatef batzit-tzit.

בָּרוּךְ אַתָּה יהוה , אֱלֹהֵינוּ , מֶלֶךְ הָעוֹלָם, אֲשֶׁר קִדְּשָׁנוּ בְּמִצְוֹתָיו, וְצִוָּנוּ לְהִתְעַתֵּף בַּצִיצִת.

Blessed are You, O יהוה our Elohim, King of the Universe, who has consecrated us by His Mitzvot, and has commanded us concerning the donning of the tzit-tzit. *(BaMidbar 15:38-41)*

Vayomer יהוה el Moshe l'mor.

וַיֹּאמֶר יהוה אֶל מֹשֶׁה לֵּאמֹר:

Daber el b'nei Yisra'el, v'amarta aleihem, v'asu lahem tzit-tzit al kanfei vigdeihem l'dorotam; v'natnu al tzit-tzit hakanaf petil tekḥelet.

דַּבֵּר אֶל בְּנֵי יִשְׂרָאֵל וְאָמַרְתָּ אֲלֵהֶם וְעָשׂוּ לָהֶם צִיצִת עַל כַּנְפֵי בִגְדֵיהֶם לְדֹרֹתָם; וְנָתְנוּ עַל צִיצִת הַכָּנָף פְּתִיל תְּכֵלֶת.

V'hayah lakḥem l'tzit-tzit, ure'item oto uz'kḥartem et kol mitzvot יהוה , va'asitem otam; v'lo taturu akḥarei l'vavkḥem, v'akḥarei eineikḥem, asher atem zonim akḥareihem.

וְהָיָה לָכֶם לְצִיצִת וּרְאִיתֶם אֹתוֹ. וּזְכַרְתֶּם אֶת כָּל מִצְוֹת יהוה וַעֲשִׂיתֶם אֹתָם; וְלֹא תָתוּרוּ אַחֲרֵי לְבַבְכֶם וְאַחֲרֵי עֵינֵיכֶם אֲשֶׁר אַתֶּם זֹנִים אַחֲרֵיהֶם.

L'ma'an tizk'ru va'asitem et kol mitzvotai; vihitem k'doshim l'Eloheikḥem.

לְמַעַן תִּזְכְּרוּ וַעֲשִׂיתֶם אֶת כָּל מִצְוֹתָי; וִהְיִיתֶם קְדֹשִׁים לֵאלֹהֵיכֶם.

Ani יהוה Eloheikhem, asher hotzeti etkhem m'eretz Mitzrayim, lihyot lakhem l'Elohim: Ani יהוה Eloheikhem.

אֲנִי יהוה אֱלֹהֵיכֶם אֲשֶׁר הוֹצֵאתִי אֶתְכֶם מֵאֶרֶץ מִצְרַיִם לִהְיוֹת לָכֶם לֵאלֹהִים: אֲנִי יהוה אֱלֹהֵיכֶם.

G'dilim ta'aseh lakh, al arbah kanfot k'sut'kha asher t'khaseh bah.

גְּדִלִים תַּעֲשֶׂה לָּךְ עַל אַרְבַּע כַּנְפוֹת כְּסוּתְךָ אֲשֶׁר תְּכַסֶּה בָּהּ.

And יהוה spoke unto Moshe, saying, "Speak unto B'nei Yisra'el, and bid them that they make them throughout their generations tzit-tzit in the kanfot of their garments, and that they put with the Tzit-tzit HaKanaf a thread of Tekhelet.

And it shall be unto you for a tzit-tzit, that you may look upon it, and remember all the Mitzvot of יהוה , and do them; and that you go not about after your own heart and your own eyes after which you use to go astray; that you may remember and do all My Mitzvot, and be kadosh unto your Elohim. I am יהוה your Elohim, who brought you out of the land of Mitzrayim, to be your Elohim: I am יהוה your Elohim."

"You shall make yourself twisted cords upon the four corners of your covering, wherewith you cover yourself." *(BaMidbar 15:38-41, D'varim 22:12)*

## Ma Yakar

Ma yakar khasd'kha, Elohim: u'vnei adam b'tzel k'nafeikha yekhesayun.

מַה יָּקָר חַסְדְּךָ, אֱלֹהִים: וּבְנֵי אָדָם בְּצֵל כְּנָפֶיךָ יֶחֱסָיוּן.

Yirveyun mideshen beiteikha, v'nakhal adaneikha tashkem.

יִרְוְיֻן מִדֶּשֶׁן בֵּיתֶךָ; וְנַחַל עֲדָנֶיךָ תַשְׁקֵם.

Ki im'**kha** m'**kor kha**yim, כִּי עִמְּךָ מְקוֹר חַיִּים; בְּאוֹרְךָ
b'or**kha** ni**rei** or. נִרְאֶה אוֹר.

**Meshokh** khasd'**kha** מְשֹׁךְ חַסְדְּךָ לְיֹדְעֶיךָ;
l'yo**deikha**, v'tzidka**teikha** וְצִדְקָתְךָ, לְיִשְׁרֵי לֵב.
lish**rei** lev.

How precious is Your compassion, O Elohim! and the children of men take refuge in the shadow of Your wings. They are abundantly satisfied with the abundance of Your House; and You make them drink of the river of Your pleasures. For with You is the fountain of Khayim; in Your light do we see light. O continue Your compassion unto them that know You; and Your tzedaka to the upright in heart.

## Shakharit

V'eras**tikh** li, le'o**lam**; וְאֵרַשְׂתִּיךְ לִי לְעוֹלָם;
v'eras**tikh** li b'**tzedek** וְאֵרַשְׂתִּיךְ לִי בְּצֶדֶק
uvmish**pat**, uv'**khesed** וּבְמִשְׁפָּט וּבְחֶסֶד
uv'rakha**mim**. וּבְרַחֲמִים.

V'eras**tikh** li, b'emu**nah**; וְאֵרַשְׂתִּיךְ לִי בֶּאֱמוּנָה;
v'yada'at et יהוה. וְיָדַעַתְּ אֶת יהוה .

And I will betroth you unto Me forever; yes, I will betroth you unto Me in righteousness, and in fairness, and in compassion, and in mercies. And I will betroth you unto Me in faithfulness; and you shall know יהוה . ( *Hoshe'ah 2:21-22* )

## Tehillah 100
Transitioning from the ordinary into the sacred, through
thankfulness and through song.
*Hebrew first, then English*

Miz**mor** l'to**dah**: Hari**yu** la אמִזְמוֹר לְתוֹדָה: הָרִיעוּ
יהוה , kol ha'**aretz**! לַיהוה כָּל הָאָרֶץ.

Ivdu et יהוה besimkḥah; bo'u l'fanav birnanah.

עִבְדוּ אֶת יהוה בְּשִׂמְחָה; בֹּאוּ לְפָנָיו בִּרְנָנָה.

De'u ki יהוה , hu Elohim. Hu asanu, v'lo anakḥnu; amo, v'tzon maritoh.

דְּעוּ כִּי יהוה הוּא אֱלֹהִים: הוּא עָשָׂנוּ וְלֹא אֲנַחְנוּ עַמּוֹ וְצֹאן מַרְעִיתוֹ.

Bo'u sh'arav b'todah, khatzerotav bit'hilah; hodu lo, barkḥu sh'mo

בֹּאוּ שְׁעָרָיו בְּתוֹדָה חֲצֵרֹתָיו בִּתְהִלָּה; הוֹדוּ לוֹ בָּרְכוּ שְׁמוֹ.

Ki tov יהוה , l'olam kḥasdo; v'ad dor vador emunatoh.

כִּי טוֹב יהוה לְעוֹלָם חַסְדּוֹ; וְעַד דֹּר וָדֹר אֱמוּנָתוֹ.

A Mizmor [song/melody] of thanksgiving.

Shout unto יהוה , all the earth. Serve יהוה with gladness; come before His presence with singing. Know that יהוה , He is Elohim; it is He that has made us, and not we ourselves; we are His people, and the flock of His pasture.

Enter into His gates with thanksgiving, and into His courts with praise; give thanks unto Him, and bless His Name. For יהוה is good; His compassion endures forever; and His faithfulness unto all generations.

## Tefillat HaTalmidim: The Disciples' Prayer
*Hebrew first, then English*

Avinu sh'bashamayim, yitkadesh shimkḥa. Tavo malkḥuteikḥa, y'aseh retzonkḥa k'vahshamayim gam ba'aretz.

אָבִנוּ שֶׁבַּשָּׁמַיִם, יִתְקַדֵּשׁ שְׁמֶךָ, תָּבוֹא מַלְכוּתֶךָ , יֵעָשֶׂה רְצוֹנְךָ כְּבַשָּׁמַיִם גַּם בָּאָרֶץ.

103

Ten lanu et lekhem tzarkenu hayom, Um'khol lanu et khovoteinu kemo shegam anakhnu makholnu l'khayaveinu.

תֵּן לָנוּ אֶת לֶחֶם צָרְכֵּנוּ הַיּוֹם, וּמְחַל לָנוּ אֶת חוֹבוֹתֵינוּ כְּמוֹ שֶׁגַּם אֲנַחְנוּ מָחַלְנוּ לְחַיָּבֵינוּ.

V'al tevi'enu lidei nisayon, elah hatzileinu min hara, ki shelkha hi hamalkhut v'hagevurah v'hatifarah l'olemei olamim.

וְאַל תְּבִיאֵנוּ לִידֵי נִסָּיוֹן, אֶלָּא הַצִּילֵנוּ מִן הָרָע, כִּי שֶׁלְּךָ הִיא הַמַּלְכוּת וְהַגְּבוּרָה וְהַתִּפְאָרָה לְעוֹלְמֵי עוֹלָמִים.

'Avinu Sh'bah Shamayim, may Your Name be made kadosh. May Your Kingdom come. May Your will be done, as in Heaven, so on earth.

Give us the bread we need today. And forgive us our offenses, as we have forgiven our offenders;

And do not lead us into the power of testing, but deliver us from the Evil One. Because Yours is HaMalkhut, and the power, and the glory, for ever and ever. Amein.' *( Matai 6:9-13 )*

## Justification – The Blood of Messiah
Recognizing the need of forgiveness and imparted innocence from יהוה , and our attainment of it through trust in Messiah Yeshua's shed blood.
*Hebrew first, then English*

Reishit khokhma yirat יהוה , sekhel tov l'khol oseihem; tehilatoh omedet la'ad.

ראשִׁית חָכְמָה יִרְאַת יהוה שֵׂכֶל טוֹב לְכָל עֹשֵׂיהֶם; תְּהִלָּתוֹ עֹמֶדֶת לָעַד.

V'hu rakhum y'khaper avohn, v'lo yash'khit: V'hirbah l'hashiv apoh; v'lo ya'ir kol khamatoh.

לחוְהוּא רַחוּם יְכַפֵּר עָוֹן וְלֹא יַשְׁחִית: וְהִרְבָּה לְהָשִׁיב אַפּוֹ; וְלֹא יָעִיר כָּל חֲמָתוֹ.

Im no**mar** ki yesh **lanu** shuta**fut** imo, u'mithal'**khim** Anu ba**kh**oshe**kh**, shakra**nim** Anu v'**lo** ba'e**met** mitnaha**lim**. A**val** im mit'hal'**khim** Anu ba'**or**, k'a**sher hu** va'**or**, yesh lanu shuta**fut** zeh im zeh, v'**dam** Yeshua B'no y'taha**reinu** mi'**kol** khata'**einu**.

אִם נֹאמַר כִּי יֵשׁ לָנוּ שֻׁתָּפוּת עִמּוֹ וּמִתְהַלְּכִים אָנוּ בַּחֹשֶׁךְ, שַׁקְרָנִים אָנוּ וְלֹא בָּאֱמֶת מִתְנַהֲלִים. ⁷אֲבָל אִם מִתְהַלְּכִים אָנוּ בָּאוֹר כַּאֲשֶׁר הוּא בָאוֹר יֵשׁ לָנוּ שֻׁתָּפוּת זֶה עִם זֶה וְדַם יֵשׁוּעַ בְּנוֹ יְטַהֲרֵנוּ מִכָּל חֲטָאֵינוּ.

V'**im** no**mar** sh'**ein banu kh**et, mat'im ana**kh**nu et atz**meinu** v'ha'e**met** eine**inah banu**. A**val** im nitva**deh** et khata'**einu**, ne'e**man** hu v'tza**dik** lislo'a**kh** et khata'**einu**, u'leta**reinu** mi'**kol** avla**teinu**.

⁸וְאָם נֹאמַר שָׁאֵין בָּנוּ חֵטְא מַתְעִים אֲנַחְנוּ אֶת עַצְמֵנוּ וְהָאֱמֶת אֵינֶנָּה בָּנוּ. ⁹אֲבָל אִם נִתְוַדֶּה אֶת חֲטָאֵינוּ נֶאֱמָן הוּא וְצַדִּיק לִסְלֹחַ אֶת חֲטָאֵינוּ וּלְטַהֲרֵנוּ מִכָּל עַוְלָתֵנוּ.

The fear of יהוה is the beginning of wisdom; a good understanding have all they that do thereafter; His praise endures forever. But He, being full of mercy, atones for iniquity and destroys not; often does He turn His anger away, and does not stir up all His wrath. If we say that we have fellowship with Him and yet walk in darkness, we lie and do not follow the truth; but if we walk in the light as He is in the light, we have fellowship with one another, and the blood of Yeshua, His Son, cleanses us from all sin. If we say that we have no sin, we deceive ourselves and the truth is not in us. If we confess our sins, He is faithful and just to forgive us our sins, and to cleanse us from all our iniquity.

# Consecration – Obedience to His Commands

Setting ourselves apart from this world by His power, the power of His Word.

*Hebrew first, then English*

Aba, kadesh Otam ba'amite**kḥa**, ki d'vare'**kḥa** shel'**kḥa** emet hu.

"אַבָּא, קַדֵּשׁ אוֹתָם בַּאֲמִתֶּךָ, כִּי דְבָרְךָ שֶׁלְּךָ אֱמֶת הוּא.

B'**kḥol** libi d'rashtik**ḥa**; al tash**gei**ni mi'mitzvotei**kḥa**.

בְּכָל לִבִּי דְרַשְׁתִּיךָ; אַל תַּשְׁגֵּנִי מִמִּצְוֹתֶיךָ.

O Abba, consecrate them in Your truth, because Your Davar is truth. *(Yokhanan 17:17)* With my whole heart have I sought You; O let me not err from Your Mitzvot. *(Tehillim 119:10)*

# Attributes of Mercy

Leader and Congregation together

Known as the "Thirteen Attributes of Elohim," declared when He put Moshe in the cleft of the Rock. Each of us is placed in the cleft of the rock, Messiah's wounds.

*Hebrew first, then English*

יהוה , יהוה , El rak**ḥum** v'k**ḥanun**; erek**ḥ** apayim, v'rav k**ḥe**sed v'**emet**.

יהוה יהוה אֵל רַחוּם וְחַנּוּן. אֶרֶךְ אַפַּיִם וְרַב חֶסֶד וֶאֱמֶת.

Notzer k**ḥe**sed la'ala**fim**, no**seh** avon vafe**sha** v'k**ḥa**ta'**ah**, v'nakeh.

נֹצֵר חֶסֶד לָאֲלָפִים נֹשֵׂא עָוֹן וָפֶשַׁע וְחַטָאָה וְנַקֵּה.

יהוה , יהוה , El, merciful and gracious, longsuffering, and abundant in compassion and truth; guardian of compassion unto the thousandth generation; forgiving iniquity, and transgression, and sin, and pardoning. *(Shemot 34:6-7)*

# Unto Him Who Is Able

Leader and Congregation together
*Hebrew first, then English*

V'**Lo** haya**kḥol** lishmar'**kḥem** mimikḥ'**shol** ul'ha'**amid** et**kḥem** bli mum,

כד**וְלוֹ** הַיָּכוֹל לְשָׁמְרְכֶם מִמִּכְשׁוֹל וּלְהַעֲמִיד אֶתְכֶם בְּלִי מוּם

lif**nei** tifar**to** b'sim**kḥa**, a**sher** hu l'va**do** ha'Elo**him** haMo**shiah** o**tanu** b'Yeshu**a** HaMashi'a**kḥ** Ado**neinu**. Lo haka**vod**, hashil**ton** v'hai**kar** v'hagdu**lah**, lif**nei** k**ḥol** o**lam**, gam **ata** gam l'ola**mei** ola**mim**. A**mein**.

כה**לִפְנֵי** תִּפְאַרְתּוֹ בְּשִׂמְחָה אֲשֶׁר הוּא לְבַדּוֹ הָאֱלֹהִים הַמּוֹשִׁיעַ אֹתָנוּ בְּיֵשׁוּעַ הַמָּשִׁיחַ אֲדֹנֵינוּ. לוֹ הַכָּבוֹד, הַשִּׁלְטוֹן וְהַיְקָר וְהַגְּדֻלָּה לִפְנֵי כָל עוֹלָם גַּם עַתָּה גַּם לְעוֹלְמֵי עוֹלָמִים. אָמֵן.

Now to Him who is able to keep you from falling and to present you faultless before the presence of His Majesty with exceeding joy, to the only Elohim our Savior, through Yeshua HaMashi'akh Adoneinu, be glory, and majesty, dominion, and power, both now and in all the ages. Amein. *(Yehudah 1:24-25)*

# Yetzer Hara

Baru**kḥ** **Atah**, יהוה , Elo**heinu**, **Melekḥ** HaO**lam**, Hama'a**vir** she**nah** m'ei**nai** utnu**mah** m'afa**pai**. Vihi ra**tzon** milfanei**kḥa** יהוה Elo**heinu** velo**hei** Avo**teinu** sh'targi**lenu** b'toratei**kḥa** v'dabe**kenu** b'mitzvotei**kḥa**.

בָּרוּךְ אַתָּה יהוה , אֱלֹהֵינוּ, מֶלֶךְ הָעוֹלָם. הַמַּעֲבִיר שֵׁנָה מֵעֵינַי וּתְנוּמָה מֵעַפְעַפָּי: וִיהִי רָצוֹן מִלְּפָנֶיךָ, יהוה אֱלֹהֵינוּ, וֵאלֹהֵי אֲבוֹתֵינוּ. שֶׁתַּרְגִּילֵנוּ בְּתוֹרָתֶךָ, וְדַבְּקֵנוּ בְּמִצְוֹתֶיךָ.

| | |
|---|---|
| V'al tevi'enu lidei khet. | וְאַל תְּבִיאֵנוּ לִידֵי חֵטְא. |
| V'lo lidei averah v'avon. | וְלֹא לִידֵי עֲבֵרָה וְעָוֹן. וְלֹא |
| V'lo lidei nisayon. V'lo | לִידֵי נִסָּיוֹן. וְלֹא לִידֵי בִזָּיוֹן. |
| lidei vizayon. V'al tashlet | |
| banu yetzer hara. | וְאַל תַּשְׁלֶט בָּנוּ יֵצֶר הָרָע. |

Blessed are You, O יהוה our Elohim, King of the universe, who removes sleep from my eyes and slumber from my eyelids. May it be your will, יהוה our Eloheinu, Elohei Avoteinu, to accustom us to your Torah and attach us to your mitzvot. Do not lead us into the hands of sin, the hands of pride or perversity, the hands of temptation, nor into the hands of shame. And do not let the evil inclination rule over us.

# Ma Tovu (How Lovely)

Recognizing the oneness and beauty of the spiritual House of Elohim and Yisra'el, and the proper attitude in approaching our Elohim

*Hebrew first, then English*

| | |
|---|---|
| Ma tovu ohaleikha, Ya'akov; mishkenoteikha, Yisra'el! | מַה טֹּבוּ אֹהָלֶיךָ יַעֲקֹב; מִשְׁכְּנֹתֶיךָ יִשְׂרָאֵל. |
| Va'ani berov khasd'kha, avoh veiteikha; eshtakhaveh el heikhal kodsheikha, b'ir'ateikha. | וַאֲנִי בְּרֹב חַסְדְּךָ אָבוֹא בֵיתֶךָ; אֶשְׁתַּחֲוֶה אֶל הֵיכַל קָדְשְׁךָ בְּיִרְאָתֶךָ. |
| יהוה ahavti me'on beiteikha; um'kom, mishkan kevodeikha. | יהוה אָהַבְתִּי מְעוֹן בֵּיתֶךָ; וּמְקוֹם מִשְׁכַּן כְּבוֹדֶךָ. |
| Va'ani eshtakhaveh v'ekhra'a. Evr'kha lifnei יהוה osi. | וַאֲנִי אֶשְׁתַּחֲוֶה וְאֶכְרָעָה אֶבְרְכָה לִפְנֵי יהוה עֹשִׂי. |

Va'ani tefilati lekḥa יהוה, et ratzon, Elohim b'rov khasdeiḥa, aneni b'emet Yisheiḥa.

וַאֲנִי תְפִלָּתִי לְךָ יהוה עֵת רָצוֹן אֱלֹהִים בְּרָב חַסְדֶּךָ עֲנֵנִי בֶּאֱמֶת יִשְׁעֶךָ.

How lovely are your tents, O Ya'akov, your dwelling places, O Yisra'el! But as for me, in the abundance of Your compassion will I come into Your house; I will bow down toward Your Heikhal Kadosh in the fear of You. *(BaMidbar 24:5, Tehillah 5:8)*

יהוה , I love the habitation of Your House, and the place where Your Kavod dwells. I will bow down and bend the knee; I will kneel before יהוה my maker. *(Tehillah 26:8, 95:6)*

But as for me, let my tefilah be unto You, O יהוה , in an acceptable time; O Elohim, in the abundance of Your compassion, answer me with the truth of Your Salvation. *( Tehillah 69:14 )*

## Torah Blessing

Barukḥ Atah, יהוה , Eloheinu, Melekḥ ha'olam, asher kidshanu b'mitzvotav, v'tzivanu la'asok b'divrei Torah.

בָּרוּךְ אַתָּה יהוה , אֱלֹהֵינוּ, מֶלֶךְ הָעוֹלָם, אֲשֶׁר קִדְּשָׁנוּ בְּמִצְוֹתָיו, וְצִוָּנוּ לַעֲסוֹק בְּדִבְרֵי תוֹרָה.

Barukḥ Atah, יהוה , Eloheinu, Melekḥ ha'olam, asher bakḥar banu mikol ha'amim v'natan lanu et torato. Barukḥ Atah יהוה , noten haTorah.

בָּרוּךְ אַתָּה יהוה , אֱלֹהֵינוּ, מֶלֶךְ הָעוֹלָם, אֲשֶׁר בָּחַר בָּנוּ מִכָּל הָעַמִּים וְנָתַן לָנוּ אֶת תּוֹרָתוֹ. בָּרוּךְ אַתָּה יהוה , נוֹתֵן הַתּוֹרָה.

Blessed are You, O יהוה our Elohim, King of the Universe, who has consecrated us with Your Mitzvot, and commanded us to be occupied with the words of Torah.

Blessed are You, O יהוה our Elohim, King of the Universe, Who

has chosen us from all peoples, and has given us Your Torah. Blessed are You O יהוה , giver of the Torah.

# Kaddish: A Song of Praise
*Hebrew first, then English*

Yitga**dal** v'yitka**dash** she**meh** ra**ba**. Be'al**ma** di ve**ra** khir'u**teh** v'yam**likh** mal**khu**teh, b'khaiyei**khon** uv'yomei**khon** uvkha**iyei** d'**khol** beit Yisra'el ba'aga**la** uviz**man** ka**riv**. V'im**ru**, A**mein**.

יִתְגַּדֵל וְיִתְקַדַּשׁ שְׁמֵהּ רַבָּא. בְּעָלְמָא דִּי בְרָא כִרְעוּתֵהּ וְיַמְלִיךְ מַלְכוּתֵהּ, בְּחַיֵּיכוֹן וּבְיוֹמֵיכוֹן וּבְחַיֵּי דְכָל בֵּית יִשְׂרָאֵל בַּעֲגָלָא וּבִזְמַן קָרִיב. וְאִמְרוּ, אָמֵן.

Ye**heh** she**meh** ra**ba** m'va**rakh** l'o**lam** ul'ale**mei** alema**iya'**. V'im**ru**, A**mein**.

יְהֵא שְׁמֵהּ רַבָּא מְבָרַךְ לְעָלַם וּלְעָלְמֵי עָלְמַיָּא. וְאִמְרוּ, אָמֵן.

Yitba**rakh** v'yishta**bakh** v'yitpa'**ar** v'yitro**mam** v'yitna**seh** v'yitha**dar** v'yit'a**leh** v'yit'ha**lal** she**meh** d'kud**sha'**, ba**rikh** hu l'e**la** min kol bor**khata** v'**shir**ata, tushb'**khatah**, v'**nekh**emata, da'ami**ran** b'al**ma**. V'im**ru**, A**mein**.

יִתְבָּרַךְ וְיִשְׁתַּבַּח וְיִתְפָּאַר וְיִתְרוֹמַם וְיִתְנַשֵּׂא וְיִתְהַדָּר וְיִתְעַלֶּה וְיִתְהַלָּל שְׁמֵהּ דְּקֻדְשָׁא בְּרִיךְ הוּא לְעֵלָּא מִן כָּל בִּרְכָתָא וְשִׁירָתָא תֻּשְׁבְּחָתָא וְנֶחֱמָתָא דַּאֲמִירָן בְּעָלְמָא. וְאִמְרוּ, אָמֵן.

Oseh sha**lom** bimro**mav**, hu ya'**aseh** sha**lom** alei**nu** v'**al** kal Yisra'el. V'im**ru**, A**mein**.

עֹשֶׂה שָׁלוֹם בִּמְרוֹמָיו, הוּא יַעֲשֶׂה שָׁלוֹם עָלֵינוּ וְעַל כָּל יִשְׂרָאֵל. וְאִמְרוּ, אָמֵן.

Magnified and sanctified be His great Name in the world which He has created according to His will. May He establish His kingdom during our lifetime, and during our days, and during the life of the whole house of Yisra'el, even swiftly and soon, And

all say, "Amein." *(Divrei HaYamim 22:10)*

Let His great name be blessed forever and to all eternity, And all say, "Amein." *(Tehillah 113:2)*

Blessed, praised, glorified, exalted, extolled and honored, magnified and lauded be the name of the Holy One, blessed be He, though He is high above all blessings and songs, praise and consolations which are uttered in the world, And all say, "Amein." *(Neh 9:5)* He who makes peace in His heights, may He make peace upon us, and upon all Yisra'el. And all say, "Amein." *(Iyov 25:2)*

## Ashrei: Happy Are They!
### *Hebrew first, then English*

Ashrei yoshvei veiteikḥa, od yehalelukḥa, Selah.

אַשְׁרֵי יוֹשְׁבֵי בֵיתֶךָ עוֹד יְהַלְלוּךָ סֶּלָה.

Ashrei ha'am sh'kakḥah lo. Ashrei ha'am sheh Elohaiv.

אַשְׁרֵי הָעָם שֶׁכָּכָה לּוֹ: אַשְׁרֵי הָעָם שֶׁיהוה אֱלֹהָיו. יהוה

Happy are those who dwell in Your house, they are ever praising You! Selah. *(Tehillah 84:5)*

Happy is the people that is in such a state. Yes, happy is the people whose Elohim is יהוה . *(Tehillah 144:15)*

## Tehillah 145
### *Hebrew first, then English*

Tehillah l'David. Aromimkḥa Elohai hamelekḥ; Va'avarekḥah shimkḥa, l'olam va'ed.

תְּהִלָּה לְדָוִד: אֲרוֹמִמְךָ אֱלוֹהַי הַמֶּלֶךְ; וַאֲבָרְכָה שִׁמְךָ לְעוֹלָם וָעֶד.

B'khol yom avarekhekha;
Va'ahalelah shimkha
l'olam va'ed.

בְּכָל יוֹם אֲבָרְכֶךָ; וַאֲהַלְלָה שִׁמְךָ לְעוֹלָם וָעֶד.

Gadol יהוה um'hullal
me'od; V'ligdullato ein
kheker.

גָּדוֹל יהוה וּמְהֻלָּל מְאֹד; וְלִגְדֻלָּתוֹ אֵין חֵקֶר.

Dor l'dor, yeshabakh
ma'aseikha; Ugvuroteikha
yagidu.

דּוֹר לְדוֹר יְשַׁבַּח מַעֲשֶׂיךָ; וּגְבוּרֹתֶיךָ יַגִּידוּ.

Hadar k'vod hodekha,
v'divrei nifl'oteikha
asikhah.

הֲדַר כְּבוֹד הוֹדֶךָ וְדִבְרֵי נִפְלְאֹתֶיךָ אָשִׂיחָה.

V'ezuz norotekha yomeru;
ugdulatekha asaprenah.

וֶעֱזוּז נוֹרְאֹתֶיךָ יֹאמֵרוּ; וגדלותיך (וּגְדֻלָּתְךָ) אֲסַפְּרֶנָּה.

Zekher rav tuv'kha yabi'u;
v'tzidkatekha yeranenu.

זֵכֶר רַב טוּבְךָ יַבִּיעוּ; וְצִדְקָתְךָ יְרַנֵּנוּ.

Khanun v'rakhum יהוה ;
erekh apaiyim ugdal
khased.

חַנּוּן וְרַחוּם יהוה ; אֶרֶךְ אַפַּיִם וּגְדָל חָסֶד.

Tov יהוה lakol;
V'rakhamav, al kol
ma'asav.

טוֹב יהוה לַכֹּל; וְרַחֲמָיו עַל כָּל מַעֲשָׂיו.

Yodukha יהוה , kol
ma'aseikha; vakhasidekha
yevar'khukhah.

יוֹדוּךָ יהוה כָּל מַעֲשֶׂיךָ; וַחֲסִידֶיךָ יְבָרְכוּכָה.

K'vod malkhutkha yomeru; Ugvuratekha yedaberu.

יא כְּבוֹד מַלְכוּתְךָ יֹאמֵרוּ; וּגְבוּרָתְךָ יְדַבֵּרוּ.

L'hodiya, liv'nei ha'adam g'vurotav; ukhvod, hadar malkhuto.

יב לְהוֹדִיעַ לִבְנֵי הָאָדָם גְּבוּרֹתָיו; וּכְבוֹד הֲדַר מַלְכוּתוֹ.

Malkhutkha malkhut kol olamim; umemshaltekha, bekhol dor vador.

יג מַלְכוּתְךָ מַלְכוּת כָּל עֹלָמִים; וּמֶמְשַׁלְתְּךָ בְּכָל דּוֹר וָדֹר.

Somekh יהוה , l'khol hanoflim; V'zokef l'khol hak'fufim.

יד סוֹמֵךְ יהוה לְכָל הַנֹּפְלִים; וְזוֹקֵף לְכָל הַכְּפוּפִים.

Einei khol eleikha y'saberu; v'atah noten lahem et okhlam b'itoh.

טו עֵינֵי כֹל אֵלֶיךָ יְשַׂבֵּרוּ; וְאַתָּה נוֹתֵן לָהֶם אֶת אָכְלָם בְּעִתּוֹ.

Pote'akh et yadekha umasbi'a l'khol khai ratzon.

טז פּוֹתֵחַ אֶת יָדֶךָ; וּמַשְׂבִּיעַ לְכָל חַי רָצוֹן.

Tzadik יהוה , b'khol d'rakhav; v'khasid b'khol ma'asav.

יז צַדִּיק יהוה בְּכָל דְּרָכָיו; וְחָסִיד בְּכָל מַעֲשָׂיו.

Karov יהוה l'khol kor'av, l'khol asher yikra'uhu v'emet.

יח קָרוֹב יהוה לְכָל קֹרְאָיו לְכֹל אֲשֶׁר יִקְרָאֻהוּ בֶאֱמֶת.

Retzon yere'av ya'aseh; ve'et shavatam yishma, v'yoshi'em.

יט רְצוֹן יְרֵאָיו יַעֲשֶׂה; וְאֶת שַׁוְעָתָם יִשְׁמַע וְיוֹשִׁיעֵם.

Shomer יהוה , et kol ohavav; v'et kol haresha'im yashmid.

כ שׁוֹמֵר יהוה אֶת כָּל אֹהֲבָיו; וְאֵת כָּל הָרְשָׁעִים יַשְׁמִיד.

Tehillat יהוה yedaber pi: Vivarekh kol basar, shem kodshoh l'olam va'ed.

כא תְּהִלַּת יהוה יְדַבֶּר פִּי: וִיבָרֵךְ כָּל בָּשָׂר שֵׁם קָדְשׁוֹ לְעוֹלָם וָעֶד.

A Tehillah of David. I will extol You, my Elohim, O Melekh; and I will bless Your Name forever and ever.

Every day will I bless You; and I will praise Your Name forever and ever. Great is יהוה , and highly to be praised; and His greatness is unsearchable. One generation shall laud Your works to another, and shall declare Your mighty acts.

The glorious splendor of Your majesty, and Your wondrous works, will I rehearse. And men shall speak of the might of Your tremendous acts; and I will tell of Your greatness.

They shall utter the fame of Your great goodness, and shall sing of Your tzedaka. יהוה is gracious, and full of mercy; slow to anger, and of great compassion. יהוה is good to all; and His tender mercies are over all His works.

All Your works shall praise You, O יהוה ; and Your Khasidim shall bless You. They shall speak of the Kavod of Your Malkhut, and talk of Your might; to make known to the sons of men His mighty acts, and the glory of the majesty of His kingdom.

Your Malkhut is a kingdom for all ages, and Your dominion endures throughout all generations. יהוה upholds all that fall, and raises up all those that are bowed down. The eyes of all wait for You, and You give them their food in its time. O open Your hand, and satisfy every living thing with favor. יהוה is righteous in all His ways, and gracious in all His works.

יהוה is nigh unto all them that call upon Him, to all that call upon Him in truth. He will fulfill the desire of them that fear Him; He also will hear their cry, and will save them. יהוה preserves all them that love Him; but all the wicked will He destroy. My mouth shall speak the

114

praise of יהוה , and let all flesh bless His consecrated name forever and ever.

## Yishtabakḥ

Yishtabakḥ shimkḥa la'ad malkeinu. Ha'el hamelekḥ hagadol v'hakadosh bashamayim uva'aretz. Ki lekḥa na'eh יהוה Eloheinu v'Elohei Avoteinu. Shir ush'vakḥah hallel v'zimrah, oz umemshalah netzakḥ g'dulah ug'vurah tehillah vetiferet kedushah umalkḥut, berakḥot v'hoda'ot m'otah ve'ad olam.

יִשְׁתַּבַּח שִׁמְךָ לָעַד מַלְכֵּנוּ. הָאֵל הַמֶּלֶךְ הַגָּדוֹל וְהַקָּדוֹשׁ בַּשָּׁמַיִם וּבָאָרֶץ. כִּי לְךָ נָאֶה יהוה אֱלֹהֵינוּ וֵאלֹהֵי אֲבוֹתֵינוּ, שִׁיר וּשְׁבָחָה, הַלֵּל וְזִמְרָה, עֹז וּמֶמְשָׁלָה, נֶצַח גְּדֻלָּה וּגְבוּרָה, תְּהִלָּה וְתִפְאֶרֶת, קְדֻשָּׁה וּמַלְכוּת: בְּרָכוֹת וְהוֹדָאוֹת, מֵעוֹתָּה וְעַד עוֹלָם.

Barukḥ Atah יהוה El Melekḥ gadol umhulal batishbakḥot. El hahoda'ot. Adon hanifla'ot. Habokḥer b'shirei zimrah, Melekḥ, El kḥei ha'olamim. Amein.

בָּרוּךְ אַתָּה יהוה אֵל מֶלֶךְ גָּדוֹל וּמְהֻלָּל בַּתִּשְׁבָּחוֹת. אֵל הַהוֹדָאוֹת. אֲדוֹן הַנִּפְלָאוֹת. הַבּוֹחֵר בְּשִׁירֵי זִמְרָה, מֶלֶךְ אֵל חֵי הָעוֹלָמִים: אָמֵן.

May Your Name be praised forever – Elohim, the great and holy King, who is in heaven and on earth. For to You is fitting – יהוה , our Elohim and the Elohim of our forefathers – song and praise, tribute and singing, strength and dominion, eternal greatness and triumph, glory and splendor, holiness and kingdom, blessings and thanksgiving from now to eternity. Blessed are You, O יהוה , Elohim, King exalted through praises, Elohim of thanksgiving, Master of wonders, Who chooses musical songs of praise, King, Elohim, Lifegiver of the world. Amein.

# Kadosh: Consecrated

Vekara zeh el zeh ve'amar, "Kadosh Kadosh Kadosh יהוה Tzeva'ot." Melo khol ha'aretz k'vodo.

וְקָרָא זֶה אֶל זֶה וְאָמַר קָדוֹשׁ קָדוֹשׁ קָדוֹשׁ יהוה צְבָאוֹת; מְלֹא כָל הָאָרֶץ כְּבוֹדוֹ.

Vatisa'eni ru'akh va'eshma akharai, kol ra'ash gadol. Barukh k'vod יהוה , mim'komo.

וַתִּשָּׂאֵנִי רוּחַ וָאֶשְׁמַע אַחֲרַי קוֹל רַעַשׁ גָּדוֹל: בָּרוּךְ כְּבוֹד יהוה מִמְּקוֹמוֹ.

And they called to each other, and said, "Kadosh, Kadosh, Kadosh, is יהוה Tzeva'ot; the whole earth is full of His Kavod." *(Yesha-Yahu 6:3)*
Then a Ru'akh lifted me up, and I heard behind me the voice of a great rushing, "Blessed is the Kavod יהוה from His place" *(Yekhezkel 3:12)*

# Aharon's Blessing

Y'varekhekha יהוה , v'yishmerekha.

יְבָרֶכְךָ יהוה וְיִשְׁמְרֶךָ.

Ya'er יהוה panav eleikha vikhunekha.

יָאֵר יהוה פָּנָיו אֵלֶיךָ וִיחֻנֶּךָּ.

Yisah יהוה panav eleikha v'yasem lekha shalom.

יִשָּׂא יהוה פָּנָיו אֵלֶיךָ וְיָשֵׂם לְךָ שָׁלוֹם.

יהוה bless you, and keep you; יהוה make His face to shine upon you, and be gracious unto you; יהוה lift up His countenance upon you, and give you shalom.

# Shemah! The Greatest of Commandments

Shema, Yisra'el: יהוה שְׁמַע יִשְׂרָאֵל יהוה אֱלֹהֵינוּ
Eloheinu, יהוה Ekḥad.  יהוה אֶחָד.

V'ahavta, et יהוה וְאָהַבְתָּ אֵת יהוה אֱלֹהֶיךָ
Eloheikḥa, b'kḥol בְּכָל לְבָבְךָ וּבְכָל נַפְשְׁךָ
l'vavekḥa uv'kḥol וּבְכָל מְאֹדֶךָ.
nafshekḥa, uv'kḥol
me'odeikḥa.

V'hayu had'varim ha'eleh, וְהָיוּ הַדְּבָרִים הָאֵלֶּה אֲשֶׁר
asher anokḥi metzav'kḥa אָנֹכִי מְצַוְּךָ הַיּוֹם עַל לְבָבֶךָ.
hayom, al levavekḥa.

V'shinantam l'vaneikḥa, וְשִׁנַּנְתָּם לְבָנֶיךָ וְדִבַּרְתָּ בָּם
v'dibarta bam, b'shivtekḥa בְּשִׁבְתְּךָ בְּבֵיתֶךָ וּבְלֶכְתְּךָ
b'veiteikḥa uvlekḥtekḥa בַדֶּרֶךְ וּבְשָׁכְבְּךָ וּבְקוּמֶךָ.
vaderekḥ, uvshokḥbekḥa
uvkumeikḥa.

Ukshartam l'oht, al וּקְשַׁרְתָּם לְאוֹת עַל יָדֶךָ
yadeikḥa; v'hayu l'totafot וְהָיוּ לְטֹטָפֹת בֵּין עֵינֶיךָ.
bein eineikḥa.

Ukḥtavtam al mezuzot וּכְתַבְתָּם עַל מְזֻזוֹת בֵּיתֶךָ
beiteikḥa uvish'areikḥa. וּבִשְׁעָרֶיךָ.

V'ahavta lere'akḥa וְאָהַבְתָּ לְרֵעֲךָ כָּמוֹךָ.
kamokḥa.

117

V'hayah, im shamoah tishme'u el mitzvotai, asher anokhi metzaveh etkhem hayom, l'ahavah et יהוה Eloheikhem, u'le'avdo b'khol levavkhem, u'vekhol nafshekhem

יֹּוְהָיָה אִם שָׁמֹעַ תִּשְׁמְעוּ אֶל מִצְוֹתַי אֲשֶׁר אָנֹכִי מְצַוֶּה אֶתְכֶם הַיּוֹם לְאַהֲבָה אֶת יהוה אֱלֹהֵיכֶם וּלְעָבְדוֹ בְּכָל לְבַבְכֶם וּבְכָל נַפְשְׁכֶם.

V'natati metar artzekhem b'itoh, yoreh umalkosh; v'asaftah deganeikha, v'tirohshekha v'yitzhareikha

יֹּדוְנָתַתִּי מְטַר אַרְצְכֶם בְּעִתּוֹ יוֹרֶה וּמַלְקוֹשׁ וְאָסַפְתָּ דְגָנֶךָ וְתִירֹשְׁךָ וְיִצְהָרֶךָ.

V'natati esev b'sadekha, Liv'hemteikha; v'akhalta, v'savata

יֹּוְנָתַתִּי עֵשֶׂב בְּשָׂדְךָ לִבְהֶמְתֶּךָ וְאָכַלְתָּ וְשָׂבָעְתָּ.

Hishamru lakhem, pen yifteh levavkhem; v'sartem, va'a'va'de'tem elohim akharim, v'hishtakhavitem lahem

יֹּהִשָּׁמְרוּ לָכֶם פֶּן יִפְתֶּה לְבַבְכֶם וְסַרְתֶּם וַעֲבַדְתֶּם אֱלֹהִים אֲחֵרִים וְהִשְׁתַּחֲוִיתֶם לָהֶם.

V'harah af יהוה bakhem, v'atzar et hashamayim v'lo yihyeh matar, v'ha'a'damah, lo titen et yevulah; va'avadtem me'herah, me'al ha'aretz hatovah, asher יהוה noten lakhem

יֹּוְחָרָה אַף יהוה בָּכֶם וְעָצַר אֶת הַשָּׁמַיִם וְלֹא יִהְיֶה מָטָר וְהָאֲדָמָה לֹא תִתֵּן אֶת יְבוּלָהּ וַאֲבַדְתֶּם מְהֵרָה מֵעַל הָאָרֶץ הַטֹּבָה אֲשֶׁר יהוה נֹתֵן לָכֶם.

118

V'samtem et d'varai eleh al levav'khem v'al nafsh'khem; ukshartem otam l'ot al yedkhem, v'hayu l'totafot bein einekhem

יחוְשַׂמְתֶּם אֶת דְּבָרַי אֵלֶּה עַל לְבַבְכֶם וְעַל נַפְשְׁכֶם וּקְשַׁרְתֶּם אֹתָם לְאוֹת עַל יֶדְכֶם וְהָיוּ לְטוֹטָפֹת בֵּין עֵינֵיכֶם.

V'limadtem otam et beneikhem, l'daber bam, b'shivtekha b'veiteikha uv'lekhtekha vaderekh, uv'shokhbekha uv'kumeikha

יטוְלִמַּדְתֶּם אֹתָם אֶת בְּנֵיכֶם לְדַבֵּר בָּם בְּשִׁבְתְּךָ בְּבֵיתֶךָ וּבְלֶכְתְּךָ בַדֶּרֶךְ וּבְשָׁכְבְּךָ וּבְקוּמֶךָ.

Ukh'tavtam al mezuzot beiteikha uvish'areikha

כוּכְתַבְתָּם עַל מְזוּזוֹת בֵּיתֶךָ וּבִשְׁעָרֶיךָ.

L'ma'an yirbu yemekhem, vi'mei v'nekhem, al ha'adamah, asher nishbah יהוה la'avoht'khem latet lahem kimei hashamayim, al ha'aretz.

כאלְמַעַן יִרְבּוּ יְמֵיכֶם וִימֵי בְנֵיכֶם עַל הָאֲדָמָה אֲשֶׁר נִשְׁבַּע יהוה לַאֲבֹתֵיכֶם לָתֵת לָהֶם כִּימֵי הַשָּׁמַיִם עַל הָאָרֶץ.

**Shema, Yisra'el: יהוה is our Elohim, יהוה is Ekhad.**

And you shall love יהוה your Elohim with all your heart, and with all your soul, and with all your might. And these words, which I command you this day, shall be upon your heart; and you shall impress them upon your children, and shall talk of them when you sit in your house, and when you walk by the way, and when you lie down, and when you rise up. And you shall bind them for a sign upon your hand, and they shall be for frontlets between your eyes. And you shall write them upon the door-posts of your house, and upon your gates.

And you shall love your neighbor as yourself. And it shall come

119

to pass, if you shall hearken diligently unto My Mitzvot which I command you this day, to love יהוה your Elohim, and to serve Him with all your heart and with all your soul, that I will give the rain of your land in its season, the former rain and the latter rain, that you may gather in your grain, and your choice wine, and your oil.

And I will give grass in your fields for your cattle, and you shall eat and be satisfied. Take heed to yourselves, lest your heart be deceived, and you turn aside, and serve other gods, and worship them; and the anger of יהוה be kindled against you, and He shut up the heaven, so that there shall be no rain, and the ground shall not yield her fruit; and you perish quickly from off the good land which יהוה gives you.

Therefore shall you lay up these My words in your heart and in your soul; and you shall bind them for a sign upon your hand, and they shall be for frontlets between your eyes. And you shall teach them to your children, talking of them, when you sit in your house, and when you walk by the way, and when you lie down, and when you rise up. And you shall write them upon the door-posts of your house, and upon your gates; that your days may be multiplied, and the days of your children, upon the land which יהוה swore unto your fathers to give them, as the days of the heavens above the earth.

## Mi Kamokḥa: Who is Like You

Mi kamokḥa ba'elim יהוה ?    מִי כָמֹכָה בָּאֵלִם יהוה
Mi kamokḥa, ne'edar    מִי כָמֹכָה נֶאְדָּר בַּקֹּדֶשׁ;
bakodesh; nora tehilot,    נוֹרָא תְהִלֹת עֹשֵׂה פֶלֶא.
oseh feleh.

Who is like unto You, O יהוה , among the gods? Who is like unto You, glorious in kodesh, awesome in praises, doing wonders? *(Shemot 15:11)*

# Sh'monei Esrei: Amidah

*Hebrew first, then English*

**THE AMIDAH OPENING**

Adonai, sefatai tiftakḥ; ufi yagid tehillateikḥa.

אֲדֹנָי, שְׂפָתַי תִּפְתָּח; וּפִי יַגִּיד תְּהִלָּתֶךָ.

O Adonai, open  my lips, and my mouth shall declare Your praise.

**1. Avot (Fathers)**

Barukḥ Atah, יהוה , Eloheinu v'Elohei avoteinu. Elohei Avraham. Elohei Yitz'khak. V'Elohei Ya'akov.

בָּרוּךְ אַתָּה יהוה , אֱלֹהֵינוּ, וֵאלֹהֵי אֲבוֹתֵינוּ. אֱלֹהֵי אַבְרָהָם. אֱלֹהֵי יִצְחָק. וֵאלֹהֵי יַעֲקֹב.

Ha'El hagadol hagibor v'hanora, El Elyon. Gomel khasadim tovim, V'koneh hakol.

הָאֵל הַגָּדוֹל הַגִּבּוֹר וְהַנּוֹרָא. אֵל עֶלְיוֹן. גּוֹמֵל חֲסָדִים טוֹבִים, וְקוֹנֵה הַכֹּל.

V'zokḥer kḥas'dei avot. Umevi go'el livnei v'neihem l'ma'an shemo b'ahavah.

וְזוֹכֵר חַסְדֵּי אָבוֹת, וּמֵבִיא גוֹאֵל לִבְנֵי בְנֵיהֶם לְמַעַן שְׁמוֹ בְּאַהֲבָה.

Melekḥ ozer umoshiya, umagen. Barukḥ Atah, יהוה , Magen Avraham.

מֶלֶךְ עוֹזֵר וּמוֹשִׁיעַ וּמָגֵן: בָּרוּךְ אַתָּה יהוה , מָגֵן אַבְרָהָם.

Blessed are You, O יהוה , our Elohim, and Elohim of our fathers, Elohim of Av'raham, Elohim of Yitz'khak and Elohim of Ya'akov, the great, mighty and awesome Elohim, the Most High God, who bestows compassion and creates all, and remembers the kindnesses of the fathers, and brings a redeemer to their children's children, for His name's sake with love. O King, helper, savior, and shield, blessed are You, יהוה , Shield of Av'raham.

## 2. Gibor (Might)

Atah gibor l'olam Adonai mekhaiyeh metim. Atah rav l'hoshia.

אַתָּה גִּבּוֹר לְעוֹלָם אֲדֹנָי, מְחַיֶּה מֵתִים. אַתָּה רַב לְהוֹשִׁיעַ.

Mekhalkel khaiyim b'khesed. Mekhaiyeh metim berakhamim rabim. Somekh noflim v'rofeh kholim uMatir asurim. Um'kaiyem emunato lishnei afar.

מְכַלְכֵּל חַיִּים בְּחֶסֶד. מְחַיֶּה מֵתִים בְּרַחֲמִים רַבִּים. סוֹמֵךְ נוֹפְלִים וְרוֹפֵא חוֹלִים וּמַתִּיר אֲסוּרִים. וּמְקַיֵּם אֱמוּנָתוֹ לִישֵׁנֵי עָפָר.

Mi kamokha ba'al gevurot, umi domeh lakh. Melekh memit um'khaiyeh umatzmi'akh Yeshua[h]?

מִי כָמוֹךָ בַּעַל גְּבוּרוֹת, וּמִי דוֹמֶה לָּךְ. מֶלֶךְ מֵמִית וּמְחַיֶּה וּמַצְמִיחַ יְשׁוּעָה?

V'ne'eman Atah l'hakhaiyot metim. Barukh Atah, יהוה , mekhaiyeh hametim.

וְנֶאֱמָן אַתָּה לְהַחֲיוֹת מֵתִים: בָּרוּךְ אַתָּה יהוה , מְחַיֶּה הַמֵּתִים.

You are eternally mighty, Adonai, the Resurrector of the dead are You; great in salvation. Who sustains the living with kindness, resurrects the dead with great mercy, supports the fallen, heals the sick, releases the confined, and keeps His faith to those asleep in the dust.

Who is like You, O master of mighty deeds, and who is comparable to You, O King, who causes death and restores life and makes salvation sprout? And You are faithful to resurrect the dead. Blessed are You, O יהוה , who resurrects the dead.

### 3. Kadosh et Hashem יהוה (Holiness of the Name of יהוה)

אַתָּה קָדוֹשׁ וְשִׁמְךָ קָדוֹשׁ
וּקְדוֹשִׁים בְּכָל יוֹם, יְהַלְלוּךָ
סֶלָה. בָּרוּךְ אַתָּה יהוה ,
הָאֵל הַקָּדוֹשׁ:

Atah kadosh v'shimkḥa
kadosh uk'doshim b'kḥol
yom y'hallelukḥa, Selah.
Barukḥ Atah, יהוה , Ha'El
hakadosh.

You are holy and your Name is holy, and every day holy ones
will praise You. Selah. Blessed are You, יהוה , the holy God.

### 4. Binah (Insight)

אַתָּה חוֹנֵן לְאָדָם דַּעַת.
וּמְלַמֵּד לֶאֱנוֹשׁ בִּינָה: וְחָנֵּנוּ
מֵאִתְּךָ חָכְמָה בִּינָה וָדָעַת;
בָּרוּךְ אַתָּה יהוה , חוֹנֵן
הַדָּעַת.

Atah khonen l'adam
da'at. Um'lamed l'enosh
binah. V'kḥanenu
me'itkḥa khakḥmah binah
vada'at. Barukḥ Atah,
יהוה , khonen hada'at.

You show favor to a man of knowledge and teach understanding
to a mortal man. Be gracious to us; a mind of understanding and
intellect is from You. Blessed are You, יהוה , who favors the
knowledge.

### 5. Teshuvah (Repentance)

הֲשִׁיבֵנוּ אָבִינוּ לְתוֹרָתֶךָ.
וְקָרְבֵנוּ מַלְכֵּנוּ לַעֲבוֹדָתֶךָ.
וְהַחֲזִירֵנוּ בִּתְשׁוּבָה שְׁלֵמָה
לְפָנֶיךָ: בָּרוּךְ אַתָּה יהוה ,
הָרוֹצֶה בִּתְשׁוּבָה.

Hashivenu Avinu
l'torateikḥa. V'karvenu
Malkeinu la'avodateikḥa.
V'hakḥazirenu bitshuvah
shelemah lefaneikḥa.
Barukḥ Atah, יהוה ,
harotzeh bitshuvah.

Bring us back, our Father, to Your Torah, and bring us closer, our
King, to Your service, and make us return in complete
repentance before You. Blessed are You, O יהוה , who desires
repentance.

## 6. Selakḥ (Forgiveness)

Selakḥ lanu Avinu, ki khatanu. Makḥol lanu malkeinu ki fashanu. Ki El tov v'salakḥ Atah. Barukḥ Atah יהוה , khanun hamarbeh lislo'akḥ.

סְלַח לָנוּ, אָבִינוּ, כִּי חָטָאנוּ. מְחַל לָנוּ מַלְכֵּנוּ, כִּי פָשָׁעְנוּ. כִּי אֵל טוֹב וְסַלָּח אָתָּה. בָּרוּךְ אַתָּה יהוה , חַנּוּן הַמַּרְבֶּה לִסְלֹחַ.

Forgive us, our Father, for we have erred; pardon us, our King, for we have intentionally sinned, for You pardon and forgive. Blessed are You, יהוה , the Compassionate One, who pardons abundantly.

## 7. Ge'ulah (Redemption)

Re'eh na v'anyeinu. V'rivah rivenu. Ug'alenu ge'ulah sh'lemah meherah l'ma'an sh'meikḥa. Ki El go'el khazak Atah. Barukḥ Atah, יהוה , go'el Yisra'el.

רְאֵה נָא בְעָנְיֵנוּ. וְרִיבָה רִיבֵנוּ. וּגְאָלֵנוּ גְאֻלָה שְׁלֵמָה מְהֵרָה לְמַעַן שְׁמֶךָ. כִּי אֵל גּוֹאֵל חָזָק אָתָּה. בָּרוּךְ אַתָּה יהוה , גּוֹאֵל יִשְׂרָאֵל.

Behold our affliction, take up our grievance, and save us soon for the sake of Your Name, for You are a powerful redeemer. Blessed are You, O יהוה , the redeemer of Yisra'el.

## 8. Refu'ah (Healing and Health)

Refa'enu יהוה v'nerafeh'. Hoshi'einu v'nivashe'ah. Ki tehilatenu Atah. V'ha'aleh arukḥah umarpeh l'khol takḥalu'enu ul'khol makḥovenu ul'khol makotenu.

רְפָאֵנוּ יהוה וְנֵרָפֵא. הוֹשִׁיעֵנוּ וְנִוָּשֵׁעָה, כִּי תְהִלָּתֵנוּ אָתָּה. וְהַעֲלֵה אֲרוּכָה וּמַרְפֵּא לְכָל תַּחֲלוּאֵינוּ, וּלְכָל מַכְאוֹבֵינוּ, וּלְכָל מַכּוֹתֵינוּ.

| | |
|---|---|
| Yehi ratzon milfaneikha, יהוה Elohai v'Elohei Avotai. Sh'tishlakh meherah refu'ah shel'mah min hashamayim. Refu'at hanefesh urefu'at haguf l'kholeh b'tokh she'ar kholei Yisra'el. | יְהִי רָצוֹן מִלְפָנֶיךָ יהוה אֱלֹהַי וֵאלֹהֵי אֲבוֹתַי, שֶׁתִּשְׁלַח מְהֵרָה רְפוּאָה שְׁלֵמָה מִן הַשָּׁמַיִם. רְפוּאַת הַנֶּפֶשׁ, וּרְפוּאַת הַגּוּף, לְחוֹלֶה בְּתוֹךְ שְׁאָר חוֹלֵי יִשְׂרָאֵל. |
| Ki El Melekh rofeh ne'eman v'rakhaman Atah. Barukh Atah, יהוה , rofeh kholei amo Yisra'el. | כִּי אֵל מֶלֶךְ רוֹפֵא נֶאֱמָן וְרַחֲמָן אָתָּה. בָּרוּךְ אַתָּה יהוה , רוֹפֵא חוֹלֵי עַמּוֹ יִשְׂרָאֵל. |

Heal us יהוה , and we shall be healed, save us, and we shall be saved, for You are our praise. And bring complete recovery for all our sicknesses, our diseases, and all our wounds. May it be Your will, יהוה , my Elohim, and the Elohim of my forefathers, that You quickly send a complete recovery from heaven, spiritual healing and physical healing to the patient (son or daughter) of (mother or father's name) among the other patients of Yisra'el, for You are Elohim, Melekh, the faithful and merciful healer. Blessed are You, O יהוה , who heals the sick of His people Yisra'el.

### 9. Birkat HaShanim (Blessings of the Years)

| | |
|---|---|
| Barekh aleinu, יהוה Eloheinu, et hashanah hazot v'et kol minei tevu'atah l'tovah v'et berakhah al p'nei ha'adamah, v'sabeinu mituvah. Uvarekh shenatenu kashanim hatovot. Barukh Atah, יהוה , mevarekh hashanim. | בָּרֵךְ עָלֵינוּ, יהוה אֱלֹהֵינוּ, אֶת הַשָּׁנָה הַזֹּאת וְאֶת כָּל מִינֵי תְבוּאָתָהּ לְטוֹבָה וְאֶת בִּרְכָה עַל פְּנֵי הָאֲדָמָה, וְשַׂבְּעֵנוּ מִטּוּבָהּ. וּבָרֵךְ שְׁנָתֵנוּ כַּשָּׁנִים הַטוֹבוֹת. בָּרוּךְ אַתָּה יהוה , מְבָרֵךְ הַשָּׁנִים. |

Bless for us, יהוה , our Elohim, this year and its crops. Give us a

blessing, and give dew and rain for blessing on the face of the earth, and satisfy us from Your goodness, and bless our year like the other good years. Blessed are You, O יהוה , who blesses the years.

### 10. Kibbutz Galuyot (Ingathering of Exiles)

Teka b'sho**far** ga**dol** le**kh**erutenu. V'**sheh** nes leka**betz** galuyotenu. V'kobe**tz**enu ya**kh**ad meher**ah** me'ar**bah kan'fot** ha'aretz l'artzeinu. Baru**kh** Atah, יהוה , meka**betz** nid**kh**ei ah**mo** Yisra'**el**.

תְּקַע בְּשׁוֹפָר גָּדוֹל לְחֵרוּתֵנוּ. וְשָׂא נֵס לְקַבֵּץ גָּלֻיּוֹתֵינוּ. וְקַבְּצֵנוּ יַחַד מְהֵרָה מֵאַרְבַּע כַּנְפוֹת הָאָרֶץ לְאַרְצֵנוּ: בָּרוּךְ אַתָּה יהוה , מְקַבֵּץ נִדְחֵי עַמּוֹ יִשְׂרָאֵל.

Sound the great shofar for our freedom, and raise a standard to gather our exiles, and gather us from the four corners of the earth. Blessed are You, O יהוה , who gathers the dispersed of His people Yisra'el.

### 11. Birkat HaDin (Restoration of Justice)

Hashiva**h** shof**teinu** k'varisho**nah**. V'yoatzeinu kevat'**kh**ilah. V'haser mimeinu ya**gon** va'ana**kh**ah. U'mele**kh** aleinu meher**ah**. Atah יהוה le'vad'**kha** b'**kh**esed uvra**kh**amim. V'tzadkenu b'**tze**dek uv'mish**pat**. Baru**kh** Atah, יהוה , **Me**lekh ohev tzeda**kah** umish**pat**.

הָשִׁיבָה שׁוֹפְטֵינוּ כְּבָרִאשׁוֹנָה. וְיוֹעֲצֵינוּ כְּבַתְּחִלָּה. וְהָסֵר מִמֶּנּוּ יָגוֹן וַאֲנָחָה. וּמְלֹךְ עָלֵינוּ מְהֵרָה. אַתָּה יהוה לְבַדְּךָ בְּחֶסֶד וּבְרַחֲמִים. וְצַדְּקֵנוּ בְּצֶדֶק וּבְמִשְׁפָּט. בָּרוּךְ אַתָּה יהוה , מֶלֶךְ אוֹהֵב צְדָקָה וּמִשְׁפָּט.

Restore our judges as in early times, and our counselors as at first; remove from us our sorrows and troubles; we want you, יהוה , alone, to rule over us with kindness and compassion and to justify us in justice. Blessed are You, O יהוה , King who loves righteousness and justice.

## 12. Tzadikim (The Righteous)

Al hatzadikim v'al hakhasidim. V'al ziknei she'erit ahm'kha Beit Yisra'el. V'al peleitat sofrehem. V'al gerei hatzedek. V'aleinu, yehemu nah rakhameikha, יהוה Eloheinu. V'ten shekhar tov lekhol habot'khim b'shimkha b'emet.

עַל הַצַּדִּיקִים וְעַל הַחֲסִידִים. וְעַל זִקְנֵי שְׁאֵרִית עַמְּךָ בֵּית יִשְׂרָאֵל. וְעַל פְּלֵיטַת סוֹפְרֵיהֶם. וְעַל גֵּרֵי הַצֶּדֶק. וְעָלֵינוּ, יֶהֱמוּ נָא רַחֲמֶיךָ יהוה אֱלֹהֵינוּ. וְתֵן שָׂכָר טוֹב לְכָל הַבּוֹטְחִים בְּשִׁמְךָ בֶּאֱמֶת.

V'sim khelkeinu imahem. Ul'olam lo nevosh ki v'kha vatakhnu. V'al khasd'kha hagadol b'emet (uv'tamim) nish'anenu. Barukh Atah, יהוה , mishan umivtakh latzadikim.

וְשִׂים חֶלְקֵנוּ עִמָּהֶם. וּלְעוֹלָם לֹא נֵבוֹשׁ כִּי בְךָ בָּטָחְנוּ. וְעַל חַסְדְּךָ הַגָּדוֹל בֶּאֱמֶת (וּבְתָמִים) נִשְׁעָנֶנוּ: בָּרוּךְ אַתָּה יהוה , מִשְׁעָן וּמִבְטָח לַצַּדִּיקִים.

On the righteous, on the devout, on the elders of Your people, the house of Yisra'el, on the remnant of their scribes, on the righteous converts and on us. May Your compassion be aroused, יהוה , our Elohim, and give good reward to all those who truly trust Your Name. May You put our share among them, and we shall not be ashamed forever, for You we trust. And upon your compassion we rely. Blessed are You, O יהוה , who supports and safeguards the righteous.

### 13. Binyan Yerushulayim (Rebuilding Yerushalayim)

V'liyrushalayim irkḥa
b'rakḥamim tashuv.
V'tishkon b'tokḥah
ka'asher dibarta. Uvneh
otah b'karov b'yameinu
binyan olam. V'kḥiseh
David avdekḥa meherah
l'tokḥah takḥin. Barukḥ
Atah, יהוה , boneh
Yerushalayim.

וְלִירוּשָׁלַיִם עִירְךָ בְּרַחֲמִים
תָּשׁוּב. וְתִשְׁכֹּן בְּתוֹכָהּ
כַּאֲשֶׁר דִּבַּרְתָּ. וּבְנֵה אוֹתָהּ
בְּקָרוֹב בְּיָמֵינוּ בִּנְיַן עוֹלָם.
וְכִסֵּא דָוִד עַבְדְּךָ מְהֵרָה
לְתוֹכָהּ תָּכִין. בָּרוּךְ אַתָּה
יהוה , בּוֹנֵה יְרוּשָׁלָיִם.

And to Yerushalayim Your city You shall return with mercy, and You shall dwell in it, as You have spoken. May You rebuild it soon in our days for eternity, and may You establish the throne of David within it. Blessed are You, O יהוה , the Builder of Yerushalayim.

### 14. Malkḥut Beit David (Davidic Reign)

Et tzemakḥ David
avdekḥa m'herah
tatzmiakḥ. V'karno tarum
bishuatekḥa. Ki lishuatekḥa
kivinu kal hayom. Barukḥ
Atah, יהוה , matzimiakḥ
keren yeshuah.

אֶת צֶמַח דָּוִד עַבְדְּךָ מְהֵרָה
תַצְמִיחַ. וְקַרְנוֹ תָּרוּם
בִּישׁוּעָתֶךָ. כִּי לִישׁוּעָתְךָ
קִוִּינוּ כָּל הַיּוֹם: בָּרוּךְ אַתָּה
יהוה , מַצְמִיחַ קֶרֶן יְשׁוּעָה.

May the offspring of David, Your servant, flourish speedily and exalt his honor with Your salvation. For Your salvation (Yeshua) we hope all day long. Blessed are You, O יהוה , who makes the horn of salvation to flourish.

## 15. Tefillah (Acceptance of Prayer)

Shema kolenu, יהוה Eloheinu. Khus v'rakhem aleinu. V'kabel b'rakhamim uv'ratzon et tefilatenu. Ki El shome'a tefilot v'takhanunim Atah. U'milfaneikha malkeinu reikam al teshivenu, ki Atah shome'a tefilat ahm'kha Yisra'el berakhamim. Barukh Atah, יהוה shome'a tefilah.

שְׁמַע קוֹלֵנוּ, יהוה אֱלֹהֵינוּ. חוּס וְרַחֵם עָלֵינוּ. וְקַבֵּל בְּרַחֲמִים וּבְרָצוֹן אֶת תְּפִלָּתֵנוּ. כִּי אֵל שׁוֹמֵעַ תְּפִלּוֹת וְתַחֲנוּנִים אָתָּה. וּמִלְּפָנֶיךָ מַלְכֵּנוּ רֵיקָם אַל תְּשִׁיבֵנוּ. כִּי אַתָּה שׁוֹמֵעַ תְּפִלַּת עַמְּךָ יִשְׂרָאֵל בְּרַחֲמִים. בָּרוּךְ אַתָּה יהוה , שׁוֹמֵעַ תְּפִלָּה.

Hear our voice, יהוה , our Elohim. Have mercy and compassion for us, and accept our prayers mercifully and willingly, for You are Elohim who listens to prayers and supplications. From before Yourself, our King, turn us not away empty handed, for You hear the prayer of Your people Yisra'el mercifully. Blessed are You, O יהוה , who hears prayers.

## 16. Avodah (Restoration of Temple Service)

Retzeh יהוה Eloheinu b'amekha Yisra'el v'litfilatam. V'hashev et ha'avodah lidvir beitekha.

רְצֵה יהוה אֱלֹהֵינוּ בְּעַמְּךָ יִשְׂרָאֵל וְלִתְפִלָּתָם. וְהָשֵׁב אֶת הָעֲבוֹדָה לִדְבִיר בֵּיתֶךָ.

V'ishei Yisra'el ut'filatam meherah b'ahavah tekabel b'ratzon. Utehi l'ratzon tamid avodat Yisra'el ahmei'kha. V'tekhezeinah eineinu b'shuvkha l'Tzion b'rakhamim. Barukh Atah, יהוה , hamakhazir shekhinato l'Tzion.

וְאִשֵּׁי יִשְׂרָאֵל וּתְפִלָּתָם מְהֵרָה בְּאַהֲבָה תְקַבֵּל בְּרָצוֹן. וּתְהִי לְרָצוֹן תָּמִיד עֲבוֹדַת יִשְׂרָאֵל עַמֶּךָ: וְתֶחֱזֶינָה עֵינֵינוּ בְּשׁוּבְךָ לְצִיּוֹן בְּרַחֲמִים. בָּרוּךְ אַתָּה יהוה , הַמַּחֲזִיר שְׁכִינָתוֹ לְצִיּוֹן.

129

Be favorable, יהוה our Elohim, toward Your people Yisra'el and their prayer, and restore the most holy service of Your house. Accept in love the offerings and prayers of Yisra'el, and may the service of Your people, Yisra'el, always be favorable to You. May our eyes behold Your return to Tzion in mercy. Blessed are You, O יהוה , who restores His presence to Tzion.

### 17. Modim (Thanksgiving)

Modim anakhnu lakh. Sha'atah Hu יהוה Eloheinu v'Elohei Avoteinu l'olam va'ed, tzur khaiyeinu, magen yisheinu atah Hu ledor vador. Nodeh l'kha un'saper tehilatekha al khaiyeinu hamesurim b'yadekha. V'al nishmoteinu hap'kudot lakh. V'al niseikha sh'bekhol yom imanu. V'al nifloteikha v'tovoteikha sh'bekhol et. Erev vavoker v'tzohorayim.

מוֹדִים אֲנַחְנוּ לָךְ. שָׁאַתָּה הוּא יהוה אֱלֹהֵינוּ וֵאלֹהֵי אֲבוֹתֵינוּ לְעוֹלָם וָעֶד, צוּר חַיֵּינוּ, מָגֵן יִשְׁעֵנוּ אַתָּה הוּא לְדוֹר וָדוֹר. נוֹדֶה לְךָ וּנְסַפֵּר תְּהִלָּתֶךָ עַל חַיֵּינוּ הַמְּסוּרִים בְּיָדֶךָ. וְעַל נִשְׁמוֹתֵינוּ הַפְּקוּדוֹת לָךְ. וְעַל נִסֶּיךָ שֶׁבְּכָל יוֹם עִמָּנוּ. וְעַל נִפְלְאוֹתֶיךָ וְטוֹבוֹתֶיךָ שֶׁבְּכָל עֵת. עֶרֶב וָבֹקֶר וְצָהֳרָיִם.

Hatov ki lo khalu rakhameikha v'hamerakhem. ki lo tamu khasadeikha. Ki me'olam kivinu lakh.

הַטּוֹב כִּי לֹא כָלוּ רַחֲמֶיךָ. וְהַמְרַחֵם כִּי לֹא תַמּוּ חֲסָדֶיךָ. כִּי מֵעוֹלָם קִוִּינוּ לָךְ.

V'al kulam yitbarekh v'yitromem shimkha, malkenu, tamid l'olam va'ed. V'khol hakhaiyim yodukha selah. Vihalelu vivarkhu et shimkha hagadol b'emet l'olam, ki tov. Ha'el yeshu'ateinu v'ezrateinu, selah.

וְעַל כֻּלָּם יִתְבָּרֵךְ וְיִתְרוֹמֵם שִׁמְךָ מַלְכֵּנוּ תָּמִיד לְעוֹלָם וָעֶד: וְכֹל הַחַיִּים יוֹדוּךָ סֶּלָה. וִיהַלְלוּ וִיבָרְכוּ אֶת שִׁמְךָ הַגָּדוֹל בֶּאֱמֶת לְעוֹלָם כִּי טוֹב. הָאֵל יְשׁוּעָתֵנוּ וְעֶזְרָתֵנוּ, סֶלָה.

Barukh Atah יהוה hatov shimkha ulekha na'eh lehodot.

בָּרוּךְ אַתָּה יהוה , הַטּוֹב שִׁמְךָ וּלְךָ נָאֶה לְהוֹדוֹת.

We thank You, for You are יהוה , our Elohim and the Elohim of our forefathers forever and ever. The rock of our lives, the shield of our salvation, You are in every generation. We shall thank You and tell Your glory for our lives which are in Your hands, and for our souls that are entrusted to You, and for Your miracles that are with us every day, and for Your wonders and favors that happen all the time, evening and morning and noon.

The Good One, for Your compassion was not exhausted, and the Compassionate One, for Your merciful deeds have not ended; always have we put our hope in You. For all these, may Your Name be blessed and exalted, our King, always, forever and ever; and all the living will thank You – Selah – and praise Your Name truly, O Elohim, our salvation and help – Selah! Blessed are You, O יהוה , the Good One is Your Name, and You are proper to thank.

### 18. Sim Shalom (Establish Peace)

Sim shalom tovah uv'rakhah. Khen vakhesed verakhamim aleinu v'al kal Yisra'el ahm'kha. Barkheinu, Avinu, kulanu k'ekhad b'or paneikha. Ki v'or paneikha natata lanu, יהוה Eloheinu, torat khaiyim v'ahavat khesed. Utzdakah v'rakhamim v'khaiyim v'shalom.

שִׂים שָׁלוֹם טוֹבָה וּבְרָכָה. חֵן וָחֶסֶד וְרַחֲמִים עָלֵינוּ וְעַל כָּל יִשְׂרָאֵל עַמֶּךָ. בָּרְכֵנוּ אָבִינוּ כֻּלָּנוּ כְּאֶחָד בְּאוֹר פָּנֶיךָ. כִּי בְאוֹר פָּנֶיךָ נָתַתָּ לָּנוּ יהוה אֱלֹהֵינוּ תּוֹרַת חַיִּים וְאַהֲבַת חֶסֶד. וּצְדָקָה וְרַחֲמִים וְחַיִּים וְשָׁלוֹם.

V'tov b'eineikha l'varekh et kol ameikha Yisra'el b'khol et uv'khol sha'ah bishlomekha. Barukh Atah, יהוה , hamevarekh et amo Yisra'el bashalom.

וְטוֹב בְּעֵינֶיךָ לְבָרֵךְ אֶת כָּל עַמְּךָ יִשְׂרָאֵל בְּכָל עֵת וּבְכָל שָׁעָה בִּשְׁלוֹמֶךָ: בָּרוּךְ אַתָּה יהוה , הַמְבָרֵךְ אֶת עַמּוֹ יִשְׂרָאֵל בַּשָּׁלוֹם.

Oseh shalom bimromav, hu ya'aseh shalom aleinu v'al kol Yisra'el.

עֹשֶׂה שָׁלוֹם בִּמְרוֹמָיו, הוּא יַעֲשֶׂה שָׁלוֹם עָלֵינוּ וְעַל כָּל יִשְׂרָאֵל

Establish shalom, goodness, and blessing, graciousness, kindness, and compassion upon us, and upon all Yisra'el Your people. Bless us our Father, all of us as one, with the light of Your countenance; for with the light of Your countenance You gave us, יהוה our Elohim, the Torah of Life, and a love of kindness, righteousness, blessing, compassion, life and peace.

May it be good in Your eyes to bless Your people Yisra'el, in every season and in every hour with Your peace. Blessed are You, O יהוה , who blesses His people Yisra'el with peace. He who makes shalom in His heights, may He make shalom upon us, and upon all Yisra'el.

**CONCLUDING PRAYER**

Netzor leshonekha merah, us'fateikha, midaber mirmah.

נְצֹר לְשׁוֹנְךָ מֵרָע; וּשְׂפָתֶיךָ מִדַּבֵּר מִרְמָה.

Yihyu l'ratzon imrei fi, v'hegyon libi l'faneikha. יהוה, tzuri v'go'eli.

יִהְיוּ לְרָצוֹן אִמְרֵי פִי וְהֶגְיוֹן לִבִּי לְפָנֶיךָ. יהוה צוּרִי וְגֹאֲלִי.

Guard your tongue from evil, and your lips from speaking deceitfully. May the expressions of my mouth and the thoughts of my heart find favor before You, יהוה , my Rock and my Redeemer.

# Adon Olam: Master of the Universe
*Hebrew first, then English*

Adon Olam asher malakh, b'terem kol yetzir nivra, le'et na'asah v'kheftzo kol, azai melekh shemoh nikra; v'akharei kikhlot hakol, l'vado yimlokh nora. V'hu hayah v'hu hoveh v'hu yihyeh b'tifarah.

אֲדוֹן עוֹלָם אֲשֶׁר מָלַךְ, בְּטֶרֶם כָּל יְצִיר נִבְרָא. לְעֵת נַעֲשָׂה בְחֶפְצוֹ כֹּל, אֲזַי מֶלֶךְ שְׁמוֹ נִקְרָא. וְאַחֲרֵי כִּכְלוֹת הַכֹּל, לְבַדּוֹ יִמְלוֹךְ נוֹרָא. וְהוּא הָיָה, וְהוּא הֹוֶה, וְהוּא יִהְיֶה בְּתִפְאָרָה

V'hu ekhad v'ein sheni, l'hamshil lo l'hakhbirah; bli reshit, bli takhlit v'lo ha'oz v'hamisrah; v'hu Eli v'khai goeli, v'tzur khevli b'yom tzarah.

וְהוּא אֶחָד וְאֵין שֵׁנִי, לְהַמְשִׁיל לוֹ לְהַחְבִּירָה. בְּלִי רֵאשִׁית בְּלִי תַכְלִית וְלוֹ הָעֹז וְהַמִּשְׂרָה. וְהוּא אֵלִי וְחַי גּוֹאֲלִי, וְצוּר חֶבְלִי בְּיוֹם צָרָה.

| | |
|---|---|
| V'**hu** **nissi** u**manos** li, me**nat** **kosi** b'**yom** e**krah**; b'yado afkid rukhi, b'et ishan v'a'irah; v'im rukhi geviyati, Adonai li v'lo ira. | וְהוּא נִסִּי וּמָנוֹס לִי, מְנָת כּוֹסִי בְּיוֹם אֶקְרָא. בְּיָדוֹ אַפְקִיד רוּחִי, בְּעֵת אִישָׁן וְאָעִירָה. וְעִם רוּחִי גְוִיָּתִי, אֲדֹנָי לִי וְלֹא אִירָא. |

Master of the Universe who has reigned before anything was created, at the time that everything was created at His will, then "King" was His Name proclaimed.

After all has ceased to exist, He, the Awesome One, will reign alone. And He was and He is, and He shall be in Glory! And He is One, and there is no second to compare to Him, to declare as His equal.

Without beginning, without end, He has the might and dominion. And He is my Elohim and my living Redeemer, and the Rock of my Salvation in time of trouble.

And He is my standard and a refuge for me, the portion of my cup on the day I call. In His hand I will deposit my spirit, when I am asleep, and I shall awaken, and with my spirit shall my body remain. Adonai is with me and I shall not fear.

# Daily Tehillim

Tehillah 100 is read daily. There are certain Tehillim that are customarily read on each of the days of the week, one for each day. These were read in the Beit HaMikdash at the time of the offerings. They follow in the immediate pages starting on 135, and they are:

Yom Reishon: Tehillah 24
Yom Sh'ni: Tehillah 48
Yom Sh'lishi: Tehillah 82
Yom Revi'i: Tehillah 94
Yom Khamishi: Tehillah 81
Yom Shishi: Tehillah 93
Yom HaShabbat: Tehillah 92

## Tehillah 24 (First Day)

L'David, Mizmor: la יהוה , ha'aretz umlo'ah tevel v'yoshvei vah.

אלְדָוִד מִזְמוֹר: לַיהוה הָאָרֶץ וּמְלוֹאָהּ; תֵּבֵל וְיֹשְׁבֵי בָהּ.

Ki Hu al yamim yesadah, v'al neharot, y'khoneneiha.

בכִּי הוּא עַל יַמִּים יְסָדָהּ; וְעַל נְהָרוֹת יְכוֹנְנֶהָ.

Mi ya'aleh v'har יהוה ? umi yakum, bimkom kodsho?

גמִי יַעֲלֶה בְהַר יהוה ; וּמִי יָקוּם בִּמְקוֹם קָדְשׁוֹ.

Neki khapayim uvar l'vav, asher lo nasa lashav nafshi; v'lo nishba l'mirma.

דנְקִי כַפַּיִם וּבַר לֵבָב: אֲשֶׁר לֹא נָשָׂא לַשָּׁוְא נַפְשִׁי; וְלֹא נִשְׁבַּע לְמִרְמָה.

Yisa verakhah me'et יהוה , utz'dakah, m'Elohei yish'o.

היִשָּׂא בְרָכָה מֵאֵת יהוה ; וּצְדָקָה מֵאֱלֹהֵי יִשְׁעוֹ.

Zeh dor dorshav mevakshei faneikha Ya'akov. Selah.

וזֶה דּוֹר דֹּרְשָׁו; מְבַקְשֵׁי פָנֶיךָ יַעֲקֹב סֶלָה.

Se'u sh'arim, rashekhem v'hinasu, pitkhei olam, v'yavo Melekh HaKavod.

זשְׂאוּ שְׁעָרִים רָאשֵׁיכֶם וְהִנָּשְׂאוּ פִּתְחֵי עוֹלָם; וְיָבוֹא מֶלֶךְ הַכָּבוֹד.

Mi zeh, Melekh HaKavod? יהוה , izzuz v'gibor, יהוה , gibor milkhamah.

חמִי זֶה מֶלֶךְ הַכָּבוֹד: יהוה עִזּוּז וְגִבּוֹר; יהוה גִּבּוֹר מִלְחָמָה.

Se'u sh'arim ra'shekhem use'u, pitkhei olam; v'yavo Melekh HaKavod.

טשְׂאוּ שְׁעָרִים רָאשֵׁיכֶם וּשְׂאוּ פִּתְחֵי עוֹלָם; וְיָבֹא מֶלֶךְ הַכָּבוֹד.

135

Mi hu zeh, **Melekh** HaKavod? יהוה Tzeva'ot Hu **Melekh** HaKavod! **Se**lah.

מִי הוּא זֶה מֶלֶךְ הַכָּבוֹד: יהוה צְבָאוֹת הוּא מֶלֶךְ הַכָּבוֹד סֶלָה.

[1]A Mizmor of David. The earth belongs to יהוה , and the fullness thereof; the world, and they that dwell therein. [2]For He has founded it upon the seas, and established it upon the floods.

[3]Who shall ascend into Har יהוה ? And who shall stand in His consecrated place? [4]He that has clean hands, and a pure heart; who has not taken My Name in vain, and has not sworn deceitfully. [5]He shall receive a blessing from יהוה , and tzedaka from the Elohim of his Salvation. [6]Such is the generation of them that seek after Him, that seek Your face, even Ya'akov. Selah.

[7]Lift up your heads, O you gates, and be lifted up, O you everlasting doors; that the Melekh HaKavod may come in. [8]"Who is this Melekh HaKavod?" " יהוה strong and mighty, יהוה mighty in battle." [9]Lift up your heads, O you gates, yes, lift them up, O you everlasting doors; that the Melekh HaKavod may come in. [10]"Who then is this Melekh HaKavod?" " יהוה Tzeva'ot; He is Melekh HaKavod." Selah.

## Tehillah 48 (Second Day)

Shir miz**mor**, liv**nei** **Kora**kh

א‎שִׁיר מִזְמוֹר לִבְנֵי קֹרַח.

Gadol יהוה umhu**lal** me'od be'**ir** Elo**hei**nu, har kod**shoh**

ב‎גָּדוֹל יהוה וּמְהֻלָּל מְאֹד בְּעִיר אֱלֹהֵינוּ הַר קָדְשׁוֹ.

Ye**feh** nof, me**sos** kol ha'**a**retz. Har Tzi**on**, yark'**tei** tza**fon**, kir**yat me**lekh rav.

ג‎יְפֵה נוֹף מְשׂוֹשׂ כָּל הָאָרֶץ: הַר צִיּוֹן יַרְכְּתֵי צָפוֹן; קִרְיַת מֶלֶךְ רָב.

Elohim b'armenoteiha, noda l'misgav.

יֱאלֹהִים בְּאַרְמְנוֹתֶיהָ נוֹדַע לְמִשְׂגָּב.

Ki hineh hamelakhim no'adu. Av'ru yakhdav.

הּכִּי הִנֵּה הַמְּלָכִים נוֹעֲדוּ; עָבְרוּ יַחְדָּו.

Hemah ra'u ken tamahu. Nivhalu nekh'pazu.

וּהֵמָה רָאוּ כֵּן תָּמָהוּ; נִבְהֲלוּ נֶחְפָּזוּ.

Re'adah, akhazatam sham, khil kayoledah.

זּרְעָדָה אֲחָזָתַם שָׁם; חִיל כַּיּוֹלֵדָה.

B'ru'akh kadim teshaber, oniyot tarshish

חּבְּרוּחַ קָדִים תְּשַׁבֵּר אֳנִיּוֹת תַּרְשִׁישׁ.

Ka'asher shamanu, ken ra'inu be'ir יהוה Tzeva'ot, be'ir Eloheinu: Elohim yekhoneneha ad olam. Selah.

טּכַּאֲשֶׁר שָׁמַעְנוּ כֵּן רָאִינוּ בְּעִיר יהוה צְבָאוֹת בְּעִיר אֱלֹהֵינוּ: אֱלֹהִים יְכוֹנְנֶהָ עַד עוֹלָם סֶלָה.

Diminu Elohim khasdeikha, b'kerev, heikhalekha.

יּדִּמִּינוּ אֱלֹהִים חַסְדֶּךָ בְּקֶרֶב הֵיכָלֶךָ.

K'shimkha Elohim, ken tehilatekha, al katzvei eretz. Tzedek, mal'ah y'minekha.

יאּכְּשִׁמְךָ אֱלֹהִים כֵּן תְּהִלָּתְךָ עַל קַצְוֵי אֶרֶץ; צֶדֶק מָלְאָה יְמִינֶךָ.

Yismakh, Har Tzion, tagelnah b'not Yehudah. L'ma'an mishpatekha.

יבּיִשְׂמַח הַר צִיּוֹן תָּגֵלְנָה בְּנוֹת יְהוּדָה: לְמַעַן מִשְׁפָּטֶיךָ.

Sobu Tzion, vehakifuha; Sifru migdaleha.

יגּסֹבּוּ צִיּוֹן וְהַקִּיפוּהָ; סִפְרוּ מִגְדָּלֶיהָ.

Shitu libkhem lekheilah, pas'gu armenoteha. Lema'an t'saperu l'dor akharon.

שִׁיתוּ לִבְּכֶם לְחֵילָה פַּסְגוּ אַרְמְנוֹתֶיהָ: לְמַעַן תְּסַפְּרוּ לְדוֹר אַחֲרוֹן.

Ki zeh Elohim Eloheinu olam va'ed. Hu y'nahageinu al mut.

כִּי זֶה אֱלֹהִים אֱלֹהֵינוּ עוֹלָם וָעֶד; הוּא יְנַהֲגֵנוּ עַל מוּת.

[1]A Song; a Mizmor for the sons of Korakh. [2]Great is יהוה , and highly to be praised, in the city of our Elohim, His Har Kadosh, [3]Fair in situation, the joy of the whole earth; even Har Tzion, the uttermost parts of the north, the city of Melekh Rav.

[4]Elohim in her palaces has made Himself known for a stronghold. [5]For, lo, the kings assembled themselves, they came onward together. [6]They saw, straightway they were amazed; they were terrified, they hasted away. [7]Trembling took hold of them there, pangs, as of a woman in travail. [8]With the east wind You break the ships of Tarshish.

[9]As we have heard, so have we seen; in the city of יהוה Tzeva'ot, in the city of our Elohim. Elohim establishes it forever. Selah.

[10]We have thought on Your compassion, O Elohim, in the midst of Your Heikhal. [11]As is Your Name, O Elohim, so is Your praise unto the ends of the earth; Your right hand is full of righteousness.

[12]Let Har Tzion be glad, let the daughters of Yehudah rejoice, because of Your judgments. [13]Walk about Tzion, and go round about her; count the towers thereof. [14]Mark well her ramparts, traverse her palaces; that you may tell it to the generation following. [15]For such is Elohim, our Elohim, forever and ever; He will guide us even in death.

# Tehillah 82 (Third Day)

Mizmor, l'Asaf. Elohim, nitzav ba'adat El. B'kerev Elohim yishpot.

אמִזְמוֹר לְאָסָף: אֱלֹהִים נִצָּב בַּעֲדַת אֵל; בְּקֶרֶב אֱלֹהִים יִשְׁפֹּט.

Ad matai tishpetu avel, ufnei resha'im tis'u. Selah.

בעַד מָתַי תִּשְׁפְּטוּ עָוֶל; וּפְנֵי רְשָׁעִים תִּשְׂאוּ סֶלָה.

Shiftu dal v'yatom. Ani varash hatz'diku.

גשִׁפְטוּ דַל וְיָתוֹם; עָנִי וָרָשׁ הַצְדִּיקוּ.

Pal'tu dal v'evyon. Miyad resha'im hatzilu.

דפַּלְּטוּ דַל וְאֶבְיוֹן; מִיַּד רְשָׁעִים הַצִּילוּ.

Lo yade'u, velo yavinu. Bakhash'khah yithalakhu; yimotu, kol mos'dei aretz.

הלֹא יָדְעוּ וְלֹא יָבִינוּ בַּחֲשֵׁכָה יִתְהַלָּכוּ; יִמּוֹטוּ כָּל מוֹסְדֵי אָרֶץ.

Ani amarti, Elohim atem. Uvnei Elyon kul'khem.

ואֲנִי אָמַרְתִּי אֱלֹהִים אַתֶּם; וּבְנֵי עֶלְיוֹן כֻּלְּכֶם.

Akhen, k'adam t'mutun, ukha'akhad hasarim tipolu.

זאָכֵן כְּאָדָם תְּמוּתוּן; וּכְאַחַד הַשָּׂרִים תִּפֹּלוּ.

Kumah Elohim, shaf'tah ha'aretz. Ki Atah tinkhal, b'khol hagoyim.

חקוּמָה אֱלֹהִים שָׁפְטָה הָאָרֶץ: כִּי אַתָּה תִנְחַל בְּכָל הַגּוֹיִם.

[1]A Mizmor of Asaf. Elohim stands in the assembly of God; in the midst of Mighty Ones He will judge: [2]"How long will you judge unjustly, and respect the persons of the wicked? Selah.

[3]Judge the poor and fatherless; do justice to the afflicted and destitute. [4]Rescue the poor and needy; deliver them out of the hand of the wicked. [5]They know not, neither do they understand;

139

they go about in darkness; all the foundations of the earth are moved.

[6]I said, "You are gods, and all of you B'nei Elyon. [7]Nevertheless you shall die like men, and fall like one of the princes." [8]Arise, O Elohim, judge the earth; for You shall possess all the nations.

## Tehillah 94 (Fourth Day)

El nekamot יהוה , El nekamot hofia.

אֵל נְקָמוֹת יהוה ; אֵל נְקָמוֹת הוֹפִיעַ.

Hinase shofet ha'aretz. Hashev gemul, al ge'im.

הִנָּשֵׂא שֹׁפֵט הָאָרֶץ; הָשֵׁב גְּמוּל עַל גֵּאִים.

Ad matai resha'im יהוה , ad matai resha'im ya'alozu?

עַד מָתַי רְשָׁעִים יהוה : עַד מָתַי רְשָׁעִים יַעֲלֹזוּ.

Yabiu yedab'ru atak. Yitameru kol po'alei aven.

יַבִּיעוּ יְדַבְּרוּ עָתָק; יִתְאַמְּרוּ כָּל פֹּעֲלֵי אָוֶן.

Amekha יהוה yedake'u, v'nakhalatekha y'anu.

עַמְּךָ יהוה יְדַכְּאוּ; וְנַחֲלָתְךָ יְעַנּוּ.

Almanah v'ger yaharogu. Vitomim y'ratzekhu.

אַלְמָנָה וְגֵר יַהֲרֹגוּ; וִיתוֹמִים יְרַצֵּחוּ.

Vaiyom'ru, lo yireh Yah, v'lo yavin, Elohei Ya'akov.

וַיֹּאמְרוּ לֹא יִרְאֶה יָּה; וְלֹא יָבִין אֱלֹהֵי יַעֲקֹב.

Binu bo'arim ba'am ukh'silim, matai taskilu.

בִּינוּ בֹּעֲרִים בָּעָם; וּכְסִילִים מָתַי תַּשְׂכִּילוּ.

Hanota ozen halo yishma? im yotzer ayin, halo yabit?

הֲנֹטַע אֹזֶן הֲלֹא יִשְׁמָע; אִם יֹצֵר עַיִן הֲלֹא יַבִּיט.

Hayoser goyim, halo yokhiakh. Ham'lamed adam da'at

יְהַיֹּסֵר גּוֹיִם הֲלֹא יוֹכִיחַ׃ הַמְלַמֵּד אָדָם דָּעַת.

יהוה yode'a, makhshevot adam. Ki hemah havel.

י״א יהוה יֹדֵעַ מַחְשְׁבוֹת אָדָם׃ כִּי הֵמָּה הָבֶל.

Ashrei, hagever asher teyas'renu Yah, umitoratekha telamdeinu.

י״ב אַשְׁרֵי הַגֶּבֶר אֲשֶׁר תְּיַסְּרֶנּוּ יָּהּ; וּמִתּוֹרָתְךָ תְלַמְּדֶנּוּ.

L'hashkit lo mimei ra, ad yikareh larasha shakhat.

י״ג לְהַשְׁקִיט לוֹ מִימֵי רָע עַד יִכָּרֶה לָרָשָׁע שָׁחַת.

Ki lo yitosh יהוה amo. V'nakhalato, lo ya'azov.

י״ד כִּי לֹא יִטֹּשׁ יהוה עַמּוֹ; וְנַחֲלָתוֹ לֹא יַעֲזֹב.

Ki ad tzedek yashuv mishpat v'akharav, kol yishrei lev.

ט״ו כִּי עַד צֶדֶק יָשׁוּב מִשְׁפָּט; וְאַחֲרָיו כָּל יִשְׁרֵי לֵב.

Mi yakum li, im mere'im. Mi yityatzev li, im po'alei aven?

ט״ז מִי יָקוּם לִי עִם מְרֵעִים; מִי יִתְיַצֵּב לִי עִם פֹּעֲלֵי אָוֶן.

Lulei יהוה ezrata li, kim'at, shakh'nah duma nafshi.

י״ז לוּלֵי יהוה עֶזְרָתָה לִּי כִּמְעַט שָׁכְנָה דוּמָה נַפְשִׁי.

Im amarti, mata ragli, khasd'kha יהוה , yisadeni.

י״ח אִם אָמַרְתִּי מָטָה רַגְלִי; חַסְדְּךָ יהוה יִסְעָדֵנִי.

B'rov sarapai bekirbi, tankhumeikha yesha'ashu nafshi.

י״ט בְּרֹב שַׂרְעַפַּי בְּקִרְבִּי תַּנְחוּמֶיךָ יְשַׁעַשְׁעוּ נַפְשִׁי.

Haikhovrekha kiseh hav'ot, yotzer amal alei khok.

כ׳ הַיְחָבְרְךָ כִּסֵּא הַוּוֹת; יֹצֵר עָמָל עֲלֵי חֹק.

141

Yagodu, al **ne**fesh tza**dik**, כּאיָגוֹדוּ עַל נֶפֶשׁ צַדִּיק; וְדָם
v'**dam** naki yarshi'u. נָקִי יַרְשִׁיעוּ.

Vaye**hi** יהוה li l'misga**v**, כּבוַיְהִי יהוה לִי לְמִשְׂגָּב;
v'Elo**hai** l'**tzur** makḥsi. וֵאלֹהַי לְצוּר מַחְסִי.

Vaya**shev** alei**hem**, et כּגוַיָּשֶׁב עֲלֵיהֶם אֶת אוֹנָם
o**nam**, uvra'**atam** וּבְרָעָתָם יַצְמִיתֵם; יַצְמִיתֵם
yatzmi**tem**. Yatzmi**tem** יהוה יהוה אֱלֹהֵינוּ.
Elo**hei**nu.

[1]God of vegeance, יהוה , God of vengeance, shine forth. [2]Lift up Yourself, O Judge of the earth; render to the proud their recompense. [3] יהוה , how long shall the wicked, how long shall the wicked exult?

[4]They gush out, they speak arrogance; all the workers of iniquity bear themselves loftily. [5]They crush Your people, O יהוה , and afflict Your heritage. [6]They slay the widow and the stranger, and murder the fatherless. [7]And they say, "Yah will not see, neither will the Elohim of Ya'akov give heed."

[8]Consider, you brutish among the people; and you fools, when will you understand? [9]He that planted the ear, shall He not hear? He that formed the eye, shall He not see? [10]He that instructs nations, shall not He correct? Even He that teaches man knowledge?

[11] יהוה knows the thoughts of man, that they are vanity. [12]Happy is the man whom You instruct, O יהוה , and teach out of Your Torah; [13]That You may give him rest from the days of evil, until the pit is digged for the wicked. [14]For יהוה will not cast off His people, neither will He forsake His inheritance.

[15]For eternal righteousness will return justice, and all the upright in heart shall follow it. [16]Who will rise up for me against the evil-doers? Who will stand up for me against the workers of iniquity?

[17]Unless יהוה had been my help, my soul would have soon dwelt in silence. [18]If I say, "My foot slips", Your compassion, O יהוה, holds me up. [19]When my cares are many within me, Your comforts delight my soul. [20]Shall the seat of wickedness have fellowship with You, which frames mischief by statute?

[21]They gather themselves together against the soul of a Tzadik, and condemn innocent blood. [22]But יהוה has been my high tower, and my Elohim the Rock of my refuge. [23]And He has brought upon them their own iniquity, and will cut them off in their own evil; יהוה our Elohim will cut them off.

# Tehillah 81 (Fifth Day)

| | |
|---|---|
| Lamnatze'akḥ al hagitit l'Asaf. | אֿלַמְנַצֵּחַ עַל הַגִּתִּית לְאָסָף. |
| Harninu, l'Elohim uzenu. Hari'u l'Elohei Ya'akov. | בֿהַרְנִינוּ לֵאלֹהִים עוּזֵּנוּ; הָרִיעוּ לֵאלֹהֵי יַעֲקֹב. |
| Se'u zimrah, ut'nu tof. Kinor na'im im navel. | גֿשְׂאוּ זִמְרָה וּתְנוּ תֹף; כִּנּוֹר נָעִים עִם נָבֶל. |
| Tiku vakḥodesh shofar. Bakeseh, l'yom kḥagenu. | דֿתִּקְעוּ בַחֹדֶשׁ שׁוֹפָר; בַּכֵּסֶה לְיוֹם חַגֵּנוּ. |
| Ki kḥok l'Yisra'el hu, mishpat l'Elohei Ya'akov. | הֿכִּי חֹק לְיִשְׂרָאֵל הוּא; מִשְׁפָּט לֵאלֹהֵי יַעֲקֹב. |
| Edut, biYosef samoh, b'tzetoh al eretz Mitzrayim; Sefat lo yadati eshma. | וֿעֵדוּת בִּיהוֹסֵף שָׂמוֹ בְּצֵאתוֹ עַל אֶרֶץ מִצְרָיִם; שְׂפַת לֹא יָדַעְתִּי אֶשְׁמָע. |
| Hasiroti misevel shikḥmo; kapav midud ta'avornah. | זֿהֲסִירוֹתִי מִסֵּבֶל שִׁכְמוֹ; כַּפָּיו מִדּוּד תַּעֲבֹרְנָה. |

Batzarah karata,
va'akḥal'tzekḥa e'en'kḥa
b'seter ra'am; ev'kḥonkḥa
al mei Merivah. Selah.

ח בַּצָּרָה קָרָאתָ וָאֲחַלְּצֶךָ;
אֶעֶנְךָ בְּסֵתֶר רַעַם; אֶבְחָנְךָ
עַל מֵי מְרִיבָה סֶלָה.

Shema ami, ve'a'idah
bakḥ; Yisra'el, im tishma
li.

ט שְׁמַע עַמִּי וְאָעִידָה בָּךְ;
יִשְׂרָאֵל אִם תִּשְׁמַע לִי.

Lo yiyeh vekḥa el zar; v'lo
tishtakḥaveh l'el nekḥar.

לֹא יִהְיֶה בְךָ אֵל זָר; וְלֹא
תִשְׁתַּחֲוֶה לְאֵל נֵכָר.

Anokḥi יהוה Eloheikḥa,
hama'al'kḥa me'eretz
Mitzrayim. Harkḥev
pikḥa, va'amale'eihu.

יא אָנֹכִי יהוה אֱלֹהֶיךָ הַמַּעַלְךָ
מֵאֶרֶץ מִצְרָיִם; הַרְחֶב פִּיךָ
וַאֲמַלְאֵהוּ.

Velo shama ami l'koli;
v'Yisra'el, lo avah li.

יב וְלֹא שָׁמַע עַמִּי לְקוֹלִי;
וְיִשְׂרָאֵל לֹא אָבָה לִי.

Va'ashalekḥehu bishrirut
libam; yel'kḥu,
b'mo'atzvoteihem.

יג וָאֲשַׁלְּחֵהוּ בִּשְׁרִירוּת לִבָּם;
יֵלְכוּ בְּמוֹעֲצוֹתֵיהֶם.

Lu ami shome'a li;
Yisra'el bidrakḥai
y'halekḥu.

יד לוּ עַמִּי שֹׁמֵעַ לִי; יִשְׂרָאֵל
בִּדְרָכַי יְהַלֵּכוּ.

Kim'at oyveihem akḥniya
v'al tzareihem, ashiv yadi.

טו כִּמְעַט אוֹיְבֵיהֶם אַכְנִיעַ;
וְעַל צָרֵיהֶם אָשִׁיב יָדִי.

Mesane'ei יהוה ,
yekḥakḥashu lo, vihi itam
l'olam.

טז מְשַׂנְאֵי יהוה יְכַחֲשׁוּ לוֹ;
וִיהִי עִתָּם לְעוֹלָם.

144

Vaya'akhilehu, mekhelev khitah umitzur d'vash asbi'ekha.

"וַיַּאֲכִילֵהוּ מֵחֵלֶב חִטָּה; וּמִצּוּר דְּבַשׁ אַשְׂבִּיעֶךָ.

[1]For the Leader; upon the Gitit. By Asaf. [2]Sing aloud unto Elohim our strength; shout unto the Elohim of Ya'akov. [3]Take up the melody, and sound the timbrel, the sweet Kinor with the Nevel.

[4]Blast the shofar at the khodesh, at the full moon for our Khag. [5]For it is a statute for Yisra'el, an ordinance of the Elohim of Ya'akov. [6]He appointed it in Yosef for a testimony, when He went forth against the land of Mitzrayim.

The speech of one that I knew not did I hear: [7]"I removed his shoulder from the burden; his hands were freed from the basket. [8]You did call in trouble, and I rescued you; I answered you in the secret place of thunder; I proved you at the waters of Merivah. Selah.

[9]Hear, O My people, and I will admonish you: O Yisra'el, if you would hearken unto Me! [10]There shall no strange god be in you; neither shall you worship any foreign god. [11]I am יהוה your Elohim, who brought you up out of the land of Mitzrayim; open your mouth wide, and I will fill it.

[12]But My people hearkened not to My voice; and Yisra'el would not love Me. [13]So I let them go after the stubbornness of their heart, that they might walk in their own counsels.

[14]Oh that My people would hearken unto Me, that Yisra'el would walk in My ways! [15]I would soon subdue their enemies, and turn My hand against their adversaries. [16]The haters of יהוה would dwindle away before Him; and their punishment would endure forever. [17]They would also be fed with the fat of wheat; and with honey out of the Rock would I satisfy you."

145

## Tehillah 93 (Sixth Day)

יהוה malakḥ; g'ut lavesh. Lavesh יהוה oz hitazar. Af tikon tevel, bal timot.

יהוה מָלָךְ גֵּאוּת לָבֵשׁ: לָבֵשׁ יהוה עֹז הִתְאַזָּר; אַף תִּכּוֹן תֵּבֵל בַּל תִּמּוֹט.

Nakḥon kisakḥa m'az; M'olam Atah.

נָכוֹן כִּסְאֲךָ מֵאָז; מֵעוֹלָם אָתָּה.

Nase'u neharot, יהוה , nase'u neharot kolam; Yisu neharot dakḥyam.

נָשְׂאוּ נְהָרוֹת יהוה נָשְׂאוּ נְהָרוֹת קוֹלָם; יִשְׂאוּ נְהָרוֹת דָּכְיָם.

Mikolot mayim rabim adirim mishberei yam; adir bamarom יהוה.

מִקֹּלוֹת מַיִם רַבִּים אַדִּירִים מִשְׁבְּרֵי יָם; אַדִּיר בַּמָּרוֹם יהוה .

Edoteikḥa n'emnu me'od leveitekḥa na'avah kodesh. יהוה l'orekḥ yamim.

עֵדֹתֶיךָ נֶאֶמְנוּ מְאֹד לְבֵיתְךָ נַאֲוָה קֹדֶשׁ: יהוה לְאֹרֶךְ יָמִים.

[1] יהוה reigns; He is clothed in majesty; יהוה is clothed, He has girded Himself with strength; yes, the world is established, that it cannot be moved. [2]Your throne is established of old; You are from everlasting.

[3]The floods have lifted up, O יהוה , the floods have lifted up their voice; the floods lift up their roaring. [4]Above the voices of many waters, the mighty breakers of the sea, יהוה on high is mighty. [5]Your testimonies are very sure, kodesh becomes Your house, O יהוה , forevermore.

## Tehillah 92 (Shabbat)

Mizmor shir, l'yom hashabbat.

מִזְמוֹר שִׁיר, לְיוֹם הַשַּׁבָּת.

Tov l'ho**dot** la יהוה .
Ul'**zamer** l'shim**kḥa** El**yon**.

²טוֹב לְהֹדוֹת לַיהוה; וּלְזַמֵּר
לְשִׁמְךָ עֶלְיוֹן.

L'ha**gid** ba**boker**
kḥas'**deikḥa**, v'emunatei**kḥa**
bale**ilot**.

³לְהַגִּיד בַּבֹּקֶר חַסְדֶּךָ;
וֶאֱמוּנָתְךָ בַּלֵּילוֹת.

A**lei** a**sor**, va'a**lei** **nah**vel;
a**lei** higa**yon** bekḥi**nor**.

⁴עֲלֵי עָשׂוֹר וַעֲלֵי נָבֶל; עֲלֵי
הִגָּיוֹן בְּכִנּוֹר.

Ki sima**kḥtani** יהוה
befo'a**leikḥa**; b'ma'a**sei**
ya**deikḥa** ara**nen**.

⁵כִּי שִׂמַּחְתַּנִי יהוה בְּפָעֳלֶךָ;
בְּמַעֲשֵׂי יָדֶיךָ אֲרַנֵּן.

Ma gad**lu** ma'asei**kḥa** יהוה ;
me'**od** am**ku**
makḥshevotei**kḥa**

⁶מַה גָּדְלוּ מַעֲשֶׂיךָ יהוה;
מְאֹד עָמְקוּ מַחְשְׁבֹתֶיךָ.

Ish **ba**'ar lo ye**da**; ukḥ**sil** lo
ya**vin** et zot,

⁷אִישׁ בַּעַר לֹא יֵדָע; וּכְסִיל
לֹא יָבִין אֶת זֹאת.

Bifroa**kḥ** resha'**im** kemo
esev, vayatzi**tzu** kol po'a**lei**
a**ven**. L'hishsham'**dam** a**dei**
ad.

⁸בִּפְרֹחַ רְשָׁעִים כְּמוֹ עֵשֶׂב
וַיָּצִיצוּ כָּל פֹּעֲלֵי אָוֶן:
לְהִשָּׁמְדָם עֲדֵי עַד.

V'a**tah** ma**rom** l'o**lam**, יהוה
.

⁹וְאַתָּה מָרוֹם לְעֹלָם יהוה.

Ki hi**neh** oyevei**kḥa**, יהוה ,
ki hi**neh** oyevei**kḥa** yove**du**.
Yitpare**du**, kol po'a**lei** a**ven**.

¹⁰כִּי הִנֵּה אֹיְבֶיךָ, יהוה , כִּי
הִנֵּה אֹיְבֶיךָ יֹאבֵדוּ: יִתְפָּרְדוּ
כָּל פֹּעֲלֵי אָוֶן.

Vata**rem** kire'**eim** **karni**;
balo**ti** b'she**men** ra'a**nan**.

¹¹וַתָּרֶם כִּרְאֵים קַרְנִי; בַּלֹּתִי
בְּשֶׁמֶן רַעֲנָן.

147

Vatabet eini beshurai. יַ״וַתַּבֵּט עֵינִי בְּשׁוּרָי:
Bakamim alai mere'im, בַּקָּמִים עָלַי מְרֵעִים
tishmanah oznai. תִּשְׁמַעְנָה אָזְנָי.

Tzadik katamar yifrakh; יַ״צַדִּיק כַּתָּמָר יִפְרָח; כְּאֶרֶז
k'erez balevanon yisgeh. בַּלְּבָנוֹן יִשְׂגֶּה.

Shetulim b'veit יהוה ; יַ״שְׁתוּלִים בְּבֵית יהוה;
b'khatzrot Eloheinu בְּחַצְרוֹת אֱלֹהֵינוּ יַפְרִיחוּ.
yafrikhu.

Od y'nuvun b'seivah; טַ״עוֹד יְנוּבוּן בְּשֵׂיבָה;
d'shenim v'ra'ananim דְּשֵׁנִים וְרַעֲנַנִּים יִהְיוּ.
yihyu.

L'hagid, ki yashar יהוה ; טַ״לְהַגִּיד כִּי יָשָׁר יהוה;
tzuri, v'lo avlatah boh. צוּרִי, וְלֹא עַוְלָתָה בּוֹ.

[1]A Mizmor, a Song. For Yom HaShabbat. [2]It is good to give thanks unto יהוה , to sing praises unto Your Name, O Eliyon; [3]to declare Your compassion in the morning, and Your faithfulness in the night seasons, [4]With an Asor, and with the Nevel; with a solemn sound upon the Kinor.

[5]For You, יהוה , have made me glad through Your work; I will exult in the works of Your hands. [6]How great are Your works, O יהוה ! Your thoughts are very deep. [7]A brutish man knows not, neither does a fool understand this. [8]When the wicked spring up as the grass, and when all the workers of iniquity do flourish; it is that they may be destroyed forever. [9]But You, O יהוה , are on high for evermore.

[10]For, lo, Your enemies, O יהוה , for, lo, Your enemies shall perish: all the workers of iniquity shall be scattered. [11]But my horn have You exalted like the horn of the wild ox; I am anointed with rich oil.

[12]My eye also has gazed on them that lie in wait for me, my ears

have heard my desire for the evil-doers that rise up against me. [13]A Tzadik shall flourish like the palm tree; he shall grow like a cedar in Levanon. [14]Planted in Beit יהוה , they shall flourish in the courts of our Elohim. [15]They shall still bring forth fruit in old age; they shall be full of sap and richness; [16]To declare that יהוה is upright, my Rock, in whom there is no unrighteousness.

# SEFIRAT HA'OMER

Blessing for counting the Omer from Reishit Omer to Shavu'ot:

Barukh Atah, יהוה , Eloheinu, Melekh haOlam, asher kidshanu b'mitzvotav v'tzivanu al sefirat ha'Omer.

בָּרוּךְ אַתָה יהוה , אֱלֹהֵינוּ, מֶלֶךְ הַעוֹלָם, אֲשֶׁר קִדְשָׁנוּ בְּמִצְוֹתָיו וְצִוָּנוּ עַל סְפִירַת הַעוֹמֶר.

"Blessed are You O יהוה our Elohim, King of the Universe, who set us apart by His Mitzvot and has commanded us to count the Omer."

Hayom, zeh yom _____ ba'Omer.

הַיוֹם, זֶה יוֹם _____ בָּעוֹמֶר

"Today is day _____ of the Omer."

At the end of the first Sabbath, after Havdalah, when the seventh day of the Omer has been counted, and at the end of each week, count the week in this manner:

after the first week:

Hayom, zeh Shabat ekhad ba'Omer.

הַיוֹם, זֶה שָׁבָת אֶחָד בָּעוֹמֶר

"Today is one Shabbat in the Omer."

after the second week:

Hayom, zeh shtei Shabbatot ba'Omer.

הַיוֹם, זֶה שתי שָׁבָתוֹת בָּעוֹמֶר

"Today is two Sabbaths in the Omer."

on each subsequent week:

Ha**yom**,   zeh   _____   שַׁבָּתוֹת _____ הַיּוֹם, זֶה
Shabba**tot**  ba'**O**mer.                              בָּעוֹמֶר

shlo**shah**, arba'**ah**, khami**shah**, shi**shah**, shi**vat**
"Today is _____ Sabbaths in the Omer."     3, 4, 5, 6, 7

# TESHUVAH

Additional prayers for the season of Teshuvah, Daniel 9:4-19 and Tehillah 27.

## Daniel 9

[4]O Adonai, the great and awful God, who keeps covenant and compassion with them that love You and keep Your mitzvot,

⁴אָנָּא אֲדֹנָי הָאֵל הַגָּדוֹל וְהַנּוֹרָא שֹׁמֵר הַבְּרִית וְהַחֶסֶד לְאֹהֲבָיו וּלְשֹׁמְרֵי מִצְוֹתָיו.

[5]we have sinned, and have dealt iniquitously, and have done wickedly, and have rebelled, and have turned aside from Your mitzvot and from Your ordinances;

⁵חָטָאנוּ וְעָוִינוּ והרשענו (הִרְשַׁעְנוּ) וּמָרָדְנוּ; וְסוֹר מִמִּצְוֹתֶךָ וּמִמִּשְׁפָּטֶיךָ.

[6]neither have we hearkened unto Your servants the Nevi'im, that spoke in Your Name to our kings, our princes, and our fathers, and to all the people of the land.

⁶וְלֹא שָׁמַעְנוּ אֶל עֲבָדֶיךָ הַנְּבִיאִים אֲשֶׁר דִּבְּרוּ בְּשִׁמְךָ אֶל מְלָכֵינוּ שָׂרֵינוּ וַאֲבֹתֵינוּ וְאֶל כָּל עַם הָאָרֶץ.

[7]Unto You, O Adonai, belongs tzedaka, but unto us shame of face, as at this day; to the men of Yehudah, and to the inhabitants of Yerushalayim, and unto all Yisra'el, that are near, and that are far off, through all the countries where You have driven them, because they dealt treacherously with You.

⁷לְךָ אֲדֹנָי הַצְּדָקָה וְלָנוּ בֹּשֶׁת הַפָּנִים כַּיּוֹם הַזֶּה; לְאִישׁ יְהוּדָה וּלְיֹשְׁבֵי יְרוּשָׁלַם וּלְכָל יִשְׂרָאֵל הַקְּרֹבִים וְהָרְחֹקִים בְּכָל הָאֲרָצוֹת אֲשֶׁר הִדַּחְתָּם שָׁם בְּמַעֲלָם אֲשֶׁר מָעֲלוּ בָךְ.

ח יהוה לָנוּ בֹּשֶׁת הַפָּנִים לִמְלָכֵינוּ לְשָׂרֵינוּ וְלַאֲבֹתֵינוּ: אֲשֶׁר חָטָאנוּ לָךְ.

[8]O יהוה , to us belongs shame of face, to our kings, to our princes, and to our fathers, because we have sinned against You.

ט לַאדֹנָי אֱלֹהֵינוּ הָרַחֲמִים וְהַסְּלִחוֹת: כִּי מָרַדְנוּ בּוֹ.

[9]To Adonai Eloheinu belongs mercies and forgivenesses; for we have rebelled against Him;

י וְלֹא שָׁמַעְנוּ בְּקוֹל יהוה אֱלֹהֵינוּ לָלֶכֶת בְּתוֹרֹתָיו אֲשֶׁר נָתַן לְפָנֵינוּ בְּיַד עֲבָדָיו הַנְּבִיאִים.

[10]neither have we hearkened to the voice of יהוה our Elohim, to walk in His instructions, which He set before us by His servants the Nevi'im.

יא וְכָל יִשְׂרָאֵל עָבְרוּ אֶת תּוֹרָתֶךָ וְסוֹר לְבִלְתִּי שְׁמוֹעַ בְּקֹלֶךָ; וַתִּתַּךְ עָלֵינוּ הָאָלָה וְהַשְּׁבֻעָה אֲשֶׁר כְּתוּבָה בְּתוֹרַת מֹשֶׁה עֶבֶד הָאֱלֹהִים כִּי חָטָאנוּ לוֹ.

[11]Yes, all Yisra'el has transgressed Your Torah, and has turned aside, so as not to hearken to Your voice; and so there have been poured out upon us the curse and the oath that is written in the Torah of Moshe the servant of Elohim; for we have sinned against Him.

<sup>12</sup>And He has confirmed His D'var, which He spoke against us, and against our judges that judged us, by bringing upon us a great evil; so that under the whole heaven has not been done as has been done upon Yerushalayim.

יבוַיָּקֶם אֶת דבריו (דְּבָרוֹ) אֲשֶׁר דִּבֶּר עָלֵינוּ וְעַל שֹׁפְטֵינוּ אֲשֶׁר שְׁפָטוּנוּ לְהָבִיא עָלֵינוּ רָעָה גְדֹלָה: אֲשֶׁר לֹא נֶעֶשְׂתָה תַּחַת כָּל הַשָּׁמַיִם כַּאֲשֶׁר נֶעֶשְׂתָה בִּירוּשָׁלָם.

<sup>13</sup>As it is written in the Torah of Moshe, all this evil is come upon us; yet have we not entreated the favor of יהוה our Elohim, that we might turn from our iniquities, and have discernment in Your truth.

יגכַּאֲשֶׁר כָּתוּב בְּתוֹרַת מֹשֶׁה אֵת כָּל הָרָעָה הַזֹּאת בָּאָה עָלֵינוּ; וְלֹא חִלִּינוּ אֶת פְּנֵי יהוה אֱלֹהֵינוּ לָשׁוּב מֵעֲוֹנֵנוּ וּלְהַשְׂכִּיל בַּאֲמִתֶּךָ.

<sup>14</sup>And so יהוה has watched over the evil, and brought it upon us; for יהוה our Elohim is righteous in all His works which He has done, and we have not hearkened to His voice.

ידוַיִּשְׁקֹד יהוה עַל הָרָעָה וַיְבִיאֶהָ עָלֵינוּ: כִּי צַדִּיק יהוה אֱלֹהֵינוּ עַל כָּל מַעֲשָׂיו אֲשֶׁר עָשָׂה וְלֹא שָׁמַעְנוּ בְּקֹלוֹ.

<sup>15</sup>And now, O Adonai Elohim, that has brought Your people forth out of the land of Mitzrayim with a mighty hand, and has gotten renown, as at this day; we have sinned, we have done wickedly.

טווְעַתָּה אֲדֹנָי אֱלֹהֵינוּ אֲשֶׁר הוֹצֵאתָ אֶת עַמְּךָ מֵאֶרֶץ מִצְרַיִם בְּיָד חֲזָקָה וַתַּעַשׂ לְךָ שֵׁם כַּיּוֹם הַזֶּה: חָטָאנוּ רָשָׁעְנוּ.

<sup>16</sup>O Adonai, according to all Your tzedaka, let Your anger and Your fury, I pray, be turned away from Your city Yerushalayim, Your Har Kodesh; because for our sins, and for the iniquities of our fathers, Yerushalayim and Your people are become a reproach to all that are about us.

טז אֲדֹנָי כְּכָל צִדְקֹתֶךָ יָשָׁב נָא אַפְּךָ וַחֲמָתְךָ מֵעִירְךָ יְרוּשָׁלַם הַר קָדְשֶׁךָ: כִּי בַחֲטָאֵינוּ וּבַעֲוֹנוֹת אֲבֹתֵינוּ יְרוּשָׁלַם וְעַמְּךָ לְחֶרְפָּה לְכָל סְבִיבֹתֵינוּ.

<sup>17</sup>Now therefore, O our Elohim, hearken unto the prayer of Your servant, and to his supplications, and cause Your face to shine upon Your Mikdash that is desolate, for Adonai's sake.

יז וְעַתָּה שְׁמַע אֱלֹהֵינוּ אֶל תְּפִלַּת עַבְדְּךָ וְאֶל תַּחֲנוּנָיו וְהָאֵר פָּנֶיךָ עַל מִקְדָּשְׁךָ הַשָּׁמֵם לְמַעַן אֲדֹנָי.

<sup>18</sup>O my Elohim, incline Your ear, and hear; open Your eyes, and behold our desolations, and the city upon which Your Name is called; for we do not present our supplications before You because of our tzedaka, but because of Your great mercies.

יח הַטֵּה אֱלֹהַי אָזְנְךָ וּשְׁמָע פְּקחה (פְּקַח) עֵינֶיךָ וּרְאֵה שֹׁמְמֹתֵינוּ וְהָעִיר אֲשֶׁר נִקְרָא שִׁמְךָ עָלֶיהָ: כִּי לֹא עַל צִדְקֹתֵינוּ אֲנַחְנוּ מַפִּילִים תַּחֲנוּנֵינוּ לְפָנֶיךָ כִּי עַל רַחֲמֶיךָ הָרַבִּים.

<sup>19</sup>O Adonai, hear, O Adonai, forgive, O Adonai, attend and do, defer not; for Your own sake, O my Elohim, because Your Name is called upon Your city and Your people."

יט אֲדֹנָי שְׁמָעָה אֲדֹנָי סְלָחָה אֲדֹנָי הַקְשִׁיבָה וַעֲשֵׂה אַל תְּאַחַר: לְמַעַנְךָ אֱלֹהַי כִּי שִׁמְךָ נִקְרָא עַל עִירְךָ וְעַל עַמֶּךָ.

# Tehillah 27 תְּהִלָּה

<sup>1</sup>By David. יהוה is my light and my Salvation; whom shall I fear? יהוה is the stronghold of my life; of whom shall I be afraid?

אלְדָוִד: יהוה אוֹרִי וְיִשְׁעִי מִמִּי אִירָא; יהוה מָעוֹז חַיַּי מִמִּי אֶפְחָד.

<sup>2</sup>When evil-doers came upon me to eat up my flesh, even my adversaries and my foes, they stumbled and fell.

בבִּקְרֹב עָלַי מְרֵעִים לֶאֱכֹל אֶת בְּשָׂרִי: צָרַי וְאֹיְבַי לִי; הֵמָּה כָשְׁלוּ וְנָפָלוּ.

<sup>3</sup>Though a host should encamp against me, my heart shall not fear; though war should rise up against me, even then will I be confident.

גאִם תַּחֲנֶה עָלַי מַחֲנֶה לֹא יִירָא לִבִּי: אִם תָּקוּם עָלַי מִלְחָמָה בְּזֹאת אֲנִי בוֹטֵחַ.

<sup>4</sup>One thing have I asked of יהוה, that will I seek after: that I may dwell in Beit יהוה all the days of my life, to behold the kindness of יהוה, and to visit early in His Heikhal.

דאַחַת שָׁאַלְתִּי מֵאֵת יהוה אוֹתָהּ אֲבַקֵּשׁ: שִׁבְתִּי בְּבֵית יהוה כָּל יְמֵי חַיַּי; לַחֲזוֹת בְּנֹעַם יהוה וּלְבַקֵּר בְּהֵיכָלוֹ.

<sup>5</sup>For He conceals me in His Sukka in the day of evil; He hides me in the covert of His Ohel; He lifts me up upon a Rock.

הכִּי יִצְפְּנֵנִי בְּסֻכֹּה בְּיוֹם רָעָה: יַסְתִּרֵנִי בְּסֵתֶר אָהֳלוֹ; בְּצוּר יְרוֹמְמֵנִי.

⁶And now shall my head be lifted up above my enemies round about me; and I will offer in His Ohel sacrifices with a blast; I will sing, yes, I will sing praises unto יהוה.

וְעַתָּה יָרוּם רֹאשִׁי עַל אֹיְבַי סְבִיבוֹתַי וְאֶזְבְּחָה בְאָהֳלוֹ זִבְחֵי תְרוּעָה; אָשִׁירָה וַאֲזַמְּרָה לַיהוה .

⁷Hear, O יהוה , when I call with my voice, and be gracious unto me, and answer me.

שְׁמַע יהוה קוֹלִי אֶקְרָא; וְחָנֵּנִי וַעֲנֵנִי.

⁸In Your behalf my heart has said, "Seek My face"; Your face, O יהוה , will I seek.

לְךָ אָמַר לִבִּי בַּקְּשׁוּ פָנָי; אֶת פָּנֶיךָ יהוה אֲבַקֵּשׁ.

⁹Hide not Your face from me; put not Your servant away in anger; You have been my help; cast me not off, neither forsake me, O Elohim of my Salvation.

אַל תַּסְתֵּר פָּנֶיךָ מִמֶּנִּי אַל תַּט בְּאַף עַבְדֶּךָ: עֶזְרָתִי הָיִיתָ; אַל תִּטְּשֵׁנִי וְאַל תַּעַזְבֵנִי אֱלֹהֵי יִשְׁעִי.

¹⁰For though my father and my mother have forsaken me, יהוה will take me up.

כִּי אָבִי וְאִמִּי עֲזָבוּנִי; וַיהוה יַאַסְפֵנִי.

¹¹Teach me Your Derekh, O יהוה ; and lead me in an even path, because of them that lie in wait for me.

הוֹרֵנִי יהוה דַּרְכֶּךָ: וּנְחֵנִי בְּאֹרַח מִישׁוֹר לְמַעַן שׁוֹרְרָי.

¹²Deliver me not over unto the will of my adversaries; for false witnesses are risen up against me, and such as breathe out violence.

אַל תִּתְּנֵנִי בְּנֶפֶשׁ צָרָי: כִּי קָמוּ בִי עֵדֵי שֶׁקֶר וִיפֵחַ חָמָס.

157

¹³If I had not believed to look upon the goodness of יהוה in the land of the living!

לּוּלֵא הֶאֱמַנְתִּי לִרְאוֹת
בְּטוּב יהוה : בְּאֶרֶץ חַיִּים.

¹⁴Wait for יהוה ; be strong, and let your heart take courage; yes, wait for יהוה .

קַוֵּה אֶל יהוה : חֲזַק וְיַאֲמֵץ
לִבֶּךָ; וְקַוֵּה אֶל יהוה .

# הת'ערו TERU'AH

## The Kingship of Messiah

יהוה yimlok̲ h l'olam va'ed.

יהוה יִמְלֹךְ לְעֹלָם וָעֶד.

יהוה shall reign forever and ever. *(Shemot 15:18)*

Lo hibit aven b'Ya'akov, v'lo ra'ah amal b'Yisra'el; יהוה Elohaiv imo, uteru'at Melek̲ h bo.

לֹא הִבִּיט אָוֶן בְּיַעֲקֹב וְלֹא רָאָה עָמָל בְּיִשְׂרָאֵל; יהוה אֱלֹהָיו עִמּוֹ, וּתְרוּעַת מֶלֶךְ בּוֹ.

None has beheld iniquity in Ya'akov, neither has one seen perverseness in Yisra'el; יהוה his Elohim is with him, and the shouting of a Melekh is among them. *(BaMidbar 23:21)*

Vayehi v'Yeshurun Melek̲ h, b'hitasef rashei am, yak̲ had shivtei Yisra'el.

וַיְהִי בִישֻׁרוּן מֶלֶךְ בְּהִתְאַסֵּף רָאשֵׁי עָם יַחַד שִׁבְטֵי יִשְׂרָאֵל.

[5]And there was a Melekh in Yeshurun, when the heads of the people were gathered, all the tribes of Yisra'el together. *(D'varim 33:5)*

Yizk'ru v'yashuvu el יהוה ; kol afsei aretz; v'yishtak̲ havu l'faneik̲ ha kol mishpak̲ hot goyim.

יִזְכְּרוּ וְיָשֻׁבוּ אֶל יהוה; כָּל אַפְסֵי אָרֶץ; וְיִשְׁתַּחֲווּ לְפָנֶיךָ כָּל מִשְׁפְּחוֹת גּוֹיִם.

Ki la יהוה ham'luk̲ ha; umoshel bagoyim.

כִּי לַיהוה הַמְּלוּכָה; וּמֹשֵׁל בַּגּוֹיִם.

All the ends of the earth shall remember and turn unto יהוה ; and

all the kindreds of the goyim shall worship before You. For HaM'lukha belongs to יהוה ; and He is the ruler over the goyim. *(Tehillah 22:28-29)*

יהוה malakḥ, ge'ut lavesh: lavesh יהוה , oz hitazar; af tikon tevel, bal timot.

יהוה מָלָךְ גֵּאוּת לָבֵשׁ: לָבֵשׁ יהוה עֹז הִתְאַזָּר; אַף תִּכּוֹן תֵּבֵל בַּל תִּמּוֹט.

Nakḥon kisakḥa m'az; m'olam Atah.

נָכוֹן כִּסְאֲךָ מֵאָז; מֵעוֹלָם אָתָּה.

יהוה reigns; He is clothed in majesty; יהוה is clothed, He has girded Himself with strength; yes, the world is established, that it cannot be moved. Your throne is established of old; You are from everlasting. *(Tehillah 93:1-2)*

Se'u, She'arim, rashekḥem, v'hinasu pitkḥei olam, v'yavo Melekḥ HaKavod!

שְׂאוּ שְׁעָרִים, רָאשֵׁיכֶם, וְהִנָּשְׂאוּ פִּתְחֵי עוֹלָם; וְיָבוֹא, מֶלֶךְ הַכָּבוֹד.

Mi zeh, Melekḥ HaKavod: יהוה , izuz v'gibor; יהוה , gibor milkḥamah.

מִי זֶה, מֶלֶךְ הַכָּבוֹד: יהוה עִזּוּז וְגִבּוֹר; יהוה גִּבּוֹר מִלְחָמָה.

Se'u, She'arim, rashekḥem, use'u pitkḥei olam, v'yavo Melekḥ HaKavod!

שְׂאוּ שְׁעָרִים רָאשֵׁיכֶם, וּשְׂאוּ פִּתְחֵי עוֹלָם; וְיָבֹא, מֶלֶךְ הַכָּבוֹד.

Mi hu zeh, Melekḥ HaKavod? יהוה Tzeva'ot, Hu Melekḥ HaKavod: Selah.

מִי הוּא זֶה מֶלֶךְ הַכָּבוֹד: יהוה צְבָאוֹת; הוּא מֶלֶךְ הַכָּבוֹד סֶלָה.

Lift up your heads, O you gates, and be lifted up, O you everlasting doors; that the Melekh HaKavod may come in. "Who

is this Melekh HaKavod?" " יהוה strong and mighty, יהוה mighty in battle."

Lift up your heads, O you gates, yes, lift them up, O you everlasting doors; that the Melekh HaKavod may come in. "Who then is this Melekh HaKavod?" " יהוה Tzeva'ot; He is Melekh HaKavod." Selah. *(Tehillah 24:7-10)*

Ko **amar** יהוה **Melekh** Yisra'**el** v'go'**elo**, יהוה Tzeva'**ot**: **Ani** **rishon** va'**Ani** akh**aron**, u'mibala**dai** ein elo**him**.

כֹּה אָמַר יהוה מֶלֶךְ יִשְׂרָאֵל וְגֹאֲלוֹ יהוה צְבָאוֹת: אֲנִי רִאשׁוֹן וַאֲנִי אַחֲרוֹן וּמִבַּלְעָדַי אֵין אֱלֹהִים.

"Thus says יהוה , Melekh Yisra'el, and His Redeemer, יהוה Tzeva'ot, 'I am the first, and I am the last, and beside Me there are no gods." *(Yesha'Yahu 44:6)*

V'**alu** moshi'**im** b'**Har** Tz**ion**, lish**pot** et har E**sav**; v'hayi**ta** la יהוה , hamlukh**a**.

וְעָלוּ מוֹשִׁעִים בְּהַר צִיּוֹן לִשְׁפֹּט אֶת הַר עֵשָׂו; וְהָיְתָה לַיהוה, הַמְּלוּכָה.

And saviors shall come up on Har Tzion to judge the mount of Esav; and HaMalkhut shall belong to יהוה . *(Ovad-Yah 1:21)*

V'h**aya** יהוה l'**Melekh**, al kol ha'**aretz** ba**yom** ha**hu**, yih**yeh** יהוה **Ekhad**, ush'**mo** **Ekhad**.

וְהָיָה יהוה לְמֶלֶךְ עַל כָּל הָאָרֶץ; בַּיּוֹם הַהוּא יִהְיֶה יהוה אֶחָד וּשְׁמוֹ אֶחָד.

And יהוה shall be Melekh over all the earth; in that day shall יהוה be Ekhad, and His Name Ekhad. *(Zekhar-Yah 14:9)*

# Avinu Malkeinu

Avinu Malkeinu, Shema koleinu

אָבִינוּ מַלְכֵּנוּ שְׁמַע קוֹלֵנוּ.

Avinu Malkeinu, khatanu l'faneikha

אָבִינוּ מַלְכֵּנוּ חָטָאנוּ לְפָנֶיךָ.

Avinu Malkeinu ein lanu melekh ela Atah.

אָבִינוּ מַלְכֵּנוּ אֵין לָנוּ מֶלֶךְ אֶלָּא אָתָּה.

Avinu Malkeinu aseh imanu l'ma'an sh'mekha.

אָבִינוּ מַלְכֵּנוּ עֲשֵׂה עִמָּנוּ לְמַעַן שְׁמֶךָ.

Avinu Malkeinu khadesh aleinu shana tova.

אָבִינוּ מַלְכֵּנוּ חַדֵּשׁ עָלֵינוּ שָׁנָה טוֹבָה.

Avinu Malkeinu batel m'aleinu kol g'zerot kashot.

אָבִינוּ מַלְכֵּנוּ בַּטֵּל מֵעָלֵינוּ כָּל גְּזֵרוֹת קָשׁוֹת.

Avinu Malkeinu batel makhshevot soneinu.

אָבִינוּ מַלְכֵּנוּ בַּטֵּל מַחְשְׁבוֹת שׂוֹנְאֵינוּ.

Avinu Malkeinu hafer atzat oyveinu

אָבִינוּ מַלְכֵּנוּ הָפֵר עֲצַת אוֹיְבֵינוּ.

Avinu Malkeinu kale kol tzar u'mastin m'aleinu

אָבִינוּ מַלְכֵּנוּ כַּלֵּה כָּל צַר וּמַשְׂטִין מֵעָלֵינוּ.

Avinu Malkeinu s'tom piyot mastineinu u'mekatregeinu.

אָבִינוּ מַלְכֵּנוּ סְתֹם פִּיּוֹת מַשְׂטִינֵינוּ וּמְקַטְרְגֵנוּ.

Avinu Malkeinu koleh dever v'kherev v'ra'av ush'vi umashkhit ushmad mib'nei b'riteikha.

אָבִינוּ מַלְכֵּנוּ כַּלֵּה דֶּבֶר וְחֶרֶב וְרָעָב וּשְׁבִי וּמַשְׁחִית (וְעָוֹן) וּשְׁמָד מִבְּנֵי בְּרִיתֶךָ.

163

Avinu Malkeinu m'na magefa minakhalateikha.

אָבִינוּ מַלְכֵּנוּ מְנַע מַגֵּפָה מִנַּחֲלָתֶךָ.

Avinu Malkeinu s'lakh umakhol l'khol avonoteinu.

אָבִינוּ מַלְכֵּנוּ סְלַח וּמְחַל לְכָל עֲוֹנוֹתֵינוּ.

Avinu Malkeinu m'kheh v'ha'aver p'sha'einu v'khatoteinu mineged eineikha.

אָבִינוּ מַלְכֵּנוּ מְחֵה וְהַעֲבֵר פְּשָׁעֵינוּ וְחַטֹּאתֵינוּ מִנֶּגֶד עֵינֶיךָ.

Avinu Malkeinu m'khok b'rakhameikha harabim kol shitrai khovoteinu.

אָבִינוּ מַלְכֵּנוּ מְחֹק בְּרַחֲמֶיךָ הָרַבִּים כָּל שִׁטְרֵי חוֹבוֹתֵינוּ.

Avinu Malkeinu hakhazireinu bit'shuvah sh'lema l'faneikha.

אָבִינוּ מַלְכֵּנוּ הַחֲזִירֵנוּ בִּתְשׁוּבָה שְׁלֵמָה לְפָנֶיךָ.

Avinu Malkeinu shelakh refu'ah sh'lemah l'kholei ameikha

אָבִינוּ מַלְכֵּנוּ שְׁלַח רְפוּאָה שְׁלֵמָה לְחוֹלֵי עַמֶּךָ.

Avinu Malkeinu k'ra ro'ah g'zar dinenu.

אָבִינוּ מַלְכֵּנוּ קְרַע רֹעַ גְּזַר דִּינֵנוּ.

Avinu Malkeinu zakhreinu b'zikron tov l'faneikha.

אָבִינוּ מַלְכֵּנוּ זָכְרֵנוּ בְּזִכָּרוֹן טוֹב לְפָנֶיךָ.

Avinu Malkeinu kotveinu b'sefer khayim tovim.

אָבִינוּ מַלְכֵּנוּ כתבנו בְּסֵפֶר חיים טוֹבים.

Our Father, Our King, hear our voice.
Our Father, Our King, we have sinned before You.
Our Father, Our King, there is no King for us but You.
Our Father, Our King, deal kindly with us for Your Name's sake.
Our Father, Our King, inaugurate upon us a good year.

Our Father, Our King, nullify all harsh decrees upon us.

Our Father, Our King, nullify the thoughts of those who hate us.

Our Father, Our King, thwart the counsel of our enemies.

Our Father, Our King, exterminate every foe and adversary from upon us.

Our Father, Our King, seal the mouths of our adversaries and accusers.

Our Father, Our King, exterminate pestilence, sword, famine, captivity, destruction, iniquity, and eradication from the members of Your covenant.

Our Father, Our King, withhold the plague from Your heritage.

Our Father, Our King, forgive and pardon all our iniquities.

Our Father, Our King, wipe away and remove our willful sins and errors from Your sight.

Our Father, Our King, erase through Your abundant compassion all records of our guilt.

Our Father, Our King, return us to You in perfect repentance.

Our Father, Our King, send complete recovery to the sick among Your people.

Our Father, Our King, tear up the evil decree of our verdict.

Our Father, Our King, remember us with a favorable memory before You.

Our Father, Our King, inscribe us in the book of good Life.

## Kaddish: A Song of Praise
### Congregation and Mourners
*Hebrew first, then English*

יִתְגַדַל וְיִתְקַדַשׁ שְׁמֵהּ רַבָּא. בְּעָלְמָא דִּי בְרָא כִרְעוּתֵהּ וְיַמְלִיךְ מַלְכוּתֵהּ, בְּחַיֵּיכוֹן וּבְיוֹמֵיכוֹן וּבְחַיֵּי דְכָל בֵּית יִשְׂרָאֵל בַּעֲגָלָא וּבִזְמַן קָרִיב. וְאִמְרוּ, אָמֵן.

Yitgadal v'yitkadash shemeh raba. Be'alma di vera khir'uteh v'yamlikh malkhuteh, b'khaiyeikhon uv'yomeikhon uvkhaiyei d'khol beit Yisra'el ba'agala uvizman kariv. V'imru, Amein.

165

| Yeheh shemeh raba m'varakh l'olam ul'alemei alemaiya'. V'imru, Amein. | יְהֵא שְׁמֵהּ רַבָּא מְבָרַךְ לְעָלַם וּלְעָלְמֵי עָלְמַיָּא.וְאִמְרוּ, אָמֵן. |
|---|---|
| Yitbarakh v'yishtabakh v'yitpa'ar v'yitromam v'yitnaseh v'yithadar v'yit'aleh v'yit'halal shemeh d'kudsha', barikh hu l'ela min kol borkhata v'shirata, tushb'khatah, v'nekhemata, da'amiran b'alma. V'imru, Amein. | יִתְבָּרַךְ וְיִשְׁתַּבַּח וְיִתְפָּאַר וְיִתְרוֹמַם וְיִתְנַשֵּׂא וְיִתְהַדָּר וְיִתְעַלֶּה וְיִתְהַלָּל שְׁמֵהּ דְּקֻדְשָׁא בְּרִיךְ הוּא לְעֵלָא מִן כָּל בִּרְכָתָא וְשִׁירָתָא תֻּשְׁבְּחָתָא וְנֶחֱמָתָא דַּאֲמִירָן בְּעָלְמָא. וְאִמְרוּ, אָמֵן. |
| Oseh shalom bimromav, hu ya'aseh shalom aleinu v'al kal Yisra'el. V'imru, Amein. | עֹשֶׂה שָׁלוֹם בִּמְרוֹמָיו, הוּא יַעֲשֶׂה שָׁלוֹם עָלֵינוּ וְעַל כָּל יִשְׂרָאֵל. וְאִמְרוּ, אָמֵן. |

Magnified and sanctified be His great Name in the world which He has created according to His will. May He establish His kingdom during our lifetime, and during our days, and during the life of the whole house of Yisra'el, even swiftly and soon, And all say, "Amein." *(Divrei HaYamim 22:10)* Let His great name be blessed forever and to all eternity, And all say, "Amein." *(Tehillah 113:2)*

Blessed, praised, glorified, exalted, extolled and honored, magnified and lauded be the name of the Holy One, blessed be He, though He is high above all blessings and songs, praise and consolations which are uttered in the world, And all say, "Amein." *(Neh 9:5)* He who makes peace in His heights, may He make peace upon us, and upon all Yisra'el. And all say, "Amein." *(Iyov 25:2)*

# Aleinu: It is Our Duty
Congregation Rises :: Leader and Congregation together
*Hebrew then English*

Aleinu l'shabeakḥ la'adon hakol. Latet gedulah l'yotzer b'reshiit. Sh'lo asanu k'goyei ha'aratzot. V'lo samanu k'mishpekḥot ha'adamah. Sh'lo sam kḥelkenu kahem v'goralenu k'kḥol hamonam.

עָלֵינוּ לְשַׁבֵּחַ לַאֲדוֹן הַכֹּל. לָתֵת גְּדֻלָּה לְיוֹצֵר בְּרֵאשִׁית. שֶׁלֹּא עָשָׂנוּ כְּגוֹיֵי הָאֲרָצוֹת. וְלֹא שָׂמָנוּ כְּמִשְׁפְּחוֹת הָאֲדָמָה. שֶׁלֹּא שָׂם חֶלְקֵנוּ כָּהֶם וְגוֹרָלֵנוּ כְּכָל הֲמוֹנָם:

Sh'hem mishtakḥavim l'hevel varik umitpalelim el el lo moshei'a. Va'anakḥnu kore'im umishtakḥavim umodim lifnei Melekḥ Malkḥei hammelakḥim, hakodosh barukḥ Hu'.

שֶׁהֵם מִשְׁתַּחֲוִים לְהֶבֶל וָרִיק וּמִתְפַּלְלִים אֶל אֵל לֹא מוֹשִׁיעַ: וַאֲנַחְנוּ כּוֹרְעִים וּמִשְׁתַּחֲוִים וּמוֹדִים לִפְנֵי מֶלֶךְ מַלְכֵי הַמְּלָכִים הַקָּדוֹשׁ בָּרוּךְ הוּא:

Sh'Hu noteh shamayim v'yosed aretz umoshav. Y'karo bashamayim mima'al ush'kḥinat uzzo b'gav'hei m'romim Hu Eloheinu ein od.

שֶׁהוּא נוֹטֶה שָׁמַיִם וְיוֹסֵד אֶרֶץ וּמוֹשָׁב. יְקָרוֹ בַּשָּׁמַיִם מִמַּעַל. וּשְׁכִינַת עֻזּוֹ בְּגָבְהֵי מְרוֹמִים: הוּא אֱלֹהֵינוּ אֵין עוֹד:

Emet malkenu. Efes zulato kakatuv betoratoh. V'yadatah hayom v'hashevota el levavekḥa ki יהוה Hu ha'elohim bashamayim mim'al v'al ha'aretz mitakḥat ein od.

אֱמֶת מַלְכֵּנוּ. אֶפֶס זוּלָתוֹ. כַּכָּתוּב בְּתוֹרָתוֹ. וְיָדַעְתָּ הַיּוֹם וַהֲשֵׁבֹתָ אֶל לְבָבֶךָ. כִּי יהוה הוּא הָאֱלֹהִים בַּשָּׁמַיִם מִמַּעַל וְעַל הָאָרֶץ מִתָּחַת. אֵין עוֹד:

Vehayah יהוה l'melekh al kol ha'aretz bayom hahu, yiyeh יהוה ekhad, ushmo ekhad.

וְהָיָה יהוה לְמֶלֶךְ, עַל כָּל הָאָרֶץ; בַּיּוֹם הַהוּא, יִהְיֶה יהוה אֶחָדוּשְׁמוֹ אֶחָד.

It is our duty to praise the Master of all, to ascribe greatness to the Molder of Creation, for He has not made us like the nations of the lands, and has not placed us like families of the earth. For He has not assigned our portion like theirs, nor our fate like all their crowds. For they bow down to vanity and emptiness and pray to a god who does not save. But we kneel, and bow and acknowledge our thanks, before the King who reigns over kings, the Holy One. He stretches out heaven and establishes earth (Isaiah 51:13); the seat of His glory is in the heavens above, and His powerful presence is in the loftiest heights. He is our Elohim and there is none other.

True is our King, there is nothing beside Him, as it is written in His Torah: "Know this day, and lay it to your heart, that יהוה , He is Elohim in heaven above and upon the earth beneath; there is none else." And it is said: "And יהוה shall be Melekh over all the earth; in that day shall יהוה be Ekhad, and His Name Ekhad."

## Adon Olam: Master of the Universe
*Hebrew first, then English*

Adon Olam asher malakh, b'terem kol yetzir nivra, le'et na'asah v'kheftzo kol, azai melekh shemoh nikra; v'akharei kikhlot hakol, l'vado yimlokh nora. V'hu hayah v'hu hoveh v'hu yihyeh b'tifarah.

אֲדוֹן עוֹלָם אֲשֶׁר מָלַךְ, בְּטֶרֶם כָּל יְצִיר נִבְרָא. לְעֵת נַעֲשָׂה בְחֶפְצוֹ כֹּל, אֲזַי מֶלֶךְ שְׁמוֹ נִקְרָא. וְאַחֲרֵי כִּכְלוֹת הַכֹּל, לְבַדּוֹ יִמְלוֹךְ נוֹרָא. וְהוּא הָיָה, וְהוּא הֹוֶה, וְהוּא יִהְיֶה בְּתִפְאָרָה

V'hu ekḥad v'ein sheni, l'hamshil lo l'hakḥbirah; bli reshit, bli takḥlit v'lo ha'oz v'hamisrah; v'hu Eli v'kḥai goeli, v'tzur kḥevli b'yom tzarah.

וְהוּא אֶחָד וְאֵין שֵׁנִי, לְהַמְשִׁיל לוֹ לְהַחְבִּירָה. בְּלִי רֵאשִׁית בְּלִי תַכְלִית וְלוֹ הָעֹז וְהַמִּשְׂרָה. וְהוּא אֵלִי וְחַי גּוֹאֲלִי, וְצוּר חֶבְלִי בְּיוֹם צָרָה.

V'hu nissi umanos li, menat kosi b'yom ekrah; b'yado afkid rukḥi, b'et ishan v'a'irah; v'im rukḥi geviyati, Adonai li v'lo ira.

וְהוּא נִסִּי וּמָנוֹס לִי, מְנָת כּוֹסִי בְּיוֹם אֶקְרָא. בְּיָדוֹ אַפְקִיד רוּחִי, בְּעֵת אִישָׁן וְאָעִירָה. וְעִם רוּחִי גְוִיָּתִי, אֲדֹנָי לִי וְלֹא אִירָא.

Master of the Universe who has reigned before anything was created, at the time that everything was created at His will, then "King" was His Name proclaimed.

After all has ceased to exist, He, the Awesome One, will reign alone. And He was and He is, and He shall be in Glory! And He is One, and there is no second to compare to Him, to declare as His equal.

Without beginning, without end, He has the might and dominion. And He is my Elohim and my living Redeemer, and the Rock of my Salvation in time of trouble.

And He is my standard and a refuge for me, the portion of my cup on the day I call. In His hand I will deposit my spirit, when I am asleep, and I shall awaken, and with my spirit shall my body remain. Adonai is with me and I shall not fear.

# Ein K'Eloheinu
*Hebrew first, then English*

| | |
|---|---|
| Ein K'Eloheinu, ein k'adoneinu, ein k'malkeinu, ein k'moshi'einu, | אין כאלהינו. אין כאדונינו. אין כמלכנו. אין כמושיענו. |
| mi k'eloheinu, mi k'adoneinu, mi k'malkeinu, mi k'moshi`einu, | מי כאלהינו. מי כאדונינו. מי כמלכנו. מי כמושיענו. |
| Nodeh l'eloheinu, nodeh l'adoneinu, nodeh l'malkeinu, nodeh l'moshi`einu, | נודה לאלהינו. נודה לאדונינו. נודה למלכנו. נודה למושיענו. |
| Barukh Eloheinu, Barukh Adoneinu, Barukh Malkeinu, Barukh Moshi'einu, | ברוך אלהינו. ברוך אדונינו. ברוך מלכנו. ברוך מושיענו. |
| Atah Hu Eloheinu, Atah Hu Adoneinu, Atah Hu Malkeinu, Atah Hu Moshi'einu, | אתה הוא אלהינו. אתה הוא אדונינו. אתה הוא מלכנו. אתה הוא מושיענו. |
| Atah Hu shehiktiru avoteinu, l'faneikha et ketoret hasamim. | אתה הוא שהקטירו אבותינו לפניך את קטרת הסמים. |
| Atah tushi'einu. Atah tokum t'rakhem Tzion, ki et l'khen'nah, ki va mo'ed. | אתה תושיענו. אתה תקום תרחם ציון, כי עת לחננה כי בא מועד. |

There is none like our Elohim, There is none like our Master, There is none like our King, There is none like our Savior.

Who is like our Elohim?, Who is like our Master?, Who is like

our King?, Who is like our Savior?

Let us thank our Elohim, Let us thank our Master, Let us thank our King, Let us thank our Savior.

Blessed be our Elohim, Blessed be our Master, Blessed be our King, Blessed be our Savior.

You are our Elohim, You are our Master, You are our King, You are our Savior.

You are the one before whom our fathers burned the incense of spice.

You will save us. You will arise and show mercy to Tzion, for it will be the time to favor her, for the appointed time is coming.

## Tefillat HaTalmidim: The Disciples' Prayer
*Hebrew first, then English*

Avinu sh'bashamayim, yitkadesh shimkha. Tavoh malkhutekha, y'aseh retzon'kha k'vahshamayim gam ba'aretz.

אָבִנוּ שֶׁבַּשָּׁמַיִם, יִתְקַדֵּשׁ שְׁמֶךָ, תָּבוֹא מַלְכוּתֶךָ, יֵעָשֶׂה רְצוֹנְךָ כְּבַשָּׁמַיִם גַּם בָּאָרֶץ.

Ten lanu et lekhem tzarkenu hayom, Um'khol lanu et khovoteinu kemo shegam anakhnu makholnu l'khayaveinu.

תֵּן לָנוּ אֶת לֶחֶם צָרְכֵּנוּ הַיּוֹם, וּמְחַל לָנוּ אֶת חוֹבוֹתֵינוּ כְּמוֹ שֶׁגַּם אֲנַחְנוּ מָחַלְנוּ לְחַיָּבֵינוּ.

V'al tevi'enu lidei nisayon, elah hatzileinu min hara, ki shelkha hi hamalkhut v'hagevurah v'hatifarah l'olemei olamim.

וְאַל תְּבִיאֵנוּ לִידֵי נִסָּיוֹן, אֶלָּא הַצִּילֵנוּ מִן הָרַע, כִּי שֶׁלְּךָ הִיא הַמַּלְכוּת וְהַגְּבוּרָה וְהַתִּפְאָרָה לְעוֹלְמֵי עוֹלָמִים.

171

'Avinu Sh'bah Shamayim, may Your Name be made kadosh. May Your Kingdom come. May Your will be done, as in Heaven, so on earth. Give us the bread we need today. And forgive us our offenses, as we have forgiven our offenders;
And do not lead us into the power of testing, but deliver us from the Evil One. Because Yours is HaMalkhut, and the power, and the glory, for ever and ever. Amein.' ( *Matai 6:9-13* )

## The Ten Remembrances

Vayiz**kor** El**ohim** et No'a**kh**, v'**et** kol hakhaiya v'et kol hab'he**ma**, as**her** i**to** ba**teva**. Vaya'aver Elo**him** ru'ak**h** al ha'**aretz** vayas**ku** ham**ayim**.

וַיִּזְכֹּר אֱלֹהִים אֶת נֹחַ וְאֵת כָּל הַחַיָּה וְאֶת כָּל הַבְּהֵמָה אֲשֶׁר אִתּוֹ בַּתֵּבָה; וַיַּעֲבֵר אֱלֹהִים רוּחַ עַל הָאָרֶץ וַיָּשֹׁכּוּ הַמָּיִם.

And Elohim remembered No'akh, and every living thing, and all the cattle that were with him in the ark; and Elohim made a wind to pass over the earth, and the waters assuaged. *(B'reshit 8:1)*

Vayish**ma** El**ohim** et na'aka**tam**, vayiz**kor** Elo**him** et bri**to**, et Avra**ham**, et Yitz'k**hak**, v'**et** Ya'akov.

וַיִּשְׁמַע אֱלֹהִים אֶת נַאֲקָתָם; וַיִּזְכֹּר אֱלֹהִים אֶת בְּרִיתוֹ אֶת אַבְרָהָם אֶת יִצְחָק וְאֶת יַעֲקֹב.

And Elohim heard their groaning, and Elohim remembered His Brit with Avraham, with Yitz'khak, and with Ya'akov. *(Shemot 2:24)*

V'zak**har**ti et bri**ti** Ya'akov; V'**af** et bri**ti** Yitz'k**hak** v'**af** et bri**ti** Avra**ham**, ez**kor**, v'ha'**aretz** ez**kor**.

וְזָכַרְתִּי אֶת בְּרִיתִי יַעֲקוֹב; וְאַף אֶת בְּרִיתִי יִצְחָק וְאַף אֶת בְּרִיתִי אַבְרָהָם אֶזְכֹּר וְהָאָרֶץ אֶזְכֹּר.

172

I remember My Brit with Ya'akov, and also My Brit with Yitz'khak, and also My Brit with Avraham will I remember; and I will remember the land. *(VaYikra 26:42)*

Z'kher asa l'nifl'otav; khanun v'rakhum יהוה.

זֵכֶר עָשָׂה לְנִפְלְאוֹתָיו; חַנּוּן וְרַחוּם יהוה.

He has made a memorial for His wonderful works; יהוה is gracious and full of mercy. *(Tehillah 111:4)*

Teref natan lirei'av; yizkor l'olam brito.

טֶרֶף נָתַן לִירֵאָיו; יִזְכֹּר לְעוֹלָם בְּרִיתוֹ.

He has given food unto them that fear Him; He will ever be mindful of His Brit. *(Tehillah 111:5)*

Vayizkor lahem brito; vayinakhem, k'rov khasadav.

וַיִּזְכֹּר לָהֶם בְּרִיתוֹ; וַיִּנָּחֵם כְּרֹב חֲסָדָו.

And He remembered for them His Brit, and relented according to the multitude of His compassions. *(Tehillah 106:45)*

Halokh v'karata v'aznei Yerushalayim l'mor: Ko amar יהוה , zakharti lakh khesed n'ura'ikh, ahavat k'lulota'ikh; l'kh'teikh akharai bamidbar, b'eretz lo z'rua.

הָלֹךְ וְקָרָאתָ בְאָזְנֵי יְרוּשָׁלַם לֵאמֹר כֹּה אָמַר יהוה זָכַרְתִּי לָךְ חֶסֶד נְעוּרַיִךְ אַהֲבַת כְּלוּלֹתָיִךְ; לֶכְתֵּךְ אַחֲרַי בַּמִּדְבָּר, בְּאֶרֶץ לֹא זְרוּעָה.

Go, and cry in the ears of Yerushalayim, saying thus says יהוה , 'I remember for you the affection of your youth, the love of your espousals; how you went after Me in the wilderness, in a land that was not sown. *(Yirme-Yahu 2:2)*

173

V'zakḥarti Ani et briti otakḥ bimei nura'ikḥ; vahakimoti lakḥ, brit olam.

וְזָכַרְתִּי אֲנִי אֶת בְּרִיתִי אוֹתָךְ בִּימֵי נְעוּרָיִךְ; וַהֲקִימוֹתִי לָךְ בְּרִית עוֹלָם.

Nevertheless I will remember My Brit with you in the days of your youth, and I will establish unto you a Brit Olam. *(Yekhezkel 16:60)*

Ha'ven yakir li Efrayim, im yeled sh'ashu'im; ki midei dab'ri bo, zakḥar ezk'reinu od; al ken hamu me'ai lo; rakḥam arakḥameinu, ne'um יהוה.

הֲבֵן יַקִּיר לִי אֶפְרַיִם אִם יֶלֶד שַׁעֲשֻׁעִים; כִּי מִדֵּי דַבְּרִי בּוֹ זָכֹר אֶזְכְּרֶנּוּ עוֹד; עַל כֵּן הָמוּ מֵעַי לוֹ; רַחֵם אֲרַחֲמֶנּוּ נְאֻם יהוה.

Is Efrayim a darling son unto Me? Is he a child that is dandled? For as often as I speak of him, I do earnestly remember him still; therefore My heart yearns for him, I will surely have compassion upon him, says יהוה . *(Yirme-Yahu 31:19)*

V'zakḥarti lahem brit rishonim: asher hotzeti otam m'eretz Mitzrayim l'einei hagoyim liyot lahem l'Elohim: Ani יהוה.

וְזָכַרְתִּי לָהֶם בְּרִית רִאשֹׁנִים: אֲשֶׁר הוֹצֵאתִי אֹתָם מֵאֶרֶץ מִצְרַיִם לְעֵינֵי הַגּוֹיִם לִהְיוֹת לָהֶם לֵאלֹהִים אֲנִי יהוה.

But I will for their sakes remember the Brit of their ancestors, whom I brought forth out of the land of Mitzrayim in the sight of the nations, that I might be their Elohim: I am יהוה '. *(VaYikra 26:45)*

# The Power of the Shofar

Daber el B'**nei** Yisra'**el**, l'**mor**: bakḥodesh hashevi'**i** b'ekḥad lakḥodesh, yihyeh lakḥem shabatton; zikron teruah, mikra kodesh.

דַּבֵּר אֶל בְּנֵי יִשְׂרָאֵל לֵאמֹר: בַּחֹדֶשׁ הַשְּׁבִיעִי בְּאֶחָד לַחֹדֶשׁ יִהְיֶה לָכֶם שַׁבָּתוֹן; זִכְרוֹן תְּרוּעָה מִקְרָא קֹדֶשׁ.

Kol m'**lekḥet** avodah, lo ta'asu; v'hikravtem isheh la יהוה.

כָּל מְלֶאכֶת עֲבֹדָה לֹא תַעֲשׂוּ; וְהִקְרַבְתֶּם אִשֶּׁה לַיהוה.

Speak unto B'nei Yisra'el, saying, 'In the seventh khodesh, in the first day of the khodesh, shall be a Shabbaton unto you, a Zikhron Teru'ah, a Mikra Kodesh. You shall do no manner of regular work; and you shall bring a karban of fire unto יהוה. *(VaYikra 23:24-25)*

V'**kḥi** tavo'u milkḥama b'artzeikḥem, al hatzar hatzorer etkḥem; v'hare'otem, bakḥatzotzrot; v'nizkartem lifnei יהוה Eloheikḥem, v'nosha'etem, m'oyveikḥem.

וְכִי תָבֹאוּ מִלְחָמָה בְּאַרְצְכֶם, עַל הַצַּר הַצֹּרֵר אֶתְכֶם; וַהֲרֵעֹתֶם בַּחֲצֹצְרֹת; וְנִזְכַּרְתֶּם לִפְנֵי יהוה אֱלֹהֵיכֶם וְנוֹשַׁעְתֶּם מֵאֹיְבֵיכֶם.

U'vayom simakḥtekḥem uv'moadeikḥem, uv'rashei kḥad'sheikḥem: ut'ka'etem bakḥatzotzrot al oloteikḥem, v'al zivkḥei shalmeikḥem; v'hayu lakḥem l'zikaron lifnei Eloheikḥem, Ani יהוה Eloheikḥem.

וּבְיוֹם שִׂמְחַתְכֶם וּבְמוֹעֲדֵיכֶם, וּבְרָאשֵׁי חָדְשֵׁיכֶם וּתְקַעְתֶּם בַּחֲצֹצְרֹת עַל עֹלֹתֵיכֶם, וְעַל זִבְחֵי שַׁלְמֵיכֶם; וְהָיוּ לָכֶם לְזִכָּרוֹן לִפְנֵי אֱלֹהֵיכֶם אֲנִי יהוה אֱלֹהֵיכֶם.

And when you go to war in your land against the adversary that

175

oppresses you, then you shall sound a Teru'ah with the trumpets; and you shall be remembered before יהוה your Elohim, and you shall be saved from your enemies.

Also in the day of your gladness, and in your Mo'edim, and in your khadashim, you shall blow with the trumpets over your Olot, and over the sacrifices of your Sh'lamim; and they shall be to you for a memorial before your Elohim: I am יהוה your Elohim. *(BaMidbar 10:9-10)*

| | |
|---|---|
| **Tiku** vakhodesh sho**far**; bake**seh** l'**yom** khageinu. | תִּקְעוּ בַחֹדֶשׁ שׁוֹפָר; בַּכֵּסֶה לְיוֹם חַגֵּנוּ. |

| | |
|---|---|
| Ki khok l'Yisra'**el** hu; mish**pat** l'Elo**hei** Ya'a**kov**. | כִּי חֹק לְיִשְׂרָאֵל הוּא; מִשְׁפָּט לֵאלֹהֵי יַעֲקֹב. |

Blast the shofar at the khodesh, at the full moon for our Khag. For it is a statute for Yisra'el, an ordinance of the Elohim of Ya'akov. *(Tehillah 81:4-5)*

| | |
|---|---|
| B'**rega** ek**had** k'**heref** ayin kit'**ko**'ah hasho**far** ha'ak**haron** ki yita**ka**; v'hame**tim** ya**ku**mu bli khila**yon**, v'ana**kh**nu nitkha**laf**! | בְּרֶגַע אֶחָד כְּהֶרֶף עַיִן כִּתְקֹעַ הַשּׁוֹפָר הָאַחֲרוֹן כִּי יִתָּקַע, וְהַמֵּתִים יָקוּמוּ בְּלִי כִלָּיוֹן וַאֲנַחְנוּ נִתְחַלָּף. |

In a moment, in the twinkling of an eye, at the Last Shofar; for the shofar shall sound, and the dead shall be raised incorruptible, and we shall be changed! *(Korinti'im Alef 15:52)*

| | |
|---|---|
| Bakhatzotz**rot** sho**far**, hariu HaMe**lekh** יהוה ! | v'**kol** lif**nei** | בַּחֲצֹצְרוֹת וְקוֹל שׁוֹפָר הָרִיעוּ לִפְנֵי הַמֶּלֶךְ יהוה . |

With trumpets and the sound of the shofar, shout before HaMelekh, יהוה ! *(Tehillah 98:6)*

Barukh Atah, יהוה , אֱלֹהֵינוּ, בָּרוּךְ אַתָּה יהוה , אֱלֹהֵינוּ,
Eloheinu, Melekh מֶלֶךְ הָעוֹלָם, אֲשֶׁר קִדְּשָׁנוּ
HaOlam, asher kid'shanu
b'mitzvotav, v'tzivanu בְּמִצְוֹתָיו, וְצִוָּנוּ לשמוע קוֹל
lishmoa kol hashofar. השפר.

Barukh Atah, יהוה , אֱלֹהֵינוּ, בָּרוּךְ אַתָּה יהוה , אֱלֹהֵינוּ,
Eloheinu, Melekh מֶלֶךְ הָעוֹלָם, שֶׁהֶחֱיָנוּ
HaOlam sh'hekheyanu
v'kimanu v'higi'anu וְקִיְּמָנוּ, וְהִגִּיעָנוּ לַזְּמָן הַזֶּה.
lazman hazeh. Amein.

Blessed are You, O יהוה Eloheinu, King of the Universe, who has
consecrated us in His Mitzvot and commanded us to hear the
voice of the Shofar. Blessed are You, O יהוה Eloheinu, King of
the Universe, who has kept us in life and has preserved us, and
has enabled us to reach this season. Amein.

# The Voice of the Shofar

The congregation rises. Each of the thirty (30) calls is announced and then
blown. The congregation contemplates the sound of the Shofar. The Tekiah is
a long, single blast, to awaken those who sleep. The Shevarim are three (3)
short blasts, crying out for relief from distress. The Teruah is a series of nine
(9) blasts, sounding the alarm, to call the congregation to assemble, and to
battle. The Tekiah HaG'dolah is the final blast. The leader and the
congregation conduct the Baalim HaShofarim together in the blasts.

| | | |
|---|---|---|
| TEKI**AH**! SHEVA**RIM**! TERU**AH**! | תקיעה! שברים! תרועה! | |
| TEKI**AH**! | | |
| TEKI**AH**! SHEVA**RIM**! TERU**AH**! | תקיעה! תקיעה! שברים! | |
| TEKI**AH**! | | |
| TEKI**AH**! SHEVA**RIM**! TERU**AH**! | תרועה! תקיעה! תקיעה! | |
| TEKI**AH**! | | |
| | שברים! תרועה! תקיעה! | |

| | |
|---|---|
| TEKI**AH**! SHEVA**RIM**! TEKI**AH**! | תקיעה! שברים! תקיעה! |
| TEKI**AH**! SHEVA**RIM**! TEKI**AH**! | תקיעה! שברים! תקיעה! |
| TEKI**AH**! SHEVA**RIM**! TEKI**AH**! | תקיעה! שברים! תקיעה! |

| | |
|---|---|
| | תקיעה! תרועה! תקיעה! |
| TEKI**AH**! TERU**AH**! TEKI**AH**! | תקיעה! תרועה! תקיעה! |
| TEKI**AH**! TERU**AH**! TEKI**AH**! | |
| TEKI**AH**! TERU**AH**! TEKI**AH** | תקיעה! תרועה! תקיעה |
| HAG'DO**LAH**! | הגדולה!! |

# הַמֶּלֶךְ!
## יֹשֵׁב עַל כִּסֵּא, רָם וְנִשָּׂא!

HaMelekḥ! Yoshev al kiseh, Ram v'Nisah!

# The King!
# Sitting on the throne!
# High and Lifted up!

Everyone who holds a shofar blows the shofar together, for as long as can be maintained, until the leader signals to cease. Everyone who is not holding a shofar participates with shouting. This anticipates the Shofar that will awaken the dead, and will reveal our Messiah Yeshua to us visibly for the first time since we came to believe in Him.

# שפר האחרון!
**Shofar HaAkharon**

# *DRASH*

*Service concludes starting on page 71*

# תוֹרָקוּ HaKiוּעֶמ תהסצ

Akh b'asor lakhodesh
hashevi'i hazeh Yom
HaKipurim hu, mikra
kodesh yihyeh lakhem,
v'initem et nafshoteikhem;
v'hikravtem isheh la יהוה.

אַךְ בֶּעָשׂוֹר לַחֹדֶשׁ הַשְּׁבִיעִי
הַזֶּה יוֹם הַכִּפֻּרִים הוּא
מִקְרָא קֹדֶשׁ יִהְיֶה לָכֶם,
וְעִנִּיתֶם אֶת נַפְשֹׁתֵיכֶם;
וְהִקְרַבְתֶּם אִשֶּׁה לַיהוה.

V'khol m'lakha lo ta'asu,
b'etzem hayom hazeh: ki
Yom Kipurim hu, l'khaper
aleikhem lifnei יהוה
Eloheikhem.

וְכָל מְלָאכָה לֹא תַעֲשׂוּ
בְּעֶצֶם הַיּוֹם הַזֶּה: כִּי יוֹם
כִּפֻּרִים, הוּא לְכַפֵּר עֲלֵיכֶם
לִפְנֵי יהוה אֱלֹהֵיכֶם.

But on the tenth day of this seventh khodesh is Yom
HaKippurim; there shall be a Mikra Kodesh unto you, and you
shall afflict your souls; and you shall bring a karban of fire unto
יהוה . And you shall do no manner of work in that same day; for
it is Yom HaKippurim, to make atonement for you before יהוה
your Elohim. *(VaYikra 23:27-28)*

V'hitvadu et avonam v'et
avon Avotam, b'ma'alam
asher ma'alu vi, v'af asher
hal'khu imi b'keri.

וְהִתְוַדּוּ אֶת עֲוֹנָם וְאֶת עֲוֹן
אֲבֹתָם בְּמַעֲלָם אֲשֶׁר מָעֲלוּ
בִי וְאַף אֲשֶׁר הָלְכוּ עִמִּי
בְּקֶרִי.

Af Ani elekh imam b'keri
v'heveti otam, b'eretz
oiveihem; o'az yikana,
l'vavam he'arel, v'az yirtzu
et avonam.

אַף אֲנִי אֵלֵךְ עִמָּם בְּקֶרִי
וְהֵבֵאתִי אֹתָם בְּאֶרֶץ
אֹיְבֵיהֶם; אוֹאָז יִכָּנַע לְבָבָם
הֶעָרֵל וְאָז יִרְצוּ אֶת עֲוֹנָם.

V'zakḥarti et b'riti
Ya'akov; V'af et b'riti
Yitz'kḥak v'af et b'riti
Avraham, ezkor,
v'ha'aretz ezkor.

וְזָכַרְתִּי אֶת בְּרִיתִי יַעֲקוֹב;
וְאַף אֶת בְּרִיתִי יִצְחָק וְאַף
אֶת בְּרִיתִי אַבְרָהָם אֶזְכֹּר
וְהָאָרֶץ אֶזְכֹּר.

And they shall confess their iniquity, and the iniquity of their
fathers, in their treachery which they committed against Me, and
also that they have walked contrary unto Me. I also will walk
contrary unto them, and bring them into the land of their
enemies; if then perchance their uncircumcised heart is humbled,
and they then be paid the punishment of their iniquity, then will I
remember My Brit with Ya'akov, and also My Brit with
Yitz'khak, and also My Brit with Avraham will I remember; and I
will remember the land. _(VaYikra 26:40-42)_

Anokḥi, Anokḥi hu
mokḥeh f'sha'eikḥa,
l'ma'ani: v'kḥatoteikḥa lo
ezkor.

אָנֹכִי אָנֹכִי הוּא מֹחֶה
פְּשָׁעֶיךָ לְמַעֲנִי: וְחַטֹּאתֶיךָ
לֹא אֶזְכֹּר.

Haz'kireini nishaf'ta
yakḥad; sahfer atah,
l'ma'an titz'dak.

הַזְכִּירֵנִי נִשָּׁפְטָה יָחַד; סַפֵּר
אַתָּה, לְמַעַן תִּצְדָּק.

I, even I, am He that blots out your transgressions for My own
sake; and your sins I will not remember. Put Me in
remembrance, let us plead together; declare, that you may be
justified. _(Yesha-Yahu 43:25-26)_

Ki im dahm se'irim
va'agalim v'efer ha'eglah
asher yuzeh al hat'me'im
y'kadshem l'taher
b'saram,

כִּי אִם דַּם שְׂעִירִים וַעֲגָלִים
וְאֵפֶר הָעֶגְלָה אֲשֶׁר יֶזֶּה עַל
הַטְּמֵאִים יְקַדֵּשׁ לְטַהֵר
בְּשָׂרָם

Af ki dahm haMashi'akh asher hikriv et atzmo l'Elohim b'Ru'akh Olam u'vli mum y'taher lib'khem mima'asei mavet, k'dei sh'nesharet et Elohim khayim.

אַף כִּי דַם הַמָּשִׁיחַ אֲשֶׁר הִקְרִיב אֶת עַצְמוֹ לֵאלֹהִים בְּרוּחַ עוֹלָם וּבְלִי מוּם יְטַהֵר לִבְּכֶם מִמַּעֲשֵׂי מָוֶת כְּדֵי שֶׁנְּשָׁרֵת אֶת אֱלֹהִים חַיִּים.

For if the blood of goats and calves and the ashes of a heifer sprinkled on those who were defiled consecrated them even to the cleansing of their flesh, how much more will the blood of Mashi'akh, who through the eternal Ru'akh offered Himself without blemish to Elohim, purify our conscience from dead works so that we may serve the living Elohim? *(Ivrim 9:13-14)*

Aval im nitvadeh et khata'einu, ne'eman hu v'tzadik lislo'akh et khata'einu, u'letareinu mi'kol avlateinu.

אֲבָל אִם נִתְוַדֶּה אֶת חֲטָאֵינוּ נֶאֱמָן הוּא וְצַדִּיק לִסְלֹחַ אֶת חֲטָאֵינוּ וּלְטַהֲרֵנוּ מִכָּל עַוְלָתֵנוּ.

If we confess our sins, he is faithful and just to forgive us our sins, and to cleanse us from all our iniquity. *( Yokhanan Alef 1:9)*

## Kadosh: Consecrated
### *Hebrew first, then English*

V'kara zeh el zeh v'amar, Kadosh kadosh kadosh יהוה Tzeva'ot. Melo khol ha'aretz k'vodoh.

וְקָרָא זֶה אֶל זֶה וְאָמַר, קָדוֹשׁ קָדוֹשׁ קָדוֹשׁ יהוה צְבָאוֹת; מְלֹא כָל הָאָרֶץ, כְּבוֹדוֹ.

Va'yikre'u b'kol gadol b'ahmrahm: haYeshu'ah l'Eloheinu, hayoshev al hakiseh, v'laSeh.

וַיִּקְרְאוּ בְּקוֹל גָּדוֹל בְּאָמְרָם: הַיְשׁוּעָה לֵאלֹהֵנוּ, הַיּוֹשֵׁב עַל הַכִּסֵּא וְלַשֶׂה.

Na'**eh** La**Seh** HaTavu**akh**,
l'ka**bel** ko'a**kh** v'o**sher**
v'**kh**o**kh**ma v'**oz** vi**kar**
v'tiferet uv'ra**kh**a.

נָאֶה לַשֶּׂה הַטָּבוּחַ לְקַבֵּל
כֹּחַ וְעֹשֶׁר וְחָכְמָה וְעֹז וִיקָר
וְתִפְאֶרֶת וּבְרָכָה.

La**yoshev** al haki**seh**
v'la**seh**, hab'ra**kha** v'hai**kar**
v'hatiferet v'hashil**ton**
l'ola**mei** ola**mim**.

לַיּוֹשֵׁב עַל הַכִּסֵּא וְלַשֶּׂה
הַבְּרָכָה וְהַיְקָר וְהַתִּפְאֶרֶת
וְהַשִּׁלְטוֹן לְעוֹלְמֵי עוֹלָמִים.

And they called to each other, and said, "Kadosh, Kadosh,
Kadosh, is יהוה Tzeva'ot; the whole earth is full of His Kavod"
*(Yesha-Yahu 6:3)* and cried with a loud voice, saying, "Yeshua[h]
belongs to our Elohim, who sits upon the throne, and to HaSeh."
*(Hitgalut 7:10)*

[And they cried] "Worthy is HaSeh that was slain, to receive
power, and riches, and wisdom, and might, and honor, and glory
and blessing." *(Hitgalut 5:12)*

"To Him who sits on the throne, and to HaSeh, be blessing, and
honor, and glory, and dominion, forever and ever." *(Hitgalut 5:13)*

# Vidui Al Khayit

*Leader and Congregation together*

For the sins which we have committed against You under duress
or willingly, and for the sins which we have committed against
You by hard-heartedness.
For the sins which we have committed against You inadvertently,
and for the sins which we have committed against You with an
utterance of the lips.

For the sins which we have committed against You with
immorality, and for the sins which we have committed against
You openly or secretly.

For the sins which we have committed against You with

knowledge and with deceit, and for the sins which we have committed against You through speech.

For the sins which we have committed against You by deceiving a fellow man, and for the sins which we have committed against You by improper thoughts.

For the sins which we have committed against You by a gathering of lewdness, and for the sins which we have committed against You by verbal, insincere confession.

For the sins which we have committed against You by disrespect for parents and teachers, and for the sins which we have committed against You intentionally or unintentionally.

For the sins which we have committed against You by using coercion, and for the sins which we have committed against You by desecrating the Divine Name.

For the sins which we have committed against You by impurity of speech, and for the sins which we have committed against You by foolish talk.

For the sins which we have committed against You with the evil inclination, and for the sins which we have committed against You knowingly or unknowingly.

For all these, Elohim who pardons, pardon us, forgive us, atone for us.

For the sins which we have committed against You by false denial and lying, and for the sins which we have committed against You by a bribe-taking or a bribe-giving hand.

For the sins which we have committed against You by scoffing, and for the sins which we have committed against You by evil talk about another.

For the sins which we have committed against You in business dealings, and for the sins which we have committed against You by eating and drinking.

For the sins which we have committed against You by taking or giving interest and by usury, and for the sins which we have committed against You by a haughty demeanor.

For the sins which we have committed against You by the prattle of our lips, and for the sins which we have committed against You by a glance of the eye.

For the sins which we have committed against You with proud looks, and for the sins which we have committed against You with impudence.

For all these, Elohim who pardons, pardon us, forgive us, atone for us.

For the sins which we have committed against You by casting off the yoke of Heaven, and for the sins which we have committed against You in passing judgment.

For the sins which we have committed against You by scheming against a fellow man, and for the sins which we have committed against You by a begrudging eye.

For the sins which we have committed against You by frivolity, and for the sins which we have committed against You by obduracy.

For the sins which we have committed against You by running to do evil, and for the sins which we have committed against You by tale-bearing.

For the sins which we have committed against You by swearing in vain, and for the sins which we have committed against You by causeless hatred.

For the sins which we have committed against You by embezzlement, and for the sins which we have committed against You by a confused heart.

For all these, Elohim who pardons, pardon us, forgive us, atone for us.

For the sins for which we are obligated to bring a burnt offering.
For the sins for which we are obligated to bring a sin offering.
For the sins for which we are obligated to bring a varying offering .
For the sins for which we are obligated to bring a guilt offering for a certain or doubtful trespass.

For the sins for which we incur the penalty of lashing for rebelliousness.
For the sins for which we incur the penalty of forty lashes, and for the sins for which we incur the penalty of death by the hand of Heaven.
For the sins for which we incur the penalty of excision and childlessness.

For transgressing positive and negative mitzvot, whether the prohibitions can be rectified by a specifically prescribed act or not, those of which we are aware and those of which we are not aware; those of which we are aware, we have already declared them before You and confessed them to You, and those of which we are not aware before You they are revealed and known, as it is stated: The hidden things belong to יהוה Eloheinu, but the revealed things are for us and for our children forever, that we may carry out all the words of this Torah. For You are the Pardoner of Yisra'el and the Forgiver of the tribes of Yeshurun in every generation, and aside from You we have no King who forgives and pardons.

Barkhi nafshi, et יהוה; v'khol k'ravai, et shem kodsho.

בָּרְכִי נַפְשִׁי, אֶת יהוה; וְכָל קְרָבַי, אֶת שֵׁם קָדְשׁוֹ.

Barkhi nafshi, et יהוה; v'al tishk'khi, kol g'mulav.

בָּרְכִי נַפְשִׁי, אֶת יהוה; וְאַל תִּשְׁכְּחִי, כָּל גְּמוּלָיו.

Hasole'akh l'khol avonekhi; harofeh l'khol takhalu'aikhi.

הַסֹּלֵחַ לְכָל עֲוֹנֵכִי; הָרֹפֵא, לְכָל תַּחֲלוּאָיְכִי.

Hago'el mishakhat khaiyaikhi; hame'atrekhi khesed v'rakhamim.

הַגּוֹאֵל מִשַּׁחַת חַיָּיְכִי; הַמְעַטְּרֵכִי, חֶסֶד וְרַחֲמִים.

Bless יהוה, O my soul; and all that is within me, bless His consecrated name. Bless יהוה, O my soul, and forget not all His benefits; Who forgives all your iniquity; who heals all your diseases; Who redeems your life from the pit; who encompasses you with compassion and tender mercies; *(Tehillah 103:1-4)*

## B'khol Birkhot
*Hebrew first, then English*

Barukh HaElohim Avi Adoneinu Yeshua HaMashi'akh, asher ber'khanu b'khol birkhot haRu'akh bashamayim baMashi'akh.

בָּרוּךְ הָאֱלֹהִים אֲבִי אֲדֹנֵינוּ יֵשׁוּעַ הַמָּשִׁיחַ אֲשֶׁר בֵּרְכָנוּ בְּכָל בִּרְכוֹת הָרוּחַ בַּשָּׁמַיִם בַּמָּשִׁיחַ.

K'fi shehikdim uv'kharanu bo lifnei mos'dot olam liyot k'doshim uv'li mum l'fanav,

כְּפִי שֶׁהִקְדִּים וּבָחָרָנוּ בּוֹ לִפְנֵי מוֹסְדוֹת עוֹלָם לִהְיוֹת קְדוֹשִׁים וּבְלִי מוּם לְפָנָיו,

Uv'ahavah hikdim v'tziyen otanu lo v'sam otanu l'vanim b'Yeshua HaMashi'akh katov b'enei r'tzonoh,

וּבְאַהֲבָה הִקְדִּים וְצִיֵּן אוֹתָנוּ לוֹ וְשָׂם אוֹתָנוּ לְבָנִים בְּיֵשׁוּעַ הַמָּשִׁיחַ כַּטּוֹב בְּעֵינֵי רְצוֹנוֹ,

L'ma'an yishtabakh k'vod khasdo asher hishpiah aleinu al yedei ahuvoh.

לְמַעַן יִשְׁתַּבַּח כְּבוֹד חַסְדּוֹ אֲשֶׁר הִשְׁפִּיעַ עָלֵינוּ עַל יְדֵי אֲהוּבוֹ:

asher bo yesh lanu pedut, uv'damoh slikhat hakhata'im k'osher khasdoh:

אֲשֶׁר בּוֹ יֵשׁ לָנוּ פְּדוּת, וּבְדָמוֹ סְלִיחַת הַחֲטָאִים כְּעֹשֶׁר חַסְדּוֹ:

asher shafah banu b'khol khakhmah uv'khol binah rukhanit

אֲשֶׁר שָׁפַע בָּנוּ בְּכָל חָכְמָה וּבְכָל בִּינָה רוּחָנִית

v'hodianu et sod r'tzonoh asher m'rosh kavah l'hotzi lapo'al bo:

וְהוֹדִיעָנוּ אֶת סוֹד רְצוֹנוֹ אֲשֶׁר מֵרֹאשׁ קָבַע לְהוֹצִיא לַפֹּעַל בּוֹ:

l'hesder m'loht ha'yamim, sh'kol mah sh'bashamayim uva'aretz shuv yitkhadash baMashi'akh,

לְהֶסְדֵּר מְלֹאת הָעִתִּים, שֶׁכָּל מַה שֶׁבַּשָּׁמַיִם וּבָאָרֶץ שׁוּב יִתְחַדֵּשׁ בַּמָּשִׁיחַ,

Lo hayakhol bigvurah la'asoht l'ma'aneinu yoter mikol, v'yoter mimah sh'anu m'vakshim v'khoshvim, k'fi kokho hapo'el b'kirbeinu,

לוֹ הַיָכוֹל בִּגְבוּרָה לַעֲשׂוֹת לְמַעֲנֵנוּ יוֹתֵר מִכֹּל, וְיוֹתֵר מִמַּה שֶׁאָנוּ מְבַקְשִׁים וְחוֹשְׁבִים, כְּפִי כֹּחוֹ הַפּוֹעֵל בְּקִרְבֵּנוּ,

Lo hakavod b'kerev adato b'Yeshua HaMashi'akh, l'dor vador olamei haolamim, Amein.

לוֹ הַכָּבוֹד בְּקֶרֶב עֲדָתוֹ בִּישׁוּעַ הַמָּשִׁיחַ, לְדֹר וָדֹר עוֹלְמֵי הָעוֹלָמִים, אָמֵן.

Barukh Elohim, HaAv of Adoneinu Yeshua HaMashi'akh, who has blessed us with all spiritual blessings in heaven through Mashi'akh. Since, as from the beginning, He has chosen us

188

through Him before the foundation of the world, that we may become consecrated and without blemish before Him, in love, as at the first, for Himself. And He marked us for Him, and appointed us to be sons through Yeshua HaMashi'akh, as was the pleasure of His will, to the praise of the glory of His compassion that He has poured upon us by His beloved one. In Him we have redemption, and in His blood, forgiveness of sins, according to the richness of His compassion which has abounded in us in all wisdom and spiritual understanding. And He has made known to us the Sod of His will, that He has ordained from the very beginning, to work through it. He did so in the stewardship of the fullness of times, that all things might be made new in heaven and on earth through Mashi'akh.

Now to Him who is able by power to do for us more than anyone else, and to do for us more than we ask or think, according to His mighty power that works in us, unto Him be glory in His assembly by Yeshua HaMashi'akh throughout all ages, forever and ever. Amein.*(Efisim 1:3-10, 3:20-21)*

Ki et asher lo yadah קִּי אֶת אֲשֶׁר לֹא יָדַע חֲטָאָה
khata'**ah**, hu na'asah הוּא נַעֲשָׂה לַחֲטָאת בַּעֲדֵנוּ
l'khatat, k'**dei** anakhnu לְמַעַן נִהְיֶה בּוֹ אֲנַחְנוּ לְצִדְקַת
ni**yeh** bo l'tzid**kat** Elo**him**. אֱלֹהִים.

For He who did not know sin, for our sakes He became a Khatat, that we may through Him be made the tzedaka of Elohim. *(Korinti'im Bet 5:21)*

V'**amar** Yeshua, hito**ded** וְאָמַר יֵשׁוּעַ, הִתְעוֹדֵד בְּנִי,
B'**ni**, nisl'**khu** l'**kha** נִסְלְחוּ לְךָ חֲטָאֶיךָ.
khata'**eikha**.

And Yeshua said, "Be of good cheer, My son, your sins are forgiven you." *(Maai 9:2)*

***Service concludes starting on page 71***

# Sukkot

Daber el B'nei Yisra'el l'emor: bakhamisha asar yom, lakhodesh hashevi'i hazeh, khag hasukkot shivat yamim la יהוה.

דַּבֵּר אֶל בְּנֵי יִשְׂרָאֵל לֵאמֹר: בַּחֲמִשָּׁה עָשָׂר יוֹם, לַחֹדֶשׁ הַשְּׁבִיעִי הַזֶּה חַג הַסֻּכּוֹת שִׁבְעַת יָמִים _ לַיהוה.

B'yom harishon mikra kodesh; kol m'lekhet avodah, lo ta'asu.

בַּיּוֹם הָרִאשׁוֹן מִקְרָא קֹדֶשׁ; כָּל מְלֶאכֶת עֲבֹדָה לֹא תַעֲשׂוּ.

Shivat yamim takrivu isha la יהוה ; bayom hashmini mikra kodesh yihyeh lakhem v'hikravtem isheh la יהוה , atzeret hi; kol m'lekhet avodah, lo ta'asu.

שִׁבְעַת יָמִים תַּקְרִיבוּ אִשֶּׁה לַיהוה; בַּיּוֹם הַשְּׁמִינִי מִקְרָא קֹדֶשׁ יִהְיֶה לָכֶם וְהִקְרַבְתֶּם אִשֶּׁה לַיהוה עֲצֶרֶת הִוא כָּל מְלֶאכֶת עֲבֹדָה לֹא תַעֲשׂוּ.

Speak unto B'nei Yisra'el, saying, 'On the fifteenth day of this seventh khodesh is Khag HaSukkot, Shivat Yamim unto יהוה . On the first day shall be a Mikra Kodesh; you shall do no manner of regular work. Seven days you shall bring a karban of fire unto יהוה ; on the eighth day shall be a Mikra Kodesh unto you; and you shall bring a karban of fire unto יהוה ; it is a festive assembly; you shall do no manner of regular work. *(VaYikra 23:34-36)*

BaSukkot teshvu, shivat yamim; kol ha'azrakh b'Yisrael, yeshvu basukkot.

בַּסֻּכֹּת תֵּשְׁבוּ, שִׁבְעַת יָמִים; כָּל הָאֶזְרָח, בְּיִשְׂרָאֵל, יֵשְׁבוּ בַּסֻּכֹּת.

L'ma'an yed'u dorotekhem, ki basukkot hoshavti et B'nei Yisra'el, b'hotzi'i otam m'eretz Mitzrayim: Ani יהוה Eloheikhem.

לְמַעַן יֵדְעוּ דֹרֹתֵיכֶם כִּי בַסֻּכּוֹת הוֹשַׁבְתִּי אֶת בְּנֵי יִשְׂרָאֵל בְּהוֹצִיאִי אוֹתָם מֵאֶרֶץ מִצְרָיִם: אֲנִי יהוה אֱלֹהֵיכֶם.

You shall dwell in sukkot seven days; all that spring forth in Yisra'el shall dwell in sukkot; that your generations may know that I made B'nei Yisra'el to dwell in sukkot, when I brought them out of the land of Mitzrayim: I am יהוה your Elohim'. *(VaYikra 23:42-43)*

U'vara יהוה al kol m'khon Har Tzion v'al mikra'eha, anan yomam v'ashan, v'nogah esh l'hava laila: ki al kol kavod khuppa.

וּבָרָא יהוה עַל כָּל מְכוֹן הַרצִיּוֹן וְעַל מִקְרָאֶהָ עָנָן יוֹמָם וְעָשָׁן וְנֹגַה אֵשׁ לֶהָבָה לָיְלָה: כִּי עַל כָּל כָּבוֹד חֻפָּה.

V'sukka tiyeh l'tzel yomam, m'khorev; ul'makhseh, ul'mistor, mizerem, umimatar.

וְסֻכָּה תִּהְיֶה לְצֵל יוֹמָם מֵחֹרֶב; וּלְמַחְסֶה וּלְמִסְתּוֹר מִזֶּרֶם וּמִמָּטָר.

And יהוה will create over the whole habitation of Har Tzion, and over her assemblies, a cloud and smoke by day, and the shining of a flaming fire by night; for over all the glory shall be a canopy. [6]And there shall be a sukka for a shadow in the day-time from the heat, and for a refuge, and for a covert from storm and from rain. *(Yesha-Yahu 4:5-6)*

Ki Yitzp'neni b'sukko; b'yom ra'a: Yastireni b'seter ohalo; b'tzur, y'rom'meni.

כִּי יִצְפְּנֵנִי בְּסֻכֹּה; בְּיוֹם רָעָה: יַסְתִּרֵנִי בְּסֵתֶר אָהֳלוֹ; בְּצוּר יְרוֹמְמֵנִי.

V'**ata** y**arum** r**oshi**, al o**ivai** s'**vivotai**, v'**ezbekha** v'**ohalo**, z**ivkhei** teru**ah**; **ashira** v'**azam'ra**, la יהוה .

וְעַתָּה יָרוּם רֹאשִׁי עַל אֹיְבַי סְבִיבוֹתַי וְאֶזְבְּחָה בְאָהֳלֹו זִבְחֵי תְרוּעָה; אָשִׁירָה וַאֲזַמְּרָה לַיהוה.

For He conceals me in His Sukka in the day of evil; He hides me in the covert of His Ohel; He lifts me up upon a Rock. And now shall my head be lifted up above my enemies round about me; and I will offer in His Ohel sacrifices with a blast; I will sing, yes, I will sing praises unto יהוה . *(Tehillah 27:5-6)*

Vayetze'**u** ha'**am**, vayavi'**u**, vaya'**asu** lah**em** suk**kot** ish al ga**go** uv'**khatzroteihem**, uv'**khatzrot** beit haElo**him**; uvirk**hov** sha'ar hama**yim**, uvirk**hov** sha'ar Efra**im**.

וַיֵּצְאוּ הָעָם וַיָּבִיאוּ וַיַּעֲשׂוּ לָהֶם סֻכּוֹת אִישׁ עַל גַּגּוֹ וּבְחַצְרֹתֵיהֶם וּבְחַצְרוֹת בֵּית הָאֱלֹהִים וּבִרְחוֹב שַׁעַר הַמַּיִם וּבִרְחוֹב שַׁעַר אֶפְרָיִם.

Vaya'asu k**hol** haka**hal** hashav**im** min hash'**vi** suk**kot** vayeshvu ki lo **asu** mi**mei** Yeshu**a** Bin Nun ken B'**nei** Yisra'**el** ad ha**yom** hah**u**; vateh**i** sim**kha** g'dolah me'**od**.

וַיַּעֲשׂוּ כָל הַקָּהָל הַשָּׁבִים מִן הַשְּׁבִי סֻכּוֹת וַיֵּשְׁבוּ בַסֻּכּוֹת כִּי לֹא עָשׂוּ מִימֵי יֵשׁוּעַ בִּן נוּן כֵּן בְּנֵי יִשְׂרָאֵל עַד הַיּוֹם הַהוּא; וַתְּהִי שִׂמְחָה גְדוֹלָה מְאֹד.

VaYikra b'**sefer** To**rat** HaElo**him** yom b'**yom** min ha**yom** harish**on** ad ha**yom** ha'akhar**on**; vaya'asu khag shi**vat** ya**mim** uva**yom** hashmi**ni** atzeret kamish**pat**.

וַיִּקְרָא בְּסֵפֶר תּוֹרַת הָאֱלֹהִים יוֹם בְּיוֹם מִן הַיּוֹם הָרִאשׁוֹן עַד הַיּוֹם הָאַחֲרוֹן; וַיַּעֲשׂוּ חָג שִׁבְעַת יָמִים וּבַיּוֹם הַשְּׁמִינִי עֲצֶרֶת כַּמִּשְׁפָּט.

So the people went forth, and brought them, and made themselves sukkot, every one upon the roof of his house, and in

their courts, and in the courts of Beit HaElohim, and in the broad
place of the water gate, and in the broad place of the gate of
Efrayim. And all the congregation of them that were come back
out of the captivity made sukkot, and dwelt in the sukkot; for
since the days of Yeshua Bin Nun unto that day had not B'nei
Yisra'el done so. And there was very great gladness. Also day by
day, from the first day unto the last day, he read in the book of
the Torah of Elohim. And they kept the Khag seven days; and on
the eighth day [Sh'mini] Atzeret, according unto the ordinance.
*(Neh 8:16-18)*

V'haDavar niyeh Vasar וְהַדְּבָר נִהְיָה בָּשָׂר וְשָׁכַן
v'sha**kh**an banu. בָּנוּ.

And HaDavar became a Body and dwelt among us. *(Yokhanan
1:14)*

On 1 Sukkot, read the first seven Psalms of Ascent; on Simkḥat Torah/The
Eighth Day, read the last eight Psalms of Ascent.

On Shabbat Sukkot [the ordinary sabbath that occurs during Sukkot], read
Yekhezkel 37-39.

# ENTERING THE SUKKA

Baru**kh** Atah יהוה , בָּרוּךְ אַתָּה יהוה , אֱלֹהֵינוּ,
Elo**he**inu, Mele**kh** מֶלֶךְ הָעוֹלָם, אֲשֶׁר קִדְּשָׁנוּ
HaOlam, asher kid'shanu בְּמִצְוֹתָיו, וְצִוָּנוּ לָשֶׁבֶת
b'mitzvo**tav** v'tzivanu בַּסֻּכּוֹת.
la**she**vet basu**kkot**.

Blessed are You, O יהוה our Elohim, King of the Universe, who
has consecrated us by His Mitzvot and commanded us to sit in
booths.

*on the first night only add:*

Barukḥ Atah יהוה , Eloheinu, Melekḥ HaOlam, sh'hekḥeyanu v'kimanu v'higi'anu lazman hazeh. Amein.

בָּרוּךְ אַתָּה יהוה , אֱלֹהֵינוּ, מֶלֶךְ הָעוֹלָם, שֶׁהֶחֱיָנוּ וְקִיְּמָנוּ, וְהִגִּיעָנוּ לַזְמַן הַזֶּה.

Blessed are You, O יהוה our Elohim, King of the Universe, who has kept us in life and has preserved us, and has enabled us to reach this season. Amein.

Blessing for waving the Lulav

Barukḥ Atah יהוה , Eloheinu, Melekḥ HaOlam, asher kid'shanu b'mitzvotav v'tzivanu al netilat lulav.

בָּרוּךְ אַתָּה יהוה , אֱלֹהֵינוּ, מֶלֶךְ הָעוֹלָם, אֲשֶׁר קִדְּשָׁנוּ בְּמִצְוֹתָיו, וְצִוָּנוּ עַל נְתִלַת לוּלָב.

Blessed are You, O יהוה our Elohim, King of the Universe, who has consecrated us by His Mitzvot and commanded us concerning using the Lulav.

# Messiah Born in the Sukka

Yosef also went up from Natzrat, a city of the Galil, to Y'hudah, to the city of David, which is called Beit Lekhem; because he was of the house and family of David, with his betrothed, Miryam, while she was with child, that they might be registered there. And it came to pass while they were there that her days to be delivered were fulfilled. And she gave birth to her first-born son; and she wrapped Him in strips of cloth and laid Him in a **sukka**, because there was no room for them for lodging. Now there were shepherds in that region where they were staying, and they were watching their flocks at night. And behold, a Malakh of Elohim came to them, and the Kavod יהוה shone on them; and they were seized with a great fear. And a Malakh said to them, "Do not be afraid; for behold, I bring you glad tidings of great joy, which will be to the entire world. For this day is born to you in the city of David, a Moshi'ah, who is יהוה HaMashi'akh. And this is a sign for you: you will find the babe wrapped in strips of cloth and lying in a sukka."

וַיַּעַל גַּם יוֹסֵף מִן הַגָּלִיל מֵעִיר נָצְרַת אֶל יְהוּדָה לְעִיר דָּוִד הַנִּקְרֵאת בֵּית לֶחֶם כִּי הָיָה מִבֵּית דָּוִד וּמִמִּשְׁפַּחְתּוֹ עִם מִרְיָם אֲרוּסָתוֹ בִּהְיוֹתָהּ הָרָה, לְהִתְפָּקֵד עִם מִרְיָם הַמְאֹרָשָׂה לוֹ וְהִיא הָרָה. וַיְהִי בִּהְיוֹתָם שָׁם וַיִּמְלְאוּ יָמֶיהָ לָלֶדֶת. וַתֵּלֶד אֶת בְּנָהּ הַבְּכוֹר וַתְּחַתְּלֵהוּ וַתַּשְׁכִּיבֵהוּ בַסֻּכָּה כִּי לֹא הָיָה לָהֶם מָקוֹם לְהִתְאַכְּסֵן. וְרֹעִים הָיוּ בָאָרֶץ הַהִיא לָנִים בַּשָּׂדֶה וְשֹׁמְרִים אֶת מִשְׁמְרוֹת הַלַּיְלָה עַל עֶדְרָם. וְהִנֵּה מַלְאַךְ יהוה נִצָּב עֲלֵיהֶם וּכְבוֹד יהוה הוֹפִיעַ עֲלֵיהֶם מִסָּבִיב וְהֵם פָּחֲדוּ פַּחַד רָב. וַיֹּאמֶר אֲלֵיהֶם הַמַּלְאָךְ אַל תִּפְחֲדוּ כִּי הִנְנִי מְבַשֵּׂר אֶתְכֶם שִׂמְחָה גְדוֹלָה אֲשֶׁר תִּהְיֶה לְכָל הָעוֹלָם. כִּי הַיּוֹם יֻלַּד לָכֶם בְּעִיר דָּוִד מוֹשִׁיעַ אֲשֶׁר הוּא יהוה הַמָּשִׁיחַ. וְזֶה לָכֶם הָאוֹת אֲשֶׁר תִּמְצְאוּן תִּינוֹק מְחֻתָּל וּמֻנָּח בַּסֻּכָּה.

195

And suddenly there appeared with the Malakh a host of heaven, praising Elohim and saying, "Glory to Elohim in the highest, and on earth Shalom, and good hope for the sons of men." And it came to pass when the Malakhim departed from them and went to Heaven, that the shepherds spoke to one another, saying, "Let us go to Beit Lekhem and see this thing that has happened as יהוה has shown to us." And they came hurriedly, and found Miryam and Yosef and the babe at rest in the sukka. When they had seen, they made known the word which was spoken to them concerning the boy. And all who heard it were amazed at the things which were spoken by the shepherds. But Miryam treasured all these things and pondered them in her heart. And the shepherds returned, glorifying and praising Elohim for all that they had seen and heard, as it was spoken to them. And when eight days were fulfilled to circumcise the child, His Name was called Yeshua; for He was named by the Malakh before he was conceived in the womb.

וּפִתְאֹם הָיָה אֵצֶל הַמַּלְאָךְ הֲמוֹנֵי צְבָאוֹת הַשָּׁמַיִם וְהֵם מְשַׁבְּחִים אֶת הָאֱלֹהִים וְאֹמְרִים, כָּבוֹד לֵאלֹהִים בַּמְּרוֹמִים, וְעַל הָאָרֶץ שָׁלוֹם וְתִקְוָה טוֹבָה לִבְנֵי אָדָם. וַיְהִי כַּאֲשֶׁר עָלוּ מֵעֲלֵיהֶם הַמַּלְאָכִים הַשָּׁמַיְמָה וַיֹּאמְרוּ הָרֹעִים אִישׁ אֶל רֵעֵהוּ נֵלֵךְ עַד בֵּית לֶחֶם וְנִרְאֶה אֶת הַדָּבָר הַזֶּה אֲשֶׁר קָרָה, כְּפִי שֶׁיהוה הוֹדִיעַ לָנוּ. וַיְמַהֲרוּ וַיָּבֹאוּ וַיִּמְצְאוּ אֶת מִרְיָם וְאֶת יוֹסֵף וְאֶת הַתִּינוֹק הַמֻּנָּח בַּסֻּכָּה. וַיִּרְאוּ וַיַּשְׁמִיעוּ אֶת הַדָּבָר הַנֶּאֱמָר אֲלֵיהֶם עַל הַיֶּלֶד הַזֶּה. וְכָל הַשֹּׁמְעִים הִתְפַּלְאוּ עַל הַדְּבָרִים שֶׁסִּפְּרוּ אֲלֵיהֶם הָרֹעִים. וּמִרְיָם שָׁמְרָה אֶת הַדְּבָרִים הָאֵלֶּה וְשָׁקְלָה אוֹתָן בְּלִבָּהּ. וַיָּשׁוּבוּ הָרֹעִים וְהֵם מְהַלְּלִים וּמְשַׁבְּחִים אֶת הָאֱלֹהִים עַל כֹּל אֲשֶׁר שָׁמְעוּ וְרָאוּ כְּפִי שֶׁדֻּבַּר אֲלֵיהֶם. וַיְהִי בִּמְלֹאת הַיֶּלֶד שְׁמֹנָה יָמִים וַיִּמּוֹל וַיִּקָּרֵא שְׁמוֹ יֵשׁוּעַ כַּשֵּׁם אֲשֶׁר קָרָא לוֹ הַמַּלְאָךְ בְּטֶרֶם הֹרָה בַּבֶּטֶן.

*(Luka 2:4 - 21)*

Akḥarei khen ashuv v'akim et sukkat David hanofelet v'evneh et asher nafal mimenah va'akimeinah.

אַחֲרֵי כֵן אָשׁוּב וְאָקִים אֶת סֻכַּת דָּוִד הַנּוֹפֶלֶת, וְאֶבְנֶה אֶת אֲשֶׁר נָפַל מִמֶּנָּה וַאֲקִימֶנָּה,

L'ma'an yidreshu sh'erit b'nei ha'adam et יהוה v'khol hagoyim asher nikra shmi aleihem, ne'um יהוה , asher asah khol eleh.

לְמַעַן יִדְרְשׁוּ שְׁאֵרִית בְּנֵי הָאָדָם אֶת יהוה , וְכָל הַגּוֹיִים אֲשֶׁר נִקְרָא שְׁמִי עֲלֵיהֶם; נְאֻם יהוה אֲשֶׁר עָשָׂה כָּל אֵלֶּה.

Noda'im l'Elohim m'olam kol ma'asav.

נוֹדָעִים לֵאלֹהִים מֵעוֹלָם כָּל מַעֲשָׂיו.

'After this I will return, and I will set up again the Sukka of David which has fallen down; and I will repair what has fallen from it, and I will set it up, so that a remnant of the sons of Man may seek after יהוה , and also all the Goyim upon whom My Name is called; so said יהוה , who does all these things.' The works of Elohim are known from the very beginning. *(Ma'Asei HaShlikhim 15:16-18)*

# FAREWELL TO THE SUKKA

Vaya'asu khol hakahal hashavim min hashvi sukkot, vayeshvu basukkot; ki lo asu mimei Yeshua Bin Nun ken B'nei Yisra'el, ad hayom hahu; vat'hi simkḥa g'dolah me'od.

וַיַּעֲשׂוּ כָל הַקָּהָל הַשָּׁבִים מִן הַשְּׁבִי סֻכּוֹת וַיֵּשְׁבוּ בַסֻּכּוֹת כִּי לֹא עָשׂוּ מִימֵי יֵשׁוּעַ בֶּן נוּן כֵּן בְּנֵי יִשְׂרָאֵל עַד הַיּוֹם הַהוּא; וַתְּהִי שִׂמְחָה, גְּדוֹלָה מְאֹד.

197

VaYikra b'sefer torat haElo**him**, yom b'**yom**; min ha**yom** hari**shon**, ad ha**yom** ha'ak̄**aron**; vaya'**asu** k̄ag shi**vat** ya**mim**, uva**yom** hashmi**ni** a**tze**ret kamish**pat**.

תּוֹרַת בְּסֵפֶר וַיִּקְרָא הָאֱלֹהִים יוֹם בְּיוֹם מִן הַיּוֹם הָרִאשׁוֹן, עַד הַיּוֹם הָאַחֲרוֹן; וַיַּעֲשׂוּ חָג שִׁבְעַת יָמִים וּבַיּוֹם הַשְּׁמִינִי עֲצֶרֶת כַּמִּשְׁפָּט.

And all the congregation of them that were come back out of the captivity made sukkot, and dwelt in the sukkot; for since the days of Yeshua Bin Nun unto that day had not B'nei Yisra'el done so. And there was very great gladness.

Also day by day, from the first day unto the last day, he read in the book of the Torah of Elohim. And they kept the Khag seven days; and on the eighth day [Sh'mini] Atzeret, according unto the ordinance. *(Nekhem-Yah 8:17-18)*

# KHANUKAH

Ha'am haholkḥim bakḥoshekḥ ra'u or gadol: Yoshvei b'eretz tzalmavet, or naga aleihem.

הָעָם הַהֹלְכִים בַּחֹשֶׁךְ רָאוּ אוֹר גָּדוֹל: יֹשְׁבֵי בְּאֶרֶץ צַלְמָוֶת אוֹר נָגַה עֲלֵיהֶם.

Hirbita hagoy, lo higdalta hasimkḥa; sam'khu l'faneikḥa k'simkḥat bakatzir, ka'asher yagilu b'kḥalkam shalal.

הִרְבִּיתָ הַגּוֹי לוֹ הִגְדַּלְתָּ הַשִּׂמְחָה; שָׂמְחוּ לְפָנֶיךָ כְּשִׂמְחַת בַּקָּצִיר כַּאֲשֶׁר יָגִילוּ בְּחַלְּקָם שָׁלָל.

Ki et ol subolo, v'et mateh shikḥmo, shevet, hanoges bo; hakḥitota k'yom Midyan.

כִּי אֶת עֹל סֻבֳּלוֹ וְאֶת מַטֵּה שִׁכְמוֹ שֵׁבֶט הַנֹּגֵשׂ בּוֹ; הַחִתֹּתָ, כְּיוֹם מִדְיָן.

"The people that walked in darkness have seen a great light; they that dwelt in the land of Tzal-Mavet, upon them has the light shined. You have multiplied the nation, You have increased their joy; they joy before You according to the joy in harvest, as men rejoice when they divide the spoil. For the yoke of his burden, and the staff of his shoulder, the rod of his oppressor, You have broken as in the day of Midyan. *(Yesha-Yahu 9:1-3)*

יהוה ori v'yishi, mimi irah? יהוה ma'oz khaiyai, mimi efkḥad?

יהוה אוֹרִי וְיִשְׁעִי מִמִּי אִירָא; יהוה מָעוֹז חַיַּי מִמִּי אֶפְחָד.

יהוה is my light and my Salvation; whom shall I fear? יהוה is the stronghold of my life; of whom shall I be afraid? *(Tehillah 27:1)*

Or zaru'**ah** latzadik; אוֹר זָרֻעַ לַצַּדִּיק; וּלְיִשְׁרֵי לֵב
ul'yish**rei** lev sim**kha**! שִׂמְחָה.

Sim**khu**, tzadi**kim**, ba יהוה ; שִׂמְחוּ צַדִּיקִים בַּיהוה ;
; v'ho**du** l'**zekh**er kod'**sho**. וְהוֹדוּ, לְזֵכֶר קָדְשׁוֹ.

Light is sown for HaTzadik, and gladness for the upright in
heart. Be glad in יהוה , you Tzadikim; and give thanks to His
consecrated Name. *(Tehillah 97:11-12)*

**Ani** or ha'o**lam**, kol אֲנִי אוֹר הָעוֹלָם כָּל הַהֹלֵךְ
haho**lekh** ak**harai** lo אַחֲרַי לֹא יִתְהַלֵּךְ בַּחֲשֵׁכָה
yitha**lekh** bakhashe**kha**, ki כִּי אוֹר הַחַיִּים יִהְיֶה לוֹ.
or' hak**hay**im yih**yeh** lo.

"I am the light of the world; he who follows me shall not walk in
darkness, but He shall find for himself the light of life."
*(Yokhanan 8:12)*

Baru**kh** Atah, יהוה , בָּרוּךְ אַתָּה יהוה , אֱלֹהֵינוּ,
Elo**heinu**, Mele**kh** מֶלֶךְ הָעוֹלָם, אֲשֶׁר בָּחַר בָּנוּ
HaOlam, asher ba**khar** מִכָּל הָעַמִּים וְנָתַן לָנוּ אֶת
banu mi**kol** ha'a**mim**, חַגִּים, חֻקּוֹת, וּמוֹעֲדִים
v'**nat**an **lanu** et **kha**gim, לְשִׂמְחָה, לִכְבוֹד יֵשׁוּעַ
**khu**kot, umo'a**dim**, הַמָּשִׁיחַ אֲדוֹנֵינוּ, אוֹר
l'sim**kha** lik**hvod** Yeshua הָעוֹלָם.
HaMashi'a**kh** Ado**neinu**, or
HaO**lam**.

Blessed are You, O יהוה our Elohim, King of the Universe, who
has chosen us from among the peoples, and given us feasts,
statutes, and appointed times, for joy, for the glory of Our
Master, Messiah Yeshua, the Light of the World.

on the first night only add:

Barukh Atah, יהוה , אֱלֹהֵינוּ ,
Eloheinu, Melekh
HaOlam, asher
sh'hekheyanu v'kimanu
v'higi'anu lazman hazeh.
Amein.

בָּרוּךְ אַתָּה יהוה , אֱלֹהֵינוּ,
מֶלֶךְ הָעוֹלָם, שֶׁהֶחֱיָנוּ,
וְקִימָנוּ, וְהִגִיעָנוּ לַזְמָן הַזֶה.

Blessed are You, O יהוה Eloheinu, King of the Universe, who has kept us in life and has preserved us, and has enabled us to reach this season. Amein.

## Ma'oz Tzur
### Rock of Salvation

Ma'oz Tzur Yeshu'ati, lekha na'eh leshabe'akh. Tikon beit tefilati, v'sham toda nezabe'akh. Le'et takhin matbe'akh mitzar hamnabe'akh. Az egmor b'shir mizmor khanukat hamizbe'akh.

מָעוֹז צוּר יְשׁוּעָתִי, לְךָ נָאֶה
לְשַׁבֵּחַ. תִּכּוֹן בֵּית תְּפִלָתִי,
וְשָׁם תּוֹדָה נְזַבֵּחַ. לְעֵת תָּכִין
מַטְבֵּחַ מִצָּר הַמְנַבֵּחַ. אָז
אֶגְמוֹר בְּשִׁיר מִזְמוֹר חֲנֻכַּת
הַמִזְבֵּחַ.

Ra'ot sav'ah nafshi, b'yagon kokhi kala. Khayai mer'ru v'koshi, beshi'bud malkhut egla. Uv'yado hag'dola hotzi et has'gula. Kha'il par'o v'khol zar'o yardu k'even bimtzula.

רָעוֹת שָׂבְעָה נַפְשִׁי, בְּיָגוֹן
כֹּחִי כָּלָה חַיֵּי מֵרְרוּ בְקֹשִׁי,
בְּשִׁעְבּוּד מַלְכוּת עֶגְלָה
וּבְיָדוֹ הַגְדוֹלָה הוֹצִיא אֶת
הַסְגֻלָה חֵיל פַּרְעֹה וְכָל
זַרְעוֹ יָרְדוּ כְּאֶבֶן בִּמְצוּלָה .

202

D'vir kodsho hevi'ani, vegam sham lo shakateti. Uva noges vehiglani, ki zarim avad'ti. V'yein ra'al masakhti, kim'at she'avarti. Ketz Bavel Zerubavel, leketz shiv'im nosha'ati.

דְּבִיר קָדְשׁוֹ הֱבִיאַנִי, וְגַם שָׁם לֹא שָׁקַטְתִּי וּבָא נוֹגֵשׂ וְהִגְלַנִי, כִּי זָרִים עָבַדְתִּי וְיֵין רַעַל מָסַכְתִּי, כִּמְעַט שֶׁעָבַרְתִּי קֵץ בָּבֶל זְרֻבָּבֶל, לְקֵץ שִׁבְעִים נוֹשַׁעְתִּי.

K'rot komat b'rosh bikesh, Agagi ben Hamedatah. v'nihyata lo lefakh ul'mokesh, v'ga'avato nishbata. Rosh yemini niseta, v'oyev sh'mo makhita. Rov banav v'kinyanav al ha'etz talita.

כְּרוֹת קוֹמַת בְּרוֹשׁ בִּקֵּשׁ, אֲגָגִי בֶּן הַמְּדָתָא וְנִהְיָתָה לוֹ לְפַח וּלְמוֹקֵשׁ, וְגַאֲוָתוֹ נִשְׁבָּתָה רֹאשׁ יְמִינִי נִשֵּׂאתָ, וְאוֹיֵב שְׁמוֹ מָחִיתָ רֹב בָּנָיו וְקִנְיָנָיו עַל הָעֵץ תָּלִיתָ.

Y'vanim nikbetzu alai, azai bimei Khashmanim. Ufartzu khomot migdalai, v'tim'u kol hash'manim. Uminotar kankanim na'asa nes lashoshanim. B'nei vina yemei sh'mona kav'u shir urenanim.

יְוָנִים נִקְבְּצוּ עָלַי, אֲזַי בִּימֵי חַשְׁמַנִּים. וּפָרְצוּ חוֹמוֹת מִגְדָּלַי, וְטִמְּאוּ כָּל הַשְּׁמָנִים וּמִנּוֹתַר קַנְקַנִּים נַעֲשָׂה נֵס לַשּׁוֹשַׁנִּים. בְּנֵי בִינָה יְמֵי שְׁמוֹנָה קָבְעוּ שִׁיר וּרְנָנִים

Hasof z'roa kodshekha, v'karev ketz hayeshu'ah. N'kom nikmat avadeikha me'uma haresha'a. Ki arkha hasha'a, ve'ein ketz limei hara'a. D'kheh admon b'tzel tzalmon, hakem lanu ro'im shiv'a.

חֲשׂוֹף זְרוֹעַ קָדְשֶׁךָ וְקָרֵב קֵץ הַיְשׁוּעָה נְקֹם נִקְמַת עֲבָדֶיךָ מֵאֻמָּה הָרְשָׁעָה כִּי אָרְכָה הַשָּׁעָה וְאֵין קֵץ לִימֵי הָרָעָה דְּחֵה אַדְמוֹן בְּצֵל צַלְמוֹן הָקֵם לָנוּ רוֹעִים שִׁבְעָה

Refuge, Rock of my salvation! 'Tis pleasant to sing your praises. Let our house of prayer be restored, and there we will offer You our thanks. When You will have utterly silenced the

loudmouthed foe, then we will celebrate, with song and psalm, the dedication of the altar.

My soul was sated with misery, my strength was spent with grief. They embittered my life with hardship, when enslaved under the rule of Mitzrayim. But Elohim with his mighty power brought out His treasured people, while Paroh's host and followers sank like a stone into the deep.

He brought me to His holy abode; even there, I found no rest. The oppressor came and exiled me, because I served strange gods, and drank poisonous wine. Yet scarcely had I gone into exile, when Bavel fell and Zerubavel took charge; within seventy years I was saved.

The Agagite, son of Hammedatha, plotted to cut down the lofty fir tree; but it proved a snare to him, and his insolence was silenced. You raised the head of the Benjamite, but the enemy's name You blotted out. His numerous sons and his household You hanged upon the gallows.

The Greeks gathered against me, in Hasmonian days . They broke down the walls of my towers, and defiled all the oils. But from the last remaining flask a miracle was wrought for the Lilies [Jews, or the flowers under each bowl on the Menorah, which were lilies]. Therefore the sages of the day ordained these eight nights for songs of praise.

O bare Your holy arm, and hasten the time of salvation. Wreak vengeance upon the wicked nation, on behalf of your faithful servants. For deliverance has too long been delayed; and the evil days are endless. O thrust the enemy into the shadows of death, and set up for us the seven Shepherds.

# Tehillim תְּהִלִּים

*The Tehillim, or Psalms, were written as prayers and as songs of praise. The Tehillim were an integral part of Temple worship, and synagogue worship. Worshipping Elohim is "service" to Him. One of the ways in which we serve Him is through prayer. There are prescribed prayers for the prescribed parashot. During the moedim (feast seasons) including one for each Shabbat, there are certain tehillim that are offered in prayer. As such, we have provided all of the tehillim for use in our service to Elohim.*

## Tehillah 1 תְּהִלָּה

¹Happy is the man that has not walked in the counsel of the wicked, nor stood in the way of sinners, nor sat in the seat of the scornful.

אַשְׁרֵי הָאִישׁ אֲשֶׁר לֹא הָלַךְ בַּעֲצַת רְשָׁעִים; וּבְדֶרֶךְ חַטָּאִים לֹא עָמָד וּבְמוֹשַׁב לֵצִים לֹא יָשָׁב.

²But his delight is in the Torah of יהוה ; and in His Torah does he meditate day and night.

כִּי אִם בְּתוֹרַת יהוה חֶפְצוֹ; וּבְתוֹרָתוֹ יֶהְגֶּה יוֹמָם וָלָיְלָה.

³And he shall be like a tree planted by streams of water, that brings forth its fruit in its season, and whose leaf does not wither; and in whatever he does he shall prosper.

וְהָיָה כְּעֵץ שָׁתוּל עַל פַּלְגֵי מָיִם: אֲשֶׁר פִּרְיוֹ יִתֵּן בְּעִתּוֹ וְעָלֵהוּ לֹא יִבּוֹל; וְכֹל אֲשֶׁר יַעֲשֶׂה יַצְלִיחַ.

⁴Not so the wicked; but they are like the chaff which the wind drives away.

לֹא כֵן הָרְשָׁעִים: כִּי אִם כַּמֹּץ אֲשֶׁר תִּדְּפֶנּוּ רוּחַ.

⁵Therefore the wicked shall not stand in the judgment, nor sinners in the assembly of the Tzadikim.

הֵעַל כֵּן לֹא יָקֻמוּ רְשָׁעִים בַּמִּשְׁפָּט; וְחַטָּאִים בַּעֲדַת צַדִּיקִים.

⁶For יהוה knows the way of the Tzadikim; but the way of the wicked shall perish.

וכִּי יוֹדֵעַ יהוה דֶּרֶךְ צַדִּיקִים; וְדֶרֶךְ רְשָׁעִים תֹּאבֵד.

# תְּהִלָּה Tehillah 2

¹Why do the nations rage? And the peoples plot in vain?

אלָמָה רָגְשׁוּ גוֹיִם; וּלְאֻמִּים יֶהְגּוּ רִיק.

²The kings of the earth revolt, and the rulers take counsel together, against יהוה , and against His Mashi'akh!

ביִתְיַצְּבוּ מַלְכֵי אֶרֶץ וְרוֹזְנִים נוֹסְדוּ יָחַד: עַל יהוה וְעַל מְשִׁיחוֹ.

³"Let us break their bands asunder, and cast away their cords from us."

גנְנַתְּקָה אֶת מוֹסְרוֹתֵימוֹ; וְנַשְׁלִיכָה מִמֶּנּוּ עֲבֹתֵימוֹ.

⁴He that sits in heaven will laugh, Adonai has them in derision.

דיוֹשֵׁב בַּשָּׁמַיִם יִשְׂחָק: אֲדֹנָי יִלְעַג לָמוֹ.

⁵Then will He speak unto them in His wrath, and frighten them in His sore displeasure:

האָז יְדַבֵּר אֵלֵימוֹ בְאַפּוֹ; וּבַחֲרוֹנוֹ יְבַהֲלֵמוֹ.

⁶"Truly it is I that have established My Melekh upon Tzion, My Har Kodesh.

ווַאֲנִי נָסַכְתִּי מַלְכִּי: עַל צִיּוֹן הַר קָדְשִׁי.

<sup>7</sup>I will tell of the decree: יהוה said unto me, "You are My son, this day have I begotten you.

אֲסַפְּרָה אֶל חֹק: יהוה אָמַר אֵלַי בְּנִי אַתָּה אֲנִי הַיּוֹם יְלִדְתִּיךָ.

<sup>8</sup>Ask of Me, and I will give the nations for your inheritance, and the ends of the earth for your possession.

שְׁאַל מִמֶּנִּי וְאֶתְּנָה גוֹיִם נַחֲלָתֶךָ; וַאֲחֻזָּתְךָ אַפְסֵי אָרֶץ.

<sup>9</sup>You shall break them with a rod of iron; you shall dash them in pieces like a potter's vessel."

תְּרֹעֵם בְּשֵׁבֶט בַּרְזֶל: כִּכְלִי יוֹצֵר תְּנַפְּצֵם.

<sup>10</sup>Now therefore, O you kings, be wise; be admonished, you judges of the earth.

וְעַתָּה מְלָכִים הַשְׂכִּילוּ; הִוָּסְרוּ שֹׁפְטֵי אָרֶץ.

<sup>11</sup>Serve יהוה with fear, and rejoice with trembling.

עִבְדוּ אֶת יהוה בְּיִרְאָה; וְגִילוּ בִּרְעָדָה.

<sup>12</sup>Kiss the Son, lest He be angry, and you perish in the way, when suddenly His wrath is kindled. Happy are all they that take refuge in Him.

נַשְּׁקוּ בַר פֶּן יֶאֱנַף וְתֹאבְדוּ דֶרֶךְ כִּי יִבְעַר כִּמְעַט אַפּוֹ: אַשְׁרֵי כָּל חוֹסֵי בוֹ.

# תְּהִלָּה 3 Tehillah

<sup>1</sup>A Mizmor of David, when he fled from Avshalom his son.

מִזְמוֹר לְדָוִד: בְּבָרְחוֹ מִפְּנֵי אַבְשָׁלוֹם בְּנוֹ.

208

[2] יהוה , how many are my adversaries become! Many are they that rise up against me.

ב יהוה מָה רַבּוּ צָרָי; רַבִּים קָמִים עָלָי.

[3]Many there are that say of my soul, "There is no Salvation for him in Elohim." Selah.

ג רַבִּים אֹמְרִים לְנַפְשִׁי: אֵין יְשׁוּעָתָה לּוֹ בֵאלֹהִים סֶלָה.

[4]But you, O יהוה , are a shield about me; my glory, and the lifter up of my head.

ד וְאַתָּה יהוה מָגֵן בַּעֲדִי; כְּבוֹדִי וּמֵרִים רֹאשִׁי.

[5]With my voice I call unto יהוה , and He answers me out of Har Kodsho. Selah.

ה קוֹלִי אֶל יהוה אֶקְרָא; וַיַּעֲנֵנִי מֵהַר קָדְשׁוֹ סֶלָה.

[6]I lay me down, and I sleep; I awake, for יהוה sustains me.

ו אֲנִי שָׁכַבְתִּי וָאִישָׁנָה; הֱקִיצוֹתִי כִּי יהוה יִסְמְכֵנִי.

[7]I am not afraid of ten thousands of people, that have set themselves against me round about.

ז לֹא אִירָא מֵרִבְבוֹת עָם אֲשֶׁר סָבִיב שָׁתוּ עָלָי.

[8]Arise, O יהוה ; save me, O my Elohim; for You have smitten all my enemies upon the cheek, You have broken the teeth of the wicked.

ח קוּמָה יהוה הוֹשִׁיעֵנִי אֱלֹהַי כִּי הִכִּיתָ אֶת כָּל אֹיְבַי לֶחִי; שִׁנֵּי רְשָׁעִים שִׁבַּרְתָּ.

[9]Salvation belongs unto יהוה . May Your blessing be upon Your people. Selah.

ט לַיהוה הַיְשׁוּעָה; עַל עַמְּךָ בִרְכָתֶךָ סֶלָה.

# Tehillah 4 תְּהִלָּה

<sup>1</sup>For the Leader; with string-music. A Mizmor of David.

אלַמְנַצֵּחַ בִּנְגִינוֹת מִזְמוֹר לְדָוִד.

<sup>2</sup>Answer me when I call, O Elohim of my righteousness, You who did set me free when I was in distress; be gracious unto me, and hear my prayer.

בְּקָרְאִי עֲנֵנִי אֱלֹהֵי צִדְקִי בַּצָּר הִרְחַבְתָּ לִּי; חָנֵּנִי וּשְׁמַע תְּפִלָּתִי.

<sup>3</sup>O you sons of men, how long shall my glory be put to shame, in that you love vanity, and seek after falsehood? Selah.

גבְּנֵי אִישׁ עַד מֶה כְבוֹדִי לִכְלִמָּה תֶּאֱהָבוּן רִיק; תְּבַקְשׁוּ כָזָב סֶלָה.

<sup>4</sup>But know that יהוה has consecrated the Khasid as His own; יהוה will hear when I call unto Him.

דוּדְעוּ כִּי הִפְלָה יהוה חָסִיד לוֹ; יהוה יִשְׁמַע בְּקָרְאִי אֵלָיו.

<sup>5</sup>Tremble, and sin not; commune with your own heart upon your bed, and be still. Selah.

הרִגְזוּ וְאַל תֶּחֱטָאוּ: אִמְרוּ בִלְבַבְכֶם עַל מִשְׁכַּבְכֶם; וְדֹמּוּ סֶלָה.

<sup>6</sup>Offer righteous sacrifices, and put your trust in יהוה .

וזִבְחוּ זִבְחֵי צֶדֶק; וּבִטְחוּ אֶל יהוה .

<sup>7</sup>Many there are that say, "Oh that we could see some good!" יהוה , lift up the light of Your countenance upon us.

זרַבִּים אֹמְרִים מִי יַרְאֵנוּ טוֹב: נְסָה עָלֵינוּ אוֹר פָּנֶיךָ יהוה .

<sup>8</sup>You have put gladness in my heart, more than when their grain and their wine increase.

נָתַתָּה שִׂמְחָה בְלִבִּי; מֵעֵת דְּגָנָם וְתִירוֹשָׁם רָבּוּ.

<sup>9</sup>In perfect shalom will I lay me down and sleep; for You alone, יהוה , make me dwell in safety.

בְּשָׁלוֹם יַחְדָּו אֶשְׁכְּבָה וְאִישָׁן: כִּי אַתָּה יהוה לְבָדָד; לָבֶטַח תּוֹשִׁיבֵנִי.

# תְּהִלָּה 5 Tehillah

<sup>1</sup>For the Leader; upon the Nekhilot. A Mizmor of David.

לַמְנַצֵּחַ אֶל הַנְּחִילוֹת מִזְמוֹר לְדָוִד.

<sup>2</sup>Give ear to my words, O יהוה , consider my meditation.

אֲמָרַי הַאֲזִינָה יהוה ; בִּינָה הֲגִיגִי.

<sup>3</sup>Hearken unto the voice of my cry, my Melekh, and my Elohim; for unto You do I pray.

הַקְשִׁיבָה לְקוֹל שַׁוְעִי מַלְכִּי וֵאלֹהָי: כִּי אֵלֶיךָ אֶתְפַּלָּל.

<sup>4</sup>O יהוה , in the morning shall You hear my voice; in the morning will I order my prayer unto You, and will look forward.

יהוה בֹּקֶר תִּשְׁמַע קוֹלִי; בֹּקֶר אֶעֱרָךְ לְךָ וַאֲצַפֶּה.

<sup>5</sup>For You are not a God that has pleasure in wickedness; evil shall not sojourn with You.

כִּי לֹא אֵל חָפֵץ רֶשַׁע אָתָּה: לֹא יְגֻרְךָ רָע.

<sup>6</sup>The boasters shall not stand in Your sight; You hate all workers of iniquity.

לֹא יִתְיַצְּבוּ הוֹלְלִים לְנֶגֶד עֵינֶיךָ; שָׂנֵאתָ כָּל פֹּעֲלֵי אָוֶן.

⁷You destroy them that speak falsehood; יהוה abhors the man of blood and of deceit.

תְּאַבֵּד דֹּבְרֵי כָזָב: אִישׁ דָּמִים וּמִרְמָה יְתָעֵב יהוה.

⁸But as for me, in the abundance of Your compassion will I come into Your house; I will bow down toward Your Heikhal Kadosh in the fear of You.

וַאֲנִי בְּרֹב חַסְדְּךָ אָבוֹא בֵיתֶךָ; אֶשְׁתַּחֲוֶה אֶל הֵיכַל קָדְשְׁךָ בְּיִרְאָתֶךָ.

⁹O יהוה , lead me in Your tzedaka because of them that lie in wait for me; make Your way straight before my face.

יהוה נְחֵנִי בְצִדְקָתֶךָ לְמַעַן שׁוֹרְרָי; הוֹשַׁר (הַיְשַׁר) לְפָנַי דַּרְכֶּךָ.

¹⁰For there is no sincerity in their mouth; their inward part is a yawning gulf, their throat is an open grave; they make smooth their tongue.

כִּי אֵין בְּפִיהוּ נְכוֹנָה קִרְבָּם הַוּוֹת: קֶבֶר פָּתוּחַ גְּרֹנָם; לְשׁוֹנָם יַחֲלִיקוּן.

¹¹Hold them guilty, O Elohim, let them fall by their own counsels; cast them down in the multitude of their transgressions; for they have rebelled against You.

הַאֲשִׁימֵם אֱלֹהִים יִפְּלוּ מִמֹּעֲצוֹתֵיהֶם: בְּרֹב פִּשְׁעֵיהֶם הַדִּיחֵמוֹ כִּי מָרוּ בָךְ.

¹²So shall all those that take refuge in You rejoice, they shall ever shout for joy, and You shall shelter them; let them also that love Your Name exult in You.

וְיִשְׂמְחוּ כָל חוֹסֵי בָךְ לְעוֹלָם יְרַנֵּנוּ וְתָסֵךְ עָלֵימוֹ; וְיַעְלְצוּ בְךָ אֹהֲבֵי שְׁמֶךָ.

¹³For You do bless a Tzadik; O יהוה, You do crown him with good will as with a shield.

כִּי־אַתָּה תְּבָרֵךְ צַדִּיק: יהוה כַּצִּנָּה רָצוֹן תַּעְטְרֶנּוּ.

# תְּהִלָּה Tehillah 6

¹For the Leader; with string-music; on the Sh'minit. A Mizmor of David.

לַמְנַצֵּחַ בִּנְגִינוֹת עַל הַשְּׁמִינִית; מִזְמוֹר לְדָוִד.

²O יהוה, rebuke me not in Your anger, neither chasten me in Your wrath.

יהוה אַל־בְּאַפְּךָ תוֹכִיחֵנִי; וְאַל־בַּחֲמָתְךָ תְיַסְּרֵנִי.

³Be gracious unto me, O יהוה, for I languish away; heal me, O יהוה, for my bones are terrified.

חָנֵּנִי יהוה כִּי אֻמְלַל אָנִי: רְפָאֵנִי יהוה כִּי נִבְהֲלוּ עֲצָמָי.

⁴My soul also is very terrified; and You, O יהוה, how long?

וְנַפְשִׁי נִבְהֲלָה מְאֹד; וְאַתְּ (וְאַתָּה) יהוה עַד־מָתָי.

⁵Return, O יהוה, deliver my soul; save me for Your compassion's sake.

שׁוּבָה יהוה חַלְּצָה נַפְשִׁי; הוֹשִׁיעֵנִי לְמַעַן חַסְדֶּךָ.

⁶For in Mavet there is no remembrance of You; in She'ol who will give You thanks?

כִּי אֵין בַּמָּוֶת זִכְרֶךָ; בִּשְׁאוֹל מִי יוֹדֶה־לָּךְ.

<sup>7</sup>I am weary with my groaning; every night I make my bed to swim; I melt away my couch with my tears.

יָגַעְתִּי בְּאַנְחָתִי אַשְׂחֶה בְכָל לַיְלָה מִטָּתִי; בְּדִמְעָתִי עַרְשִׂי אַמְסֶה.

<sup>8</sup>My eye is dimmed because of vexation; it waxes old because of all my adversaries.

עָשְׁשָׁה מִכַּעַס עֵינִי; עָתְקָה בְּכָל צוֹרְרָי.

<sup>9</sup>Depart from me, all you workers of iniquity, for יהוה has heard the voice of my weeping.

סוּרוּ מִמֶּנִּי כָּל פֹּעֲלֵי אָוֶן: כִּי שָׁמַע יהוה קוֹל בִּכְיִי.

<sup>10</sup> יהוה has heard my supplication; יהוה receives my prayer.

שָׁמַע יהוה תְּחִנָּתִי; יהוה תְּפִלָּתִי יִקָּח.

<sup>11</sup>All my enemies shall be ashamed and very terrified; they shall turn back, they shall be ashamed suddenly.

יֵבֹשׁוּ וְיִבָּהֲלוּ מְאֹד כָּל אֹיְבָי; יָשֻׁבוּ יֵבֹשׁוּ רָגַע.

# Tehillah 7 תְּהִלָּה

<sup>1</sup>Shigayon of David, which he sang unto יהוה , concerning Khush, a Ben Yemini.

שִׁגָּיוֹן לְדָוִד: אֲשֶׁר שָׁר לַיהוה עַל דִּבְרֵי כוּשׁ בֶּן יְמִינִי.

<sup>2</sup>O יהוה my Elohim, in You have I taken refuge; save me from all them that pursue me, and deliver me;

יהוה אֱלֹהַי בְּךָ חָסִיתִי; הוֹשִׁיעֵנִי מִכָּל רֹדְפַי וְהַצִּילֵנִי.

³Lest he tears my soul like a lion, rending it in pieces, while there is none to deliver.

גּפֶּן יִטְרֹף כְּאַרְיֵה נַפְשִׁי; פֹּרֵק וְאֵין מַצִּיל.

⁴O יהוה my Elohim, if I have done this, if there is iniquity in my hands,

ד יהוה אֱלֹהַי אִם עָשִׂיתִי זֹּאת; אִם יֶשׁ עָוֶל בְּכַפָּי.

⁵If I have requited him that did evil unto me, or spoiled my adversary unto emptiness,

האִם גָּמַלְתִּי שׁוֹלְמִי רָע; וָאֲחַלְּצָה צוֹרְרִי רֵיקָם.

⁶Let the enemy pursue my soul, and overtake it, and tread my life down to the earth; yes, let him lay my glory in the dust. Selah.

ויִרַדֹּף אוֹיֵב נַפְשִׁי וְיַשֵּׂג וְיִרְמֹס לָאָרֶץ חַיָּי; וּכְבוֹדִי לֶעָפָר יַשְׁכֵּן סֶלָה.

⁷Arise, O יהוה , in Your anger, lift up Yourself in indignation against my adversaries; yes, awake for me at the judgment which You have commanded.

זקוּמָה יהוה בְּאַפֶּךָ הִנָּשֵׂא בְּעַבְרוֹת צוֹרְרָי; וְעוּרָה אֵלַי מִשְׁפָּט צִוִּיתָ.

⁸And let the assembly of the peoples encompass You about, and over them may You return on high.

חוַעֲדַת לְאֻמִּים תְּסוֹבְבֶךָ; וְעָלֶיהָ לַמָּרוֹם שׁוּבָה.

⁹O יהוה , who ministers judgment to the peoples, judge me, O יהוה , according to my tzedaka, and according to my integrity that is in me.

ט יהוה יָדִין עַמִּים: שָׁפְטֵנִי יהוה ; כְּצִדְקִי וּכְתֻמִּי עָלָי.

<sup>10</sup>Oh that a full measure of evil might come upon the wicked, and that You would establish the Tzadik; for Elohim the Tzadik tries the heart and reins.

יִגְמָר נָא רַע רְשָׁעִים וּתְכוֹנֵן צַדִּיק; וּבֹחֵן לִבּוֹת וּכְלָיוֹת אֱלֹהִים צַדִּיק.

<sup>11</sup>My Magen is with Elohim, Moshi'ah of the upright in heart.

אָמָגִנִּי עַל אֱלֹהִים; מוֹשִׁיעַ יִשְׁרֵי לֵב.

<sup>12</sup>Elohim is a righteous judge, yes, a God that has indignation every day:

בֱאֱלֹהִים שׁוֹפֵט צַדִּיק; וְאֵל זֹעֵם בְּכָל יוֹם.

<sup>13</sup>If a man turns not, He will whet His sword, He has bent His bow, and made it ready;

גאִם לֹא יָשׁוּב חַרְבּוֹ יִלְטוֹשׁ; קַשְׁתּוֹ דָרַךְ וַיְכוֹנְנֶהָ.

<sup>14</sup>He has also prepared for him the weapons of death, yes, His arrows which He made sharp.

דוְלוֹ הֵכִין כְּלֵי מָוֶת; חִצָּיו לְדֹלְקִים יִפְעָל.

<sup>15</sup>Behold, he travails with iniquity; yes, he conceives mischief, and brings forth falsehood.

טוהִנֵּה יְחַבֶּל אָוֶן; וְהָרָה עָמָל וְיָלַד שָׁקֶר.

<sup>16</sup>He has digged a pit, and hollowed it, and is fallen into the ditch which he made.

טזבּוֹר כָּרָה וַיַּחְפְּרֵהוּ; וַיִּפֹּל בְּשַׁחַת יִפְעָל.

<sup>17</sup>His mischief shall return upon his own head, and his violence shall come down upon his own pate.

יזיָשׁוּב עֲמָלוֹ בְרֹאשׁוֹ; וְעַל קָדְקֳדוֹ חֲמָסוֹ יֵרֵד.

<sup>18</sup>I will give thanks unto יהוה according to His righteousness; and will sing praise to the Name of יהוה Elyon.

אוֹדֶה יהוה כְּצִדְקוֹ; וַאֲזַמְּרָה שֵׁם יהוה עֶלְיוֹן.

# תְּהִלָּה 8 Tehillah

<sup>1</sup>For the Leader; upon the Gitit. A Mizmor of David.

לַמְנַצֵּחַ עַל הַגִּתִּית מִזְמוֹר לְדָוִד.

<sup>2</sup>O יהוה , our Adonai, how mighty is Your Name in all the earth! Whose majesty is rehearsed above the heavens.

יהוה אֲדֹנֵינוּ מָה אַדִּיר שִׁמְךָ בְּכָל הָאָרֶץ; אֲשֶׁר תְּנָה הוֹדְךָ עַל הַשָּׁמָיִם.

<sup>3</sup>Out of the mouth of babes and sucklings have You founded strength, because of Your adversaries; that You might still the enemy and the avenger.

מִפִּי עוֹלְלִים וְיֹנְקִים יִסַּדְתָּ עֹז: לְמַעַן צוֹרְרֶיךָ; לְהַשְׁבִּית אוֹיֵב וּמִתְנַקֵּם.

<sup>4</sup>When I behold Your heavens, the work of Your fingers, the moon and the stars, which You have established;

כִּי אֶרְאֶה שָׁמֶיךָ מַעֲשֵׂה אֶצְבְּעֹתֶיךָ יָרֵחַ וְכוֹכָבִים אֲשֶׁר כּוֹנָנְתָּה.

<sup>5</sup>What is man, that You are mindful of him? And the son of man, that You think of him?

מָה אֱנוֹשׁ כִּי תִזְכְּרֶנּוּ; וּבֶן אָדָם כִּי תִפְקְדֶנּוּ.

217

⁶Yet You have made him but a little lower than the gods, and have crowned him with glory and splendor.

וַתְּחַסְּרֵהוּ מְּעַט מֵאֱלֹהִים; וְכָבוֹד וְהָדָר תְּעַטְּרֵהוּ.

⁷You have made him to have dominion over the works of Your hands; You have put all things under his feet:

תַּמְשִׁילֵהוּ בְּמַעֲשֵׂי יָדֶיךָ; כֹּל שַׁתָּה תַחַת רַגְלָיו.

⁸Sheep and oxen, all of them, yes, and the beasts of the field;

צֹנֶה וַאֲלָפִים כֻּלָּם; וְגַם בַּהֲמוֹת שָׂדָי.

⁹The fowl of the air, and the fish of the sea; whatever passes through the paths of the seas.

צִפּוֹר שָׁמַיִם וּדְגֵי הַיָּם; עֹבֵר אָרְחוֹת יַמִּים.

¹⁰O יהוה , our Adonai, how mighty is Your Name in all the earth!

יהוה אֲדֹנֵינוּ: מָה אַדִּיר שִׁמְךָ בְּכָל הָאָרֶץ.

# Tehillah 9 תְּהִלָּה

¹For the Leader; upon Mut Laben. A Mizmor of David.

לַמְנַצֵּחַ עַל מוּת לַבֵּן; מִזְמוֹר לְדָוִד.

²I will give thanks unto יהוה with my whole heart; I will tell of all Your marvelous works.

אוֹדֶה יהוה בְּכָל לִבִּי; אֲסַפְּרָה כָּל נִפְלְאוֹתֶיךָ.

³I will be glad and exult in You; I will sing praise to Your Name, O Elyon:

אֶשְׂמְחָה וְאֶעֶלְצָה בָךְ; אֲזַמְּרָה שִׁמְךָ עֶלְיוֹן.

⁴When my enemies are turned back, they stumble and perish at Your presence;

בְּשׁוּב אוֹיְבַי אָחוֹר; יִכָּשְׁלוּ וְיֹאבְדוּ מִפָּנֶיךָ.

⁵For You have maintained my right and my cause; You sat upon the throne as the righteous Judge.

כִּי עָשִׂיתָ מִשְׁפָּטִי וְדִינִי; יָשַׁבְתָּ לְכִסֵּא שׁוֹפֵט צֶדֶק.

⁶You have rebuked the nations, You have destroyed the wicked, You have blotted out their name forever and ever.

גָּעַרְתָּ גוֹיִם אִבַּדְתָּ רָשָׁע; שְׁמָם מָחִיתָ לְעוֹלָם וָעֶד.

⁷O you enemy, the waste places are come to an end forever; and the cities which you did uproot, their very memorial is perished.

הָאוֹיֵב תַּמּוּ חֳרָבוֹת לָנֶצַח; וְעָרִים נָתַשְׁתָּ אָבַד זִכְרָם הֵמָּה.

⁸But יהוה is enthroned forever; He has established His throne for judgment.

וַיהוה לְעוֹלָם יֵשֵׁב; כּוֹנֵן לַמִּשְׁפָּט כִּסְאוֹ.

⁹And He will judge the world in righteousness, He will minister judgment to the peoples with equity.

וְהוּא יִשְׁפֹּט תֵּבֵל בְּצֶדֶק; יָדִין לְאֻמִּים בְּמֵישָׁרִים.

¹⁰ יהוה also will be a high tower for the oppressed, a high tower in times of trouble;

וִיהִי יהוה מִשְׂגָּב לַדָּךְ; מִשְׂגָּב לְעִתּוֹת בַּצָּרָה.

¹¹And they that know Your Name will put their trust in You; for You, יהוה , have not forsaken them that seek You.

וְיִבְטְחוּ בְךָ יוֹדְעֵי שְׁמֶךָ: כִּי לֹא עָזַבְתָּ דֹרְשֶׁיךָ יהוה .

219

¹²Sing praises to יהוה , who dwells in Tzion; declare among the peoples His doings.

יבזַמְּרוּ לַיהוה יֹשֵׁב צִיּוֹן; הַגִּידוּ בָעַמִּים עֲלִילוֹתָיו.

¹³For He that avenges blood has remembered them; He has not forgotten the cry of the humble.

יגכִּי דֹרֵשׁ דָּמִים אוֹתָם זָכָר; לֹא שָׁכַח צַעֲקַת עניים (עֲנָוִים).

¹⁴Be gracious unto me, O יהוה , behold my affliction at the hands of them that hate me; You that lift me up from the gates of Mavet;

ידחָנְנֵנִי יהוה רְאֵה עָנְיִי מִשֹּׂנְאָי; מְרוֹמְמִי מִשַּׁעֲרֵי מָוֶת.

¹⁵That I may tell of all Your praise in the gates of the daughter of Tzion, that I may rejoice in Your Salvation.

טולְמַעַן אֲסַפְּרָה כָּל תְּהִלָּתֶיךָ: בְּשַׁעֲרֵי בַת צִיּוֹן אָגִילָה בִּישׁוּעָתֶךָ.

¹⁶The nations are sunk down in the pit that they made; in the net which they hid is their own foot taken.

טזטָבְעוּ גוֹיִם בְּשַׁחַת עָשׂוּ; בְּרֶשֶׁת זוּ טָמָנוּ נִלְכְּדָה רַגְלָם.

¹⁷ יהוה has made Himself known, He has executed judgment, the wicked is snared in the work of his own hands. Higayon. Selah.

יזנוֹדַע יהוה מִשְׁפָּט עָשָׂה: בְּפֹעַל כַּפָּיו נוֹקֵשׁ רָשָׁע; הִגָּיוֹן סֶלָה.

¹⁸The wicked shall return to She'ol, even all the nations that forget Elohim.

יחיָשׁוּבוּ רְשָׁעִים לִשְׁאוֹלָה: כָּל גּוֹיִם שְׁכֵחֵי אֱלֹהִים.

¹⁹For the needy shall not always be forgotten, nor the expectation of the poor perish forever.

טּכִּי לֹא לָנֶצַח יִשָּׁכַח אֶבְיוֹן; תִּקְוַת עֲנוים (עֲנִיּים) תֹּאבַד לָעַד.

²⁰Arise, O יהוה , let not man prevail; let the nations be judged in Your sight.

כקוּמָה יהוה אַל יָעֹז אֱנוֹשׁ; יִשָּׁפְטוּ גוֹים עַל פָּנֶיךָ.

²¹Set terror over them, O יהוה ; let the nations know they are but men. Selah.

כאשִׁיתָה יהוה מוֹרָה לָהֶם: יֵדְעוּ גוֹים אֱנוֹשׁ הֵמָּה סֶּלָה.

# Tehillah 10 תְּהִלָּה

¹Why do You stand far off, O יהוה ? Why do You hide Yourself in times of trouble?

אלָמָה יהוה תַּעֲמֹד בְּרָחוֹק; תַּעְלִים לְעִתּוֹת בַּצָּרָה.

²Through the pride of the wicked the poor is hotly pursued, they are taken in the devices that they have imagined.

בבְּגַאֲוַת רָשָׁע יִדְלַק עָנִי; יִתָּפְשׂוּ בִּמְזִמּוֹת זוּ חָשָׁבוּ.

³For the wicked boasts of his heart's desire, and the covetous vaunts himself, though he shows יהוה contempt.

גכִּי הִלֵּל רָשָׁע עַל תַּאֲוַת נַפְשׁוֹ; וּבֹצֵעַ בֵּרֵךְ נִאֵץ יהוה .

⁴The wicked, in the pride of his countenance [says], "He will not require"; all his thoughts are, "There is no Elohim."

דרָשָׁע כְּגֹבַהּ אַפּוֹ בַּל יִדְרֹשׁ; אֵין אֱלֹהִים כָּל מְזִמּוֹתָיו.

⁵His ways prosper at all times; Your judgments are far above, out of his sight; as for all his adversaries, he puffs at them.

היָחִילוּ דְרָכָו בְּכָל עֵת מָרוֹם מִשְׁפָּטֶיךָ מִנֶּגְדּוֹ; כָּל צוֹרְרָיו יָפִיחַ בָּהֶם.

⁶He says in his heart, "I shall not be moved; I, who to all generations shall not be in adversity."

יאָמַר בְּלִבּוֹ בַּל אֶמּוֹט; לְדֹר וָדֹר אֲשֶׁר לֹא בְרָע.

⁷His mouth is full of cursing and deceit and oppression; under his tongue is mischief and iniquity.

זאָלָה פִּיהוּ מָלֵא וּמִרְמוֹת וָתֹךְ; תַּחַת לְשׁוֹנוֹ עָמָל וָאָוֶן.

⁸He sits in the lurking-places of the villages; in secret places does he slay the innocent; his eyes are on the watch for the helpless.

חיֵשֵׁב בְּמַאְרַב חֲצֵרִים בַּמִּסְתָּרִים יַהֲרֹג נָקִי; עֵינָיו לְחֵלְכָה יִצְפֹּנוּ.

⁹He lies in wait in a secret place as a lion in his lair, he lies in wait to catch the poor; he does catch the poor, when he draws him up in his net.

טיֶאֱרֹב בַּמִּסְתָּר כְּאַרְיֵה בְסֻכֹּה יֶאֱרֹב לַחֲטוֹף עָנִי; יַחְטֹף עָנִי בְּמָשְׁכוֹ בְרִשְׁתּוֹ.

¹⁰He crouches, he bows down, and the helpless fall into his mighty claws.

יודכה (יִדְכֶּה) יָשֹׁחַ; וְנָפַל בַּעֲצוּמָיו חלכאים (חֵל כָּאִים).

¹¹He has said in his heart, "Elohim has forgotten; He hides His face; He will never see."

יאאָמַר בְּלִבּוֹ שָׁכַח אֵל; הִסְתִּיר פָּנָיו בַּל רָאָה לָנֶצַח.

<sup>12</sup>Arise, O יהוה ; O God, lift up Your hand; forget not the humble.

יבקוּמָה יהוה אֵל נְשָׂא יָדֶךָ; אַל תִּשְׁכַּח עניים (עֲנָוִים).

<sup>13</sup>Why does the wicked show contempt for Elohim, and say in his heart, "You will not require"?

יגעַל מֶה נִאֵץ רָשָׁע אֱלֹהִים; אָמַר בְּלִבּוֹ לֹא תִדְרֹשׁ.

<sup>14</sup>You have seen; for You behold trouble and vexation, to requite them with Your hand; unto You the helpless commits himself; You have been the helper of the fatherless.

ידרָאִתָה כִּי אַתָּה עָמָל וָכַעַס תַּבִּיט לָתֵת בְּיָדֶךָ: עָלֶיךָ יַעֲזֹב חֵלֵכָה; יָתוֹם אַתָּה הָיִיתָ עוֹזֵר.

<sup>15</sup>Break the arm of the wicked; and as for the evil man, search out his wickedness, till none is found.

טושְׁבֹר זְרוֹעַ רָשָׁע; וָרָע תִּדְרוֹשׁ רִשְׁעוֹ בַל תִּמְצָא.

<sup>16</sup> יהוה is Melekh forever and ever; the nations are perished out of His land.

טז יהוה מֶלֶךְ עוֹלָם וָעֶד; אָבְדוּ גוֹיִם מֵאַרְצוֹ.

<sup>17</sup> יהוה , You have heard the desire of the humble: You will direct their heart, You will cause Your ear to attend;

יזתַּאֲוַת עֲנָוִים שָׁמַעְתָּ יהוה ; תָּכִין לִבָּם תַּקְשִׁיב אָזְנֶךָ.

<sup>18</sup>To right the fatherless and the oppressed, that man, who is of the earth, may be terrible no more.

יחלִשְׁפֹּט יָתוֹם וָדָךְ: בַל יוֹסִיף עוֹד לַעֲרֹץ אֱנוֹשׁ מִן הָאָרֶץ.

# תְּהִלָּה 11 Tehillah

<sup>1</sup>For the Leader. By David. In יהוה have I taken refuge; how do you say to my soul, "Flee! To your mountain, you birds!"?

אלַמְנַצֵּחַ לְדָוִד: בַּיהוה חָסִיתִי אֵיךְ תֹּאמְרוּ לְנַפְשִׁי; נוּדוּ (נוּדִי) הַרְכֶם צִפּוֹר.

<sup>2</sup>For, lo, the wicked bend the bow, they have made ready their arrow upon the string, that they may shoot in darkness at the upright in heart.

בכִּי הִנֵּה הָרְשָׁעִים יִדְרְכוּן קֶשֶׁת כּוֹנְנוּ חִצָּם עַל יֶתֶר לִירוֹת בְּמוֹ אֹפֶל לְיִשְׁרֵי לֵב.

<sup>3</sup>When the foundations are destroyed, O, Tzadik, what a wonder?

גכִּי הַשָּׁתוֹת יֵהָרֵסוּן צַדִּיק מַה פָּעָל.

<sup>4</sup>יהוה is in His Heikhal Kadosh, יהוה, His throne is in heaven; His eyes behold, His eyelids try the children of men.

ד יהוה בְּהֵיכַל קָדְשׁוֹ יהוה בַּשָּׁמַיִם כִּסְאוֹ: עֵינָיו יֶחֱזוּ עַפְעַפָּיו יִבְחֲנוּ בְּנֵי אָדָם.

<sup>5</sup>יהוה tries a Tzadik; but the wicked and him that loves violence His soul hates.

ה יהוה צַדִּיק יִבְחָן: וְרָשָׁע וְאֹהֵב חָמָס שָׂנְאָה נַפְשׁוֹ.

<sup>6</sup>Upon the wicked He will cause to rain coals; fire and brimstone and burning wind shall be the portion of their cup.

ויַמְטֵר עַל רְשָׁעִים פַּחִים: אֵשׁ וְגָפְרִית וְרוּחַ זִלְעָפוֹת מְנָת כּוֹסָם.

<sup>7</sup>For יהוה is a Tzadik, He loves righteous acts; the upright shall behold His face.

זכִּי צַדִּיק יהוה צְדָקוֹת אָהֵב; יָשָׁר יֶחֱזוּ פָנֵימוֹ.

# תְּהִלָּה 12 Tehillah

¹For the Leader; on the Sh'minit. A Mizmor of David.

אֲלַמְנַצֵּחַ עַל הַשְּׁמִינִית מִזְמוֹר לְדָוִד.

²Help, יהוה ; for the Khasid ceases; for the faithful fail from among the children of men.

בהוֹשִׁיעָה יהוה כִּי גָמַר חָסִיד: כִּי פַסּוּ אֱמוּנִים מִבְּנֵי אָדָם.

³They speak falsehood, everyone with his neighbor; with flattering lip, and with a double heart do they speak.

גשָׁוְא יְדַבְּרוּ אִישׁ אֶת רֵעֵהוּ: שְׂפַת חֲלָקוֹת בְּלֵב וָלֵב יְדַבֵּרוּ.

⁴May יהוה cut off all flattering lips, the tongue that speaks proud things!

דיַכְרֵת יהוה כָּל שִׂפְתֵי חֲלָקוֹת לָשׁוֹן מְדַבֶּרֶת גְּדֹלוֹת.

⁵Who have said, "Our tongue will we make mighty; our lips are with us: who is Adon over us?"

האֲשֶׁר אָמְרוּ לִלְשֹׁנֵנוּ נַגְבִּיר שְׂפָתֵינוּ אִתָּנוּ: מִי אָדוֹן לָנוּ.

⁶"For the oppression of the poor, for the sighing of the needy, now will I arise", says יהוה ; "I will set him in safety at whom they puff."

ומִשֹּׁד עֲנִיִּים מֵאַנְקַת אֶבְיוֹנִים: עַתָּה אָקוּם יֹאמַר יהוה ; אָשִׁית בְּיֵשַׁע יָפִיחַ לוֹ.

⁷The words of יהוה are pure words, as silver tried in a crucible on the earth, refined seven times.

זאִמְרוֹת יהוה אֲמָרוֹת טְהֹרוֹת: כֶּסֶף צָרוּף בַּעֲלִיל לָאָרֶץ; מְזֻקָּק שִׁבְעָתָיִם.

<sup>8</sup>You will keep them, O יהוה ; You will preserve us from this generation forever.

חאַתָּה יהוה תִּשְׁמְרֵם; תִּצְּרֶנּוּ מִן הַדּוֹר זוּ לְעוֹלָם.

<sup>9</sup>The wicked walk on every side, when vileness is exalted among the sons of men.

טסָבִיב רְשָׁעִים יִתְהַלָּכוּן; כְּרֻם זֻלּוּת לִבְנֵי אָדָם.

# Tehillah 13 תְּהִלָּה

<sup>1</sup>For the Leader. A Mizmor of David.

אלַמְנַצֵּחַ מִזְמוֹר לְדָוִד.

<sup>2</sup>Until when, O יהוה , will You forget me forever? Until when will You hide Your face from me?

בעַד אָנָה יהוה תִּשְׁכָּחֵנִי נֶצַח; עַד אָנָה תַּסְתִּיר אֶת פָּנֶיךָ מִמֶּנִּי.

<sup>3</sup>Until when shall I take counsel in my soul, having sorrow in my heart by day? Until when shall my enemy be exalted over me?

געַד אָנָה אָשִׁית עֵצוֹת בְּנַפְשִׁי יָגוֹן בִּלְבָבִי יוֹמָם; עַד אָנָה יָרוּם אֹיְבִי עָלָי.

<sup>4</sup>Behold, and answer me, O יהוה my Elohim; lighten my eyes, lest I sleep the sleep of Mavet;

דהַבִּיטָה עֲנֵנִי יהוה אֱלֹהָי; הָאִירָה עֵינַי פֶּן אִישַׁן הַמָּוֶת.

<sup>5</sup>Lest my enemy says, "I have prevailed against him"; lest my adversaries rejoice when I am moved.

הפֶּן יֹאמַר אֹיְבִי יְכָלְתִּיו; צָרַי יָגִילוּ כִּי אֶמּוֹט.

⁶But as for me, in Your compassion do I trust; my heart shall rejoice in Your Salvation. I will sing unto יהוה , because He has dealt bountifully with me.

וַאֲנִי בְּחַסְדְּךָ בָטַחְתִּי יָגֵל לִבִּי בִּישׁוּעָתֶךָ: אָשִׁירָה לַיהוה כִּי גָמַל עָלָי.

# תְּהִלָּה 14 Tehillah

¹For the Leader. By David. The fool has said in his heart, "There is no Elohim"; they have dealt corruptly, they have done abominably; there is none that does good.

לַמְנַצֵּחַ לְדָוִד: אָמַר נָבָל בְּלִבּוֹ אֵין אֱלֹהִים; הִשְׁחִיתוּ הִתְעִיבוּ עֲלִילָה אֵין עֹשֵׂה טוֹב.

² יהוה looked forth from heaven upon the children of men, to see if there was a man of understanding, that did seek after Elohim.

יהוה מִשָּׁמַיִם הִשְׁקִיף עַל בְּנֵי אָדָם: לִרְאוֹת הֲיֵשׁ מַשְׂכִּיל דֹּרֵשׁ אֶת אֱלֹהִים.

³They are all corrupt, they are together become impure; there is none that does good, no, not one.

הַכֹּל סָר יַחְדָּו נֶאֱלָחוּ: אֵין עֹשֵׂה טוֹב אֵין גַּם אֶחָד.

⁴"Shall not all the workers of iniquity know it, who eat up My people as they eat bread, and call not upon יהוה ?"

הֲלֹא יָדְעוּ כָּל פֹּעֲלֵי אָוֶן: אֹכְלֵי עַמִּי אָכְלוּ לֶחֶם; יהוה לֹא קָרָאוּ.

⁵There are they in great fear; for Elohim is with the righteous generation.

שָׁם פָּחֲדוּ פָחַד: כִּי אֱלֹהִים בְּדוֹר צַדִּיק.

<sup>6</sup>You would put to shame the counsel of the poor, but יהוה is his refuge.

<sup>7</sup>Oh that the Salvation of Yisra'el were come out of Tzion! When יהוה turns the captivity of His people, let Ya'akov rejoice, let Yisra'el be glad.

ⁱעֲצַת עָנִי תָבִישׁוּ: כִּי יהוה מַחְסֵהוּ.

ⁱמִי יִתֵּן מִצִּיּוֹן יְשׁוּעַת יִשְׂרָאֵל: בְּשׁוּב יהוה שְׁבוּת עַמּוֹ; יָגֵל יַעֲקֹב יִשְׂמַח יִשְׂרָאֵל.

# Tehillah 15 תְּהִלָּה

<sup>1</sup>A Mizmor of David. יהוה , who shall sojourn in Your tent? Who shall dwell upon Your Har Kodesh?

ⁿמִזְמוֹר לְדָוִד: יהוה מִי יָגוּר בְּאָהֳלֶךָ; מִי יִשְׁכֹּן בְּהַר קָדְשֶׁךָ.

<sup>2</sup>He that walks uprightly, and works righteously, and speaks truth in his heart;

ᵇהוֹלֵךְ תָּמִים וּפֹעֵל צֶדֶק; וְדֹבֵר אֱמֶת בִּלְבָבוֹ.

<sup>3</sup>That has no slander upon his tongue, nor does evil to his fellow, nor takes up a reproach against his neighbor;

ᵍלֹא רָגַל עַל לְשֹׁנוֹ לֹא עָשָׂה לְרֵעֵהוּ רָעָה; וְחֶרְפָּה לֹא נָשָׂא עַל קְרֹבוֹ.

<sup>4</sup>In whose eyes a vile person is despised, but he honors them that fear יהוה ; he that swears to his own hurt, and changes not;

ᵈנִבְזֶה בְּעֵינָיו נִמְאָס וְאֶת יִרְאֵי יהוה יְכַבֵּד; נִשְׁבַּע לְהָרַע וְלֹא יָמִר.

<sup>5</sup>He that puts not out his money on interest, nor takes a bribe against the innocent. He that does these things shall never be moved.

ʰכַּסְפּוֹ לֹא נָתַן בְּנֶשֶׁךְ וְשֹׁחַד עַל נָקִי לֹא לָקָח: עֹשֵׂה אֵלֶּה לֹא יִמּוֹט לְעוֹלָם.

# Tehillah 16 תְּהִלָּה

¹Mikhtam of David. Keep me, O God; for I have taken refuge in You.

אמִכְתָּם לְדָוִד: שָׁמְרֵנִי אֵל כִּי חָסִיתִי בָךְ.

²I have said unto יהוה , "You are Adonai; I have no good but in You";

באָמַרְתְּ לַיהוה אֲדֹנָי אָתָּה; טוֹבָתִי בַּל עָלֶיךָ.

³As for the K'doshim that are in the earth, they are the excellent in whom is all my delight.

גלִקְדוֹשִׁים אֲשֶׁר בָּאָרֶץ הֵמָּה; וְאַדִּירֵי כָּל חֶפְצִי בָם.

⁴Let the idols of them be multiplied that make suit unto another; their drink offerings of blood will I not offer, nor take their names upon my lips.

דיִרְבּוּ עַצְּבוֹתָם אַחֵר מָהָרוּ: בַּל אַסִּיךְ נִסְכֵּיהֶם מִדָּם; וּבַל אֶשָּׂא אֶת שְׁמוֹתָם עַל שְׂפָתָי.

⁵O יהוה , the portion of my inheritance and of my cup, You maintain my lot.

ה יהוה מְנָת חֶלְקִי וְכוֹסִי אַתָּה תּוֹמִיךְ גּוֹרָלִי.

⁶The lines are fallen unto me in pleasant places; yes, I have a beautiful heritage.

וחֲבָלִים נָפְלוּ לִי בַּנְּעִמִים; אַף נַחֲלָת שָׁפְרָה עָלָי.

⁷I will bless יהוה , who has given me counsel; yes, in the night seasons my reins instruct me.

זאֲבָרֵךְ אֶת יהוה אֲשֶׁר יְעָצָנִי; אַף לֵילוֹת יִסְּרוּנִי כִלְיוֹתָי.

⁸I have set יהוה always before me; surely He is at my right hand, I shall not be moved.

חשִׁוִּיתִי יהוה לְנֶגְדִּי תָמִיד: כִּי מִימִינִי בַּל אֶמּוֹט.

⁹Therefore my heart is glad, and my glory rejoices; my flesh also dwells in safety;

ט לָכֵן שָׂמַח לִבִּי וַיָּגֶל כְּבוֹדִי; אַף בְּשָׂרִי יִשְׁכֹּן לָבֶטַח.

¹⁰For You will not abandon my soul to She'ol; neither will You suffer Your Khasid to see the pit.

י כִּי לֹא תַעֲזֹב נַפְשִׁי לִשְׁאוֹל; לֹא תִתֵּן חֲסִידְךָ לִרְאוֹת שָׁחַת.

¹¹You make me to know the path of life; in Your presence is fullness of joy, in Your right hand is bliss for evermore.

יא תּוֹדִיעֵנִי אֹרַח חַיִּים: שֹׂבַע שְׂמָחוֹת אֶת פָּנֶיךָ; נְעִמוֹת בִּימִינְךָ נֶצַח.

# Tehillah 17 תְּהִלָּה

¹A Tefilah of David. Hear the right, O יהוה , attend unto my cry; give ear unto my prayer from lips without deceit.

א תְּפִלָּה לְדָוִד: שִׁמְעָה יהוה צֶדֶק הַקְשִׁיבָה רִנָּתִי הַאֲזִינָה תְפִלָּתִי; בְּלֹא שִׂפְתֵי מִרְמָה.

²Let my judgment come forth from Your presence; let Your eyes behold equity.

ב מִלְּפָנֶיךָ מִשְׁפָּטִי יֵצֵא; עֵינֶיךָ תֶּחֱזֶינָה מֵישָׁרִים.

³You have tried my heart, You have visited it in the night; You have tested me, and You find not that I had a thought which should not pass my mouth.

ג בָּחַנְתָּ לִבִּי פָּקַדְתָּ לַּיְלָה צְרַפְתַּנִי בַל תִּמְצָא; זַמֹּתִי בַל יַעֲבָר פִּי.

⁴As for the doings of men, by the word of Your lips I have kept myself from the ways of the violent.

ד לִפְעֻלּוֹת אָדָם בִּדְבַר שְׂפָתֶיךָ אֲנִי שָׁמַרְתִּי אָרְחוֹת פָּרִיץ.

230

⁵My steps have held fast to Your paths, my feet have not slipped.

הׇתׇּמֹךְ אֲשֻׁרַי בְּמַעְגְּלוֹתֶיךָ; בַּל נָמוֹטוּ פְעָמָי.

⁶As for me, I call upon You, for You will answer me, O God; incline Your ear unto me, hear my speech.

וֹאֲנִי קְרָאתִיךָ כִי תַעֲנֵנִי אֵל; הַט אָזְנְךָ לִי שְׁמַע אִמְרָתִי.

⁷Make your compassions work wonderfully, O You that save by Your right hand from assailants them that take refuge in You.

הַפְלֵה חֲסָדֶיךָ מוֹשִׁיעַ חוֹסִים מִמִּתְקוֹמְמִים בִּימִינֶךָ.

⁸Keep me as the Ishon Ayin, hide me in the shadow of Your wings,

חַשָׁמְרֵנִי כְּאִישׁוֹן בַּת עָיִן; בְּצֵל כְּנָפֶיךָ תַּסְתִּירֵנִי.

⁹From the wicked that oppresses, my deadly enemies, that encompass me about.

טׇמִפְּנֵי רְשָׁעִים זוּ שַׁדּוּנִי; אֹיְבַי בְּנֶפֶשׁ יַקִּיפוּ עָלָי.

¹⁰Their gross heart they have shut tight, with their mouth they speak proudly.

יׇחֶלְבָּמוֹ סָגְרוּ; פִּימוֹ דִּבְּרוּ בְגֵאוּת.

¹¹At our every step they have now encompassed us; they set their eyes to cast us down to the earth.

אׇיׇאַשֻּׁרֵינוּ עַתָּה סְבָבוּנִי (סְבָבוּנוּ); עֵינֵיהֶם יָשִׁיתוּ לִנְטוֹת בָּאָרֶץ.

¹²He is like a lion that is eager to tear in pieces, and like a young lion lurking in secret places.

יׇבׇּדִּמְיֹנוֹ כְּאַרְיֵה יִכְסוֹף לִטְרֹף; וְכִכְפִיר יֹשֵׁב בְּמִסְתָּרִים.

231

<sup>13</sup>Arise, O יהוה , confront him, cast him down; deliver my soul from the wicked by Your sword;

יגקוּמָה יהוה קַדְּמָה פָנָיו הַכְרִיעֵהוּ; פַּלְּטָה נַפְשִׁי מֵרָשָׁע חַרְבֶּךָ.

<sup>14</sup>From men, by Your hand, O יהוה , from men of the world, whose portion is in this life, and whose belly You fill with Your treasure; who have children in plenty, and leave their abundance to their babes.

ידמִמְתִים יָדְךָ יהוה מִמְתִים מֵחֶלֶד חֶלְקָם בַּחַיִּים וּצְפִינך (וּצְפוּנְךָ) תְּמַלֵּא בִטְנָם: יִשְׂבְּעוּ בָנִים וְהִנִּיחוּ יִתְרָם לְעוֹלְלֵיהֶם.

<sup>15</sup>As for me, I shall behold Your face in righteousness; I shall be satisfied, when I awake with Your likeness.

טואֲנִי בְּצֶדֶק אֶחֱזֶה פָנֶיךָ; אֶשְׂבְּעָה בְהָקִיץ תְּמוּנָתֶךָ.

# תְּהִלָּה 18 Tehillah

<sup>1</sup>For the Leader, by David, the servant of יהוה , who spoke unto יהוה the words of this song in the day that יהוה delivered him from the hand of all his enemies, and from the hand of Sha'ul;

אלַמְנַצֵּחַ לְעֶבֶד יהוה לְדָוִד: אֲשֶׁר דִּבֶּר לַיהוה אֶת דִּבְרֵי הַשִּׁירָה הַזֹּאת בְּיוֹם הִצִּיל יהוה אוֹתוֹ מִכַּף כָּל אֹיְבָיו וּמִיַּד שָׁאוּל.

<sup>2</sup>And he said: I love You, O יהוה , my strength.

בוַיֹּאמַר אֶרְחָמְךָ יהוה חִזְקִי.

<sup>3</sup> יהוה is my rock, and my fortress, and my deliverer; my God, my rock, in Him I take refuge; my shield, and my horn of Salvation, my high tower.

ג יהוה סַלְעִי וּמְצוּדָתִי וּמְפַלְּטִי: אֵלִי צוּרִי אֶחֱסֶה בּוֹ; מָגִנִּי וְקֶרֶן יִשְׁעִי מִשְׂגַּבִּי.

⁴Praised, I cry, is יהוה , and I am saved from my enemies.

מְהֻלָּל אֶקְרָא יהוה ; וּמִן אֹיְבַי אִוָּשֵׁעַ׃

⁵The cords of Mavet encompassed me, and the floods of Bliya'al assailed me.

אֲפָפוּנִי חֶבְלֵי מָוֶת; וְנַחֲלֵי בְלִיַּעַל יְבַעֲתוּנִי׃

⁶The cords of She'ol surrounded me; the snares of Mavet confronted me.

חֶבְלֵי שְׁאוֹל סְבָבוּנִי; קִדְּמוּנִי מוֹקְשֵׁי מָוֶת׃

⁷In my distress I called upon יהוה , and cried unto my Elohim; out of His Heikhal He heard my voice, and my cry came before Him unto His ears.

בַּצַּר לִי אֶקְרָא יהוה וְאֶל אֱלֹהַי אֲשַׁוֵּעַ: יִשְׁמַע מֵהֵיכָלוֹ קוֹלִי; וְשַׁוְעָתִי לְפָנָיו תָּבוֹא בְאָזְנָיו׃

⁸Then the earth did shake and quake, the foundations also of the mountains did tremble; they were shaken, because He was wroth.

וַתִּגְעַשׁ וַתִּרְעַשׁ הָאָרֶץ וּמוֹסְדֵי הָרִים יִרְגָּזוּ; וַיִּתְגָּעֲשׁוּ כִּי חָרָה לוֹ׃

⁹Smoke arose up in His nostrils, and fire out of His mouth did devour; coals flamed forth from Him.

עָלָה עָשָׁן בְּאַפּוֹ וְאֵשׁ מִפִּיו תֹּאכֵל; גֶּחָלִים בָּעֲרוּ מִמֶּנּוּ׃

¹⁰He bowed the heavens also, and came down; and thick darkness was under His feet.

וַיֵּט שָׁמַיִם וַיֵּרַד; וַעֲרָפֶל תַּחַת רַגְלָיו׃

¹¹And He rode upon a keruv, and flew; yes, He did swoop down upon the wings of the wind.

וַיִּרְכַּב עַל כְּרוּב וַיָּעֹף; וַיֵּדֶא עַל כַּנְפֵי רוּחַ׃

<sup>12</sup>He made darkness His hiding-place, His sukka round about Him; darkness of waters, thick clouds of the skies.

יביָשֶׁת חֹשֶׁךְ סִתְרוֹ סְבִיבוֹתָיו סֻכָּתוֹ; חֶשְׁכַת מַיִם עָבֵי שְׁחָקִים.

<sup>13</sup>At the brightness before Him, there passed through His thick clouds hailstones and coals of fire.

יגמִנֹּגַהּ נֶגְדּוֹ: עָבָיו עָבְרוּ בָּרָד וְגַחֲלֵי אֵשׁ.

<sup>14</sup>יהוה also thundered in the heavens, and Elyon gave forth His voice; hailstones and coals of fire.

ידוַיַּרְעֵם בַּשָּׁמַיִם יהוה וְעֶלְיוֹן יִתֵּן קֹלוֹ; בָּרָד וְגַחֲלֵי אֵשׁ.

<sup>15</sup>And He sent out His arrows, and scattered them; and He shot forth lightnings, and discomfited them.

טווַיִּשְׁלַח חִצָּיו וַיְפִיצֵם; וּבְרָקִים רָב וַיְהֻמֵּם.

<sup>16</sup>And the channels of waters appeared, and the foundations of the world were laid bare, at Your rebuke, O יהוה, at the blast of the breath of Your nostrils.

טזוַיֵּרָאוּ אֲפִיקֵי מַיִם וַיִּגָּלוּ מוֹסְדוֹת תֵּבֵל: מִגַּעֲרָתְךָ יהוה מִנִּשְׁמַת רוּחַ אַפֶּךָ.

<sup>17</sup>He sent from on high, He took me; He drew me out of many waters.

יזיִשְׁלַח מִמָּרוֹם יִקָּחֵנִי; יַמְשֵׁנִי מִמַּיִם רַבִּים.

<sup>18</sup>He delivered me from my enemy most strong, and from them that hated me, for they were too mighty for me.

יחיַצִּילֵנִי מֵאֹיְבִי עָז; וּמִשֹּׂנְאַי כִּי אָמְצוּ מִמֶּנִּי.

¹⁹They confronted me in the day of my calamity; but יהוה was a stay unto me.

יְקַדְּמוּנִי בְיוֹם אֵידִי; וַיְהִי יהוה לְמִשְׁעָן לִי.

²⁰He brought me forth also into a large place; He delivered me, because He delighted in me.

וַיּוֹצִיאֵנִי לַמֶּרְחָב; יְחַלְּצֵנִי כִּי חָפֵץ בִּי.

²¹ יהוה rewarded me according to my righteousness; according to the cleanness of my hands has He recompensed me.

יִגְמְלֵנִי יהוה כְּצִדְקִי; כְּבֹר יָדַי יָשִׁיב לִי.

²²For I have kept the ways of יהוה , and have not wickedly departed from my Elohim.

כִּי שָׁמַרְתִּי דַּרְכֵי יהוה ; וְלֹא רָשַׁעְתִּי מֵאֱלֹהָי.

²³For all His ordinances were before me, and I put not away His statutes from me.

כִּי כָל מִשְׁפָּטָיו לְנֶגְדִּי; וְחֻקֹּתָיו לֹא אָסִיר מֶנִּי.

²⁴And I was single-hearted with Him, and I kept myself from my iniquity.

וָאֱהִי תָמִים עִמּוֹ; וָאֶשְׁתַּמֵּר מֵעֲוֹנִי.

²⁵Therefore has יהוה recompensed me according to my righteousness, according to the cleanness of my hands in His eyes.

וַיָּשֶׁב יהוה לִי כְצִדְקִי; כְּבֹר יָדַי לְנֶגֶד עֵינָיו.

²⁶With the Khasid You show Yourself compassionate, with the upright man You show Yourself upright;

עִם חָסִיד תִּתְחַסָּד; עִם גְּבַר תָּמִים תִּתַּמָּם.

235

<sup>27</sup>With the pure You show Yourself pure; and with the crooked You show Yourself subtle.

כּ"עִם נָבָר תִּתְבָּרָר; וְעִם עִקֵּשׁ תִּתְפַּתָּל.

<sup>28</sup>For You save the afflicted people; but the haughty eyes You humble.

כּ"כִּי אַתָּה עַם עָנִי תוֹשִׁיעַ; וְעֵינַיִם רָמוֹת תַּשְׁפִּיל.

<sup>29</sup>For You light my lamp; יהוה my Elohim lightens my darkness.

כּ"כִּי אַתָּה תָּאִיר נֵרִי; יהוה אֱלֹהַי יַגִּיהַּ חָשְׁכִּי.

<sup>30</sup>For by You I run upon a troop; and by my Elohim do I scale a wall.

כּ"כִּי בְךָ אָרֻץ גְּדוּד; וּבֵאלֹהַי אֲדַלֶּג שׁוּר.

<sup>31</sup>As for God, His way is perfect; the word of יהוה is tried; He is a shield unto all them that take refuge in Him.

ל"הָאֵל תָּמִים דַּרְכּוֹ: אִמְרַת יהוה צְרוּפָה; מָגֵן הוּא לְכֹל הַחֹסִים בּוֹ.

<sup>32</sup>For who is Elo'ah, save יהוה ? And who is a Rock, except our Elohim?

ל"כִּי מִי אֱלוֹהַּ מִבַּלְעֲדֵי יהוה; וּמִי צוּר זוּלָתִי אֱלֹהֵינוּ.

<sup>33</sup>The God that girds me with strength, and makes my way straight;

ל"הָאֵל הַמְאַזְּרֵנִי חָיִל; וַיִּתֵּן תָּמִים דַּרְכִּי.

<sup>34</sup>Who makes my feet like hinds', and sets me upon my high places;

ל"מְשַׁוֶּה רַגְלַי כָּאַיָּלוֹת; וְעַל בָּמֹתַי יַעֲמִידֵנִי.

<sup>35</sup>Who trains my hands for war, so that my arms do bend a bow of brass.

ל"מְלַמֵּד יָדַי לַמִּלְחָמָה; וְנִחֲתָה קֶשֶׁת נְחוּשָׁה זְרוֹעֹתָי.

³⁶You have also given me Your shield of Salvation, and Your right hand has held me up; and Your gentleness has made me great.

לֹּוַתִּתֶּן לִי מָגֵן יִשְׁעֶךָ: וִימִינְךָ תִסְעָדֵנִי; וְעַנְוַתְךָ תַרְבֵּנִי.

³⁷You have enlarged my steps under me, and my feet have not slipped.

לֹּתַרְחִיב צַעֲדִי תַחְתָּי; וְלֹא מָעֲדוּ קַרְסֻלָּי.

³⁸I have pursued my enemies, and overtaken them; neither did I turn back till they were consumed.

לֹּאֶרְדּוֹף אוֹיְבַי וְאַשִּׂיגֵם; וְלֹא אָשׁוּב עַד כַּלּוֹתָם.

³⁹I have smitten them through, so that they are not able to rise; they are fallen under my feet.

לטֹאֶמְחָצֵם וְלֹא יֻכְלוּ קוּם; יִפְּלוּ תַּחַת רַגְלָי.

⁴⁰For You have girded me with strength unto the battle; You have subdued under me those that rose up against me.

מֹוַתְּאַזְּרֵנִי חַיִל לַמִּלְחָמָה; תַּכְרִיעַ קָמַי תַּחְתָּי.

⁴¹You have also made my enemies turn their backs unto me, and I did cut off them that hate me.

מאֹוְאֹיְבַי נָתַתָּה לִּי עֹרֶף; וּמְשַׂנְאַי אַצְמִיתֵם.

⁴²They cried, but there was none to save; even unto יהוה , but He answered them not.

מבֹיְשַׁוְּעוּ וְאֵין מוֹשִׁיעַ; עַל יהוה וְלֹא עָנָם.

⁴³Then did I beat them small as the dust before the wind; I did cast them out as the mire of the streets.

מג וְאֶשְׁחָקֵם כְּעָפָר עַל פְּנֵי רוּחַ; כְּטִיט חוּצוֹת אֲרִיקֵם.

⁴⁴You have delivered me from the contentions of the people; You have made me the head of the nations; a people whom I have not known serve me.

מד תְּפַלְּטֵנִי מֵרִיבֵי עָם: תְּשִׂימֵנִי לְרֹאשׁ גּוֹיִם; עַם לֹא יָדַעְתִּי יַעַבְדוּנִי.

⁴⁵As soon as they hear of me, they obey me; the sons of the stranger dwindle away before me.

מה לְשֵׁמַע אֹזֶן יִשָּׁמְעוּ לִי; בְּנֵי נֵכָר יְכַחֲשׁוּ לִי.

⁴⁶The sons of the stranger fade away, and come trembling out of their close places.

מו בְּנֵי נֵכָר יִבֹּלוּ; וְיַחְרְגוּ מִמִּסְגְּרוֹתֵיהֶם.

⁴⁷ יהוה lives, and blessed is my Rock; and exalted be the Elohim of my Salvation;

מז חַי יהוה וּבָרוּךְ צוּרִי; וְיָרוּם אֱלוֹהֵי יִשְׁעִי.

⁴⁸Even the God that executes vengeance for me, and subdues peoples under me.

מח הָאֵל הַנּוֹתֵן נְקָמוֹת לִי; וַיַּדְבֵּר עַמִּים תַּחְתָּי.

⁴⁹He delivers me from my enemies; yes, You lift me up above them that rise up against me; You deliver me from the violent man.

מט מְפַלְּטִי מֵאֹיְבָי: אַף מִן קָמַי תְּרוֹמְמֵנִי; מֵאִישׁ חָמָס תַּצִּילֵנִי.

⁵⁰Therefore I will give thanks unto You, O יהוה, among the nations, and will sing praises unto Your Name.

ⁿ עַל כֵּן אוֹדְךָ בַגּוֹיִם יהוה; וּלְשִׁמְךָ אֲזַמֵּרָה.

⁵¹Great Salvations does He give to His king; and shows compassion to His Mashi'akh, to David and to his seed, for evermore.

נא מַגְדִּל יְשׁוּעוֹת מַלְכּוֹ: וְעֹשֶׂה חֶסֶד לִמְשִׁיחוֹ לְדָוִד וּלְזַרְעוֹ; עַד עוֹלָם.

# Tehillah 19 תְּהִלָּה

¹For the Leader. A Mizmor of David.

א לַמְנַצֵּחַ מִזְמוֹר לְדָוִד.

²The heavens declare the glory of Elohim, and the firmament shows His handiwork;

ב הַשָּׁמַיִם מְסַפְּרִים כְּבוֹד אֵל; וּמַעֲשֵׂה יָדָיו מַגִּיד הָרָקִיעַ.

³Day unto day utters speech, and night unto night reveals knowledge;

ג יוֹם לְיוֹם יַבִּיעַ אֹמֶר; וְלַיְלָה לְלַיְלָה יְחַוֶּה דָּעַת.

⁴There is no speech, there are no words, neither is their voice heard.

ד אֵין אֹמֶר וְאֵין דְּבָרִים: בְּלִי נִשְׁמָע קוֹלָם.

⁵Their line is gone out through all the earth, and their words to the end of the world. In them has He set an Ohel for the sun,

ה בְּכָל הָאָרֶץ יָצָא קַוָּם וּבִקְצֵה תֵבֵל מִלֵּיהֶם; לַשֶּׁמֶשׁ שָׂם אֹהֶל בָּהֶם.

239

⁶Which is as a bridegroom coming out of his Khupah, and rejoices as a strong man to run his course.

וְהוּא כְּחָתָן יֹצֵא מֵחֻפָּתוֹ; יָשִׂישׂ כְּגִבּוֹר לָרוּץ אֹרַח.

⁷His going forth is from the end of the heaven, and his circuit unto the ends of it; and there is nothing hidden from the heat thereof.

מִקְצֵה הַשָּׁמַיִם מוֹצָאוֹ וּתְקוּפָתוֹ עַל קְצוֹתָם; וְאֵין נִסְתָּר מֵחַמָּתוֹ.

⁸The Torah of יהוה is perfect, restoring the soul; the testimony of יהוה is sure, making wise the simple.

תּוֹרַת יהוה תְּמִימָה מְשִׁיבַת נָפֶשׁ; עֵדוּת יהוה נֶאֱמָנָה מַחְכִּימַת פֶּתִי.

⁹The precepts of יהוה are right, rejoicing the heart; the Mitzvah of יהוה is pure, enlightening the eyes.

פִּקּוּדֵי יהוה יְשָׁרִים מְשַׂמְּחֵי לֵב; מִצְוַת יהוה בָּרָה מְאִירַת עֵינָיִם.

¹⁰The fear of יהוה is clean, enduring forever; the ordinances of יהוה are true, they are righteous altogether;

יִרְאַת יהוה טְהוֹרָה עוֹמֶדֶת לָעַד: מִשְׁפְּטֵי יהוה אֱמֶת; צָדְקוּ יַחְדָּו.

¹¹More to be desired are they than gold, yes, than much fine gold; sweeter also than honey, and the honeycomb.

הַנֶּחֱמָדִים מִזָּהָב וּמִפַּז רָב; וּמְתוּקִים מִדְּבַשׁ וְנֹפֶת צוּפִים.

¹²Moreover, by them is Your servant warned; in keeping of them there is great reward.

גַּם עַבְדְּךָ נִזְהָר בָּהֶם; בְּשָׁמְרָם עֵקֶב רָב.

240

<sup>13</sup>Who can discern his errors? Clear me from hidden faults.

יּגְשִׁיאוֹת מִי יָבִין; מִנִּסְתָּרוֹת נַקֵּנִי.

<sup>14</sup>Keep back Your servant also from presumptuous sins, that they may not have dominion over me; then shall I be faultless, and I shall be clear from great transgression.

ידּגַּם מִזֵּדִים חֲשֹׂךְ עַבְדֶּךָ אַל יִמְשְׁלוּ בִי אָז אֵיתָם; וְנִקֵּיתִי מִפֶּשַׁע רָב.

<sup>15</sup>Let the words of my mouth and the meditation of my heart be acceptable before You, O יהוה , my Rock, and my Redeemer.

טוּיִהְיוּ לְרָצוֹן אִמְרֵי פִי וְהֶגְיוֹן לִבִּי לְפָנֶיךָ: יהוה צוּרִי וְגֹאֲלִי.

# תְּהִלָּה 20 Tehillah

<sup>1</sup>For the Leader. A Mizmor of David.

אּלַמְנַצֵּחַ מִזְמוֹר לְדָוִד.

<sup>2</sup>May יהוה answer you in the day of trouble. May the Name of the Elohim of Ya'akov set you up on high;

בּיַעַנְךָ יהוה בְּיוֹם צָרָה; יְשַׂגֶּבְךָ שֵׁם אֱלֹהֵי יַעֲקֹב.

<sup>3</sup>May He send forth your help from the Mikdash, and support you out of Tzion;

גּיִשְׁלַח עֶזְרְךָ מִקֹּדֶשׁ; וּמִצִּיּוֹן יִסְעָדֶךָּ.

<sup>4</sup>May He receive the memorial of all your Minkhot, and accept the fat of your Olah; Selah.

דּיִזְכֹּר כָּל מִנְחֹתֶךָ; וְעוֹלָתְךָ יְדַשְּׁנֶה סֶלָה.

⁵May He grant you according to your own heart, and fulfill all your counsel.

יִתֶּן לְךָ כִלְבָבֶךָ; וְכָל עֲצָתְךָ יְמַלֵּא.

⁶We will shout for joy in your victory, and in the Name of our Elohim we will set up our standards; may יהוה fulfill all your petitions.

נְרַנְּנָה בִּישׁוּעָתֶךָ וּבְשֵׁם אֱלֹהֵינוּ נִדְגֹּל; יְמַלֵּא יהוה כָּל מִשְׁאֲלוֹתֶיךָ.

⁷Now I know that יהוה saves His Mashi'akh; He will answer him from His consecrated heaven with the mighty acts of His saving right hand.

עַתָּה יָדַעְתִּי כִּי הוֹשִׁיעַ יהוה מְשִׁיחוֹ: יַעֲנֵהוּ מִשְּׁמֵי קָדְשׁוֹ בִּגְבֻרוֹת יֵשַׁע יְמִינוֹ.

⁸Some trust in chariots, and some in horses; but we will make mention of the Name of יהוה our Elohim.

אֵלֶּה בָרֶכֶב וְאֵלֶּה בַסּוּסִים; וַאֲנַחְנוּ בְּשֵׁם יהוה אֱלֹהֵינוּ נַזְכִּיר.

⁹They are bowed down and fallen; but we are risen, and stand upright.

הֵמָּה כָּרְעוּ וְנָפָלוּ; וַאֲנַחְנוּ קַמְנוּ וַנִּתְעוֹדָד.

¹⁰Save, O יהוה ! Let HaMelekh answer us in the day that we call.

יהוה הוֹשִׁיעָה: הַמֶּלֶךְ יַעֲנֵנוּ בְיוֹם קָרְאֵנוּ.

# תְּהִלָּה Tehillah 21

¹For the Leader. A Mizmor of David.

לַמְנַצֵּחַ מִזְמוֹר לְדָוִד.

²O יהוה , in Your strength the Melekh rejoices; and in Your Salvation, how greatly does he exult!

בְּ יהוה בְּעָזְּךָ יִשְׂמַח מֶלֶךְ; וּבִישׁוּעָתְךָ מַה יָגִיל (יָגֶל) מְאֹד.

³You have given him his heart's desire, and the request of his lips You have not withheld. Selah.

גַּ תַּאֲוַת לִבּוֹ נָתַתָּה לּוֹ; וַאֲרֶשֶׁת שְׂפָתָיו בַּל מָנַעְתָּ סֶּלָה.

⁴For You meet him with choicest blessings; You set a crown of fine gold on his head.

דַּ כִּי תְקַדְּמֶנּוּ בִּרְכוֹת טוֹב; תָּשִׁית לְרֹאשׁוֹ עֲטֶרֶת פָּז.

⁵He asked life of You, You gave it to him; even length of days forever and ever.

הַ חַיִּים שָׁאַל מִמְּךָ נָתַתָּה לּוֹ; אֹרֶךְ יָמִים עוֹלָם וָעֶד.

⁶His glory is great through Your Salvation; honor and majesty do You lay upon him.

וַ גָּדוֹל כְּבוֹדוֹ בִּישׁוּעָתֶךָ; הוֹד וְהָדָר תְּשַׁוֶּה עָלָיו.

⁷For You make him most blessed forever; You make him glad with joy in Your presence.

זַ כִּי תְשִׁיתֵהוּ בְרָכוֹת לָעַד; תְּחַדֵּהוּ בְשִׂמְחָה אֶת פָּנֶיךָ.

⁸For HaMelekh trusts in יהוה , yes, in the compassion of Elyon; he shall not be moved.

חַ כִּי הַמֶּלֶךְ בֹּטֵחַ בַּיהוה ; וּבְחֶסֶד עֶלְיוֹן בַּל יִמּוֹט.

⁹Your hand shall be equal to all your enemies; your right hand shall overtake those that hate you.

טַ תִּמְצָא יָדְךָ לְכָל אֹיְבֶיךָ; יְמִינְךָ תִּמְצָא שֹׂנְאֶיךָ.

¹⁰You shall make them as a fiery furnace in the time of your anger; יהוה shall swallow them up in His wrath, and the fire shall devour them.

'תְּשִׁיתֵמוֹ כְּתַנּוּר אֵשׁ לְעֵת פָּנֶיךָ: יהוה בְּאַפּוֹ יְבַלְּעֵם; וְתֹאכְלֵם אֵשׁ.

¹¹Their fruit shall you destroy from the earth, and their seed from among the children of men.

א"פִּרְיָמוֹ מֵאֶרֶץ תְּאַבֵּד; וְזַרְעָם מִבְּנֵי אָדָם.

¹²For they intended evil against you, they imagined a device, wherewith they shall not prevail.

ב"כִּי נָטוּ עָלֶיךָ רָעָה; חָשְׁבוּ מְזִמָּה בַּל יוּכָלוּ.

¹³For you shall make them turn their back, you shall make ready with your bowstrings against the face of them.

ג"כִּי תְּשִׁיתֵמוֹ שֶׁכֶם; בְּמֵיתָרֶיךָ תְּכוֹנֵן עַל פְּנֵיהֶם.

¹⁴Be exalted, O יהוה, in Your strength; so will we sing and praise Your power.

ד"רוּמָה יהוה בְּעֻזֶּךָ; וְנָזְמְרָה גְבוּרָתֶךָ.

# תְּהִלָּה Tehillah 22

¹For the Leader; upon Ayelet HaShakhar. A Mizmor of David.

א"לַמְנַצֵּחַ עַל אַיֶּלֶת הַשַּׁחַר; מִזְמוֹר לְדָוִד.

²Eli, Eli, why have You forsaken me, and are far from my Salvation at the words of my cry?

ב"אֵלִי אֵלִי לָמָה עֲזַבְתָּנִי; רָחוֹק מִישׁוּעָתִי דִּבְרֵי שַׁאֲגָתִי.

³O my Elohim, I call by day, but You answer not; and at night, and there is no silence for me.

גאֱלֹהַי אֶקְרָא יוֹמָם וְלֹא תַעֲנֶה; וְלַיְלָה וְלֹא דֻמִיָּה לִי.

⁴Yet You are Kadosh, O You that are enthroned upon the praises of Yisra'el.

דוְאַתָּה קָדוֹשׁ יוֹשֵׁב תְּהִלּוֹת יִשְׂרָאֵל.

⁵In You did our fathers trust; they trusted, and You did deliver them.

הבְּךָ בָּטְחוּ אֲבֹתֵינוּ; בָּטְחוּ וַתְּפַלְּטֵמוֹ.

⁶Unto You they cried, and escaped; in You did they trust, and were not ashamed.

ואֵלֶיךָ זָעֲקוּ וְנִמְלָטוּ; בְּךָ בָטְחוּ וְלֹא בוֹשׁוּ.

⁷But I am a worm, and no man; a reproach of men, and despised of the people.

זוְאָנֹכִי תוֹלַעַת וְלֹא אִישׁ; חֶרְפַּת אָדָם וּבְזוּי עָם.

⁸All they that see me laugh me to scorn; they shoot out the lip, they shake the head:

חכָּל רֹאַי יַלְעִגוּ לִי; יַפְטִירוּ בְשָׂפָה יָנִיעוּ רֹאשׁ.

⁹"Let him commit himself unto יהוה ! Let Him rescue him; let Him deliver him, seeing He delights in him."

טגֹּל אֶל יהוה יְפַלְּטֵהוּ; יַצִּילֵהוּ כִּי חָפֵץ בּוֹ.

¹⁰For You are He that took me out of the womb; You made me trust when I was upon my mother's breasts.

יכִּי אַתָּה גֹחִי מִבָּטֶן; מַבְטִיחִי עַל שְׁדֵי אִמִּי.

¹¹Upon You I have been cast from my birth; You are my Elohim from my mother's womb.

יאעָלֶיךָ הָשְׁלַכְתִּי מֵרָחֶם; מִבֶּטֶן אִמִּי אֵלִי אָתָּה.

245

<sup>12</sup>Be not far from me; for trouble is near; for there is none to help.

יב אַל תִּרְחַק מִמֶּנִּי כִּי צָרָה קְרוֹבָה: כִּי אֵין עוֹזֵר.

<sup>13</sup>Many bulls have encompassed me; strong bulls of Bashan have beset me round about.

יג סְבָבוּנִי פָּרִים רַבִּים; אַבִּירֵי בָשָׁן כִּתְּרוּנִי.

<sup>14</sup>They open wide their mouth against me, as a ravening and a roaring lion.

יד פָּצוּ עָלַי פִּיהֶם; אַרְיֵה טֹרֵף וְשֹׁאֵג.

<sup>15</sup>I am poured out like water, and all my bones are out of joint; my heart is become like wax; it is melted in my inmost parts.

טו כַּמַּיִם נִשְׁפַּכְתִּי וְהִתְפָּרְדוּ כָּל עַצְמוֹתָי: הָיָה לִבִּי כַּדּוֹנָג; נָמֵס בְּתוֹךְ מֵעָי.

<sup>16</sup>My strength is dried up like a potsherd; and my tongue cleaves to my throat; and You lay me in the dust of Mavet.

טז יָבֵשׁ כַּחֶרֶשׂ כֹּחִי וּלְשׁוֹנִי מֻדְבָּק מַלְקוֹחָי; וְלַעֲפַר מָוֶת תִּשְׁפְּתֵנִי.

<sup>17</sup>For dogs have encompassed me; a company of evil-doers have enclosed me; like a lion, they are at my hands and my feet.

יז כִּי סְבָבוּנִי כְּלָבִים: עֲדַת מְרֵעִים הִקִּיפוּנִי; כָּאֲרִי יָדַי וְרַגְלָי.

<sup>18</sup>I may count all my bones; they look and gloat over me.

יח אֲסַפֵּר כָּל עַצְמוֹתָי; הֵמָּה יַבִּיטוּ יִרְאוּ בִי.

<sup>19</sup>They part my garments among them, and for my vesture do they cast lots.

יט יְחַלְּקוּ בְגָדַי לָהֶם; וְעַל לְבוּשִׁי יַפִּילוּ גוֹרָל.

<sup>20</sup>But You, O יהוה , be not far off; O You my strength, hasten to help me.

כוְאַתָּה יהוה אַל תִּרְחָק; אֱיָלוּתִי לְעֶזְרָתִי חוּשָׁה.

<sup>21</sup>Deliver my soul from the sword; my only one from the power of the dog.

כאהַצִּילָה מֵחֶרֶב נַפְשִׁי; מִיַּד כֶּלֶב יְחִידָתִי.

<sup>22</sup>Save me from the lion's mouth; yes, from the horns of the wild-oxen do You answer me.

כבהוֹשִׁיעֵנִי מִפִּי אַרְיֵה; וּמִקַּרְנֵי רֵמִים עֲנִיתָנִי.

<sup>23</sup>I will declare Your Name unto my brethren; in the midst of the congregation will I praise You.

כגאֲסַפְּרָה שִׁמְךָ לְאֶחָי; בְּתוֹךְ קָהָל אֲהַלְלֶךָ.

<sup>24</sup>"You that fear יהוה , praise Him; all you the seed of Ya'akov, glorify Him; and stand in awe of Him, all you the seed of Yisra'el.

כדיִרְאֵי יהוה הַלְלוּהוּ כָּל זֶרַע יַעֲקֹב כַּבְּדוּהוּ; וְגוּרוּ מִמֶּנּוּ כָּל זֶרַע יִשְׂרָאֵל.

<sup>25</sup>For He has not despised nor abhorred the lowliness of the poor; neither has He hidden His face from him; but when he cried unto Him, He heard."

כהכִּי לֹא בָזָה וְלֹא שִׁקַּץ עֱנוּת עָנִי וְלֹא הִסְתִּיר פָּנָיו מִמֶּנּוּ; וּבְשַׁוְּעוֹ אֵלָיו שָׁמֵעַ.

<sup>26</sup>From You comes my praise in the great congregation; I will pay my vows before them that fear Him.

כומֵאִתְּךָ תְהִלָּתִי: בְּקָהָל רָב נְדָרַי אֲשַׁלֵּם נֶגֶד יְרֵאָיו.

247

[27]Let the humble eat and be satisfied; let them praise יהוה that seek after Him; may your heart be quickened forever!

כז יֹאכְלוּ עֲנָוִים וְיִשְׂבָּעוּ יְהַלְלוּ יהוה דֹּרְשָׁיו; יְחִי לְבַבְכֶם לָעַד.

[28]All the ends of the earth shall remember and turn unto יהוה ; and all the kindreds of the goyim shall worship before You.

כח יִזְכְּרוּ וְיָשֻׁבוּ אֶל יהוה כָּל אַפְסֵי אָרֶץ; וְיִשְׁתַּחֲווּ לְפָנֶיךָ כָּל מִשְׁפְּחוֹת גּוֹיִם.

[29]For HaM'lukha belongs to יהוה ; and He is the ruler over the goyim.

כט כִּי לַיהוה הַמְּלוּכָה; וּמֹשֵׁל בַּגּוֹיִם.

[30]All the fat ones of the earth shall eat and worship; all they that go down to the dust shall kneel before Him, even he that cannot keep his soul alive.

ל אָכְלוּ וַיִּשְׁתַּחֲווּ כָּל דִּשְׁנֵי אֶרֶץ לְפָנָיו יִכְרְעוּ כָּל יוֹרְדֵי עָפָר; וְנַפְשׁוֹ לֹא חִיָּה.

[31]A seed shall serve him; it shall be told of Adonai unto the next generation.

לא זֶרַע יַעַבְדֶנּוּ; יְסֻפַּר לַאדֹנָי לַדּוֹר.

[32]They shall come and shall declare His righteousness unto a people that shall be born, that He has done it.

לב יָבֹאוּ וְיַגִּידוּ צִדְקָתוֹ: לְעַם נוֹלָד כִּי עָשָׂה.

# Tehillah 23 תְּהִלָּה

[1]A Mizmor of David. יהוה is my shepherd; I shall not want.

א מִזְמוֹר לְדָוִד: יהוה רֹעִי לֹא אֶחְסָר.

²He makes me to lie down in green pastures; He leads me beside the still waters.

ᵇבִּנְאוֹת דֶּשֶׁא יַרְבִּיצֵנִי; עַל מֵי מְנֻחוֹת יְנַהֲלֵנִי.

³He restores my soul; He guides me in straight paths for His Name's sake.

ᵍנַפְשִׁי יְשׁוֹבֵב; יַנְחֵנִי בְמַעְגְּלֵי צֶדֶק לְמַעַן שְׁמוֹ.

⁴Yes, even though I walk through the valley of Tzal-Mavet, I will fear no evil, for You are with me; Your rod and Your staff, they comfort me.

ᵈגַּם כִּי אֵלֵךְ בְּגֵיא צַלְמָוֶת לֹא אִירָא רָע כִּי אַתָּה עִמָּדִי; שִׁבְטְךָ וּמִשְׁעַנְתֶּךָ הֵמָּה יְנַחֲמֻנִי.

⁵You prepare a table before me in the presence of my enemies; You have anointed my head with oil; my cup overflows.

ᵉתַּעֲרֹךְ לְפָנַי שֻׁלְחָן נֶגֶד צֹרְרָי; דִּשַּׁנְתָּ בַשֶּׁמֶן רֹאשִׁי כּוֹסִי רְוָיָה.

⁶Surely goodness and compassion shall follow me all the days of my life; and I shall dwell in Beit יהוה forever.

ᵛאַךְ טוֹב וָחֶסֶד יִרְדְּפוּנִי כָּל יְמֵי חַיָּי; וְשַׁבְתִּי בְּבֵית יהוה לְאֹרֶךְ יָמִים.

# תְּהִלָּה Tehillah 24

¹A Mizmor of David. The earth belongs to יהוה , and the fullness thereof; the world, and they that dwell therein.

ᵃלְדָוִד מִזְמוֹר: לַיהוה הָאָרֶץ וּמְלוֹאָהּ; תֵּבֵל וְיֹשְׁבֵי בָהּ.

²For He has founded it upon the seas, and established it upon the floods.

ᵇכִּי הוּא עַל יַמִּים יְסָדָהּ; וְעַל נְהָרוֹת יְכוֹנְנֶהָ.

³Who shall ascend into Har יהוה ? And who shall stand in His consecrated place?

³מִי יַעֲלֶה בְהַר יהוה ; וּמִי יָקוּם בִּמְקוֹם קָדְשׁוֹ.

⁴He that has clean hands, and a pure heart; who has not taken My Name in vain, and has not sworn deceitfully.

⁴נְקִי כַפַּיִם וּבַר לֵבָב: אֲשֶׁר לֹא נָשָׂא לַשָּׁוְא נַפְשִׁי; וְלֹא נִשְׁבַּע לְמִרְמָה.

⁵He shall receive a blessing from יהוה , and tzedaka from the Elohim of his Salvation.

⁵יִשָּׂא בְרָכָה מֵאֵת יהוה ; וּצְדָקָה מֵאֱלֹהֵי יִשְׁעוֹ.

⁶Such is the generation of them that seek after Him, that seek Your face, even Ya'akov. Selah.

⁶זֶה דּוֹר דֹּרְשָׁו; מְבַקְשֵׁי פָנֶיךָ יַעֲקֹב סֶלָה.

⁷Lift up your heads, O you gates, and be lifted up, O you everlasting doors; that the Melekh HaKavod may come in.

⁷שְׂאוּ שְׁעָרִים רָאשֵׁיכֶם וְהִנָּשְׂאוּ פִּתְחֵי עוֹלָם; וְיָבוֹא מֶלֶךְ הַכָּבוֹד.

⁸"Who is this Melekh HaKavod?" " יהוה strong and mighty, יהוה mighty in battle."

⁸מִי זֶה מֶלֶךְ הַכָּבוֹד: יהוה עִזּוּז וְגִבּוֹר; יהוה גִּבּוֹר מִלְחָמָה.

⁹Lift up your heads, O you gates, yes, lift them up, O you everlasting doors; that the Melekh HaKavod may come in.

⁹שְׂאוּ שְׁעָרִים רָאשֵׁיכֶם וּשְׂאוּ פִּתְחֵי עוֹלָם; וְיָבֹא מֶלֶךְ הַכָּבוֹד.

<sup>10</sup>"Who then is this Melekh HaKavod?" " יהוה Tzeva'ot; He is Melekh HaKavod." Selah.

מִי הוּא זֶה מֶלֶךְ הַכָּבוֹד: יהוה צְבָאוֹת הוּא מֶלֶךְ הַכָּבוֹד סֶלָה.

# תְּהִלָּה 25 Tehillah

<sup>1</sup>By David. Unto You, O יהוה , do I lift up my soul.

לְדָוִד: אֵלֶיךָ יהוה נַפְשִׁי אֶשָּׂא.

<sup>2</sup>O my Elohim, in You have I trusted, let me not be ashamed; let not my enemies triumph over me.

אֱלֹהַי בְּךָ בָטַחְתִּי אַל אֵבוֹשָׁה; אַל יַעַלְצוּ אוֹיְבַי לִי.

<sup>3</sup>Yes, none that wait for You shall be ashamed; they shall be ashamed that deal treacherously without cause.

גַּם כָּל קוֶֹיךָ לֹא יֵבֹשׁוּ; יֵבֹשׁוּ הַבּוֹגְדִים רֵיקָם.

<sup>4</sup>Show me Your ways, O יהוה ; teach me Your paths.

דְּרָכֶיךָ יהוה הוֹדִיעֵנִי; אֹרְחוֹתֶיךָ לַמְּדֵנִי.

<sup>5</sup>Guide me in Your truth, and teach me; for You are the Elohim of my Salvation; for You do I wait all the day.

הַדְרִיכֵנִי בַאֲמִתֶּךָ וְלַמְּדֵנִי כִּי אַתָּה אֱלֹהֵי יִשְׁעִי; אוֹתְךָ קוִּיתִי כָּל הַיּוֹם.

<sup>6</sup>Remember, O יהוה , Your mercies and Your compassions; for they have been from of old.

זְכֹר רַחֲמֶיךָ יהוה וַחֲסָדֶיךָ כִּי מֵעוֹלָם הֵמָּה.

251

⁷Remember not the sins of my youth, nor my transgressions; according to Your compassion remember me, for Your goodness' sake, O יהוה .

ʒחַטֹּאות נְעוּרַי וּפְשָׁעַי אַל תִּזְכֹּר: כְּחַסְדְּךָ זְכָר לִי אַתָּה לְמַעַן טוּבְךָ יהוה .

⁸Good and upright is יהוה ; therefore does He instruct sinners in HaDerekh.

ʒטוֹב וְיָשָׁר יהוה ; עַל כֵּן יוֹרֶה חַטָּאִים בַּדָּרֶךְ.

⁹He guides the humble in justice; and He teaches the humble His Derekh.

ʒיַדְרֵךְ עֲנָוִים בַּמִּשְׁפָּט; וִילַמֵּד עֲנָוִים דַּרְכּוֹ.

¹⁰All the paths of יהוה are mercy and truth unto such as keep His Brit, and His testimonies.

ʒכָּל אָרְחוֹת יהוה חֶסֶד וֶאֱמֶת לְנֹצְרֵי בְרִיתוֹ וְעֵדֹתָיו.

¹¹For Your Name's sake, O יהוה , pardon my iniquity, for it is great.

ʒלְמַעַן שִׁמְךָ יהוה ; וְסָלַחְתָּ לַעֲוֹנִי כִּי רַב הוּא.

¹²What man is he that fears יהוה ? Him will He instruct in HaDerekh, which he should choose.

ʒמִי זֶה הָאִישׁ יְרֵא יהוה יוֹרֶנּוּ בְּדֶרֶךְ יִבְחָר.

¹³His soul shall abide in prosperity; and his seed shall inherit the land.

ʒנַפְשׁוֹ בְּטוֹב תָּלִין; וְזַרְעוֹ יִירַשׁ אָרֶץ.

¹⁴The counsel of יהוה is with them that fear Him; and His Brit, to make them know it.

ʒסוֹד יהוה לִירֵאָיו; וּבְרִיתוֹ לְהוֹדִיעָם.

¹⁵My eyes are ever toward יהוה ; for He will bring forth my feet out of the net.

ʒעֵינַי תָּמִיד אֶל יהוה : כִּי הוּא יוֹצִיא מֵרֶשֶׁת רַגְלָי.

<sup>16</sup>Turn unto me, and be gracious unto me; for I am solitary and afflicted.

פְּנֵה אֵלַי וְחָנֵּנִי: כִּי יָחִיד וְעָנִי אָנִי.

<sup>17</sup>The troubles of my heart are enlarged; O bring me out of my distresses.

צָרוֹת לְבָבִי הִרְחִיבוּ; מִמְּצוּקוֹתַי הוֹצִיאֵנִי.

<sup>18</sup>See my affliction and my travail; and forgive all my sins.

רְאֵה עָנְיִי וַעֲמָלִי; וְשָׂא לְכָל חַטֹּאותָי.

<sup>19</sup>Consider how many are my enemies, and the cruel hatred wherewith they hate me.

רְאֵה אֹיְבַי כִּי רָבּוּ; וְשִׂנְאַת חָמָס שְׂנֵאוּנִי.

<sup>20</sup>O keep my soul, and deliver me; let me not be ashamed, for I have taken refuge in You.

שָׁמְרָה נַפְשִׁי וְהַצִּילֵנִי; אַל אֵבוֹשׁ כִּי חָסִיתִי בָךְ.

<sup>21</sup>Let integrity and uprightness preserve me, because I wait for You.

תֹּם וָיֹשֶׁר יִצְּרוּנִי: כִּי קִוִּיתִיךָ.

<sup>22</sup>Redeem Yisra'el, O Elohim, out of all his troubles.

פְּדֵה אֱלֹהִים אֶת יִשְׂרָאֵל מִכֹּל צָרוֹתָיו.

## Tehillah 26 תְּהִלָּה

<sup>1</sup>By David. Judge me, O יהוה , for I have walked in my integrity, and I have trusted in יהוה without wavering.

לְדָוִד: שָׁפְטֵנִי יהוה כִּי אֲנִי בְּתֻמִּי הָלַכְתִּי; וּבַיהוה בָּטַחְתִּי לֹא אֶמְעָד.

²Examine me, O יהוה , and try me; test my reins and my heart.

בְּחָנֵנִי יהוה וְנַסֵּנִי; צְרוּפָה (צְרָפָה) כִלְיוֹתַי וְלִבִּי.

³For Your compassion is before my eyes; and I have walked in Your truth.

כִּי חַסְדְּךָ לְנֶגֶד עֵינָי; וְהִתְהַלַּכְתִּי בַּאֲמִתֶּךָ.

⁴I have not sat with men of falsehood; neither will I go in with dissemblers.

לֹא יָשַׁבְתִּי עִם מְתֵי שָׁוְא; וְעִם נַעֲלָמִים לֹא אָבוֹא.

⁵I hate the gathering of evil doers, and will not sit with the wicked.

שָׂנֵאתִי קְהַל מְרֵעִים; וְעִם רְשָׁעִים לֹא אֵשֵׁב.

⁶I will wash my hands in innocence; so will I encompass Your Mizbe'akh, O יהוה ,

אֶרְחַץ בְּנִקָּיוֹן כַּפָּי; וַאֲסֹבְבָה אֶת מִזְבַּחֲךָ יהוה .

⁷That I may make the voice of thanksgiving to be heard, and tell of all Your wondrous works.

לַשְׁמִעַ בְּקוֹל תּוֹדָה; וּלְסַפֵּר כָּל נִפְלְאוֹתֶיךָ.

⁸ יהוה , I love the habitation of Your House, and the place where Your Kavod dwells.

יהוה אָהַבְתִּי מְעוֹן בֵּיתֶךָ; וּמְקוֹם מִשְׁכַּן כְּבוֹדֶךָ.

⁹Gather not my soul with sinners, nor my life with men of blood;

אַל תֶּאֱסֹף עִם חַטָּאִים נַפְשִׁי; וְעִם אַנְשֵׁי דָמִים חַיָּי.

¹⁰In whose hands is craftiness, and their right hand is full of bribes.

אֲשֶׁר בִּידֵיהֶם זִמָּה; וִימִינָם מָלְאָה שֹּׁחַד.

¹¹But as for me, I will walk in my integrity; redeem me, and be gracious unto me.

יאוַאֲנִי בְּתֻמִּי אֵלֵךְ; פְּדֵנִי וְחָנֵּנִי.

¹²My foot stands in an even place; in the congregations will I bless יהוה.

יברַגְלִי עָמְדָה בְמִישׁוֹר; בְּמַקְהֵלִים אֲבָרֵךְ יהוה.

# תְּהִלָּה 27 Tehillah

¹By David. יהוה is my light and my Salvation; whom shall I fear? יהוה is the stronghold of my life; of whom shall I be afraid?

אלְדָוִד: יהוה אוֹרִי וְיִשְׁעִי מִמִּי אִירָא; יהוה מָעוֹז חַיַּי מִמִּי אֶפְחָד.

²When evil-doers came upon me to eat up my flesh, even my adversaries and my foes, they stumbled and fell.

בבִּקְרֹב עָלַי מְרֵעִים לֶאֱכֹל אֶת בְּשָׂרִי: צָרַי וְאֹיְבַי לִי; הֵמָּה כָשְׁלוּ וְנָפָלוּ.

³Though a host should encamp against me, my heart shall not fear; though war should rise up against me, even then will I be confident.

גאִם תַּחֲנֶה עָלַי מַחֲנֶה לֹא יִירָא לִבִּי: אִם תָּקוּם עָלַי מִלְחָמָה בְּזֹאת אֲנִי בוֹטֵחַ.

⁴One thing have I asked of יהוה, that will I seek after: that I may dwell in Beit יהוה all the days of my life, to behold the kindness of יהוה, and to visit early in His Heikhal.

דאַחַת שָׁאַלְתִּי מֵאֵת יהוה אוֹתָהּ אֲבַקֵּשׁ: שִׁבְתִּי בְּבֵית יהוה כָּל יְמֵי חַיַּי; לַחֲזוֹת בְּנֹעַם יהוה וּלְבַקֵּר בְּהֵיכָלוֹ.

⁵For He conceals me in His Sukka in the day of evil; He hides me in the covert of His Ohel; He lifts me up upon a Rock.

ⁿכִּי יִצְפְּנֵנִי בְּסֻכֹּה בְּיוֹם רָעָה:
יַסְתִּרֵנִי בְּסֵתֶר אָהֳלוֹ; בְּצוּר
יְרוֹמְמֵנִי.

⁶And now shall my head be lifted up above my enemies round about me; and I will offer in His Ohel sacrifices with a blast; I will sing, yes, I will sing praises unto יהוה .

ⁱוְעַתָּה יָרוּם רֹאשִׁי עַל אֹיְבַי
סְבִיבוֹתַי וְאֶזְבְּחָה בְאָהֳלוֹ
זִבְחֵי תְרוּעָה; אָשִׁירָה
וַאֲזַמְּרָה לַיהוה .

⁷Hear, O יהוה , when I call with my voice, and be gracious unto me, and answer me.

ⁱשְׁמַע יהוה קוֹלִי אֶקְרָא;
וְחָנֵּנִי וַעֲנֵנִי.

⁸In Your behalf my heart has said, "Seek My face"; Your face, O יהוה , will I seek.

ⁿלְךָ אָמַר לִבִּי בַּקְשׁוּ פָנָי;
אֶת פָּנֶיךָ יהוה אֲבַקֵּשׁ.

⁹Hide not Your face from me; put not Your servant away in anger; You have been my help; cast me not off, neither forsake me, O Elohim of my Salvation.

ⁱאַל תַּסְתֵּר פָּנֶיךָ מִמֶּנִּי אַל
תַּט בְּאַף עַבְדֶּךָ: עֶזְרָתִי
הָיִיתָ; אַל תִּטְּשֵׁנִי וְאַל
תַּעַזְבֵנִי אֱלֹהֵי יִשְׁעִי.

¹⁰For though my father and my mother have forsaken me, יהוה will take me up.

ⁱכִּי אָבִי וְאִמִּי עֲזָבוּנִי; וַיהוה
יַאַסְפֵנִי.

¹¹Teach me Your Derekh, O יהוה ; and lead me in an even path, because of them that lie in wait for me.

ⁱⁱהוֹרֵנִי יהוה דַּרְכֶּךָ: וּנְחֵנִי
בְּאֹרַח מִישׁוֹר לְמַעַן שׁוֹרְרָי.

¹²Deliver me not over unto the will of my adversaries; for false witnesses are risen up against me, and such as breathe out violence.

יבֿאַל תִּתְּנֵנִי בְּנֶפֶשׁ צָרָי: כִּי קָמוּ בִי עֵדֵי שֶׁקֶר וִיפֵחַ חָמָס.

¹³If I had not believed to look upon the goodness of יהוה in the land of the living!

יגֿלוּלֵא הֶאֱמַנְתִּי לִרְאוֹת בְּטוּב יהוה : בְּאֶרֶץ חַיִּים.

¹⁴Wait for יהוה ; be strong, and let your heart take courage; yes, wait for יהוה .

ידֿקַוֵּה אֶל יהוה : חֲזַק וְיַאֲמֵץ לִבֶּךָ; וְקַוֵּה אֶל יהוה .

# Tehillah 28 תְּהִלָּה

¹By David. Unto you, O יהוה , do I call; my Rock, be not deaf unto me; lest, if You are silent unto me, I become like them that go down into the pit.

אֿלְדָוִד אֵלֶיךָ יהוה אֶקְרָא צוּרִי אַל תֶּחֱרַשׁ מִמֶּנִּי: פֶּן תֶּחֱשֶׁה מִמֶּנִּי; וְנִמְשַׁלְתִּי עִם יוֹרְדֵי בוֹר.

²Hear the voice of my supplications, when I cry unto You, when I lift up my hands toward Your D'vir Kadosh.

בֿשְׁמַע קוֹל תַּחֲנוּנַי בְּשַׁוְּעִי אֵלֶיךָ; בְּנָשְׂאִי יָדַי אֶל דְּבִיר קָדְשֶׁךָ.

³Draw me not away with the wicked, and with the workers of iniquity; who speak shalom with their neighbors, but evil is in their hearts.

גֿאַל תִּמְשְׁכֵנִי עִם רְשָׁעִים וְעִם פֹּעֲלֵי אָוֶן: דֹּבְרֵי שָׁלוֹם עִם רֵעֵיהֶם; וְרָעָה בִּלְבָבָם.

⁴Give them according to their deeds, and according to the evil of their endeavors; give them after the work of their hands; render to them what they deserve.

תֵּן לָהֶם כְּפָעֳלָם וּכְרֹעַ מַעַלְלֵיהֶם: כְּמַעֲשֵׂה יְדֵיהֶם תֵּן לָהֶם; הָשֵׁב גְּמוּלָם לָהֶם.

⁵Because they give no heed to the works of יהוה , nor to the operation of His hands; He will break them down and not build them up.

הכִּי לֹא יָבִינוּ אֶל פְּעֻלֹּת יהוה וְאֶל מַעֲשֵׂה יָדָיו; יֶהֶרְסֵם וְלֹא יִבְנֵם.

⁶Blessed is יהוה , because He has heard the voice of my supplications.

ובָּרוּךְ יהוה : כִּי שָׁמַע קוֹל תַּחֲנוּנָי.

⁷ יהוה is my strength, and my Magen, in Him has my heart trusted, and I am helped; therefore my heart greatly rejoices, and with my song will I praise Him.

ז יהוה עֻזִּי וּמָגִנִּי בּוֹ בָטַח לִבִּי וְנֶעֱזָרְתִּי: וַיַּעֲלֹז לִבִּי; וּמִשִּׁירִי אֲהוֹדֶנּוּ.

⁸ יהוה is a strength unto them; and He is a stronghold of Salvation to His Mashi'akh.

ח יהוה עֹז לָמוֹ; וּמָעוֹז יְשׁוּעוֹת מְשִׁיחוֹ הוּא.

⁹Save Your people, and bless Your inheritance; and tend them, and carry them forever.

טהוֹשִׁיעָה אֶת עַמֶּךָ וּבָרֵךְ אֶת נַחֲלָתֶךָ; וּרְעֵם וְנַשְּׂאֵם עַד הָעוֹלָם.

# תְּהִלָּה 29 Tehillah

¹A Mizmor of David. Ascribe unto יהוה, O you sons of might, ascribe unto יהוה glory and strength.

²Ascribe unto יהוה the glory due unto His Name; worship יהוה in the beauty of Kodesh.

³The voice of יהוה is upon the waters; the Elohim of Kavod thunders, even יהוה upon many waters.

⁴The voice of יהוה is powerful; the voice of יהוה is full of majesty.

⁵The voice of יהוה breaks the cedars; yes, יהוה breaks in pieces the cedars of Levanon.

⁶He makes them also to skip like a calf; Levanon and Siryon like a young wild ox.

⁷The voice of יהוה hews out flames of fire.

⁸The voice of יהוה shakes the wilderness; יהוה shakes the wilderness of Kadesh.

אמִזְמוֹר לְדָוִד: הָבוּ לַיהוה בְּנֵי אֵלִים; הָבוּ לַיהוה כָּבוֹד וָעֹז.

בהָבוּ לַיהוה כְּבוֹד שְׁמוֹ; הִשְׁתַּחֲווּ לַיהוה בְּהַדְרַת קֹדֶשׁ.

גקוֹל יהוה עַל הַמָּיִם: אֵל הַכָּבוֹד הִרְעִים; יהוה עַל מַיִם רַבִּים.

דקוֹל יהוה בַּכֹּחַ; קוֹל יהוה בֶּהָדָר.

הקוֹל יהוה שֹׁבֵר אֲרָזִים; וַיְשַׁבֵּר יהוה אֶת אַרְזֵי הַלְּבָנוֹן.

ווַיַּרְקִידֵם כְּמוֹ עֵגֶל; לְבָנוֹן וְשִׂרְיֹן כְּמוֹ בֶן רְאֵמִים.

זקוֹל יהוה חֹצֵב; לַהֲבוֹת אֵשׁ.

חקוֹל יהוה יָחִיל מִדְבָּר; יָחִיל יהוה מִדְבַּר קָדֵשׁ.

⁹The voice of יהוה makes the hinds to calve, and strips the forests bare; and in His Heikhal all say, "Kavod!"

טקוֹל יהוה יְחוֹלֵל אַיָּלוֹת וַיֶּחֱשֹׂף יְעָרוֹת: וּבְהֵיכָלוֹ כֻּלּוֹ אֹמֵר כָּבוֹד.

¹⁰ יהוה sat enthroned at the flood; yes, יהוה sits as Melekh forever.

י יהוה לַמַּבּוּל יָשָׁב; וַיֵּשֶׁב יהוה מֶלֶךְ לְעוֹלָם.

¹¹ יהוה will give strength unto His people; יהוה will bless his people with shalom.

יא יהוה עֹז לְעַמּוֹ יִתֵּן; יהוה יְבָרֵךְ אֶת עַמּוֹ בַשָּׁלוֹם.

# Tehillah 30 תְּהִלָּה

¹A Mizmor; a Shir, at the Dedication of HaBa'it; by David.

אמִזְמוֹר: שִׁיר חֲנֻכַּת הַבַּיִת לְדָוִד.

²I will extol you, O יהוה, for You have raised me up, and have not suffered my enemies to rejoice over me.

באֲרוֹמִמְךָ יהוה כִּי דִלִּיתָנִי; וְלֹא שִׂמַּחְתָּ אֹיְבַי לִי.

³O יהוה my Elohim, I cried unto You, and You did heal me;

ג יהוה אֱלֹהָי שִׁוַּעְתִּי אֵלֶיךָ וַתִּרְפָּאֵנִי.

⁴O יהוה, You brought up my soul from She'ol; You did keep me alive, that I should not go down to the pit.

ד יהוה הֶעֱלִיתָ מִן שְׁאוֹל נַפְשִׁי; חִיִּיתַנִי מיורדי (מִיָּרְדִי) בוֹר.

⁵Sing praise unto יהוה, O you His Khasidim, and give thanks to His Kadosh Name.

הזַמְּרוּ לַיהוה חֲסִידָיו; וְהוֹדוּ לְזֵכֶר קָדְשׁוֹ.

<sup>6</sup>For His anger is but for a moment, His favor is for a life-time; weeping may tarry for the night, but rejoicing comes in the morning.

<sup>7</sup>Now I had said in my security, "I shall never be moved."

<sup>8</sup>You had established, O יהוה , in Your favor, my mountain as a stronghold. You did hide Your face; I was terrified.

<sup>9</sup>Unto You, O יהוה , did I call, and unto יהוה I made supplication:

<sup>10</sup>"What profit is there in my blood, when I go down to the pit? Shall the dust praise You? Shall it declare Your truth?

<sup>11</sup>Hear, O יהוה , and be gracious unto me; יהוה , be my helper."

<sup>12</sup>You did turn for me my mourning into dancing; You did loose my sackcloth, and gird me with gladness;

<sup>13</sup>So that my glory may sing praise to You, and not be silent; O יהוה my Elohim, I will give thanks unto You forever.

‎א כִּי רֶגַע בְּאַפּוֹ חַיִּים בִּרְצוֹנוֹ: בָּעֶרֶב יָלִין בֶּכִי; וְלַבֹּקֶר רִנָּה.

‎ז וַאֲנִי אָמַרְתִּי בְשַׁלְוִי בַּל אֶמּוֹט לְעוֹלָם.

‎ח יהוה בִּרְצוֹנְךָ הֶעֱמַדְתָּה לְהַרְרִי עֹז: הִסְתַּרְתָּ פָנֶיךָ; הָיִיתִי נִבְהָל.

‎ט אֵלֶיךָ יהוה אֶקְרָא; וְאֶל אֲדֹנָי אֶתְחַנָּן.

‎י מַה בֶּצַע בְּדָמִי בְּרִדְתִּי אֶל שָׁחַת: הֲיוֹדְךָ עָפָר; הֲיַגִּיד אֲמִתֶּךָ.

‎יא שְׁמַע יהוה וְחָנֵּנִי; יהוה הֱיֵה עֹזֵר לִי.

‎יב הָפַכְתָּ מִסְפְּדִי לְמָחוֹל לִי: פִּתַּחְתָּ שַׂקִּי; וַתְּאַזְּרֵנִי שִׂמְחָה.

‎יג לְמַעַן יְזַמֶּרְךָ כָבוֹד וְלֹא יִדֹּם: יהוה אֱלֹהַי לְעוֹלָם אוֹדֶךָ.

261

# Tehillah 31 תְּהִלָּה

<sup>1</sup>For the Leader. A Mizmor of David.

לַמְנַצֵּחַ מִזְמוֹר לְדָוִד.

<sup>2</sup>In you, O יהוה , have I taken refuge; let me never be ashamed; deliver me in Your tzedaka.

בְּךָ יהוה חָסִיתִי אַל אֵבוֹשָׁה לְעוֹלָם; בְּצִדְקָתְךָ פַלְּטֵנִי.

<sup>3</sup>Incline Your ear unto me, deliver me speedily; be to me a Rock of refuge, even a fortress of defense, to save me.

הַטֵּה אֵלַי אָזְנְךָ מְהֵרָה הַצִּילֵנִי: הֱיֵה לִי לְצוּר מָעוֹז לְבֵית מְצוּדוֹת; לְהוֹשִׁיעֵנִי.

<sup>4</sup>For You are my Rock and my fortress; therefore for Your Name's sake lead me and guide me.

כִּי סַלְעִי וּמְצוּדָתִי אָתָּה; וּלְמַעַן שִׁמְךָ תַּנְחֵנִי וּתְנַהֲלֵנִי.

<sup>5</sup>Bring me forth out of the net that they have hidden for me; for You are my stronghold.

תּוֹצִיאֵנִי מֵרֶשֶׁת זוּ טָמְנוּ לִי: כִּי אַתָּה מָעוּזִּי.

<sup>6</sup>Into Your hand I commit my spirit; You have redeemed me, O יהוה , You, El Emet.

בְּיָדְךָ אַפְקִיד רוּחִי: פָּדִיתָ אוֹתִי יהוה אֵל אֱמֶת.

<sup>7</sup>I hate them that regard lying vanities; but I trust in יהוה .

שָׂנֵאתִי הַשֹּׁמְרִים הַבְלֵי שָׁוְא; וַאֲנִי אֶל יהוה בָּטָחְתִּי.

<sup>8</sup>I will be glad and rejoice in Your compassion; for You have seen my affliction, You have taken cognizance of the troubles of my soul,

אָגִילָה וְאֶשְׂמְחָה בְּחַסְדֶּךָ: אֲשֶׁר רָאִיתָ אֶת עָנְיִי; יָדַעְתָּ בְּצָרוֹת נַפְשִׁי.

⁹And You have not given me over into the hand of the enemy; You have set my feet in a broad place.

טְוְלֹא הִסְגַּרְתַּנִי בְּיַד אוֹיֵב; הֶעֱמַדְתָּ בַמֶּרְחָב רַגְלָי.

¹⁰Be gracious unto me, O יהוה , for I am in distress; my eye wastes away with vexation, yes, my soul and my body.

יחָנֵּנִי יהוה כִּי צַר לִי: עָשְׁשָׁה בְכַעַס עֵינִי; נַפְשִׁי וּבִטְנִי.

¹¹For my life is spent in sorrow, and my years in sighing; my strength fails because of my iniquity, and my bones are wasted away.

יאכִּי כָלוּ בְיָגוֹן חַיַּי וּשְׁנוֹתַי בַּאֲנָחָה: כָּשַׁל בַּעֲוֹנִי כֹחִי; וַעֲצָמַי עָשֵׁשׁוּ.

¹²Because of all my adversaries I am become a reproach, yes, unto my neighbors exceedingly, and a dread to my acquaintance; they that see me without flee from me.

יבמִכָּל צֹרְרַי הָיִיתִי חֶרְפָּה וְלִשְׁכֵנַי מְאֹד וּפַחַד לִמְיֻדָּעָי: רֹאַי בַּחוּץ נָדְדוּ מִמֶּנִּי.

¹³I am forgotten as a dead man out of mind; I am like a useless vessel.

יגנִשְׁכַּחְתִּי כְּמֵת מִלֵּב; הָיִיתִי כִּכְלִי אֹבֵד.

¹⁴For I have heard the whispering of many, terror on every side; while they took counsel together against me, they devised to take away my life.

ידכִּי שָׁמַעְתִּי דִּבַּת רַבִּים מָגוֹר מִסָּבִיב: בְּהִוָּסְדָם יַחַד עָלַי; לָקַחַת נַפְשִׁי זָמָמוּ.

¹⁵But as for me, I have trusted in You, O יהוה ; I have said, "You are my Elohim."

טווַאֲנִי עָלֶיךָ בָטַחְתִּי יהוה ; אָמַרְתִּי אֱלֹהַי אָתָּה.

[16]My times are in Your hand; deliver me from the hand of my enemies, and from them that persecute me.

טזבְּיָדְךָ עִתֹּתָי; הַצִּילֵנִי מִיַּד אוֹיְבַי וּמֵרֹדְפָי.

[17]Make Your face to shine upon Your servant; save me in Your compassion.

יזהָאִירָה פָנֶיךָ עַל עַבְדֶּךָ; הוֹשִׁיעֵנִי בְחַסְדֶּךָ.

[18]O יהוה , let me not be ashamed, for I have called upon You; let the wicked be ashamed, let them be put to silence in She'ol.

יח יהוה אַל אֵבוֹשָׁה כִּי קְרָאתִיךָ; יֵבֹשׁוּ רְשָׁעִים יִדְּמוּ לִשְׁאוֹל.

[19]Let the lying lips be dumb, which speak arrogantly against a Tzadik, with pride and contempt.

יטתֵּאָלַמְנָה שִׂפְתֵי שָׁקֶר: הַדֹּבְרוֹת עַל צַדִּיק עָתָק בְּגַאֲוָה וָבוּז.

[20]Oh how abundant is Your goodness, which You have laid up for them that fear You; which You have wrought for them that take their refuge in You, in the sight of the sons of men!

כמָה רַב טוּבְךָ אֲשֶׁר צָפַנְתָּ לִּירֵאֶיךָ: פָּעַלְתָּ לַחֹסִים בָּךְ; נֶגֶד בְּנֵי אָדָם.

[21]You hide them in the secret place of Your presence from the plottings of man; You conceal them in a Sukka, from the strife of tongues.

כאתַּסְתִּירֵם בְּסֵתֶר פָּנֶיךָ מֵרֻכְסֵי אִישׁ: תִּצְפְּנֵם בְּסֻכָּה; מֵרִיב לְשֹׁנוֹת.

²²Blessed is יהוה ; for He has shown me His wondrous compassion in an entrenched city.

כּג בָּרוּךְ יהוה : כִּי הִפְלִיא חַסְדּוֹ לִי בְּעִיר מָצוֹר.

²³As for me, I said in my haste, "I am cut off from before Your eyes"; nevertheless, You heard the voice of my supplications when I cried unto You.

כג וַאֲנִי אָמַרְתִּי בְחָפְזִי נִגְרַזְתִּי מִנֶּגֶד עֵינֶיךָ: אָכֵן שָׁמַעְתָּ קוֹל תַּחֲנוּנַי; בְּשַׁוְּעִי אֵלֶיךָ.

²⁴O love יהוה , all you His Khasidim; יהוה preserves the faithful, and plentifully repays him that acts haughtily.

כד אֶהֱבוּ אֶת יהוה כָּל חֲסִידָיו: אֱמוּנִים נֹצֵר יהוה ; וּמְשַׁלֵּם עַל יֶתֶר עֹשֵׂה גַאֲוָה.

²⁵Be strong, and let your heart take courage, all you that wait for יהוה .

כה חִזְקוּ וְיַאֲמֵץ לְבַבְכֶם כָּל הַמְיַחֲלִים לַיהוה .

# Tehillah 32 תְּהִלָּה

¹By David. A Maskil. Happy is he whose transgression is forgiven, whose sin is pardoned.

א לְדָוִד מַשְׂכִּיל: אַשְׁרֵי נְשׂוּי פֶּשַׁע; כְּסוּי חֲטָאָה.

²Happy is the man unto whom יהוה counts not iniquity, and in whose spirit there is no guile.

ב אַשְׁרֵי אָדָם לֹא יַחְשֹׁב יהוה לוֹ עָוֺן; וְאֵין בְּרוּחוֹ רְמִיָּה.

³When I kept silence, my bones wore away through my groaning all the day long.

ג כִּי הֶחֱרַשְׁתִּי בָּלוּ עֲצָמָי בְּשַׁאֲגָתִי כָּל הַיּוֹם.

⁴For day and night Your hand was heavy upon me; my sap was turned as in the droughts of summer. Selah.

ⁿכִּי יוֹמָם וָלַיְלָה תִּכְבַּד עָלַי יָדֶךָ: נֶהְפַּךְ לְשַׁדִּי בְּחַרְבֹנֵי קַיִץ סֶלָה.

⁵I acknowledged my sin unto You, and my iniquity have I not hidden; I said, "I will make confession concerning my transgressions unto יהוה;" and You, You forgave the iniquity of my sin. Selah.

ⁿחַטָּאתִי אוֹדִיעֲךָ וַעֲוֹנִי לֹא כִסִּיתִי אָמַרְתִּי אוֹדֶה עֲלֵי פְשָׁעַי לַיהוה; וְאַתָּה נָשָׂאתָ עֲוֹן חַטָּאתִי סֶלָה.

⁶For this let every Khasid pray unto You in a time when You may be found; surely, when the great waters overflow, they will not reach unto him.

ⁿעַל זֹאת יִתְפַּלֵּל כָּל חָסִיד אֵלֶיךָ לְעֵת מְצֹא: רַק לְשֵׁטֶף מַיִם רַבִּים אֵלָיו לֹא יַגִּיעוּ.

⁷You are my hiding-place; You will preserve me from the adversary; with songs of deliverance You will encompass me about. Selah.

ⁿאַתָּה סֵתֶר לִי מִצַּר תִּצְּרֵנִי: רָנֵּי פַלֵּט; תְּסוֹבְבֵנִי סֶלָה.

⁸"I will cause you to understand, and guide you in this Derekh in which you shall go; I will give counsel, My eye being upon you."

ⁿאַשְׂכִּילְךָ וְאוֹרְךָ בְּדֶרֶךְ זוּ תֵלֵךְ; אִיעֲצָה עָלֶיךָ עֵינִי.

⁹Be not as the horse, or as the mule, which have no understanding; whose mouth must be held in with bit and bridle, that they come not near unto you.

ⁿאַל תִּהְיוּ כְּסוּס כְּפֶרֶד אֵין הָבִין: בְּמֶתֶג וָרֶסֶן עֶדְיוֹ לִבְלוֹם; בַּל קְרֹב אֵלֶיךָ.

<sup>10</sup>Many are the sorrows of the wicked; but he that trusts in יהוה , compassion encompasses him.

רַבִּים מַכְאוֹבִים לָרָשָׁע: וְהַבּוֹטֵחַ בַּיהוה חֶסֶד יְסוֹבְבֶנּוּ.

<sup>11</sup>Be glad in יהוה , and rejoice, you Tzadikim; and shout for joy, all you that are upright in heart.

שִׂמְחוּ בַיהוה וְגִילוּ צַדִּיקִים; וְהַרְנִינוּ כָּל יִשְׁרֵי לֵב.

# תְהִלָּה Tehillah 33

<sup>1</sup>Rejoice in יהוה , O you Tzadikim, praise is comely for the upright.

רַנְּנוּ צַדִּיקִים בַּיהוה ; לַיְשָׁרִים נָאוָה תְהִלָּה.

<sup>2</sup>Give thanks unto יהוה with a Kinor, sing praises unto Him with the Nevel of ten strings.

הוֹדוּ לַיהוה בְּכִנּוֹר; בְּנֵבֶל עָשׂוֹר זַמְּרוּ לוֹ.

<sup>3</sup>Sing unto Him a new song; play skilfully amid shouts of joy.

שִׁירוּ לוֹ שִׁיר חָדָשׁ; הֵיטִיבוּ נַגֵּן בִּתְרוּעָה.

<sup>4</sup>For the D'var יהוה is upright; and all His work is done in faithfulness.

כִּי יָשָׁר דְּבַר יהוה ; וְכָל מַעֲשֵׂהוּ בֶּאֱמוּנָה.

<sup>5</sup>He loves tzedaka and justice; the earth is full of the compassion of יהוה .

אֹהֵב צְדָקָה וּמִשְׁפָּט; חֶסֶד יהוה מָלְאָה הָאָרֶץ.

<sup>6</sup>By the D'var יהוה were the heavens made; and all the host of them by the breath of His mouth.

בִּדְבַר יהוה שָׁמַיִם נַעֲשׂוּ; וּבְרוּחַ פִּיו כָּל צְבָאָם.

267

<sup>7</sup>He gathers the waters of the sea together as a heap; He lays up the deeps in storehouses.

כֹּנֵס כַּנֵּד מֵי הַיָּם; נֹתֵן בְּאוֹצָרוֹת תְּהוֹמוֹת.

<sup>8</sup>Let all the earth fear יהוה ; let all the inhabitants of the world stand in awe of Him.

יִירְאוּ מֵיהוה כָּל הָאָרֶץ; מִמֶּנּוּ יָגוּרוּ כָּל יֹשְׁבֵי תֵבֵל.

<sup>9</sup>For He spoke, and it was; He commanded, and it stood.

כִּי הוּא אָמַר וַיֶּהִי; הוּא צִוָּה וַיַּעֲמֹד.

<sup>10</sup> יהוה brings the counsel of the goyim to nought; He makes the thoughts of the peoples to be of no effect.

יהוה הֵפִיר עֲצַת גּוֹיִם; הֵנִיא מַחְשְׁבוֹת עַמִּים.

<sup>11</sup>The counsel of יהוה stands forever, the thoughts of His heart to all generations.

עֲצַת יהוה לְעוֹלָם תַּעֲמֹד; מַחְשְׁבוֹת לִבּוֹ לְדֹר וָדֹר.

<sup>12</sup>Happy is the nation whose Elohim is יהוה ; the people whom He has chosen for His own inheritance.

אַשְׁרֵי הַגּוֹי אֲשֶׁר יהוה אֱלֹהָיו; הָעָם בָּחַר לְנַחֲלָה לוֹ.

<sup>13</sup> יהוה looks from heaven; He beholds all the sons of men;

מִשָּׁמַיִם הִבִּיט יהוה ; רָאָה אֶת כָּל בְּנֵי הָאָדָם.

<sup>14</sup>From the place of His habitation He looks intently upon all the inhabitants of the earth;

מִמְּכוֹן שִׁבְתּוֹ הִשְׁגִּיחַ אֶל כָּל יֹשְׁבֵי הָאָרֶץ.

<sup>15</sup>He that fashions the hearts of them all, that considers all their doings.

הַיֹּצֵר יַחַד לִבָּם; הַמֵּבִין אֶל כָּל מַעֲשֵׂיהֶם.

<sup>16</sup>HaMelekh is not saved by the multitude of a host; a mighty man is not delivered by great strength.

טז אֵין הַמֶּלֶךְ נוֹשָׁע בְּרָב־חָיִל; גִּבּוֹר לֹא יִנָּצֵל בְּרָב־כֹּחַ.

<sup>17</sup>A horse is a vain thing for safety; neither does it afford escape by its great strength.

יז שֶׁקֶר הַסּוּס לִתְשׁוּעָה; וּבְרֹב חֵילוֹ לֹא יְמַלֵּט.

<sup>18</sup>Behold, the eye of יהוה is toward them that fear Him, toward them that wait for His compassion;

יח הִנֵּה עֵין יהוה אֶל־יְרֵאָיו; לַמְיַחֲלִים לְחַסְדּוֹ.

<sup>19</sup>To deliver their soul from death, and to keep them alive in famine.

יט לְהַצִּיל מִמָּוֶת נַפְשָׁם; וּלְחַיּוֹתָם בָּרָעָב.

<sup>20</sup>Our soul has waited for יהוה ; He is our help and our Magen.

כ נַפְשֵׁנוּ חִכְּתָה לַיהוה ; עֶזְרֵנוּ וּמָגִנֵּנוּ הוּא.

<sup>21</sup>For in Him does our heart rejoice, because we have trusted in His Kadosh Name.

כא כִּי־בוֹ יִשְׂמַח לִבֵּנוּ: כִּי בְשֵׁם קָדְשׁוֹ בָטָחְנוּ.

<sup>22</sup>Let Your mercy, O יהוה , be upon us, according as we have waited for You.

כב יְהִי־חַסְדְּךָ יהוה עָלֵינוּ: כַּאֲשֶׁר יִחַלְנוּ לָךְ.

# Tehillah 34 תְּהִלָּה

<sup>1</sup>By David; when he changed his demeanor before Avimelekh, who drove him away, and he departed.

א לְדָוִד בְּשַׁנּוֹתוֹ אֶת־טַעְמוֹ לִפְנֵי אֲבִימֶלֶךְ; וַיְגָרְשֵׁהוּ וַיֵּלַךְ.

269

²I will bless יהוה at all times; His praise shall continually be in my mouth.

³My soul shall glory in יהוה ; the humble shall hear thereof, and be glad.

⁴O magnify יהוה with me, and let us exalt His Name together.

⁵I sought יהוה , and He answered me, and delivered me from all my fears.

⁶They looked unto Him, and were radiant; and their faces shall never be abashed.

⁷This poor man cried, and יהוה heard, and saved him out of all his troubles.

⁸Malakh יהוה encamps round about them that fear Him, and delivers them.

⁹O taste and see that יהוה is good; happy is the man that takes refuge in Him.

¹⁰O fear יהוה , you His K'doshim; for there is no want to them that fear Him.

¹¹The young lions do lack, and suffer hunger; but they that seek יהוה want not any good thing.

ᵇאֲבָרְכָה אֶת יהוה בְּכָל עֵת; תָּמִיד תְּהִלָּתוֹ בְּפִי.

ᵍבַּיהוה תִּתְהַלֵּל נַפְשִׁי; יִשְׁמְעוּ עֲנָוִים וְיִשְׂמָחוּ.

ᵈגַּדְּלוּ לַיהוה אִתִּי; וּנְרוֹמְמָה שְׁמוֹ יַחְדָּו.

ʰדָּרַשְׁתִּי אֶת יהוה וְעָנָנִי; וּמִכָּל מְגוּרוֹתַי הִצִּילָנִי.

ʷהִבִּיטוּ אֵלָיו וְנָהָרוּ; וּפְנֵיהֶם אַל יֶחְפָּרוּ.

ᶻזֶה עָנִי קָרָא וַיהוה שָׁמֵעַ; וּמִכָּל צָרוֹתָיו הוֹשִׁיעוֹ.

ᶜחֹנֶה מַלְאַךְ יהוה סָבִיב לִירֵאָיו; וַיְחַלְּצֵם.

ᵗטַעֲמוּ וּרְאוּ כִּי טוֹב יהוה ; אַשְׁרֵי הַגֶּבֶר יֶחֱסֶה בּוֹ.

ʸיְראוּ אֶת יהוה קְדֹשָׁיו: כִּי אֵין מַחְסוֹר לִירֵאָיו.

ᵏכְּפִירִים רָשׁוּ וְרָעֵבוּ; וְדֹרְשֵׁי יהוה לֹא יַחְסְרוּ כָל טוֹב.

¹²Come, you children, hearken unto me; I will teach you the fear of יהוה.

יבלְכוּ בָנִים שִׁמְעוּ לִי; יִרְאַת יהוה אֲלַמֶּדְכֶם.

¹³Who is the man that desires life, and loves days, that he may see good therein?

יגמִי הָאִישׁ הֶחָפֵץ חַיִּים; אֹהֵב יָמִים לִרְאוֹת טוֹב.

¹⁴Keep your tongue from evil, and your lips from speaking guile.

ידנְצֹר לְשׁוֹנְךָ מֵרָע; וּשְׂפָתֶיךָ מִדַּבֵּר מִרְמָה.

¹⁵Depart from evil, and do good; seek shalom, and pursue it.

טוסוּר מֵרָע וַעֲשֵׂה טוֹב; בַּקֵּשׁ שָׁלוֹם וְרָדְפֵהוּ.

¹⁶The eyes of יהוה are toward the Tzadikim, and His ears are open unto their cry.

טזעֵינֵי יהוה אֶל צַדִּיקִים; וְאָזְנָיו אֶל שַׁוְעָתָם.

¹⁷The face of יהוה is against them that do evil, to cut off the remembrance of them from the earth.

יזפְּנֵי יהוה בְּעֹשֵׂי רָע; לְהַכְרִית מֵאֶרֶץ זִכְרָם.

¹⁸They cried, and יהוה heard, and delivered them out of all their troubles.

יחצָעֲקוּ וַיהוה שָׁמֵעַ; וּמִכָּל צָרוֹתָם הִצִּילָם.

¹⁹ יהוה is nigh unto them that are of a broken heart, and saves such as are of a contrite spirit.

יטקָרוֹב יהוה לְנִשְׁבְּרֵי לֵב; וְאֶת דַּכְּאֵי רוּחַ יוֹשִׁיעַ.

²⁰Many are the adversities of a Tzadik, but יהוה delivers him out of them all.

כרַבּוֹת רָעוֹת צַדִּיק; וּמִכֻּלָּם יַצִּילֶנּוּ יהוה.

271

²¹He keeps all his bones; not one of them is broken.

כא שֹׁמֵר כָּל עַצְמוֹתָיו; אַחַת מֵהֵנָּה לֹא נִשְׁבָּרָה.

²²Evil shall kill the wicked; and they that hate a Tzadik shall be held guilty.

כב תְּמוֹתֵת רָשָׁע רָעָה; וְשֹׂנְאֵי צַדִּיק יֶאְשָׁמוּ.

²³יהוה redeems the soul of His servants; and none of them that take refuge in Him shall be held guilty.

כג פֹּדֶה יהוה נֶפֶשׁ עֲבָדָיו; וְלֹא יֶאְשְׁמוּ כָּל הַחֹסִים בּוֹ.

# תְּהִלָּה Tehillah 35

¹A Mizmor of David. Strive, O יהוה , with them that strive with me; fight against them that fight against me.

א לְדָוִד: רִיבָה יהוה אֶת יְרִיבַי; לְחַם אֶת לֹחֲמָי.

²Take hold of shield and buckler, and rise up to my help.

ב הַחֲזֵק מָגֵן וְצִנָּה; וְקוּמָה בְּעֶזְרָתִי.

³Draw out also the spear, and the battle-axe, against them that pursue me; say unto my soul, "I am your Salvation."

ג וְהָרֵק חֲנִית וּסְגֹר לִקְרַאת רֹדְפָי; אֱמֹר לְנַפְשִׁי יְשֻׁעָתֵךְ אָנִי.

⁴Let them be ashamed and brought to confusion that seek after my soul; let them be turned back and be abashed that devise my hurt.

ד יֵבֹשׁוּ וְיִכָּלְמוּ מְבַקְשֵׁי נַפְשִׁי: יִסֹּגוּ אָחוֹר וְיַחְפְּרוּ חֹשְׁבֵי רָעָתִי.

⁵Let them be as chaff before the wind, Malakh יהוה thrusting them.

ה יִהְיוּ כְּמֹץ לִפְנֵי רוּחַ; וּמַלְאַךְ יהוה דּוֹחֶה.

[6]Let their way be dark and slippery, Malakh יהוה pursuing them.

יְהִי דַרְכָּם חֹשֶׁךְ וַחֲלַקְלַקֹּת; וּמַלְאַךְ יהוה רֹדְפָם.

[7]For without cause have they hidden for me the pit, even their net, without cause have they digged for my soul.

כִּי חִנָּם טָמְנוּ לִי שַׁחַת רִשְׁתָּם; חִנָּם חָפְרוּ לְנַפְשִׁי.

[8]Let destruction come upon him unawares; and let his net that he has hidden catch himself; with destruction let him fall therein.

תְּבוֹאֵהוּ שׁוֹאָה לֹא יֵדָע: וְרִשְׁתּוֹ אֲשֶׁר טָמַן תִּלְכְּדוֹ; בְּשׁוֹאָה יִפָּל בָּהּ.

[9]And my soul shall be joyful in יהוה ; it shall rejoice in His Salvation.

וְנַפְשִׁי תָּגִיל בַּיהוה ; תָּשִׂישׂ בִּישׁוּעָתוֹ.

[10]All my bones shall say, " יהוה , who is like unto You, who delivers the poor from him that is too strong for him, yes, the poor and the needy from him that spoils him?"

כָּל עַצְמוֹתַי תֹּאמַרְנָה יהוה מִי כָמוֹךָ: מַצִּיל עָנִי מֵחָזָק מִמֶּנּוּ; וְעָנִי וְאֶבְיוֹן מִגֹּזְלוֹ.

[11]Unrighteous witnesses rise up; they ask me of things that I know not.

יְקוּמוּן עֵדֵי חָמָס: אֲשֶׁר לֹא יָדַעְתִּי יִשְׁאָלוּנִי.

[12]They repay me evil for good; bereavement is come to my soul.

יְשַׁלְּמוּנִי רָעָה תַּחַת טוֹבָה: שְׁכוֹל לְנַפְשִׁי.

273

<sup>13</sup>But as for me, when they were sick, my clothing was sackcloth, I afflicted my soul with fasting; and my prayer, may it return into my own bosom.

יגוַאֲנִי בַּחֲלוֹתָם לְבוּשִׁי שָׂק עִנֵּיתִי בַצּוֹם נַפְשִׁי; וּתְפִלָּתִי עַל חֵיקִי תָשׁוּב.

<sup>14</sup>I went about as though it had been my friend or my brother; I bowed down mournful, as one that mourns for his mother.

ידכְּרֵעַ כְּאָח לִי הִתְהַלָּכְתִּי; כַּאֲבֶל אֵם קֹדֵר שַׁחוֹתִי.

<sup>15</sup>But when I halt they rejoice, and gather themselves together; the abjects gather themselves together against me, and those whom I know not; they tear me, and cease not;

טווּבְצַלְעִי שָׂמְחוּ וְנֶאֱסָפוּ; נֶאֶסְפוּ עָלַי נֵכִים וְלֹא יָדַעְתִּי, קָרְעוּ וְלֹא דָמּוּ.

<sup>16</sup>With the profanest mockeries of backbiting they gnash at me with their teeth.

טזבְּחַנְפֵי לַעֲגֵי מָעוֹג חָרֹק עָלַי שִׁנֵּימוֹ.

<sup>17</sup>Adonai, how long will You look on? Rescue my soul from their destructions, my only one from the lions.

יזאֲדֹנָי כַּמָּה תִּרְאֶה: הָשִׁיבָה נַפְשִׁי מִשֹּׁאֵיהֶם; מִכְּפִירִים יְחִידָתִי.

<sup>18</sup>I will give You thanks in the great congregation; I will praise You among a numerous people.

יחאוֹדְךָ בְּקָהָל רָב; בְּעַם עָצוּם אֲהַלְלֶךָּ.

<sup>19</sup>Let not them that are wrongfully my enemies rejoice over me; neither let them wink with the eye that hate me without a cause.

יט‏אַל יִשְׂמְחוּ לִי אֹיְבַי שֶׁקֶר; שֹׂנְאַי חִנָּם יִקְרְצוּ עָיִן.

<sup>20</sup>For they speak not shalom; but they devise deceitful matters against them that are quiet in the land.

כ‏כִּי לֹא שָׁלוֹם יְדַבֵּרוּ: וְעַל רִגְעֵי אֶרֶץ דִּבְרֵי מִרְמוֹת יַחֲשֹׁבוּן.

<sup>21</sup>Yes, they open their mouth wide against me; they say, "Aha, aha, our eye has seen it."

כא‏וַיַּרְחִיבוּ עָלַי פִּיהֶם: אָמְרוּ הֶאָח הֶאָח; רָאֲתָה עֵינֵנוּ.

<sup>22</sup>You have seen, O יהוה ; keep not silence; O Adonai, be not far from me.

כב‏רָאִיתָה יהוה אַל תֶּחֱרַשׁ; אֲדֹנָי אַל תִּרְחַק מִמֶּנִּי.

<sup>23</sup>Rouse Yourself, and awake to my judgment, even unto my cause, my Elohim and Adonai.

כג‏הָעִירָה וְהָקִיצָה לְמִשְׁפָּטִי; אֱלֹהַי וַאדֹנָי לְרִיבִי.

<sup>24</sup>Judge me, O יהוה my Elohim, according to Your righteousness; and let them not rejoice over me.

כד‏שָׁפְטֵנִי כְצִדְקְךָ יהוה אֱלֹהָי; וְאַל יִשְׂמְחוּ לִי.

<sup>25</sup>Let them not say in their heart, "Aha, we have our desire"; let them not say, "We have swallowed him up."

כה‏אַל יֹאמְרוּ בְלִבָּם הֶאָח נַפְשֵׁנוּ; אַל יֹאמְרוּ בִּלַּעֲנוּהוּ.

²⁶Let them be ashamed and abashed together that rejoice at my hurt; let them be clothed with shame and confusion that magnify themselves against me.

כּוֹיֵבֹשׁוּ וְיַחְפְּרוּ יַחְדָּו שְׂמֵחֵי רָעָתִי: יִלְבְּשׁוּ בֹשֶׁת וּכְלִמָּה הַמַּגְדִּילִים עָלָי.

²⁷Let them shout for joy, and be glad, that delight in my righteousness; yes, let them say continually, "Magnified is יהוה , who delights in the shalom of His servant."

כּוֹיָרֹנּוּ וְיִשְׂמְחוּ חֲפֵצֵי צִדְקִי: וְיֹאמְרוּ תָמִיד יִגְדַּל יהוה ; הֶחָפֵץ שְׁלוֹם עַבְדּוֹ.

²⁸And my tongue shall speak of Your Tzedaka, and of Your praise all the day.

כּחוּלְשׁוֹנִי תֶּהְגֶּה צִדְקֶךָ; כָּל הַיּוֹם תְּהִלָּתֶךָ.

# תְּהִלָּה Tehillah 36

¹For the Leader. By David, the servant of יהוה .

אלַמְנַצֵּחַ לְעֶבֶד יהוה לְדָוִד.

²Transgression speaks to the wicked; in the depth of my heart, there is no fear of Elohim before his eyes.

בנְאֻם פֶּשַׁע לָרָשָׁע בְּקֶרֶב לִבִּי; אֵין פַּחַד אֱלֹהִים לְנֶגֶד עֵינָיו.

³For it flatters him in his eyes, until his iniquity is found, and he is hated.

גכִּי הֶחֱלִיק אֵלָיו בְּעֵינָיו; לִמְצֹא עֲוֹנוֹ לִשְׂנֹא.

⁴The words of his mouth are iniquity and deceit; he has left off to be wise, to do good.

דדִּבְרֵי פִיו אָוֶן וּמִרְמָה; חָדַל לְהַשְׂכִּיל לְהֵיטִיב.

276

<sup>5</sup>He devises iniquity upon his bed; he sets himself in a way that is not good; he abhors not evil.

הֿאָוֶן יַחְשֹׁב עַל מִשְׁכָּבוֹ: יִתְיַצֵּב עַל דֶּרֶךְ לֹא טוֹב; רָע לֹא יִמְאָס.

<sup>6</sup>Your compassion, O יהוה , is in the heavens; Your faithfulness reaches unto the skies.

וֿ יהוה בְּהַשָּׁמַיִם חַסְדֶּךָ; אֱמוּנָתְךָ עַד שְׁחָקִים.

<sup>7</sup>Your righteousness is like the mighty mountains; Your judgments are like the great deep; man and beast You preserve, O יהוה .

זֿצִדְקָתְךָ כְּהַרְרֵי אֵל מִשְׁפָּטֶיךָ תְּהוֹם רַבָּה; אָדָם וּבְהֵמָה תוֹשִׁיעַ יהוה .

<sup>8</sup>How precious is Your compassion, O Elohim! and the children of men take refuge in the shadow of Your wings.

חֿמַה יָּקָר חַסְדְּךָ אֱלֹהִים: וּבְנֵי אָדָם בְּצֵל כְּנָפֶיךָ יֶחֱסָיוּן.

<sup>9</sup>They are abundantly satisfied with the abundance of Your House; and You make them drink of the river of Your pleasures.

טֿיִרְוְיֻן מִדֶּשֶׁן בֵּיתֶךָ; וְנַחַל עֲדָנֶיךָ תַשְׁקֵם.

<sup>10</sup>For with You is the fountain of Khayim; in Your light do we see light.

יֿכִּי עִמְּךָ מְקוֹר חַיִּים; בְּאוֹרְךָ נִרְאֶה אוֹר.

<sup>11</sup>O continue Your compassion unto them that know You; and Your tzedaka to the upright in heart.

יאֿמְשֹׁךְ חַסְדְּךָ לְיֹדְעֶיךָ; וְצִדְקָתְךָ לְיִשְׁרֵי לֵב.

277

¹²Let not the foot of pride overtake me, and let not the hand of the wicked drive me away.

יבאַל תְּבוֹאֵנִי רֶגֶל גַּאֲוָה; וְיַד רְשָׁעִים אַל תְּנִדֵנִי.

¹³There are the workers of iniquity fallen; they are thrust down, and are not able to rise.

יגשָׁם נָפְלוּ פֹּעֲלֵי אָוֶן; דֹּחוּ וְלֹא יָכְלוּ קוּם.

# תְּהִלָּה 37 Tehillah

¹By David. Fret not yourself because of evil-doers, neither be envious against them that work iniquity.

אלְדָוִד: אַל תִּתְחַר בַּמְּרֵעִים; אַל תְּקַנֵּא בְּעֹשֵׂי עַוְלָה.

²For they shall soon wither like the grass, and fade as the green herb.

בכִּי כֶחָצִיר מְהֵרָה יִמָּלוּ; וּכְיֶרֶק דֶּשֶׁא יִבּוֹלוּן.

³Trust in יהוה , and do good; dwell in the land, and cherish faithfulness.

גבְּטַח בַּיהוה וַעֲשֵׂה טוֹב; שְׁכָן אֶרֶץ וּרְעֵה אֱמוּנָה.

⁴So shall you delight yourself in יהוה ; and He shall give you the petitions of your heart.

דוְהִתְעַנַּג עַל יהוה ; וְיִתֶּן לְךָ מִשְׁאֲלֹת לִבֶּךָ.

⁵Commit your way unto יהוה ; trust also in Him, and He will bring it to pass.

הגּוֹל עַל יהוה דַּרְכֶּךָ; וּבְטַח עָלָיו וְהוּא יַעֲשֶׂה.

⁶And He will make your righteousness to go forth as the light, and your right as the noonday.

ווְהוֹצִיא כָאוֹר צִדְקֶךָ; וּמִשְׁפָּטֶךָ כַּצָּהֳרָיִם.

[7]Resign yourself unto יהוה , and wait patiently for Him; fret not yourself because of him who prospers in his way, because of the man who brings wicked devices to pass.

דּוֹם לַיהוה וְהִתְחוֹלֵל לוֹ: אַל תִּתְחַר בְּמַצְלִיחַ דַּרְכּוֹ; בְּאִישׁ עֹשֶׂה מְזִמּוֹת.

[8]Cease from anger, and forsake wrath; fret not yourself, it tends only to evil-doing.

הֶרֶף מֵאַף וַעֲזֹב חֵמָה; אַל תִּתְחַר אַךְ לְהָרֵעַ.

[9]For evil-doers shall be cut off; but those that wait for יהוה , they shall inherit the earth.

כִּי מְרֵעִים יִכָּרֵתוּן; וְקֹוֵי יהוה הֵמָּה יִירְשׁוּ אָרֶץ.

[10]And yet a little while, and there will be no more wicked; yes, you shall look well at his place, and he will not exist.

וְעוֹד מְעַט וְאֵין רָשָׁע; וְהִתְבּוֹנַנְתָּ עַל מְקוֹמוֹ וְאֵינֶנּוּ.

[11]But the humble shall inherit the earth, and delight themselves in the abundance of shalom.

וַעֲנָוִים יִירְשׁוּ אָרֶץ; וְהִתְעַנְּגוּ עַל רֹב שָׁלוֹם.

[12]The wicked plots against HaTzadik, and gnashes at him with his teeth.

זֹמֵם רָשָׁע לַצַּדִּיק; וְחֹרֵק עָלָיו שִׁנָּיו.

[13]Adonai does laugh at him; for He sees that his day is coming.

אֲדֹנָי יִשְׂחַק לוֹ: כִּי רָאָה כִּי יָבֹא יוֹמוֹ.

[14]The wicked have drawn out the sword, and have bent their bow; to cast down the poor and needy, to slay such as are upright in HaDerekh;

חֶרֶב פָּתְחוּ רְשָׁעִים וְדָרְכוּ קַשְׁתָּם: לְהַפִּיל עָנִי וְאֶבְיוֹן; לִטְבוֹחַ יִשְׁרֵי דָרֶךְ.

[15]Their sword shall enter into their own heart, and their bows shall be broken.

חַרְבָּם תָּבוֹא בְלִבָּם; וְקַשְּׁתוֹתָם תִּשָּׁבַרְנָה.

[16]Better is a little that HaTzadik has than the abundance of many wicked.

טוֹב מְעַט לַצַּדִּיק מֵהֲמוֹן רְשָׁעִים רַבִּים.

[17]For the arms of the wicked shall be broken; but יהוה upholds the Tzadikim.

כִּי זְרוֹעוֹת רְשָׁעִים תִּשָּׁבַרְנָה; וְסוֹמֵךְ צַדִּיקִים יהוה.

[18] יהוה knows the days of them that are wholehearted; and their inheritance shall be forever.

יוֹדֵעַ יהוה יְמֵי תְמִימִם; וְנַחֲלָתָם לְעוֹלָם תִּהְיֶה.

[19]They shall not be ashamed in the time of evil; and in the days of famine they shall be satisfied.

לֹא יֵבֹשׁוּ בְּעֵת רָעָה; וּבִימֵי רְעָבוֹן יִשְׂבָּעוּ.

[20]For the wicked shall perish, and the enemies of יהוה shall be as the fat of lambs; they shall pass away in smoke, they shall pass away.

כִּי רְשָׁעִים יֹאבֵדוּ וְאֹיְבֵי יהוה כִּיקַר כָּרִים; כָּלוּ בֶעָשָׁן כָּלוּ.

[21]The wicked borrows, and pays not; but a Tzadik deals graciously, and gives.

לֹוֶה רָשָׁע וְלֹא יְשַׁלֵּם; וְצַדִּיק חוֹנֵן וְנוֹתֵן.

280

<sup>22</sup>For such as are blessed of Him shall inherit the earth; and they that are cursed of Him shall be cut off.

כבכִּי מְבֹרָכָיו יִירְשׁוּ אָרֶץ; וּמְקֻלָּלָיו יִכָּרֵתוּ.

<sup>23</sup>It is of יהוה that a man's goings are established; and He delighted in his way.

כגמֵיהוה מִצְעֲדֵי גֶבֶר כּוֹנָנוּ; וְדַרְכּוֹ יֶחְפָּץ.

<sup>24</sup>Though he falls, he shall not be utterly cast down; for יהוה upholds his hand.

כדכִּי יִפֹּל לֹא יוּטָל: כִּי יהוה סוֹמֵךְ יָדוֹ.

<sup>25</sup>I have been young, and now am old; yet have I not seen a Tzadik forsaken, nor his seed begging for bread.

כהנַעַר הָיִיתִי גַּם זָקַנְתִּי: וְלֹא רָאִיתִי צַדִּיק נֶעֱזָב; וְזַרְעוֹ מְבַקֶּשׁ לָחֶם.

<sup>26</sup>All the day long he deals graciously, and lends; and his seed is blessed.

כוכָּל הַיּוֹם חוֹנֵן וּמַלְוֶה; וְזַרְעוֹ לִבְרָכָה.

<sup>27</sup>Depart from evil, and do good; and dwell for evermore.

כזסוּר מֵרָע וַעֲשֵׂה טוֹב; וּשְׁכֹן לְעוֹלָם.

<sup>28</sup>For יהוה loves justice, and forsakes not His Khasidim; they are preserved forever; but the seed of the wicked shall be cut off.

כחכִּי יהוה אֹהֵב מִשְׁפָּט וְלֹא יַעֲזֹב אֶת חֲסִידָיו לְעוֹלָם נִשְׁמָרוּ; וְזֶרַע רְשָׁעִים נִכְרָת.

<sup>29</sup>The Tzadikim shall inherit the earth, and dwell therein forever.

כטצַדִּיקִים יִירְשׁוּ אָרֶץ; וְיִשְׁכְּנוּ לָעַד עָלֶיהָ.

<sup>30</sup>The mouth of a Tzadik utters wisdom, and his tongue speaks justice.

לפִּי צַדִּיק יֶהְגֶּה חָכְמָה; וּלְשׁוֹנוֹ תְּדַבֵּר מִשְׁפָּט.

³¹The Torah of his Elohim is in his heart; none of his steps slide.

תּוֹרַת אֱלֹהָיו בְּלִבּוֹ; לֹא תִמְעַד אֲשֻׁרָיו.

³²The wicked watches the righteous, and seeks to slay him.

צוֹפֶה רָשָׁע לַצַּדִּיק; וּמְבַקֵּשׁ לַהֲמִיתוֹ.

³³ יהוה will not leave him in his hand, nor suffer him to be condemned when he is judged.

יְהוָה לֹא יַעַזְבֶנּוּ בְיָדוֹ; וְלֹא יַרְשִׁיעֶנּוּ בְּהִשָּׁפְטוֹ.

³⁴Wait for יהוה, and keep His Derekh, and He will exalt you to inherit the earth; when the wicked are cut off, you shall see it.

קַוֵּה אֶל יהוה וּשְׁמֹר דַּרְכּוֹ וִירוֹמִמְךָ לָרֶשֶׁת אָרֶץ; בְּהִכָּרֵת רְשָׁעִים תִּרְאֶה.

³⁵I have seen the wicked in great power, and spreading himself like an evergreen tree in its native soil.

רָאִיתִי רָשָׁע עָרִיץ; וּמִתְעָרֶה כְּאֶזְרָח רַעֲנָן.

³⁶But one passed by, and, lo, he was not; yes, I sought him, but he could not be found.

וַיַּעֲבֹר וְהִנֵּה אֵינֶנּוּ; וָאֲבַקְשֵׁהוּ וְלֹא נִמְצָא.

³⁷Mark the man of integrity, and behold the upright; for there is a future for the man of shalom.

שְׁמָר תָּם וּרְאֵה יָשָׁר: כִּי אַחֲרִית לְאִישׁ שָׁלוֹם.

³⁸But transgressors shall be destroyed together; the future of the wicked shall be cut off.

וּפֹשְׁעִים נִשְׁמְדוּ יַחְדָּו; אַחֲרִית רְשָׁעִים נִכְרָתָה.

³⁹But the Salvation of the Tzadikim is from יהוה ; He is their stronghold in the time of trouble.

לטוּתְשׁוּעַת צַדִּיקִים מֵיהוה; מָעוּזָּם בְּעֵת צָרָה.

⁴⁰And יהוה helps them, and delivers them; He delivers them from the wicked, and saves them, because they have taken refuge in Him.

מוַיַּעְזְרֵם יהוה וַיְפַלְּטֵם: יְפַלְּטֵם מֵרְשָׁעִים וְיוֹשִׁיעֵם כִּי חָסוּ בוֹ.

# תְּהִלָּה Tehillah 38

¹A Mizmor of David, to make memorial.

אמִזְמוֹר לְדָוִד לְהַזְכִּיר.

²O יהוה , rebuke me not in Your anger; neither chasten me in Your wrath.

ב יהוה אַל בְּקֶצְפְּךָ תוֹכִיחֵנִי; וּבַחֲמָתְךָ תְיַסְּרֵנִי.

³For Your arrows are gone deep into me, and Your hand is come down upon me.

גכִּי חִצֶּיךָ נִחֲתוּ בִי; וַתִּנְחַת עָלַי יָדֶךָ.

⁴There is no soundness in my flesh because of Your indignation; neither is there any health in my bones because of my sin.

דאֵין מְתֹם בִּבְשָׂרִי מִפְּנֵי זַעְמֶךָ; אֵין שָׁלוֹם בַּעֲצָמַי מִפְּנֵי חַטָּאתִי.

⁵For my iniquities are gone over my head; as a heavy burden they are too heavy for me.

הכִּי עֲוֹנֹתַי עָבְרוּ רֹאשִׁי; כְּמַשָּׂא כָבֵד יִכְבְּדוּ מִמֶּנִּי.

⁶My wounds are noisome, they fester, because of my foolishness.

והִבְאִישׁוּ נָמַקּוּ חַבּוּרֹתָי: מִפְּנֵי אִוַּלְתִּי.

<sup>7</sup>I am bent and bowed down greatly; I go mourning all the day.

נַעֲוֵיתִי שַׁחֹתִי עַד מְאֹד; כָּל הַיּוֹם קֹדֵר הִלָּכְתִּי.

<sup>8</sup>For my loins are filled with burning; and there is no soundness in my flesh.

כִּי כְסָלַי מָלְאוּ נִקְלֶה; וְאֵין מְתֹם בִּבְשָׂרִי.

<sup>9</sup>I am benumbed and sore crushed; I groan by reason of the moaning of my heart.

נְפוּגוֹתִי וְנִדְכֵּיתִי עַד מְאֹד; שָׁאַגְתִּי מִנַּהֲמַת לִבִּי.

<sup>10</sup>Adonai, all my desire is before You; and my sighing is not hidden from You.

אֲדֹנָי נֶגְדְּךָ כָל תַּאֲוָתִי; וְאַנְחָתִי מִמְּךָ לֹא נִסְתָּרָה.

<sup>11</sup>My heart flutters, my strength fails me; as for the light of my eyes, it also is gone from me.

לִבִּי סְחַרְחַר עֲזָבַנִי כֹחִי; וְאוֹר עֵינַי גַּם הֵם אֵין אִתִּי.

<sup>12</sup>My friends and my companions stand aloof from my plague; and my kinsmen stand afar off.

אֹהֲבַי וְרֵעַי מִנֶּגֶד נִגְעִי יַעֲמֹדוּ; וּקְרוֹבַי מֵרָחֹק עָמָדוּ.

<sup>13</sup>They also that seek after my life lay snares for me; and they that seek my hurt speak crafty devices, and utter deceits all the day.

וַיְנַקְשׁוּ מְבַקְשֵׁי נַפְשִׁי וְדֹרְשֵׁי רָעָתִי דִּבְּרוּ הַוּוֹת; וּמִרְמוֹת כָּל הַיּוֹם יֶהְגּוּ.

<sup>14</sup>But I am as a deaf man, I hear not; and I am as a dumb man that opens not his mouth.

וַאֲנִי כְחֵרֵשׁ לֹא אֶשְׁמָע; וּכְאִלֵּם לֹא יִפְתַּח פִּיו.

<sup>15</sup>Yes, I am become as a man that hears not, and in whose mouth are no arguments.

וָאֱהִי כְּאִישׁ אֲשֶׁר לֹא שֹׁמֵעַ; וְאֵין בְּפִיו תּוֹכָחוֹת.

<sup>16</sup>For in You, O יהוה , do I hope; You will answer, O Adonai, my Elohim.

טזכִּי לְךָ יהוה הוֹחָלְתִּי; אַתָּה תַעֲנֶה אֲדֹנָי אֱלֹהָי.

<sup>17</sup>For I said, "Lest they rejoice over me; when my foot slips, they magnify themselves against me."

יזכִּי אָמַרְתִּי פֶּן יִשְׂמְחוּ לִי; בְּמוֹט רַגְלִי עָלַי הִגְדִּילוּ.

<sup>18</sup>For I am ready to halt, and my pain is continually before me.

יחכִּי אֲנִי לְצֶלַע נָכוֹן; וּמַכְאוֹבִי נֶגְדִּי תָמִיד.

<sup>19</sup>For I do declare my iniquity; I am full of care because of my sin.

יטכִּי עֲוֹנִי אַגִּיד; אֶדְאַג מֵחַטָּאתִי.

<sup>20</sup>But my enemies are strong in health; and they that hate me wrongfully are multiplied.

כוְאֹיְבַי חַיִּים עָצֵמוּ; וְרַבּוּ שֹׂנְאַי שָׁקֶר.

<sup>21</sup>They also that repay evil for good are adversaries unto me, because I pursue goodness.

כאוּמְשַׁלְּמֵי רָעָה תַּחַת טוֹבָה יִשְׂטְנוּנִי תַּחַת רדוֹפִי (רָדְפִי) טוֹב.

<sup>22</sup>Forsake me not, O יהוה; O my Elohim, be not far from me.

כבאַל תַּעַזְבֵנִי יהוה : אֱלֹהַי אַל תִּרְחַק מִמֶּנִּי.

<sup>23</sup>Make haste to help me, O Adonai, my Salvation.

כגחוּשָׁה לְעֶזְרָתִי: אֲדֹנָי תְּשׁוּעָתִי.

# Tehillah 39 תְּהִלָּה

<sup>1</sup>For the Leader, for Yedutun. A Mizmor of David.

אלַמְנַצֵּחַ לידיתון (לִידוּתוּן) מִזְמוֹר לְדָוִד.

285

<sup>2</sup>I said, "I will take heed to my ways, that I sin not with my tongue; I will keep a bridle upon my mouth, while the wicked is before me."

אָמַרְתִּי אֶשְׁמְרָה דְרָכַי מֵחֲטוֹא בִלְשׁוֹנִי: אֶשְׁמְרָה לְפִי מַחְסוֹם בְּעֹד רָשָׁע לְנֶגְדִּי.

<sup>3</sup>I was dumb with silence; I held my peace, I had no comfort; and my pain was held in check.

נֶאֱלַמְתִּי דוּמִיָּה הֶחֱשֵׁיתִי מִטּוֹב; וּכְאֵבִי נֶעְכָּר.

<sup>4</sup>My heart waxed hot within me; while I was musing, the fire kindled; then I spoke with my tongue:

חַם לִבִּי בְּקִרְבִּי בַּהֲגִיגִי תִבְעַר אֵשׁ; דִּבַּרְתִּי בִּלְשׁוֹנִי.

<sup>5</sup>"יהוה , make me to know my end, and the measure of my days, what it is; let me know how short-lived I am.

הוֹדִיעֵנִי יהוה קִצִּי וּמִדַּת יָמַי מַה הִיא; אֵדְעָה מֶה חָדֵל אָנִי.

<sup>6</sup>Behold, You have made my days as hand-breadths; and my age is as nothing before You; surely every man at his best estate is altogether vanity. Selah.

הִנֵּה טְפָחוֹת נָתַתָּה יָמַי וְחֶלְדִּי כְאַיִן נֶגְדֶּךָ; אַךְ כָּל הֶבֶל כָּל אָדָם נִצָּב סֶלָה.

<sup>7</sup>Surely man walks as a mere semblance; surely for vanity they are in turmoil; he heaps up riches, and knows not who shall gather them.

אַךְ בְּצֶלֶם יִתְהַלֶּךְ אִישׁ אַךְ הֶבֶל יֶהֱמָיוּן; יִצְבֹּר וְלֹא יֵדַע מִי אֹסְפָם.

<sup>8</sup>And now, Adonai, what do I wait for? My hope, it is in You.

וְעַתָּה מַה קִוִּיתִי אֲדֹנָי תּוֹחַלְתִּי לְךָ הִיא.

⁹Deliver me from all my transgressions; make me not the reproach of the base.

ⁱⁿמִכָּל פְּשָׁעַי הַצִּילֵנִי; חֶרְפַּת נָבָל אַל תְּשִׂימֵנִי.

¹⁰I am dumb, I open not my mouth; because You have done it.

ⁱנֶאֱלַמְתִּי לֹא אֶפְתַּח פִּי: כִּי אַתָּה עָשִׂיתָ.

¹¹Remove Your stroke from off me; I am consumed by the blow of Your hand.

ⁱᵃהָסֵר מֵעָלַי נִגְעֶךָ; מִתִּגְרַת יָדְךָ אֲנִי כָלִיתִי.

¹²With rebukes do You chasten man for iniquity, and like a moth You make his beauty to consume away; surely every man is vanity. Selah.

ⁱᵇבְּתוֹכָחוֹת עַל עָוֹן יִסַּרְתָּ אִישׁ וַתֶּמֶס כָּעָשׁ חֲמוּדוֹ; אַךְ הֶבֶל כָּל אָדָם סֶלָה.

¹³Hear my prayer, O יהוה, and give ear unto my cry; keep not silence at my tears; for I am a stranger with You, a sojourner, as all my fathers were.

ⁱᵍשִׁמְעָה תְפִלָּתִי יהוה וְשַׁוְעָתִי הַאֲזִינָה אֶל דִּמְעָתִי אַל תֶּחֱרַשׁ: כִּי גֵר אָנֹכִי עִמָּךְ; תּוֹשָׁב כְּכָל אֲבוֹתָי.

¹⁴Look away from me, that I may take comfort, before I go hence, and am no more."

ⁱᵈהָשַׁע מִמֶּנִּי וְאַבְלִיגָה בְּטֶרֶם אֵלֵךְ וְאֵינֶנִּי.

# Tehillah 40 תְּהִלָּה

¹For the Leader. A Mizmor of David.

ᵃלַמְנַצֵּחַ לְדָוִד מִזְמוֹר.

²I waited patiently for יהוה; and He inclined unto me, and heard my cry.

ᵇקַוֹּה קִוִּיתִי יהוה; וַיֵּט אֵלַי וַיִּשְׁמַע שַׁוְעָתִי.

[3]He brought me up also out of the tumultuous pit, out of the miry clay; and He set my feet upon a Rock, He established my goings.

וַיַּעֲלֵנִי מִבּוֹר שָׁאוֹן מִטִּיט הַיָּוֵן: וַיָּקֶם עַל סֶלַע רַגְלַי; כּוֹנֵן אֲשֻׁרָי.

[4]And He has put a new song in my mouth, even praise unto our Elohim; many shall see, and fear, and shall trust in יהוה .

וַיִּתֵּן בְּפִי שִׁיר חָדָשׁ תְּהִלָּה לֵאלֹהֵינוּ: יִרְאוּ רַבִּים וְיִירָאוּ; וְיִבְטְחוּ בַּיהוה .

[5]Happy is the man that has made יהוה his trust, and has not turned unto the arrogant, nor unto such as fall away treacherously.

אַשְׁרֵי הַגֶּבֶר אֲשֶׁר שָׂם יהוה מִבְטַחוֹ; וְלֹא פָנָה אֶל רְהָבִים וְשָׂטֵי כָזָב.

[6]Many things have You done, O יהוה my Elohim, even Your wonderful works, and Your thoughts toward us; there is none to be compared unto You! If I would declare and speak of them, they are more than can be told.

רַבּוֹת עָשִׂיתָ אַתָּה יהוה אֱלֹהַי נִפְלְאֹתֶיךָ וּמַחְשְׁבֹתֶיךָ אֵלֵינוּ: אֵין עֲרֹךְ אֵלֶיךָ אַגִּידָה וַאֲדַבֵּרָה; עָצְמוּ מִסַּפֵּר.

[7]Zevakh and Minkhah You have no delight in; ["A Body have you prepared for me" (from the Aramaic Targums)] my ears have You opened; Olah and Khata'ah have You not required.

זֶבַח וּמִנְחָה לֹא חָפַצְתָּ אָזְנַיִם כָּרִיתָ לִּי; עוֹלָה וַחֲטָאָה לֹא שָׁאָלְתָּ.

<sup>8</sup>Then said I, "Lo, I am come! In the scroll, a Sefer is written concerning me;

ח אָז אָמַרְתִּי הִנֵּה בָאתִי: בִּמְגִלַּת סֵפֶר כָּתוּב עָלָי.

<sup>9</sup>I delight to do Your will, O my Elohim; yes, Your Torah is in my inmost parts."

ט לַעֲשׂוֹת רְצוֹנְךָ אֱלֹהַי חָפָצְתִּי; וְתוֹרָתְךָ בְּתוֹךְ מֵעָי.

<sup>10</sup>I have declared righteousness in the great congregation, lo, I did not refrain my lips; O יהוה, You know.

י בִּשַּׂרְתִּי צֶדֶק בְּקָהָל רָב הִנֵּה שְׂפָתַי לֹא אֶכְלָא: יהוה אַתָּה יָדָעְתָּ.

<sup>11</sup>I have not hidden Your tzedaka within my heart; I have declared Your faithfulness and Your Salvation; I have not concealed Your compassion and Your truth from the great congregation.

יא צִדְקָתְךָ לֹא כִסִּיתִי בְּתוֹךְ לִבִּי אֱמוּנָתְךָ וּתְשׁוּעָתְךָ אָמָרְתִּי; לֹא כִחַדְתִּי חַסְדְּךָ וַאֲמִתְּךָ לְקָהָל רָב.

<sup>12</sup>You, O יהוה, will not withhold Your mercies from me; let Your compassion and Your truth continually preserve me.

יב אַתָּה יהוה לֹא תִכְלָא רַחֲמֶיךָ מִמֶּנִּי; חַסְדְּךָ וַאֲמִתְּךָ תָּמִיד יִצְּרוּנִי.

<sup>13</sup>For innumerable evils have encompassed me, my iniquities have overtaken me, so that I am not able to look up; they are more than the hairs of my head, and my heart has failed me.

יג כִּי אָפְפוּ עָלַי רָעוֹת עַד אֵין מִסְפָּר הִשִּׂיגוּנִי עֲוֹנֹתַי וְלֹא יָכֹלְתִּי לִרְאוֹת; עָצְמוּ מִשַּׂעֲרוֹת רֹאשִׁי וְלִבִּי עֲזָבָנִי.

<sup>14</sup>Be pleased, O יהוה, to deliver me; O יהוה, make haste to help me.

יד רְצֵה יהוה לְהַצִּילֵנִי; יהוה לְעֶזְרָתִי חוּשָׁה.

<sup>15</sup>Let them be ashamed and abashed together that seek after my soul to sweep it away; let them be turned backward and brought to confusion that delight in my hurt.

ט<sup>ו</sup>יֵבֹשׁוּ וְיַחְפְּרוּ יַחַד מְבַקְשֵׁי נַפְשִׁי לִסְפּוֹתָהּ: יִסֹּגוּ אָחוֹר וְיִכָּלְמוּ חֲפֵצֵי רָעָתִי.

<sup>16</sup>Let them be appalled by reason of their shame that say unto me, "Aha, aha."

ט<sup>ז</sup>יָשֹׁמּוּ עַל עֵקֶב בָּשְׁתָּם הָאֹמְרִים לִי הֶאָח הֶאָח.

<sup>17</sup>Let all those that seek You rejoice and be glad in You; let such as love Your Salvation say continually, "יהוה be magnified."

<sup>יז</sup>יָשִׂישׂוּ וְיִשְׂמְחוּ בְּךָ כָּל מְבַקְשֶׁיךָ: יֹאמְרוּ תָמִיד יִגְדַּל יהוה אֹהֲבֵי תְּשׁוּעָתֶךָ.

<sup>18</sup>But, as for me, that am poor and needy, Adonai will account it unto me; You are my help and my deliverer; O my Elohim, tarry not.

<sup>יח</sup>וַאֲנִי עָנִי וְאֶבְיוֹן אֲדֹנָי יַחֲשָׁב לִי: עֶזְרָתִי וּמְפַלְטִי אַתָּה; אֱלֹהַי אַל תְּאַחַר.

# Tehillah 41 תְּהִלָּה

<sup>1</sup>For the Leader. A Mizmor of David.

<sup>א</sup>לַמְנַצֵּחַ מִזְמוֹר לְדָוִד.

<sup>2</sup>Happy is he that considers the poor; יהוה will deliver him in the day of evil.

<sup>ב</sup>אַשְׁרֵי מַשְׂכִּיל אֶל דָּל; בְּיוֹם רָעָה יְמַלְּטֵהוּ יהוה.

<sup>3</sup>יהוה, preserve him, and keep him alive, let him be called happy in the land; and do not deliver him unto the greed of his enemies.

<sup>ג</sup> יהוה יִשְׁמְרֵהוּ וִיחַיֵּהוּ יֻאַשַּׁר (וְאֻשַּׁר) בָּאָרֶץ; וְאַל תִּתְּנֵהוּ בְּנֶפֶשׁ אֹיְבָיו.

290

<sup>4</sup> יהוה , support him upon the bed of illness; may You turn all his lying down in his sickness.

ד יהוה יִסְעָדֶנּוּ עַל עֶרֶשׂ דְּוָי; כָּל מִשְׁכָּבוֹ הָפַכְתָּ בְחָלְיוֹ.

<sup>5</sup>As for me, I said, "O יהוה , be gracious unto me; heal my soul; for I have sinned against You."

ה אֲנִי אָמַרְתִּי יהוה חָנֵּנִי; רְפָאָה נַפְשִׁי כִּי חָטָאתִי לָךְ.

<sup>6</sup>My enemies speak evil of me, "When shall he die, and his name perish?"

ו אוֹיְבַי יֹאמְרוּ רַע לִי; מָתַי יָמוּת וְאָבַד שְׁמוֹ.

<sup>7</sup>And if one comes to see me, he speaks falsehood; his heart gathers iniquity to itself; when he goes abroad, he speaks of it.

ז וְאִם בָּא לִרְאוֹת שָׁוְא יְדַבֵּר לִבּוֹ יִקְבָּץ אָוֶן לוֹ; יֵצֵא לַחוּץ יְדַבֵּר.

<sup>8</sup>All that hate me whisper together against me, against me do they devise my hurt:

ח יַחַד עָלַי יִתְלַחֲשׁוּ כָּל שֹׂנְאָי; עָלַי יַחְשְׁבוּ רָעָה לִי.

<sup>9</sup>"An evil thing cleaves fast unto him; and now that he lies, he shall rise up no more."

ט דְּבַר בְּלִיַּעַל יָצוּק בּוֹ; וַאֲשֶׁר שָׁכַב לֹא יוֹסִיף לָקוּם.

<sup>10</sup>Yes, my own familiar friend, in whom I trusted, who did eat of my bread, has lifted up his heel against me.

י גַּם אִישׁ שְׁלוֹמִי אֲשֶׁר בָּטַחְתִּי בוֹ אוֹכֵל לַחְמִי; הִגְדִּיל עָלַי עָקֵב.

<sup>11</sup>But You, O יהוה , be gracious unto me, and raise me up, that I may requite them.

יא וְאַתָּה יהוה חָנֵּנִי וַהֲקִימֵנִי; וַאֲשַׁלְּמָה לָהֶם.

291

[12]By this I know that You delight in me, that my enemy does not triumph over me.

יᵇבְּזֹאת יָדַעְתִּי כִּי חָפַצְתָּ בִּי: כִּי לֹא יָרִיעַ אֹיְבִי עָלָי.

[13]And as for me, You uphold me because of my integrity, and set me before Your face forever.

יᵍוַאֲנִי בְּתֻמִּי תָּמַכְתָּ בִּי; וַתַּצִּיבֵנִי לְפָנֶיךָ לְעוֹלָם.

[14]Blessed is יהוה Elohei Yisra'el, from everlasting and to everlasting. Amein, and Amein.

יᵈבָּרוּךְ יהוה אֱלֹהֵי יִשְׂרָאֵל מֵהָעוֹלָם וְעַד הָעוֹלָם: אָמֵן וְאָמֵן.

# Tehillah 42 תְּהִלָּה

[1]For the Leader; A Maskil for the sons of Korakh.

אᵃלַמְנַצֵּחַ מַשְׂכִּיל לִבְנֵי קֹרַח.

[2]As the dear pants after the water brooks, so pants my soul after You, O Elohim.

בᵇכְּאַיָּל תַּעֲרֹג עַל אֲפִיקֵי מָיִם כֵּן נַפְשִׁי תַעֲרֹג אֵלֶיךָ אֱלֹהִים.

[3]My soul thirsts for Elohim, for El Khai: "When shall I come and appear before Elohim?"

גᵍצָמְאָה נַפְשִׁי לֵאלֹהִים לְאֵל חָי: מָתַי אָבוֹא; וְאֵרָאֶה פְּנֵי אֱלֹהִים.

[4]My tears have been my food day and night, while they say unto me all the day, "Where is your Elohim?"

דᵈהָיְתָה לִּי דִמְעָתִי לֶחֶם יוֹמָם וָלָיְלָה; בֶּאֱמֹר אֵלַי כָּל הַיּוֹם אַיֵּה אֱלֹהֶיךָ.

<sup>5</sup>These things I remember, and pour out my soul within me, how I passed on with the throng, and led them to Beit Elohim, with the voice of joy and praise, a multitude celebrating the Khag.

<sup>6</sup>Why are you cast down, O my soul? And why do you moan within me? Hope in Elohim; for I shall yet praise Him for the Salvation of His countenance.

<sup>7</sup>O my Elohim, my soul is cast down within me; therefore do I remember You from the land of Yarden, and the Khermonim, from Har Mitzar.

<sup>8</sup>Deep calls unto deep at the voice of Your downpouring; all Your waves and Your billows are gone over me.

<sup>9</sup>By day יהוה will command His compassion, and in the night His song shall be with me, even a prayer unto the Elohim of my life.

ה‏אֵלֶּה אֶזְכְּרָה וְאֶשְׁפְּכָה עָלַי נַפְשִׁי כִּי אֶעֱבֹר בַּסָּךְ אֶדַּדֵּם עַד בֵּית אֱלֹהִים: בְּקוֹל רִנָּה וְתוֹדָה; הָמוֹן חוֹגֵג.

ו‏מַה תִּשְׁתּוֹחֲחִי נַפְשִׁי וַתֶּהֱמִי עָלַי: הוֹחִלִי לֵאלֹהִים כִּי עוֹד אוֹדֶנּוּ יְשׁוּעוֹת פָּנָיו.

ז‏אֱלֹהַי עָלַי נַפְשִׁי תִּשְׁתּוֹחָח: עַל כֵּן אֶזְכָּרְךָ מֵאֶרֶץ יַרְדֵּן; וְחֶרְמוֹנִים מֵהַר מִצְעָר.

ח‏תְּהוֹם אֶל תְּהוֹם קוֹרֵא לְקוֹל צִנּוֹרֶיךָ; כָּל מִשְׁבָּרֶיךָ וְגַלֶּיךָ עָלַי עָבָרוּ.

ט‏יוֹמָם יְצַוֶּה יהוה חַסְדּוֹ וּבַלַּיְלָה שִׁירֹה עִמִּי תְּפִלָּה לְאֵל חַיָּי.

[10]I will say unto Elohim my Rock, "Why have You forgotten me? Why do I go mourning under the oppression of the enemy?"

אֹומְרָה לְאֵל סַלְעִי לָמָה שְׁכַחְתָּנִי: לָמָה קֹדֵר אֵלֵךְ בְּלַחַץ אֹויֵב.

[11]As with a crushing in my bones, my adversaries taunt me; while they say unto me all the day, "Where is your Elohim?"

בְּרֶצַח בְּעַצְמֹותַי חֵרְפוּנִי צֹורְרָי; בְּאָמְרָם אֵלַי כָּל הַיֹּום אַיֵּה אֱלֹהֶיךָ.

[12]Why are you cast down, O my soul? And why do you moan within me? Hope in Elohim; for I shall yet praise Him, the Salvation of my countenance, and my Elohim.

מַה תִּשְׁתֹּוחֲחִי נַפְשִׁי וּמַה תֶּהֱמִי עָלָי: הֹוחִילִי לֵאלֹהִים כִּי עֹוד אֹודֶנּוּ יְשׁוּעֹת פָּנַי וֵאלֹהָי.

# Tehillah 43 תְּהִלָּה

[1]Be my judge, O Elohim, and plead my cause against an ungodly nation; O deliver me from the deceitful and unjust man.

שָׁפְטֵנִי אֱלֹהִים וְרִיבָה רִיבִי מִגֹּוי לֹא חָסִיד; מֵאִישׁ מִרְמָה וְעַוְלָה תְפַלְּטֵנִי.

[2]For You are the Elohim of my strength; why have You cast me off? Why do I go mourning under the oppression of the enemy?

כִּי אַתָּה אֱלֹהֵי מָעוּזִּי לָמָה זְנַחְתָּנִי: לָמָה קֹדֵר אֶתְהַלֵּךְ בְּלַחַץ אֹויֵב.

³O send out Your light and Your truth; let them lead me; let them bring me unto Your Har Kodesh, and to Your dwelling-places.

שְׁלַח אוֹרְךָ וַאֲמִתְּךָ הֵמָּה יַנְחוּנִי; יְבִיאוּנִי אֶל הַר קָדְשְׁךָ וְאֶל מִשְׁכְּנוֹתֶיךָ.

⁴Then will I go unto the Mizbe'akh of Elohim, unto Elohim, my exceeding joy, and praise You upon the Kinor, O Elohim, my Elohim.

וְאָבוֹאָה אֶל מִזְבַּח אֱלֹהִים אֶל אֵל שִׂמְחַת גִּילִי: וְאוֹדְךָ בְכִנּוֹר אֱלֹהִים אֱלֹהָי.

⁵Why are you cast down, O my soul? And why do you moan within me? Hope in Elohim; for I shall yet praise Him, the Salvation of my countenance, and my Elohim.

מַה תִּשְׁתּוֹחֲחִי נַפְשִׁי וּמַה תֶּהֱמִי עָלָי: הוֹחִילִי לֵאלֹהִים כִּי עוֹד אוֹדֶנּוּ יְשׁוּעֹת פָּנַי וֵאלֹהָי.

# תְּהִלָּה 44 Tehillah

¹For the Leader; for the sons of Korakh. A Maskil.

לַמְנַצֵּחַ לִבְנֵי קֹרַח מַשְׂכִּיל.

²O Elohim, we have heard with our ears, our fathers have told us; a work You did in their days, in the days of old.

אֱלֹהִים בְּאָזְנֵינוּ שָׁמַעְנוּ אֲבוֹתֵינוּ סִפְּרוּ לָנוּ: פֹּעַל פָּעַלְתָּ בִימֵיהֶם בִּימֵי קֶדֶם.

³You with Your hand did drive out the nations, and did plant them; You did break the peoples, and did spread them abroad.

אַתָּה יָדְךָ גּוֹיִם הוֹרַשְׁתָּ וַתִּטָּעֵם; תָּרַע לְאֻמִּים וַתְּשַׁלְּחֵם.

295

⁴For not by their own sword did they get the land in possession, neither did their own arm save them; but Your right hand, and Your arm, and the light of Your countenance, because You were favorable unto them.

זּכִּי לֹא בְחַרְבָּם יָרְשׁוּ אָרֶץ וּזְרוֹעָם לֹא הוֹשִׁיעָה לָּמוֹ: כִּי יְמִינְךָ וּזְרוֹעֲךָ וְאוֹר פָּנֶיךָ כִּי רְצִיתָם.

⁵You are my Melekh, O Elohim; command the Salvations of Ya'akov.

הּאַתָּה הוּא מַלְכִּי אֱלֹהִים; צַוֵּה יְשׁוּעוֹת יַעֲקֹב.

⁶Through You do we push down our adversaries; through Your Name do we tread them under that rise up against us.

וּבְךָ צָרֵינוּ נְנַגֵּחַ; בְּשִׁמְךָ נָבוּס קָמֵינוּ.

⁷For I trust not in my bow, neither can my sword save me.

זכִּי לֹא בְקַשְׁתִּי אֶבְטָח; וְחַרְבִּי לֹא תוֹשִׁיעֵנִי.

⁸But You have saved us from our adversaries, and have put them to shame that hate us.

חכִּי הוֹשַׁעְתָּנוּ מִצָּרֵינוּ; וּמְשַׂנְאֵינוּ הֱבִישׁוֹתָ.

⁹In Elohim have we gloried all the day, and we will give thanks unto Your Name forever. Selah.

טבֵּאלֹהִים הִלַּלְנוּ כָל הַיּוֹם; וְשִׁמְךָ לְעוֹלָם נוֹדֶה סֶלָה.

¹⁰Yet You have cast off, and brought us to confusion; and go not forth with our hosts.

יאַף זָנַחְתָּ וַתַּכְלִימֵנוּ; וְלֹא תֵצֵא בְּצִבְאוֹתֵינוּ.

<sup>11</sup>You make us to turn back from the adversary; and they that hate us spoil at their will.

<sup>יא</sup>תְּשִׁיבֵנוּ אָחוֹר מִנִּי צָר; וּמְשַׂנְאֵינוּ שָׁסוּ לָמוֹ.

<sup>12</sup>You have given us like sheep to be eaten; and have scattered us among the goyim.

<sup>יב</sup>תִּתְּנֵנוּ כְּצֹאן מַאֲכָל; וּבַגּוֹיִם זֵרִיתָנוּ.

<sup>13</sup>You sell Your people for small gain, and have not set their prices high.

<sup>יג</sup>תִּמְכֹּר עַמְּךָ בְלֹא הוֹן; וְלֹא רִבִּיתָ בִּמְחִירֵיהֶם.

<sup>14</sup>You make us a taunt to our neighbors, a scorn and a derision to them that are round about us.

<sup>יד</sup>תְּשִׂימֵנוּ חֶרְפָּה לִשְׁכֵנֵינוּ; לַעַג וָקֶלֶס לִסְבִיבוֹתֵינוּ.

<sup>15</sup>You make us a byword among the nations, a shaking of the head among the peoples.

<sup>טו</sup>תְּשִׂימֵנוּ מָשָׁל בַּגּוֹיִם; מְנוֹד רֹאשׁ בַּלְאֻמִּים.

<sup>16</sup>All the day is my confusion before me, and the shame of my face has covered me,

<sup>טז</sup>כָּל הַיּוֹם כְּלִמָּתִי נֶגְדִּי; וּבֹשֶׁת פָּנַי כִּסָּתְנִי.

<sup>17</sup>For the voice of him that taunts and blasphemes; by reason of the enemy and the vengeful.

<sup>יז</sup>מִקּוֹל מְחָרֵף וּמְגַדֵּף; מִפְּנֵי אוֹיֵב וּמִתְנַקֵּם.

<sup>18</sup>All this is come upon us; yet have we not forgotten You, neither have we been false to Your Brit.

<sup>יח</sup>כָּל זֹאת בָּאַתְנוּ וְלֹא שְׁכַחֲנוּךָ; וְלֹא שִׁקַּרְנוּ בִּבְרִיתֶךָ.

<sup>19</sup>Our heart is not turned back, neither have our steps declined from Your path;

יט‏לֹא נָסוֹג אָחוֹר לִבֵּנוּ; וַתֵּט אֲשֻׁרֵינוּ מִנִּי אָרְחֶךָ.

<sup>20</sup>Though You have crushed us into a place of jackals, and covered us with Tzal-Mavet.

כ‏כִּי דִכִּיתָנוּ בִּמְקוֹם תַּנִּים; וַתְּכַס עָלֵינוּ בְצַלְמָוֶת.

<sup>21</sup>If we had forgotten the Name of our Elohim, or spread forth our hands to a strange god;

כא‏אִם שָׁכַחְנוּ שֵׁם אֱלֹהֵינוּ; וַנִּפְרֹשׂ כַּפֵּינוּ לְאֵל זָר.

<sup>22</sup>Would not Elohim search this out? For He knows the secrets of the heart.

כב‏הֲלֹא אֱלֹהִים יַחֲקָר זֹאת: כִּי הוּא יֹדֵעַ תַּעֲלֻמוֹת לֵב.

<sup>23</sup>Nay, but for Your sake are we killed all the day; we are accounted as sheep for the slaughter.

כג‏כִּי עָלֶיךָ הֹרַגְנוּ כָל הַיּוֹם; נֶחְשַׁבְנוּ כְּצֹאן טִבְחָה.

<sup>24</sup>Awake, why do You sleep, O Adonai? Arouse Yourself, cast not off forever.

כד‏עוּרָה לָמָּה תִישַׁן אֲדֹנָי; הָקִיצָה אַל תִּזְנַח לָנֶצַח.

<sup>25</sup>Why do You hide Your face, and forget our affliction and our oppression?

כה‏לָמָּה פָנֶיךָ תַסְתִּיר; תִּשְׁכַּח עָנְיֵנוּ וְלַחֲצֵנוּ.

<sup>26</sup>For our soul is bowed down to the dust; our belly cleaves unto the earth.

כו‏כִּי שָׁחָה לֶעָפָר נַפְשֵׁנוּ; דָּבְקָה לָאָרֶץ בִּטְנֵנוּ.

<sup>27</sup>Arise for our help, and redeem us for Your compassion's sake.

כז‏קוּמָה עֶזְרָתָה לָּנוּ; וּפְדֵנוּ לְמַעַן חַסְדֶּךָ.

# תְּהִלָּה 45 Tehillah

<sup>1</sup>For the Leader; upon Shoshannim; for the sons of Korakh. A Maskil. A Song of loves.

אלַמְנַצֵּחַ עַל שֹׁשַׁנִּים לִבְנֵי קֹרַח; מַשְׂכִּיל שִׁיר יְדִידֹת.

<sup>2</sup>My heart overflows with a goodly matter; I say, "My work is concerning a Melekh"; my tongue is the pen of a ready writer.

ברָחַשׁ לִבִּי דָּבָר טוֹב אֹמֵר אָנִי מַעֲשַׂי לְמֶלֶךְ; לְשׁוֹנִי עֵט סוֹפֵר מָהִיר.

<sup>3</sup>You are fairer than the children of men; grace is poured upon your lips; therefore Elohim has blessed you forever.

גיָפְיָפִיתָ מִבְּנֵי אָדָם הוּצַק חֵן בְּשְׂפְתוֹתֶיךָ; עַל כֵּן בֵּרַכְךָ אֱלֹהִים לְעוֹלָם.

<sup>4</sup>Gird your sword upon your thigh, O mighty one, your glory and your majesty.

דחֲגוֹר חַרְבְּךָ עַל יָרֵךְ גִּבּוֹר הוֹדְךָ וַהֲדָרֶךָ.

<sup>5</sup>And in your majesty prosper, ride on, in behalf of truth and meekness and righteousness; and let your right hand teach you tremendous things.

הוַהֲדָרְךָ צְלַח רְכַב עַל דְּבַר אֱמֶת וְעַנְוָה צֶדֶק; וְתוֹרְךָ נוֹרָאוֹת יְמִינֶךָ.

<sup>6</sup>Your arrows are sharp; the peoples fall under you; [they sink] into the heart of the enemies of HaMelekh.

וחִצֶּיךָ שְׁנוּנִים: עַמִּים תַּחְתֶּיךָ יִפְּלוּ; בְּלֵב אוֹיְבֵי הַמֶּלֶךְ.

<sup>7</sup>Your throne given of Elohim is forever and ever; a scepter of equity is the scepter of your Malkhut.

זכִּסְאֲךָ אֱלֹהִים עוֹלָם וָעֶד; שֵׁבֶט מִישֹׁר שֵׁבֶט מַלְכוּתֶךָ.

⁸You have loved righteousness, and hated wickedness; therefore Elohim, your Elohim, has anointed you with the oil of gladness above your fellows.

חאָהַבְתָּ צֶּדֶק וַתִּשְׂנָא רֶשַׁע: עַל כֵּן מְשָׁחֲךָ אֱלֹהִים אֱלֹהֶיךָ שֶׁמֶן שָׂשׂוֹן מֵחֲבֵרֶךָ.

⁹Myrrh, and aloes, and cassia are all your garments; out of ivory palaces stringed instruments have made you glad.

טמֹר וַאֲהָלוֹת קְצִיעוֹת כָּל בִּגְדֹתֶיךָ; מִן הֵיכְלֵי שֵׁן מִנִּי שִׂמְּחוּךָ.

¹⁰Kings' daughters are among your favorites; at your right hand does stand the queen in gold of Ofir.

יבְּנוֹת מְלָכִים בְּיִקְּרוֹתֶיךָ; נִצְּבָה שֵׁגַל לִימִינְךָ בְּכֶתֶם אוֹפִיר.

¹¹"Hearken, O daughter, and consider, and incline your ear; forget also your own people, and your father's house;

יאשִׁמְעִי בַת וּרְאִי וְהַטִּי אָזְנֵךְ; וְשִׁכְחִי עַמֵּךְ וּבֵית אָבִיךְ.

¹²So shall HaMelekh desire your beauty; for he is your Adonai; and do homage unto him.

יבוְיִתְאָו הַמֶּלֶךְ יָפְיֵךְ: כִּי הוּא אֲדֹנַיִךְ וְהִשְׁתַּחֲוִי לוֹ.

¹³And, O daughter of Tzor, the richest of the people shall entreat your favor with a gift."

יגוּבַת צֹר: בְּמִנְחָה פָּנַיִךְ יְחַלּוּ עֲשִׁירֵי עָם.

300

¹⁴All glorious is the daughter of HaMelekh within the palace; her raiment is of chequer work inwrought with gold.

כָּל־כְּבוּדָּה בַת־מֶלֶךְ פְּנִימָה; מִמִּשְׁבְּצוֹת זָהָב לְבוּשָׁהּ.

¹⁵She shall be led unto HaMelekh on richly woven stuff; the virgins, her companions in her train, being brought unto you.

לִרְקָמוֹת תּוּבַל לַמֶּלֶךְ: בְּתוּלוֹת אַחֲרֶיהָ רֵעוֹתֶיהָ מוּבָאוֹת לָךְ.

¹⁶They shall be led with gladness and rejoicing; they shall enter into the palace of HaMelekh.

תּוּבַלְנָה בִּשְׂמָחֹת וָגִיל; תְּבֹאֶינָה בְּהֵיכַל מֶלֶךְ.

¹⁷Instead of your fathers shall be your sons, whom you shall make princes in all the land.

תַּחַת אֲבֹתֶיךָ יִהְיוּ בָנֶיךָ; תְּשִׁיתֵמוֹ לְשָׂרִים בְּכָל־הָאָרֶץ.

¹⁸I will make your name to be remembered in all generations; therefore shall the peoples praise you forever and ever.

אַזְכִּירָה שִׁמְךָ בְּכָל־דֹּר וָדֹר; עַל־כֵּן עַמִּים יְהוֹדֻךָ לְעֹלָם וָעֶד.

# Tehillah 46 תְּהִלָּה

¹For the Leader; for the sons of Korakh; upon Alamot. A Song.

לַמְנַצֵּחַ לִבְנֵי־קֹרַח עַל־עֲלָמוֹת שִׁיר.

²Elohim is our refuge and strength, a very present help in trouble.

אֱלֹהִים לָנוּ מַחֲסֶה וָעֹז; עֶזְרָה בְצָרוֹת נִמְצָא מְאֹד.

301

³Therefore will we not fear, though the earth does change, and though the mountains are moved into the heart of the seas;

געַל כֵּן לֹא נִירָא בְּהָמִיר אָרֶץ; וּבְמוֹט הָרִים בְּלֵב יַמִּים.

⁴Though the waters thereof roar and foam, though the mountains shake at the swelling thereof. Selah.

דיֶהֱמוּ יֶחְמְרוּ מֵימָיו; יִרְעֲשׁוּ הָרִים בְּגַאֲוָתוֹ סֶלָה.

⁵There is a river, the streams whereof make glad the city of Elohim, the Kadosh dwelling-place of Elyon.

הנָהָר פְּלָגָיו יְשַׂמְּחוּ עִיר אֱלֹהִים; קְדֹשׁ מִשְׁכְּנֵי עֶלְיוֹן.

⁶Elohim is in the midst of her, she shall not be moved; Elohim shall help her, at the approach of morning.

ואֱלֹהִים בְּקִרְבָּהּ בַּל תִּמּוֹט; יַעְזְרֶהָ אֱלֹהִים לִפְנוֹת בֹּקֶר.

⁷Nations were in tumult, kingdoms were moved; He uttered His voice, the earth melted.

זהָמוּ גוֹיִם מָטוּ מַמְלָכוֹת; נָתַן בְּקוֹלוֹ תָּמוּג אָרֶץ.

⁸ יהוה Tzeva'ot is with us; the Elohim of Ya'akov is our high tower. Selah.

ח יהוה צְבָאוֹת עִמָּנוּ; מִשְׂגָּב לָנוּ אֱלֹהֵי יַעֲקֹב סֶלָה.

⁹Come, behold the works of יהוה , who has made desolations in the earth.

טלְכוּ חֲזוּ מִפְעֲלוֹת יהוה אֲשֶׁר שָׂם שַׁמּוֹת בָּאָרֶץ.

¹⁰He makes wars to cease unto the end of the earth; He breaks the bow, and cuts the spear asunder; He burns the chariots in the fire.

ימַשְׁבִּית מִלְחָמוֹת עַד קְצֵה הָאָרֶץ: קֶשֶׁת יְשַׁבֵּר וְקִצֵּץ חֲנִית; עֲגָלוֹת יִשְׂרֹף בָּאֵשׁ.

<sup>11</sup>"Let it be, and know that I am Elohim; I will be exalted among the goyim, I will be exalted in the earth."

יאהַרְפּוּ וּדְעוּ כִּי אָנֹכִי אֱלֹהִים; אָרוּם בַּגּוֹיִם אָרוּם בָּאָרֶץ.

<sup>12</sup> יהוה Tzeva'ot is with us; the Elohim of Ya'akov is our high tower. Selah.

יב יהוה צְבָאוֹת עִמָּנוּ; מִשְׂגָּב לָנוּ אֱלֹהֵי יַעֲקֹב סֶלָה.

# Tehillah 47 תְּהִלָּה

<sup>1</sup>For the Leader; a Mizmor for the sons of Korakh.

אלַמְנַצֵּחַ לִבְנֵי קֹרַח מִזְמוֹר.

<sup>2</sup>O clap your hands, all you peoples; shout unto Elohim with the voice of triumph.

בכָּל הָעַמִּים תִּקְעוּ כָף; הָרִיעוּ לֵאלֹהִים בְּקוֹל רִנָּה.

<sup>3</sup>For יהוה is Elyon, full of awe; a great Melekh over all the earth.

גכִּי יהוה עֶלְיוֹן נוֹרָא; מֶלֶךְ גָּדוֹל עַל כָּל הָאָרֶץ.

<sup>4</sup>He subdues peoples under us, and nations under our feet.

דיַדְבֵּר עַמִּים תַּחְתֵּינוּ; וּלְאֻמִּים תַּחַת רַגְלֵינוּ.

<sup>5</sup>He chooses our inheritance for us, the pride of Ya'akov whom He loves. Selah.

היִבְחַר לָנוּ אֶת נַחֲלָתֵנוּ; אֶת גְּאוֹן יַעֲקֹב אֲשֶׁר אָהֵב סֶלָה.

<sup>6</sup>Elohim is gone up amidst shouting, יהוה amidst the voice of the shofar.

ועָלָה אֱלֹהִים בִּתְרוּעָה; יהוה בְּקוֹל שׁוֹפָר.

<sup>7</sup>Sing praises to Elohim, sing praises; sing praises unto our Melekh, sing praises.

זזַמְּרוּ אֱלֹהִים זַמֵּרוּ; זַמְּרוּ לְמַלְכֵּנוּ זַמֵּרוּ.

<sup>8</sup>For Elohim is Melekh of all the earth; sing praises in a skillful song.

<sup>ח</sup>כִּי מֶלֶךְ כָּל הָאָרֶץ אֱלֹהִים זַמְּרוּ מַשְׂכִּיל.

<sup>9</sup>Elohim reigns over the goyim; Elohim sits upon His consecrated throne.

<sup>ט</sup>מָלַךְ אֱלֹהִים עַל גּוֹיִם; אֱלֹהִים יָשַׁב עַל כִּסֵּא קָדְשׁוֹ.

<sup>10</sup>The princes of the peoples are gathered together, the people of the Elohim of Avraham; for unto Elohim belong the shields of the earth; He is greatly exalted.

<sup>י</sup>נְדִיבֵי עַמִּים נֶאֱסָפוּ עַם אֱלֹהֵי אַבְרָהָם: כִּי לֵאלֹהִים מָגִנֵּי אֶרֶץ מְאֹד נַעֲלָה.

# תְּהִלָּה 48 Tehillah

<sup>1</sup>A Song; a Mizmor for the sons of Korakh.

<sup>א</sup>שִׁיר מִזְמוֹר לִבְנֵי קֹרַח.

<sup>2</sup>Great is יהוה , and highly to be praised, in the city of our Elohim, His Har Kadosh,

<sup>ב</sup>גָּדוֹל יהוה וּמְהֻלָּל מְאֹד בְּעִיר אֱלֹהֵינוּ הַר קָדְשׁוֹ.

<sup>3</sup>Fair in situation, the joy of the whole earth; even Har Tzion, the uttermost parts of the north, the city of Melekh Rav.

<sup>ג</sup>יְפֵה נוֹף מְשׂוֹשׂ כָּל הָאָרֶץ: הַר צִיּוֹן יַרְכְּתֵי צָפוֹן; קִרְיַת מֶלֶךְ רָב.

<sup>4</sup>Elohim in her palaces has made Himself known for a stronghold.

<sup>ד</sup>אֱלֹהִים בְּאַרְמְנוֹתֶיהָ נוֹדַע לְמִשְׂגָּב.

<sup>5</sup>For, lo, the kings assembled themselves, they came onward together.

<sup>ה</sup>כִּי הִנֵּה הַמְּלָכִים נוֹעֲדוּ; עָבְרוּ יַחְדָּו.

⁶They saw, straightway they were amazed; they were terrified, they hasted away.

הֵמָּה רָאוּ כֵּן תָּמָהוּ; נִבְהֲלוּ נֶחְפָּזוּ.

⁷Trembling took hold of them there, pangs, as of a woman in travail.

רְעָדָה אֲחָזָתַם שָׁם; חִיל כַּיּוֹלֵדָה.

⁸With the east wind You break the ships of Tarshish.

בְּרוּחַ קָדִים תְּשַׁבֵּר אֳנִיּוֹת תַּרְשִׁישׁ.

⁹As we have heard, so have we seen; in the city of יהוה Tzeva'ot, in the city of our Elohim. Elohim establishes it forever. Selah.

כַּאֲשֶׁר שָׁמַעְנוּ כֵּן רָאִינוּ בְּעִיר יהוה צְבָאוֹת בְּעִיר אֱלֹהֵינוּ: אֱלֹהִים יְכוֹנְנֶהָ עַד עוֹלָם סֶלָה.

¹⁰We have thought on Your compassion, O Elohim, in the midst of Your Heikhal.

דִּמִּינוּ אֱלֹהִים חַסְדֶּךָ בְּקֶרֶב הֵיכָלֶךָ.

¹¹As is Your Name, O Elohim, so is Your praise unto the ends of the earth; Your right hand is full of righteousness.

כְּשִׁמְךָ אֱלֹהִים כֵּן תְּהִלָּתְךָ עַל קַצְוֵי אֶרֶץ; צֶדֶק מָלְאָה יְמִינֶךָ.

¹²Let Har Tzion be glad, let the daughters of Yehudah rejoice, because of Your judgments.

יִשְׂמַח הַר צִיּוֹן תָּגֵלְנָה בְּנוֹת יְהוּדָה: לְמַעַן מִשְׁפָּטֶיךָ.

¹³Walk about Tzion, and go round about her; count the towers thereof.

סֹבּוּ צִיּוֹן וְהַקִּיפוּהָ; סִפְרוּ מִגְדָּלֶיהָ.

¹⁴Mark well her ramparts, traverse her palaces; that you may tell it to the generation following.

שִׁיתוּ לִבְּכֶם לְחֵילָה פַּסְּגוּ אַרְמְנוֹתֶיהָ: לְמַעַן תְּסַפְּרוּ לְדוֹר אַחֲרוֹן.

<sup>15</sup>For such is Elohim, our Elohim, forever and ever; He will guide us even in death.

טּכִּי זֶה אֱלֹהִים אֱלֹהֵינוּ עוֹלָם וָעֶד; הוּא יְנַהֲגֵנוּ עַל מוּת.

# תְּהִלָּה 49 Tehillah

<sup>1</sup>For the Leader; a Mizmor for the sons of Korakh.

אלַמְנַצֵּחַ לִבְנֵי קֹרַח מִזְמוֹר.

<sup>2</sup>Hear this, all you peoples; give ear, all you inhabitants of the world,

בשִׁמְעוּ זֹאת כָּל הָעַמִּים; הַאֲזִינוּ כָּל יֹשְׁבֵי חָלֶד.

<sup>3</sup>Both low and high, rich and poor together.

גגַּם בְּנֵי אָדָם גַּם בְּנֵי אִישׁ יַחַד עָשִׁיר וְאֶבְיוֹן.

<sup>4</sup>My mouth shall speak wisdom, and the meditation of my heart shall be understanding.

דפִּי יְדַבֵּר חָכְמוֹת; וְהָגוּת לִבִּי תְבוּנוֹת.

<sup>5</sup>I will incline my ear to a mashal; I will open my dark saying upon the Kinor.

האַטֶּה לְמָשָׁל אָזְנִי; אֶפְתַּח בְּכִנּוֹר חִידָתִי.

<sup>6</sup>Why should I fear in the days of evil, when the iniquity of my supplanters ecompass me,

ולָמָּה אִירָא בִּימֵי רָע עֲוֹן עֲקֵבַי יְסוּבֵּנִי.

<sup>7</sup>Of them that trust in their wealth, and boast themselves in the multitude of their riches?

זהַבֹּטְחִים עַל חֵילָם; וּבְרֹב עָשְׁרָם יִתְהַלָּלוּ.

<sup>8</sup>No man can by any means redeem his brother, nor give to Elohim an atonement for him;

חאָח לֹא פָדֹה יִפְדֶּה אִישׁ; לֹא יִתֵּן לֵאלֹהִים כָּפְרוֹ.

⁹For too costly is the redemption of their soul, and must be let alone forever.

ⁱⁱⁱⁱⁱⁱ ⁱ טְוִיקַר פִּדְיוֹן נַפְשָׁם; וְחָדַל לְעוֹלָם.

¹⁰That he should still live always, that he should not see the pit.

ⁱוִיחִי עוֹד לָנֶצַח; לֹא יִרְאֶה הַשָּׁחַת.

¹¹For he sees that wise men die, the fool and the brutish together perish, and leave their wealth to others.

ⁱⁱכִּי יִרְאֶה חֲכָמִים יָמוּתוּ יַחַד כְּסִיל וָבַעַר יֹאבֵדוּ; וְעָזְבוּ לַאֲחֵרִים חֵילָם.

¹²Their inward thought is that their houses shall continue forever, and their dwelling-places to all generations; they call their lands after their own names.

ⁱⁱקִרְבָּם בָּתֵּימוֹ לְעוֹלָם מִשְׁכְּנֹתָם לְדוֹר וָדֹר; קָרְאוּ בִשְׁמוֹתָם עֲלֵי אֲדָמוֹת.

¹³But man abides not in honor; he is like the beasts that perish.

ⁱוְאָדָם בִּיקָר בַּל יָלִין; נִמְשַׁל כַּבְּהֵמוֹת נִדְמוּ.

¹⁴This is the way of them that are foolish, and of those who after them approve their sayings. Selah.

ⁱזֶה דַרְכָּם כֵּסֶל לָמוֹ; וְאַחֲרֵיהֶם בְּפִיהֶם יִרְצוּ סֶלָה.

¹⁵Like sheep they are appointed for She'ol; Mavet shall be their shepherd; and the upright shall have dominion over them in the morning; and their form shall be for She'ol to wear away, that there may be no habitation for it.

טְכַּצֹּאן לִשְׁאוֹל שַׁתּוּ מָוֶת יִרְעֵם: וַיִּרְדּוּ בָם יְשָׁרִים לַבֹּקֶר וצירם (וְצוּרָם) לְבַלּוֹת שְׁאוֹל; מִזְּבֻל לוֹ.

<sup>16</sup>But Elohim will redeem my soul from the power of She'ol; for He shall receive me. Selah.

ט<sup>ז</sup>אַךְ אֱלֹהִים יִפְדֶּה נַפְשִׁי מִיַּד שְׁאוֹל: כִּי יִקָּחֵנִי סֶלָה.

<sup>17</sup>Be not afraid when one waxes rich, when the wealth of his house is increased;

<sup>יז</sup>אַל תִּירָא כִּי יַעֲשִׁר אִישׁ: כִּי יִרְבֶּה כְּבוֹד בֵּיתוֹ.

<sup>18</sup>For when he dies he shall carry nothing away; his wealth shall not descend after him.

<sup>יח</sup>כִּי לֹא בְמוֹתוֹ יִקַּח הַכֹּל; לֹא יֵרֵד אַחֲרָיו כְּבוֹדוֹ.

<sup>19</sup>Though while he lived he blessed his soul, "Men will praise you, when you shall do well to yourself,"

<sup>יט</sup>כִּי נַפְשׁוֹ בְּחַיָּיו יְבָרֵךְ; וְיוֹדֻךָ כִּי תֵיטִיב לָךְ.

<sup>20</sup>It shall go to the generation of his fathers; they shall never see the light.

<sup>כ</sup>תָּבוֹא עַד דּוֹר אֲבוֹתָיו; עַד נֵצַח לֹא יִרְאוּ אוֹר.

<sup>21</sup>Man that is in honor understands not; he is like the beasts that perish.

<sup>כא</sup>אָדָם בִּיקָר וְלֹא יָבִין; נִמְשַׁל כַּבְּהֵמוֹת נִדְמוּ.

# Tehillah 50 תְּהִלָּה

<sup>1</sup>A Mizmor for Asaf. God, Elohim, יהוה , has spoken, and called the earth from the rising of the sun unto the going down thereof.

<sup>א</sup>מִזְמוֹר לְאָסָף: אֵל אֱלֹהִים יהוה דִּבֶּר וַיִּקְרָא אָרֶץ; מִמִּזְרַח שֶׁמֶשׁ עַד מְבֹאוֹ.

<sup>2</sup>Out of Tzion, the perfection of beauty, Elohim has shined forth.

<sup>ב</sup>מִצִּיּוֹן מִכְלַל יֹפִי אֱלֹהִים הוֹפִיעַ.

<sup>3</sup>Our Elohim comes, and does not keep silence; a fire devours before Him, and round about Him it storms mightily.

ג**יָבֹא אֱלֹהֵינוּ וְאַל יֶחֱרַשׁ: אֵשׁ לְפָנָיו תֹּאכֵל; וּסְבִיבָיו נִשְׂעֲרָה מְאֹד.**

<sup>4</sup>He calls to the heavens above, and to the earth, that He may judge His people:

ד**יִקְרָא אֶל הַשָּׁמַיִם מֵעָל; וְאֶל הָאָרֶץ לָדִין עַמּוֹ.**

<sup>5</sup>"Gather My Khasidim together unto Me; those that have made a Brit with Me by sacrifice."

ה**אִסְפוּ לִי חֲסִידָי כֹּרְתֵי בְרִיתִי עֲלֵי זָבַח.**

<sup>6</sup>And the heavens declare His righteousness; for Elohim, He is judge. Selah.

ו**וַיַּגִּידוּ שָׁמַיִם צִדְקוֹ: כִּי אֱלֹהִים שֹׁפֵט הוּא סֶלָה.**

<sup>7</sup>"Hear, O My people, and I will speak; O Yisra'el, and I will testify against you: Elohim, your Elohim, am I.

ז**שִׁמְעָה עַמִּי וַאֲדַבֵּרָה יִשְׂרָאֵל וְאָעִידָה בָּךְ: אֱלֹהִים אֱלֹהֶיךָ אָנֹכִי.**

<sup>8</sup>I will not reprove you for your sacrifices; and your Olot are continually before Me.

ח**לֹא עַל זְבָחֶיךָ אוֹכִיחֶךָ; וְעוֹלֹתֶיךָ לְנֶגְדִּי תָמִיד.**

<sup>9</sup>I will take no bullock out of your house, nor he-goats out of your folds.

ט**לֹא אֶקַּח מִבֵּיתְךָ פָר; מִמִּכְלְאֹתֶיךָ עַתּוּדִים.**

<sup>10</sup>For every beast of the forest is Mine, and the cattle upon a thousand hills.

י**כִּי לִי כָל חַיְתוֹ יָעַר; בְּהֵמוֹת בְּהַרְרֵי אָלֶף.**

<sup>11</sup>I know all the fowls of the mountains; and the wild beasts of the field are Mine.

יא**יָדַעְתִּי כָּל עוֹף הָרִים; וְזִיז שָׂדַי עִמָּדִי.**

<sup>12</sup>If I were hungry, I would not tell you; for the world is Mine, and the fullness thereof.

יבאִם־אֶרְעַב לֹא־אֹמַר לָךְ: כִּי־לִי תֵבֵל וּמְלֹאָהּ.

<sup>13</sup>Do I eat the flesh of bulls, or drink the blood of goats?

יגהַאוֹכַל בְּשַׂר אַבִּירִים; וְדַם עַתּוּדִים אֶשְׁתֶּה.

<sup>14</sup>Offer unto Elohim the Zevakh Todah; and pay your Nederim unto Elyon;

ידזְבַח לֵאלֹהִים תּוֹדָה; וְשַׁלֵּם לְעֶלְיוֹן נְדָרֶיךָ.

<sup>15</sup>And call upon Me in the day of trouble; I will deliver you, and you shall honor Me."

טווּקְרָאֵנִי בְּיוֹם צָרָה; אֲחַלֶּצְךָ וּתְכַבְּדֵנִי.

<sup>16</sup>But unto the wicked Elohim says, "What have you to do to declare My statutes, and that you have taken My Brit in your mouth?

טזוְלָרָשָׁע אָמַר אֱלֹהִים מַה־לְּךָ לְסַפֵּר חֻקָּי; וַתִּשָּׂא בְרִיתִי עֲלֵי פִיךָ.

<sup>17</sup>Seeing you hate instruction, and cast My D'varim behind you.

יזוְאַתָּה שָׂנֵאתָ מוּסָר; וַתַּשְׁלֵךְ דְּבָרַי אַחֲרֶיךָ.

<sup>18</sup>When you saw a thief, you had company with him, and with adulterers was your portion.

יחאִם־רָאִיתָ גַנָּב וַתִּרֶץ עִמּוֹ; וְעִם מְנָאֲפִים חֶלְקֶךָ.

<sup>19</sup>You have let loose your mouth for evil, and your tongue frames deceit.

יטפִּיךָ שָׁלַחְתָּ בְרָעָה; וּלְשׁוֹנְךָ תַּצְמִיד מִרְמָה.

<sup>20</sup>You sit and speak against your brother; you slander your own mother's son.

כתֵּשֵׁב בְּאָחִיךָ תְדַבֵּר; בְּבֶן אִמְּךָ תִּתֶּן דֹּפִי.

²¹These things have you done, and should I have kept silence? You had thought that I was altogether such a one as yourself? But I will reprove you, and set the cause before your eyes.

כאאֵלֶּה עָשִׂיתָ וְהֶחֱרַשְׁתִּי דִּמִּיתָ הֱיוֹת אֶהְיֶה כָמוֹךָ; אוֹכִיחֲךָ וְאֶעֶרְכָה לְעֵינֶיךָ.

²²Now consider this, you that forget Elohim, lest I tear in pieces, and there be none to deliver.

כבבִּינוּ נָא זֹאת שֹׁכְחֵי אֱלוֹהַּ: פֶּן אֶטְרֹף וְאֵין מַצִּיל.

²³Whoever offers the Zevakh Todah honors Me; and to him that orders his way aright will I show the Salvation of Elohim."

כגזֹבֵחַ תּוֹדָה יְכַבְּדָנְנִי: וְשָׂם דֶּרֶךְ אַרְאֶנּוּ בְּיֵשַׁע אֱלֹהִים.

# תְּהִלָּה 51 Tehillah

¹For the Leader. A Mizmor of David.

אלַמְנַצֵּחַ מִזְמוֹר לְדָוִד.

²When Natan HaNavi came unto him, after he had gone in to Bat Sheva.

בבְּבוֹא אֵלָיו נָתָן הַנָּבִיא כַּאֲשֶׁר בָּא אֶל בַּת שָׁבַע.

³Be gracious unto me, O Elohim, according to Your compassion; according to the multitude of Your mercies blot out my transgressions.

גחָנֵּנִי אֱלֹהִים כְּחַסְדֶּךָ; כְּרֹב רַחֲמֶיךָ מְחֵה פְשָׁעָי.

⁴Wash me thoroughly from my iniquity, and cleanse me from my sin.

דהרבה (הֶרֶב) כַּבְּסֵנִי מֵעֲוֹנִי; וּמֵחַטָּאתִי טַהֲרֵנִי.

311

⁵For I know my transgressions; and my sin is ever before me.

הּכִּי פְשָׁעַי אֲנִי אֵדָע; וְחַטָּאתִי נֶגְדִּי תָמִיד.

⁶Against You, You only, have I sinned, and done that which is evil in Your sight; that You may be justified when You speak, and be in the right when You judge.

וּלְךָ לְבַדְּךָ חָטָאתִי וְהָרַע בְּעֵינֶיךָ עָשִׂיתִי: לְמַעַן תִּצְדַּק בְּדָבְרֶךָ תִּזְכֶּה בְשָׁפְטֶךָ.

⁷Behold, I was brought forth in iniquity, and in sin did my mother conceive me.

זהֵן בְּעָווֹן חוֹלָלְתִּי; וּבְחֵטְא יֶחֱמַתְנִי אִמִּי.

⁸Behold, You desire truth in the inward parts; make me, therefore, to know wisdom in my inmost heart.

חהֵן אֱמֶת חָפַצְתָּ בַטֻּחוֹת; וּבְסָתֻם חָכְמָה תוֹדִיעֵנִי.

⁹Purge me with hyssop, and I shall be clean; wash me, and I shall be whiter than snow.

טתְּחַטְּאֵנִי בְאֵזוֹב וְאֶטְהָר; תְּכַבְּסֵנִי וּמִשֶּׁלֶג אַלְבִּין.

¹⁰Make me to hear joy and gladness; that the bones which You have crushed may rejoice.

יתַּשְׁמִיעֵנִי שָׂשׂוֹן וְשִׂמְחָה; תָּגֵלְנָה עֲצָמוֹת דִּכִּיתָ.

¹¹Hide Your face from my sins, and blot out all my iniquities.

יאהַסְתֵּר פָּנֶיךָ מֵחֲטָאָי; וְכָל עֲוֹנֹתַי מְחֵה.

¹²Create for me a clean heart, O Elohim; and renew a stedfast ru'akh within me.

יבלֵב טָהוֹר בְּרָא לִי אֱלֹהִים; וְרוּחַ נָכוֹן חַדֵּשׁ בְּקִרְבִּי.

¹³Cast me not away from Your presence; and take not Your Ru'akh HaKodesh from me.

יגאַל תַּשְׁלִיכֵנִי מִלְּפָנֶיךָ; וְרוּחַ קָדְשְׁךָ אַל תִּקַּח מִמֶּנִּי.

¹⁴Restore unto me the joy of Your Salvation; and let a willing Ru'akh uphold me.

ידהָשִׁיבָה לִי שְׂשׂוֹן יִשְׁעֶךָ; וְרוּחַ נְדִיבָה תִסְמְכֵנִי.

¹⁵Then will I teach transgressors Your ways; and sinners shall return unto You.

טואֲלַמְּדָה פֹשְׁעִים דְּרָכֶיךָ; וְחַטָּאִים אֵלֶיךָ יָשׁוּבוּ.

¹⁶Deliver me from bloodguiltiness, O Elohim, You, O Elohim of my Salvation; so shall my tongue sing aloud of Your tzedaka.

טזהַצִּילֵנִי מִדָּמִים אֱלֹהִים אֱלֹהֵי תְשׁוּעָתִי: תְּרַנֵּן לְשׁוֹנִי צִדְקָתֶךָ.

¹⁷O Adonai, open my lips; and my mouth shall declare Your praise.

יזאֲדֹנָי שְׂפָתַי תִּפְתָּח; וּפִי יַגִּיד תְּהִלָּתֶךָ.

¹⁸For You delight not in sacrifice, else would I give it; You have no pleasure in Olot.

יחכִּי לֹא תַחְפֹּץ זֶבַח וְאֶתֵּנָה; עוֹלָה לֹא תִרְצֶה.

¹⁹The sacrifices of Elohim are a broken spirit; a broken and a contrite heart, O Elohim, You will not despise.

יטזִבְחֵי אֱלֹהִים רוּחַ נִשְׁבָּרָה: לֵב נִשְׁבָּר וְנִדְכֶּה אֱלֹהִים לֹא תִבְזֶה.

²⁰Do good in Your favor unto Tzion; build the walls of Yerushalayim.

כהֵיטִיבָה בִרְצוֹנְךָ אֶת צִיּוֹן; תִּבְנֶה חוֹמוֹת יְרוּשָׁלָםִ.

<sup>21</sup>Then will You delight in the sacrifices of righteousness, in Olot and whole offering; then will they offer bullocks upon Your Mizbe'akh.

כאאָז תַּחְפֹּץ זִבְחֵי צֶדֶק עוֹלָה וְכָלִיל; אָז יַעֲלוּ עַל מִזְבַּחֲךָ פָרִים.

# תְּהִלָּה 52 Tehillah

<sup>1</sup>For the Leader. A Maskil of David;

אלַמְנַצֵּחַ מַשְׂכִּיל לְדָוִד.

<sup>2</sup>when Do'eg the Adomi came and told Sha'ul, and said unto him, "David is come to the house of Akhimelekh."

בבְּבוֹא דּוֹאֵג הָאֲדֹמִי וַיַּגֵּד לְשָׁאוּל: וַיֹּאמֶר לוֹ בָּא דָוִד אֶל בֵּית אֲחִימֶלֶךְ.

<sup>3</sup>Why do you boast yourself of evil, O mighty man? The compassion of Elohim endures continually.

גמַה תִּתְהַלֵּל בְּרָעָה הַגִּבּוֹר; חֶסֶד אֵל כָּל הַיּוֹם.

<sup>4</sup>Your tongue devises destruction; like a sharp razor, working deceitfully.

דהַוּוֹת תַּחְשֹׁב לְשׁוֹנֶךָ; כְּתַעַר מְלֻטָּשׁ עֹשֵׂה רְמִיָּה.

<sup>5</sup>You love evil more than good; falsehood rather than speaking righteousness. Selah.

האָהַבְתָּ רָּע מִטּוֹב; שֶׁקֶר מִדַּבֵּר צֶדֶק סֶלָה.

<sup>6</sup>You love all devouring words, the deceitful tongue.

ואָהַבְתָּ כָל דִּבְרֵי בָלַע; לְשׁוֹן מִרְמָה.

⁷Elohim will likewise break you forever; He will take you up, and pluck you out of your tent, and root you out of the land of the living. Selah.

גַּם אֵל יִתָּצְךָ לָנֶצַח: יַחְתְּךָ וְיִסָּחֲךָ מֵאֹהֶל; וְשֵׁרֶשְׁךָ מֵאֶרֶץ חַיִּים סֶלָה.

⁸The Tzadikim also shall see, and fear, and shall laugh at him:

וְיִרְאוּ צַדִּיקִים וְיִירָאוּ; וְעָלָיו יִשְׂחָקוּ.

⁹"Lo, this is the man that made not Elohim his stronghold, but trusted in the abundance of his riches, and strengthened himself in his wickedness?"

הִנֵּה הַגֶּבֶר לֹא יָשִׂים אֱלֹהִים מָעוּזּוֹ: וַיִּבְטַח בְּרֹב עָשְׁרוֹ; יָעֹז בְּהַוָּתוֹ.

¹⁰But as for me, I am like a leafy olive tree in Beit Elohim; I trust in the compassion of Elohim forever and ever.

וַאֲנִי כְּזַיִת רַעֲנָן בְּבֵית אֱלֹהִים; בָּטַחְתִּי בְחֶסֶד אֱלֹהִים עוֹלָם וָעֶד.

¹¹I will give You thanks forever, because You have done it; and I will wait for Your Name, for it is good, in the presence of Your Khasidim.

אוֹדְךָ לְעוֹלָם כִּי עָשִׂיתָ; וַאֲקַוֶּה שִׁמְךָ כִי טוֹב נֶגֶד חֲסִידֶיךָ.

# Tehillah 53 תְּהִלָּה

¹For the Leader; upon Makhalat. A Maskil of David.

לַמְנַצֵּחַ עַל מָחֲלַת מַשְׂכִּיל לְדָוִד.

315

²The fool has said in his heart, "There is no Elohim"; they have dealt corruptly, and have done abominable iniquity; there is none that does good.

בֶּאָמַר נָבָל בְּלִבּוֹ אֵין אֱלֹהִים; הִשְׁחִיתוּ וְהִתְעִיבוּ עָוֶל אֵין עֹשֵׂה טוֹב.

³Elohim looked forth from heaven upon the children of men, to see if there was any man of understanding, that did seek after Elohim.

גֱאלֹהִים מִשָּׁמַיִם הִשְׁקִיף עַל בְּנֵי אָדָם: לִרְאוֹת הֲיֵשׁ מַשְׂכִּיל דֹּרֵשׁ אֶת אֱלֹהִים.

⁴Every one of them is unclean, they are together become impure; there is none that does good, no, not one.

דֱכֻּלּוֹ סָג יַחְדָּו נֶאֱלָחוּ: אֵין עֹשֵׂה טוֹב; אֵין גַּם אֶחָד.

⁵"Shall not the workers of iniquity know it, who eat up My people as they eat bread, and call not upon Elohim?"

הֱהֲלֹא יָדְעוּ פֹּעֲלֵי אָוֶן: אֹכְלֵי עַמִּי אָכְלוּ לֶחֶם; אֱלֹהִים לֹא קָרָאוּ.

⁶There are they in great fear, where no fear was; for Elohim has scattered the bones of him that encamps against you; You have put them to shame, because Elohim has rejected them.

וֱשָׁם פָּחֲדוּ פַחַד לֹא הָיָה פָחַד: כִּי אֱלֹהִים פִּזַּר עַצְמוֹת חֹנָךְ; הֱבִשֹׁתָה כִּי אֱלֹהִים מְאָסָם.

⁷Oh that the Salvation of Yisra'el were come out of Tzion! When Elohim turns the captivity of His people, let Ya'akov rejoice; let Yisra'el be glad.

זֱמִי יִתֵּן מִצִּיּוֹן יְשֻׁעוֹת יִשְׂרָאֵל: בְּשׁוּב אֱלֹהִים שְׁבוּת עַמּוֹ; יָגֵל יַעֲקֹב יִשְׂמַח יִשְׂרָאֵל.

# Tehillah 54 תְּהִלָּה

¹For the Leader; with string-music. A Maskil of David.

אלַמְנַצֵּחַ בִּנְגִינֹת מַשְׂכִּיל לְדָוִד.

²When the Zifim came and said to Sha'ul, "Does not David hide himself with us?"

בבְּבֹא הַזִּיפִים וַיֹּאמְרוּ לְשָׁאוּל: הֲלֹא דָוִד מִסְתַּתֵּר עִמָּנוּ.

³O Elohim, save me by Your Name, and right me by Your might.

גאֱלֹהִים בְּשִׁמְךָ הוֹשִׁיעֵנִי; וּבִגְבוּרָתְךָ תְדִינֵנִי.

⁴O Elohim, hear my tefilah; give ear to the words of my mouth.

דאֱלֹהִים שְׁמַע תְּפִלָּתִי; הַאֲזִינָה לְאִמְרֵי פִי.

⁵For strangers are risen up against me, and violent men have sought after my soul; they have not set Elohim before them. Selah.

הכִּי זָרִים קָמוּ עָלַי וְעָרִיצִים בִּקְשׁוּ נַפְשִׁי; לֹא שָׂמוּ אֱלֹהִים לְנֶגְדָּם סֶלָה.

⁶Behold, Elohim is my helper; Adonai is for me as the upholder of my soul.

והִנֵּה אֱלֹהִים עֹזֵר לִי; אֲדֹנָי בְּסֹמְכֵי נַפְשִׁי.

⁷He will requite the evil unto them that lie in wait for me; destroy them in Your truth.

זישוב (יָשִׁיב) הָרַע לְשֹׁרְרָי; בַּאֲמִתְּךָ הַצְמִיתֵם.

⁸With a Nedavah will I sacrifice unto You; I will give thanks unto Your Name, O יהוה , for it is good.

חבִּנְדָבָה אֶזְבְּחָה לָּךְ; אוֹדֶה שִׁמְךָ יהוה כִּי טוֹב.

⁹For He has delivered me out of all trouble; and my eye has gazed upon my enemies.

ט כִּי מִכָּל צָרָה הִצִּילָנִי; וּבְאֹיְבַי רָאֲתָה עֵינִי.

# תְּהִלָּה 55 Tehillah

¹For the Leader; with string-music. A Maskil of David.

א לַמְנַצֵּחַ בִּנְגִינֹת מַשְׂכִּיל לְדָוִד.

²Give ear, O Elohim, to my tefilah; and hide not Yourself from my supplication.

ב הַאֲזִינָה אֱלֹהִים תְּפִלָּתִי; וְאַל תִּתְעַלַּם מִתְּחִנָּתִי.

³Attend unto me, and hear me; I am distraught in my complaint, and will moan;

ג הַקְשִׁיבָה לִּי וַעֲנֵנִי; אָרִיד בְּשִׂיחִי וְאָהִימָה.

⁴Because of the voice of the enemy, because of the oppression of the wicked; for they cast mischief upon me, and in anger they persecute me.

ד מִקּוֹל אוֹיֵב מִפְּנֵי עָקַת רָשָׁע: כִּי יָמִיטוּ עָלַי אָוֶן וּבְאַף יִשְׂטְמוּנִי.

⁵My heart does writhe within me; and the terrors of Mavet are fallen upon me.

ה לִבִּי יָחִיל בְּקִרְבִּי; וְאֵימוֹת מָוֶת נָפְלוּ עָלָי.

⁶Fear and trembling come upon me, and horror has overwhelmed me.

ו יִרְאָה וָרַעַד יָבֹא בִי; וַתְּכַסֵּנִי פַּלָּצוּת.

⁷And I said, "Oh that I had wings like a dove! Then would I fly away, and be at rest.

ז וָאֹמַר מִי יִתֶּן לִי אֵבֶר כַּיּוֹנָה: אָעוּפָה וְאֶשְׁכֹּנָה.

⁸Lo, then would I wander far off, I would lodge in the wilderness. Selah.

ᶜהִנֵּה אַרְחִיק נְדֹד; אָלִין בַּמִּדְבָּר סֶלָה.

⁹I would haste me to a shelter from the stormy wind and tempest."

ᵗאָחִישָׁה מִפְלָט לִי מֵרוּחַ סֹעָה מִסָּעַר.

¹⁰Destroy, O Adonai, and divide their tongue; for I have seen violence and strife in the city.

ᶦבַּלַּע אֲדֹנָי פַּלַּג לְשׁוֹנָם: כִּי רָאִיתִי חָמָס וְרִיב בָּעִיר.

¹¹Day and night they go about it upon the walls thereof; iniquity also, and mischief, are in the midst of it.

ᵃᶦיוֹמָם וָלַיְלָה יְסוֹבְבֻהָ עַל חוֹמֹתֶיהָ; וְאָוֶן וְעָמָל בְּקִרְבָּהּ.

¹²Wickedness is in the midst thereof; oppression and guile depart not from her broad place.

ᵇᶦהַוּוֹת בְּקִרְבָּהּ; וְלֹא יָמִישׁ מֵרְחֹבָהּ תֹּךְ וּמִרְמָה.

¹³For it was not an enemy that taunted me, then I could have borne it; neither was it my adversary that did magnify himself against me, then I would have hidden myself from him.

ᵍᶦכִּי לֹא אוֹיֵב יְחָרְפֵנִי וְאֶשָּׂא: לֹא מְשַׂנְאִי עָלַי הִגְדִּיל; וְאֶסָּתֵר מִמֶּנּוּ.

¹⁴But it was you, a man my equal, my companion, and my familiar friend;

ᵈᶦוְאַתָּה אֱנוֹשׁ כְּעֶרְכִּי; אַלּוּפִי וּמְיֻדָּעִי.

¹⁵We took sweet counsel together, in Beit Elohim we walked with the throng.

ᵗᶦאֲשֶׁר יַחְדָּו נַמְתִּיק סוֹד; בְּבֵית אֱלֹהִים נְהַלֵּךְ בְּרָגֶשׁ.

<sup>16</sup>May He incite Mavet against them, let them go down alive into She'ol; for evil is in their dwelling, and within them.

ט״יַשִּׁימוֹת (יַשִּׁי מָוֶת) עָלֵימוֹ יֵרְדוּ שְׁאוֹל חַיִּים: כִּי רָעוֹת בִּמְגוּרָם בְּקִרְבָּם.

<sup>17</sup>As for me, I will call upon Elohim; and יהוה shall save me.

י״אֲנִי אֶל אֱלֹהִים אֶקְרָא; וַיהוה יוֹשִׁיעֵנִי.

<sup>18</sup>Evening, and morning, and at noon, will I complain, and moan; and He has heard my voice.

י״עֶרֶב וָבֹקֶר וְצָהֳרַיִם אָשִׂיחָה וְאֶהֱמֶה; וַיִּשְׁמַע קוֹלִי.

<sup>19</sup>He has redeemed my soul in shalom from those nearby to me; for they were many that strove with me.

י״פָּדָה בְשָׁלוֹם נַפְשִׁי מִקְּרָב לִי: כִּי בְרַבִּים הָיוּ עִמָּדִי.

<sup>20</sup>Elohim shall hear, and humble them, even He that is enthroned of old, Selah, such as have no changes, and fear not Elohim.

כ״יִשְׁמַע אֵל וְיַעֲנֵם וְיֹשֵׁב קֶדֶם סֶלָה: אֲשֶׁר אֵין חֲלִיפוֹת לָמוֹ; וְלֹא יָרְאוּ אֱלֹהִים.

<sup>21</sup>He has put forth his hands against them that were at shalom with him; he has profaned his Brit.

כא״שָׁלַח יָדָיו בִּשְׁלֹמָיו; חִלֵּל בְּרִיתוֹ.

<sup>22</sup>Smoother than cream were the speeches of his mouth, but his heart was war; his words were softer than oil, yet were they keen-edged swords.

כב״חָלְקוּ מַחְמָאֹת פִּיו וּקְרָב לִבּוֹ: רַכּוּ דְבָרָיו מִשֶּׁמֶן; וְהֵמָּה פְתִחוֹת.

²³Cast your burden upon יהוה , and He will sustain you; He will never suffer HaTzadik to be moved.

כג הַשְׁלֵךְ עַל יהוה יְהָבְךָ וְהוּא יְכַלְכְּלֶךָ: לֹא יִתֵּן לְעוֹלָם מוֹט לַצַּדִּיק.

²⁴But You, O Elohim, will bring them down into the nethermost pit; men of blood and deceit shall not live out half their days; but as for me, I will trust in You.

כד וְאַתָּה אֱלֹהִים תּוֹרִדֵם לִבְאֵר שַׁחַת אַנְשֵׁי דָמִים וּמִרְמָה לֹא יֶחֱצוּ יְמֵיהֶם;

# Tehillah 56 תְּהִלָּה

¹For the Leader; upon Yonat Elem Rekhokim. For David; A Mikhtam; when the P'lishtim took him in Gat.

א לַמְנַצֵּחַ עַל יוֹנַת אֵלֶם רְחֹקִים לְדָוִד מִכְתָּם: בֶּאֱחֹז אוֹתוֹ פְלִשְׁתִּים בְּגַת.

²Be gracious unto me, O Elohim, for man would swallow me up; all the day he, with fighting, oppresses me.

ב חָנֵּנִי אֱלֹהִים כִּי שְׁאָפַנִי אֱנוֹשׁ; כָּל הַיּוֹם לֹחֵם יִלְחָצֵנִי.

³They that lie in wait for me would swallow me up all the day; for they are many that fight against me, O Exalted One.

ג שָׁאֲפוּ שׁוֹרְרַי כָּל הַיּוֹם: כִּי רַבִּים לֹחֲמִים לִי מָרוֹם.

⁴In the day that I am afraid, I will put my trust in You.

ד יוֹם אִירָא אֲנִי אֵלֶיךָ אֶבְטָח.

<sup>5</sup>In Elohim, I will praise His D'var. In Elohim do I trust, I will not be afraid; what can flesh do unto me?

בֵּאלֹהִים אֲהַלֵּל דְּבָרוֹ: בֵּאלֹהִים בָּטַחְתִּי לֹא אִירָא; מַה יַּעֲשֶׂה בָשָׂר לִי.

<sup>6</sup>All the day they trouble my affairs; all their thoughts are against me for evil.

כָּל הַיּוֹם דְּבָרַי יְעַצֵּבוּ; עָלַי כָּל מַחְשְׁבֹתָם לָרָע.

<sup>7</sup>They gather themselves together, they hide themselves, they mark my steps; according as they have waited for my soul.

יָגוּרוּ יצפינו (יִצְפּוֹנוּ) הֵמָּה עֲקֵבַי יִשְׁמֹרוּ: כַּאֲשֶׁר קִוּוּ נַפְשִׁי.

<sup>8</sup>Because of iniquity cast them out; in anger bring down the peoples, O Elohim.

עַל אָוֶן פַּלֶּט לָמוֹ; בְּאַף עַמִּים הוֹרֵד אֱלֹהִים.

<sup>9</sup>You have counted my wanderings; put my tears into Your bottle; are they not in Your Sefer?

נֹדִי סָפַרְתָּה אָתָּה: שִׂימָה דִמְעָתִי בְנֹאדֶךָ; הֲלֹא בְּסִפְרָתֶךָ.

<sup>10</sup>Then shall my enemies turn back in the day that I call; this I know, that Elohim is for me.

אָז יָשׁוּבוּ אוֹיְבַי אָחוֹר בְּיוֹם אֶקְרָא; זֶה יָדַעְתִּי כִּי אֱלֹהִים לִי.

<sup>11</sup>In Elohim, I will praise His D'var. In יהוה, I will praise His D'var.

בֵּאלֹהִים אֲהַלֵּל דָּבָר; בַּיהוה אֲהַלֵּל דָּבָר.

<sup>12</sup>In Elohim do I trust, I will not be afraid; what can man do unto me?

בֵּאלֹהִים בָּטַחְתִּי לֹא אִירָא; מַה יַּעֲשֶׂה אָדָם לִי.

<sup>13</sup>Your vows are upon me, O Elohim; I will render Todah offerings unto You.

"עָלַי אֱלֹהִים נְדָרֶיךָ; אֲשַׁלֵּם תּוֹדֹת לָךְ.

<sup>14</sup>For You have delivered my soul from Mavet; have You not delivered my feet from stumbling, that I may walk before Elohim in Or HaKhayim?

"כִּי הִצַּלְתָּ נַפְשִׁי מִמָּוֶת הֲלֹא רַגְלַי מִדֶּחִי: לְהִתְהַלֵּךְ לִפְנֵי אֱלֹהִים בְּאוֹר הַחַיִּים.

# Tehillah 57 תְּהִלָּה

<sup>1</sup>For the Leader; Al Tashkhet. By David; A Mikhtam; when he fled from Sha'ul, in the cave.

"לַמְנַצֵּחַ אַל תַּשְׁחֵת לְדָוִד מִכְתָּם בְּבָרְחוֹ מִפְּנֵי שָׁאוּל בַּמְּעָרָה.

<sup>2</sup>Be gracious unto me, O Elohim, be gracious unto me, for in You has my soul taken refuge; yes, in the shadow of Your wings will I take refuge, until calamities are overpast.

"חָנֵּנִי אֱלֹהִים חָנֵּנִי כִּי בְךָ חָסָיָה נַפְשִׁי: וּבְצֵל כְּנָפֶיךָ אֶחְסֶה עַד יַעֲבֹר הַוּוֹת.

<sup>3</sup>I will cry unto Elohim, Elyon; unto Elohim that accomplishes it for me.

"אֶקְרָא לֵאלֹהִים עֶלְיוֹן; לָאֵל גֹּמֵר עָלָי.

<sup>4</sup>He will send from heaven, and save me, when he that would swallow me up taunts; Selah. Elohim shall send forth His compassion and His truth.

"יִשְׁלַח מִשָּׁמַיִם וְיוֹשִׁיעֵנִי חֵרֵף שֹׁאֲפִי סֶלָה; יִשְׁלַח אֱלֹהִים חַסְדּוֹ וַאֲמִתּוֹ.

323

⁵My soul is among lions, I do lie down among them that are aflame; even the sons of men, whose teeth are spears and arrows, and their tongue a sharp sword.

ⁿנַפְשִׁי בְּתוֹךְ לְבָאִם אֶשְׁכְּבָה לֹהֲטִים: בְּנֵי אָדָם שִׁנֵּיהֶם חֲנִית וְחִצִּים; וּלְשׁוֹנָם חֶרֶב חַדָּה.

⁶Be exalted, O Elohim, above the heavens; Your Kavod is above all the earth.

ⁱרוּמָה עַל הַשָּׁמַיִם אֱלֹהִים; עַל כָּל הָאָרֶץ כְּבוֹדֶךָ.

⁷They have prepared a net for my steps, my soul is bowed down; they have digged a pit before me, they are fallen into the midst thereof themselves. Selah.

ⁱרֶשֶׁת הֵכִינוּ לִפְעָמַי כָּפַף נַפְשִׁי: כָּרוּ לְפָנַי שִׁיחָה; נָפְלוּ בְתוֹכָהּ סֶלָה.

⁸My heart is stedfast, O Elohim, my heart is stedfast; I will sing, yes, I will sing praises.

ⁿנָכוֹן לִבִּי אֱלֹהִים נָכוֹן לִבִּי; אָשִׁירָה וַאֲזַמֵּרָה.

⁹Awake, my glory; awake, Nevel and Kinor; I will awaken the dawn.

ⁱעוּרָה כְבוֹדִי עוּרָה הַנֵּבֶל וְכִנּוֹר; אָעִירָה שָּׁחַר.

¹⁰I will give thanks unto You, O Adonai, among the peoples; I will sing praises unto You among the nations.

ⁱאוֹדְךָ בָעַמִּים אֲדֹנָי; אֲזַמֶּרְךָ בַּלְאֻמִּים.

¹¹For Your compassion is great unto the heavens, and Your truth unto the skies.

ⁱⁿכִּי גָדֹל עַד שָׁמַיִם חַסְדֶּךָ; וְעַד שְׁחָקִים אֲמִתֶּךָ.

¹²Be exalted, O Elohim, above the heavens; Your glory is above all the earth.

יֵרוּמָה עַל שָׁמַיִם אֱלֹהִים; עַל כָּל הָאָרֶץ כְּבוֹדֶךָ.

# תְּהִלָּה 58 Tehillah

¹For the Leader; Al Tashkhet. By David; A Mikhtam.

אַלַמְנַצֵּחַ אַל תַּשְׁחֵת לְדָוִד מִכְתָּם.

²Do you indeed speak as a righteous company? Do you judge with equity the sons of men?

בַּהַאֻמְנָם אֵלֶם צֶדֶק תְּדַבֵּרוּן; מֵישָׁרִים תִּשְׁפְּטוּ בְּנֵי אָדָם.

³Yes, in heart you work wickedness; you weigh out in the earth the violence of your hands.

גַּאַף בְּלֵב עוֹלֹת תִּפְעָלוּן: בָּאָרֶץ חֲמַס יְדֵיכֶם תְּפַלֵּסוּן.

⁴The wicked are estranged from the womb; the speakers of lies go astray as soon as they are born.

דֹזֹרוּ רְשָׁעִים מֵרָחֶם; תָּעוּ מִבֶּטֶן דֹּבְרֵי כָזָב.

⁵Their venom is like the venom of a serpent; they are like the deaf asp that stops her ear;

הֹחֲמַת לָמוֹ כִּדְמוּת חֲמַת נָחָשׁ; כְּמוֹ פֶתֶן חֵרֵשׁ יַאְטֵם אָזְנוֹ.

⁶Which hearkens not to the voice of charmers, or of the most cunning binder of spells.

ואַשֶׁר לֹא יִשְׁמַע לְקוֹל מְלַחֲשִׁים; חוֹבֵר חֲבָרִים מְחֻכָּם.

⁷Break their teeth, O Elohim, in their mouth; break out the cheek-teeth of the young lions, O יהוה .

זאֱלֹהִים הֲרָס שִׁנֵּימוֹ בְּפִימוֹ; מַלְתְּעוֹת כְּפִירִים נְתֹץ יהוה .

⁸Let them melt away as water that runs apace; when he aims his arrows, let them be as though they were cut off.

חיִמָּאֲסוּ כְמוֹ מַיִם יִתְהַלְכוּ לָמוֹ; יִדְרֹךְ חִצּוֹ כְּמוֹ יִתְמֹלָלוּ.

⁹Let them be as a snail which melts and passes away; like the untimely births of a woman, that have not seen the sun.

טכְּמוֹ שַׁבְּלוּל תֶּמֶס יַהֲלֹךְ; נֵפֶל אֵשֶׁת בַּל חָזוּ שָׁמֶשׁ.

¹⁰Before your pots can feel the thorns, He will sweep it away with a whirlwind, the raw and the burning alike.

יבְּטֶרֶם יָבִינוּ סִירֹתֵכֶם אָטָד; כְּמוֹ חַי כְּמוֹ חָרוֹן יִשְׂעָרֶנּוּ.

¹¹A Tzadik shall rejoice when he sees the vengeance; he shall wash his feet in the blood of the wicked.

יאיִשְׂמַח צַדִּיק כִּי חָזָה נָקָם; פְּעָמָיו יִרְחַץ בְּדַם הָרָשָׁע.

¹²And men shall say, "Indeed there is a reward for HaTzadik; indeed there is an Elohim that judges in the earth."

יבוְיֹאמַר אָדָם אַךְ פְּרִי לַצַּדִּיק; אַךְ יֵשׁ אֱלֹהִים שֹׁפְטִים בָּאָרֶץ.

# Tehillah 59 תְּהִלָּה

¹For the Leader; Al Tashkhet. By David; A Mikhtam; when Sha'ul sent, and they watched the house to kill him.

אלַמְנַצֵּחַ אַל תַּשְׁחֵת לְדָוִד מִכְתָּם: בִּשְׁלֹחַ שָׁאוּל; וַיִּשְׁמְרוּ אֶת הַבַּיִת לַהֲמִיתוֹ.

²Deliver me from my enemies, O my Elohim; set me on high from them that rise up against me.

גהַצִּילֵנִי מֵאֹיְבַי אֱלֹהָי; מִמִּתְקוֹמְמַי תְּשַׂגְּבֵנִי.

³Deliver me from the workers of iniquity, and save me from the men of blood.

דהַצִּילֵנִי מִפֹּעֲלֵי אָוֶן; וּמֵאַנְשֵׁי דָמִים הוֹשִׁיעֵנִי.

⁴For, lo, they lie in wait for my soul; the impudent gather themselves together against me; not for my transgression, nor for my sin, O יהוה.

הכִּי הִנֵּה אָרְבוּ לְנַפְשִׁי יָגוּרוּ עָלַי עַזִּים; לֹא פִשְׁעִי וְלֹא חַטָּאתִי יהוה.

⁵Without my fault, they run and prepare themselves; awake to help me, and behold.

הבְּלִי עָוֹן יְרֻצוּן וְיִכּוֹנָנוּ; עוּרָה לִקְרָאתִי וּרְאֵה.

⁶You therefore, O יהוה Elohim Tzeva'ot, the Elohim of Yisra'el, arouse Yourself to punish all the nations; show no grace to any iniquitous traitors. Selah.

וְאַתָּה יהוה אֱלֹהִים צְבָאוֹת אֱלֹהֵי יִשְׂרָאֵל הָקִיצָה לִפְקֹד כָּל הַגּוֹיִם; אַל תָּחֹן כָּל בֹּגְדֵי אָוֶן סֶלָה.

⁷They return at evening, they howl like a dog, and go round about the city.

זיָשׁוּבוּ לָעֶרֶב יֶהֱמוּ כַכָּלֶב; וִיסוֹבְבוּ עִיר.

⁸Behold, they belch out with their mouth; swords are in their lips, "For who does hear?"

חהִנֵּה יַבִּיעוּן בְּפִיהֶם חֲרָבוֹת בְּשִׂפְתוֹתֵיהֶם: כִּי מִי שֹׁמֵעַ.

<sup>9</sup>But You, O יהוה , shall laugh at them; You shall have all the goyim in derision.

ט וְאַתָּה יהוה תִּשְׂחַק לָמוֹ; תִּלְעַג לְכָל גּוֹיִם.

<sup>10</sup>Because of his strength, I will wait for You; for Elohim is my high tower.

י עֻזּוֹ אֵלֶיךָ אֶשְׁמֹרָה: כִּי אֱלֹהִים מִשְׂגַּבִּי.

<sup>11</sup>The Elohim of my compassion will come to meet me; Elohim will let me gaze upon my adversaries.

יא אֱלֹהֵי חסדו (חַסְדִּי) יְקַדְּמֵנִי; אֱלֹהִים יַרְאֵנִי בְשֹׁרְרָי.

<sup>12</sup>Slay them not, lest my people forget, make them wander to and fro by Your power, and bring them down, O Adonai our Magen.

יב אַל תַּהַרְגֵם פֶּן יִשְׁכְּחוּ עַמִּי הֲנִיעֵמוֹ בְחֵילְךָ וְהוֹרִידֵמוֹ: מָגְנֵּנוּ אֲדֹנָי.

<sup>13</sup>For the sin of their mouth, and the words of their lips, let them even be taken in their pride, and for cursing and lying which they speak.

יג חַטַּאת פִּימוֹ דְּבַר שְׂפָתֵימוֹ: וְיִלָּכְדוּ בִגְאוֹנָם; וּמֵאָלָה וּמִכַּחַשׁ יְסַפֵּרוּ.

<sup>14</sup>Consume them in wrath, consume them, that they shall be no more; and let them know that Elohim rules in Ya'akov, unto the ends of the earth. Selah.

יד כַּלֵּה בְחֵמָה כַּלֵּה וְאֵינֵמוֹ: וְיֵדְעוּ כִּי אֱלֹהִים מֹשֵׁל בְּיַעֲקֹב; לְאַפְסֵי הָאָרֶץ סֶלָה.

<sup>15</sup>And they return at evening, they howl like a dog, and go round about the city;

טו וְיָשֻׁבוּ לָעֶרֶב יֶהֱמוּ כַכָּלֶב; וִיסוֹבְבוּ עִיר.

<sup>16</sup>They wander up and down to devour, and tarry all night if they have not their fill.

ט״הֵמָּה יְנוּעוּן (יְנִיעוּן) לֶאֱכֹל אִם לֹא יִשְׂבְּעוּ וַיָּלִינוּ.

<sup>17</sup>But as for me, I will sing of Your strength; yes, I will sing aloud of Your compassion in the morning; for You have been my high tower, and a refuge in the day of my distress.

י״וַאֲנִי אָשִׁיר עֻזֶּךָ וַאֲרַנֵּן לַבֹּקֶר חַסְדֶּךָ: כִּי הָיִיתָ מִשְׂגָּב לִי; וּמָנוֹס בְּיוֹם צַר לִי.

<sup>18</sup>O my strength, unto You will I sing praises; for Elohim is my high tower, the Elohim of my compassion.

י״חעֻזִּי אֵלֶיךָ אֲזַמֵּרָה: כִּי אֱלֹהִים מִשְׂגַּבִּי אֱלֹהֵי חַסְדִּי.

# Tehillah 60 תְּהִלָּה

<sup>1</sup>For the Leader; upon Shushan Edut; A Mikhtam of David, to teach.

א״לַמְנַצֵּחַ עַל שׁוּשַׁן עֵדוּת; מִכְתָּם לְדָוִד לְלַמֵּד.

<sup>2</sup>When he strove with Aram Naharayim and with Aram Tzovah, and Yo'av returned, and smote of Edom in the Valley of Salt twelve thousand.

ב״בְּהַצּוֹתוֹ אֶת אֲרַם נַהֲרַיִם וְאֶת אֲרַם צוֹבָה: וַיָּשָׁב יוֹאָב וַיַּךְ אֶת אֱדוֹם בְּגֵיא מֶלַח שְׁנֵים עָשָׂר אָלֶף.

<sup>3</sup>O Elohim, You have cast us off, You have broken us down; You have been angry; O restore us.

ג״אֱלֹהִים זְנַחְתָּנוּ פְרַצְתָּנוּ; אָנַפְתָּ תְּשׁוֹבֵב לָנוּ.

⁴You have made the land to shake, You have cleft it; heal the breaches thereof; for it totters.

הִרְעַשְׁתָּה אֶרֶץ פְּצַמְתָּהּ; רְפָה שְׁבָרֶיהָ כִי מָטָה.

⁵You have made Your people to see hard things; You have made us to drink the wine of staggering.

הִרְאִיתָ עַמְּךָ קָשָׁה; הִשְׁקִיתָנוּ יַיִן תַּרְעֵלָה.

⁶You have given a banner to them that fear You, that it may be displayed because of the truth. Selah.

נָתַתָּה לִּירֵאֶיךָ נֵּס לְהִתְנוֹסֵס מִפְּנֵי קֹשֶׁט סֶלָה.

⁷That Your beloved may be delivered, save with Your right hand, and answer me.

לְמַעַן יֵחָלְצוּן יְדִידֶיךָ; הוֹשִׁיעָה יְמִינְךָ וענני (וַעֲנֵנִי).

⁸Elohim spoke in His Kodesh, that I would exult; that I would divide Shekhem, and mete out the valley of Sukkot.

אֱלֹהִים דִּבֶּר בְּקָדְשׁוֹ אֶעְלֹזָה: אֲחַלְּקָה שְׁכֶם; וְעֵמֶק סֻכּוֹת אֲמַדֵּד.

⁹"Gilad is Mine, and Menasheh is Mine; Efrayim also is the head of my defense; Yehudah is my scepter.

לִי גִלְעָד וְלִי מְנַשֶּׁה וְאֶפְרַיִם מָעוֹז רֹאשִׁי; יְהוּדָה מְחֹקְקִי.

¹⁰Mo'av is My washpot; upon Edom do I cast My shoe; Peleshet, cry aloud because of Me!"

מוֹאָב סִיר רַחְצִי עַל אֱדוֹם אַשְׁלִיךְ נַעֲלִי; עָלַי פְּלֶשֶׁת הִתְרוֹעָעִי.

¹¹Who will bring me into the fortified city? Who will lead me unto Edom?

מִי יֹבְלֵנִי עִיר מָצוֹר; מִי נָחַנִי עַד אֱדוֹם.

<sup>12</sup>Have not You, O Elohim, cast us off? And You go not forth, O Elohim, with our hosts.

יֹבַהֲלֹא אַתָּה אֱלֹהִים זְנַחְתָּנוּ; וְלֹא תֵצֵא אֱלֹהִים בְּצִבְאוֹתֵינוּ.

<sup>13</sup>Give us help against the adversary; for vain is the help of man.

יֹגהָבָה לָּנוּ עֶזְרָת מִצָּר; וְשָׁוְא תְּשׁוּעַת אָדָם.

<sup>14</sup>Through Elohim we shall do valiantly; for He it is that will tread down our adversaries.

יֹדבֵּאלֹהִים נַעֲשֶׂה חָיִל; וְהוּא יָבוּס צָרֵינוּ.

# Tehillah 61 תְּהִלָּה

<sup>1</sup>For the Leader; with string-music. By David.

אלַמְנַצֵּחַ עַל נְגִינַת לְדָוִד.

<sup>2</sup>Hear my cry, O Elohim; attend unto my prayer.

בשִׁמְעָה אֱלֹהִים רִנָּתִי; הַקְשִׁיבָה תְּפִלָּתִי.

<sup>3</sup>From the end of the earth will I call unto You, when my heart faints; lead me to a Rock that is higher than I.

גמִקְצֵה הָאָרֶץ אֵלֶיךָ אֶקְרָא בַּעֲטֹף לִבִּי; בְּצוּר יָרוּם מִמֶּנִּי תַנְחֵנִי.

<sup>4</sup>For You have been a refuge for me, a tower of strength in the face of the enemy.

דכִּי הָיִיתָ מַחְסֶה לִי; מִגְדַּל עֹז מִפְּנֵי אוֹיֵב.

<sup>5</sup>I will dwell in Your Ohel forever; I will take refuge in the shadow of Your wings. Selah.

האָגוּרָה בְאָהָלְךָ עוֹלָמִים; אֶחֱסֶה בְסֵתֶר כְּנָפֶיךָ סֶּלָה.

<sup>6</sup>For You, O Elohim, have heard my vows; You have granted the heritage of those that fear Your Name.

וכִּי אַתָּה אֱלֹהִים שָׁמַעְתָּ לִנְדָרָי; נָתַתָּ יְרֻשַּׁת יִרְאֵי שְׁמֶךָ.

⁷May You add days unto the days of the Melekh! May his years be as many generations!

יָמִים עַל יְמֵי מֶלֶךְ תּוֹסִיף; שְׁנוֹתָיו כְּמוֹ דֹר וָדֹר.

⁸May he be enthroned before Elohim forever! Appoint compassion and truth, that they may preserve him.

יֵשֵׁב עוֹלָם לִפְנֵי אֱלֹהִים; חֶסֶד וֶאֱמֶת מַן יִנְצְרֻהוּ.

⁹So will I sing praise unto Your Name forever, that I may daily perform my vows.

כֵּן אֲזַמְּרָה שִׁמְךָ לָעַד לְשַׁלְּמִי נְדָרַי יוֹם יוֹם.

# תְּהִלָּה Tehillah 62

¹For the Leader; for Yedutun. A Mizmor of David.

לַמְנַצֵּחַ עַל יְדוּתוּן מִזְמוֹר לְדָוִד.

²Only for Elohim does my soul wait in stillness; from Him comes my Salvation.

אַךְ אֶל אֱלֹהִים דּוּמִיָּה נַפְשִׁי; מִמֶּנּוּ יְשׁוּעָתִי.

³He only is my Rock and my Salvation, my high tower, I shall not be greatly moved.

אַךְ הוּא צוּרִי וִישׁוּעָתִי; מִשְׂגַּבִּי לֹא אֶמּוֹט רַבָּה.

⁴How long will you set upon a man, that you may slay him, all of you, as a leaning wall, a tottering fence?

עַד אָנָה תְּהוֹתְתוּ עַל אִישׁ תְּרָצְּחוּ כֻלְּכֶם: כְּקִיר נָטוּי; גָּדֵר הַדְּחוּיָה.

332

⁵They only devise to thrust him down from his height, delighting in lies; they bless with their mouth, but they curse inwardly. Selah.

ᵓאַךְ מִשְּׂאֵתוֹ יָעֲצוּ לְהַדִּיחַ יִרְצוּ כָזָב: בְּפִיו יְבָרֵכוּ; וּבְקִרְבָּם יְקַלְלוּ סֶלָה.

⁶Only for Elohim wait in stillness, my soul; for from Him comes my hope.

ᵓאַךְ לֵאלֹהִים דּוֹמִי נַפְשִׁי: כִּי מִמֶּנּוּ תִּקְוָתִי.

⁷He only is my Rock and my Salvation, my high tower, I shall not be moved.

ᵓאַךְ הוּא צוּרִי וִישׁוּעָתִי; מִשְׂגַּבִּי לֹא אֶמּוֹט.

⁸Upon Elohim rests my Salvation and my glory; the Rock of my strength, and my refuge, is in Elohim.

ᵓעַל אֱלֹהִים יִשְׁעִי וּכְבוֹדִי; צוּר עֻזִּי מַחְסִי בֵּאלֹהִים.

⁹Trust in Him at all times, you people; pour out your heart before Him; Elohim is a refuge for us. Selah.

ᵗבִּטְחוּ בוֹ בְכָל עֵת עָם שִׁפְכוּ לְפָנָיו לְבַבְכֶם; אֱלֹהִים מַחֲסֶה לָנוּ סֶלָה.

¹⁰Men of low degree are vanity, and men of high degree are a lie; if they are laid in the balances, they are together lighter than vanity.

ᵓאַךְ הֶבֶל בְּנֵי אָדָם כָּזָב בְּנֵי אִישׁ: בְּמֹאזְנַיִם לַעֲלוֹת; הֵמָּה מֵהֶבֶל יָחַד.

¹¹Trust not in oppression, and put not vain hope in robbery; if riches increase, set not your heart thereon.

ᵃᵓאַל תִּבְטְחוּ בְעֹשֶׁק וּבְגָזֵל אַל תֶּהְבָּלוּ: חַיִל כִּי יָנוּב אַל תָּשִׁיתוּ לֵב.

¹²Elohim has spoken once, twice have I heard this: that strength belongs unto Elohim;

ᵇᵓאַחַת דִּבֶּר אֱלֹהִים שְׁתַּיִם זוּ שָׁמָעְתִּי: כִּי עֹז לֵאלֹהִים.

[13]Also unto You, O Adonai, belongs compassion; for You render to every man according to what he does.

יִּלְךָ אֲדֹנָי חָסֶד: כִּי אַתָּה תְשַׁלֵּם לְאִישׁ כְּמַעֲשֵׂהוּ.

# תְּהִלָּה 63 Tehillah

[1]A Mizmor of David, when he was in the wilderness of Yehudah.

מִזְמוֹר לְדָוִד; בִּהְיוֹתוֹ בְּמִדְבַּר יְהוּדָה.

[2]O Elohim, You are my God, earnestly will I seek You; my soul thirsts for You, my flesh longs for You, in a dry and weary land, where no water is.

אֱלֹהִים אֵלִי אַתָּה אֲשַׁחֲרֶךָ; צָמְאָה לְךָ נַפְשִׁי כָּמַהּ לְךָ בְשָׂרִי; בְּאֶרֶץ צִיָּה וְעָיֵף בְּלִי מָיִם.

[3]So have I looked for You in the Kodesh, to see Your power and Your Kavod.

כֵּן בַּקֹּדֶשׁ חֲזִיתִךָ לִרְאוֹת עֻזְּךָ וּכְבוֹדֶךָ.

[4]For Your compassion is better than life; my lips shall praise You.

כִּי טוֹב חַסְדְּךָ מֵחַיִּים; שְׂפָתַי יְשַׁבְּחוּנְךָ.

[5]So will I bless You as long as I live; in Your Name will I lift up my hands.

כֵּן אֲבָרֶכְךָ בְחַיָּי; בְּשִׁמְךָ אֶשָּׂא כַפָּי.

[6]My soul is satisfied as with marrow and fatness; and my mouth does praise You with joyful lips;

כְּמוֹ חֵלֶב וָדֶשֶׁן תִּשְׂבַּע נַפְשִׁי; וְשִׂפְתֵי רְנָנוֹת יְהַלֶּל פִּי.

[7]When I remember You upon my couch, and meditate on You in the night-watches.

אִם זְכַרְתִּיךָ עַל יְצוּעָי בְּאַשְׁמֻרוֹת אֶהְגֶּה בָּךְ.

⁸For You have been my help, and in the shadow of Your wings do I rejoice.

חכִּי הָיִיתָ עֶזְרָתָה לִּי; וּבְצֵל כְּנָפֶיךָ אֲרַנֵּן.

⁹My soul cleaves unto You; Your right hand holds me fast.

טדָּבְקָה נַפְשִׁי אַחֲרֶיךָ; בִּי תָּמְכָה יְמִינֶךָ.

¹⁰But those that seek my soul, to destroy it, shall go into the nethermost parts of the earth.

יוְהֵמָּה לְשׁוֹאָה יְבַקְשׁוּ נַפְשִׁי; יָבֹאוּ בְּתַחְתִּיּוֹת הָאָרֶץ.

¹¹They shall be hurled to the power of the sword; they shall be a portion for foxes.

יאיַגִּירֻהוּ עַל יְדֵי חָרֶב; מְנָת שֻׁעָלִים יִהְיוּ.

¹²But HaMelekh shall rejoice in Elohim; every one that swears by Him shall glory; for the mouth of them that speak lies shall be stopped.

יבוְהַמֶּלֶךְ יִשְׂמַח בֵּאלֹהִים: יִתְהַלֵּל כָּל הַנִּשְׁבָּע בּוֹ כִּי יִסָּכֵר פִּי דוֹבְרֵי שָׁקֶר.

# Tehillah 64 תְּהִלָּה

¹For the Leader. A Mizmor of David.

אלַמְנַצֵּחַ מִזְמוֹר לְדָוִד.

²Hear my voice, O Elohim, in my complaint; preserve my life from the terror of the enemy.

בשְׁמַע אֱלֹהִים קוֹלִי בְשִׂיחִי; מִפַּחַד אוֹיֵב תִּצֹּר חַיָּי.

³Hide me from the council of evil-doers; from the tumult of the workers of iniquity;

גתַּסְתִּירֵנִי מִסּוֹד מְרֵעִים; מֵרִגְשַׁת פֹּעֲלֵי אָוֶן.

⁴Who have whet their tongue like a sword, and have aimed their arrow, a poisoned word;

דֲאֲשֶׁר שָׁנְנוּ כַחֶרֶב לְשׁוֹנָם; דָּרְכוּ חִצָּם דָּבָר מָר.

⁵That they may shoot in secret places at the blameless; suddenly do they shoot at him, and fear not.

הלִירֹת בַּמִּסְתָּרִים תָּם; פִּתְאֹם יֹרֻהוּ וְלֹא יִירָאוּ.

⁶They encourage one another in an evil matter; they converse of laying snares secretly; they ask, "Who would see them?"

ויְחַזְּקוּ לָמוֹ דָּבָר רָע יְסַפְּרוּ לִטְמוֹן מוֹקְשִׁים; אָמְרוּ מִי יִרְאֶה לָּמוֹ.

⁷They search out iniquities, they have accomplished a diligent search; even in the inward thought of every one, and the deep heart.

זיַחְפְּשׂוּ עוֹלֹת תַּמְנוּ חֵפֶשׂ מְחֻפָּשׂ; וְקֶרֶב אִישׁ וְלֵב עָמֹק.

⁸But Elohim does shoot at them with an arrow suddenly; thence are their wounds.

חוַיֹּרֵם אֱלֹהִים: חֵץ פִּתְאוֹם הָיוּ מַכּוֹתָם.

⁹So they make their own tongue a stumbling unto themselves; all that see them shake the head.

טוַיַּכְשִׁילוּהוּ עָלֵימוֹ לְשׁוֹנָם; יִתְנֹדְדוּ כָּל רֹאֵה בָם.

¹⁰And all men fear; and they declare the work of Elohim, and understand His doing.

יוַיִּירְאוּ כָּל אָדָם: וַיַּגִּידוּ פֹּעַל אֱלֹהִים; וּמַעֲשֵׂהוּ הִשְׂכִּילוּ.

¹¹A Tzadik shall be glad in יהוה , and shall take refuge in Him; and all the upright in heart shall glory.

יאיִשְׂמַח צַדִּיק בַּיהוה וְחָסָה בוֹ; וְיִתְהַלְלוּ כָּל יִשְׁרֵי לֵב.

# תְּהִלָּה 65 Tehillah

¹For the Leader. A Mizmor. A Song of David.

אלַמְנַצֵּחַ מִזְמוֹר לְדָוִד שִׁיר.

²Praise waits for You, O Elohim, in Tzion; and unto You the vow is performed.

בלְךָ דֻמִיָּה תְהִלָּה אֱלֹהִים בְּצִיּוֹן; וּלְךָ יְשֻׁלַּם נֶדֶר.

³O You that hears prayer, unto You does all flesh come.

גשֹׁמֵעַ תְּפִלָּה עָדֶיךָ כָּל בָּשָׂר יָבֹאוּ.

⁴The tale of iniquities is too heavy for me; as for our transgressions, You will pardon them.

דדִּבְרֵי עֲוֺנֹת גָּבְרוּ מֶנִּי; פְּשָׁעֵינוּ אַתָּה תְכַפְּרֵם.

⁵Happy is the man whom You choose, and bring near, that he may dwell in Your courts; may we be satisfied with the goodness of Your house, the Kadosh of Your Heikhal!

האַשְׁרֵי תִּבְחַר וּתְקָרֵב יִשְׁכֹּן חֲצֵרֶיךָ: נִשְׂבְּעָה בְּטוּב בֵּיתֶךָ, קְדֹשׁ הֵיכָלֶךָ.

⁶With wondrous works do You answer us in righteousness, O Elohim of our Salvation; You, the confidence of all the ends of the earth, and of the far distant seas;

ונוֹרָאוֹת בְּצֶדֶק תַּעֲנֵנוּ אֱלֹהֵי יִשְׁעֵנוּ; מִבְטָח כָּל קַצְוֵי אֶרֶץ וְיָם רְחֹקִים.

⁷Who by Your strength set fast the mountains, who are girded about with might;

זמֵכִין הָרִים בְּכֹחוֹ; נֶאְזָר בִּגְבוּרָה.

337

[8]Who stills the roaring of the seas, the roaring of their waves, and the tumult of the peoples;

חמַשְׁבִּיחַ שְׁאוֹן יַמִּים שְׁאוֹן גַּלֵּיהֶם; וַהֲמוֹן לְאֻמִּים.

[9]So that they that dwell in the uttermost parts stand in awe of Your signs; You make the outgoings of the morning and evening to rejoice.

טוַיִּירְאוּ יֹשְׁבֵי קְצָוֹת מֵאוֹתֹתֶיךָ; מוֹצָאֵי בֹקֶר וָעֶרֶב תַּרְנִין.

[10]You have remembered the earth, and watered her, greatly enriching her with the river of Elohim that is full of water; You prepare them grain, for so do You prepare her.

יפָּקַדְתָּ הָאָרֶץ וַתְּשֹׁקְקֶהָ רַבַּת תַּעְשְׁרֶנָּה פֶּלֶג אֱלֹהִים מָלֵא מָיִם; תָּכִין דְּגָנָם כִּי כֵן תְּכִינֶהָ.

[11]Watering her ridges abundantly, settling down the furrows thereof, You make her soft with showers; You bless the growth thereof.

יאתְּלָמֶיהָ רַוֵּה נַחֵת גְּדוּדֶהָ; בִּרְבִיבִים תְּמֹגְגֶנָּה צִמְחָהּ תְּבָרֵךְ.

[12]You crown the year with Your goodness; and Your paths drop fatness.

יבעִטַּרְתָּ שְׁנַת טוֹבָתֶךָ; וּמַעְגָּלֶיךָ יִרְעֲפוּן דָּשֶׁן.

[13]The pastures of the wilderness do drop; and the hills are girded with joy.

יגיִרְעֲפוּ נְאוֹת מִדְבָּר; וְגִיל גְּבָעוֹת תַּחְגֹּרְנָה.

<sup>14</sup>The meadows are clothed with flocks; the valleys also are covered over with grain; they shout for joy, yes, they sing.

ᵈלָבְשׁוּ כָרִים הַצֹּאן וַעֲמָקִים יַעַטְפוּ בָר; יִתְרוֹעֲעוּ אַף יָשִׁירוּ.

# תְּהִלָּה Tehillah 66

<sup>1</sup>For the Leader. A Song, a Mizmor. Shout unto Elohim, all the earth;

אלַמְנַצֵּחַ שִׁיר מִזְמוֹר: הָרִיעוּ לֵאלֹהִים כָּל הָאָרֶץ.

<sup>2</sup>Sing praises unto the glory of His Name; make His praise glorious.

בזַמְּרוּ כְבוֹד שְׁמוֹ; שִׂימוּ כָבוֹד תְּהִלָּתוֹ.

<sup>3</sup>Say unto Elohim, "How tremendous is Your work! Through the greatness of Your power shall Your enemies dwindle away before You.

גאִמְרוּ לֵאלֹהִים מַה נּוֹרָא מַעֲשֶׂיךָ; בְּרֹב עֻזְּךָ יְכַחֲשׁוּ לְךָ אֹיְבֶיךָ.

<sup>4</sup>All the earth shall worship You, and shall sing praises unto You; they shall sing praises to Your Name." Selah.

דכָּל הָאָרֶץ יִשְׁתַּחֲווּ לְךָ וִיזַמְּרוּ לָךְ; יְזַמְּרוּ שִׁמְךָ סֶלָה.

<sup>5</sup>Come, and see the works of Elohim; He is awesome in His doings toward the children of men.

הלְכוּ וּרְאוּ מִפְעֲלוֹת אֱלֹהִים; נוֹרָא עֲלִילָה עַל בְּנֵי אָדָם.

<sup>6</sup>He turned the sea into dry land; they went through the river on foot; there let us rejoice in Him!

והָפַךְ יָם לְיַבָּשָׁה בַּנָּהָר יַעַבְרוּ בְרָגֶל; שָׁם נִשְׂמְחָה בּוֹ.

⁷Who rules by His might forever; His eyes keep watch upon the nations; let not the rebellious exalt themselves. Selah.

ⁱמֹשֵׁל בִּגְבוּרָתוֹ עוֹלָם עֵינָיו בַּגּוֹיִם תִּצְפֶּינָה; הַסּוֹרְרִים אַל ירימו (יָרוּמוּ) לָמוֹ סֶלָה.

⁸Bless our Elohim, you peoples, and make the voice of His praise to be heard;

חבָּרְכוּ עַמִּים אֱלֹהֵינוּ; וְהַשְׁמִיעוּ קוֹל תְּהִלָּתוֹ.

⁹Who has set our soul in life, and suffered not our foot to be moved,

טהַשָּׂם נַפְשֵׁנוּ בַּחַיִּים; וְלֹא נָתַן לַמּוֹט רַגְלֵנוּ.

¹⁰For You, O Elohim, have tried us; You have refined us, as silver is refined.

יכִּי בְחַנְתָּנוּ אֱלֹהִים; צְרַפְתָּנוּ כִּצְרָף כָּסֶף.

¹¹You did bring us into the hold; You did lay constraint upon our loins.

יאהֲבֵאתָנוּ בַמְּצוּדָה; שַׂמְתָּ מוּעָקָה בְמָתְנֵינוּ.

¹²You have caused men to ride over our heads; we went through fire and through water; but You did bring us out unto abundance.

יבהִרְכַּבְתָּ אֱנוֹשׁ לְרֹאשֵׁנוּ: בָּאנוּ בָאֵשׁ וּבַמַּיִם; וַתּוֹצִיאֵנוּ לָרְוָיָה.

¹³I will come into Your house with Olot, I will perform unto You my vows,

יגאָבוֹא בֵיתְךָ בְעוֹלוֹת; אֲשַׁלֵּם לְךָ נְדָרָי.

¹⁴Which my lips have uttered, and my mouth has spoken, when I was in distress.

ידאֲשֶׁר פָּצוּ שְׂפָתָי; וְדִבֶּר פִּי בַּצַּר לִי.

<sup>15</sup>I will offer unto You Olot of fatlings, with the sweet smoke of rams; I will offer bullocks with goats. Selah.

ט״עֹלוֹת מֵיחִים אַעֲלֶה לָּךְ עִם קְטֹרֶת אֵילִים; אֶעֱשֶׂה בָקָר עִם עַתּוּדִים סֶלָה.

<sup>16</sup>Come, and hearken, all you that fear Elohim, and I will declare what He has done for my soul.

ט״לְכוּ שִׁמְעוּ וַאֲסַפְּרָה כָּל יִרְאֵי אֱלֹהִים: אֲשֶׁר עָשָׂה לְנַפְשִׁי.

<sup>17</sup>I cried unto Him with my mouth, and He was extolled with my tongue.

י״אֵלָיו פִּי קָרָאתִי; וְרוֹמַם תַּחַת לְשׁוֹנִי.

<sup>18</sup>If I had regarded iniquity in my heart, Adonai would not hear;

י״חָאָוֶן אִם רָאִיתִי בְלִבִּי לֹא יִשְׁמַע אֲדֹנָי.

<sup>19</sup>But indeed, Elohim has heard; He has attended to the voice of my tefilah.

י״טאָכֵן שָׁמַע אֱלֹהִים; הִקְשִׁיב בְּקוֹל תְּפִלָּתִי.

<sup>20</sup>Blessed is Elohim, who has not turned away my tefilah, nor His mercy from me.

כבָּרוּךְ אֱלֹהִים אֲשֶׁר לֹא הֵסִיר תְּפִלָּתִי וְחַסְדּוֹ מֵאִתִּי.

# Tehillah 67 תְּהִלָּה

<sup>1</sup>For the Leader; with N'ginot. A Mizmor, a Song.

אלַמְנַצֵּחַ בִּנְגִינֹת מִזְמוֹר שִׁיר.

<sup>2</sup>Elohim be gracious unto us, and bless us; may He cause His face to shine toward us; Selah.

באֱלֹהִים יְחָנֵּנוּ וִיבָרְכֵנוּ; יָאֵר פָּנָיו אִתָּנוּ סֶלָה.

³That Your way may be known upon earth, Your Salvation among all goyim.

לָדַעַת בָּאָרֶץ דַּרְכֶּךָ; בְּכָל גּוֹיִם יְשׁוּעָתֶךָ.

⁴Let the peoples give thanks unto You, O Elohim; let the peoples give thanks unto You, all of them.

יוֹדוּךָ עַמִּים אֱלֹהִים: יוֹדוּךָ עַמִּים כֻּלָּם.

⁵O let the goyim be glad and sing for joy; for You will judge the peoples with equity, and lead the goyim upon earth. Selah.

יִשְׂמְחוּ וִירַנְּנוּ לְאֻמִּים: כִּי תִשְׁפֹּט עַמִּים מִישֹׁר; וּלְאֻמִּים בָּאָרֶץ תַּנְחֵם סֶלָה.

⁶Let the peoples give thanks unto You, O Elohim; let the peoples give thanks unto You, all of them.

יוֹדוּךָ עַמִּים אֱלֹהִים: יוֹדוּךָ עַמִּים כֻּלָּם.

⁷The earth has yielded her increase; may Elohim, our own Elohim, bless us.

אֶרֶץ נָתְנָה יְבוּלָהּ; יְבָרְכֵנוּ אֱלֹהִים אֱלֹהֵינוּ.

⁸May Elohim bless us; and let all the ends of the earth fear Him.

יְבָרְכֵנוּ אֱלֹהִים; וְיִירְאוּ אוֹתוֹ כָּל אַפְסֵי אָרֶץ.

# Tehillah 68 תְּהִלָּה

¹For the Leader. A Mizmor of David, a Song.

לַמְנַצֵּחַ לְדָוִד מִזְמוֹר שִׁיר.

²Let Elohim arise, let His enemies be scattered; and let them that hate Him flee from before Him.

יָקוּם אֱלֹהִים יָפוּצוּ אוֹיְבָיו; וְיָנוּסוּ מְשַׂנְאָיו מִפָּנָיו.

³As smoke is driven away, so drive them away; as wax melts before the fire, so let the wicked perish at the presence of Elohim.

ᵍכְּהִנְדֹּף עָשָׁן תִּנְדֹּף: כְּהִמֵּס דּוֹנַג מִפְּנֵי אֵשׁ יֹאבְדוּ רְשָׁעִים מִפְּנֵי אֱלֹהִים.

⁴But let the Tzadikim be glad, let them exult before Elohim; yes, let them rejoice with gladness.

ᵈוְצַדִּיקִים יִשְׂמְחוּ יַעַלְצוּ לִפְנֵי אֱלֹהִים; וְיָשִׂישׂוּ בְשִׂמְחָה.

⁵Sing unto Elohim, sing praises to His Name; extol Him that rides upon the skies, whose Name is Yah; and exult before Him.

ʰשִׁירוּ לֵאלֹהִים זַמְּרוּ שְׁמוֹ: סֹלּוּ לָרֹכֵב בָּעֲרָבוֹת בְּיָהּ שְׁמוֹ; וְעִלְזוּ לְפָנָיו.

⁶A father of the fatherless, and a judge of the widows, is Elohim in His consecrated habitation.

ᵛאֲבִי יְתוֹמִים וְדַיַּן אַלְמָנוֹת אֱלֹהִים בִּמְעוֹן קָדְשׁוֹ.

⁷Elohim makes the solitary to dwell in a house; He brings out the prisoners into prosperity; the rebellious dwell but in a parched land.

ᶻאֱלֹהִים מוֹשִׁיב יְחִידִים בַּיְתָה מוֹצִיא אֲסִירִים בַּכּוֹשָׁרוֹת; אַךְ סוֹרְרִים שָׁכְנוּ צְחִיחָה.

⁸O Elohim, when You went forth before Your people, when You did march through the wilderness, Selah,

ᶜʰאֱלֹהִים בְּצֵאתְךָ לִפְנֵי עַמֶּךָ; בְּצַעְדְּךָ בִישִׁימוֹן סֶלָה.

⁹The earth trembled, the heavens also dropped at the presence of Elohim; even yon Sinai trembled at the presence of Elohim, the Elohim of Yisra'el.

ᵗאֶרֶץ רָעָשָׁה אַף שָׁמַיִם נָטְפוּ מִפְּנֵי אֱלֹהִים: זֶה סִינַי מִפְּנֵי אֱלֹהִים אֱלֹהֵי יִשְׂרָאֵל.

<sup>10</sup>A bounteous rain did You pour down, O Elohim; when Your inheritance was weary, You did confirm it.

גֶּשֶׁם נְדָבוֹת תָּנִיף אֱלֹהִים; נַחֲלָתְךָ וְנִלְאָה אַתָּה כוֹנַנְתָּה.

<sup>11</sup>Your flock settled therein; You did prepare in Your goodness for the poor, O Elohim.

יאחַיָּתְךָ יָשְׁבוּ בָהּ; תָּכִין בְּטוֹבָתְךָ לֶעָנִי אֱלֹהִים.

<sup>12</sup>Adonai gives the word; those who declare the good news are a great army.

יבאֲדֹנָי יִתֶּן אֹמֶר; הַמְבַשְּׂרוֹת צָבָא רָב.

<sup>13</sup>Kings of armies flee, they flee; and she that tarries at home divides the spoil.

יגמַלְכֵי צְבָאוֹת יִדֹּדוּן יִדֹּדוּן; וּנְוַת בַּיִת תְּחַלֵּק שָׁלָל.

<sup>14</sup>When you lie among the sheepfolds, the wings of the dove are covered with silver, and her pinions with the shimmer of gold.

ידאִם תִּשְׁכְּבוּן בֵּין שְׁפַתָּיִם: כַּנְפֵי יוֹנָה נֶחְפָּה בַכֶּסֶף; וְאֶבְרוֹתֶיהָ בִּירַקְרַק חָרוּץ.

<sup>15</sup>When Shadai scatters kings therein, it snows in Tzalmon.

טובְּפָרֵשׁ שַׁדַּי מְלָכִים בָּהּ תַּשְׁלֵג בְּצַלְמוֹן.

<sup>16</sup>A mountain of Elohim is the mountain of Bashan; a mountain of peaks is the mountain of Bashan.

טזהַר אֱלֹהִים הַר בָּשָׁן: הַר גַּבְנֻנִּים הַר בָּשָׁן.

<sup>17</sup>Why do you look askance, you mountains of peaks, at the mountain which Elohim has desired for His abode? Yes, יהוה will dwell therein forever.

יזלָמָּה תְּרַצְּדוּן הָרִים גַּבְנֻנִּים: הָהָר חָמַד אֱלֹהִים לְשִׁבְתּוֹ; אַף יהוה יִשְׁכֹּן לָנֶצַח.

<sup>18</sup>The chariots of Elohim are myriads, even thousands upon thousands; Adonai is among them, as in Sinai, in Kodesh.

יח רֶכֶב אֱלֹהִים רִבֹּתַיִם אַלְפֵי שִׁנְאָן; אֲדֹנָי בָם סִינַי בַּקֹּדֶשׁ.

<sup>19</sup>You have ascended on high, You have recaptured the captives; You have taken gifts to mankind. And even among the rebellious, Yah, Elohim, is to dwell.

יט עָלִיתָ לַמָּרוֹם שָׁבִיתָ שֶּׁבִי לָקַחְתָּ מַתָּנוֹת בָּאָדָם; וְאַף סוֹרְרִים לִשְׁכֹּן יָהּ אֱלֹהִים.

<sup>20</sup>Blessed is Adonai, day by day He bears our burden, even the Elohim who is our Salvation. Selah.

כ בָּרוּךְ אֲדֹנָי יוֹם יוֹם: יַעֲמָס לָנוּ הָאֵל יְשׁוּעָתֵנוּ סֶלָה.

<sup>21</sup>God is unto us a God of Salvations; and unto יהוה Adonai belong the issues of Mavet.

כא הָאֵל לָנוּ אֵל לְמוֹשָׁעוֹת: וְלֵיהוָה אֲדֹנָי לַמָּוֶת תֹּצָאוֹת.

<sup>22</sup>Surely Elohim will smite through the head of His enemies, the hairy scalp of him that goes about in his guiltiness.

כב אַךְ אֱלֹהִים יִמְחַץ רֹאשׁ אֹיְבָיו: קָדְקֹד שֵׂעָר מִתְהַלֵּךְ בַּאֲשָׁמָיו.

<sup>23</sup>Adonai said, "I will bring back from Bashan, I will bring them back from the depths of the sea;

כג אָמַר אֲדֹנָי מִבָּשָׁן אָשִׁיב; אָשִׁיב מִמְּצֻלוֹת יָם.

<sup>24</sup>That your foot may wade through blood, that the tongue of your dogs may have its portion from your enemies."

כד לְמַעַן תִּמְחַץ רַגְלְךָ בְּדָם: לְשׁוֹן כְּלָבֶיךָ מֵאֹיְבִים מִנֵּהוּ.

²⁵They see Your goings, O Elohim, even the goings of my Elohim, my Melekh, in Kodesh.

כּהרָאוּ הֲלִיכוֹתֶיךָ אֱלֹהִים; הֲלִיכוֹת אֵלִי מַלְכִּי בַקֹּדֶשׁ.

²⁶The singers go before, the minstrels follow after, in the midst of damsels playing upon timbrels.

כּוקִדְּמוּ שָׁרִים אַחַר נֹגְנִים; בְּתוֹךְ עֲלָמוֹת תּוֹפֵפוֹת.

²⁷"Bless Elohim in full assemblies, even Adonai, you that are from the fountain of Yisra'el."

כּזבְּמַקְהֵלוֹת בָּרְכוּ אֱלֹהִים; אֲדֹנָי מִמְּקוֹר יִשְׂרָאֵל.

²⁸There is Binyamin, the youngest, ruling them, the princes of Yehudah their council, the princes of Zevulun, the princes of Naftali.

כּחשָׁם בִּנְיָמִן צָעִיר רֹדֵם שָׂרֵי יְהוּדָה רִגְמָתָם; שָׂרֵי זְבֻלוּן שָׂרֵי נַפְתָּלִי.

²⁹Your Elohim has commanded your strength; be strong, O Elohim, You that have wrought for us

כּטצִוָּה אֱלֹהֶיךָ עֻזֶּךָ: עוּזָּה אֱלֹהִים זוּ פָּעַלְתָּ לָּנוּ.

³⁰Out of Your Heikhal at Yerushalayim, where kings shall bring presents unto You.

למֵהֵיכָלֶךָ עַל יְרוּשָׁלָם לָךְ יוֹבִילוּ מְלָכִים שָׁי.

³¹Rebuke the wild beast of the reeds, the multitude of the bulls, with the calves of the peoples, every one submitting himself with pieces of silver; He has scattered the peoples that delight in war!

לאגְּעַר חַיַּת קָנֶה עֲדַת אַבִּירִים בְּעֶגְלֵי עַמִּים מִתְרַפֵּס בְּרַצֵּי כָסֶף; בִּזַּר עַמִּים קְרָבוֹת יֶחְפָּצוּ.

³²Nobles shall come out of Mitzrayim; Kush shall hasten to stretch out her hands unto Elohim.

לביֶאֱתָיוּ חַשְׁמַנִּים מִנִּי מִצְרָיִם; כּוּשׁ תָּרִיץ יָדָיו לֵאלֹהִים.

³³Sing unto Elohim, you kingdoms of the earth; O sing praises unto Adonai; Selah.

לגמַמְלְכוֹת הָאָרֶץ שִׁירוּ לֵאלֹהִים; זַמְּרוּ אֲדֹנָי סֶלָה.

³⁴To Him that rides upon the heaven of heavens, which are of old; lo, He utters His voice, a mighty voice.

לדלָרֹכֵב בִּשְׁמֵי שְׁמֵי קֶדֶם הֵן יִתֵּן בְּקוֹלוֹ קוֹל עֹז.

³⁵Ascribe strength unto Elohim; His majesty is over Yisra'el, and His strength is in the skies.

להתְּנוּ עֹז לֵאלֹהִים: עַל יִשְׂרָאֵל גַּאֲוָתוֹ; וְעֻזּוֹ בַּשְּׁחָקִים.

³⁶Awesome is Elohim out of your Mikdashim; the Elohim of Yisra'el, He gives strength and power unto the people; blessed is Elohim.

לונוֹרָא אֱלֹהִים מִמִּקְדָּשֶׁיךָ: אֵל יִשְׂרָאֵל הוּא נֹתֵן עֹז וְתַעֲצֻמוֹת לָעָם; בָּרוּךְ אֱלֹהִים.

# תְּהִלָּה 69 Tehillah

¹For the Leader; upon Shoshannim. By David.

אלַמְנַצֵּחַ עַל שׁוֹשַׁנִּים לְדָוִד.

²Save me, O Elohim; for the waters are come in even unto the soul.

בהוֹשִׁיעֵנִי אֱלֹהִים כִּי בָאוּ מַיִם עַד נָפֶשׁ.

³I am sunk in deep mire, where there is no standing; I am come into deep waters, and the flood overwhelms me.

גטָבַעְתִּי בִּיוֵן מְצוּלָה וְאֵין מָעֳמָד; בָּאתִי בְמַעֲמַקֵּי מַיִם וְשִׁבֹּלֶת שְׁטָפָתְנִי.

⁴I am weary of my crying; my throat is dried; my eyes fail while I wait for my Elohim.

דיָגַעְתִּי בְקָרְאִי נִחַר גְּרוֹנִי: כָּלוּ עֵינַי מְיַחֵל לֵאלֹהָי.

⁵They that hate me without a cause are more than the hairs of my head; they that would cut me off, being my enemies wrongfully, are many; should I restore that which I did not take away?

הרַבּוּ מִשַּׂעֲרוֹת רֹאשִׁי שֹׂנְאַי חִנָּם: עָצְמוּ מַצְמִיתַי אֹיְבַי שֶׁקֶר אֲשֶׁר לֹא גָזַלְתִּי אָז אָשִׁיב.

⁶O Elohim, You know my folly; and my trespasses are not hidden from You.

ואֱלֹהִים אַתָּה יָדַעְתָּ לְאִוַּלְתִּי; וְאַשְׁמוֹתַי מִמְּךָ לֹא נִכְחָדוּ.

⁷Let not them that wait for You be ashamed through me, O Adonai יהוה Tzeva'ot; let not those that seek You be brought to confusion through me, O Elohim of Yisra'el.

זאַל יֵבֹשׁוּ בִי קוֶֹיךָ אֲדֹנָי יהוה צְבָאוֹת: אַל יִכָּלְמוּ בִי מְבַקְשֶׁיךָ אֱלֹהֵי יִשְׂרָאֵל.

⁸Because for Your sake I have borne reproach; confusion has covered my face.

⁹I am become a stranger unto my brethren, and an alien unto my mother's children.

¹⁰Because zeal for Your house has consumed me, and the reproaches of them that reproach You are fallen upon me.

¹¹And I wept with my soul fasting, and that became unto me a reproach.

¹²I made sackcloth also my garment, and I became a byword unto them.

¹³They that sit in the gate talk of me; and I am the song of the drunkards.

¹⁴But as for me, let my tefilah be unto You, O יהוה , in an acceptable time; O Elohim, in the abundance of Your compassion, answer me with the truth of Your Salvation.

ח‏כִּי עָלֶיךָ נָשָׂאתִי חֶרְפָּה; כִּסְּתָה כְלִמָּה פָנָי.

ט‏מוּזָר הָיִיתִי לְאֶחָי; וְנָכְרִי לִבְנֵי אִמִּי.

י‏כִּי קִנְאַת בֵּיתְךָ אֲכָלָתְנִי; וְחֶרְפּוֹת חוֹרְפֶיךָ נָפְלוּ עָלָי.

יא‏וָאֶבְכֶּה בַצּוֹם נַפְשִׁי; וַתְּהִי לַחֲרָפוֹת לִי.

יב‏וָאֶתְּנָה לְבוּשִׁי שָׂק; וָאֱהִי לָהֶם לְמָשָׁל.

יג‏יָשִׂיחוּ בִי יֹשְׁבֵי שָׁעַר; וּנְגִינוֹת שׁוֹתֵי שֵׁכָר.

יד‏וַאֲנִי תְפִלָּתִי לְךָ יהוה עֵת רָצוֹן אֱלֹהִים בְּרָב חַסְדֶּךָ; עֲנֵנִי בֶּאֱמֶת יִשְׁעֶךָ.

<sup>15</sup>Deliver me out of the mire, and let me not sink; let me be delivered from them that hate me, and out of the deep waters.

<sup>טו</sup>הַצִּילֵנִי מִטִּיט וְאַל אֶטְבָּעָה; אִנָּצְלָה מִשֹּׂנְאַי וּמִמַּעֲמַקֵּי מָיִם.

<sup>16</sup>Let not the waterflood overwhelm me, neither let the deep swallow me up; and let not the pit shut her mouth upon me.

<sup>טז</sup>אַל תִּשְׁטְפֵנִי שִׁבֹּלֶת מַיִם וְאַל תִּבְלָעֵנִי מְצוּלָה; וְאַל תֶּאְטַר עָלַי בְּאֵר פִּיהָ.

<sup>17</sup>Answer me, O יהוה , for Your compassion is good; according to the multitude of Your mercies turn unto me.

<sup>יז</sup>עֲנֵנִי יהוה כִּי טוֹב חַסְדֶּךָ; כְּרֹב רַחֲמֶיךָ פְּנֵה אֵלָי.

<sup>18</sup>And hide not Your face from Your servant; for I am in distress; answer me speedily.

<sup>יח</sup>וְאַל תַּסְתֵּר פָּנֶיךָ מֵעַבְדֶּךָ: כִּי צַר לִי מַהֵר עֲנֵנִי.

<sup>19</sup>Draw nigh unto my soul, and redeem it; ransom me because of my enemies.

<sup>יט</sup>קָרְבָה אֶל נַפְשִׁי גְאָלָהּ; לְמַעַן אֹיְבַי פְּדֵנִי.

<sup>20</sup>You know my reproach, and my shame, and my confusion; my adversaries are all before You.

<sup>כ</sup>אַתָּה יָדַעְתָּ חֶרְפָּתִי וּבָשְׁתִּי וּכְלִמָּתִי; נֶגְדְּךָ כָּל צוֹרְרָי.

<sup>21</sup>Reproach has broken my heart; and I am sore sick; and I looked for some to show compassion, but there was none; and for comforters, but I found none.

<sup>כא</sup>חֶרְפָּה שָׁבְרָה לִבִּי וָאָנוּשָׁה: וָאֲקַוֶּה לָנוּד וָאַיִן; וְלַמְנַחֲמִים וְלֹא מָצָאתִי.

350

²²Yes, they put poison into my food; and in my thirst they gave me vinegar to drink.

כב וַיִּתְּנוּ בְּבָרוּתִי רֹאשׁ; וְלִצְמָאִי יַשְׁקוּנִי חֹמֶץ.

²³Let their table before them become a snare; and when they are in shalom, let it become a trap.

כג יְהִי שֻׁלְחָנָם לִפְנֵיהֶם לְפָח; וְלִשְׁלוֹמִים לְמוֹקֵשׁ.

²⁴Let their eyes be darkened, that they see not; and make their loins continually to totter.

כד תֶּחְשַׁכְנָה עֵינֵיהֶם מֵרְאוֹת; וּמָתְנֵיהֶם תָּמִיד הַמְעַד.

²⁵Pour out Your indignation upon them, and let the fierceness of Your anger overtake them.

כה שְׁפָךְ עֲלֵיהֶם זַעְמֶךָ; וַחֲרוֹן אַפְּךָ יַשִּׂיגֵם.

²⁶Let their encampment be desolate; let none dwell in their tents.

כו תְּהִי טִירָתָם נְשַׁמָּה; בְּאָהֳלֵיהֶם אַל יְהִי יֹשֵׁב.

²⁷For they persecute him whom You have smitten; and they tell of the pain of those whom You have wounded.

כז כִּי אַתָּה אֲשֶׁר הִכִּיתָ רָדָפוּ; וְאֶל מַכְאוֹב חֲלָלֶיךָ יְסַפֵּרוּ.

²⁸Add iniquity unto their iniquity; and let them not come into Your tzedaka.

כח תְּנָה עָוֹן עַל עֲוֹנָם; וְאַל יָבֹאוּ בְּצִדְקָתֶךָ.

²⁹Let them be blotted out of the Sefer Khayim, and not be written with the Tzadikim.

כט יִמָּחוּ מִסֵּפֶר חַיִּים; וְעִם צַדִּיקִים אַל יִכָּתֵבוּ.

<sup>30</sup>But I am afflicted and in pain; let Your Salvation, O Elohim, set me up on high.

<sup>ל</sup>וַאֲנִי עָנִי וְכוֹאֵב; יְשׁוּעָתְךָ אֱלֹהִים תְּשַׂגְּבֵנִי.

<sup>31</sup>I will praise the Name of Elohim with a song, and will magnify Him with thanksgiving.

<sup>לא</sup>אֲהַלְלָה שֵׁם אֱלֹהִים בְּשִׁיר; וַאֲגַדְּלֶנּוּ בְתוֹדָה.

<sup>32</sup>And it shall please יהוה better than a bullock that has horns and hoofs.

<sup>לב</sup>וְתִיטַב לַיהוה מִשּׁוֹר פָּר; מַקְרִן מַפְרִיס.

<sup>33</sup>The humble shall see it, and be glad; you that seek after Elohim, let your heart revive.

<sup>לג</sup>רָאוּ עֲנָוִים יִשְׂמָחוּ; דֹּרְשֵׁי אֱלֹהִים וִיחִי לְבַבְכֶם.

<sup>34</sup>For יהוה hearkens unto the needy, and despises not His prisoners.

<sup>לד</sup>כִּי שֹׁמֵעַ אֶל אֶבְיוֹנִים יהוה; וְאֶת אֲסִירָיו לֹא בָזָה.

<sup>35</sup>Let heaven and earth praise Him, the seas, and every thing that moves therein.

<sup>לה</sup>יְהַלְלוּהוּ שָׁמַיִם וָאָרֶץ; יַמִּים וְכָל רֹמֵשׂ בָּם.

<sup>36</sup>For Elohim will save Tzion, and build the cities of Yehudah; and they shall abide there, and have it in possession.

<sup>לו</sup>כִּי אֱלֹהִים יוֹשִׁיעַ צִיּוֹן וְיִבְנֶה עָרֵי יְהוּדָה; וְיָשְׁבוּ שָׁם וִירֵשׁוּהָ.

<sup>37</sup>The seed also of His servants shall inherit it; and they that love His Name shall dwell therein.

<sup>לז</sup>וְזֶרַע עֲבָדָיו יִנְחָלוּהָ; וְאֹהֲבֵי שְׁמוֹ יִשְׁכְּנוּ בָהּ.

# תְּהִלָּה 70 Tehillah

¹For the Leader. By David; to make memorial.

אלַמְנַצֵּחַ לְדָוִד לְהַזְכִּיר.

²O Elohim, to deliver me, O יהוה , to help me, make haste.

באֱלֹהִים לְהַצִּילֵנִי, יהוה לְעֶזְרָתִי חוּשָׁה.

³Let them be ashamed and abashed that seek after my soul; let them be turned backward and brought to confusion that delight in my hurt.

גיֵבֹשׁוּ וְיַחְפְּרוּ מְבַקְשֵׁי נַפְשִׁי: יִסֹּגוּ אָחוֹר וְיִכָּלְמוּ; חֲפֵצֵי רָעָתִי.

⁴Let them be turned back by reason of their shame that say, "Aha, aha."

דיָשׁוּבוּ עַל עֵקֶב בָּשְׁתָּם הָאֹמְרִים הֶאָח הֶאָח.

⁵Let all those that seek You rejoice and be glad in You; and let such as love Your Salvation say continually, "Let Elohim be magnified."

היָשִׂישׂוּ וְיִשְׂמְחוּ בְּךָ כָּל מְבַקְשֶׁיךָ: וְיֹאמְרוּ תָמִיד יִגְדַּל אֱלֹהִים אֹהֲבֵי יְשׁוּעָתֶךָ.

⁶But I am poor and needy; O Elohim, make haste unto me; You are my help and my deliverer; O יהוה , tarry not.

ווַאֲנִי עָנִי וְאֶבְיוֹן אֱלֹהִים חוּשָׁה לִּי: עֶזְרִי וּמְפַלְטִי אַתָּה; יהוה אַל תְּאַחַר.

# תְּהִלָּה 71 Tehillah

¹In You, O יהוה , have I taken refuge; let me never be ashamed.

אבְּךָ יהוה חָסִיתִי; אַל אֵבוֹשָׁה לְעוֹלָם.

²Deliver me in Your tzedaka, and rescue me; incline Your ear unto me, and save me.

בְּצִדְקָתְךָ תַּצִּילֵנִי וּתְפַלְּטֵנִי; הַטֵּה אֵלַי אָזְנְךָ וְהוֹשִׁיעֵנִי.

³Be to me a sheltering Rock, whereunto I may continually resort, which You have appointed to save me; for You are my Rock and my fortress.

הֱיֵה לִי לְצוּר מָעוֹן לָבוֹא תָּמִיד צִוִּיתָ לְהוֹשִׁיעֵנִי: כִּי סַלְעִי וּמְצוּדָתִי אָתָּה.

⁴O my Elohim, rescue me out of the hand of the wicked, out of the grasp of the unrighteous and ruthless man.

אֱלֹהַי פַּלְּטֵנִי מִיַּד רָשָׁע; מִכַּף מְעַוֵּל וְחוֹמֵץ.

⁵For You are my hope; O Adonai יהוה, my trust from my youth.

כִּי אַתָּה תִקְוָתִי; אֲדֹנָי יהוה מִבְטַחִי מִנְּעוּרָי.

⁶Upon You have I stayed myself from birth; You are He that took me out of my mother's womb; my praise is continually of You.

עָלֶיךָ נִסְמַכְתִּי מִבֶּטֶן מִמְּעֵי אִמִּי אַתָּה גוֹזִי; בְּךָ תְהִלָּתִי תָמִיד.

⁷I am as a wonder unto many; but You are my strong refuge.

כְּמוֹפֵת הָיִיתִי לְרַבִּים; וְאַתָּה מַחֲסִי עֹז.

⁸My mouth shall be filled with Your praise, and with Your glory all the day.

יִמָּלֵא פִי תְּהִלָּתֶךָ; כָּל הַיּוֹם תִּפְאַרְתֶּךָ.

⁹Cast me not off in the time of old age; when my strength fails, forsake me not.

אַל תַּשְׁלִיכֵנִי לְעֵת זִקְנָה; כִּכְלוֹת כֹּחִי אַל תַּעַזְבֵנִי.

<sup>10</sup>For my enemies speak concerning me, and they that watch for my soul take counsel together,

כִּי אָמְרוּ אוֹיְבַי לִי; וְשֹׁמְרֵי נַפְשִׁי נוֹעֲצוּ יַחְדָּו.

<sup>11</sup>Saying, "Elohim has forsaken him; pursue and take him; for there is none to deliver."

לֵאמֹר אֱלֹהִים עֲזָבוֹ; רִדְפוּ וְתִפְשׂוּהוּ כִּי אֵין מַצִּיל.

<sup>12</sup>O Elohim, be not far from me; O my Elohim, make haste to help me.

אֱלֹהִים אַל תִּרְחַק מִמֶּנִּי; אֱלֹהַי לְעֶזְרָתִי חִישָׁה (חוּשָׁה).

<sup>13</sup>Let them be ashamed and consumed that are adversaries to my soul; let them be covered with reproach and confusion that seek my hurt.

יֵבֹשׁוּ יִכְלוּ שֹׂטְנֵי נַפְשִׁי: יַעֲטוּ חֶרְפָּה וּכְלִמָּה מְבַקְשֵׁי רָעָתִי.

<sup>14</sup>But as for me, I will hope continually, and I will praise You yet more and more.

וַאֲנִי תָּמִיד אֲיַחֵל; וְהוֹסַפְתִּי עַל כָּל תְּהִלָּתֶךָ.

<sup>15</sup>My mouth shall tell of Your tzedaka, and of Your Salvation all the day; for I know not the numbers thereof.

פִּי יְסַפֵּר צִדְקָתֶךָ כָּל הַיּוֹם תְּשׁוּעָתֶךָ: כִּי לֹא יָדַעְתִּי סְפֹרוֹת.

<sup>16</sup>I will come with Your mighty acts, O Adonai יהוה ; I will make mention of Your tzedaka, Yours alone.

אָבוֹא בִּגְבֻרוֹת אֲדֹנָי יהוה ; אַזְכִּיר צִדְקָתְךָ לְבַדֶּךָ.

<sup>17</sup>O Elohim, You have taught me from my youth; and until now do I declare Your wondrous works.

אֱלֹהִים לִמַּדְתַּנִי מִנְּעוּרָי; וְעַד הֵנָּה אַגִּיד נִפְלְאוֹתֶיךָ.

<sup>18</sup>And even unto old age and gray hairs, O Elohim, forsake me not; until I have declared Your Zero'ah unto the next generation, Your might to everyone that is to come.

וְגַם עַד זִקְנָה וְשֵׂיבָה אֱלֹהִים אַל תַּעַזְבֵנִי: עַד אַגִּיד זְרוֹעֲךָ לְדוֹר; לְכָל יָבוֹא גְּבוּרָתֶךָ.

<sup>19</sup>Your tzedaka also, O Elohim, which reaches unto high heaven; You who have done great things, O Elohim, who is like unto You?

וְצִדְקָתְךָ אֱלֹהִים עַד מָרוֹם: אֲשֶׁר עָשִׂיתָ גְדֹלוֹת; אֱלֹהִים מִי כָמוֹךָ.

<sup>20</sup>You, who have made me to see many and sore troubles, will quicken me again, and bring me up again from the depths of the earth.

אֲשֶׁר הראיתנו (הִרְאִיתַנִי) צָרוֹת רַבּוֹת וְרָעוֹת: תָּשׁוּב תחינו (תְּחַיֵּנִי); וּמִתְּהֹמוֹת הָאָרֶץ תָּשׁוּב תַּעֲלֵנִי.

<sup>21</sup>You will increase my greatness, and turn and comfort me.

תֶּרֶב גְּדֻלָּתִי; וְתִסֹּב תְּנַחֲמֵנִי.

<sup>22</sup>I also will give thanks unto You with the Nevel, even unto Your truth, O my Elohim; I will sing praises unto You with the Kinor, O You, Kadosh One of Yisra'el.

גַּם אֲנִי אוֹדְךָ בִכְלִי נֶבֶל אֲמִתְּךָ אֱלֹהָי: אֲזַמְּרָה לְךָ בְכִנּוֹר קְדוֹשׁ יִשְׂרָאֵל.

<sup>23</sup>My lips shall greatly rejoice when I sing praises unto You; and my soul, which You have redeemed.

כג תְּרַנֵּנָּה שְׂפָתַי כִּי אֲזַמְּרָה לָךְ; וְנַפְשִׁי אֲשֶׁר פָּדִיתָ.

<sup>24</sup>My tongue also shall tell of Your tzedaka all the day; for they are ashamed, for they are abashed, that seek my hurt.

כד גַּם לְשׁוֹנִי כָּל הַיּוֹם תֶּהְגֶּה צִדְקָתֶךָ: כִּי בֹשׁוּ כִי חָפְרוּ מְבַקְשֵׁי רָעָתִי.

# תְּהִלָּה Tehillah 72

<sup>1</sup>For Shlomo. Give the Melekh Your judgments, O Elohim, and Your tzedaka unto the king's son;

א לִשְׁלֹמֹה: אֱלֹהִים מִשְׁפָּטֶיךָ לְמֶלֶךְ תֵּן; וְצִדְקָתְךָ לְבֶן מֶלֶךְ.

<sup>2</sup>That he may judge Your people righteously, and Your poor with justice.

ב יָדִין עַמְּךָ בְצֶדֶק; וַעֲנִיֶּיךָ בְמִשְׁפָּט.

<sup>3</sup>Let the mountains bear shalom to the people, and the hills, through tzedaka.

ג יִשְׂאוּ הָרִים שָׁלוֹם לָעָם; וּגְבָעוֹת בִּצְדָקָה.

<sup>4</sup>May he judge the poor of the people, and save the children of the needy, and crush the oppressor.

ד יִשְׁפֹּט עֲנִיֵּי עָם יוֹשִׁיעַ לִבְנֵי אֶבְיוֹן; וִידַכֵּא עוֹשֵׁק.

<sup>5</sup>They shall fear You while the sun endures, and as long as the moon is, throughout all generations.

ה יִירָאוּךָ עִם שָׁמֶשׁ; וְלִפְנֵי יָרֵחַ דּוֹר דּוֹרִים.

357

<sup>6</sup>May he come down like rain upon the mown grass, as showers that water the earth.

יֵרֵד כְּמָטָר עַל גֵּז; כִּרְבִיבִים זַרְזִיף אָרֶץ.

<sup>7</sup>In his days let a Tzadik flourish, and abundance of shalom, till the moon is no more.

יִפְרַח בְּיָמָיו צַדִּיק; וְרֹב שָׁלוֹם עַד בְּלִי יָרֵחַ.

<sup>8</sup>May he have dominion also from sea to sea, and from the River unto the ends of the earth.

וְיֵרְדְּ מִיָּם עַד יָם; וּמִנָּהָר עַד אַפְסֵי אָרֶץ.

<sup>9</sup>Let them that dwell in the wilderness bow before him; and his enemies lick the dust.

לְפָנָיו יִכְרְעוּ צִיִּים; וְאֹיְבָיו עָפָר יְלַחֵכוּ.

<sup>10</sup>The kings of Tarshish and of the isles shall render tribute; the kings of Sheva and Seva shall offer gifts.

מַלְכֵי תַרְשִׁישׁ וְאִיִּים מִנְחָה יָשִׁיבוּ; מַלְכֵי שְׁבָא וּסְבָא אֶשְׁכָּר יַקְרִיבוּ.

<sup>11</sup>Yes, all kings shall prostrate themselves before him; all nations shall serve him.

וְיִשְׁתַּחֲווּ לוֹ כָל מְלָכִים; כָּל גּוֹיִם יַעַבְדוּהוּ.

<sup>12</sup>For he will deliver the needy when he cries; the poor also, and him that has no helper.

כִּי יַצִּיל אֶבְיוֹן מְשַׁוֵּעַ; וְעָנִי וְאֵין עֹזֵר לוֹ.

<sup>13</sup>He will have pity on the poor and needy, and the souls of the needy he will save.

יָחֹס עַל דַּל וְאֶבְיוֹן; וְנַפְשׁוֹת אֶבְיוֹנִים יוֹשִׁיעַ.

<sup>14</sup>He will redeem their soul from oppression and violence, and precious will their blood be in his sight;

יד מִתּוֹךְ וּמֵחָמָס יִגְאַל נַפְשָׁם; וְיֵיקַר דָּמָם בְּעֵינָיו.

<sup>15</sup>That they may live, and that he may give them of the gold of Sheva, that they may pray for him continually, yes, bless him all the day.

טו וִיחִי וְיִתֶּן לוֹ מִזְּהַב שְׁבָא: וְיִתְפַּלֵּל בַּעֲדוֹ תָמִיד; כָּל הַיּוֹם יְבָרְכֶנְהוּ.

<sup>16</sup>May he be as a rich field of grain in the land upon the top of the mountains; may his fruit rustle like Levanon; and may they blossom out of the city like grass of the earth.

טז יְהִי פִסַּת בַּר בָּאָרֶץ בְּרֹאשׁ הָרִים: יִרְעַשׁ כַּלְּבָנוֹן פִּרְיוֹ; וְיָצִיצוּ מֵעִיר כְּעֵשֶׂב הָאָרֶץ.

<sup>17</sup>May his name endure forever; may his name be continued as long as the sun; may men also bless themselves by him; may all nations call him happy.

יז יְהִי שְׁמוֹ לְעוֹלָם לִפְנֵי שֶׁמֶשׁ יָנִין (יִנּוֹן) שְׁמוֹ: וְיִתְבָּרְכוּ בוֹ; כָּל גּוֹיִם יְאַשְּׁרוּהוּ.

<sup>18</sup>Blessed is יהוה Elohim, Elohei Yisra'el, who alone does wondrous things;

יח בָּרוּךְ יהוה אֱלֹהִים אֱלֹהֵי יִשְׂרָאֵל: עֹשֵׂה נִפְלָאוֹת לְבַדּוֹ.

<sup>19</sup>And blessed is His glorious Name forever; and let the whole earth be filled with His Kavod. Amein, and Amein.

יט וּבָרוּךְ שֵׁם כְּבוֹדוֹ לְעוֹלָם: וְיִמָּלֵא כְבוֹדוֹ אֶת כֹּל הָאָרֶץ אָמֵן וְאָמֵן.

<sup>20</sup>The prayers of David Ben Yishai are ended.

כֻּלּוּ תְפִלּוֹת דָּוִד בֶּן יִשָׁי. <sup>כ</sup>

# Tehillah 73 תְּהִלָּה

<sup>1</sup>A Mizmor of Asaf. Surely Elohim is good to Yisra'el, even to such as are pure in heart.

מִזְמוֹר לְאָסָף: אַךְ טוֹב לְיִשְׂרָאֵל אֱלֹהִים לְבָרֵי לֵבָב. <sup>א</sup>

<sup>2</sup>But as for me, my feet were almost gone; my steps had well nigh slipped.

וַאֲנִי כִּמְעַט נטוי (נָטָיוּ) רַגְלָי; כְּאַיִן שפכה (שֻׁפְּכוּ) אֲשֻׁרָי. <sup>ב</sup>

<sup>3</sup>For I was envious at the arrogant, when I saw the prosperity of the wicked.

כִּי קִנֵּאתִי בַּהוֹלְלִים; שְׁלוֹם רְשָׁעִים אֶרְאֶה. <sup>ג</sup>

<sup>4</sup>For there are no pangs at their death, and their body is sound.

כִּי אֵין חַרְצֻבּוֹת לְמוֹתָם; וּבָרִיא אוּלָם. <sup>ד</sup>

<sup>5</sup>In the trouble of man they are not; neither are they plagued like men.

בַּעֲמַל אֱנוֹשׁ אֵינֵמוֹ; וְעִם אָדָם לֹא יְנֻגָּעוּ. <sup>ה</sup>

<sup>6</sup>Therefore pride is as a chain about their neck; violence covers them as a garment.

לָכֵן עֲנָקַתְמוֹ גַאֲוָה; יַעֲטָף שִׁית חָמָס לָמוֹ. <sup>ו</sup>

<sup>7</sup>Their eyes stand forth from fatness; they are gone beyond the imaginations of their heart.

יָצָא מֵחֵלֶב עֵינֵמוֹ; עָבְרוּ מַשְׂכִּיּוֹת לֵבָב. <sup>ז</sup>

[8]They scoff, and in wickedness utter oppression; they speak as if there were none on high.

יָמִיקוּ וִידַבְּרוּ בְרָע עֹשֶׁק; מִמָּרוֹם יְדַבֵּרוּ.

[9]They have set their mouth against the heavens, and their tongue walks through the earth.

שַׁתּוּ בַשָּׁמַיִם פִּיהֶם; וּלְשׁוֹנָם תִּהֲלַךְ בָּאָרֶץ.

[10]Therefore His people return hither; and waters of fullness are drained out by them.

לָכֵן ישיב (יָשׁוּב) עַמּוֹ הֲלֹם; וּמֵי מָלֵא יִמָּצוּ לָמוֹ.

[11]And they say, "How does God know? And is there knowledge in Elyon?"

וְאָמְרוּ אֵיכָה יָדַע אֵל; וְיֵשׁ דֵּעָה בְעֶלְיוֹן.

[12]Behold, such are the wicked; and they that are always at ease increase riches.

הִנֵּה אֵלֶּה רְשָׁעִים; וְשַׁלְוֵי עוֹלָם הִשְׂגּוּ חָיִל.

[13]Surely in vain have I cleansed my heart, and washed my hands in innocence;

אַךְ רִיק זִכִּיתִי לְבָבִי; וָאֶרְחַץ בְּנִקָּיוֹן כַּפָּי.

[14]For all the day have I been plagued, and my chastisement came every morning.

וָאֱהִי נָגוּעַ כָּל הַיּוֹם; וְתוֹכַחְתִּי לַבְּקָרִים.

[15]If I had said, "I will speak thus", behold, I would have been faithless to the generation of Your children.

אִם אָמַרְתִּי אֲסַפְּרָה כְמוֹ; הִנֵּה דוֹר בָּנֶיךָ בָגָדְתִּי.

¹⁶And when I pondered how I might know this, it was wearisome in my eyes;

טזוָאֲחַשְּׁבָה לָדַעַת זֹאת; עָמָל הִיא (הוּא) בְעֵינָי.

¹⁷Until I entered into the Mikdash of God, and considered their end.

יזעַד אָבוֹא אֶל מִקְדְּשֵׁי אֵל; אָבִינָה לְאַחֲרִיתָם.

¹⁸Surely You set them in slippery places; You hurl them down to utter ruin.

יחאַךְ בַּחֲלָקוֹת תָּשִׁית לָמוֹ; הִפַּלְתָּם לְמַשּׁוּאוֹת.

¹⁹How are they become a desolation in a moment! They are wholly consumed by terrors.

יטאֵיךְ הָיוּ לְשַׁמָּה כְרָגַע; סָפוּ תַמּוּ מִן בַּלָּהוֹת.

²⁰As a dream when one awakes, so, O Adonai, when You arouse Yourself, You will despise their semblance.

ככַּחֲלוֹם מֵהָקִיץ אֲדֹנָי בָּעִיר צַלְמָם תִּבְזֶה.

²¹For my heart was in a ferment, and I was pricked in my reins.

כאכִּי יִתְחַמֵּץ לְבָבִי; וְכִלְיוֹתַי אֶשְׁתּוֹנָן.

²²But I was brutish, and ignorant; I was as a beast before You.

כבוַאֲנִי בַעַר וְלֹא אֵדָע; בְּהֵמוֹת הָיִיתִי עִמָּךְ.

²³Nevertheless I am continually with You; You hold my right hand.

כגוַאֲנִי תָמִיד עִמָּךְ; אָחַזְתָּ בְּיַד יְמִינִי.

²⁴You will guide me with Your counsel, and afterward receive me with glory.

כדבַּעֲצָתְךָ תַנְחֵנִי; וְאַחַר כָּבוֹד תִּקָּחֵנִי.

²⁵Whom have I in heaven but You? And beside You I desire none upon earth.

כה מִי לִי בַשָּׁמָיִם; וְעִמְּךָ לֹא חָפַצְתִּי בָאָרֶץ.

²⁶My flesh and my heart fails; but Elohim is the Rock of my heart and my portion forever.

כו כָּלָה שְׁאֵרִי וּלְבָבִי: צוּר לְבָבִי וְחֶלְקִי אֱלֹהִים לְעוֹלָם.

²⁷For, lo, they that go far from You shall perish; You do destroy all them that go astray from You.

כז כִּי הִנֵּה רְחֵקֶיךָ יֹאבֵדוּ; הִצְמַתָּה כָּל זוֹנֶה מִמֶּךָּ.

²⁸But as for me, the nearness of Elohim is my good; I have made Adonai יהוה my refuge, that I may tell of all Your works.

כח וַאֲנִי קִרְבַת אֱלֹהִים לִי טוֹב: שַׁתִּי בַּאדֹנָי יהוה מַחְסִי; לְסַפֵּר כָּל מַלְאֲכוֹתֶיךָ.

# Tehillah 74 תְּהִלָּה

¹A Maskil of Asaf. Why, O Elohim, have You cast us off forever? Why does Your anger smoke against the flock of Your pasture?

א מַשְׂכִּיל לְאָסָף: לָמָה אֱלֹהִים זָנַחְתָּ לָנֶצַח; יֶעְשַׁן אַפְּךָ בְּצֹאן מַרְעִיתֶךָ.

²Remember Your assembly, which You have gotten of old, which You have redeemed to be the tribe of Your inheritance; and Har Tzion, wherein You have dwelt.

ב זְכֹר עֲדָתְךָ קָנִיתָ קֶּדֶם גָּאַלְתָּ שֵׁבֶט נַחֲלָתֶךָ; הַר צִיּוֹן זֶה שָׁכַנְתָּ בּוֹ.

<sup>3</sup>Lift up Your steps because of the perpetual ruins, even all the evil that the enemy has done in HaKodesh.

הָרִימָה פְעָמֶיךָ לְמַשֻּׁאוֹת נֶצַח; כָּל הֵרַע אוֹיֵב בַּקֹּדֶשׁ.

<sup>4</sup>Your adversaries have roared in the midst of Your meeting-place; they have set up their own signs for signs.

שָׁאֲגוּ צֹרְרֶיךָ בְּקֶרֶב מוֹעֲדֶךָ; שָׂמוּ אוֹתֹתָם אֹתוֹת.

<sup>5</sup>It seemed as when men wield upwards axes in a thicket of trees.

יִוָּדַע כְּמֵבִיא לְמָעְלָה; בִּסְבָךְ עֵץ קַרְדֻּמּוֹת.

<sup>6</sup>And now all the carved work thereof together they strike down with hatchet and hammers.

ועת (וְעַתָּה) פִּתּוּחֶיהָ יָּחַד בְּכַשִּׁיל וְכֵילַפּוֹת יַהֲלֹמוּן.

<sup>7</sup>They have set Your Mikdash on fire; they have profaned the dwelling-place of Your Name even to the ground.

שִׁלְחוּ בָאֵשׁ מִקְדָּשֶׁךָ; לָאָרֶץ חִלְּלוּ מִשְׁכַּן שְׁמֶךָ.

<sup>8</sup>They said in their heart, "Let us make havoc of them altogether"; they have burned up all the Mo'edim of God in the land.

אָמְרוּ בְלִבָּם נִינָם יָחַד; שָׂרְפוּ כָל מוֹעֲדֵי אֵל בָּאָרֶץ.

<sup>9</sup>We see not our signs; there is no more any navi; neither is there among us any that knows how long.

אוֹתֹתֵינוּ לֹא רָאִינוּ: אֵין עוֹד נָבִיא; וְלֹא אִתָּנוּ יֹדֵעַ עַד מָה.

<sup>10</sup>How long, O Elohim, shall the troubler reproach? Shall the enemy blaspheme Your Name forever?

עַד מָתַי אֱלֹהִים יְחָרֶף צָר; יְנָאֵץ אוֹיֵב שִׁמְךָ לָנֶצַח.

¹¹Why do You withdraw Your hand, even Your right hand? Draw it out of Your bosom and consume them.

יא לָמָה תָשִׁיב יָדְךָ וִימִינֶךָ; מִקֶּרֶב חוקד (חֵיקְךָ) כַלֵּה.

¹²Yet Elohim is my Melekh of old, working Salvations in the midst of the earth.

יב וֵאלֹהִים מַלְכִּי מִקֶּדֶם; פֹּעֵל יְשׁוּעוֹת בְּקֶרֶב הָאָרֶץ.

¹³You did break the sea in pieces by Your strength; You did shatter the heads of the sea-monsters in the waters.

יג אַתָּה פוֹרַרְתָּ בְעָזְּךָ יָם; שִׁבַּרְתָּ רָאשֵׁי תַנִּינִים עַל הַמָּיִם.

¹⁴You did crush the heads of Livyatan, You gave him to be food to the folk inhabiting the wilderness.

יד אַתָּה רִצַּצְתָּ רָאשֵׁי לִוְיָתָן; תִּתְּנֶנּוּ מַאֲכָל לְעָם לְצִיִּים.

¹⁵You did cleave fountain and brook; You dried up ever-flowing rivers.

טו אַתָּה בָקַעְתָּ מַעְיָן וָנָחַל; אַתָּה הוֹבַשְׁתָּ נַהֲרוֹת אֵיתָן.

¹⁶Yours is the day, Yours also the night; You have established luminary and sun.

טז לְךָ יוֹם אַף לְךָ לָיְלָה; אַתָּה הֲכִינוֹתָ מָאוֹר וָשָׁמֶשׁ.

¹⁷You have set all the borders of the earth; You have made summer and winter.

יז אַתָּה הִצַּבְתָּ כָּל גְּבוּלוֹת אָרֶץ; קַיִץ וָחֹרֶף אַתָּה יְצַרְתָּם.

¹⁸Remember this, how the enemy has reproached יהוה , and how a base people have blasphemed Your Name.

יח זְכָר זֹאת אוֹיֵב חֵרֵף יהוה; וְעַם נָבָל נִאֲצוּ שְׁמֶךָ.

[19]O deliver not the soul of Your turtle-dove unto the wild beast; forget not the life of Your poor forever.

יט‏אַל תִּתֵּן לְחַיַּת נֶפֶשׁ תּוֹרֶךָ; חַיַּת עֲנִיֶּיךָ אַל תִּשְׁכַּח לָנֶצַח.

[20]Look upon the Brit; for the dark places of the land are full of the habitations of violence.

כ‏הַבֵּט לַבְּרִית: כִּי מָלְאוּ מַחֲשַׁכֵּי אֶרֶץ נְאוֹת חָמָס.

[21]O let not the oppressed turn back in confusion; let the poor and needy praise Your Name.

כא‏אַל יָשׁב דַּךְ נִכְלָם; עָנִי וְאֶבְיוֹן יְהַלְלוּ שְׁמֶךָ.

[22]Arise, O Elohim, plead Your own cause; remember Your reproach all the day at the hand of the base man.

כב‏קוּמָה אֱלֹהִים רִיבָה רִיבֶךָ; זְכֹר חֶרְפָּתְךָ מִנִּי נָבָל כָּל הַיּוֹם.

[23]Forget not the voice of Your adversaries, the tumult of those that rise up against You, which ascends continually.

כג‏אַל תִּשְׁכַּח קוֹל צֹרְרֶיךָ; שְׁאוֹן קָמֶיךָ עֹלֶה תָמִיד.

# Tehillah 75 תְּהִלָּה

[1]For the Leader; Al Tashkhet. A Mizmor of Asaf; a Song.

א‏לַמְנַצֵּחַ אַל תַּשְׁחֵת; מִזְמוֹר לְאָסָף שִׁיר.

[2]We give thanks unto You, O Elohim, we give thanks, and Your Name is near; men tell of Your wondrous works.

ב‏הוֹדִינוּ לְךָ אֱלֹהִים הוֹדִינוּ וְקָרוֹב שְׁמֶךָ; סִפְּרוּ נִפְלְאוֹתֶיךָ.

³"When I take the Mo'ed, I Myself will judge with equity.

ג כִּי אֶקַּח מוֹעֵד; אֲנִי מֵישָׁרִים אֶשְׁפֹּט.

⁴When the earth and all the inhabitants thereof are dissolved, I Myself establish the pillars of it." Selah.

ד נְמֹגִים אֶרֶץ וְכָל יֹשְׁבֶיהָ; אָנֹכִי תִכַּנְתִּי עַמּוּדֶיהָ סֶּלָה.

⁵I say unto the arrogant, "Deal not arrogantly"; and to the wicked, "Lift not up the horn."

ה אָמַרְתִּי לַהוֹלְלִים אַל תָּהֹלּוּ; וְלָרְשָׁעִים אַל תָּרִימוּ קָרֶן.

⁶Lift not up your horn on high; speak not insolence with a haughty neck.

ו אַל תָּרִימוּ לַמָּרוֹם קַרְנְכֶם; תְּדַבְּרוּ בְצַוָּאר עָתָק.

⁷For neither from the east, nor from the west, nor yet from the wilderness, comes lifting up.

ז כִּי לֹא מִמּוֹצָא וּמִמַּעֲרָב; וְלֹא מִמִּדְבַּר הָרִים.

⁸For Elohim is judge; He puts down one, and lifts up another.

ח כִּי אֱלֹהִים שֹׁפֵט; זֶה יַשְׁפִּיל וְזֶה יָרִים.

⁹For in the hand of יהוה there is a cup, with foaming wine, full of mixture, and He pours out of the same; surely the dregs thereof, all the wicked of the earth shall drain them, and drink them.

ט כִּי כוֹס בְּיַד יהוה וְיַיִן חָמַר מָלֵא מֶסֶךְ וַיַּגֵּר מִזֶּה: אַךְ שְׁמָרֶיהָ יִמְצוּ יִשְׁתּוּ; כֹּל רִשְׁעֵי אָרֶץ.

¹⁰But as for me, I will declare forever, I will sing praises to the Elohim of Ya'akov.

י וַאֲנִי אַגִּיד לְעֹלָם; אֲזַמְּרָה לֵאלֹהֵי יַעֲקֹב.

[11]All the horns of the wicked also will I cut off; but the horns of a Tzadik shall be lifted up.

וְכָל קַרְנֵי רְשָׁעִים אֲגַדֵּעַ; תְּרוֹמַמְנָה קַרְנוֹת צַדִּיק.

# תְּהִלָּה Tehillah 76

[1]For the Leader; with string-music. A Mizmor of Asaf, a Song.

לַמְנַצֵּחַ בִּנְגִינֹת; מִזְמוֹר לְאָסָף שִׁיר.

[2]In Yehudah is Elohim known; His Name is great in Yisra'el.

נוֹדָע בִּיהוּדָה אֱלֹהִים; בְּיִשְׂרָאֵל גָּדוֹל שְׁמוֹ.

[3]In Shalem also is set His Sukka, and His dwelling-place in Tzion.

וַיְהִי בְשָׁלֵם סוּכּוֹ; וּמְעוֹנָתוֹ בְצִיּוֹן.

[4]There He broke the fiery shafts of the bow; the shield, and the sword, and the battle. Selah.

שָׁמָּה שִׁבַּר רִשְׁפֵי קָשֶׁת; מָגֵן וְחֶרֶב וּמִלְחָמָה סֶלָה.

[5]Glorious are You and excellent, coming down from the mountains of prey.

נָאוֹר אַתָּה אַדִּיר מֵהַרְרֵי טָרֶף.

[6]The stout-hearted are bereft of sense, they sleep their sleep; and none of the men of might have found their hands.

אֶשְׁתּוֹלְלוּ אַבִּירֵי לֵב נָמוּ שְׁנָתָם; וְלֹא מָצְאוּ כָל אַנְשֵׁי חַיִל יְדֵיהֶם.

[7]At Your rebuke, O Elohim of Ya'akov, they are cast into a dead sleep, the riders also, and the horses.

מִגַּעֲרָתְךָ אֱלֹהֵי יַעֲקֹב; נִרְדָּם וְרֶכֶב וָסוּס.

⁸You, even You, are awesome; and who may stand in Your sight when once You are angry?

חאַתָּה נוֹרָא אַתָּה וּמִי יַעֲמֹד לְפָנֶיךָ; מֵאָז אַפֶּךָ.

⁹You did cause sentence to be heard from heaven; the earth feared, and was still,

טמִשָּׁמַיִם הִשְׁמַעְתָּ דִּין; אֶרֶץ יָרְאָה וְשָׁקָטָה.

¹⁰When Elohim arose to judgment, to save all the humble of the earth. Selah.

יבְּקוּם לַמִּשְׁפָּט אֱלֹהִים לְהוֹשִׁיעַ כָּל עַנְוֵי אֶרֶץ סֶלָה.

¹¹Surely the wrath of man shall praise You; the residue of wrath shall You gird upon You.

יאכִּי חֲמַת אָדָם תּוֹדֶךָּ; שְׁאֵרִית חֵמֹת תַּחְגֹּר.

¹²Vow, and pay unto יהוה your Elohim; let all that are round about Him bring gifts unto Him that is to be feared;

יבנִדְרוּ וְשַׁלְּמוּ לַיהוה אֱלֹהֵיכֶם: כָּל סְבִיבָיו יֹבִילוּ שַׁי לַמּוֹרָא.

¹³He cuts off the spirit of princes; He strikes awe in the kings of the earth.

יגיִבְצֹר רוּחַ נְגִידִים; נוֹרָא לְמַלְכֵי אָרֶץ.

# תְּהִלָּה 77 Tehillah

¹For the Leader; for Yedutun. A Mizmor of Asaf.

אלַמְנַצֵּחַ עַל יְדִיתוּן (יְדוּתוּן); לְאָסָף מִזְמוֹר.

²I will lift up my voice unto Elohim, and cry; I will lift up my voice unto Elohim, that He may give ear unto me.

בקוֹלִי אֶל אֱלֹהִים וְאֶצְעָקָה; קוֹלִי אֶל אֱלֹהִים וְהַאֲזִין אֵלָי.

<sup>3</sup>In the day of my trouble I seek Adonai; with my hand uplifted, [my eye] streams in the night without ceasing; my soul refuses to be comforted.

בְּיוֹם צָרָתִי אֲדֹנָי דָּרָשְׁתִּי: יָדִי לַיְלָה נִגְּרָה וְלֹא תָפוּג; מֵאֲנָה הִנָּחֵם נַפְשִׁי.

<sup>4</sup>When I think thereon, O Elohim, I must moan; when I muse thereon, my spirit faints. Selah.

אֶזְכְּרָה אֱלֹהִים וְאֶהֱמָיָה; אָשִׂיחָה וְתִתְעַטֵּף רוּחִי סֶלָה.

<sup>5</sup>You hold fast the lids of my eyes; I am troubled, and cannot speak.

אָחַזְתָּ שְׁמֻרוֹת עֵינָי; נִפְעַמְתִּי וְלֹא אֲדַבֵּר.

<sup>6</sup>I have pondered the days of old, the years of ancient times.

חִשַּׁבְתִּי יָמִים מִקֶּדֶם שְׁנוֹת עוֹלָמִים.

<sup>7</sup>In the night I will call to remembrance my song; I will commune with my own heart; and my spirit makes diligent search:

אֶזְכְּרָה נְגִינָתִי בַּלָּיְלָה: עִם לְבָבִי אָשִׂיחָה; וַיְחַפֵּשׂ רוּחִי.

<sup>8</sup>"Will Adonai cast off forever? And will He be favorable no more?

הַלְעוֹלָמִים יִזְנַח אֲדֹנָי; וְלֹא יֹסִיף לִרְצוֹת עוֹד.

<sup>9</sup>Is His mercy clean gone forever? Is His promise come to an end for evermore?

הֶאָפֵס לָנֶצַח חַסְדּוֹ; גָּמַר אֹמֶר לְדֹר וָדֹר.

<sup>10</sup>Has Elohim forgotten to be gracious? Has He in anger shut up his mercies?" Selah.

הֲשָׁכַח חַנּוֹת אֵל; אִם קָפַץ בְּאַף רַחֲמָיו סֶלָה.

¹¹And I say, "This is my weakness, that the right hand of Elyon could change.

יֹא וָאֹמַר חַלּוֹתִי הִיא שְׁנוֹת יְמִין עֶלְיוֹן.

¹²I will make mention of the deeds of Yah; yes, I will remember Your wonders of old.

יֹב אַזְכִּיר (אֶזְכּוֹר) מַעַלְלֵי יה : כִּי אֶזְכְּרָה מִקֶּדֶם פִּלְאֶךָ.

¹³I will meditate also upon all Your work, and muse on Your doings."

יֹג וְהָגִיתִי בְכָל פָּעֳלֶךָ; וּבַעֲלִילוֹתֶיךָ אָשִׂיחָה.

¹⁴O Elohim, Your way is in HaKodesh; who is a great God like unto Elohim?

יֹד אֱלֹהִים בַּקֹּדֶשׁ דַּרְכֶּךָ; מִי אֵל גָּדוֹל כֵּאלֹהִים.

¹⁵You are the Elohim that does wonders; You have made known Your strength among the peoples.

יֹה אַתָּה הָאֵל עֹשֵׂה פֶלֶא; הוֹדַעְתָּ בָעַמִּים עֻזֶּךָ.

¹⁶You have with Your arm redeemed Your people, B'nei Ya'akov and Yosef. Selah.

יֹו גָּאַלְתָּ בִּזְרוֹעַ עַמֶּךָ; בְּנֵי יַעֲקֹב וְיוֹסֵף סֶלָה.

¹⁷The waters saw You, O Elohim; the waters saw You, they were in pain; the depths also trembled.

יֹז רָאוּךָ מַּיִם אֱלֹהִים רָאוּךָ מַּיִם יָחִילוּ; אַף יִרְגְּזוּ תְהֹמוֹת.

¹⁸The clouds flooded forth waters; the skies sent out a sound; Your arrows also went abroad.

יֹח זֹרְמוּ מַיִם עָבוֹת קוֹל נָתְנוּ שְׁחָקִים; אַף חֲצָצֶיךָ יִתְהַלָּכוּ.

[19]The voice of Your thunder was in the whirlwind; the lightnings lighted up the world; the earth trembled and shook.

יטקוֹל רַעַמְךָ בַּגַּלְגַּל הֵאִירוּ בְרָקִים תֵּבֵל; רָגְזָה וַתִּרְעַשׁ הָאָרֶץ.

[20]Your way was in the sea, and Your path in the great waters, and Your footsteps were not known.

כבַּיָּם דַּרְכֶּךָ וּשְׁבִילֶיךָ (וּשְׁבִילְךָ) בְּמַיִם רַבִּים; וְעִקְּבוֹתֶיךָ לֹא נֹדָעוּ.

[21]You did lead Your people like a flock, by the hand of Moshe and Aharon.

כאנָחִיתָ כַצֹּאן עַמֶּךָ בְּיַד מֹשֶׁה וְאַהֲרֹן.

# תְּהִלָּה 78 Tehillah

[1]A Maskil of Asaf. Give ear, O my people, to my Torah; incline your ears to the words of my mouth.

אמַשְׂכִּיל לְאָסָף: הַאֲזִינָה עַמִּי תּוֹרָתִי; הַטּוּ אָזְנְכֶם לְאִמְרֵי פִי.

[2]I will open my mouth with a mashal; I will utter dark sayings concerning days of old;

באֶפְתְּחָה בְמָשָׁל פִּי; אַבִּיעָה חִידוֹת מִנִּי קֶדֶם.

[3]That which we have heard and known, and our fathers have told us,

גאֲשֶׁר שָׁמַעְנוּ וַנֵּדָעֵם; וַאֲבוֹתֵינוּ סִפְּרוּ לָנוּ.

[4]We will not hide from their children, telling to the generation to come the praises of יהוה , and His strength, and His wondrous works that He has done.

דלֹא נְכַחֵד מִבְּנֵיהֶם לְדוֹר אַחֲרוֹן מְסַפְּרִים תְּהִלּוֹת יהוה ; וֶעֱזוּזוֹ וְנִפְלְאֹתָיו אֲשֶׁר עָשָׂה.

⁵For He established a testimony in Ya'akov, and appointed a Torah in Yisra'el, which He commanded our fathers, that they should make them known to their children;

וַיָּקֶם עֵדוּת בְּיַעֲקֹב וְתוֹרָה שָׂם בְּיִשְׂרָאֵל: אֲשֶׁר צִוָּה אֶת אֲבוֹתֵינוּ לְהוֹדִיעָם לִבְנֵיהֶם.

⁶That the generation to come might know them, even the children that should be born; who should arise and tell them to their children,

לְמַעַן יֵדְעוּ דּוֹר אַחֲרוֹן בָּנִים יִוָּלֵדוּ; יָקֻמוּ וִיסַפְּרוּ לִבְנֵיהֶם.

⁷That they might put their confidence in Elohim, and not forget the works of Elohim, but keep His Mitzvot;

וְיָשִׂימוּ בֵאלֹהִים כִּסְלָם: וְלֹא יִשְׁכְּחוּ מַעַלְלֵי אֵל; וּמִצְוֹתָיו יִנְצֹרוּ.

⁸And might not be as their fathers, a stubborn and rebellious generation; a generation that set not their heart aright, and whose spirit was not stedfast with Elohim.

וְלֹא יִהְיוּ כַּאֲבוֹתָם דּוֹר סוֹרֵר וּמֹרֶה: דּוֹר לֹא הֵכִין לִבּוֹ; וְלֹא נֶאֶמְנָה אֶת אֵל רוּחוֹ.

⁹B'nei Efrayim were as archers handling the bow, that turned back in the day of battle.

בְּנֵי אֶפְרַיִם נוֹשְׁקֵי רוֹמֵי קָשֶׁת; הָפְכוּ בְּיוֹם קְרָב.

¹⁰They kept not the Brit of Elohim, and refused to walk in His Torah;

לֹא שָׁמְרוּ בְּרִית אֱלֹהִים; וּבְתוֹרָתוֹ מֵאֲנוּ לָלֶכֶת.

<sup>11</sup>And they forgot His doings, and His wondrous works that He had shown them.

<sup>יא</sup>וַיִּשְׁכְּחוּ עֲלִילוֹתָיו;
וְנִפְלְאוֹתָיו אֲשֶׁר הֶרְאָם.

<sup>12</sup>Marvellous things did He in the sight of their fathers, in the land of Mitzrayim, in the field of Tzo'an.

<sup>יב</sup>נֶגֶד אֲבוֹתָם עָשָׂה פֶלֶא;
בְּאֶרֶץ מִצְרַיִם שְׂדֵה צֹעַן.

<sup>13</sup>He cleaved the sea, and caused them to pass through; and He made the waters to stand as a heap.

<sup>יג</sup>בָּקַע יָם וַיַּעֲבִירֵם; וַיַּצֶּב מַיִם
כְּמוֹ נֵד.

<sup>14</sup>By day also He led them with a cloud, and all the night with a light of fire.

<sup>יד</sup>וַיַּנְחֵם בֶּעָנָן יוֹמָם; וְכָל
הַלַּיְלָה בְּאוֹר אֵשׁ.

<sup>15</sup>He cleaved rocks in the wilderness, and gave them drink abundantly as out of the great deep.

<sup>טו</sup>יְבַקַּע צֻרִים בַּמִּדְבָּר; וַיַּשְׁקְ
כִּתְהֹמוֹת רַבָּה.

<sup>16</sup>He brought streams also out of the Rock, and caused waters to run down like rivers.

<sup>טז</sup>וַיּוֹצִא נוֹזְלִים מִסָּלַע; וַיּוֹרֶד
כַּנְּהָרוֹת מָיִם.

<sup>17</sup>Yet they went on still to sin against Him, to rebel against Elyon in the desert.

<sup>יז</sup>וַיּוֹסִיפוּ עוֹד לַחֲטֹא לוֹ
לַמְרוֹת עֶלְיוֹן בַּצִּיָּה.

<sup>18</sup>And they tried God in their heart by asking food for their craving.

<sup>יח</sup>וַיְנַסּוּ אֵל בִּלְבָבָם לִשְׁאָל
אֹכֶל לְנַפְשָׁם.

<sup>19</sup>Yes, they spoke against Elohim; they said, "Can God prepare a table in the wilderness?

<sup>יט</sup>וַיְדַבְּרוּ בֵּאלֹהִים: אָמְרוּ
הֲיוּכַל אֵל לַעֲרֹךְ שֻׁלְחָן
בַּמִּדְבָּר.

374

²⁰Behold, He smote the Rock, that waters gushed out, and streams overflowed; can He give bread also? Or will He provide flesh for His people?"

כ הֵן הִכָּה צוּר וַיָּזוּבוּ מַיִם וּנְחָלִים יִשְׁטֹפוּ: הֲגַם לֶחֶם יוּכַל תֵּת; אִם יָכִין שְׁאֵר לְעַמּוֹ.

²¹Therefore יהוה heard, and was wroth; and a fire was kindled against Ya'akov, and anger also went up against Yisra'el;

כא לָכֵן שָׁמַע יהוה וַיִּתְעַבָּר: וְאֵשׁ נִשְּׂקָה בְיַעֲקֹב; וְגַם אַף עָלָה בְיִשְׂרָאֵל.

²²Because they believed not in Elohim, and trusted not in His Salvation.

כב כִּי לֹא הֶאֱמִינוּ בֵּאלֹהִים; וְלֹא בָטְחוּ בִּישׁוּעָתוֹ.

²³And He commanded the skies above, and opened the doors of heaven;

כג וַיְצַו שְׁחָקִים מִמָּעַל; וְדַלְתֵי שָׁמַיִם פָּתָח.

²⁴And He caused manna to rain upon them for food, and gave them of the grain of heaven.

כד וַיַּמְטֵר עֲלֵיהֶם מָן לֶאֱכֹל; וּדְגַן שָׁמַיִם נָתַן לָמוֹ.

²⁵Man did eat the bread of the mighty; He sent them provisions to the full.

כה לֶחֶם אַבִּירִים אָכַל אִישׁ; צֵידָה שָׁלַח לָהֶם לָשֹׂבַע.

²⁶He caused the east wind to set forth in heaven; and by His power He brought on the south wind.

כו יַסַּע קָדִים בַּשָּׁמָיִם; וַיְנַהֵג בְּעֻזּוֹ תֵימָן.

²⁷He caused flesh also to rain upon them as the dust, and winged fowl as the sand of the seas;

כז וַיַּמְטֵר עֲלֵיהֶם כֶּעָפָר שְׁאֵר; וּכְחוֹל יַמִּים עוֹף כָּנָף.

[28]And He let it fall in the midst of their camp, round about their dwellings.

כחוַיַּפֵּל בְּקֶרֶב מַחֲנֵהוּ; סָבִיב לְמִשְׁכְּנֹתָיו.

[29]So they did eat, and were well filled; and He gave them that which they craved.

כטוַיֹּאכְלוּ וַיִּשְׂבְּעוּ מְאֹד; וְתַאֲוָתָם יָבִא לָהֶם.

[30]They were not estranged from their craving, their food was yet in their mouths,

ללֹא זָרוּ מִתַּאֲוָתָם; עוֹד אָכְלָם בְּפִיהֶם.

[31]When the anger of Elohim went up against them, and slew of the lustiest among them, and smote down the young men of Yisra'el.

לאוְאַף אֱלֹהִים עָלָה בָהֶם וַיַּהֲרֹג בְּמִשְׁמַנֵּיהֶם; וּבַחוּרֵי יִשְׂרָאֵל הִכְרִיעַ.

[32]For all this they sinned still, and believed not in His wondrous works.

לבבְּכָל זֹאת חָטְאוּ עוֹד; וְלֹא הֶאֱמִינוּ בְּנִפְלְאוֹתָיו.

[33]Therefore He ended their days as a breath, and their years in terror.

לגוַיְכַל בַּהֶבֶל יְמֵיהֶם; וּשְׁנוֹתָם בַּבֶּהָלָה.

[34]When He slew them, then they would inquire after Him, and turn back and seek Elohim earnestly.

לדאִם הֲרָגָם וּדְרָשׁוּהוּ; וְשָׁבוּ וְשִׁחֲרוּ אֵל.

[35]And they remembered that Elohim was their Rock, and El Elyon their redeemer.

להוַיִּזְכְּרוּ כִּי אֱלֹהִים צוּרָם; וְאֵל עֶלְיוֹן גֹּאֲלָם.

[36]But they beguiled Him with their mouth, and lied unto Him with their tongue.

לווַיְפַתּוּהוּ בְּפִיהֶם; וּבִלְשׁוֹנָם יְכַזְּבוּ לוֹ.

³⁷For their heart was not stedfast with Him, neither were they faithful in His Brit.

לֹּזוְלִבָּם לֹא נָכוֹן עִמּוֹ; וְלֹא נֶאֶמְנוּ בִּבְרִיתוֹ.

³⁸But He, being full of mercy, atones for iniquity, and destroys not; often does He turn His anger away, and does not stir up all His wrath.

לֹּחוְהוּא רַחוּם יְכַפֵּר עָוֹן וְלֹא יַשְׁחִית: וְהִרְבָּה לְהָשִׁיב אַפּוֹ; וְלֹא יָעִיר כָּל חֲמָתוֹ.

³⁹So He remembered that they were but flesh, a wind that passes away, and comes not again.

לֹטוַיִּזְכֹּר כִּי בָשָׂר הֵמָּה; רוּחַ הוֹלֵךְ וְלֹא יָשׁוּב.

⁴⁰How often did they rebel against Him in the wilderness, and grieve Him in the desert!

מכַּמָּה יַמְרוּהוּ בַמִּדְבָּר; יַעֲצִיבוּהוּ בִּישִׁימוֹן.

⁴¹And still again they tried God, and set bounds for the Kadosh One of Yisra'el.

מאוַיָּשׁוּבוּ וַיְנַסּוּ אֵל; וּקְדוֹשׁ יִשְׂרָאֵל הִתְווּ.

⁴²They remembered not His hand, nor the day when He redeemed them from the adversary.

מבלֹא זָכְרוּ אֶת יָדוֹ; יוֹם אֲשֶׁר פָּדָם מִנִּי צָר.

⁴³How He set His signs in Mitzrayim, and His wonders in the field of Tzo'an;

מגאֲשֶׁר שָׂם בְּמִצְרַיִם אֹתוֹתָיו; וּמוֹפְתָיו בִּשְׂדֵה צֹעַן.

⁴⁴And turned their rivers into blood, so that they could not drink their streams.

מדוַיַּהֲפֹךְ לְדָם יְאֹרֵיהֶם; וְנֹזְלֵיהֶם בַּל יִשְׁתָּיוּן.

<sup>45</sup>He sent among them swarms of flies, which devoured them; and frogs, which destroyed them.

מה‏יְשַׁלַּח בָּהֶם עָרֹב וַיֹּאכְלֵם; וּצְפַרְדֵּעַ וַתַּשְׁחִיתֵם.

<sup>46</sup>He gave also their increase unto the caterpillar, and their labor unto the locust.

מו‏וַיִּתֵּן לֶחָסִיל יְבוּלָם; וִיגִיעָם לָאַרְבֶּה.

<sup>47</sup>He destroyed their vines with hail, and their sycamore trees with frost.

מז‏יַהֲרֹג בַּבָּרָד גַּפְנָם; וְשִׁקְמוֹתָם בַּחֲנָמַל.

<sup>48</sup>He gave over their cattle also to the hail, and their flocks to fiery bolts.

מח‏וַיַּסְגֵּר לַבָּרָד בְּעִירָם; וּמִקְנֵיהֶם לָרְשָׁפִים.

<sup>49</sup>He sent forth upon them the fierceness of His anger, wrath, and indignation, and trouble, a sending of messengers of evil.

מט‏יְשַׁלַּח בָּם חֲרוֹן אַפּוֹ עֶבְרָה וָזַעַם וְצָרָה; מִשְׁלַחַת מַלְאֲכֵי רָעִים.

<sup>50</sup>He levelled a path for His anger; He spared not their soul from death, but gave their life over to the pestilence;

נ‏יְפַלֵּס נָתִיב לְאַפּוֹ: לֹא חָשַׂךְ מִמָּוֶת נַפְשָׁם; וְחַיָּתָם לַדֶּבֶר הִסְגִּיר.

<sup>51</sup>And smote all the first-born in Mitzrayim, the first-fruits of their strength in the tents of Kham;

נא‏וַיַּךְ כָּל בְּכוֹר בְּמִצְרָיִם; רֵאשִׁית אוֹנִים בְּאָהֳלֵי חָם.

<sup>52</sup>But He made His own people to go forth like sheep, and guided them in the wilderness like a flock.

נב‏וַיַּסַּע כַּצֹּאן עַמּוֹ; וַיְנַהֲגֵם כַּעֵדֶר בַּמִּדְבָּר.

⁵³And He led them safely, and they feared not; but the sea overwhelmed their enemies.

ⁿᵍוַיַּנְחֵם לָבֶטַח וְלֹא פָחָדוּ; וְאֶת אוֹיְבֵיהֶם כִּסָּה הַיָּם.

⁵⁴And He brought them to His consecrated border, to the Har which His right hand had gotten.

ⁿᵈוַיְבִיאֵם אֶל גְּבוּל קָדְשׁוֹ; הַר זֶה קָנְתָה יְמִינוֹ.

⁵⁵He drove out the nations also before them, and allotted them for an inheritance by line, and made the tribes of Yisra'el to dwell in their tents.

ⁿᵉוַיְגָרֶשׁ מִפְּנֵיהֶם גּוֹיִם וַיַּפִּילֵם בְּחֶבֶל נַחֲלָה; וַיַּשְׁכֵּן בְּאָהֳלֵיהֶם שִׁבְטֵי יִשְׂרָאֵל.

⁵⁶Yet they tried and provoked Elohim, Elyon, and kept not His testimonies;

ⁿᵂוַיְנַסּוּ וַיַּמְרוּ אֶת אֱלֹהִים עֶלְיוֹן; וְעֵדוֹתָיו לֹא שָׁמָרוּ.

⁵⁷But turned back, and dealt treacherously like their fathers; they were turned aside like a deceitful bow.

ⁿᶻוַיִּסֹּגוּ וַיִּבְגְּדוּ כַּאֲבוֹתָם; נֶהְפְּכוּ כְּקֶשֶׁת רְמִיָּה.

⁵⁸For they provoked Him with their high places, and moved Him to jealousy with their graven images.

ⁿᶜוַיַּכְעִיסוּהוּ בְּבָמוֹתָם; וּבִפְסִילֵיהֶם יַקְנִיאוּהוּ.

⁵⁹Elohim heard, and was wroth, and He greatly abhorred Yisra'el;

ⁿᵗשָׁמַע אֱלֹהִים וַיִּתְעַבָּר; וַיִּמְאַס מְאֹד בְּיִשְׂרָאֵל.

⁶⁰And He forsook the Mishkan of Shiloh, the tent which He had made to dwell among men;

ᵉוַיִּטֹּשׁ מִשְׁכַּן שִׁלוֹ; אֹהֶל שִׁכֵּן בָּאָדָם.

⁶¹And delivered His strength into captivity, and His glory into the adversary's hand.

סא‏וַיִּתֵּן לַשְּׁבִי עֻזּוֹ; וְתִפְאַרְתּוֹ בְיַד צָר.

⁶²He gave His people over also unto the sword; and was wroth with His inheritance.

סב‏וַיַּסְגֵּר לַחֶרֶב עַמּוֹ; וּבְנַחֲלָתוֹ הִתְעַבָּר.

⁶³Fire devoured their young men; and their virgins had no marriage-song.

סג‏בַּחוּרָיו אָכְלָה אֵשׁ; וּבְתוּלֹתָיו לֹא הוּלָּלוּ.

⁶⁴Their priests fell by the sword; and their widows made no lamentation.

סד‏כֹּהֲנָיו בַּחֶרֶב נָפָלוּ; וְאַלְמְנֹתָיו לֹא תִבְכֶּינָה.

⁶⁵Then Adonai awaked as one asleep, like a mighty man recovering from wine.

סה‏וַיִּקַץ כְּיָשֵׁן אֲדֹנָי; כְּגִבּוֹר מִתְרוֹנֵן מִיָּיִן.

⁶⁶And He smote His adversaries backward; He put upon them a perpetual reproach.

סו‏וַיַּךְ צָרָיו אָחוֹר; חֶרְפַּת עוֹלָם נָתַן לָמוֹ.

⁶⁷Moreover He abhorred the Ohel of Yosef, and chose not the tribe of Efrayim;

סז‏וַיִּמְאַס בְּאֹהֶל יוֹסֵף; וּבְשֵׁבֶט אֶפְרַיִם לֹא בָחָר.

⁶⁸But chose the tribe of Yehudah, Har Tzion which He loved.

סח‏וַיִּבְחַר אֶת שֵׁבֶט יְהוּדָה; אֶת הַר צִיּוֹן אֲשֶׁר אָהֵב.

⁶⁹And He built His Mikdash like the heights, like the earth which He has founded forever.

סט‏וַיִּבֶן כְּמוֹ רָמִים מִקְדָּשׁוֹ; כְּאֶרֶץ יְסָדָהּ לְעוֹלָם.

⁷⁰He chose David also His servant, and took him from the sheepfolds;

עׄוַיִּבְחַר בְּדָוִד עַבְדּוֹ; וַיִּקָּחֵהוּ מִמִּכְלְאֹת צֹאן.

⁷¹From following the ewes that nurse He brought him, to be shepherd over Ya'akov His people, and Yisra'el His inheritance.

עׄאמֵאַחַר עָלוֹת הֱבִיאוֹ: לִרְעוֹת בְּיַעֲקֹב עַמּוֹ; וּבְיִשְׂרָאֵל נַחֲלָתוֹ.

⁷²So he shepherded them according to the integrity of his heart; and lead them by the skillfulness of his hands.

עׄבוַיִּרְעֵם כְּתֹם לְבָבוֹ; וּבִתְבוּנוֹת כַּפָּיו יַנְחֵם.

# Tehillah 79 תְּהִלָּה

¹A Mizmor of Asaf. O Elohim, the heathen are come into Your inheritance; they have defiled Your Heikhal Kadosh; they have made Yerushalayim into heaps.

אׄמִזְמוֹר לְאָסָף: אֱלֹהִים בָּאוּ גוֹיִם בְּנַחֲלָתֶךָ טִמְּאוּ אֶת הֵיכַל קָדְשֶׁךָ; שָׂמוּ אֶת יְרוּשָׁלַם לְעִיִּים.

²They have given the dead bodies of Your servants to be food unto the fowls of the heaven, the flesh of Your Khasidim unto the beasts of the earth.

בׄנָתְנוּ אֶת נִבְלַת עֲבָדֶיךָ מַאֲכָל לְעוֹף הַשָּׁמָיִם; בְּשַׂר חֲסִידֶיךָ לְחַיְתוֹ אָרֶץ.

³They have shed their blood like water round about Yerushalayim, with none to bury them.

גׄשָׁפְכוּ דָמָם כַּמַּיִם סְבִיבוֹת יְרוּשָׁלָם; וְאֵין קוֹבֵר.

⁴We are become a taunt to our neighbors, a scorn and derision to them that are round about us.

⁷הָיִינוּ חֶרְפָּה לִשְׁכֵנֵינוּ; לַעַג וָקֶלֶס לִסְבִיבוֹתֵינוּ.

⁵How long, O יהוה ? Will You be angry forever? How long will Your jealousy burn like fire?

⁷עַד מָה יהוה תֶּאֱנַף לָנֶצַח; תִּבְעַר כְּמוֹ אֵשׁ קִנְאָתֶךָ.

⁶Pour out Your wrath upon the nations that know You not, and upon the kingdoms that call not upon Your Name.

יִשְׁפֹךְ חֲמָתְךָ אֶל הַגּוֹיִם אֲשֶׁר לֹא יְדָעוּךָ: וְעַל מַמְלָכוֹת אֲשֶׁר בְּשִׁמְךָ לֹא קָרָאוּ.

⁷For they have devoured Ya'akov, and laid waste his habitation.

יכִּי אָכַל אֶת יַעֲקֹב; וְאֶת נָוֵהוּ הֵשַׁמּוּ.

⁸Remember not against us the iniquities of our forefathers; let Your mercies speedily come to meet us; for we are brought very low.

חאַל תִּזְכָּר לָנוּ עֲוֹנֹת רִאשֹׁנִים: מַהֵר יְקַדְּמוּנוּ רַחֲמֶיךָ כִּי דַלּוֹנוּ מְאֹד.

⁹Help us, O Elohim of our Salvation, for the sake of the glory of Your Name; and deliver us, and forgive our sins, for Your Name's sake.

טעָזְרֵנוּ אֱלֹהֵי יִשְׁעֵנוּ עַל דְּבַר כְּבוֹד שְׁמֶךָ; וְהַצִּילֵנוּ וְכַפֵּר עַל חַטֹּאתֵינוּ לְמַעַן שְׁמֶךָ.

<sup>10</sup>Why should the nations say, "Where is their Elohim?" Let the avenging of Your servants' blood that is shed be made known among the nations in our sight.

לָמָּה יֹאמְרוּ הַגּוֹיִם אַיֵּה אֱלֹהֵיהֶם: יִוָּדַע בַּגּיִים לְעֵינֵינוּ; נִקְמַת דַּם עֲבָדֶיךָ הַשָּׁפוּךְ.

<sup>11</sup>Let the groaning of the prisoner come before You; according to the greatness of Your power set free those that are mortals;

תָּבוֹא לְפָנֶיךָ אֶנְקַת אָסִיר: כְּגֹדֶל זְרוֹעֲךָ הוֹתֵר בְּנֵי תְמוּתָה.

<sup>12</sup>And render unto our neighbors sevenfold into their bosom their reproach, wherewith they have reproached You, O Adonai.

וְהָשֵׁב לִשְׁכֵנֵינוּ שִׁבְעָתַיִם אֶל חֵיקָם; חֶרְפָּתָם אֲשֶׁר חֵרְפוּךָ אֲדֹנָי.

<sup>13</sup>So we that are Your people and the flock of Your pasture will give You thanks forever; we will tell of Your praise to all generations.

וַאֲנַחְנוּ עַמְּךָ וְצֹאן מַרְעִיתֶךָ נוֹדֶה לְּךָ לְעוֹלָם: לְדוֹר וָדֹר נְסַפֵּר תְּהִלָּתֶךָ.

# תְּהִלָּה 80 Tehillah

<sup>1</sup>For the Leader; upon Shoshannim. A testimony. A Mizmor of Asaf.

לַמְנַצֵּחַ אֶל שֹׁשַׁנִּים; עֵדוּת לְאָסָף מִזְמוֹר.

<sup>2</sup>Give ear, O Shepherd of Yisra'el, You that lead Yosef like a flock; You that are enthroned upon the Keruvim, shine forth.

רֹעֵה יִשְׂרָאֵל הַאֲזִינָה נֹהֵג כַּצֹּאן יוֹסֵף; יֹשֵׁב הַכְּרוּבִים הוֹפִיעָה.

³Before Efrayim and Binyamin and Menasheh, stir up Your might, and come to save us.

לִפְנֵי אֶפְרַיִם וּבִנְיָמִן וּמְנַשֶּׁה עוֹרְרָה אֶת גְּבוּרָתֶךָ; וּלְכָה לִישֻׁעָתָה לָנוּ.

⁴O Elohim, restore us; and cause Your face to shine, and we shall be saved.

אֱלֹהִים הֲשִׁיבֵנוּ; וְהָאֵר פָּנֶיךָ וְנִוָּשֵׁעָה.

⁵O יהוה Elohim Tzeva'ot, how long will You be angry against the tefilah of Your people?

ה יהוה אֱלֹהִים צְבָאוֹת עַד מָתַי עָשַׁנְתָּ בִּתְפִלַּת עַמֶּךָ.

⁶You have fed them with the bread of tears, and given them tears to drink in large measure.

הֶאֱכַלְתָּם לֶחֶם דִּמְעָה; וַתַּשְׁקֵמוֹ בִּדְמָעוֹת שָׁלִישׁ.

⁷You make us a strife unto our neighbors; and our enemies mock as they please.

תְּשִׂימֵנוּ מָדוֹן לִשְׁכֵנֵינוּ; וְאֹיְבֵינוּ יִלְעֲגוּ לָמוֹ.

⁸O Elohim Tzeva'ot, restore us; and cause Your face to shine, and we shall be saved.

אֱלֹהִים צְבָאוֹת הֲשִׁיבֵנוּ; וְהָאֵר פָּנֶיךָ וְנִוָּשֵׁעָה.

⁹You did pluck up a vine out of Mitzrayim; You did drive out the nations, and did plant it.

גֶּפֶן מִמִּצְרַיִם תַּסִּיעַ; תְּגָרֵשׁ גּוֹיִם וַתִּטָּעֶהָ.

¹⁰You did clear a place before it, and it took deep root, and filled the land.

פִּנִּיתָ לְפָנֶיהָ; וַתַּשְׁרֵשׁ שָׁרָשֶׁיהָ וַתְּמַלֵּא אָרֶץ.

<sup>11</sup>The mountains were covered with the shadow of it, and the mighty cedars with the boughs thereof.

יאכָּסוּ הָרִים צִלָּהּ; וַעֲנָפֶיהָ אַרְזֵי־אֵל.

<sup>12</sup>She sent out her branches unto the sea, and her shoots unto the River.

יבתְּשַׁלַּח קְצִירֶהָ עַד־יָם; וְאֶל־נָהָר יוֹנְקוֹתֶיהָ.

<sup>13</sup>Why have You broken down her fences, so that all they that pass by the way do pluck her?

יגלָמָּה פָּרַצְתָּ גְדֵרֶיהָ; וְאָרוּהָ כָּל־עֹבְרֵי דָרֶךְ.

<sup>14</sup>The boar out of the wood does ravage it, that which moves in the field feeds on it.

ידיְכַרְסְמֶנָּה חֲזִיר מִיָּעַר; וְזִיז שָׂדַי יִרְעֶנָּה.

<sup>15</sup>O Elohim Tzeva'ot, return, we beseech You; look from heaven, and behold, and be mindful of this vine,

טואֱלֹהִים צְבָאוֹת שׁוּב נָא: הַבֵּט מִשָּׁמַיִם וּרְאֵה; וּפְקֹד גֶּפֶן זֹאת.

<sup>16</sup>And of the stock which Your right hand has planted, and the Son that You made strong for Yourself.

טזוְכַנָּה אֲשֶׁר נָטְעָה יְמִינֶךָ; וְעַל־בֵּן אִמַּצְתָּה לָּךְ.

<sup>17</sup>It is burned with fire, it is cut down; they perish at the rebuke of Your countenance.

יזשְׂרֻפָה בָאֵשׁ כְּסוּחָה; מִגַּעֲרַת פָּנֶיךָ יֹאבֵדוּ.

<sup>18</sup>Let Your hand be upon the man of Your right hand, upon Ben Adam, whom You made strong for Yourself.

יחתְּהִי־יָדְךָ עַל־אִישׁ יְמִינֶךָ; עַל־בֶּן־אָדָם אִמַּצְתָּ לָּךְ.

[19]So shall we not turn back from You; quicken us, and we will call upon Your Name.

יטוְלֹא נָסוֹג מִמֶּךָּ; תְּחַיֵּנוּ וּבְשִׁמְךָ נִקְרָא.

[20]O יהוה Elohim Tzeva'ot, restore us; cause Your face to shine, and we shall be saved.

כ יהוה אֱלֹהִים צְבָאוֹת הֲשִׁיבֵנוּ; הָאֵר פָּנֶיךָ וְנִוָּשֵׁעָה.

# Tehillah 81 תְּהִלָּה

[1]For the Leader; upon the Gitit. By Asaf.

אלַמְנַצֵּחַ עַל הַגִּתִּית לְאָסָף.

[2]Sing aloud unto Elohim our strength; shout unto the Elohim of Ya'akov.

בהַרְנִינוּ לֵאלֹהִים עוּזֵּנוּ; הָרִיעוּ לֵאלֹהֵי יַעֲקֹב.

[3]Take up the melody, and sound the timbrel, the sweet Kinor with the Nevel.

גשְׂאוּ זִמְרָה וּתְנוּ תֹף; כִּנּוֹר נָעִים עִם נָבֶל.

[4]Blast the shofar at the khodesh, at the full moon for our Khag.

דתִּקְעוּ בַחֹדֶשׁ שׁוֹפָר; בַּכֵּסֶה לְיוֹם חַגֵּנוּ.

[5]For it is a statute for Yisra'el, an ordinance of the Elohim of Ya'akov.

הכִּי חֹק לְיִשְׂרָאֵל הוּא; מִשְׁפָּט לֵאלֹהֵי יַעֲקֹב.

[6]He appointed it in Yosef for a testimony, when He went forth against the land of Mitzrayim. The speech of one that I knew not did I hear:

ועֵדוּת בִּיהוֹסֵף שָׂמוֹ בְּצֵאתוֹ עַל אֶרֶץ מִצְרָיִם; שְׂפַת לֹא יָדַעְתִּי אֶשְׁמָע.

⁷"I removed his shoulder from the burden; his hands were freed from the basket.

זהֲסִירוֹתִי מִסֵּבֶל שִׁכְמוֹ; כַּפָּיו מִדּוּד תַּעֲבֹרְנָה.

⁸You did call in trouble, and I rescued you; I answered you in the secret place of thunder; I proved you at the waters of Merivah. Selah.

חבַּצָּרָה קָרָאתָ וָאֲחַלְּצֶךָּ; אֶעֶנְךָ בְּסֵתֶר רַעַם; אֶבְחָנְךָ עַל מֵי מְרִיבָה סֶלָה.

⁹Hear, O My people, and I will admonish you: O Yisra'el, if you would hearken unto Me!

טשְׁמַע עַמִּי וְאָעִידָה בָּךְ; יִשְׂרָאֵל אִם תִּשְׁמַע לִי.

¹⁰There shall no strange god be in you; neither shall you worship any foreign god.

ילֹא יִהְיֶה בְךָ אֵל זָר; וְלֹא תִשְׁתַּחֲוֶה לְאֵל נֵכָר.

¹¹I am יהוה your Elohim, who brought you up out of the land of Mitzrayim; open your mouth wide, and I will fill it.

יאאָנֹכִי יהוה אֱלֹהֶיךָ הַמַּעַלְךָ מֵאֶרֶץ מִצְרָיִם; הַרְחֶב פִּיךָ וַאֲמַלְאֵהוּ.

¹²But My people hearkened not to My voice; and Yisra'el would not love Me.

יבוְלֹא שָׁמַע עַמִּי לְקוֹלִי; וְיִשְׂרָאֵל לֹא אָבָה לִי.

¹³So I let them go after the stubbornness of their heart, that they might walk in their own counsels.

יגוָאֲשַׁלְּחֵהוּ בִּשְׁרִירוּת לִבָּם; יֵלְכוּ בְּמוֹעֲצוֹתֵיהֶם.

¹⁴Oh that My people would hearken unto Me, that Yisra'el would walk in My ways!

ידלוּ עַמִּי שֹׁמֵעַ לִי; יִשְׂרָאֵל בִּדְרָכַי יְהַלֵּכוּ.

¹⁵I would soon subdue their enemies, and turn My hand against their adversaries.

ט״וּכִמְעַט אוֹיְבֵיהֶם אַכְנִיעַ; וְעַל צָרֵיהֶם אָשִׁיב יָדִי.

¹⁶The haters of יהוה would dwindle away before Him; and their punishment would endure forever.

ט״זמְשַׂנְאֵי יהוה יְכַחֲשׁוּ לוֹ; וִיהִי עִתָּם לְעוֹלָם.

¹⁷They would also be fed with the fat of wheat; and with honey out of the Rock would I satisfy you."

י״זוַיַּאֲכִילֵהוּ מֵחֵלֶב חִטָּה; וּמִצּוּר דְּבַשׁ אַשְׂבִּיעֶךָ.

# Tehillah 82 תְּהִלָּה

¹A Mizmor of Asaf. Elohim stands in the assembly of God; in the midst of Mighty Ones He will judge:

אמִזְמוֹר לְאָסָף: אֱלֹהִים נִצָּב בַּעֲדַת אֵל; בְּקֶרֶב אֱלֹהִים יִשְׁפֹּט.

²"How long will you judge unjustly, and respect the persons of the wicked? Selah.

בעַד מָתַי תִּשְׁפְּטוּ עָוֶל; וּפְנֵי רְשָׁעִים תִּשְׂאוּ סֶלָה.

³Judge the poor and fatherless; do justice to the afflicted and destitute.

גשִׁפְטוּ דַל וְיָתוֹם; עָנִי וָרָשׁ הַצְדִּיקוּ.

⁴Rescue the poor and needy; deliver them out of the hand of the wicked.

דפַּלְּטוּ דַל וְאֶבְיוֹן; מִיַּד רְשָׁעִים הַצִּילוּ.

⁵They know not, neither do they understand; they go about in darkness; all the foundations of the earth are moved.

הלֹא יָדְעוּ וְלֹא יָבִינוּ בַּחֲשֵׁכָה יִתְהַלָּכוּ; יִמּוֹטוּ כָּל מוֹסְדֵי אָרֶץ.

⁶I said, "You are gods, and all of you B'nei Elyon. ⁶אֲנִי אָמַרְתִּי אֱלֹהִים אַתֶּם; וּבְנֵי עֶלְיוֹן כֻּלְּכֶם.

⁷Nevertheless you shall die like men, and fall like one of the princes." ⁷אָכֵן כְּאָדָם תְּמוּתוּן; וּכְאַחַד הַשָּׂרִים תִּפֹּלוּ.

⁸Arise, O Elohim, judge the earth; for You shall possess all the nations. ⁸קוּמָה אֱלֹהִים שָׁפְטָה הָאָרֶץ: כִּי אַתָּה תִנְחַל בְּכָל הַגּוֹיִם.

# Tehillah 83 תְּהִלָּה

¹A Song, a Mizmor of Asaf. ¹שִׁיר מִזְמוֹר לְאָסָף.

²O Elohim, keep not silent; hold not Your peace, and be not still, O Elohim. ²אֱלֹהִים אַל דֳּמִי לָךְ; אַל תֶּחֱרַשׁ וְאַל תִּשְׁקֹט אֵל.

³For, lo, Your enemies are in an uproar; and they that hate You have lifted up the head. ³כִּי הִנֵּה אוֹיְבֶיךָ יֶהֱמָיוּן; וּמְשַׂנְאֶיךָ נָשְׂאוּ רֹאשׁ.

⁴They hold crafty conversation against Your people, and take counsel against Your treasured ones. ⁴עַל עַמְּךָ יַעֲרִימוּ סוֹד; וְיִתְיָעֲצוּ עַל צְפוּנֶיךָ.

⁵They have said, "Come, and let us cut them off from being a nation, that the name of Yisra'el may be no more in remembrance." ⁵אָמְרוּ לְכוּ וְנַכְחִידֵם מִגּוֹי; וְלֹא יִזָּכֵר שֵׁם יִשְׂרָאֵל עוֹד.

⁶For they have consulted together with one consent; against You do they make a covenant; ⁶כִּי נוֹעֲצוּ לֵב יַחְדָּו; עָלֶיךָ בְּרִית יִכְרֹתוּ.

389

⁷The tents of Edom and the Yishma'elim; Mo'av, and the Hagrim;

אָהֳלֵי אֱדוֹם וְיִשְׁמְעֵאלִים; מוֹאָב וְהַגְרִים.

⁸Geval, and Amon, and Amalek; Peleshet, with the inhabitants of Tzor;

גְּבָל וְעַמּוֹן וַעֲמָלֵק; פְּלֶשֶׁת עִם יֹשְׁבֵי צוֹר.

⁹Ashur also is joined with them; they have been an arm to the children of Lot. Selah.

גַּם אַשּׁוּר נִלְוָה עִמָּם; הָיוּ זְרוֹעַ לִבְנֵי לוֹט סֶלָה.

¹⁰Do unto them as unto Midyan; as to Sisera, as to Yavin, at the brook Kishon;

עֲשֵׂה לָהֶם כְּמִדְיָן; כְּסִיסְרָא כְיָבִין בְּנַחַל קִישׁוֹן.

¹¹Who were destroyed at Ein Dor; they became as dung for the earth.

נִשְׁמְדוּ בְעֵין דֹּאר; הָיוּ דֹּמֶן לָאֲדָמָה.

¹²Make their nobles like Orev and Ze'ev, and like Zevakh and Tzalmuna all their princes;

שִׁיתֵמוֹ נְדִיבֵימוֹ כְּעֹרֵב וְכִזְאֵב; וּכְזֶבַח וּכְצַלְמֻנָּע כָּל נְסִיכֵימוֹ.

¹³Who said, "Let us take to ourselves in possession the habitations of Elohim."

אֲשֶׁר אָמְרוּ נִירֲשָׁה לָּנוּ אֵת נְאוֹת אֱלֹהִים.

¹⁴O my Elohim, make them like the whirling dust; as stubble before the wind.

אֱלֹהַי שִׁיתֵמוֹ כַגַּלְגַּל; כְּקַשׁ לִפְנֵי רוּחַ.

¹⁵As the fire that burns the forest, and as the flame that sets the mountains ablaze,

כְּאֵשׁ תִּבְעַר יָעַר; וּכְלֶהָבָה תְּלַהֵט הָרִים.

¹⁶So pursue them with Your tempest, and frighten them with Your storm.

כֵּן תִּרְדְּפֵם בְּסַעֲרֶךָ; וּבְסוּפָתְךָ תְבַהֲלֵם.

<sup>17</sup>Fill their faces with shame; that they may seek Your Name, O יהוה .

מַלֵּא פְנֵיהֶם קָלוֹן; וִיבַקְשׁוּ שְׁמְךָ יהוה .

<sup>18</sup>Let them be ashamed and terrified forever; yes, let them be abashed and perish;

יֵבֹשׁוּ וְיִבָּהֲלוּ עֲדֵי עַד; וְיַחְפְּרוּ וְיֹאבֵדוּ.

<sup>19</sup>That they may know that it is You alone whose Name is יהוה , Elyon over all the earth.

וְיֵדְעוּ כִּי אַתָּה שִׁמְךָ יהוה לְבַדֶּךָ: עֶלְיוֹן עַל כָּל הָאָרֶץ.

# Tehillah 84 תְּהִלָּה

<sup>1</sup>For the Leader; upon the Gitit. A Mizmor for the sons of Korakh.

לַמְנַצֵּחַ עַל הַגִּתִּית; לִבְנֵי קֹרַח מִזְמוֹר.

<sup>2</sup>How lovely are Your Mishkanim, O יהוה Tzeva'ot!

מַה יְּדִידוֹת מִשְׁכְּנוֹתֶיךָ יהוה צְבָאוֹת.

<sup>3</sup>My soul yearns, yes, even pines for the courts of יהוה ; my heart and my flesh sing for joy unto El Khai.

נִכְסְפָה וְגַם כָּלְתָה נַפְשִׁי לְחַצְרוֹת יהוה : לִבִּי וּבְשָׂרִי יְרַנְּנוּ אֶל אֵל חָי.

<sup>4</sup>Yes, the sparrow has found a house, and the swallow a nest for herself, where she may lay her young; Your Mizbekhot, O יהוה Tzeva'ot, my Melekh, and my Elohim.

גַּם צִפּוֹר מָצְאָה בַיִת וּדְרוֹר קֵן לָהּ אֲשֶׁר שָׁתָה אֶפְרֹחֶיהָ: אֶת מִזְבְּחוֹתֶיךָ יהוה צְבָאוֹת מַלְכִּי וֵאלֹהָי.

<sup>5</sup>Happy are they that dwell in Your house, they are ever praising You. Selah.

אַשְׁרֵי יוֹשְׁבֵי בֵיתֶךָ עוֹד יְהַלְלוּךָ סֶּלָה.

391

⁶Happy is the man whose strength is in You; in whose heart are the highways.

אַשְׁרֵי אָדָם עוֹז לוֹ בָךְ; מְסִלּוֹת בִּלְבָבָם.

⁷Passing through the valley of Bakha they make it a place of springs; yes, the early rain clothes it with blessings.

עֹבְרֵי בְּעֵמֶק הַבָּכָא מַעְיָן יְשִׁיתוּהוּ; גַּם בְּרָכוֹת יַעְטֶה מוֹרֶה.

⁸They go from strength to strength, every one of them appears before Elohim in Tzion.

יֵלְכוּ מֵחַיִל אֶל חָיִל; יֵרָאֶה אֶל אֱלֹהִים בְּצִיּוֹן.

⁹O יהוה Elohim Tzeva'ot, hear my tefilah; give ear, O Elohim of Ya'akov. Selah.

יהוה אֱלֹהִים צְבָאוֹת שִׁמְעָה תְפִלָּתִי; הַאֲזִינָה אֱלֹהֵי יַעֲקֹב סֶלָה.

¹⁰Behold, O Elohim our Magen, and look upon the face of Your Mashi'akh.

מָגִנֵּנוּ רְאֵה אֱלֹהִים; וְהַבֵּט פְּנֵי מְשִׁיחֶךָ.

¹¹For a day in Your courts is better than a thousand; I would rather stand at the threshold of Beit Elohai, than to dwell in the tents of wickedness.

כִּי טוֹב יוֹם בַּחֲצֵרֶיךָ מֵאָלֶף: בָּחַרְתִּי הִסְתּוֹפֵף בְּבֵית אֱלֹהַי; מִדּוּר בְּאָהֳלֵי רֶשַׁע.

¹²For יהוה Elohim is a sun and a Magen; יהוה gives grace and glory; no good thing will He withhold from them that walk uprightly.

כִּי שֶׁמֶשׁ וּמָגֵן יהוה אֱלֹהִים: חֵן וְכָבוֹד יִתֵּן יהוה; לֹא יִמְנַע טוֹב לַהֹלְכִים בְּתָמִים.

¹³O יהוה Tzeva'ot, happy is the man that trusts in You.

יהוה צְבָאוֹת אַשְׁרֵי אָדָם בֹּטֵחַ בָּךְ.

# תְּהִלָּה 85 Tehillah

<sup>1</sup>For the Leader. A Mizmor for the sons of Korakh.

אלַמְנַצֵּחַ לִבְנֵי קֹרַח מִזְמוֹר.

<sup>2</sup> יהוה , You have been favorable unto Your land, You have turned the captivity of Ya'akov.

ברָצִיתָ יהוה אַרְצֶךָ; שַׁבְתָּ שבות (שְׁבִית) יַעֲקֹב.

<sup>3</sup>You have forgiven the iniquity of Your people, You have pardoned all their sin. Selah.

גנָשָׂאתָ עֲוֹן עַמֶּךָ; כִּסִּיתָ כָל חַטָּאתָם סֶלָה.

<sup>4</sup>You have withdrawn all Your wrath; You have turned from the fierceness of Your anger.

דאָסַפְתָּ כָל עֶבְרָתֶךָ; הֱשִׁיבוֹתָ מֵחֲרוֹן אַפֶּךָ.

<sup>5</sup>Restore us, O Elohim of our Salvation, and cause Your indignation toward us to cease.

השׁוּבֵנוּ אֱלֹהֵי יִשְׁעֵנוּ; וְהָפֵר כַּעַסְךָ עִמָּנוּ.

<sup>6</sup>Will You be angry with us forever? Will You draw out Your anger to all generations?

והַלְעוֹלָם תֶּאֱנַף בָּנוּ; תִּמְשֹׁךְ אַפְּךָ לְדֹר וָדֹר.

<sup>7</sup>Will You not quicken us again, that Your people may rejoice in You?

זהֲלֹא אַתָּה תָּשׁוּב תְּחַיֵּנוּ; וְעַמְּךָ יִשְׂמְחוּ בָךְ.

<sup>8</sup>Show us Your compassion, O יהוה , and grant us Your Salvation.

חהַרְאֵנוּ יהוה חַסְדֶּךָ; וְיֶשְׁעֲךָ תִּתֶּן לָנוּ.

⁹I will hear what Elohim, יהוה, will speak; for He will speak shalom unto His people, and to His Khasidim; but let them not turn back to folly.

ט אֶשְׁמְעָה מַה יְדַבֵּר הָאֵל יהוה : כִּי יְדַבֵּר שָׁלוֹם אֶל עַמּוֹ וְאֶל חֲסִידָיו; וְאַל יָשׁוּבוּ לְכִסְלָה.

¹⁰Surely His Salvation is nigh to them that fear Him; that glory may dwell in our land.

י אַךְ קָרוֹב לִירֵאָיו יִשְׁעוֹ; לִשְׁכֹּן כָּבוֹד בְּאַרְצֵנוּ.

¹¹Compassion and truth are met together; righteousness and shalom have kissed each other.

יא חֶסֶד וֶאֱמֶת נִפְגָּשׁוּ; צֶדֶק וְשָׁלוֹם נָשָׁקוּ.

¹²Truth springs out of the earth; and righteousness has looked down from heaven.

יב אֱמֶת מֵאֶרֶץ תִּצְמָח; וְצֶדֶק מִשָּׁמַיִם נִשְׁקָף.

¹³Yes, יהוה will give that which is good; and our land shall yield her produce.

יג גַּם יהוה יִתֵּן הַטּוֹב; וְאַרְצֵנוּ תִּתֵּן יְבוּלָהּ.

¹⁴Righteousness shall go before Him, and shall make His footsteps a way.

יד צֶדֶק לְפָנָיו יְהַלֵּךְ; וְיָשֵׂם לְדֶרֶךְ פְּעָמָיו.

# Tehillah 86 תְּהִלָּה

¹A Tefilah of David. Incline Your ear, O יהוה, and answer me; for I am poor and needy.

א תְּפִלָּה לְדָוִד: הַטֵּה יהוה אָזְנְךָ עֲנֵנִי כִּי עָנִי וְאֶבְיוֹן אָנִי.

²Keep my soul, for I am a Khasid; O You my Elohim, save Your servant that trusts in You.

ב שָׁמְרָה נַפְשִׁי כִּי חָסִיד אָנִי: הוֹשַׁע עַבְדְּךָ אַתָּה אֱלֹהַי הַבּוֹטֵחַ אֵלֶיךָ.

394

³Be gracious unto me, O Adonai; for unto You do I cry all the day.

³חָנֵּנִי אֲדֹנָי: כִּי אֵלֶיךָ אֶקְרָא כָּל הַיּוֹם.

⁴Make joyful the soul of Your servant; for unto You, O Adonai, do I lift up my soul.

⁴שַׂמֵּחַ נֶפֶשׁ עַבְדֶּךָ: כִּי אֵלֶיךָ אֲדֹנָי נַפְשִׁי אֶשָּׂא.

⁵For You, Adonai, are good, and ready to pardon, and plenteous in compassion unto all them that call upon You.

⁵כִּי אַתָּה אֲדֹנָי טוֹב וְסַלָּח; וְרַב חֶסֶד לְכָל קֹרְאֶיךָ.

⁶Give ear, O יהוה, unto my prayer; and attend unto the voice of my supplications.

⁶הַאֲזִינָה יהוה תְּפִלָּתִי; וְהַקְשִׁיבָה בְּקוֹל תַּחֲנוּנוֹתָי.

⁷In the day of my trouble I call upon You; for You will answer me.

⁷בְּיוֹם צָרָתִי אֶקְרָאֶךָ: כִּי תַעֲנֵנִי.

⁸There is none like unto You among the gods, O Adonai, and there are no works like Yours.

⁸אֵין כָּמוֹךָ בָאֱלֹהִים אֲדֹנָי; וְאֵין כְּמַעֲשֶׂיךָ.

⁹All nations whom You have made shall come and prostrate themselves before You, O Adonai; and they shall glorify Your Name.

⁹כָּל גּוֹיִם אֲשֶׁר עָשִׂיתָ יָבוֹאוּ וְיִשְׁתַּחֲווּ לְפָנֶיךָ אֲדֹנָי; וִיכַבְּדוּ לִשְׁמֶךָ.

¹⁰For You are great, and do wondrous things; You are Elohim alone.

¹⁰כִּי גָדוֹל אַתָּה וְעֹשֵׂה נִפְלָאוֹת; אַתָּה אֱלֹהִים לְבַדֶּךָ.

¹¹Teach me, O יהוה, Your Derekh, that I may walk in Your truth; unify my heart to fear Your Name.

א הוֹרֵנִי יהוה דַּרְכֶּךָ אֲהַלֵּךְ בַּאֲמִתֶּךָ; יַחֵד לְבָבִי לְיִרְאָה שְׁמֶךָ.

¹²I will thank You, O Adonai my Elohim, with my whole heart; and I will glorify Your Name for evermore.

ב אוֹדְךָ אֲדֹנָי אֱלֹהַי בְּכָל לְבָבִי; וַאֲכַבְּדָה שִׁמְךָ לְעוֹלָם.

¹³For great is Your compassion toward me; and You have delivered my soul from the lowest parts of She'ol.

ג כִּי חַסְדְּךָ גָּדוֹל עָלָי; וְהִצַּלְתָּ נַפְשִׁי מִשְּׁאוֹל תַּחְתִּיָּה.

¹⁴O Elohim, the proud are risen up against me, and the company of violent men have sought after my soul, and have not set You before them.

ד אֱלֹהִים זֵדִים קָמוּ עָלַי וַעֲדַת עָרִיצִים בִּקְשׁוּ נַפְשִׁי; וְלֹא שָׂמוּךָ לְנֶגְדָּם.

¹⁵But You, O Adonai, are El, merciful and gracious, longsuffering, and abundant in compassion and truth.

טו וְאַתָּה אֲדֹנָי אֵל רַחוּם וְחַנּוּן; אֶרֶךְ אַפַּיִם וְרַב חֶסֶד וֶאֱמֶת.

¹⁶O turn unto me, and be gracious unto me; give Your strength unto Your servant, and save the son of Your handmaid.

טז פְּנֵה אֵלַי וְחָנֵּנִי: תְּנָה עֻזְּךָ לְעַבְדֶּךָ; וְהוֹשִׁיעָה לְבֶן אֲמָתֶךָ.

[17]Work in my behalf a sign for good; that they that hate me may see it, and be put to shame, because You, יהוה , have helped me, and comforted me.

עֲשֵׂה עִמִּי אוֹת לְטוֹבָה: וְיִרְאוּ שֹׂנְאַי וְיֵבֹשׁוּ כִּי אַתָּה יהוה עֲזַרְתַּנִי וְנִחַמְתָּנִי.

# תְּהִלָּה 87 Tehillah

[1]A Mizmor for the sons of Korakh; a Song. His foundation is in the consecrated mountains.

לִבְנֵי קֹרַח מִזְמוֹר שִׁיר: יְסוּדָתוֹ בְּהַרְרֵי קֹדֶשׁ.

[2] יהוה loves the gates of Tzion more than all the dwellings of Ya'akov.

אֹהֵב יהוה שַׁעֲרֵי צִיּוֹן מִכֹּל מִשְׁכְּנוֹת יַעֲקֹב.

[3]Glorious things are spoken of you, O city of Elohim. Selah.

נִכְבָּדוֹת מְדֻבָּר בָּךְ עִיר הָאֱלֹהִים סֶלָה.

[4]"I will make mention of Rahav and Bavel, as among them that know Me; behold Peleshet, and Tzor, with Kush; this one was born there."

אַזְכִּיר רַהַב וּבָבֶל לְיֹדְעָי: הִנֵּה פְלֶשֶׁת וְצֹר עִם כּוּשׁ; זֶה יֻלַּד שָׁם.

[5]But of Tzion it shall be said, "This man and that was born in her; and Elyon Himself does establish her."

וּלְצִיּוֹן יֵאָמַר אִישׁ וְאִישׁ יֻלַּד בָּהּ; וְהוּא יְכוֹנְנֶהָ עֶלְיוֹן.

[6] יהוה shall count in the register of the peoples, "This one was born there." Selah.

יהוה יִסְפֹּר בִּכְתוֹב עַמִּים: זֶה יֻלַּד שָׁם סֶלָה.

[7]And whether they sing or dance, all my thoughts are in you.

וְשָׁרִים כְּחֹלְלִים כָּל מַעְיָנַי בָּךְ.

# Tehillah 88 תְּהִלָּה

[1]A Song, a Mizmor for the sons of Korakh; for the Leader; upon Makhalat Le'anot. A Maskil of Heman the Ezrakhi.

שִׁיר מִזְמוֹר לִבְנֵי קֹרַח: לַמְנַצֵּחַ עַל מָחֲלַת לְעַנּוֹת; מַשְׂכִּיל לְהֵימָן הָאֶזְרָחִי.

[2]O יהוה , Elohim of my Salvation, whatever time I cry in the night before You,

יהוה אֱלֹהֵי יְשׁוּעָתִי יוֹם צָעַקְתִּי בַלַּיְלָה נֶגְדֶּךָ.

[3]Let my prayer come before You, incline Your ear unto my cry.

תָּבוֹא לְפָנֶיךָ תְּפִלָּתִי; הַטֵּה אָזְנְךָ לְרִנָּתִי.

[4]For my soul is sated with troubles, and my life draws nigh unto the grave.

כִּי שָׂבְעָה בְרָעוֹת נַפְשִׁי; וְחַיַּי לִשְׁאוֹל הִגִּיעוּ.

[5]I am counted with them that go down into the pit; I am become as a man that has no help;

נֶחְשַׁבְתִּי עִם יוֹרְדֵי בוֹר; הָיִיתִי כְּגֶבֶר אֵין אֱיָל.

[6]Cast out among the dead, like the slain that lie in the grave, whom You remember no more; and they are cut off from Your hand.

בַּמֵּתִים חָפְשִׁי: כְּמוֹ חֲלָלִים שֹׁכְבֵי קֶבֶר אֲשֶׁר לֹא זְכַרְתָּם עוֹד; וְהֵמָּה מִיָּדְךָ נִגְזָרוּ.

[7]You have laid me in the nethermost pit, in dark places, in the deeps.

שַׁתַּנִי בְּבוֹר תַּחְתִּיּוֹת; בְּמַחֲשַׁכִּים בִּמְצֹלוֹת.

⁸Your wrath lies hard upon me, and all Your waves You press down. Selah.

ח עָלַי סָמְכָה חֲמָתֶךָ; וְכָל מִשְׁבָּרֶיךָ עִנִּיתָ סֶּלָה.

⁹You have put my acquaintances far from me; You have made me an abomination unto them; I am shut up, and I cannot come forth.

ט הִרְחַקְתָּ מְיֻדָּעַי מִמֶּנִּי: שַׁתַּנִי תוֹעֵבוֹת לָמוֹ; כָּלֻא וְלֹא אֵצֵא.

¹⁰My eye languishes by reason of affliction; I have called upon You, O יהוה , every day, I have spread forth my hands unto You.

י עֵינִי דָאֲבָה מִנִּי עֹנִי: קְרָאתִיךָ יהוה בְּכָל יוֹם; שִׁטַּחְתִּי אֵלֶיךָ כַפָּי.

¹¹Will You work wonders for the dead? Or shall the shades arise and give You thanks? Selah.

יא הֲלַמֵּתִים תַּעֲשֶׂה פֶּלֶא: אִם רְפָאִים יָקוּמוּ יוֹדוּךָ סֶּלָה.

¹²Shall Your compassion be declared in the grave, or Your faithfulness in Abadon?

יב הַיְסֻפַּר בַּקֶּבֶר חַסְדֶּךָ; אֱמוּנָתְךָ בָּאֲבַדּוֹן.

¹³Shall Your wonders be known in the dark, and Your tzedaka in the land of forgetfulness?

יג הֲיִוָּדַע בַּחֹשֶׁךְ פִּלְאֶךָ; וְצִדְקָתְךָ בְּאֶרֶץ נְשִׁיָּה.

¹⁴But as for me, unto You, O יהוה , do I cry, and in the morning does my tefilah come to meet You.

יד וַאֲנִי אֵלֶיךָ יהוה שִׁוַּעְתִּי; וּבַבֹּקֶר תְּפִלָּתִי תְקַדְּמֶךָּ.

¹⁵ יהוה , why do You cast off my soul? Why do You hide Your face from me?

טו לָמָה יהוה תִּזְנַח נַפְשִׁי; תַּסְתִּיר פָּנֶיךָ מִמֶּנִּי.

<sup>16</sup>I am afflicted and at the point of death from my youth up; I have borne Your terrors, I am distracted.

ט"עָנִי אֲנִי וְגֹוֵעַ מִנֹּעַר; נָשָׂאתִי אֵמֶיךָ אָפוּנָה.

<sup>17</sup>Your fierce wrath is gone over me; Your terrors have cut me off.

י"עָלַי עָבְרוּ חֲרוֹנֶיךָ; בִּעוּתֶיךָ צִמְּתוּתֻנִי.

<sup>18</sup>They came round about me like water all the day; they encompassed me altogether.

י"חסַבּוּנִי כַמַּיִם כָּל הַיּוֹם; הִקִּיפוּ עָלַי יָחַד.

<sup>19</sup>Friend and companion You have put far from me, and my acquaintances into darkness.

י"טהִרְחַקְתָּ מִמֶּנִּי אֹהֵב וָרֵעַ; מְיֻדָּעַי מַחְשָׁךְ.

# Tehillah 89 תְּהִלָּה

<sup>1</sup>A Maskil of Etan the Ezrakhi.

א מַשְׂכִּיל לְאֵיתָן הָאֶזְרָחִי.

<sup>2</sup>I will sing of the compassions of יהוה forever; to all generations will I make known Your faithfulness with my mouth.

ב חַסְדֵי יהוה עוֹלָם אָשִׁירָה; לְדֹר וָדֹר אוֹדִיעַ אֱמוּנָתְךָ בְּפִי.

<sup>3</sup>For I have said, "Forever is compassion built; in the very heavens You do establish Your faithfulness.

ג כִּי אָמַרְתִּי עוֹלָם חֶסֶד יִבָּנֶה; שָׁמַיִם תָּכִן אֱמוּנָתְךָ בָהֶם.

<sup>4</sup>I have made a Brit with My chosen, I have sworn unto David My servant:

ד כָּרַתִּי בְרִית לִבְחִירִי; נִשְׁבַּעְתִּי לְדָוִד עַבְדִּי.

5"Forever will I establish your seed, and build up your throne to all generations." Selah.

עַד עוֹלָם אָכִין זַרְעֶךָ; וּבָנִיתִי לְדֹר וָדוֹר כִּסְאֲךָ סֶלָה.

6So shall the heavens praise Your wonders, O יהוה, Your faithfulness also in the congregation of the K'doshim.

וְיוֹדוּ שָׁמַיִם פִּלְאֲךָ יהוה; אַף אֱמוּנָתְךָ בִּקְהַל קְדֹשִׁים.

7For who in the skies can be compared unto יהוה, who among the sons of might can be likened unto יהוה,

כִּי מִי בַשַּׁחַק יַעֲרֹךְ לַיהוה; יִדְמֶה לַיהוה בִּבְנֵי אֵלִים.

8A God, dreaded in the great council of the K'doshim, and feared of all them that are about Him?

אֵל נַעֲרָץ בְּסוֹד קְדֹשִׁים רַבָּה; וְנוֹרָא עַל כָּל סְבִיבָיו.

9O יהוה Elohei Tzeva'ot, who is a mighty one, like unto You, O Yah? And Your faithfulness is round about You.

יהוה אֱלֹהֵי צְבָאוֹת מִי כָמוֹךָ חֲסִין יָהּ; וֶאֱמוּנָתְךָ סְבִיבוֹתֶיךָ.

10You rule the proud swelling of the sea; when the waves thereof arise, You still them.

אַתָּה מוֹשֵׁל בְּגֵאוּת הַיָּם; בְּשׂוֹא גַלָּיו אַתָּה תְשַׁבְּחֵם.

11You did crush Rahav, as one that is slain; You did scatter Your enemies with the arm of Your strength.

אַתָּה דִכִּאתָ כֶחָלָל רָהַב; בִּזְרוֹעַ עֻזְּךָ פִּזַּרְתָּ אוֹיְבֶיךָ.

<sup>12</sup>Yours are the heavens, Yours also is the earth; the world and the fullness thereof, You have founded them.

יבּלְךָ שָׁמַיִם אַף לְךָ אָרֶץ; תֵּבֵל וּמְלֹאָהּ אַתָּה יְסַדְתָּם.

<sup>13</sup>The north and the south, You have created them; Tabor and Khermon rejoice in Your Name.

יגצָפוֹן וְיָמִין אַתָּה בְרָאתָם; תָּבוֹר וְחֶרְמוֹן בְּשִׁמְךָ יְרַנֵּנוּ.

<sup>14</sup>Yours is an arm with might; strong is Your hand, and exalted is Your right hand.

ידלְךָ זְרוֹעַ עִם גְּבוּרָה; תָּעֹז יָדְךָ תָּרוּם יְמִינֶךָ.

<sup>15</sup>Righteousness and justice are the foundation of Your throne; compassion and truth go before You.

טוצֶדֶק וּמִשְׁפָּט מְכוֹן כִּסְאֶךָ; חֶסֶד וֶאֱמֶת יְקַדְּמוּ פָנֶיךָ.

<sup>16</sup>Happy is the people that know the Teru'ah; they walk, O יהוה , in the light of Your countenance.

טזאַשְׁרֵי הָעָם יוֹדְעֵי תְרוּעָה; יהוה בְּאוֹר פָּנֶיךָ יְהַלֵּכוּן.

<sup>17</sup>In Your Name do they rejoice all the day; and through Your tzedaka are they exalted.

יזבְּשִׁמְךָ יְגִילוּן כָּל הַיּוֹם; וּבְצִדְקָתְךָ יָרוּמוּ.

<sup>18</sup>For You are the glory of their strength; and in Your favor our horn is exalted.

יחכִּי תִפְאֶרֶת עֻזָּמוֹ אָתָּה; וּבִרְצוֹנְךָ תָּרִים (תָּרוּם) קַרְנֵנוּ.

<sup>19</sup>For of יהוה is our Magen; and the Kadosh One of Yisra'el is our Melekh.

יטכִּי לַיהוה מָגִנֵּנוּ; וְלִקְדוֹשׁ יִשְׂרָאֵל מַלְכֵּנוּ.

<sup>20</sup>Then You spoke in a vision to Your Khasidim, and said, "I have laid help upon one that is mighty; I have exalted one chosen out of the people.

כֹּאָז דִּבַּרְתָּ בְחָזוֹן לַחֲסִידֶיךָ וַתֹּאמֶר שִׁוִּיתִי עֵזֶר עַל גִּבּוֹר; הֲרִימוֹתִי בָחוּר מֵעָם.

<sup>21</sup>I have found David My servant; with My consecrated oil have I anointed him;

כֹּאמָצָאתִי דָּוִד עַבְדִּי; בְּשֶׁמֶן קָדְשִׁי מְשַׁחְתִּיו.

<sup>22</sup>With whom My hand shall be established; My arm also shall strengthen him.

כֹּבאֲשֶׁר יָדִי תִּכּוֹן עִמּוֹ; אַף זְרוֹעִי תְאַמְּצֶנּוּ.

<sup>23</sup>The enemy shall not exact from him; nor the son of wickedness afflict him.

כֹּגלֹא יַשִּׁיא אוֹיֵב בּוֹ; וּבֶן עַוְלָה לֹא יְעַנֶּנּוּ.

<sup>24</sup>And I will beat to pieces his adversaries before him, and smite them that hate him.

כֹּדוְכַתּוֹתִי מִפָּנָיו צָרָיו; וּמְשַׂנְאָיו אֶגּוֹף.

<sup>25</sup>But My faithfulness and My compassion shall be with him; and through My Name shall his horn be exalted.

כֹּהוֶאֱמוּנָתִי וְחַסְדִּי עִמּוֹ; וּבִשְׁמִי תָּרוּם קַרְנוֹ.

<sup>26</sup>I will set his hand also on the sea, and his right hand on the rivers.

כֹּווְשַׂמְתִּי בַיָּם יָדוֹ; וּבַנְּהָרוֹת יְמִינוֹ.

<sup>27</sup>He shall call unto Me, 'You are my Father, my Elohim, and the Rock of my Salvation.'

כֹּזהוּא יִקְרָאֵנִי אָבִי אָתָּה; אֵלִי וְצוּר יְשׁוּעָתִי.

²⁸I also will appoint him first-born, the highest of the kings of the earth.

כח אַף אָנִי בְּכוֹר אֶתְּנֵהוּ; עֶלְיוֹן לְמַלְכֵי אָרֶץ.

²⁹Forever will I keep for him My compassion, and My Brit shall stand fast with him.

כט לְעוֹלָם אשמור (אֶשְׁמָר) לוֹ חַסְדִּי; וּבְרִיתִי נֶאֱמֶנֶת לוֹ.

³⁰His seed also will I make to endure forever, and his throne as the days of heaven.

ל וְשַׂמְתִּי לָעַד זַרְעוֹ; וְכִסְאוֹ כִּימֵי שָׁמָיִם.

³¹If his children forsake My Torah, and walk not in My ordinances;

לא אִם יַעַזְבוּ בָנָיו תּוֹרָתִי; וּבְמִשְׁפָּטַי לֹא יֵלֵכוּן.

³²If they profane My statutes, and keep not My Mitzvot;

לב אִם חֻקֹּתַי יְחַלֵּלוּ; וּמִצְוֹתַי לֹא יִשְׁמֹרוּ.

³³Then will I visit their transgression with the rod, and their iniquity with strokes.

לג וּפָקַדְתִּי בְשֵׁבֶט פִּשְׁעָם; וּבִנְגָעִים עֲוֹנָם.

³⁴But My compassion will I not break off from him, nor will I be false to My faithfulness.

לד וְחַסְדִּי לֹא אָפִיר מֵעִמּוֹ; וְלֹא אֲשַׁקֵּר בֶּאֱמוּנָתִי.

³⁵My Brit will I not profane, nor alter that which is gone out of My lips.

לה לֹא אֲחַלֵּל בְּרִיתִי; וּמוֹצָא שְׂפָתַי לֹא אֲשַׁנֶּה.

³⁶Once have I sworn by My Kadesh, "Surely I will not be false unto David;

לו אַחַת נִשְׁבַּעְתִּי בְקָדְשִׁי: אִם לְדָוִד אֲכַזֵּב.

404

<sup>37</sup>His seed shall endure forever, and his throne as the sun before Me.

לזזַרְעוֹ לְעוֹלָם יִהְיֶה; וְכִסְאוֹ כַשֶּׁמֶשׁ נֶגְדִּי.

<sup>38</sup>It shall be established forever as the moon; and be stedfast as the witness in sky." Selah.

לחכְּיָרֵחַ יִכּוֹן עוֹלָם; וְעֵד בַּשַּׁחַק נֶאֱמָן סֶלָה.

<sup>39</sup>But You have cast off and rejected, You have been wroth with Your Mashi'akh.

לטוְאַתָּה זָנַחְתָּ וַתִּמְאָס; הִתְעַבַּרְתָּ עִם מְשִׁיחֶךָ.

<sup>40</sup>You have abhorred the Brit of Your servant; You have profaned his crown even to the ground.

מנֵאַרְתָּה בְּרִית עַבְדֶּךָ; חִלַּלְתָּ לָאָרֶץ נִזְרוֹ.

<sup>41</sup>You have broken down all his fences; You have brought his strongholds to ruin.

מאפָּרַצְתָּ כָל גְּדֵרֹתָיו; שַׂמְתָּ מִבְצָרָיו מְחִתָּה.

<sup>42</sup>All that pass by the way spoil him; he is become a taunt to his neighbors.

מבשַׁסֻּהוּ כָּל עֹבְרֵי דָרֶךְ; הָיָה חֶרְפָּה לִשְׁכֵנָיו.

<sup>43</sup>You have exalted the right hand of his adversaries; You have made all his enemies to rejoice.

מגהֲרִימוֹתָ יְמִין צָרָיו; הִשְׂמַחְתָּ כָּל אוֹיְבָיו.

<sup>44</sup>Yes, You turn back the edge of his sword, and have not made him to stand in the battle.

מדאַף תָּשִׁיב צוּר חַרְבּוֹ; וְלֹא הֲקֵימֹתוֹ בַּמִּלְחָמָה.

<sup>45</sup>You have made his brightness to cease, and cast his throne down to the ground.

מההִשְׁבַּתָּ מִטְּהָרוֹ; וְכִסְאוֹ לָאָרֶץ מִגַּרְתָּה.

405

⁴⁶The days of his youth have You shortened; You have covered him with shame. Selah.

מוהִקְצַרְתָּ יְמֵי עֲלוּמָיו; הֶעֱטִיתָ עָלָיו בּוּשָׁה סֶלָה.

⁴⁷How long, O יהוה , will You hide Yourself forever? How long shall Your wrath burn like fire?

מזעַד מָה יהוה תִּסָּתֵר לָנֶצַח; תִּבְעַר כְּמוֹ אֵשׁ חֲמָתֶךָ.

⁴⁸O remember how short my time is; for what vanity have You created all the children of men!

מחזְכָר אֲנִי מֶה חָלֶד; עַל מַה שָּׁוְא בָּרָאתָ כָל בְּנֵי אָדָם.

⁴⁹What man is he that lives and shall not see Mavet, that shall deliver his soul from the power of She'ol? Selah.

מטמִי גֶבֶר יִחְיֶה וְלֹא יִרְאֶה מָּוֶת; יְמַלֵּט נַפְשׁוֹ מִיַּד שְׁאוֹל סֶלָה.

⁵⁰Where are Your former compassions, O Adonai, which You did swear unto David in Your faithfulness?

נאַיֵּה חֲסָדֶיךָ הָרִאשֹׁנִים אֲדֹנָי: נִשְׁבַּעְתָּ לְדָוִד בֶּאֱמוּנָתֶךָ.

⁵¹Remember, Adonai, the taunt of Your servants; how I do bear in my bosom [the taunt of] so many peoples;

נאזְכֹר אֲדֹנָי חֶרְפַּת עֲבָדֶיךָ; שְׂאֵתִי בְחֵיקִי כָּל רַבִּים עַמִּים.

⁵²Wherewith Your enemies have taunted, O יהוה , wherewith they have taunted the footsteps of Your Mashi'akh.

נבאֲשֶׁר חֵרְפוּ אוֹיְבֶיךָ יהוה : אֲשֶׁר חֵרְפוּ עִקְּבוֹת מְשִׁיחֶךָ.

⁵³Blessed is יהוה for evermore. Amein, and Amein.

נגבָּרוּךְ יהוה לְעוֹלָם: אָמֵן וְאָמֵן.

# תְּהִלָּה 90 Tehillah

<sup>1</sup>A Tefilah of Moshe, the man of Elohim. Adonai, You have been our dwelling-place in all generations.

אתְּפִלָּה לְמֹשֶׁה אִישׁ הָאֱלֹהִים: אֲדֹנָי מָעוֹן אַתָּה הָיִיתָ לָּנוּ; בְּדֹר וָדֹר.

<sup>2</sup>Before the mountains were brought forth, or ever You had formed the earth and the world, even from everlasting to everlasting, You are Elohim.

בבְּטֶרֶם הָרִים יֻלָּדוּ וַתְּחוֹלֵל אֶרֶץ וְתֵבֵל; וּמֵעוֹלָם עַד עוֹלָם אַתָּה אֵל.

<sup>3</sup>You turn man to contrition; and say, "Return, you children of men."

גתָּשֵׁב אֱנוֹשׁ עַד דַּכָּא; וַתֹּאמֶר שׁוּבוּ בְנֵי אָדָם.

<sup>4</sup>For a thousand years in Your sight are but as yesterday when it is past, and as a watch in the night.

דכִּי אֶלֶף שָׁנִים בְּעֵינֶיךָ כְּיוֹם אֶתְמוֹל כִּי יַעֲבֹר; וְאַשְׁמוּרָה בַלָּיְלָה.

<sup>5</sup>You carry them away as with a flood; they are as a sleep; in the morning they are like grass which grows up.

הזְרַמְתָּם שֵׁנָה יִהְיוּ; בַּבֹּקֶר כֶּחָצִיר יַחֲלֹף.

<sup>6</sup>In the morning it flourishes, and grows up; in the evening it is cut down, and withers.

ובַּבֹּקֶר יָצִיץ וְחָלָף; לָעֶרֶב יְמוֹלֵל וְיָבֵשׁ.

<sup>7</sup>For we are consumed in Your anger, and by Your wrath are we hurried away.

זכִּי כָלִינוּ בְאַפֶּךָ; וּבַחֲמָתְךָ נִבְהָלְנוּ.

8You have set our iniquities before You, our secret sins in the light of Your countenance.

חשת (שַׁתָּה) עֲוֹנֹתֵינוּ לְנֶגְדֶּךָ; עֲלֻמֵנוּ לִמְאוֹר פָּנֶיךָ.

9For all our days are passed away in Your wrath; we bring our years to an end as a tale that is told.

טכִּי כָל יָמֵינוּ פָּנוּ בְעֶבְרָתֶךָ; כִּלִּינוּ שָׁנֵינוּ כְמוֹ הֶגֶה.

10The days of our years are sixty years and ten, or even by reason of strength eighty years; yet is their pride but travail and vanity; for it is speedily gone, and we fly away.

יְמֵי שְׁנוֹתֵינוּ בָהֶם שִׁבְעִים שָׁנָה וְאִם בִּגְבוּרֹת שְׁמוֹנִים שָׁנָה וְרָהְבָּם עָמָל וָאָוֶן: כִּי גָז חִישׁ וַנָּעֻפָה.

11Who knows the power of Your anger, and Your wrath according to the fear that is due unto You?

אמִי יוֹדֵעַ עֹז אַפֶּךָ; וּכְיִרְאָתְךָ עֶבְרָתֶךָ.

12So teach us to number our days, that we may get us a heart of wisdom.

יבלִמְנוֹת יָמֵינוּ כֵּן הוֹדַע; וְנָבִא לְבַב חָכְמָה.

13Return, O יהוה ; how long? And let yourself relent concerning Your servants.

יגשׁוּבָה יהוה עַד מָתָי; וְהִנָּחֵם עַל עֲבָדֶיךָ.

14O satisfy us in the morning with Your compassion; that we may rejoice and be glad all our days.

ידשַׂבְּעֵנוּ בַבֹּקֶר חַסְדֶּךָ; וּנְרַנְּנָה וְנִשְׂמְחָה בְּכָל יָמֵינוּ.

<sup>15</sup>Make us glad according to the days wherein You have afflicted us, according to the years wherein we have seen evil.

טּוְשַׂמְּחֵנוּ כִּימוֹת עִנִּיתָנוּ: שְׁנוֹת רָאִינוּ רָעָה.

<sup>16</sup>Let Your work appear unto Your servants, and Your glory upon their children.

טזיֵרָאֶה אֶל עֲבָדֶיךָ פָעֳלֶךָ; וַהֲדָרְךָ עַל בְּנֵיהֶם.

<sup>17</sup>And let the graciousness of Adonai our Elohim be upon us; establish also upon us the work of our hands; yes, the work of our hands, establish it.

יזוִיהִי נֹעַם אֲדֹנָי אֱלֹהֵינוּ עָלֵינוּ: וּמַעֲשֵׂה יָדֵינוּ כּוֹנְנָה עָלֵינוּ; וּמַעֲשֵׂה יָדֵינוּ כּוֹנְנֵהוּ.

# Tehillah 91 תְּהִלָּה

<sup>1</sup>O you that dwell in the secret place of Elyon, and abide in the shadow of Shadai;

אׁיֹשֵׁב בְּסֵתֶר עֶלְיוֹן; בְּצֵל שַׁדַּי יִתְלוֹנָן.

<sup>2</sup>I will say of יהוה , who is my refuge and my fortress, my Elohim, in whom I trust,

באֹמַר לַיהוה מַחְסִי וּמְצוּדָתִי; אֱלֹהַי אֶבְטַח בּוֹ.

<sup>3</sup>That He will deliver you from the snare of the fowler, and from the noisome pestilence.

גכִּי הוּא יַצִּילְךָ מִפַּח יָקוּשׁ; מִדֶּבֶר הַוּוֹת.

<sup>4</sup>He will cover you with His pinions, and under His wings shall you take refuge; His truth is a shield and a buckler.

דבְּאֶבְרָתוֹ יָסֶךְ לָךְ וְתַחַת כְּנָפָיו תֶּחְסֶה; צִנָּה וְסֹחֵרָה אֲמִתּוֹ.

⁵You shall not be afraid of the terror by night, nor of the arrow that flies by day;

הֹלֹא תִירָא מִפַּחַד לָיְלָה; מֵחֵץ יָעוּף יוֹמָם.

⁶Of the pestilence that walks in darkness, nor of the destruction that wastes at noonday.

וֹמִדֶּבֶר בָּאֹפֶל יַהֲלֹךְ; מִקֶּטֶב יָשׁוּד צָהֳרָיִם.

⁷A thousand may fall at your side, and ten thousand at your right hand; it shall not come nigh unto you.

יִפֹּל מִצִּדְּךָ אֶלֶף וּרְבָבָה מִימִינֶךָ: אֵלֶיךָ לֹא יִגָּשׁ.

⁸Only with your eyes shall you behold, and see the recompense of the wicked.

חֹרַק בְּעֵינֶיךָ תַבִּיט; וְשִׁלֻּמַת רְשָׁעִים תִּרְאֶה.

⁹For you have made יהוה , who is my refuge, even Elyon, your habitation.

טֹכִּי אַתָּה יהוה מַחְסִי; עֶלְיוֹן שַׂמְתָּ מְעוֹנֶךָ.

¹⁰There shall no evil befall you, neither shall any plague come nigh your tent.

יֹלֹא תְאֻנֶּה אֵלֶיךָ רָעָה; וְנֶגַע לֹא יִקְרַב בְּאָהֳלֶךָ.

¹¹For He will give His Malakhim charge over you, to keep you in all your ways.

יאֹכִּי מַלְאָכָיו יְצַוֶּה לָּךְ; לִשְׁמָרְךָ בְּכָל דְּרָכֶיךָ.

¹²They shall bear you upon their hands, lest you dash your foot against a stone.

יבֹעַל כַּפַּיִם יִשָּׂאוּנְךָ: פֶּן תִּגֹּף בָּאֶבֶן רַגְלֶךָ.

¹³You shall tread upon the lion and asp; the young lion and the serpent shall you trample under feet.

יגֹעַל שַׁחַל וָפֶתֶן תִּדְרֹךְ; תִּרְמֹס כְּפִיר וְתַנִּין.

410

<sup>14</sup>"Because he has set his love upon Me, therefore will I deliver him; I will set him on high, because he has known My Name.

יֹד כִּי בִי חָשַׁק וַאֲפַלְּטֵהוּ; אֲשַׂגְּבֵהוּ כִּי יָדַע שְׁמִי.

<sup>15</sup>He shall call upon Me, and I will answer him; I will be with him in trouble; I will rescue him, and bring him to honor.

טֹו יִקְרָאֵנִי וְאֶעֱנֵהוּ עִמּוֹ אָנֹכִי בְצָרָה; אֲחַלְּצֵהוּ וַאֲכַבְּדֵהוּ.

<sup>16</sup>With long life will I satisfy him, and make him to behold My Salvation."

טֹז אֹרֶךְ יָמִים אַשְׂבִּיעֵהוּ; וְאַרְאֵהוּ בִּישׁוּעָתִי.

# Tehillah 92 תְּהִלָּה

<sup>1</sup>A Mizmor, a Song. For Yom HaShabbat.

א מִזְמוֹר שִׁיר לְיוֹם הַשַּׁבָּת.

<sup>2</sup>It is good to give thanks unto יהוה , and to sing praises unto Your Name, O Elyon;

ב טוֹב לְהֹדוֹת לַיהוה ; וּלְזַמֵּר לְשִׁמְךָ עֶלְיוֹן.

<sup>3</sup>To declare Your compassion in the morning, and Your faithfulness in the night seasons,

ג לְהַגִּיד בַּבֹּקֶר חַסְדֶּךָ; וֶאֱמוּנָתְךָ בַּלֵּילוֹת.

<sup>4</sup>With an Asor, and with the Nevel; with a solemn sound upon the Kinor.

ד עֲלֵי עָשׂוֹר וַעֲלֵי נָבֶל; עֲלֵי הִגָּיוֹן בְּכִנּוֹר.

<sup>5</sup>For You, יהוה , have made me glad through Your work; I will exult in the works of Your hands.

ה כִּי שִׂמַּחְתַּנִי יהוה בְּפָעֳלֶךָ; בְּמַעֲשֵׂי יָדֶיךָ אֲרַנֵּן.

<sup>6</sup>How great are Your works, O יהוה ! Your thoughts are very deep.

מַה גָּדְלוּ מַעֲשֶׂיךָ יהוה ; מְאֹד עָמְקוּ מַחְשְׁבֹתֶיךָ.

<sup>7</sup>A brutish man knows not, neither does a fool understand this.

אִישׁ בַּעַר לֹא יֵדָע; וּכְסִיל לֹא יָבִין אֶת זֹאת.

<sup>8</sup>When the wicked spring up as the grass, and when all the workers of iniquity do flourish; it is that they may be destroyed forever.

בִּפְרֹחַ רְשָׁעִים כְּמוֹ עֵשֶׂב וַיָּצִיצוּ כָּל פֹּעֲלֵי אָוֶן: לְהִשָּׁמְדָם עֲדֵי עַד.

<sup>9</sup>But You, O יהוה , are on high for evermore.

וְאַתָּה מָרוֹם לְעֹלָם יהוה .

<sup>10</sup>For, lo, Your enemies, O יהוה , for, lo, Your enemies shall perish: all the workers of iniquity shall be scattered.

כִּי הִנֵּה אֹיְבֶיךָ יהוה כִּי הִנֵּה אֹיְבֶיךָ יֹאבֵדוּ: יִתְפָּרְדוּ כָּל פֹּעֲלֵי אָוֶן.

<sup>11</sup>But my horn have You exalted like the horn of the wild ox; I am anointed with rich oil.

וַתָּרֶם כִּרְאֵים קַרְנִי; בַּלֹּתִי בְּשֶׁמֶן רַעֲנָן.

<sup>12</sup>My eye also has gazed on them that lie in wait for me, my ears have heard my desire for the evil-doers that rise up against me.

וַתַּבֵּט עֵינִי בְּשׁוּרָי: בַּקָּמִים עָלַי מְרֵעִים תִּשְׁמַעְנָה אָזְנָי.

<sup>13</sup>A Tzadik shall flourish like the palm tree; he shall grow like a cedar in Levanon.

צַדִּיק כַּתָּמָר יִפְרָח; כְּאֶרֶז בַּלְּבָנוֹן יִשְׂגֶּה.

412

¹⁴Planted in Beit יהוה , they shall flourish in the courts of our Elohim.

יֹד שְׁתוּלִים בְּבֵית יהוה ; בְּחַצְרוֹת אֱלֹהֵינוּ יַפְרִיחוּ.

¹⁵They shall still bring forth fruit in old age; they shall be full of sap and richness;

טוֹעוֹד יְנוּבוּן בְּשֵׂיבָה; דְּשֵׁנִים וְרַעֲנַנִּים יִהְיוּ.

¹⁶To declare that יהוה is upright, my Rock, in whom there is no unrighteousness.

טוֹלְהַגִּיד כִּי יָשָׁר יהוה ; צוּרִי וְלֹא עלתה (עַוְלָתָה) בּוֹ.

# תְּהִלָּה 93 Tehillah

¹ יהוה reigns; He is clothed in majesty; יהוה is clothed, He has girded Himself with strength; yes, the world is established, that it cannot be moved.

א יהוה מָלָךְ גֵּאוּת לָבֵשׁ: לָבֵשׁ יהוה עֹז הִתְאַזָּר; אַף תִּכּוֹן תֵּבֵל בַּל תִּמּוֹט.

²Your throne is established of old; You are from everlasting.

בנָכוֹן כִּסְאֲךָ מֵאָז; מֵעוֹלָם אָתָּה.

³The floods have lifted up, O יהוה , the floods have lifted up their voice; the floods lift up their roaring.

גנָשְׂאוּ נְהָרוֹת יהוה נָשְׂאוּ נְהָרוֹת קוֹלָם; יִשְׂאוּ נְהָרוֹת דָּכְיָם.

⁴Above the voices of many waters, the mighty breakers of the sea, יהוה on high is mighty.

דמִקֹּלוֹת מַיִם רַבִּים אַדִּירִים מִשְׁבְּרֵי יָם; אַדִּיר בַּמָּרוֹם יהוה .

⁵Your testimonies are very sure, kodesh becomes Your house, O יהוה , forevermore.

העֵדֹתֶיךָ נֶאֶמְנוּ מְאֹד לְבֵיתְךָ נַאֲוָה קֹדֶשׁ: יהוה לְאֹרֶךְ יָמִים.

# Tehillah 94 תְּהִלָּה

[1]God of vegeance, God of vengeance, shine forth.

אֵל נְקָמוֹת יהוה ; אֵל , יהוה נְקָמוֹת הוֹפִיעַ.

[2]Lift up Yourself, O Judge of the earth; render to the proud their recompense.

הִנָּשֵׂא שֹׁפֵט הָאָרֶץ; הָשֵׁב גְּמוּל עַל גֵּאִים.

[3] יהוה , how long shall the wicked, how long shall the wicked exult?

עַד מָתַי רְשָׁעִים יהוה : עַד מָתַי רְשָׁעִים יַעֲלֹזוּ.

[4]They gush out, they speak arrogance; all the workers of iniquity bear themselves loftily.

יַבִּיעוּ יְדַבְּרוּ עָתָק; יִתְאַמְּרוּ כָּל פֹּעֲלֵי אָוֶן.

[5]They crush Your people, O יהוה , and afflict Your heritage.

עַמְּךָ יהוה יְדַכְּאוּ; וְנַחֲלָתְךָ יְעַנּוּ.

[6]They slay the widow and the stranger, and murder the fatherless.

אַלְמָנָה וְגֵר יַהֲרֹגוּ; וִיתוֹמִים יְרַצֵּחוּ.

[7]And they say, "Yah will not see, neither will the Elohim of Ya'akov give heed."

וַיֹּאמְרוּ לֹא יִרְאֶה יָּהּ; וְלֹא יָבִין אֱלֹהֵי יַעֲקֹב.

[8]Consider, you brutish among the people; and you fools, when will you understand?

בִּינוּ בֹּעֲרִים בָּעָם; וּכְסִילִים מָתַי תַּשְׂכִּילוּ.

[9]He that planted the ear, shall He not hear? He that formed the eye, shall He not see?

הֲנֹטַע אֹזֶן הֲלֹא יִשְׁמָע; אִם יֹצֵר עַיִן הֲלֹא יַבִּיט.

<sup>10</sup>He that instructs nations, shall not He correct? Even He that teaches man knowledge?

הֲיֹסֵר גּוֹיִם הֲלֹא יוֹכִיחַ: הַמְלַמֵּד אָדָם דָּעַת.

<sup>11</sup> יהוה knows the thoughts of man, that they are vanity.

יא יהוה יֹדֵעַ מַחְשְׁבוֹת אָדָם: כִּי הֵמָּה הָבֶל.

<sup>12</sup>Happy is the man whom You instruct, O יהוה , and teach out of Your Torah;

יבאַשְׁרֵי הַגֶּבֶר אֲשֶׁר תְּיַסְּרֶנּוּ יָּה; וּמִתּוֹרָתְךָ תְלַמְּדֶנּוּ.

<sup>13</sup>That You may give him rest from the days of evil, until the pit is digged for the wicked.

יגלְהַשְׁקִיט לוֹ מִימֵי רָע עַד יִכָּרֶה לָרָשָׁע שָׁחַת.

<sup>14</sup>For יהוה will not cast off His people, neither will He forsake His inheritance.

ידכִּי לֹא יִטֹּשׁ יהוה עַמּוֹ; וְנַחֲלָתוֹ לֹא יַעֲזֹב.

<sup>15</sup>For eternal righteousness will return justice, and all the upright in heart shall follow it.

טוכִּי עַד צֶדֶק יָשׁוּב מִשְׁפָּט; וְאַחֲרָיו כָּל יִשְׁרֵי לֵב.

<sup>16</sup>Who will rise up for me against the evil-doers? Who will stand up for me against the workers of iniquity?

טזמִי יָקוּם לִי עִם מְרֵעִים; מִי יִתְיַצֵּב לִי עִם פֹּעֲלֵי אָוֶן.

<sup>17</sup>Unless יהוה had been my help, my soul would have soon dwelt in silence.

יזלוּלֵי יהוה עֶזְרָתָה לִי כִּמְעַט שָׁכְנָה דוּמָה נַפְשִׁי.

<sup>18</sup>If I say, "My foot slips", Your compassion, O יהוה , holds me up.

יחאִם אָמַרְתִּי מָטָה רַגְלִי; חַסְדְּךָ יהוה יִסְעָדֵנִי.

415

[19]When my cares are many within me, Your comforts delight my soul.

טבְּרֹב שַׂרְעַפַּי בְּקִרְבִּי תַּנְחוּמֶיךָ יְשַׁעַשְׁעוּ נַפְשִׁי.

[20]Shall the seat of wickedness have fellowship with You, which frames mischief by statute?

כהַיְחָבְרְךָ כִּסֵּא הַוּוֹת; יֹצֵר עָמָל עֲלֵי חֹק.

[21]They gather themselves together against the soul of a Tzadik, and condemn innocent blood.

כאיָגוֹדּוּ עַל נֶפֶשׁ צַדִּיק; וְדָם נָקִי יַרְשִׁיעוּ.

[22]But יהוה has been my high tower, and my Elohim the Rock of my refuge.

כבוַיְהִי יהוה לִי לְמִשְׂגָּב; וֵאלֹהַי לְצוּר מַחְסִי.

[23]And He has brought upon them their own iniquity, and will cut them off in their own evil; יהוה our Elohim will cut them off.

כגוַיָּשֶׁב עֲלֵיהֶם אֶת אוֹנָם וּבְרָעָתָם יַצְמִיתֵם; יַצְמִיתֵם יהוה אֱלֹהֵינוּ.

# תְּהִלָּה 95 Tehillah

[1]O come, let us sing unto יהוה ; let us shout for joy to the Rock of our Salvation.

אלְכוּ נְרַנְּנָה לַיהוה ; נָרִיעָה לְצוּר יִשְׁעֵנוּ.

[2]Let us come before His presence with thanksgiving, let us shout for joy unto Him with songs.

בנְקַדְּמָה פָנָיו בְּתוֹדָה; בִּזְמִרוֹת נָרִיעַ לוֹ.

[3]For יהוה is El Gadol, and a great Melekh above all gods;

גכִּי אֵל גָּדוֹל יהוה ; וּמֶלֶךְ גָּדוֹל עַל כָּל אֱלֹהִים.

<sup>4</sup>In whose hand are the depths of the earth; the heights of the mountains are His also.

אֲשֶׁר בְּיָדוֹ מֶחְקְרֵי אָרֶץ; וְתוֹעֲפֹת הָרִים לוֹ.

<sup>5</sup>The sea is His, and He made it; and His hands formed the dry land.

אֲשֶׁר לוֹ הַיָּם וְהוּא עָשָׂהוּ; וְיַבֶּשֶׁת יָדָיו יָצָרוּ.

<sup>6</sup>O come, let us bow down and bend the knee; let us kneel before יהוה our Maker;

בֹּאוּ נִשְׁתַּחֲוֶה וְנִכְרָעָה; נִבְרְכָה לִפְנֵי יהוה עֹשֵׂנוּ.

<sup>7</sup>For He is our Elohim, and we are the people of His pasture, and the flock of His hand. Today, if you would but hearken to His voice!

כִּי הוּא אֱלֹהֵינוּ וַאֲנַחְנוּ עַם מַרְעִיתוֹ וְצֹאן יָדוֹ: הַיּוֹם אִם בְּקֹלוֹ תִשְׁמָעוּ.

<sup>8</sup>"Harden not your heart, as at Merivah, as in the day of Masah in the wilderness;

אַל תַּקְשׁוּ לְבַבְכֶם כִּמְרִיבָה; כְּיוֹם מַסָּה בַּמִּדְבָּר.

<sup>9</sup>When your fathers tried Me, proved Me, even though they saw My work.

אֲשֶׁר נִסּוּנִי אֲבוֹתֵיכֶם: בְּחָנוּנִי גַּם רָאוּ פָעֳלִי.

<sup>10</sup>For forty years was I wearied with that generation, and said, "It is a people that do err in their heart, and they have not known My ways;

אַרְבָּעִים שָׁנָה אָקוּט בְּדוֹר וָאֹמַר עַם תֹּעֵי לֵבָב הֵם; וְהֵם לֹא יָדְעוּ דְרָכָי.

<sup>11</sup>Therefore, I swore in My wrath, that they should not enter into My rest."

אֲשֶׁר נִשְׁבַּעְתִּי בְאַפִּי; אִם יְבֹאוּן אֶל מְנוּחָתִי.

417

# Tehillah 96 תְּהִלָּה

ⁱשִׁירוּ לַיהוה שִׁיר חָדָשׁ; שִׁירוּ לַיהוה כָּל הָאָרֶץ.

¹O sing unto יהוה a new song; sing unto יהוה , all the earth.

ᵇשִׁירוּ לַיהוה בָּרְכוּ שְׁמוֹ; בַּשְּׂרוּ מִיּוֹם לְיוֹם יְשׁוּעָתוֹ.

²Sing unto יהוה , bless His Name; proclaim His Salvation from day to day.

ᵍסַפְּרוּ בַגּוֹיִם כְּבוֹדוֹ; בְּכָל הָעַמִּים נִפְלְאוֹתָיו.

³Declare His Kavod among the nations, His marvelous works among all the peoples.

ᵈכִּי גָדוֹל יהוה וּמְהֻלָּל מְאֹד; נוֹרָא הוּא עַל כָּל אֱלֹהִים.

⁴For great is יהוה , and highly to be praised; He is to be feared above all gods.

ᵉכִּי כָּל אֱלֹהֵי הָעַמִּים אֱלִילִים; וַיהוה שָׁמַיִם עָשָׂה.

⁵For all the gods of the peoples are things of nought; but יהוה made the heavens.

ᵛהוֹד וְהָדָר לְפָנָיו; עֹז וְתִפְאֶרֶת בְּמִקְדָּשׁוֹ.

⁶Honor and majesty are before Him; strength and beauty are in His Mikdash.

ᵍהָבוּ לַיהוה מִשְׁפְּחוֹת עַמִּים; הָבוּ לַיהוה כָּבוֹד וָעֹז.

⁷Ascribe unto יהוה , you kindreds of the peoples, ascribe unto יהוה glory and strength.

ᶜהָבוּ לַיהוה כְּבוֹד שְׁמוֹ; שְׂאוּ מִנְחָה וּבֹאוּ לְחַצְרוֹתָיו.

⁸Ascribe unto יהוה the glory due unto His Name; bring an offering, and come into His courts.

ᵗהִשְׁתַּחֲווּ לַיהוה בְּהַדְרַת קֹדֶשׁ; חִילוּ מִפָּנָיו כָּל הָאָרֶץ.

⁹O worship יהוה in the beauty of kodesh; tremble before Him, all the earth.

¹⁰Say among the nations, " יהוה reigns." The world also is established that it cannot be moved; He will judge the peoples with equity.

אִמְרוּ בַגּוֹיִם יהוה מָלָךְ אַף תִּכּוֹן תֵּבֵל בַּל תִּמּוֹט; יָדִין עַמִּים בְּמֵישָׁרִים.

¹¹Let the heavens be glad, and let the earth rejoice; let the sea roar, and the fullness thereof;

יִשְׂמְחוּ הַשָּׁמַיִם וְתָגֵל הָאָרֶץ; יִרְעַם הַיָּם וּמְלֹאוֹ.

¹²Let the field exult; and all that is therein; then shall all the trees of the wood sing for joy

יַעֲלֹז שָׂדַי וְכָל אֲשֶׁר בּוֹ; אָז יְרַנְּנוּ כָּל עֲצֵי יָעַר.

¹³before יהוה , for He is come; for He is come to judge the earth; He will judge the world with righteousness, and the peoples in His faithfulness.

לִפְנֵי יהוה כִּי בָא כִּי בָא לִשְׁפֹּט הָאָרֶץ: יִשְׁפֹּט תֵּבֵל בְּצֶדֶק; וְעַמִּים בֶּאֱמוּנָתוֹ.

# Tehillah 97 תְּהִלָּה

¹ יהוה reigns; let the earth rejoice; let the multitude of isles be glad.

יהוה מָלָךְ תָּגֵל הָאָרֶץ; יִשְׂמְחוּ אִיִּים רַבִּים.

²Clouds and darkness are round about Him; righteousness and justice are the foundation of His throne.

עָנָן וַעֲרָפֶל סְבִיבָיו; צֶדֶק וּמִשְׁפָּט מְכוֹן כִּסְאוֹ.

³A fire goes before Him, and burns up His adversaries round about.

אֵשׁ לְפָנָיו תֵּלֵךְ; וּתְלַהֵט סָבִיב צָרָיו.

419

⁴His lightnings lighted up the world; the earth saw, and trembled.

הֵאִירוּ בְרָקָיו תֵּבֵל; רָאֲתָה וַתָּחֵל הָאָרֶץ.

⁵The mountains melted like wax at the Presence of יהוה, at the Presence of the Adon of the whole earth.

הָרִים כַּדּוֹנַג נָמַסּוּ מִלִּפְנֵי יהוה : מִלִּפְנֵי אֲדוֹן כָּל הָאָרֶץ.

⁶The heavens declared His righteousness, and all the peoples saw His glory.

הִגִּידוּ הַשָּׁמַיִם צִדְקוֹ; וְרָאוּ כָל הָעַמִּים כְּבוֹדוֹ.

⁷Ashamed are all they that serve graven images, that boast themselves of things of nought; bow down to Him, all you gods.

יֵבֹשׁוּ כָּל עֹבְדֵי פֶסֶל הַמִּתְהַלְלִים בָּאֱלִילִים; הִשְׁתַּחֲווּ לוֹ כָּל אֱלֹהִים.

⁸Tzion heard and was glad, and the daughters of Yehudah rejoiced; because of Your judgments, O יהוה.

שָׁמְעָה וַתִּשְׂמַח צִיּוֹן וַתָּגֵלְנָה בְּנוֹת יְהוּדָה לְמַעַן מִשְׁפָּטֶיךָ יהוה.

⁹For You, יהוה, are most high above all the earth; You are exalted far above all gods.

כִּי אַתָּה יהוה עֶלְיוֹן עַל כָּל הָאָרֶץ; מְאֹד נַעֲלֵיתָ עַל כָּל אֱלֹהִים.

¹⁰O you that love יהוה, hate evil; He preserves the souls of His Khasidim; He delivered them out of the hand of the wicked.

אֹהֲבֵי יהוה שִׂנְאוּ רָע: שֹׁמֵר נַפְשׁוֹת חֲסִידָיו; מִיַּד רְשָׁעִים יַצִּילֵם.

¹¹Light is sown for HaTzadik, and gladness for the upright in heart.

אוֹר זָרֻעַ לַצַּדִּיק; וּלְיִשְׁרֵי לֵב שִׂמְחָה.

¹²Be glad in יהוה , you Tzadikim; and give thanks to His consecrated Name.

יבשִׂמְחוּ צַדִּיקִים בַּיהוה ; וְהוֹדוּ לְזֵכֶר קָדְשׁוֹ.

# תְּהִלָּה 98 Tehillah

¹A Mizmor. O sing unto יהוה a new song; for He has done marvelous things; His right hand, and His consecrated arm, has wrought Salvation for Him.

אמִזְמוֹר שִׁירוּ לַיהוה שִׁיר חָדָשׁ כִּי נִפְלָאוֹת עָשָׂה; הוֹשִׁיעָה לּוֹ יְמִינוֹ וּזְרוֹעַ קָדְשׁוֹ.

² יהוה has made known His Salvation; His tzedaka has He revealed in the sight of the goyim.

בהוֹדִיעַ יהוה יְשׁוּעָתוֹ; לְעֵינֵי הַגּוֹיִם גִּלָּה צִדְקָתוֹ.

³He has remembered His compassion and His faithfulness toward Beit Yisra'el; all the ends of the earth have seen the Salvation of our Elohim.

גזָכַר חַסְדּוֹ וֶאֱמוּנָתוֹ לְבֵית יִשְׂרָאֵל: רָאוּ כָל אַפְסֵי אָרֶץ אֵת יְשׁוּעַת אֱלֹהֵינוּ.

⁴Shout unto יהוה , all the earth; break forth and sing for joy, yes, sing praises.

דהָרִיעוּ לַיהוה כָּל הָאָרֶץ; פִּצְחוּ וְרַנְּנוּ וְזַמֵּרוּ.

⁵Sing praises unto יהוה with the Kinor; with the Kinor and the voice of melody.

הזַמְּרוּ לַיהוה בְּכִנּוֹר; בְּכִנּוֹר וְקוֹל זִמְרָה.

⁶With trumpets and the sound of the shofar, shout before HaMelekh, יהוה .

ובַחֲצֹצְרוֹת וְקוֹל שׁוֹפָר הָרִיעוּ לִפְנֵי הַמֶּלֶךְ יהוה .

421

⁷Let the sea roar, and the fullness thereof; the world, and they that dwell therein;

יִרְעַם הַיָּם וּמְלֹאוֹ; תֵּבֵל וְיֹשְׁבֵי בָהּ.

⁸Let the floods clap their hands; let the mountains sing for joy together

נְהָרוֹת יִמְחֲאוּ כָף; יַחַד הָרִים יְרַנֵּנוּ.

⁹before יהוה , for He is come to judge the earth; He will judge the world with righteousness, and the peoples with equity.

לִפְנֵי יהוה כִּי בָא לִשְׁפֹּט הָאָרֶץ: יִשְׁפֹּט תֵּבֵל בְּצֶדֶק; וְעַמִּים בְּמֵישָׁרִים.

# Tehillah 99 תְּהִלָּה

¹ יהוה reigns; let the peoples tremble; He is enthroned upon the Keruvim; let the earth quake.

א יהוה מָלָךְ יִרְגְּזוּ עַמִּים; יֹשֵׁב כְּרוּבִים תָּנוּט הָאָרֶץ.

² יהוה is great in Tzion; and He is high above all the peoples.

ב יהוה בְּצִיּוֹן גָּדוֹל; וְרָם הוּא עַל כָּל הָעַמִּים.

³Let them praise Your Name as great and awesome; Kadosh is He.

ג יוֹדוּ שִׁמְךָ גָּדוֹל וְנוֹרָא; קָדוֹשׁ הוּא.

⁴The strength also of the Melekh who loves justice; You have established equity, You have executed justice and tzedaka in Ya'akov.

ד וְעֹז מֶלֶךְ מִשְׁפָּט אָהֵב: אַתָּה כּוֹנַנְתָּ מֵישָׁרִים; מִשְׁפָּט וּצְדָקָה בְּיַעֲקֹב אַתָּה עָשִׂיתָ.

⁵Exalt יהוה our Elohim, and prostrate yourselves at His footstool; Kadosh is He.

ה רוֹמְמוּ יהוה אֱלֹהֵינוּ וְהִשְׁתַּחֲווּ לַהֲדֹם רַגְלָיו: קָדוֹשׁ הוּא.

⁶Moshe and Aharon among His Kohanim, and Shmu'el among them that call upon His Name, did call upon יהוה , and He answered them.

מֹשֶׁה וְאַהֲרֹן בְּכֹהֲנָיו וּשְׁמוּאֵל בְּקֹרְאֵי שְׁמוֹ; קֹרְאִים אֶל יהוה וְהוּא יַעֲנֵם.

⁷He spoke unto them in the pillar of cloud; they kept His testimonies, and the statute that He gave them.

בְּעַמּוּד עָנָן יְדַבֵּר אֲלֵיהֶם; שָׁמְרוּ עֵדֹתָיו וְחֹק נָתַן לָמוֹ.

⁸O יהוה our Elohim, You did answer them; a forgiving God were You unto them, though You took vengeance of their misdeeds.

יהוה אֱלֹהֵינוּ אַתָּה עֲנִיתָם: אֵל נֹשֵׂא הָיִיתָ לָהֶם; וְנֹקֵם עַל עֲלִילוֹתָם.

⁹Exalt יהוה our Elohim, and worship at His Har Kodesh; for יהוה our Elohim is Kadosh.

רוֹמְמוּ יהוה אֱלֹהֵינוּ וְהִשְׁתַּחֲווּ לְהַר קָדְשׁוֹ: כִּי קָדוֹשׁ יהוה אֱלֹהֵינוּ.

# Tehillah 100 תְּהִלָּה

¹A Mizmor of thanksgiving. Shout unto יהוה , all the earth.

מִזְמוֹר לְתוֹדָה: הָרִיעוּ לַיהוה כָּל הָאָרֶץ.

²Serve יהוה with gladness; come before His presence with singing.

עִבְדוּ אֶת יהוה בְּשִׂמְחָה; בֹּאוּ לְפָנָיו בִּרְנָנָה.

<sup>3</sup>Know that יהוה , He is Elohim; it is He that has made us, and not we ourselves; we are His people, and the flock of His pasture.

גדְּעוּ כִּי יהוה הוּא אֱלֹהִים: הוּא עָשָׂנוּ וְלֹא אֲנַחְנוּ עַמּוֹ וְצֹאן מַרְעִיתוֹ.

<sup>4</sup>Enter into His gates with thanksgiving, and into His courts with praise; give thanks unto Him, and bless His Name.

דבֹּאוּ שְׁעָרָיו בְּתוֹדָה חֲצֵרֹתָיו בִּתְהִלָּה; הוֹדוּ לוֹ בָּרְכוּ שְׁמוֹ.

<sup>5</sup>For יהוה is good; His compassion endures forever; and His faithfulness unto all generations.

הכִּי טוֹב יהוה לְעוֹלָם חַסְדּוֹ; וְעַד דֹּר וָדֹר אֱמוּנָתוֹ.

# Tehillah 101 תְּהִלָּה

<sup>1</sup>A Mizmor of David. I will sing of compassion and justice; unto You, O יהוה , will I sing praises.

אלְדָוִד מִזְמוֹר: חֶסֶד וּמִשְׁפָּט אָשִׁירָה; לְךָ יהוה אֲזַמֵּרָה.

<sup>2</sup>I will give heed unto the way of integrity; oh when will You come unto me? I will walk within my house in the integrity of my heart.

באַשְׂכִּילָה בְּדֶרֶךְ תָּמִים מָתַי תָּבוֹא אֵלָי; אֶתְהַלֵּךְ בְּתָם לְבָבִי בְּקֶרֶב בֵּיתִי.

<sup>3</sup>I will set no base thing before my eyes; I hate the doing of things crooked; it shall not cleave unto me.

גלֹא אָשִׁית לְנֶגֶד עֵינַי דְּבַר בְּלִיָּעַל: עֲשֹׂה סֵטִים שָׂנֵאתִי; לֹא יִדְבַּק בִּי.

<sup>4</sup>A perverse heart shall depart from me; I will know no evil thing.

דלֵבָב עִקֵּשׁ יָסוּר מִמֶּנִּי; רָע לֹא אֵדָע.

⁵Whoever slanders his neighbor in secret, him will I destroy; whoever is haughty of eye and proud of heart, him will I not suffer.

הְמְלוֹשְׁנִי (מְלָשְׁנִי) בַסֵּתֶר רֵעֵהוּ אוֹתוֹ אַצְמִית: גְּבַהּ עֵינַיִם וּרְחַב לֵבָב אֹתוֹ לֹא אוּכָל.

⁶My eyes are upon the faithful of the land, that they may dwell with me; he that walks in a way of integrity, he shall minister unto me.

וֹעֵינַי בְּנֶאֶמְנֵי אֶרֶץ לָשֶׁבֶת עִמָּדִי: הֹלֵךְ בְּדֶרֶךְ תָּמִים הוּא יְשָׁרְתֵנִי.

⁷He that works deceit shall not dwell within my house; he that speaks falsehood shall not be established before my eyes.

זלֹא יֵשֵׁב בְּקֶרֶב בֵּיתִי עֹשֵׂה רְמִיָּה: דֹּבֵר שְׁקָרִים לֹא יִכּוֹן לְנֶגֶד עֵינָי.

⁸Morning by morning will I destroy all the wicked of the land; to cut off all the workers of iniquity from the City of יהוה .

חלַבְּקָרִים אַצְמִית כָּל רִשְׁעֵי אָרֶץ; לְהַכְרִית מֵעִיר יהוה כָּל פֹּעֲלֵי אָוֶן.

# תְּהִלָּה Tehillah 102

¹A tefilah of the afflicted, when he faints, and pours out his complaint before יהוה .

אתְּפִלָּה לְעָנִי כִי יַעֲטֹף וְלִפְנֵי יהוה יִשְׁפֹּךְ שִׂיחוֹ.

²O יהוה , hear my prayer, and let my cry come unto You.

ב יהוה שִׁמְעָה תְפִלָּתִי; וְשַׁוְעָתִי אֵלֶיךָ תָבוֹא.

³Hide not Your face from me in the day of my distress; incline Your ear unto me; in the day when I call, answer me speedily.

ג**אַל תַּסְתֵּר פָּנֶיךָ מִמֶּנִּי בְּיוֹם צַר לִי: הַטֵּה אֵלַי אָזְנֶךָ; בְּיוֹם אֶקְרָא מַהֵר עֲנֵנִי.**

⁴For my days are consumed like smoke, and my bones are burned as a hearth.

ד**כִּי כָלוּ בְעָשָׁן יָמָי; וְעַצְמוֹתַי כְּמוֹקֵד נִחָרוּ.**

⁵My heart is smitten like grass, and withered; for I forget to eat my bread.

ה**הוּכָּה כָעֵשֶׂב וַיִּבַשׁ לִבִּי: כִּי שָׁכַחְתִּי מֵאֲכֹל לַחְמִי.**

⁶By reason of the voice of my sighing, my bones cleave to my flesh.

ו**מִקּוֹל אַנְחָתִי דָּבְקָה עַצְמִי לִבְשָׂרִי.**

⁷I am like a pelican of the wilderness; I am become as an owl of the waste places.

ז**דָּמִיתִי לִקְאַת מִדְבָּר; הָיִיתִי כְּכוֹס חֳרָבוֹת.**

⁸I watch, and am become like a sparrow that is alone upon the housetop.

ח**שָׁקַדְתִּי וָאֶהְיֶה כְּצִפּוֹר בּוֹדֵד עַל גָּג.**

⁹My enemies taunt me all the day; they that are mad against me do curse by me.

ט**כָּל הַיּוֹם חֵרְפוּנִי אוֹיְבָי; מְהוֹלָלַי בִּי נִשְׁבָּעוּ.**

¹⁰For I have eaten ashes like bread, and mingled my drink with weeping,

י**כִּי אֵפֶר כַּלֶּחֶם אָכָלְתִּי; וְשִׁקֻּוַי בִּבְכִי מָסָכְתִּי.**

¹¹Because of Your indignation and Your wrath; for You have borne me up, and cast me away.

יא**מִפְּנֵי זַעַמְךָ וְקִצְפֶּךָ כִּי נְשָׂאתַנִי וַתַּשְׁלִיכֵנִי.**

¹²My days are like a lengthening shadow; and I am withered like grass.

יבִיָמַי כְּצֵל נָטוּי; וַאֲנִי כָּעֵשֶׂב אִיבָשׁ.

¹³But You, O יהוה , sit enthroned forever; and Your Name is unto all generations.

יגוְאַתָּה יהוה לְעוֹלָם תֵּשֵׁב; וְזִכְרְךָ לְדֹר וָדֹר.

¹⁴You will arise, and have mercy upon Tzion; for it is time to be gracious unto her, for the Mo'ed is come.

ידאַתָּה תָקוּם תְּרַחֵם צִיּוֹן: כִּי עֵת לְחֶנְנָהּ כִּי בָא מוֹעֵד.

¹⁵For Your servants take pleasure in her stones, and love her dust.

טוכִּי רָצוּ עֲבָדֶיךָ אֶת אֲבָנֶיהָ; וְאֶת עֲפָרָהּ יְחֹנֵנוּ.

¹⁶So the nations will fear the Name of יהוה , and all the kings of the earth Your glory;

טווְיִירְאוּ גוֹיִם אֶת שֵׁם יהוה ; וְכָל מַלְכֵי הָאָרֶץ אֶת כְּבוֹדֶךָ.

¹⁷When יהוה has built up Tzion, when He has appeared in His Kavod;

יזכִּי בָנָה יהוה צִיּוֹן נִרְאָה בִּכְבוֹדוֹ.

¹⁸When He has regarded the tefilah of the destitute, and has not despised their tefilah.

יחפָּנָה אֶל תְּפִלַּת הָעַרְעָר; וְלֹא בָזָה אֶת תְּפִלָּתָם.

¹⁹This shall be written for the generation to come; and a people which shall be created shall praise Yah.

יטתִּכָּתֶב זֹאת לְדוֹר אַחֲרוֹן; וְעַם נִבְרָא יְהַלֶּל יָהּ .

²⁰For He has looked down from the height of His Kodesh; from heaven did יהוה behold the earth;

ככִּי הִשְׁקִיף מִמְּרוֹם קָדְשׁוֹ; יהוה מִשָּׁמַיִם אֶל אֶרֶץ הִבִּיט.

427

²¹To hear the groaning of the prisoner; to loose those that are appointed to Mavet;

כֹּא לִשְׁמֹעַ אֶנְקַת אָסִיר; לְפַתֵּחַ בְּנֵי תְמוּתָה.

²²That men may tell of the Name of יהוה in Tzion, and His praise in Yerushalayim;

כֹּב לְסַפֵּר בְּצִיּוֹן שֵׁם יהוה ; וּתְהִלָּתוֹ בִּירוּשָׁלָם.

²³When the peoples are gathered together, and the kingdoms, to serve יהוה.

כֹּג בְּהִקָּבֵץ עַמִּים יַחְדָּו; וּמַמְלָכוֹת לַעֲבֹד אֶת יהוה .

²⁴He weakened my strength in the way; He shortened my days.

כֹּד עִנָּה בַדֶּרֶךְ כחו (כֹּחִי); קִצַּר יָמָי.

²⁵I say, "O my Elohim, take me not away in the midst of my days, You whose years endure throughout all generations.

כֹּה אֹמַר אֵלִי אַל תַּעֲלֵנִי בַּחֲצִי יָמָי: בְּדוֹר דּוֹרִים שְׁנוֹתֶיךָ.

²⁶Of old You did lay the foundation of the earth; and the heavens are the work of Your hands.

כֹּו לְפָנִים הָאָרֶץ יָסַדְתָּ; וּמַעֲשֵׂה יָדֶיךָ שָׁמָיִם.

²⁷They shall perish, but You shall endure; yes, all of them shall wax old like a garment; as a vesture shall You change them, and they shall pass away;

כֹּז הֵמָּה יֹאבֵדוּ וְאַתָּה תַעֲמֹד: וְכֻלָּם כַּבֶּגֶד יִבְלוּ; כַּלְּבוּשׁ תַּחֲלִיפֵם וְיַחֲלֹפוּ.

²⁸But You are the selfsame, and Your years shall have no end.

כֹּח וְאַתָּה הוּא; וּשְׁנוֹתֶיךָ לֹא יִתָּמּוּ.

428

²⁹The children of Your servants shall dwell securely, and their seed shall be established before You."

כט בְּנֵי עֲבָדֶיךָ יִשְׁכּוֹנוּ; וְזַרְעָם לְפָנֶיךָ יִכּוֹן.

# Tehillah 103 תְּהִלָּה

¹By David. Bless יהוה, O my soul; and all that is within me, bless His consecrated name.

א לְדָוִד: בָּרְכִי נַפְשִׁי אֶת יהוה; וְכָל קְרָבַי אֶת שֵׁם קָדְשׁוֹ.

²Bless יהוה, O my soul, and forget not all His benefits;

ב בָּרְכִי נַפְשִׁי אֶת יהוה; וְאַל תִּשְׁכְּחִי כָּל גְּמוּלָיו.

³Who forgives all your iniquity; who heals all your diseases;

ג הַסֹּלֵחַ לְכָל עֲוֹנֵכִי; הָרֹפֵא לְכָל תַּחֲלוּאָיְכִי.

⁴Who redeems your life from the pit; who encompasses you with compassion and tender mercies;

ד הַגּוֹאֵל מִשַּׁחַת חַיָּיְכִי; הַמְעַטְּרֵכִי חֶסֶד וְרַחֲמִים.

⁵Who satisfies your old age with good things; so that your youth is renewed like the eagle.

ה הַמַּשְׂבִּיעַ בַּטּוֹב עֶדְיֵךְ; תִּתְחַדֵּשׁ כַּנֶּשֶׁר נְעוּרָיְכִי.

⁶ יהוה executes tzedakot, and acts of justice for all that are oppressed.

ו עֹשֵׂה צְדָקוֹת יהוה; וּמִשְׁפָּטִים לְכָל עֲשׁוּקִים.

⁷He made known His ways unto Moshe, His doings unto B'nei Yisra'el.

ז יוֹדִיעַ דְּרָכָיו לְמֹשֶׁה; לִבְנֵי יִשְׂרָאֵל עֲלִילוֹתָיו.

[8] יהוה is full of mercy, and gracious, slow to anger, and plenteous in compassion.

<sup>ח</sup>רַחוּם וְחַנּוּן יהוה ; אֶרֶךְ אַפַּיִם וְרַב חָסֶד.

[9] He will not always contend; neither will He keep His anger forever.

<sup>ט</sup>לֹא לָנֶצַח יָרִיב; וְלֹא לְעוֹלָם יִטּוֹר.

[10] He has not dealt with us after our sins, nor requited us according to our iniquities.

<sup>י</sup>לֹא כַחֲטָאֵינוּ עָשָׂה לָנוּ; וְלֹא כַעֲוֹנֹתֵינוּ גָּמַל עָלֵינוּ.

[11] For as the heaven is high above the earth, so great is His compassion toward them that fear Him.

<sup>יא</sup>כִּי כִגְבֹהַּ שָׁמַיִם עַל הָאָרֶץ גָּבַר חַסְדּוֹ עַל יְרֵאָיו.

[12] As far as the east is from the west, so far has He removed our transgressions from us.

<sup>יב</sup>כִּרְחֹק מִזְרָח מִמַּעֲרָב הִרְחִיק מִמֶּנּוּ אֶת פְּשָׁעֵינוּ.

[13] Like as a father has mercy upon his children, so has יהוה mercy upon them that fear Him.

<sup>יג</sup>כְּרַחֵם אָב עַל בָּנִים רִחַם יהוה עַל יְרֵאָיו.

[14] For He knows our frame; He remembers that we are dust.

<sup>יד</sup>כִּי הוּא יָדַע יִצְרֵנוּ; זָכוּר כִּי עָפָר אֲנָחְנוּ.

[15] As for man, his days are as grass; as a flower of the field, so he flourishes.

<sup>טו</sup>אֱנוֹשׁ כֶּחָצִיר יָמָיו; כְּצִיץ הַשָּׂדֶה כֵּן יָצִיץ.

[16] For the wind passes over it, and it is gone; and the place thereof knows it no more.

<sup>טז</sup>כִּי רוּחַ עָבְרָה בּוֹ וְאֵינֶנּוּ; וְלֹא יַכִּירֶנּוּ עוֹד מְקוֹמוֹ.

<sup>17</sup>But the compassion of יהוה is from everlasting to everlasting upon them that fear Him, and His tzedaka unto children's children;

וְחֶסֶד יהוה מֵעוֹלָם וְעַד עוֹלָם עַל יְרֵאָיו; וְצִדְקָתוֹ לִבְנֵי בָנִים.

<sup>18</sup>To such as keep His Brit, and to those that remember His precepts to do them.

לְשֹׁמְרֵי בְרִיתוֹ; וּלְזֹכְרֵי פִקֻּדָיו לַעֲשׂוֹתָם.

<sup>19</sup> יהוה has established His throne in the heavens; and His kingdom rules over all.

יהוה בַּשָּׁמַיִם הֵכִין כִּסְאוֹ; וּמַלְכוּתוֹ בַּכֹּל מָשָׁלָה.

<sup>20</sup>Bless יהוה , you Malakhim of His, you mighty in strength, that fulfill His D'var, hearkening unto the voice of His D'var.

בָּרְכוּ יהוה מַלְאָכָיו: גִּבֹּרֵי כֹחַ עֹשֵׂי דְבָרוֹ; לִשְׁמֹעַ בְּקוֹל דְּבָרוֹ.

<sup>21</sup>Bless יהוה , all you His hosts; you ministers of His, that do His pleasure.

בָּרְכוּ יהוה כָּל צְבָאָיו מְשָׁרְתָיו עֹשֵׂי רְצוֹנוֹ.

<sup>22</sup>Bless יהוה , all you His works, in all places of His dominion; bless יהוה , O my soul.

בָּרְכוּ יהוה כָּל מַעֲשָׂיו בְּכָל מְקֹמוֹת מֶמְשַׁלְתּוֹ; בָּרְכִי נַפְשִׁי אֶת יהוה .

# Tehillah 104 תְּהִלָּה

<sup>1</sup>Bless יהוה , O my soul. O יהוה my Elohim, You are very great; You are clothed with glory and majesty.

בָּרְכִי נַפְשִׁי אֶת יהוה : יהוה אֱלֹהַי גָּדַלְתָּ מְּאֹד; הוֹד וְהָדָר לָבָשְׁתָּ.

²Who covers Yourself with light as with a garment, who stretches out the heavens like a curtain;

עֹטֶה אוֹר כַּשַּׂלְמָה; נוֹטֶה שָׁמַיִם כַּיְרִיעָה.

³Who lays the beams of Your upper chambers in the waters, who makes the clouds Your chariot, who walks upon the wings of the wind;

הַמְקָרֶה בַמַּיִם עֲלִיּוֹתָיו: הַשָּׂם עָבִים רְכוּבוֹ; הַמְהַלֵּךְ עַל כַּנְפֵי רוּחַ.

⁴Who makes winds Your messengers, the flaming fire Your ministers.

עֹשֶׂה מַלְאָכָיו רוּחוֹת; מְשָׁרְתָיו אֵשׁ לֹהֵט.

⁵Who did establish the earth upon its foundations, that it should not be moved forever and ever;

יָסַד אֶרֶץ עַל מְכוֹנֶיהָ; בַּל תִּמּוֹט עוֹלָם וָעֶד.

⁶You did cover it with the deep as with a vesture; the waters stood above the mountains.

תְּהוֹם כַּלְּבוּשׁ כִּסִּיתוֹ; עַל הָרִים יַעַמְדוּ מָיִם.

⁷At Your rebuke they fled, at the voice of Your thunder they hasted away.

מִן גַּעֲרָתְךָ יְנוּסוּן; מִן קוֹל רַעַמְךָ יֵחָפֵזוּן.

⁸The mountains rose, the valleys sank down unto the place which You had founded for them;

יַעֲלוּ הָרִים יֵרְדוּ בְקָעוֹת אֶל מְקוֹם זֶה יָסַדְתָּ לָהֶם.

⁹You did set a boundary which they should not pass over, that they might not return to cover the earth.

גְּבוּל שַׂמְתָּ בַּל יַעֲברוּן; בַּל יְשֻׁבוּן לְכַסּוֹת הָאָרֶץ.

432

<sup>10</sup>Who sends forth springs into the valleys; they run between the mountains;

הַמְשַׁלֵּחַ מַעְיָנִים בַּנְּחָלִים; בֵּין הָרִים יְהַלֵּכוּן.

<sup>11</sup>They give drink to every beast of the field, the wild donkeys quench their thirst.

יַשְׁקוּ כָּל חַיְתוֹ שָׂדָי; יִשְׁבְּרוּ פְרָאִים צְמָאָם.

<sup>12</sup>Beside them dwell the fowls of heaven, from among the branches they sing.

עֲלֵיהֶם עוֹף הַשָּׁמַיִם יִשְׁכּוֹן; מִבֵּין עֳפָאיִם יִתְּנוּ קוֹל.

<sup>13</sup>He who waters the mountains from Your upper chambers; the earth is full of the fruit of Your works.

מַשְׁקֶה הָרִים מֵעֲלִיּוֹתָיו; מִפְּרִי מַעֲשֶׂיךָ תִּשְׂבַּע הָאָרֶץ.

<sup>14</sup>He who causes the grass to spring up for the cattle, and herb for the service of man; to bring forth bread out of the earth,

מַצְמִיחַ חָצִיר לַבְּהֵמָה וְעֵשֶׂב לַעֲבֹדַת הָאָדָם; לְהוֹצִיא לֶחֶם מִן הָאָרֶץ.

<sup>15</sup>And wine that makes glad the heart of man, making the face brighter than oil, and bread that stays man's heart.

וְיַיִן יְשַׂמַּח לְבַב אֱנוֹשׁ לְהַצְהִיל פָּנִים מִשָּׁמֶן; וְלֶחֶם לְבַב אֱנוֹשׁ יִסְעָד.

<sup>16</sup>The trees of יהוה have their fill, the cedars of Levanon, which He has planted;

יִשְׂבְּעוּ עֲצֵי יהוה אַרְזֵי לְבָנוֹן אֲשֶׁר נָטָע.

<sup>17</sup>Wherein the birds make their nests; as for the stork, the fir trees are her house.

אֲשֶׁר שָׁם צִפֳּרִים יְקַנֵּנוּ; חֲסִידָה בְּרוֹשִׁים בֵּיתָהּ.

<sup>18</sup>The high mountains are for the wild goats; the rocks are a refuge for the conies.

יחהָרִים הַגְּבֹהִים לַיְּעֵלִים; סְלָעִים מַחְסֶה לַשְׁפַנִּים.

<sup>19</sup>Who appointed the moon for seasons; the sun knows his going down.

יטעָשָׂה יָרֵחַ לְמוֹעֲדִים; שֶׁמֶשׁ יָדַע מְבוֹאוֹ.

<sup>20</sup>You make darkness, and it is night, wherein all the beasts of the forest do creep forth.

כתָּשֶׁת חֹשֶׁךְ וִיהִי לָיְלָה בּוֹ תִרְמֹשׂ כָּל חַיְתוֹ יָעַר.

<sup>21</sup>The young lions roar after their prey, and seek their food from Elohim.

כאהַכְּפִירִים שֹׁאֲגִים לַטָּרֶף; וּלְבַקֵּשׁ מֵאֵל אָכְלָם.

<sup>22</sup>The sun arises, they slink away, and couch in their dens.

כבתִּזְרַח הַשֶּׁמֶשׁ יֵאָסֵפוּן; וְאֶל מְעוֹנֹתָם יִרְבָּצוּן.

<sup>23</sup>Man goes forth unto his work and to his labor until the evening.

כגיֵצֵא אָדָם לְפָעֳלוֹ; וְלַעֲבֹדָתוֹ עֲדֵי עָרֶב.

<sup>24</sup>How manifold are Your works, O יהוה ! In wisdom have You made them all; the earth is full of Your creatures.

כדמָה רַבּוּ מַעֲשֶׂיךָ יהוה כֻּלָּם בְּחָכְמָה עָשִׂיתָ; מָלְאָה הָאָרֶץ קִנְיָנֶךָ.

<sup>25</sup>Yonder sea, great and wide, therein are creeping things innumerable, living creatures, both small and great.

כהזֶה הַיָּם גָּדוֹל וּרְחַב יָדָיִם: שָׁם רֶמֶשׂ וְאֵין מִסְפָּר; חַיּוֹת קְטַנּוֹת עִם גְּדֹלוֹת.

<sup>26</sup>There go the ships; there is Livyatan, whom You have formed to sport therein.

כושָׁם אֳנִיּוֹת יְהַלֵּכוּן; לִוְיָתָן זֶה יָצַרְתָּ לְשַׂחֶק בּוֹ.

²⁷All of them wait for You, that You may give them their food in due season.

כז‏כֻּלָּם אֵלֶיךָ יְשַׂבֵּרוּן לָתֵת אָכְלָם בְּעִתּוֹ.

²⁸You give it unto them, they gather it; You open Your hand, they are satisfied with good.

כח‏תִּתֵּן לָהֶם יִלְקֹטוּן; תִּפְתַּח יָדְךָ יִשְׂבְּעוּן טוֹב.

²⁹You hide Your face, they vanish; You withdraw their breath, they perish, and return to their dust.

כט‏תַּסְתִּיר פָּנֶיךָ יִבָּהֵלוּן: תֹּסֵף רוּחָם יִגְוָעוּן; וְאֶל עֲפָרָם יְשׁוּבוּן.

³⁰You send forth Your spirit, they are created; and You renew the face of the earth.

ל‏תְּשַׁלַּח רוּחֲךָ יִבָּרֵאוּן; וּתְחַדֵּשׁ פְּנֵי אֲדָמָה.

³¹May the glory of יהוה endure forever; let יהוה rejoice in His works!

לא‏יְהִי כְבוֹד יהוה לְעוֹלָם; יִשְׂמַח יהוה בְּמַעֲשָׂיו.

³²Who looks on the earth, and it trembles; He touches the mountains, and they smoke.

לב‏הַמַּבִּיט לָאָרֶץ וַתִּרְעָד; יִגַּע בֶּהָרִים וְיֶעֱשָׁנוּ.

³³I will sing unto יהוה as long as I live; I will sing praise to my Elohim while I have any being.

לג‏אָשִׁירָה לַיהוה בְּחַיָּי; אֲזַמְּרָה לֵאלֹהַי בְּעוֹדִי.

³⁴Let my musing be sweet unto Him; as for me, I will rejoice in יהוה .

לד‏יֶעֱרַב עָלָיו שִׂיחִי; אָנֹכִי אֶשְׂמַח בַּיהוה .

³⁵Let sinners cease out of the earth, and let the wicked be no more. Bless יהוה , O my soul. Hallelu Yah!

לה‏יִתַּמּוּ חַטָּאִים מִן הָאָרֶץ וּרְשָׁעִים עוֹד אֵינָם. בָּרְכִי נַפְשִׁי אֶת יהוה ; הַלְלוּ יָהּ !

# Tehillah 105 תְּהִלָּה

¹O give thanks unto יהוה , call upon His Name; make known His doings among the peoples.

א הוֹדוּ לַיהוה קִרְאוּ בִשְׁמוֹ; הוֹדִיעוּ בָעַמִּים עֲלִילוֹתָיו.

²Sing unto Him, sing praises unto Him; speak of all His marvelous works.

ב שִׁירוּ לוֹ זַמְּרוּ לוֹ; שִׂיחוּ בְּכָל נִפְלְאוֹתָיו.

³Glory in His consecrated Name; let the heart of them rejoice that seek יהוה .

ג הִתְהַלְלוּ בְּשֵׁם קָדְשׁוֹ; יִשְׂמַח לֵב מְבַקְשֵׁי יהוה .

⁴Seek יהוה and His strength; seek His face continually.

ד דִּרְשׁוּ יהוה וְעֻזּוֹ; בַּקְּשׁוּ פָנָיו תָּמִיד.

⁵Remember His marvelous works that He has done, His wonders, and the judgments of His mouth;

ה זִכְרוּ נִפְלְאוֹתָיו אֲשֶׁר עָשָׂה; מֹפְתָיו וּמִשְׁפְּטֵי פִיו.

⁶O you seed of Avraham His servant, you B'nei Ya'akov, His chosen ones.

ו זֶרַע אַבְרָהָם עַבְדּוֹ: בְּנֵי יַעֲקֹב בְּחִירָיו.

⁷He is יהוה our Elohim; His judgments are in all the earth.

ז הוּא יהוה אֱלֹהֵינוּ; בְּכָל הָאָרֶץ מִשְׁפָּטָיו.

⁸He has remembered His Brit forever, The Davar which He commanded to a thousand generations,

ח זָכַר לְעוֹלָם בְּרִיתוֹ; דָּבָר צִוָּה לְאֶלֶף דּוֹר.

⁹[The Brit] which He made with Avraham, and His oath unto Yitz'khak;

ט אֲשֶׁר כָּרַת אֶת אַבְרָהָם; וּשְׁבוּעָתוֹ לְיִשְׂחָק.

<sup>10</sup>And He established it unto Ya'akov for a statute, to Yisra'el for a Brit Olam;

וַיַּעֲמִידֶהָ לְיַעֲקֹב לְחֹק; לְיִשְׂרָאֵל בְּרִית עוֹלָם.

<sup>11</sup>Saying, "Unto you will I give the land of Kena'an, the lot of your inheritance."

לֵאמֹר לְךָ אֶתֵּן אֶת אֶרֶץ כְּנָעַן: חֶבֶל נַחֲלַתְכֶם.

<sup>12</sup>When they were but a few men in number. Yes, very few, and sojourners in it,

בִּהְיוֹתָם מְתֵי מִסְפָּר; כִּמְעַט וְגָרִים בָּהּ.

<sup>13</sup>And when they went about from nation to nation, from one kingdom to another people,

וַיִּתְהַלְּכוּ מִגּוֹי אֶל גּוֹי; מִמַּמְלָכָה אֶל עַם אַחֵר.

<sup>14</sup>He suffered no man to do them wrong, yes, for their sake He reproved kings:

לֹא הִנִּיחַ אָדָם לְעָשְׁקָם; וַיּוֹכַח עֲלֵיהֶם מְלָכִים.

<sup>15</sup>"Touch not My anointed ones, and do My Nevi'im no harm."

אַל תִּגְּעוּ בִמְשִׁיחָי; וְלִנְבִיאַי אַל תָּרֵעוּ.

<sup>16</sup>And He called a famine upon the land; He broke the whole staff of bread.

וַיִּקְרָא רָעָב עַל הָאָרֶץ; כָּל מַטֵּה לֶחֶם שָׁבָר.

<sup>17</sup>He sent a man before them; Yosef was sold for a servant;

שָׁלַח לִפְנֵיהֶם אִישׁ; לְעֶבֶד נִמְכַּר יוֹסֵף.

<sup>18</sup>His feet they hurt with fetters, his person was laiden in iron;

עִנּוּ בַכֶּבֶל רגליו (רַגְלוֹ); בַּרְזֶל בָּאָה נַפְשׁוֹ.

<sup>19</sup>Until the time that His D'var came to pass, the word of יהוה tested him.

עַד עֵת בֹּא דְבָרוֹ אִמְרַת יהוה צְרָפָתְהוּ.

²⁰The king sent and loosed him; even the ruler of the peoples, and set him free.

שָׁלַח מֶלֶךְ וַיַּתִּירֵהוּ; מֹשֵׁל עַמִּים וַיְפַתְּחֵהוּ.

²¹He made him Adon of his house, and ruler of all his possessions;

כאשָׂמוֹ אָדוֹן לְבֵיתוֹ; וּמֹשֵׁל בְּכָל קִנְיָנוֹ.

²²To bind his princes at his pleasure, and teach his elders wisdom.

כבלֶאְסֹר שָׂרָיו בְּנַפְשׁוֹ; וּזְקֵנָיו יְחַכֵּם.

²³Yisra'el also came into Mitzrayim; and Ya'akov sojourned in the land of Kham.

כגוַיָּבֹא יִשְׂרָאֵל מִצְרָיִם; וְיַעֲקֹב גָּר בְּאֶרֶץ חָם.

²⁴And He increased His people greatly, and made them too mighty for their adversaries.

כדוַיֶּפֶר אֶת עַמּוֹ מְאֹד; וַיַּעֲצִמֵהוּ מִצָּרָיו.

²⁵He turned their heart to hate His people, to deal craftily with His servants.

כההָפַךְ לִבָּם לִשְׂנֹא עַמּוֹ; לְהִתְנַכֵּל בַּעֲבָדָיו.

²⁶He sent Moshe His servant, and Aharon whom He had chosen.

כושָׁלַח מֹשֶׁה עַבְדּוֹ; אַהֲרֹן אֲשֶׁר בָּחַר בּוֹ.

²⁷They wrought among them His manifold signs and wonders in the land of Kham.

כזשָׂמוּ בָם דִּבְרֵי אֹתוֹתָיו; וּמֹפְתִים בְּאֶרֶץ חָם.

²⁸He sent darkness, and it was dark; and they rebelled not against His word.

כחשָׁלַח חֹשֶׁךְ וַיַּחְשִׁךְ; וְלֹא מָרוּ אֶת דבריו (דְּבָרוֹ).

²⁹He turned their waters into blood, and slew their fish.

כטהָפַךְ אֶת מֵימֵיהֶם לְדָם; וַיָּמֶת אֶת דְּגָתָם.

³⁰Their land swarmed with frogs, in the chambers of their kings.

לשָׁרַץ אַרְצָם צְפַרְדְּעִים; בְּחַדְרֵי מַלְכֵיהֶם.

³¹He spoke, and there came swarms of flies, and gnats in all their borders.

לאאָמַר וַיָּבֹא עָרֹב; כִּנִּים בְּכָל גְּבוּלָם.

³²He gave them hail for rain, and flaming fire in their land.

לבנָתַן גִּשְׁמֵיהֶם בָּרָד; אֵשׁ לֶהָבוֹת בְּאַרְצָם.

³³He smote their vines also, and their fig trees; and broke the trees of their borders.

לגוַיַּךְ גַּפְנָם וּתְאֵנָתָם; וַיְשַׁבֵּר עֵץ גְּבוּלָם.

³⁴He spoke, and the locust came, and the canker-worm without number,

לדאָמַר וַיָּבֹא אַרְבֶּה; וְיֶלֶק וְאֵין מִסְפָּר.

³⁵And did eat up every herb in their land, and did eat up the fruit of their ground.

להוַיֹּאכַל כָּל עֵשֶׂב בְּאַרְצָם; וַיֹּאכַל פְּרִי אַדְמָתָם.

³⁶He smote also all the first-born in their land, the first-fruits of all their strength.

לווַיַּךְ כָּל בְּכוֹר בְּאַרְצָם; רֵאשִׁית לְכָל אוֹנָם.

³⁷And He brought them forth with silver and gold; and there was none that stumbled among His tribes.

לזוַיּוֹצִיאֵם בְּכֶסֶף וְזָהָב; וְאֵין בִּשְׁבָטָיו כּוֹשֵׁל.

³⁸Mitzrayim was glad when they departed; for the fear of them had fallen upon them.

לחשָׂמַח מִצְרַיִם בְּצֵאתָם: כִּי נָפַל פַּחְדָּם עֲלֵיהֶם.

³⁹He spread a cloud for a screen; and fire to give light in the night.

לט פָּרַשׂ עָנָן לְמָסָךְ; וְאֵשׁ לְהָאִיר לָיְלָה.

⁴⁰They asked, and He brought quails, and gave them in plenty the bread of heaven.

מ שָׁאַל וַיָּבֵא שְׂלָו; וְלֶחֶם שָׁמַיִם יַשְׂבִּיעֵם.

⁴¹He opened the Rock, and waters gushed out; they ran, a river in the dry places.

מא פָּתַח צוּר וַיָּזוּבוּ מָיִם; הָלְכוּ בַּצִּיּוֹת נָהָר.

⁴²For He remembered His D'var Kadosh unto Avraham His servant;

מב כִּי זָכַר אֶת דְּבַר קָדְשׁוֹ; אֶת אַבְרָהָם עַבְדּוֹ.

⁴³And He brought forth His people with joy, His chosen ones with singing.

מג וַיּוֹצֵא עַמּוֹ בְשָׂשׂוֹן; בְּרִנָּה אֶת בְּחִירָיו.

⁴⁴And He gave them the lands of the nations, and they took the labor of the peoples in possession;

מד וַיִּתֵּן לָהֶם אַרְצוֹת גּוֹיִם; וַעֲמַל לְאֻמִּים יִירָשׁוּ.

⁴⁵That they might keep His statutes, and observe His instructions. Hallelu Yah!

מה בַּעֲבוּר יִשְׁמְרוּ חֻקָּיו וְתוֹרֹתָיו יִנְצֹרוּ; הַלְלוּ יָהּ !

# Tehillah 106 תְּהִלָּה

¹Hallelu Yah! O give thanks unto יהוה ; for He is good; for His compassion endures forever.

א הַלְלוּ יָהּ : הוֹדוּ לַיהוה כִּי טוֹב כִּי לְעוֹלָם חַסְדּוֹ.

²Who can express the mighty acts of יהוה , or make all His praise to be heard?

מִי יְמַלֵּל גְּבוּרוֹת יהוה ; יַשְׁמִיעַ כָּל תְּהִלָּתוֹ.

³Happy are they that keep justice, that do tzedaka at all times.

אַשְׁרֵי שֹׁמְרֵי מִשְׁפָּט; עֹשֵׂה צְדָקָה בְכָל עֵת.

⁴Remember me, O יהוה , when You favor Your people; O think of me at Your Salvation;

זָכְרֵנִי יהוה בִּרְצוֹן עַמֶּךָ; פָּקְדֵנִי בִּישׁוּעָתֶךָ.

⁵That I may behold the prosperity of Your chosen, that I may rejoice in the gladness of Your nation, that I may glory with Your inheritance.

לִרְאוֹת בְּטוֹבַת בְּחִירֶיךָ לִשְׂמֹחַ בְּשִׂמְחַת גּוֹיֶךָ; לְהִתְהַלֵּל עִם נַחֲלָתֶךָ.

⁶We have sinned with our fathers, we have done iniquitously, we have dealt wickedly.

חָטָאנוּ עִם אֲבוֹתֵינוּ; הֶעֱוִינוּ הִרְשָׁעְנוּ.

⁷Our fathers in Mitzrayim gave no heed unto Your wonders; they remembered not the multitude of Your compassions; but were rebellious at the sea, even at Yam Suf.

אֲבוֹתֵינוּ בְמִצְרַיִם לֹא הִשְׂכִּילוּ נִפְלְאוֹתֶיךָ לֹא זָכְרוּ אֶת רֹב חֲסָדֶיךָ; וַיַּמְרוּ עַל יָם בְּיַם סוּף.

⁸Nevertheless, He saved them for His Name's sake, that He might make His mighty power to be known.

וַיּוֹשִׁיעֵם לְמַעַן שְׁמוֹ לְהוֹדִיעַ אֶת גְּבוּרָתוֹ.

⁹And He rebuked Yam Suf, and it was dried up; and He led them through the depths, as through a wilderness.

טוַיִּגְעַר בְּיַם סוּף וַיֶּחֱרָב; וַיּוֹלִיכֵם בַּתְּהֹמוֹת כַּמִּדְבָּר.

¹⁰And He saved them from the hand of him that hated them, and redeemed them from the hand of the enemy.

יוַיּוֹשִׁיעֵם מִיַּד שׂוֹנֵא; וַיִּגְאָלֵם מִיַּד אוֹיֵב.

¹¹And the waters covered their adversaries; there was not one of them left.

יאוַיְכַסּוּ מַיִם צָרֵיהֶם; אֶחָד מֵהֶם לֹא נוֹתָר.

¹²Then they believed His D'varim; they sang His praise.

יבוַיַּאֲמִינוּ בִדְבָרָיו; יָשִׁירוּ תְּהִלָּתוֹ.

¹³They soon forgot His works; they waited not for His counsel;

יגמִהֲרוּ שָׁכְחוּ מַעֲשָׂיו; לֹא חִכּוּ לַעֲצָתוֹ.

¹⁴But lusted exceedingly in the wilderness, and tried God in the desert.

ידוַיִּתְאַוּוּ תַאֲוָה בַּמִּדְבָּר; וַיְנַסּוּ אֵל בִּישִׁימוֹן.

¹⁵And He gave them their request; but sent leanness into their soul.

טווַיִּתֵּן לָהֶם שֶׁאֱלָתָם; וַיְשַׁלַּח רָזוֹן בְּנַפְשָׁם.

¹⁶They were jealous also of Moshe in the camp, and of Aharon, the Kadosh יהוה.

טזוַיְקַנְאוּ לְמֹשֶׁה בַּמַּחֲנֶה; לְאַהֲרֹן קְדוֹשׁ יהוה.

¹⁷The earth opened and swallowed up Datan, and covered the company of Aviram.

יזתִּפְתַּח אֶרֶץ וַתִּבְלַע דָּתָן; וַתְּכַס עַל עֲדַת אֲבִירָם.

<sup>18</sup>And a fire was kindled in their company; the flame burned up the wicked.

יחוַתִּבְעַר אֵשׁ בַּעֲדָתָם; לֶהָבָה תְּלַהֵט רְשָׁעִים.

<sup>19</sup>They made a calf in Khorev, and worshipped a molten image.

יטיַעֲשׂוּ עֵגֶל בְּחֹרֵב; וַיִּשְׁתַּחֲווּ לְמַסֵּכָה.

<sup>20</sup>Thus they exchanged their glory for the likeness of an ox that eats grass.

כוַיָּמִירוּ אֶת כְּבוֹדָם; בְּתַבְנִית שׁוֹר אֹכֵל עֵשֶׂב.

<sup>21</sup>They forgot Elohim their Moshi'ah, who had done great things in Mitzrayim;

כאשָׁכְחוּ אֵל מוֹשִׁיעָם עֹשֶׂה גְדֹלוֹת בְּמִצְרָיִם.

<sup>22</sup>Wondrous works in the land of Kham, terrible things by Yam Suf.

כבנִפְלָאוֹת בְּאֶרֶץ חָם; נוֹרָאוֹת עַל יַם סוּף.

<sup>23</sup>Therefore He said that He would destroy them, had not Moshe His chosen stood before Him in the breach, to turn back His wrath, lest He should destroy them.

כגוַיֹּאמֶר לְהַשְׁמִידָם: לוּלֵי מֹשֶׁה בְחִירוֹ עָמַד בַּפֶּרֶץ לְפָנָיו; לְהָשִׁיב חֲמָתוֹ מֵהַשְׁחִית.

<sup>24</sup>Moreover, they scorned the desirable land, they believed not His D'var;

כדוַיִּמְאֲסוּ בְּאֶרֶץ חֶמְדָּה; לֹא הֶאֱמִינוּ לִדְבָרוֹ.

<sup>25</sup>And they murmured in their tents, they hearkened not unto the voice of יהוה .

כהוַיֵּרָגְנוּ בְאָהֳלֵיהֶם; לֹא שָׁמְעוּ בְּקוֹל יהוה .

<sup>26</sup>Therefore He swore concerning them, that He would overthrow them in the wilderness;

כווַיִּשָּׂא יָדוֹ לָהֶם לְהַפִּיל אוֹתָם בַּמִּדְבָּר.

<sup>27</sup>And that He would cast out their seed among the nations, and scatter them in the lands.

כזוּלְהַפִּיל זַרְעָם בַּגּוֹיִם; וּלְזָרוֹתָם בָּאֲרָצוֹת.

<sup>28</sup>They joined themselves also unto Ba'al of Pe'or, and ate the sacrifices of the dead.

כחוַיִּצָּמְדוּ לְבַעַל פְּעוֹר; וַיֹּאכְלוּ זִבְחֵי מֵתִים.

<sup>29</sup>Thus they provoked Him with their doings, and the plague broke in upon them.

כטוַיַּכְעִיסוּ בְּמַעַלְלֵיהֶם; וַתִּפְרָץ בָּם מַגֵּפָה.

<sup>30</sup>Then stood up Pin'khas, and wrought judgment, and so the plague was stayed.

לוַיַּעֲמֹד פִּינְחָס וַיְפַלֵּל; וַתֵּעָצַר הַמַּגֵּפָה.

<sup>31</sup>And that was counted unto him for tzedaka, unto all generations forever.

לאוַתֵּחָשֶׁב לוֹ לִצְדָקָה; לְדֹר וָדֹר עַד עוֹלָם.

<sup>32</sup>They angered Him also at the waters of Merivah, and it went ill with Moshe because of them;

לבוַיַּקְצִיפוּ עַל מֵי מְרִיבָה; וַיֵּרַע לְמֹשֶׁה בַּעֲבוּרָם.

<sup>33</sup>For they embittered his spirit, and he spoke rashly with his lips.

לגכִּי הִמְרוּ אֶת רוּחוֹ; וַיְבַטֵּא בִּשְׂפָתָיו.

<sup>34</sup>They did not destroy the peoples, as יהוה commanded them;

לדלֹא הִשְׁמִידוּ אֶת הָעַמִּים אֲשֶׁר אָמַר יהוה לָהֶם.

<sup>35</sup>But mingled themselves with the nations, and learned their works;

להוַיִּתְעָרְבוּ בַגּוֹיִם; וַיִּלְמְדוּ מַעֲשֵׂיהֶם.

<sup>36</sup>And they served their idols, which became a snare unto them;

לוֹוַיַּעַבְדוּ אֶת עֲצַבֵּיהֶם; וַיִּהְיוּ לָהֶם לְמוֹקֵשׁ.

<sup>37</sup>Yes, they sacrificed their sons and their daughters unto demons,

לזוַיִּזְבְּחוּ אֶת בְּנֵיהֶם וְאֶת בְּנוֹתֵיהֶם לַשֵּׁדִים.

<sup>38</sup>And shed innocent blood, even the blood of their sons and of their daughters, whom they sacrificed unto the idols of Kena'an; and the land was polluted with blood.

לחוַיִּשְׁפְּכוּ דָם נָקִי דַּם בְּנֵיהֶם וּבְנוֹתֵיהֶם אֲשֶׁר זִבְּחוּ לַעֲצַבֵּי כְנָעַן; וַתֶּחֱנַף הָאָרֶץ בַּדָּמִים.

<sup>39</sup>Thus were they defiled with their works, and went astray in their doings.

לטוַיִּטְמְאוּ בְמַעֲשֵׂיהֶם; וַיִּזְנוּ בְּמַעַלְלֵיהֶם.

<sup>40</sup>Therefore was the wrath of יהוה kindled against His people, and He abhorred His inheritance.

מוַיִּחַר אַף יהוה בְּעַמּוֹ; וַיְתָעֵב אֶת נַחֲלָתוֹ.

<sup>41</sup>And He gave them into the hand of the nations; and they that hated them ruled over them.

מאוַיִּתְּנֵם בְּיַד גּוֹיִם; וַיִּמְשְׁלוּ בָהֶם שֹׂנְאֵיהֶם.

<sup>42</sup>Their enemies also oppressed them, and they were subdued under their hand.

מבוַיִּלְחָצוּם אוֹיְבֵיהֶם; וַיִּכָּנְעוּ תַּחַת יָדָם.

<sup>43</sup>Many times did He deliver them; but they were rebellious in their counsel, and sank low through their iniquity.

מגפְּעָמִים רַבּוֹת יַצִּילֵם: וְהֵמָּה יַמְרוּ בַעֲצָתָם; וַיָּמֹכּוּ בַּעֲוֹנָם.

<sup>44</sup>Nevertheless He looked upon their distress, when He heard their cry;

מד‎וַיַּרְא בַּצַּר לָהֶם בְּשָׁמְעוֹ אֶת רִנָּתָם.

<sup>45</sup>And He remembered for them His Brit, and relented according to the multitude of His compassions.

מה‎וַיִּזְכֹּר לָהֶם בְּרִיתוֹ; וַיִּנָּחֵם כְּרֹב חֲסָדָו.

<sup>46</sup>He made them also to be pitied of all those that carried them captive.

מו‎וַיִּתֵּן אוֹתָם לְרַחֲמִים לִפְנֵי כָּל שׁוֹבֵיהֶם.

<sup>47</sup>Save us, O יהוה our Elohim, and gather us from among the nations, that we may give thanks unto Your consecrated Name, that we may triumph in Your praise.

מז‎הוֹשִׁיעֵנוּ יהוה אֱלֹהֵינוּ וְקַבְּצֵנוּ מִן הַגּוֹיִם: לְהֹדוֹת לְשֵׁם קָדְשֶׁךָ; לְהִשְׁתַּבֵּחַ בִּתְהִלָּתֶךָ.

<sup>48</sup>Blessed is יהוה Elohei Yisra'el, from everlasting even to everlasting, and let all the people say, "Amein." Hallelu Yah!

מח‎בָּרוּךְ יהוה אֱלֹהֵי יִשְׂרָאֵל מִן הָעוֹלָם וְעַד הָעוֹלָם וְאָמַר כָּל הָעָם אָמֵן: הַלְלוּ יה !

# Tehillah 107 תְּהִלָּה

<sup>1</sup>"O give thanks unto יהוה , for He is good, for His compassion endures forever."

א‎הֹדוּ לַיהוה כִּי טוֹב: כִּי לְעוֹלָם חַסְדּוֹ.

<sup>2</sup>So let the redeemed of יהוה say, whom He has redeemed from the hand of the adversary;

ב‎יֹאמְרוּ גְּאוּלֵי יהוה אֲשֶׁר גְּאָלָם מִיַּד צָר.

446

³And gathered them out of the lands, from the east and from the west, from the north and from the sea.

ג׳וּמֵאֲרָצוֹת קִבְּצָם: מִמִּזְרָח וּמִמַּעֲרָב; מִצָּפוֹן וּמִיָּם.

⁴They wandered in the wilderness in a desert way; they found no city of habitation.

ד׳תָּעוּ בַמִּדְבָּר בִּישִׁימוֹן דָּרֶךְ; עִיר מוֹשָׁב לֹא מָצָאוּ.

⁵Hungry and thirsty, their soul fainted in them.

ה׳רְעֵבִים גַּם צְמֵאִים נַפְשָׁם בָּהֶם תִּתְעַטָּף.

⁶Then they cried unto יהוה in their trouble, and He delivered them out of their distresses.

ו׳וַיִּצְעֲקוּ אֶל יהוה בַּצַּר לָהֶם; מִמְּצוּקוֹתֵיהֶם יַצִּילֵם.

⁷And He led them by a straight way, that they might go to a city of habitation.

ז׳וַיַּדְרִיכֵם בְּדֶרֶךְ יְשָׁרָה לָלֶכֶת אֶל עִיר מוֹשָׁב.

⁸Let them give thanks unto יהוה for His compassion, and for His wonderful works to the children of men!

ח׳יוֹדוּ לַיהוה חַסְדּוֹ; וְנִפְלְאוֹתָיו לִבְנֵי אָדָם.

⁹For He has satisfied the longing soul, and the hungry soul He has filled with good.

ט׳כִּי הִשְׂבִּיעַ נֶפֶשׁ שֹׁקֵקָה; וְנֶפֶשׁ רְעֵבָה מִלֵּא טוֹב.

¹⁰Such as sat in darkness and in Tzal-Mavet, being bound in affliction and iron

י׳יֹשְׁבֵי חֹשֶׁךְ וְצַלְמָוֶת; אֲסִירֵי עֳנִי וּבַרְזֶל.

447

<sup>11</sup>because they rebelled against the words of Elohim, and showed contempt for the counsel of Elyon.

יא כִּי הִמְרוּ אִמְרֵי אֵל; וַעֲצַת עֶלְיוֹן נָאָצוּ.

<sup>12</sup>Therefore He humbled their heart with travail, they stumbled, and there was none to help.

יב וַיַּכְנַע בֶּעָמָל לִבָּם; כָּשְׁלוּ וְאֵין עֹזֵר.

<sup>13</sup>They cried unto יהוה in their trouble, and He saved them out of their distresses.

יג וַיִּזְעֲקוּ אֶל יהוה בַּצַּר לָהֶם; מִמְּצֻקוֹתֵיהֶם יוֹשִׁיעֵם.

<sup>14</sup>He brought them out of darkness and the shadow of death, and broke their bands assunder.

יד יוֹצִיאֵם מֵחֹשֶׁךְ וְצַלְמָוֶת; וּמוֹסְרוֹתֵיהֶם יְנַתֵּק.

<sup>15</sup>Let them give thanks unto יהוה for His compassion, and for His wonderful works to the children of men!

טו יוֹדוּ לַיהוה חַסְדּוֹ; וְנִפְלְאוֹתָיו לִבְנֵי אָדָם.

<sup>16</sup>For He has broken the gates of brass, and cut the bars of iron assunder.

טז כִּי שִׁבַּר דַּלְתוֹת נְחֹשֶׁת; וּבְרִיחֵי בַרְזֶל גִּדֵּעַ.

<sup>17</sup>Crazed because of the way of their transgression, and afflicted because of their iniquities,

יז אֱוִלִים מִדֶּרֶךְ פִּשְׁעָם; וּמֵעֲוֹנֹתֵיהֶם יִתְעַנּוּ.

<sup>18</sup>Their soul abhorred all manner of food, and they drew near unto the gates of death.

יח כָּל אֹכֶל תְּתַעֵב נַפְשָׁם; וַיַּגִּיעוּ עַד שַׁעֲרֵי מָוֶת.

¹⁹They cried unto יהוה in their trouble, and He saved them out of their distresses;

טּוַיִּזְעֲקוּ אֶל יהוה בַּצַּר לָהֶם; מִמְּצֻקוֹתֵיהֶם יוֹשִׁיעֵם.

²⁰He sent His D'var, and healed them, and delivered them from their graves.

כּיִשְׁלַח דְּבָרוֹ וְיִרְפָּאֵם; וִימַלֵּט מִשְּׁחִיתוֹתָם.

²¹Let them give thanks unto יהוה for His compassion, and for His wonderful works to the children of men!

כאּיוֹדוּ לַיהוה חַסְדּוֹ; וְנִפְלְאוֹתָיו לִבְנֵי אָדָם.

²²And let them offer the sacrifices of thanksgiving, and declare His works with singing.

כבּוְיִזְבְּחוּ זִבְחֵי תוֹדָה; וִיסַפְּרוּ מַעֲשָׂיו בְּרִנָּה.

²³They that go down to the sea in ships, that do business in great waters,

כגּיוֹרְדֵי הַיָּם בָּאֳנִיּוֹת; עֹשֵׂי מְלָאכָה בְּמַיִם רַבִּים.

²⁴These saw the works of יהוה, and His wonders in the deep;

כדּהֵמָּה רָאוּ מַעֲשֵׂי יהוה; וְנִפְלְאוֹתָיו בִּמְצוּלָה.

²⁵For He commanded, and raised the stormy wind, which lifted up the waves thereof;

כהּוַיֹּאמֶר וַיַּעֲמֵד רוּחַ סְעָרָה; וַתְּרוֹמֵם גַּלָּיו.

²⁶They mounted up to the heaven, they went down to the deeps; their soul melted away because of trouble;

כוּיַעֲלוּ שָׁמַיִם יֵרְדוּ תְהוֹמוֹת; נַפְשָׁם בְּרָעָה תִתְמוֹגָג.

²⁷They reeled to and fro, and staggered like a drunken man, and all their wisdom was swallowed up.

כזּיָחוֹגּוּ וְיָנוּעוּ כַּשִּׁכּוֹר; וְכָל חָכְמָתָם תִּתְבַּלָּע.

[28]They cried unto יהוה in their trouble, and He brought them out of their distresses.

כחוַיִּצְעֲקוּ אֶל יהוה בַּצַּר לָהֶם; וּמִמְּצוּקֹתֵיהֶם יוֹצִיאֵם.

[29]He made the storm a calm, so that the waves thereof were still.

כטיָקֵם סְעָרָה לִדְמָמָה; וַיֶּחֱשׁוּ גַּלֵּיהֶם.

[30]Then were they glad because they were quiet, and He led them unto their desired haven.

לוַיִּשְׂמְחוּ כִי יִשְׁתֹּקוּ; וַיַּנְחֵם אֶל מְחוֹז חֶפְצָם.

[31]Let them give thanks unto יהוה for His compassion, and for His wonderful works to the children of men!

לאיוֹדוּ לַיהוה חַסְדּוֹ; וְנִפְלְאוֹתָיו לִבְנֵי אָדָם.

[32]Let them exalt Him also in the congregation of the people, and praise Him in the seat of the elders.

לבוִירֹמְמוּהוּ בִּקְהַל עָם; וּבְמוֹשַׁב זְקֵנִים יְהַלְלוּהוּ.

[33]He turns rivers into a wilderness, and watersprings into a thirsty ground;

לגיָשֵׂם נְהָרוֹת לְמִדְבָּר; וּמֹצָאֵי מַיִם לְצִמָּאוֹן.

[34]A fruitful land into a salt waste, for the wickedness of them that dwell therein.

לדאֶרֶץ פְּרִי לִמְלֵחָה; מֵרָעַת יוֹשְׁבֵי בָהּ.

[35]He turns a wilderness into a pool of water, and a dry land into watersprings.

להיָשֵׂם מִדְבָּר לַאֲגַם מַיִם; וְאֶרֶץ צִיָּה לְמֹצָאֵי מָיִם.

³⁶And there He makes the hungry to dwell, and they establish a city of habitation; לוַיּוֹשֶׁב שָׁם רְעֵבִים; וַיְכוֹנְנוּ עִיר מוֹשָׁב.

³⁷And sow fields, and plant vineyards, which yield fruits of increase. לוַיִּזְרְעוּ שָׂדוֹת וַיִּטְּעוּ כְרָמִים; וַיַּעֲשׂוּ פְּרִי תְבוּאָה.

³⁸He blesses them also, so that they are multiplied greatly, and suffers not their cattle to decrease. לחוַיְבָרְכֵם וַיִּרְבּוּ מְאֹד; וּבְהֶמְתָּם לֹא יַמְעִיט.

³⁹Again, they are diminished and dwindle away through oppression of evil and sorrow. לטוַיִּמְעֲטוּ וַיָּשֹׁחוּ מֵעֹצֶר רָעָה וְיָגוֹן.

⁴⁰He pours contempt upon princes, and causes them to wander in the waste, where there is no way. משֹׁפֵךְ בּוּז עַל נְדִיבִים; וַיַּתְעֵם בְּתֹהוּ לֹא דָרֶךְ.

⁴¹Yet He sets the needy on high from affliction, and makes his families like a flock. מאוַיְשַׂגֵּב אֶבְיוֹן מֵעוֹנִי; וַיָּשֶׂם כַּצֹּאן מִשְׁפָּחוֹת.

⁴²The upright see it, and are glad; and all iniquity stops her mouth. מביִרְאוּ יְשָׁרִים וְיִשְׂמָחוּ; וְכָל עַוְלָה קָפְצָה פִּיהָ.

⁴³Whoever is wise, let him observe these things, and let them consider the compassions of יהוה . מגמִי חָכָם וְיִשְׁמָר אֵלֶּה; וְיִתְבּוֹנְנוּ חַסְדֵי יהוה .

451

# Tehillah 108 תְּהִלָּה

¹A Song, a Mizmor of David.

שִׁיר מִזְמוֹר לְדָוִד.ᵃ

²My heart is steadfast, O Elohim; I will sing, yes, I will sing praises, even with my glory.

נָכוֹן לִבִּי אֱלֹהִים, אָשִׁירָהᵇ וַאֲזַמְּרָה אַף כְּבוֹדִי.

³Awake, the Nevel and Kinor; I will awaken the dawn.

עוּרָה הַנֵּבֶל וְכִנּוֹר, אָעִירָהᵍ שָּׁחַר.

⁴I will give thanks unto You, O יהוה , among the peoples; and I will sing praises unto You among the nations.

אוֹדְךָ בָעַמִּים יהוה ; וַאֲזַמֶּרְךָ בַּלְאֻמִּים.ᵈ

⁵For Your compassion is great above the heavens, and Your truth reaches unto the skies.

כִּי גָדוֹל מֵעַל שָׁמַיִם חַסְדֶּךָ; וְעַד שְׁחָקִים אֲמִתֶּךָ.ʰ

⁶Be exalted, O Elohim, above the heavens; and Your Kavod above all the earth.

רוּמָה עַל שָׁמַיִם אֱלֹהִים; וְעַל כָּל הָאָרֶץ כְּבוֹדֶךָ.ᵂ

⁷That Your beloved may be delivered, save with Your right hand, and answer me.

לְמַעַן יֵחָלְצוּן יְדִידֶיךָ; הוֹשִׁיעָה יְמִינְךָ וַעֲנֵנִי.ᶻ

⁸Elohim spoke in His Kodesh, that I would exult; that I would divide Shekhem, and mete out the valley of Sukkot.

אֱלֹהִים דִּבֶּר בְּקָדְשׁוֹ אֶעְלֹזָה: אֲחַלְּקָה שְׁכֶם; וְעֵמֶק סֻכּוֹת אֲמַדֵּד.ʰ

452

⁹Gilad is mine, Menasheh is mine; Efrayim also is the defense of my head; Yehudah is my scepter.

טלִי גִלְעָד לִי מְנַשֶׁה וְאֶפְרַיִם מָעוֹז רֹאשִׁי; יְהוּדָה מְחֹקְקִי.

¹⁰Mo'av is my washpot; upon Edom do I cast my shoe; over Peleshet do I cry aloud.

ימוֹאָב סִיר רַחְצִי עַל אֱדוֹם אַשְׁלִיךְ נַעֲלִי; עֲלֵי פְּלֶשֶׁת אֶתְרוֹעָע.

¹¹Who will bring me into the fortified city? Who will lead me unto Edom?

יאמִי יֹבִלֵנִי עִיר מִבְצָר; מִי נָחַנִי עַד אֱדוֹם.

¹²Have You not cast us off, O Elohim? And do You not go forth, O Elohim, with our hosts?

יבהֲלֹא אֱלֹהִים זְנַחְתָּנוּ; וְלֹא תֵצֵא אֱלֹהִים בְּצִבְאֹתֵינוּ.

¹³Give us help against the adversary; for vain is the help of man.

יגהָבָה לָנוּ עֶזְרָת מִצָּר; וְשָׁוְא תְּשׁוּעַת אָדָם.

¹⁴Through Elohim we shall do valiantly; for He it is that will tread down our adversaries.

ידבֵּאלֹהִים נַעֲשֶׂה חָיִל; וְהוּא יָבוּס צָרֵינוּ.

# Tehillah 109 תְּהִלָּה

¹For the Leader. A Mizmor of David. O Elohim of my praise, keep not silent;

אלַמְנַצֵּחַ לְדָוִד מִזְמוֹר: אֱלֹהֵי תְהִלָּתִי אַל תֶּחֱרַשׁ.

²For the mouth of the wicked and the mouth of deceit have they opened against me; they have spoken unto me with a lying tongue.

²כִּי פִי רָשָׁע וּפִי מִרְמָה עָלַי פָּתָחוּ; דִּבְּרוּ אִתִּי לְשׁוֹן שָׁקֶר.

³They encompassed me also with words of hatred, and fought against me without a cause.

³וְדִבְרֵי שִׂנְאָה סְבָבוּנִי; וַיִּלָּחֲמוּנִי חִנָּם.

⁴In return for my love they are my adversaries; but I am all tefilah.

⁴תַּחַת אַהֲבָתִי יִשְׂטְנוּנִי; וַאֲנִי תְפִלָּה.

⁵And they have laid upon me evil for good, and hatred for my love:

⁵וַיָּשִׂימוּ עָלַי רָעָה תַּחַת טוֹבָה; וְשִׂנְאָה תַּחַת אַהֲבָתִי.

⁶"Set a wicked man over him; and let Satan stand at his right hand.

⁶הַפְקֵד עָלָיו רָשָׁע; וְשָׂטָן יַעֲמֹד עַל יְמִינוֹ.

⁷When he is judged, let him go forth condemned; and let his tefilah be turned into sin.

⁷בְּהִשָּׁפְטוֹ יֵצֵא רָשָׁע; וּתְפִלָּתוֹ תִּהְיֶה לַחֲטָאָה.

⁸Let his days be few; let another take his charge.

⁸יִהְיוּ יָמָיו מְעַטִּים; פְּקֻדָּתוֹ יִקַּח אַחֵר.

⁹Let his children be fatherless, and his wife a widow.

⁹יִהְיוּ בָנָיו יְתוֹמִים; וְאִשְׁתּוֹ אַלְמָנָה.

¹⁰Let his children be vagabonds, and beg; and let them seek their bread out of their desolate places.

¹⁰וְנוֹעַ יָנוּעוּ בָנָיו וְשִׁאֵלוּ; וְדָרְשׁוּ מֵחָרְבוֹתֵיהֶם.

[11]Let the creditor distrain all that he has; and let strangers make spoil of his labor.

יאיְנַקֵּשׁ נוֹשֶׁה לְכָל אֲשֶׁר לוֹ; וְיָבֹזּוּ זָרִים יְגִיעוֹ.

[12]Let there be none to extend kindness unto him; neither let there be any to be gracious unto his fatherless children.

יבאַל יְהִי לוֹ מֹשֵׁךְ חָסֶד; וְאַל יְהִי חוֹנֵן לִיתוֹמָיו.

[13]Let his posterity be cut off; in the generation following let their name be blotted out.

יגיְהִי אַחֲרִיתוֹ לְהַכְרִית; בְּדוֹר אַחֵר יִמַּח שְׁמָם.

[14]Let the iniquity of his fathers be brought to remembrance unto יהוה ; and let not the sin of his mother be blotted out.

ידיִזָּכֵר עֲוֹן אֲבֹתָיו אֶל יהוה ; וְחַטַּאת אִמּוֹ אַל תִּמָּח.

[15]Let them be before יהוה continually, that He may cut off the memory of them from the earth.

טויִהְיוּ נֶגֶד יהוה תָּמִיד; וְיַכְרֵת מֵאֶרֶץ זִכְרָם.

[16]Because that he remembered not to show compassion, but persecuted the poor and needy man, and the broken in heart he was ready to slay.

טזיַעַן אֲשֶׁר לֹא זָכַר עֲשׂוֹת חָסֶד: וַיִּרְדֹּף אִישׁ עָנִי וְאֶבְיוֹן וְנִכְאֵה לֵבָב; לְמוֹתֵת.

[17]Yes, he loved cursing, and it came unto him; and he delighted not in blessing, and it is far from him.

יזוַיֶּאֱהַב קְלָלָה וַתְּבוֹאֵהוּ; וְלֹא חָפֵץ בִּבְרָכָה וַתִּרְחַק מִמֶּנּוּ.

<sup>18</sup>He clothed himself also with cursing as with his raiment, and it is come into his inward parts like water, and like oil into his bones.

יחוַיִּלְבַּשׁ קְלָלָה כְּמַדּוֹ: וַתָּבֹא כַמַּיִם בְּקִרְבּוֹ; וְכַשֶּׁמֶן בְּעַצְמוֹתָיו.

<sup>19</sup>Let it be unto him as the garment which he puts on, and for the girdle wherewith he is girded continually."

יטתְּהִי לוֹ כְּבֶגֶד יַעְטֶה; וּלְמֵזַח תָּמִיד יַחְגְּרֶהָ.

<sup>20</sup>This would my adversaries effect from יהוה , and they that speak evil against my soul.

כזֹאת פְּעֻלַּת שֹׂטְנַי מֵאֵת יהוה ; וְהַדֹּבְרִים רָע עַל נַפְשִׁי.

<sup>21</sup>But You, O יהוה Adonai, deal with me for Your Name's sake; because Your compassion is good, deliver me.

כאוְאַתָּה יהוה אֲדֹנָי עֲשֵׂה אִתִּי לְמַעַן שְׁמֶךָ; כִּי טוֹב חַסְדְּךָ הַצִּילֵנִי.

<sup>22</sup>For I am poor and needy, and my heart is wounded within me.

כבכִּי עָנִי וְאֶבְיוֹן אָנֹכִי; וְלִבִּי חָלַל בְּקִרְבִּי.

<sup>23</sup>I am gone like the shadow when it lengthens; I am shaken off as the locust.

כגכְּצֵל כִּנְטוֹתוֹ נֶהֱלָכְתִּי; נִנְעַרְתִּי כָּאַרְבֶּה.

<sup>24</sup>My knees totter through fasting; and my flesh is lean, and has no fatness.

כדבִּרְכַּי כָּשְׁלוּ מִצּוֹם; וּבְשָׂרִי כָּחַשׁ מִשָּׁמֶן.

<sup>25</sup>I am become also a taunt unto them; when they see me, they shake their head.

כהוַאֲנִי הָיִיתִי חֶרְפָּה לָהֶם; יִרְאוּנִי יְנִיעוּן רֹאשָׁם.

²⁶Help me, O יהוה my Elohim; O save me according to Your compassion;

כ״עָזְרֵנִי יהוה אֱלֹהָי; הוֹשִׁיעֵנִי כְחַסְדֶּךָ.

²⁷That they may know that this is Your hand; that You, יהוה, have done it.

כ״וְיֵדְעוּ כִּי יָדְךָ זֹּאת; אַתָּה יהוה עֲשִׂיתָהּ.

²⁸Let them curse, but You, bless; when they arise, they shall be put to shame, but Your servant shall rejoice.

כ״יְקַלְלוּ הֵמָּה וְאַתָּה תְבָרֵךְ: קָמוּ וַיֵּבֹשׁוּ וְעַבְדְּךָ יִשְׂמָח.

²⁹My adversaries shall be clothed with confusion, and shall put on their own shame as a robe.

כ״יִלְבְּשׁוּ שׂוֹטְנַי כְּלִמָּה; וְיַעֲטוּ כַמְעִיל בָּשְׁתָּם.

³⁰I will give great thanks unto יהוה with my mouth; yes, I will praise Him among the multitude;

ל״אוֹדֶה יהוה מְאֹד בְּפִי; וּבְתוֹךְ רַבִּים אֲהַלְלֶנּוּ.

³¹Because He stands at the right hand of the needy, to save him from them that judge his soul.

ל״אכִּי יַעֲמֹד לִימִין אֶבְיוֹן לְהוֹשִׁיעַ מִשֹּׁפְטֵי נַפְשׁוֹ.

# Tehillah 110 תְּהִלָּה

¹A Mizmor of David. יהוה says unto my Adon, "Sit at My right hand, until I make your enemies your footstool."

א״לְדָוִד מִזְמוֹר: נְאֻם יהוה לַאדֹנִי שֵׁב לִימִינִי; עַד אָשִׁית אֹיְבֶיךָ הֲדֹם לְרַגְלֶיךָ.

²The rod of Your strength יהוה will send out of Tzion, "Rule in the midst of your enemies."

נֵמַטֵּה עֻזְּךָ יִשְׁלַח יהוה מִצִּיּוֹן; רְדֵה בְּקֶרֶב אֹיְבֶיךָ.

³Your people offer themselves willingly in the day of your warfare; in adornments of kodesh, from the womb of the dawn, yours is the dew of your youth.

גַעַמְּךָ נְדָבֹת בְּיוֹם חֵילֶךָ: בְּהַדְרֵי קֹדֶשׁ מֵרֶחֶם מִשְׁחָר; לְךָ טַל יַלְדֻתֶיךָ.

⁴ יהוה has sworn, and will not relent, "You are a Kohen forever in the order of Malki Tzedek."

דנִשְׁבַּע יהוה וְלֹא יִנָּחֵם אַתָּה כֹהֵן לְעוֹלָם; עַל דִּבְרָתִי מַלְכִּי צֶדֶק.

⁵Adonai, at your right hand, does crush kings in the day of His wrath.

האֲדֹנָי עַל יְמִינְךָ; מָחַץ בְּיוֹם אַפּוֹ מְלָכִים.

⁶He will judge among the nations; He fills it with dead bodies, He crushes the head over a wide land.

וידִין בַּגּוֹיִם מָלֵא גְוִיּוֹת; מָחַץ רֹאשׁ עַל אֶרֶץ רַבָּה.

⁷He will drink of the brook in the way; therefore will he lift up the head.

זמִנַּחַל בַּדֶּרֶךְ יִשְׁתֶּה; עַל כֵּן יָרִים רֹאשׁ.

# Tehillah 111 תְּהִלָּה

¹Hallelu Yah! I will give thanks unto יהוה with my whole heart, in the council of the upright, and in the assembly.

אהַלְלוּ יָהּ : אוֹדֶה יהוה בְּכָל לֵבָב; בְּסוֹד יְשָׁרִים וְעֵדָה.

²The works of יהוה are great, sought out of all them that have delight therein.

ᵇגְּדֹלִים מַעֲשֵׂי יהוה ; דְּרוּשִׁים לְכָל חֶפְצֵיהֶם.

³His work is glory and majesty; and His tzedaka endures forever.

ᵍהוֹד וְהָדָר פָּעֳלוֹ; וְצִדְקָתוֹ עֹמֶדֶת לָעַד.

⁴He has made a memorial for His wonderful works; יהוה is gracious and full of mercy.

ᵈזֵכֶר עָשָׂה לְנִפְלְאוֹתָיו; חַנּוּן וְרַחוּם יהוה .

⁵He has given food unto them that fear Him; He will ever be mindful of His Brit.

ᵉטֶרֶף נָתַן לִירֵאָיו; יִזְכֹּר לְעוֹלָם בְּרִיתוֹ.

⁶He has declared to His people the power of His works, in giving them the heritage of the goyim.

ᵏכֹּחַ מַעֲשָׂיו הִגִּיד לְעַמּוֹ לָתֵת לָהֶם נַחֲלַת גּוֹיִם.

⁷The works of His hands are truth and justice; all His precepts are sure.

ᵐמַעֲשֵׂי יָדָיו אֱמֶת וּמִשְׁפָּט; נֶאֱמָנִים כָּל פִּקּוּדָיו.

⁸They are established forever and ever, they are done in truth and uprightness.

ⁿסְמוּכִים לָעַד לְעוֹלָם; עֲשׂוּיִם בֶּאֱמֶת וְיָשָׁר.

⁹He has sent redemption unto His people; He has commanded His Brit forever; Kadosh and Norah is His Name.

ᵗפְּדוּת שָׁלַח לְעַמּוֹ צִוָּה לְעוֹלָם בְּרִיתוֹ; קָדוֹשׁ וְנוֹרָא שְׁמוֹ.

¹⁰The fear of יהוה is the beginning of wisdom; a good understanding have all they that do thereafter; His praise endures forever.

רֵאשִׁית חָכְמָה יְרְאַת יהוה שֵׂכֶל טוֹב לְכָל עֹשֵׂיהֶם; תְּהִלָּתוֹ עֹמֶדֶת לָעַד.

# Tehillah 112 תְּהִלָּה

¹Hallelu Yah! Happy is the man that fears יהוה, that delights greatly in His Mitzvot.

אַהַלְלוּ יה : אַשְׁרֵי אִישׁ יֵרֵא אֶת יהוה ; בְּמִצְוֹתָיו חָפֵץ מְאֹד.

²His seed shall be mighty upon earth; the generation of the upright shall be blessed.

גּגִּבּוֹר בָּאָרֶץ יִהְיֶה זַרְעוֹ; דּוֹר יְשָׁרִים יְבֹרָךְ.

³Wealth and riches are in his house; and his merit endures forever.

הּהוֹן וָעֹשֶׁר בְּבֵיתוֹ; וְצִדְקָתוֹ עֹמֶדֶת לָעַד.

⁴Unto the upright He shines as a light in the darkness, gracious, and full of mercy, and a Tzadik.

זּזָרַח בַּחֹשֶׁךְ אוֹר לַיְשָׁרִים; חַנּוּן וְרַחוּם וְצַדִּיק.

⁵Well is it with the man that deals graciously and lends, that orders his affairs rightfully.

הּטוֹב אִישׁ חוֹנֵן וּמַלְוֶה; יְכַלְכֵּל דְּבָרָיו בְּמִשְׁפָּט.

⁶For he shall never be moved; a Tzadik shall be had in everlasting remembrance.

וּכִּי לְעוֹלָם לֹא יִמּוֹט; לְזֵכֶר עוֹלָם יִהְיֶה צַדִּיק.

460

⁷He shall not be afraid of evil tidings; his heart is stedfast, trusting in יהוה .

ז מִשְׁמוּעָה רָעָה לֹא יִירָא; נָכוֹן לִבּוֹ בָּטֵחַ בַּיהוה .

⁸His heart is established, he shall not be afraid, until he gazes upon his adversaries.

ח סָמוּךְ לִבּוֹ לֹא יִירָא; עַד אֲשֶׁר יִרְאֶה בְצָרָיו.

⁹He has scattered abroad, he has given to the needy; his tzedaka endures forever; his horn shall be exalted in honor.

ט פִּזַּר נָתַן לָאֶבְיוֹנִים צִדְקָתוֹ עֹמֶדֶת לָעַד; קַרְנוֹ תָּרוּם בְּכָבוֹד.

¹⁰The wicked shall see it, and be vexed; he shall gnash with his teeth, and melt away.

י רָשָׁע יִרְאֶה וְכָעָס שִׁנָּיו יַחֲרֹק וְנָמָס; תַּאֲוַת רְשָׁעִים תֹּאבֵד.

# Tehillah 113 תְּהִלָּה

¹Hallelu Yah! Praise, O you servants of יהוה , praise the Name of יהוה .

א הַלְלוּ יָהּ : הַלְלוּ עַבְדֵי יהוה ; הַלְלוּ אֶת שֵׁם יהוה .

²Blessed is the Name of יהוה from this time forth and forever.

ב יְהִי שֵׁם יהוה מְבֹרָךְ מֵעַתָּה וְעַד עוֹלָם.

³From the rising of the sun unto the going down thereof the Name of יהוה is to be praised.

ג מִמִּזְרַח שֶׁמֶשׁ עַד מְבוֹאוֹ מְהֻלָּל שֵׁם יהוה .

⁴ יהוה is high above all nations, His Kavod is above the heavens.

ד רָם עַל כָּל גּוֹיִם יהוה ; עַל הַשָּׁמַיִם כְּבוֹדוֹ.

461

<sup>5</sup>Who is like unto יהוה our Elohim, that is enthroned on high,

המִי כַּיהוה אֱלֹהֵינוּ הַמַּגְבִּיהִי לָשָׁבֶת.

<sup>6</sup>That looks down low upon heaven and upon the earth?

יהַמַּשְׁפִּילִי לִרְאוֹת בַּשָּׁמַיִם וּבָאָרֶץ.

<sup>7</sup>Who raises up the poor out of the dust, and lifts up the needy out of the ashes;

זמְקִימִי מֵעָפָר דָּל; מֵאַשְׁפֹּת יָרִים אֶבְיוֹן.

<sup>8</sup>That He may set him with princes, even with the princes of His people.

חלְהוֹשִׁיבִי עִם נְדִיבִים; עִם נְדִיבֵי עַמּוֹ.

<sup>9</sup>Who makes the barren woman to dwell in her house as a joyful mother of children.

טמוֹשִׁיבִי עֲקֶרֶת הַבַּיִת אֵם הַבָּנִים שְׂמֵחָה: הַלְלוּ יָהּ !

# Tehillah 114 תְּהִלָּה

<sup>1</sup>When Yisra'el came forth out of Mitzrayim, Beit Ya'akov from a people of strange language;

אבְּצֵאת יִשְׂרָאֵל מִמִּצְרָיִם; בֵּית יַעֲקֹב מֵעַם לֹעֵז.

<sup>2</sup>Yehudah became His kodesh, Yisra'el His dominion.

בהָיְתָה יְהוּדָה לְקָדְשׁוֹ; יִשְׂרָאֵל מַמְשְׁלוֹתָיו.

<sup>3</sup>The sea saw it, and fled; the Yarden turned backward.

גהַיָּם רָאָה וַיָּנֹס; הַיַּרְדֵּן יִסֹּב לְאָחוֹר.

<sup>4</sup>The mountains skipped like rams, the hills like young sheep.

דהֶהָרִים רָקְדוּ כְאֵילִים; גְּבָעוֹת כִּבְנֵי צֹאן.

⁵What ails you, O you sea, that you flee? O Yarden, that you turn backward?

ⁿמַה לְּךָ הַיָּם כִּי תָנוּס; הַיַּרְדֵּן תִּסֹּב לְאָחוֹר.

⁶You mountains, that you skip like rams; you hills, like young sheep?

ⁱהֶהָרִים תִּרְקְדוּ כְאֵילִים; גְּבָעוֹת כִּבְנֵי צֹאן.

⁷Tremble, O earth, at the presence of Adon, at the presence of the Elohim of Ya'akov;

ⁱמִלִּפְנֵי אָדוֹן חוּלִי אָרֶץ; מִלִּפְנֵי אֱלוֹהַּ יַעֲקֹב.

⁸Who turned the Rock into a pool of water, the flint into His fountain of waters.

ⁿהַהֹפְכִי הַצּוּר אֲגַם מָיִם; חַלָּמִישׁ לְמַעְיְנוֹ מָיִם.

# תְּהִלָּה 115 Tehillah

¹Not unto us, O יהוה , not unto us, but unto Your Name give glory, for Your compassion, and for Your truth's sake.

אלֹא לָנוּ יהוה לֹא לָנוּ: כִּי לְשִׁמְךָ תֵּן כָּבוֹד עַל חַסְדְּךָ עַל אֲמִתֶּךָ.

²Why should the nations say, "Where is their Elohim now?"

בלָמָּה יֹאמְרוּ הַגּוֹיִם: אַיֵּה נָא אֱלֹהֵיהֶם.

³But our Elohim is in the heavens; whatever pleased Him He has done.

ⁱוֵאלֹהֵינוּ בַשָּׁמָיִם כֹּל אֲשֶׁר חָפֵץ עָשָׂה.

⁴Their idols are silver and gold, the work of men's hands.

ⁱעֲצַבֵּיהֶם כֶּסֶף וְזָהָב; מַעֲשֵׂה יְדֵי אָדָם.

⁵They have mouths, but they speak not; eyes have they, but they see not;

ⁿפֶּה לָהֶם וְלֹא יְדַבֵּרוּ; עֵינַיִם לָהֶם וְלֹא יִרְאוּ.

463

<sup>6</sup>They have ears, but they hear not; noses have they, but they smell not;

ו׳אָזְנַיִם לָהֶם וְלֹא יִשְׁמָעוּ; אַף לָהֶם וְלֹא יְרִיחוּן.

<sup>7</sup>They have hands, but they handle not; feet have they, but they walk not; neither speak they with their throat.

ז׳יְדֵיהֶם וְלֹא יְמִישׁוּן רַגְלֵיהֶם וְלֹא יְהַלֵּכוּ; לֹא יֶהְגּוּ בִּגְרוֹנָם.

<sup>8</sup>They that make them shall be like unto them; yes, every one that trusts in them.

ח׳כְּמוֹהֶם יִהְיוּ עֹשֵׂיהֶם כֹּל אֲשֶׁר בֹּטֵחַ בָּהֶם.

<sup>9</sup>O Yisra'el, trust in יהוה ! He is their help and their Magen!

ט׳יִשְׂרָאֵל בְּטַח בַּיהוה ; עֶזְרָם וּמָגִנָּם הוּא.

<sup>10</sup>O house of Aharon, trust in יהוה ! He is their help and their Magen!

י׳בֵּית אַהֲרֹן בִּטְחוּ בַיהוה ; עֶזְרָם וּמָגִנָּם הוּא.

<sup>11</sup>You that fear יהוה , trust in יהוה ! He is their help and their Magen!

יא׳יִרְאֵי יהוה בִּטְחוּ בַיהוה ; עֶזְרָם וּמָגִנָּם הוּא.

<sup>12</sup>יהוה has been mindful of us, He will bless; He will bless Beit Yisra'el; He will bless Beit Aharon.

יב׳יהוה זְכָרָנוּ יְבָרֵךְ: יְבָרֵךְ אֶת בֵּית יִשְׂרָאֵל; יְבָרֵךְ אֶת בֵּית אַהֲרֹן.

<sup>13</sup>He will bless them that fear יהוה , both small and great.

יג׳יְבָרֵךְ יִרְאֵי יהוה הַקְּטַנִּים עִם הַגְּדֹלִים.

<sup>14</sup>May יהוה increase you more and more, you and your children.

יד׳יֹסֵף יהוה עֲלֵיכֶם; עֲלֵיכֶם וְעַל בְּנֵיכֶם.

<sup>15</sup>Blessed are you of יהוה , who made heaven and earth.

טו׳בְּרוּכִים אַתֶּם לַיהוה עֹשֵׂה שָׁמַיִם וָאָרֶץ.

¹⁶The heavens are the heavens of יהוה ; but the earth has He given to the children of men.

טזהַשָּׁמַיִם שָׁמַיִם לַיהוה ; וְהָאָרֶץ נָתַן לִבְנֵי אָדָם.

¹⁷The dead praise not יהוה , neither any that go down into silence;

יזלֹא הַמֵּתִים יְהַלְלוּ יָהּ ; וְלֹא , כָּל יֹרְדֵי דוּמָה.

¹⁸But we will bless יהוה from this time forth and forever. Hallelu Yah!

יחוַאֲנַחְנוּ נְבָרֵךְ יָהּ מֵעַתָּה וְעַד עוֹלָם: הַלְלוּ יָהּ !

# תְּהִלָּה 116 Tehillah

¹I love that יהוה should hear my voice and my supplications.

אאָהַבְתִּי כִּי יִשְׁמַע יהוה אֶת קוֹלִי תַּחֲנוּנָי.

²Because He has inclined His ear unto me, therefore will I call upon Him all my days.

בכִּי הִטָּה אָזְנוֹ לִי ; וּבְיָמַי אֶקְרָא.

³The cords of Mavet encompassed me, and the straits of She'ol got hold upon me; I found trouble and sorrow.

גאֲפָפוּנִי חֶבְלֵי מָוֶת וּמְצָרֵי שְׁאוֹל מְצָאוּנִי ; צָרָה וְיָגוֹן אֶמְצָא.

⁴But I called upon the Name of יהוה , "I beseech you, O יהוה , deliver my soul."

דוּבְשֵׁם יהוה אֶקְרָא: אָנָּה יהוה מַלְּטָה נַפְשִׁי.

⁵Gracious is יהוה , and a Tzadik; yes, our Elohim is a merciful one.

החַנּוּן יהוה וְצַדִּיק ; וֵאלֹהֵינוּ מְרַחֵם.

<sup>6</sup>יהוה preserves the simple; I was brought low, and He saved me.

שׁמֵר פְּתָאיִם יהוה ; דַּלֹתִי וְלִי יְהוֹשִׁיעַ.

<sup>7</sup>Return, O my soul, unto your rest; for יהוה has dealt bountifully with you.

שׁוּבִי נַפְשִׁי לִמְנוּחָיְכִי: כִּי יהוה גָּמַל עָלָיְכִי.

<sup>8</sup>For You have delivered my soul from Mavet, my eyes from tears, and my feet from stumbling.

כִּי חִלַּצְתָּ נַפְשִׁי מִמָּוֶת: אֶת עֵינִי מִן דִּמְעָה; אֶת רַגְלִי מִדֶּחִי.

<sup>9</sup>I shall walk before יהוה in the lands of the living.

אֶתְהַלֵּךְ לִפְנֵי יהוה בְּאַרְצוֹת הַחַיִּים.

<sup>10</sup>I trusted even when I spoke, "I am greatly afflicted."

הֶאֱמַנְתִּי כִּי אֲדַבֵּר; אֲנִי עָנִיתִי מְאֹד.

<sup>11</sup>I said in my haste, "All men are liars."

אֲנִי אָמַרְתִּי בְחָפְזִי: כָּל הָאָדָם כֹּזֵב.

<sup>12</sup>How can I repay unto יהוה all His bountiful dealings toward me?

מָה אָשִׁיב לַיהוה כָּל תַּגְמוּלוֹהִי עָלָי.

<sup>13</sup>I will lift up the cup of Salvations, and call upon the Name of יהוה .

כּוֹס יְשׁוּעוֹת אֶשָּׂא; וּבְשֵׁם יהוה אֶקְרָא.

<sup>14</sup>My vows will I pay unto יהוה , yes, in the presence of all His people.

נְדָרַי לַיהוה אֲשַׁלֵּם; נֶגְדָה נָא לְכָל עַמּוֹ.

<sup>15</sup>Precious in the sight of יהוה is the death of His Khasidim.

יָקָר בְּעֵינֵי יהוה הַמָּוְתָה לַחֲסִידָיו.

<sup>16</sup>I beseech You, O יהוה , for I am Your servant; I am Your servant, the son of Your handmaid; You have loosed my bands.

ט״אָנָּה יהוה כִּי אֲנִי עַבְדֶּךָ: אֲנִי עַבְדְּךָ בֶּן אֲמָתֶךָ; פִּתַּחְתָּ לְמוֹסֵרָי.

<sup>17</sup>I will offer to you the Zevakh Todah, and will call upon the Name of י .

י״לְךָ אֶזְבַּח זֶבַח תּוֹדָה; וּבְשֵׁם יהוה אֶקְרָא.

<sup>18</sup>I will pay my vows unto יהוה , yes, in the presence of all His people;

יח״נְדָרַי לַיהוה אֲשַׁלֵּם; נֶגְדָה נָא לְכָל עַמּוֹ.

<sup>19</sup>In the courts of Beit יהוה , in the midst of you, O Yerushalayim. Hallelu Yah!

ט״בְּחַצְרוֹת בֵּית יהוה בְּתוֹכֵכִי יְרוּשָׁלָיִם: הַלְלוּ יָהּ !

# תְּהִלָּה 117 Tehillah

<sup>1</sup>O praise יהוה , all you nations; worship Him, all you peoples.

א״הַלְלוּ אֶת יהוה כָּל גּוֹיִם; שַׁבְּחוּהוּ כָּל הָאֻמִּים.

<sup>2</sup>For His compassion is great toward us; and the truth of יהוה endures forever. Hallelu Yah!

ב״כִּי גָבַר עָלֵינוּ חַסְדּוֹ וֶאֱמֶת יהוה לְעוֹלָם: הַלְלוּ יָהּ !

# תְּהִלָּה 118 Tehillah

<sup>1</sup>"O give thanks unto יהוה , for He is good, for His compassion endures forever."

א״הוֹדוּ לַיהוה כִּי טוֹב: כִּי לְעוֹלָם חַסְדּוֹ.

<sup>2</sup>So let Yisra'el now say, for His compassion endures forever,

ב״יֹאמַר נָא יִשְׂרָאֵל: כִּי לְעוֹלָם חַסְדּוֹ.

³So let the house of Aharon now say, for His compassion endures forever.

ג יֹאמְרוּ נָא בֵית אַהֲרֹן: כִּי לְעוֹלָם חַסְדּוֹ.

⁴So let them now that fear יהוה say, for His compassion endures forever.

ד יֹאמְרוּ נָא יִרְאֵי יהוה : כִּי לְעוֹלָם חַסְדּוֹ.

⁵Out of my straits I called upon יהוה ; He answered me with great enlargement.

ה מִן הַמֵּצַר קָרָאתִי יָּהּ; עָנָנִי בַמֶּרְחָב יה .

⁶ יהוה is for me; I will not fear; what can man do unto me?

ו יהוה לִי לֹא אִירָא; מַה יַּעֲשֶׂה לִי אָדָם.

⁷ יהוה is for me as my helper; and I shall gaze upon them that hate me.

ז יהוה לִי בְּעֹזְרָי; וַאֲנִי אֶרְאֶה בְשֹׂנְאָי.

⁸It is better to take refuge in יהוה than to trust in man.

ח טוֹב לַחֲסוֹת בַּיהוה מִבְּטֹחַ בָּאָדָם.

⁹It is better to take refuge in יהוה than to trust in princes.

ט טוֹב לַחֲסוֹת בַּיהוה מִבְּטֹחַ בִּנְדִיבִים.

¹⁰All nations encompass me; in the Name of יהוה I will cut them off.

י כָּל גּוֹיִם סְבָבוּנִי; בְּשֵׁם יהוה כִּי אֲמִילַם.

¹¹They encompass me, yes, they encompass me; indeed, in the Name of יהוה I will cut them off.

יא סַבּוּנִי גַם סְבָבוּנִי; בְּשֵׁם יהוה כִּי אֲמִילַם.

[12]They encompass me like bees; they are quenched as the fire of thorns; indeed, in the Name of יהוה I will cut them off.

יבסַבּוּנִי כִדְבוֹרִים דֹעֲכוּ כְּאֵשׁ קוֹצִים; בְּשֵׁם יהוה כִּי אֲמִילַם.

[13]You did thrust sore at me that I might fall; but יהוה helped me.

יגדָּחֹה דְחִיתַנִי לִנְפֹּל; וַיהוה עֲזָרָנִי.

[14] יהוה is my strength and song; and He will become Yeshua[h] for me.

ידעָזִּי וְזִמְרָת יה ; וַיְהִי לִי לִישׁוּעָה.

[15]The voice of rejoicing and Salvation is in the tents of the Tzadikim; the right hand of יהוה does valiantly.

טוקוֹל רִנָּה וִישׁוּעָה בְּאָהֳלֵי צַדִּיקִים; יְמִין יהוה עֹשָׂה חָיִל.

[16]The right hand of יהוה is exalted; the right hand of יהוה does valiantly.

טזיְמִין יהוה רוֹמֵמָה; יְמִין יהוה עֹשָׂה חָיִל.

[17]I shall not die, but live, and declare the works of יהוה .

יזלֹא אָמוּת כִּי אֶחְיֶה; וַאֲסַפֵּר מַעֲשֵׂי יה .

[18] יהוה has chastened me sore; but He has not given me over unto Mavet.

יחיַסֹּר יִסְּרַנִּי יָּהּ; וְלַמָּוֶת לֹא נְתָנָנִי.

[19]Open to me the gates of righteousness; I will enter into them, I will give thanks unto יהוה .

יטפִּתְחוּ לִי שַׁעֲרֵי צֶדֶק; אָבֹא בָם אוֹדֶה יה .

[20]This is the gate of יהוה ; the Tzadikim shall enter into it.

כזֶה הַשַּׁעַר לַיהוה ; צַדִּיקִים ; יָבֹאוּ בוֹ.

469

²¹I will give thanks unto You, for You have answered me, and have become Yeshua[h] for me.

כאאוֹדְךָ כִּי עֲנִיתָנִי; וַתְּהִי לִי לִישׁוּעָה.

²²The stone which the builders rejected is become the chief corner-stone.

כבאֶבֶן מָאֲסוּ הַבּוֹנִים הָיְתָה לְרֹאשׁ פִּנָּה.

²³This is the one which is from יהוה ; it is marvelous in our eyes.

כגמֵאֵת יהוה הָיְתָה זֹּאת; הִיא נִפְלָאת בְּעֵינֵינוּ.

²⁴This is the day which יהוה has made; we will rejoice and be glad in it.

כדזֶה הַיּוֹם עָשָׂה יהוה ; נָגִילָה וְנִשְׂמְחָה בוֹ.

²⁵We beseech You, O יהוה , Hoshi'ah Nah! We beseech You, O יהוה , make us now to prosper!

כהאָנָּא יהוה הוֹשִׁיעָה נָּא; אָנָּא יהוה הַצְלִיחָה נָּא.

²⁶Barukh Haba B'Shem יהוה ; we bless you out of Beit יהוה .

כובָּרוּךְ הַבָּא בְּשֵׁם יהוה ; בֵּרַכְנוּכֶם מִבֵּית יהוה .

²⁷ יהוה is God, and has given us light; order the Khag with boughs, even unto the horns of the Mizbe'akh.

כזאֵל יהוה וַיָּאֶר לָנוּ: אִסְרוּ חַג בַּעֲבֹתִים עַד קַרְנוֹת הַמִּזְבֵּחַ.

²⁸You are my God, and I will give thanks unto You; You are my God, I will exalt You.

כחאֵלִי אַתָּה וְאוֹדֶךָ; אֱלֹהַי אֲרוֹמְמֶךָּ.

²⁹O give thanks unto יהוה , for He is good, for His compassion endures forever.

כטהוֹדוּ לַיהוה כִּי טוֹב: כִּי לְעוֹלָם חַסְדּוֹ.

# תְּהִלָּה 119 Tehillah

**[1]Alef**. Happy are they that are upright in HaDerekh, who walk in the Torah of יהוה .

אאַשְׁרֵי תְמִימֵי דָרֶךְ הַהֹלְכִים בְּתוֹרַת יהוה .

[2]Happy are they that keep His testimonies, that seek Him with the whole heart.

באַשְׁרֵי נֹצְרֵי עֵדֹתָיו; בְּכָל לֵב יִדְרְשׁוּהוּ.

[3]Yes, they do no unrighteousness; they walk in His ways.

גאַף לֹא פָעֲלוּ עַוְלָה; בִּדְרָכָיו הָלָכוּ.

[4]You have ordained Your precepts, that we should observe them diligently.

דאַתָּה צִוִּיתָה פִקֻּדֶיךָ לִשְׁמֹר מְאֹד.

[5]Oh that my ways were directed to observe Your statutes!

האַחֲלַי יִכֹּנוּ דְרָכָי לִשְׁמֹר חֻקֶּיךָ.

[6]Then would I not be ashamed, when I have regard unto all Your Mitzvot.

ואָז לֹא אֵבוֹשׁ בְּהַבִּיטִי אֶל כָּל מִצְוֹתֶיךָ.

[7]I will give thanks unto You with uprightness of heart, when I learn Your righteous ordinances.

זאוֹדְךָ בְּיֹשֶׁר לֵבָב בְּלָמְדִי מִשְׁפְּטֵי צִדְקֶךָ.

[8]I will observe Your statutes; O forsake me not utterly.

חאֶת חֻקֶּיךָ אֶשְׁמֹר; אַל תַּעַזְבֵנִי עַד מְאֹד.

[9]**Beit**. How shall a young man keep his way pure? By taking heed thereto according to Your D'var.

טבַּמֶּה יְזַכֶּה נַּעַר אֶת אָרְחוֹ לִשְׁמֹר כִּדְבָרֶךָ.

<sup>10</sup>With my whole heart have I sought You; O let me not err from Your Mitzvot.

בְּכָל לִבִּי דְרַשְׁתִּיךָ; אַל תַּשְׁגֵּנִי מִמִּצְוֹתֶיךָ.

<sup>11</sup>Your word have I laid up in my heart, that I might not sin against You.

בְּלִבִּי צָפַנְתִּי אִמְרָתֶךָ לְמַעַן לֹא אֶחֱטָא לָךְ.

<sup>12</sup>Blessed are You, O יהוה ; teach me Your statutes.

בָּרוּךְ אַתָּה יהוה לַמְּדֵנִי חֻקֶּיךָ.

<sup>13</sup>With my lips have I told all the ordinances of Your mouth.

בִּשְׂפָתַי סִפַּרְתִּי כֹּל מִשְׁפְּטֵי פִיךָ.

<sup>14</sup>I have rejoiced in the way of Your testimonies, as much as in all riches.

בְּדֶרֶךְ עֵדְוֹתֶיךָ שַׂשְׂתִּי כְּעַל כָּל הוֹן.

<sup>15</sup>I will meditate in Your precepts, and have respect unto Your ways.

בְּפִקּוּדֶיךָ אָשִׂיחָה; וְאַבִּיטָה אֹרְחֹתֶיךָ.

<sup>16</sup>I will delight myself in Your statutes; I will not forget Your D'var.

בְּחֻקֹּתֶיךָ אֶשְׁתַּעֲשָׁע; לֹא אֶשְׁכַּח דְּבָרֶךָ.

<sup>17</sup>**Gimel**. Deal bountifully with Your servant that I may live, and I will observe Your D'var.

גְּמֹל עַל עַבְדְּךָ אֶחְיֶה; וְאֶשְׁמְרָה דְבָרֶךָ.

<sup>18</sup>Open my eyes, that I may behold wondrous things out of Your Torah.

גַּל עֵינַי וְאַבִּיטָה נִפְלָאוֹת מִתּוֹרָתֶךָ.

<sup>19</sup>I am a sojourner in the earth; hide not Your Mitzvot from me.

גֵּר אָנֹכִי בָאָרֶץ; אַל תַּסְתֵּר מִמֶּנִּי מִצְוֹתֶיךָ.

<sup>20</sup>My soul breaks for the longing that it has unto Your ordinances at all times.

כ‎גָּרְסָה נַפְשִׁי לְתַאֲבָה אֶל מִשְׁפָּטֶיךָ בְכָל עֵת.

<sup>21</sup>You have rebuked the proud that are cursed, that do err from Your Mitzvot.

כא‎גָּעַרְתָּ זֵדִים אֲרוּרִים הַשֹּׁגִים מִמִּצְוֹתֶיךָ.

<sup>22</sup>Take away from me reproach and contempt; for I have kept Your testimonies.

כב‎גַּל מֵעָלַי חֶרְפָּה וָבוּז: כִּי עֵדֹתֶיךָ נָצָרְתִּי.

<sup>23</sup>Even though princes sit and talk against me, your servant does meditate in Your statutes.

כג‎גַּם יָשְׁבוּ שָׂרִים בִּי נִדְבָּרוּ עַבְדְּךָ יָשִׂיחַ בְּחֻקֶּיךָ.

<sup>24</sup>Yes, Your testimonies are my delight, they are my counsellors.

כד‎גַּם עֵדֹתֶיךָ שַׁעֲשֻׁעָי אַנְשֵׁי עֲצָתִי.

<sup>25</sup>**Dalet**. My soul cleaves unto the dust; quicken me according to Your D'var.

כה‎דָּבְקָה לֶעָפָר נַפְשִׁי; חַיֵּנִי כִּדְבָרֶךָ.

<sup>26</sup>I told of my ways, and You did answer me; teach me Your statutes.

כו‎דְּרָכַי סִפַּרְתִּי וַתַּעֲנֵנִי; לַמְּדֵנִי חֻקֶּיךָ.

<sup>27</sup>Make me to understand the way of Your precepts, that I may talk of Your wondrous works.

כז‎דֶּרֶךְ פִּקּוּדֶיךָ הֲבִינֵנִי; וְאָשִׂיחָה בְּנִפְלְאוֹתֶיךָ.

<sup>28</sup>My soul melts away for heaviness; sustain me according unto Your D'var.

כח‎דָּלְפָה נַפְשִׁי מִתּוּגָה; קַיְּמֵנִי כִּדְבָרֶךָ.

473

²⁹Remove from me the way of falsehood; for your Torah gives grace to me.

כ⁹דֶּרֶךְ שֶׁקֶר הָסֵר מִמֶּנִּי; וְתוֹרָתְךָ חָנֵּנִי.

³⁰I have chosen the way of faithfulness; Your ordinances have I set [before me].

לדֶּרֶךְ אֱמוּנָה בָחָרְתִּי; מִשְׁפָּטֶיךָ שִׁוִּיתִי.

³¹I cleave unto Your testimonies; O יהוה, put me not to shame.

לאדָּבַקְתִּי בְעֵדְוֹתֶיךָ; יהוה אַל תְּבִישֵׁנִי.

³²I will run the way of Your Mitzvot, for You do enlarge my heart.

לבדֶּרֶךְ מִצְוֹתֶיךָ אָרוּץ: כִּי תַרְחִיב לִבִּי.

³³**Heh**. Teach me, O יהוה, the way of Your statutes; and I will keep it at every step.

להוֹרֵנִי יהוה דֶּרֶךְ חֻקֶּיךָ; וְאֶצְּרֶנָּה עֵקֶב.

³⁴Give me understanding, that I may keep Your Torah and observe it with my whole heart.

לדהֲבִינֵנִי וְאֶצְּרָה תוֹרָתֶךָ; וְאֶשְׁמְרֶנָּה בְכָל לֵב.

³⁵Make me to tread in the path of Your Mitzvot; for therein do I delight.

לההַדְרִיכֵנִי בִּנְתִיב מִצְוֹתֶיךָ: כִּי בוֹ חָפָצְתִּי.

³⁶Incline my heart unto Your testimonies, and not to covetousness.

לוהַט לִבִּי אֶל עֵדְוֹתֶיךָ; וְאַל אֶל בָּצַע.

³⁷Turn away my eyes from beholding vanity, and quicken me in Your ways.

לזהַעֲבֵר עֵינַי מֵרְאוֹת שָׁוְא; בִּדְרָכֶךָ חַיֵּנִי.

<sup>38</sup>Confirm Your word unto Your servant, which pertains unto the fear of You.

לח הָקֵם לְעַבְדְּךָ אִמְרָתֶךָ אֲשֶׁר לְיִרְאָתֶךָ.

<sup>39</sup>Turn away my reproach which I dread; for Your ordinances are good.

לט הַעֲבֵר חֶרְפָּתִי אֲשֶׁר יָגֹרְתִּי כִּי מִשְׁפָּטֶיךָ טוֹבִים.

<sup>40</sup>Behold, I have longed after Your precepts; quicken me in Your tzedaka.

מ הִנֵּה תָּאַבְתִּי לְפִקֻּדֶיךָ; בְּצִדְקָתְךָ חַיֵּנִי.

<sup>41</sup>**Vav.** Let Your mercies also come unto me, O יהוה, even Your Salvation, according to Your word;

מא וִיבֹאֻנִי חֲסָדֶךָ יהוה ; תְּשׁוּעָתְךָ כְּאִמְרָתֶךָ.

<sup>42</sup>That I may have an answer for him that taunts me; for I trust in Your word.

מב וְאֶעֱנֶה חֹרְפִי דָבָר: כִּי בָטַחְתִּי בִּדְבָרֶךָ.

<sup>43</sup>And take not the word of truth utterly out of my mouth; for I hope in Your ordinances;

מג וְאַל תַּצֵּל מִפִּי דְבַר אֱמֶת עַד מְאֹד: כִּי לְמִשְׁפָּטֶךָ יִחָלְתִּי.

<sup>44</sup>So shall I observe Your Torah continually forever and ever;

מד וְאֶשְׁמְרָה תוֹרָתְךָ תָמִיד לְעוֹלָם וָעֶד.

<sup>45</sup>And I will walk at ease, for I have sought Your precepts;

מה וְאֶתְהַלְּכָה בָרְחָבָה: כִּי פִקֻּדֶיךָ דָרָשְׁתִּי.

<sup>46</sup>I will also speak of Your testimonies before kings, and will not be ashamed.

מו וַאֲדַבְּרָה בְעֵדֹתֶיךָ נֶגֶד מְלָכִים; וְלֹא אֵבוֹשׁ.

⁴⁷And I will delight myself in Your Mitzvot, which I have loved.

מז‏וְאֶשְׁתַּעֲשַׁע בְּמִצְוֹתֶיךָ אֲשֶׁר אָהָבְתִּי.

⁴⁸I will lift up my hands also unto Your Mitzvot, which I have loved; and I will meditate in Your statutes.

מח‏וְאֶשָּׂא כַפַּי אֶל מִצְוֹתֶיךָ אֲשֶׁר אָהָבְתִּי; וְאָשִׂיחָה בְחֻקֶּיךָ.

⁴⁹**Zayin.** Remember The Davar unto Your servant, because You have made me to hope.

מט‏זְכֹר דָּבָר לְעַבְדֶּךָ עַל אֲשֶׁר יִחַלְתָּנִי.

⁵⁰This is my comfort in my affliction, that Your word has quickened me.

נ‏זֹאת נֶחָמָתִי בְעָנְיִי: כִּי אִמְרָתְךָ חִיָּתְנִי.

⁵¹The proud have had me greatly in derision; yet have I not turned aside from Your Torah.

נא‏זֵדִים הֱלִיצֻנִי עַד מְאֹד; מִתּוֹרָתְךָ לֹא נָטִיתִי.

⁵²I have remembered Your ordinances which are of old, O יהוה , and have comforted myself.

נב‏זָכַרְתִּי מִשְׁפָּטֶיךָ מֵעוֹלָם יהוה ; וָאֶתְנֶחָם.

⁵³Burning indignation has taken hold upon me, because of the wicked that forsake Your Torah.

נג‏זַלְעָפָה אֲחָזַתְנִי מֵרְשָׁעִים עֹזְבֵי תּוֹרָתֶךָ.

⁵⁴Your statutes have been my songs in the house of my pilgrimage.

נד‏זְמִרוֹת הָיוּ לִי חֻקֶּיךָ בְּבֵית מְגוּרָי.

[55]I have remembered Your Name, O יהוה, in the night, and have observed Your Torah.

נה‏זָכַרְתִּי בַלַּיְלָה שִׁמְךָ יהוה ; וָאֶשְׁמְרָה תּוֹרָתֶךָ.

[56]This I have had, that I have kept Your precepts.

נו‏זֹאת הָיְתָה לִּי: כִּי פִקֻּדֶיךָ נָצָרְתִּי.

[57]**Khet**. My portion is יהוה, I have said that I would observe Your D'varim.

נז‏חֶלְקִי יהוה אָמַרְתִּי לִשְׁמֹר דְּבָרֶיךָ.

[58]I have entreated Your favor with my whole heart; be gracious unto me according to Your word.

נח‏חִלִּיתִי פָנֶיךָ בְכָל לֵב; חָנֵּנִי כְּאִמְרָתֶךָ.

[59]I considered my ways, and turned my feet unto Your testimonies.

נט‏חִשַּׁבְתִּי דְרָכָי; וָאָשִׁיבָה רַגְלַי אֶל עֵדֹתֶיךָ.

[60]I made haste, and delayed not, to observe Your Mitzvot.

ס‏חַשְׁתִּי וְלֹא הִתְמַהְמָהְתִּי לִשְׁמֹר מִצְוֹתֶיךָ.

[61]The bands of the wicked have enclosed me; but I have not forgotten Your Torah.

סא‏חֶבְלֵי רְשָׁעִים עִוְּדֻנִי; תּוֹרָתְךָ לֹא שָׁכָחְתִּי.

[62]At midnight I will rise to give thanks unto You because of Your righteous ordinances.

סב‏חֲצוֹת לַיְלָה אָקוּם לְהוֹדוֹת לָךְ: עַל מִשְׁפְּטֵי צִדְקֶךָ.

[63]I am a companion of all them that fear You, and of them that observe Your precepts.

סג‏חָבֵר אָנִי לְכָל אֲשֶׁר יְרֵאוּךָ; וּלְשֹׁמְרֵי פִּקּוּדֶיךָ.

[64]The earth, O יהוה , is full of Your compassion; teach me Your statutes.

סדחַסְדְּךָ יהוה מָלְאָה הָאָרֶץ; חֻקֶּיךָ לַמְּדֵנִי.

[65]**Tet**. You have done goodness to Your servant, O יהוה , according unto Your word.

סהטוֹב עָשִׂיתָ עִם עַבְדְּךָ יהוה כִּדְבָרֶךָ.

[66]Teach me good discernment and knowledge; for I have believed in Your Mitzvot.

סוטוּב טַעַם וָדַעַת לַמְּדֵנִי: כִּי בְמִצְוֹתֶיךָ הֶאֱמָנְתִּי.

[67]Before I was afflicted, I did err; but now I observe Your word.

סזטֶרֶם אֶעֱנֶה אֲנִי שֹׁגֵג; וְעַתָּה אִמְרָתְךָ שָׁמָרְתִּי.

[68]You are good, and do good; teach me Your statutes.

סחטוֹב אַתָּה וּמֵטִיב; לַמְּדֵנִי חֻקֶּיךָ.

[69]The proud have forged a lie against me; but I, with my whole heart, will keep Your precepts.

סטטָפְלוּ עָלַי שֶׁקֶר זֵדִים; אֲנִי בְּכָל לֵב אֶצֹּר פִּקּוּדֶיךָ.

[70]Their heart is gross like fat; but I delight in Your Torah.

עטָפַשׁ כַּחֵלֶב לִבָּם; אֲנִי תּוֹרָתְךָ שִׁעֲשָׁעְתִּי.

[71]It is good for me that I have been afflicted, in order that I might learn Your statutes.

עאטוֹב לִי כִי עֻנֵּיתִי לְמַעַן אֶלְמַד חֻקֶּיךָ.

[72]The Torah of Your mouth is better unto me than thousands of gold and silver.

עבטוֹב לִי תוֹרַת פִּיךָ מֵאַלְפֵי זָהָב וָכָסֶף.

<sup>73</sup>**Yod**. Your hands have made me and fashioned me; give me understanding, that I may learn Your Mitzvot.

<sup>עג</sup>יָדֶיךָ עָשׂוּנִי וַיְכוֹנְנוּנִי; הֲבִינֵנִי וְאֶלְמְדָה מִצְוֹתֶיךָ.

<sup>74</sup>They that fear You shall see me and be glad, because I have hope in Your word.

<sup>עד</sup>יְרֵאֶיךָ יִרְאוּנִי וְיִשְׂמָחוּ: כִּי לִדְבָרְךָ יִחָלְתִּי.

<sup>75</sup>I know, O יהוה , that Your judgments are righteous, and that in faithfulness You have afflicted me.

<sup>עה</sup>יָדַעְתִּי יהוה כִּי צֶדֶק מִשְׁפָּטֶיךָ; וֶאֱמוּנָה עִנִּיתָנִי.

<sup>76</sup>Let, I pray You, Your compassion be ready to comfort me, according to Your promise unto Your servant.

<sup>עו</sup>יְהִי נָא חַסְדְּךָ לְנַחֲמֵנִי כְּאִמְרָתְךָ לְעַבְדֶּךָ.

<sup>77</sup>Let Your tender mercies come unto me, that I may live; for Your Torah is my delight.

<sup>עז</sup>יְבֹאוּנִי רַחֲמֶיךָ וְאֶחְיֶה: כִּי תוֹרָתְךָ שַׁעֲשֻׁעָי.

<sup>78</sup>Let the proud be put to shame, for they have distorted my cause with falsehood; but I will meditate in Your precepts.

<sup>עח</sup>יֵבֹשׁוּ זֵדִים כִּי שֶׁקֶר עִוְּתוּנִי; אֲנִי אָשִׂיחַ בְּפִקּוּדֶיךָ.

<sup>79</sup>Let those that fear You return unto me, and they that know Your testimonies.

<sup>עט</sup>יָשׁוּבוּ לִי יְרֵאֶיךָ; וידעו (וְיֹדְעֵי) עֵדֹתֶיךָ.

<sup>80</sup>Let my heart be undivided in Your statutes, in order that I may not be put to shame.

<sup>פ</sup>יְהִי לִבִּי תָמִים בְּחֻקֶּיךָ לְמַעַן לֹא אֵבוֹשׁ.

<sup>81</sup>**Kaf**. My soul pines for Your Salvation; in Your D'var do I hope.

פֿאכָּלְתָה לִתְשׁוּעָתְךָ נַפְשִׁי; לִדְבָרְךָ יִחָלְתִּי.

<sup>82</sup>My eyes fail for Your word, saying, "When will You comfort me?"

פֿבכָּלוּ עֵינַי לְאִמְרָתֶךָ לֵאמֹר מָתַי תְּנַחֲמֵנִי.

<sup>83</sup>For I am become like a wine-skin in the smoke; yet do I not forget Your statutes.

פֿגכִּי הָיִיתִי כְּנֹאד בְּקִיטוֹר חֻקֶּיךָ לֹא שָׁכָחְתִּי.

<sup>84</sup>How many are the days of Your servant? When will You execute judgment on them that persecute me?

פֿדכַּמָּה יְמֵי עַבְדֶּךָ; מָתַי תַּעֲשֶׂה בְרֹדְפַי מִשְׁפָּט.

<sup>85</sup>The proud have digged pits for me, which is not according to Your Torah.

פֿהכָּרוּ לִי זֵדִים שִׁיחוֹת אֲשֶׁר לֹא כְתוֹרָתֶךָ.

<sup>86</sup>All Your Mitzvot are faithful; they persecute me for nought; help me.

פֿוכָּל מִצְוֹתֶיךָ אֱמוּנָה; שֶׁקֶר רְדָפוּנִי עָזְרֵנִי.

<sup>87</sup>They had almost consumed me upon earth; but as for me, I forsook not Your precepts.

פֿזכִּמְעַט כִּלּוּנִי בָאָרֶץ; וַאֲנִי לֹא עָזַבְתִּי פִקֻּדֶיךָ.

<sup>88</sup>Quicken me after Your compassion, and I will observe the testimony of Your mouth.

פֿחכְּחַסְדְּךָ חַיֵּנִי; וְאֶשְׁמְרָה עֵדוּת פִּיךָ.

<sup>89</sup>**Lamed**. Forever, O יהוה , Your D'var stands fast in heaven.

פֿטלְעוֹלָם יהוה דְּבָרְךָ נִצָּב בַּשָּׁמָיִם.

[90]Your faithfulness is unto all generations; You have established the earth, and it stands.

לְדֹר וָדֹר אֱמוּנָתֶךָ; כּוֹנַנְתָּ אֶרֶץ וַתַּעֲמֹד.

[91]They stand this day according to Your ordinances; for all things are Your servants.

לְמִשְׁפָּטֶיךָ עָמְדוּ הַיּוֹם: כִּי הַכֹּל עֲבָדֶיךָ.

[92]Unless Your Torah had been my delight, I would then have perished in my affliction.

לוּלֵי תוֹרָתְךָ שַׁעֲשֻׁעָי אָז אָבַדְתִּי בְעָנְיִי.

[93]I will never forget Your precepts; for with them You have quickened me.

לְעוֹלָם לֹא אֶשְׁכַּח פִּקּוּדֶיךָ: כִּי בָם חִיִּיתָנִי.

[94]I am Yours, save me; for I have sought Your precepts.

לְךָ אֲנִי הוֹשִׁיעֵנִי: כִּי פִקּוּדֶיךָ דָרָשְׁתִּי.

[95]The wicked have waited for me to destroy me; but I will consider Your testimonies.

לִי קִוּוּ רְשָׁעִים לְאַבְּדֵנִי; עֵדֹתֶיךָ אֶתְבּוֹנָן.

[96]I have seen an end to every purpose; but Your Mitzvah is exceedingly broad.

לְכָל תִּכְלָה רָאִיתִי קֵץ; רְחָבָה מִצְוָתְךָ מְאֹד.

[97]**Mem**. O how I love Your Torah! It is my meditation all the day.

מָה אָהַבְתִּי תוֹרָתֶךָ: כָּל הַיּוֹם הִיא שִׂיחָתִי.

[98]Your Mitzvot make me wiser than my enemies: for they are ever with me.

מֵאֹיְבַי תְּחַכְּמֵנִי מִצְוֹתֶךָ: כִּי לְעוֹלָם הִיא לִי.

[99]I have more understanding than all my teachers; for Your testimonies are my meditation.

צט מִכָּל מְלַמְּדַי הִשְׂכַּלְתִּי: כִּי עֵדְוֹתֶיךָ שִׂיחָה לִי.

[100]I understand more than my elders, because I have kept Your precepts.

ק מִזְּקֵנִים אֶתְבּוֹנָן: כִּי פִקּוּדֶיךָ נָצָרְתִּי.

[101]I have refrained my feet from every evil way, in order that I might observe Your D'var.

קא מִכָּל אֹרַח רָע כָּלִאתִי רַגְלָי לְמַעַן אֶשְׁמֹר דְּבָרֶךָ.

[102]I have not turned aside from Your ordinances; for You have instructed me.

קב מִמִּשְׁפָּטֶיךָ לֹא סָרְתִּי: כִּי אַתָּה הוֹרֵתָנִי.

[103]How sweet are Your words unto my palate! Yes, sweeter than honey to my mouth!

קג מַה נִּמְלְצוּ לְחִכִּי אִמְרָתֶךָ מִדְּבַשׁ לְפִי.

[104]From Your precepts I get understanding; therefore I hate every false way.

קד מִפִּקּוּדֶיךָ אֶתְבּוֹנָן; עַל כֵּן שָׂנֵאתִי כָּל אֹרַח שָׁקֶר.

[105]**Nun**. Your D'var is a lamp unto my feet, and a light unto my path.

קה נֵר לְרַגְלִי דְבָרֶךָ; וְאוֹר לִנְתִיבָתִי.

[106]I have sworn, and have confirmed it, to observe Your righteous ordinances.

קו נִשְׁבַּעְתִּי וָאֲקַיֵּמָה לִשְׁמֹר מִשְׁפְּטֵי צִדְקֶךָ.

[107]I am afflicted very much; quicken me, O יהוה , according unto Your D'var.

קז נַעֲנֵיתִי עַד מְאֹד; יהוה חַיֵּנִי כִּדְבָרֶךָ.

[108]Accept, I beseech You, the Nid'vot of my mouth, O יהוה , and teach me Your ordinances.

קֶ"נִדְבוֹת פִּי רְצֵה נָא יהוה; וּמִשְׁפָּטֶיךָ לַמְּדֵנִי.

[109]My soul is continually in my hand; yet have I not forgotten Your Torah.

קֶ"ט נַפְשִׁי בְכַפִּי תָמִיד; וְתוֹרָתְךָ לֹא שָׁכָחְתִּי.

[110]The wicked have laid a snare for me; yet I went not astray from Your precepts.

קֶ"נָתְנוּ רְשָׁעִים פַּח לִי; וּמִפִּקּוּדֶיךָ לֹא תָעִיתִי.

[111]Your testimonies have I taken as a heritage forever; for they are the rejoicing of my heart.

קֶ"א נָחַלְתִּי עֵדְוֹתֶיךָ לְעוֹלָם: כִּי שְׂשׂוֹן לִבִּי הֵמָּה.

[112]I have inclined my heart to perform Your statutes, forever, at every step.

קֶ"ב נָטִיתִי לִבִּי לַעֲשׂוֹת חֻקֶּיךָ לְעוֹלָם עֵקֶב.

[113]**Samekh**. I hate them that are of a double mind; but Your Torah do I love.

קֶ"ג סֵעֲפִים שָׂנֵאתִי; וְתוֹרָתְךָ אָהָבְתִּי.

[114]You are my hiding place and my Magen; in Your word do I hope.

קֶ"ד סִתְרִי וּמָגִנִּי אָתָּה; לִדְבָרְךָ יִחָלְתִּי.

[115]Depart from me, you evildoers; that I may keep the Mitzvot of my Elohim.

קֶ"ט סוּרוּ מִמֶּנִּי מְרֵעִים; וְאֶצְּרָה מִצְוֹת אֱלֹהָי.

[116]Uphold me according unto Your word, that I may live; and put me not to shame in my hope.

קֶ"ט סָמְכֵנִי כְאִמְרָתְךָ וְאֶחְיֶה; וְאַל תְּבִישֵׁנִי מִשִּׂבְרִי.

[117]Support me, and I shall be saved; and I will occupy myself with Your statutes continually.

קי״זסְעָדֵנִי וְאִוָּשֵׁעָה; וְאֶשְׁעָה בְחֻקֶּיךָ תָמִיד.

[118]You have made light of all them that err from Your statutes; for their deceit is vain.

קי״חסָלִיתָ כָּל שׁוֹגִים מֵחֻקֶּיךָ: כִּי שֶׁקֶר תַּרְמִיתָם.

[119]You put away all the wicked of the earth like dross; therefore I love Your testimonies.

קי״טסִגִים הִשְׁבַּתָּ כָל רִשְׁעֵי אָרֶץ; לָכֵן אָהַבְתִּי עֵדֹתֶיךָ.

[120]My flesh shudders for fear of You; and I am afraid of Your judgments.

קכסָמַר מִפַּחְדְּךָ בְשָׂרִי; וּמִמִּשְׁפָּטֶיךָ יָרֵאתִי.

[121]**Ayin.** I have done justice and righteousness; leave me not to my oppressors.

קכ״אעָשִׂיתִי מִשְׁפָּט וָצֶדֶק; בַּל תַּנִּיחֵנִי לְעֹשְׁקָי.

[122]Be surety for Your servant for good; let not the proud oppress me.

קכ״בעֲרֹב עַבְדְּךָ לְטוֹב; אַל יַעַשְׁקֻנִי זֵדִים.

[123]My eyes fail for Your Salvation, and for Your righteous word.

קכ״געֵינַי כָּלוּ לִישׁוּעָתֶךָ; וּלְאִמְרַת צִדְקֶךָ.

[124]Deal with Your servant according unto Your mercy, and teach me Your statutes.

קכ״דעֲשֵׂה עִם עַבְדְּךָ כְחַסְדֶּךָ; וְחֻקֶּיךָ לַמְּדֵנִי.

[125]I am Your servant, give me understanding, that I may know Your testimonies.

קכ״העַבְדְּךָ אָנִי הֲבִינֵנִי; וְאֵדְעָה עֵדֹתֶיךָ.

[126]It is time for יהוה to work; they have made void Your Torah.

קכו עֵת לַעֲשׂוֹת לַיהוה הֵפֵרוּ תּוֹרָתֶךָ.

[127]Therefore I love Your Mitzvot above gold, yes, above fine gold.

קכז עַל כֵּן אָהַבְתִּי מִצְוֹתֶיךָ מִזָּהָב וּמִפָּז.

[128]Therefore I esteem all [Your] precepts concerning all things to be right; every false way I hate.

קכח עַל כֵּן כָּל פִּקּוּדֵי כֹל יִשָּׁרְתִּי; כָּל אֹרַח שֶׁקֶר שָׂנֵאתִי.

[129]Peh. Your testimonies are wonderful; therefore does my soul keep them.

קכט פְּלָאוֹת עֵדְוֹתֶיךָ; עַל כֵּן נְצָרָתַם נַפְשִׁי.

[130]The opening of Your D'varim gives light; it gives understanding unto the simple.

קל פֵּתַח דְּבָרֶיךָ יָאִיר; מֵבִין פְּתָיִים.

[131]I opened wide my mouth, and panted; for I longed for Your Mitzvot.

קלא פִּי פָעַרְתִּי וָאֶשְׁאָפָה: כִּי לְמִצְוֹתֶיךָ יָאָבְתִּי.

[132]Turn towards me, and be gracious unto me, as is Your wont to do unto those that love Your Name.

קלב פְּנֵה אֵלַי וְחָנֵּנִי כְּמִשְׁפָּט לְאֹהֲבֵי שְׁמֶךָ.

[133]Order my footsteps by Your word; and let not any iniquity have dominion over me.

קלג פְּעָמַי הָכֵן בְּאִמְרָתֶךָ; וְאַל תַּשְׁלֶט בִּי כָל אָוֶן.

[134]Redeem me from the oppression of man, and I will observe Your precepts.

קלד פְּדֵנִי מֵעֹשֶׁק אָדָם; וְאֶשְׁמְרָה פִּקּוּדֶיךָ.

<sup>135</sup>Make Your face to shine upon Your servant; and teach me Your statutes.

קלה פָּנֶיךָ הָאֵר בְּעַבְדֶּךָ; וְלַמְּדֵנִי אֶת חֻקֶּיךָ.

<sup>136</sup>My eyes run down with rivers of water, because they observe not Your Torah.

קלו פַּלְגֵי מַיִם יָרְדוּ עֵינָי עַל לֹא שָׁמְרוּ תוֹרָתֶךָ.

<sup>137</sup>**Tzadi**. A Tzadik are You, O יהוה , and upright are Your judgments.

קלז צַדִּיק אַתָּה יהוה ; וְיָשָׁר מִשְׁפָּטֶיךָ.

<sup>138</sup>You have commanded Your testimonies in righteousness and exceeding faithfulness.

קלח צִוִּיתָ צֶדֶק עֵדֹתֶיךָ; וֶאֱמוּנָה מְאֹד.

<sup>139</sup>My zeal has undone me, because my adversaries have forgotten Your D'varim.

קלט צִמְּתַתְנִי קִנְאָתִי: כִּי שָׁכְחוּ דְבָרֶיךָ צָרָי.

<sup>140</sup>Your word is tried to the uttermost, and Your servant loves it.

קמ צְרוּפָה אִמְרָתְךָ מְאֹד; וְעַבְדְּךָ אֲהֵבָהּ.

<sup>141</sup>I am small and despised; yet have I not forgotten Your precepts.

קמא צָעִיר אָנֹכִי וְנִבְזֶה; פִּקֻּדֶיךָ לֹא שָׁכָחְתִּי.

<sup>142</sup>Your tzedaka is an everlasting tzedaka, and Your Torah is truth.

קמב צִדְקָתְךָ צֶדֶק לְעוֹלָם; וְתוֹרָתְךָ אֱמֶת.

<sup>143</sup>Trouble and anguish have overtaken me; yet Your Mitzvot are my delight.

קמג צַר וּמָצוֹק מְצָאוּנִי; מִצְוֹתֶיךָ שַׁעֲשֻׁעָי.

[144]Your testimonies are righteous forever; give me understanding, and I shall live.

קמד‎צֶדֶק עֵדְוֹתֶיךָ לְעוֹלָם; הֲבִינֵנִי וְאֶחְיֶה.

[145]**Kof**. I have called with my whole heart; answer me, O יהוה ; I will keep Your statutes.

קמה‎קָרָאתִי בְכָל לֵב עֲנֵנִי יהוה ; חֻקֶּיךָ אֶצֹּרָה.

[146]I have called You, save me, and I will observe Your testimonies.

קמו‎קְרָאתִיךָ הוֹשִׁיעֵנִי; וְאֶשְׁמְרָה עֵדֹתֶיךָ.

[147]I rose early at dawn, and cried; I hoped in Your D'var.

קמז‎קִדַּמְתִּי בַנֶּשֶׁף וָאֲשַׁוֵּעָה; לדבריך (לִדְבָרְךָ) יִחָלְתִּי.

[148]My eyes forestalled the night-watches, that I might meditate in Your word.

קמח‎קִדְּמוּ עֵינַי אַשְׁמֻרוֹת לָשִׂיחַ בְּאִמְרָתֶךָ.

[149]Hear my voice according unto Your compassion; quicken me, O יהוה , as You are wont.

קמט‎קוֹלִי שִׁמְעָה כְחַסְדֶּךָ; יהוה כְּמִשְׁפָּטֶךָ חַיֵּנִי.

[150]They draw nigh that follow after wickedness; they are far from Your Torah.

קנ‎קָרְבוּ רֹדְפֵי זִמָּה; מִתּוֹרָתְךָ רָחָקוּ.

[151]You are nigh, O יהוה ; and all Your Mitzvot are truth.

קנא‎קָרוֹב אַתָּה יהוה ; וְכָל מִצְוֹתֶיךָ אֱמֶת.

[152]Of old have I known from Your testimonies that You have founded them forever.

קנב‎קֶדֶם יָדַעְתִּי מֵעֵדֹתֶיךָ: כִּי לְעוֹלָם יְסַדְתָּם.

[153]**Resh.** O see my affliction, and rescue me; for I do not forget Your Torah.

קנג‏רְאֵה עָנְיִי וְחַלְּצֵנִי: כִּי תוֹרָתְךָ לֹא שָׁכָחְתִּי.

[154]Plead my cause, and redeem me; quicken me according to Your word.

קנד‏רִיבָה רִיבִי וּגְאָלֵנִי; לְאִמְרָתְךָ חַיֵּנִי.

[155]Yeshua[h] is far from the wicked; for they seek not Your statutes.

קנה‏רָחוֹק מֵרְשָׁעִים יְשׁוּעָה: כִּי חֻקֶּיךָ לֹא דָרָשׁוּ.

[156]Great are Your compassions, O יהוה ; quicken me as You are wont.

קנו‏רַחֲמֶיךָ רַבִּים יהוה ; כְּמִשְׁפָּטֶיךָ חַיֵּנִי.

[157]Many are my persecutors and my adversaries; yet have I not turned aside from Your testimonies.

קנז‏רַבִּים רֹדְפַי וְצָרָי; מֵעֵדְוֹתֶיךָ לֹא נָטִיתִי.

[158]I beheld them that were faithless, and strove with them; because they observed not Your word.

קנח‏רָאִיתִי בֹגְדִים וָאֶתְקוֹטָטָה אֲשֶׁר אִמְרָתְךָ לֹא שָׁמָרוּ.

[159]O see how I love Your precepts; quicken me, O יהוה , according to Your compassion.

קנט‏רְאֵה כִּי פִקּוּדֶיךָ אָהָבְתִּי; יהוה כְּחַסְדְּךָ חַיֵּנִי.

[160]The beginning of Your D'var is truth; and all Your righteous ordinance endures forever.

קס‏רֹאשׁ דְּבָרְךָ אֱמֶת; וּלְעוֹלָם כָּל מִשְׁפַּט צִדְקֶךָ.

[161]**Shin**. Princes have persecuted me without a cause; but my heart stands in awe of Your D'varim.

קסא‎שָׂרִים רְדָפוּנִי חִנָּם; וּמִדְּבָרֶיךָ (וּמִדְּבָרְךָ) פָּחַד לִבִּי.

[162]I rejoice at Your word, as one that finds great spoil.

קסב‎שָׂשׂ אָנֹכִי עַל אִמְרָתֶךָ כְּמוֹצֵא שָׁלָל רָב.

[163]I hate and abhor falsehood; Your Torah do I love.

קסג‎שֶׁקֶר שָׂנֵאתִי וַאֲתַעֵבָה; תּוֹרָתְךָ אָהָבְתִּי.

[164]Seven times a day do I praise You, because of Your righteous ordinances.

קסד‎שֶׁבַע בַּיּוֹם הִלַּלְתִּיךָ עַל מִשְׁפְּטֵי צִדְקֶךָ.

[165]Great shalom have they that love Your Torah; and there is no stumbling for them.

קסה‎שָׁלוֹם רָב לְאֹהֲבֵי תוֹרָתֶךָ; וְאֵין לָמוֹ מִכְשׁוֹל.

[166]I have hoped for Your Yeshua[h], O יהוה , and have done Your Mitzvot.

קסו‎שִׂבַּרְתִּי לִישׁוּעָתְךָ יהוה ; וּמִצְוֹתֶיךָ עָשִׂיתִי.

[167]My soul has observed Your testimonies; and I love them exceedingly.

קסז‎שָׁמְרָה נַפְשִׁי עֵדֹתֶיךָ; וָאֹהֲבֵם מְאֹד.

[168]I have observed Your precepts and Your testimonies; for all my ways are before You.

קסח‎שָׁמַרְתִּי פִקּוּדֶיךָ וְעֵדֹתֶיךָ: כִּי כָל דְּרָכַי נֶגְדֶּךָ.

[169]**Tav**. Let my cry come near before You, O יהוה ; give me understanding according to Your D'var.

קסט‎תִּקְרַב רִנָּתִי לְפָנֶיךָ יהוה ; כִּדְבָרְךָ הֲבִינֵנִי.

489

[170]Let my supplication come before You; deliver me according to Your word.

קעֹתָּבוֹא תְּחִנָּתִי לְפָנֶיךָ; כְּאִמְרָתְךָ הַצִּילֵנִי.

[171]Let my lips utter praise: because You teach me Your statutes.

קעֹאתַּבַּעְנָה שְׂפָתַי תְּהִלָּה: כִּי תְלַמְּדֵנִי חֻקֶּיךָ.

[172]Let my tongue sing of Your word; for all Your Mitzvot are righteousness.

קעֹבתַּעַן לְשׁוֹנִי אִמְרָתֶךָ: כִּי כָל מִצְוֹתֶיךָ צֶּדֶק.

[173]Let Your hand be ready to help me; for I have chosen Your precepts.

קעֹגתְּהִי יָדְךָ לְעָזְרֵנִי: כִּי פִקּוּדֶיךָ בָחָרְתִּי.

[174]I have longed for Your Yeshua[h], O יהוה ; and Your Torah is my delight.

קעֹדתָּאַבְתִּי לִישׁוּעָתְךָ יהוה ; וְתוֹרָתְךָ שַׁעֲשֻׁעָי.

[175]Let my soul live, and it shall praise You; and let Your ordinances help me.

קעֹהתְּחִי נַפְשִׁי וּתְהַלְלֶךָּ; וּמִשְׁפָּטֶךָ יַעְזְרֻנִי.

[176]I have gone astray like a lost sheep; seek Your servant; for I have not forgotten Your Mitzvot.

קעֹותָּעִיתִי כְּשֶׂה אֹבֵד בַּקֵּשׁ עַבְדֶּךָ: כִּי מִצְוֹתֶיךָ לֹא שָׁכָחְתִּי.

# Tehillah 120 תְּהִלָּה

[1]Shir HaMa'alot [A Song of Ascents]. In my distress I called unto יהוה , and He answered me.

אשִׁיר הַמַּעֲלוֹת: אֶל יהוה בַּצָּרָתָה לִי קָרָאתִי וַיַּעֲנֵנִי.

[2]O יהוה , deliver my soul from lying lips, from a deceitful tongue.

ב יהוה הַצִּילָה נַפְשִׁי מִשְׂפַת שֶׁקֶר: מִלָּשׁוֹן רְמִיָּה.

³What shall be given unto you, and what shall be done more unto you, you deceitful tongue?

מַה יִּתֵּן לְךָ וּמַה יֹּסִיף לָךְ לָשׁוֹן רְמִיָּה.

⁴Sharp arrows of the mighty, with coals of broom.

חִצֵּי גִבּוֹר שְׁנוּנִים; עִם גַּחֲלֵי רְתָמִים.

⁵Woe is me, that I sojourn with Meshekh, that I dwell beside the tents of Kedar!

אוֹיָה לִי כִּי גַרְתִּי מֶשֶׁךְ; שָׁכַנְתִּי עִם אָהֳלֵי קֵדָר.

⁶My soul has full long had her dwelling with him that hates shalom.

רַבַּת שָׁכְנָה לָּהּ נַפְשִׁי עִם שׂוֹנֵא שָׁלוֹם.

⁷I am all shalom; but when I speak, they are for war.

אֲנִי שָׁלוֹם וְכִי אֲדַבֵּר; הֵמָּה לַמִּלְחָמָה.

# תְּהִלָּה 121 Tehillah

¹Shir LaMa'alot. I will lift up my eyes unto the mountains: from where does my help come?

שִׁיר לַמַּעֲלוֹת: אֶשָּׂא עֵינַי אֶל הֶהָרִים מֵאַיִן יָבֹא עֶזְרִי.

²My help comes from יהוה , who made heaven and earth.

עֶזְרִי מֵעִם יהוה עֹשֵׂה שָׁמַיִם וָאָרֶץ.

³He will not suffer your foot to be moved; He that keeps you will not slumber.

אַל יִתֵּן לַמּוֹט רַגְלֶךָ; אַל יָנוּם שֹׁמְרֶךָ.

⁴Behold, He that keeps Yisra'el does neither slumber nor sleep.

הִנֵּה לֹא יָנוּם וְלֹא יִישָׁן שׁוֹמֵר יִשְׂרָאֵל.

⁵ יהוה is your keeper; יהוה is your shade upon your right hand.

ה יהוה שֹׁמְרֶךָ; יהוה צִלְּךָ עַל יַד יְמִינֶךָ.

⁶The sun shall not smite you by day, nor the moon by night.

יוֹמָם הַשֶּׁמֶשׁ לֹא יַכֶּכָּה; וְיָרֵחַ בַּלָּיְלָה.

⁷ יהוה shall keep you from all evil; He shall keep your soul.

ז יהוה יִשְׁמָרְךָ מִכָּל רָע: יִשְׁמֹר אֶת נַפְשֶׁךָ.

⁸ יהוה shall guard your going out and your coming in, from this time forth and forever.

ח יהוה יִשְׁמָר צֵאתְךָ וּבוֹאֶךָ מֵעַתָּה וְעַד עוֹלָם.

# תְּהִלָּה Tehillah 122

¹Shir HaMa'alot; by David. I rejoiced when they said unto me, "Let us go unto Beit יהוה."

אשִׁיר הַמַּעֲלוֹת לְדָוִד: שָׂמַחְתִּי בְּאֹמְרִים לִי בֵּית יהוה נֵלֵךְ.

²Our feet are standing within your gates, O Yerushalayim;

בעֹמְדוֹת הָיוּ רַגְלֵינוּ בִּשְׁעָרַיִךְ יְרוּשָׁלָם.

³Yerushalayim, that is built as a city that is compact together;

גיְרוּשָׁלַם הַבְּנוּיָה כְּעִיר שֶׁחֻבְּרָה לָּה יַחְדָּו.

⁴Where the tribes went up, even the tribes of יהוה, as a testimony unto Yisra'el, to give thanks unto the Name of יהוה.

דשֶׁשָּׁם עָלוּ שְׁבָטִים שִׁבְטֵי יה עֵדוּת לְיִשְׂרָאֵל: לְהֹדוֹת לְשֵׁם יהוה.

⁵For there were set thrones for judgment, the thrones of Beit David.

הּכִּי שָׁמָּה יָשְׁבוּ כִסְאוֹת לְמִשְׁפָּט: כִּסְאוֹת לְבֵית דָּוִד.

⁶Pray for the shalom of Yerushalayim; may they prosper that love you.

ושַׁאֲלוּ שְׁלוֹם יְרוּשָׁלָם; יִשְׁלָיוּ אֹהֲבָיִךְ.

⁷May Shalom be within your walls, and prosperity within your palaces.

זיְהִי שָׁלוֹם בְּחֵילֵךְ; שַׁלְוָה בְּאַרְמְנוֹתָיִךְ.

⁸For my brethren and companions' sakes, I will now say, "Shalom be within you."

חלְמַעַן אַחַי וְרֵעָי אֲדַבְּרָה נָּא שָׁלוֹם בָּךְ.

⁹For the sake of Beit יהוה our Elohim I will seek your good.

טלְמַעַן בֵּית יהוה אֱלֹהֵינוּ אֲבַקְשָׁה טוֹב לָךְ.

# תְּהִלָּה 123 Tehillah

¹Shir HaMa'alot. Unto You I lift up my eyes, O You that are enthroned in the heavens.

אשִׁיר הַמַּעֲלוֹת: אֵלֶיךָ נָשָׂאתִי אֶת עֵינַי הַיֹּשְׁבִי בַּשָּׁמָיִם.

²Behold, as the eyes of servants unto the hand of their master, as the eyes of a maiden unto the hand of her mistress; so our eyes look unto יהוה our Elohim, until He shows us grace.

בהִנֵּה כְעֵינֵי עֲבָדִים אֶל יַד אֲדוֹנֵיהֶם כְּעֵינֵי שִׁפְחָה אֶל יַד גְּבִרְתָּהּ: כֵּן עֵינֵינוּ אֶל יהוה אֱלֹהֵינוּ עַד שֶׁיְחָנֵּנוּ.

³Be gracious unto us, O יהוה , be gracious unto us; for we are full sated with contempt.

ᵍחָנֵּנוּ יהוה חָנֵּנוּ: כִּי רַב שָׂבַעְנוּ בוּז.

⁴Our soul is full sated with the scorning of those that are at ease, and with the contempt of the proud oppressors.

ᵍרַבַּת שָׂבְעָה לָּהּ נַפְשֵׁנוּ: הַלַּעַג הַשַּׁאֲנַנִּים; הַבּוּז לגאיונים (לִגְאֵי יוֹנִים).

# תְּהִלָּה 124 Tehillah

¹Shir HaMa'alot; by David. "If it had not been יהוה who was for us", let Yisra'el now say;

ᵃשִׁיר הַמַּעֲלוֹת לְדָוִד: לוּלֵי יהוה שֶׁהָיָה לָנוּ יֹאמַר נָא יִשְׂרָאֵל.

²"If it had not been יהוה who was for us, when men rose up against us,

ᵇלוּלֵי יהוה שֶׁהָיָה לָנוּ בְּקוּם עָלֵינוּ אָדָם.

³Then they would have swallowed us up alive, when their wrath was kindled against us,

ᵍאֲזַי חַיִּים בְּלָעוּנוּ בַּחֲרוֹת אַפָּם בָּנוּ.

⁴Then the waters would have overwhelmed us, the stream would have gone over our soul;

ᵍאֲזַי הַמַּיִם שְׁטָפוּנוּ נַחְלָה עָבַר עַל נַפְשֵׁנוּ.

⁵Then the proud waters would have gone over our soul."

ᵍאֲזַי עָבַר עַל נַפְשֵׁנוּ הַמַּיִם הַזֵּידוֹנִים.

⁶Blessed is יהוה , who has not given us as prey to their teeth.

ᵍבָּרוּךְ יהוה שֶׁלֹּא נְתָנָנוּ טֶרֶף לְשִׁנֵּיהֶם.

⁷Our soul is escaped as a bird out of the snare of the fowlers; the snare is broken, and we are escaped.

נַפְשֵׁנוּ כְּצִפּוֹר נִמְלְטָה מִפַּח יוֹקְשִׁים: הַפַּח נִשְׁבָּר וַאֲנַחְנוּ נִמְלָטְנוּ.

⁸Our help is in the Name of יהוה , who made heaven and earth.

עֶזְרֵנוּ בְּשֵׁם יהוה עֹשֵׂה שָׁמַיִם וָאָרֶץ.

# תְהִלָּה 125 Tehillah

¹Shir HaMa'alot. They that trust in יהוה are as Har Tzion, which cannot be moved, but abides forever.

אשִׁיר הַמַּעֲלוֹת: הַבֹּטְחִים בַּיהוה כְּהַר צִיּוֹן לֹא יִמּוֹט לְעוֹלָם יֵשֵׁב.

²As the mountains are round about Yerushalayim, so יהוה is round about His people, from this time forth and forever.

בִּירוּשָׁלַם הָרִים סָבִיב לָהּ: וַיהוה סָבִיב לְעַמּוֹ מֵעַתָּה וְעַד עוֹלָם.

³For the rod of wickedness shall not rest upon the lot of the Tzadikim; that the Tzadikim put not forth their hands unto iniquity.

גכִּי לֹא יָנוּחַ שֵׁבֶט הָרֶשַׁע עַל גּוֹרַל הַצַּדִּיקִים: לְמַעַן לֹא יִשְׁלְחוּ הַצַּדִּיקִים בְּעַוְלָתָה יְדֵיהֶם.

⁴Do good, O יהוה , unto the good, and to them that are upright in their hearts.

דהֵיטִיבָה יהוה לַטּוֹבִים; וְלִישָׁרִים בְּלִבּוֹתָם.

⁵But as for such as turn aside unto their crooked ways, יהוה will lead them away with the workers of iniquity. Shalom be upon Yisra'el.

הוְהַמַּטִּים עֲקַלְקַלּוֹתָם יוֹלִיכֵם יהוה אֶת פֹּעֲלֵי הָאָוֶן: שָׁלוֹם עַל יִשְׂרָאֵל.

# Tehillah 126 תְּהִלָּה

[1]Shir HaMa'alot. When יהוה brought back those that returned to Tzion, we were like unto them that dream.

אשִׁיר הַמַּעֲלוֹת: בְּשׁוּב יהוה אֶת שִׁיבַת צִיּוֹן הָיִינוּ כְּחֹלְמִים.

[2]Then was our mouth filled with laughter, and our tongue with singing; then said they among the goyim, "יהוה has done great things with these."

באָז יִמָּלֵא שְׂחוֹק פִּינוּ וּלְשׁוֹנֵנוּ רִנָּה: אָז יֹאמְרוּ בַגּוֹיִם הִגְדִּיל יהוה לַעֲשׂוֹת עִם אֵלֶּה.

[3] יהוה has done great things with us; we are rejoiced.

גהִגְדִּיל יהוה לַעֲשׂוֹת עִמָּנוּ הָיִינוּ שְׂמֵחִים.

[4]Turn our captivity, O יהוה , as the streams in the dry land.

דשׁוּבָה יהוה אֶת שְׁבוּתֵנוּ (שְׁבִיתֵנוּ) כַּאֲפִיקִים בַּנֶּגֶב.

[5]They that sow in tears shall reap in joy.

ההַזֹּרְעִים בְּדִמְעָה בְּרִנָּה יִקְצֹרוּ.

[6]Though he goes on his way weeping that bears the measure of seed, he shall come home with joy, bearing his sheaves.

והָלוֹךְ יֵלֵךְ וּבָכֹה נֹשֵׂא מֶשֶׁךְ הַזָּרַע: בֹּא יָבֹא בְרִנָּה נֹשֵׂא אֲלֻמֹּתָיו.

# Tehillah 127 תְּהִלָּה

[1]Shir HaMa'alot; of Shlomo. Except יהוה builds the house, they labor in vain that build it; except יהוה keeps the city, the watchman wakes but in vain.

אשִׁיר הַמַּעֲלוֹת לִשְׁלֹמֹה: אִם יהוה לֹא יִבְנֶה בַיִת שָׁוְא עָמְלוּ בוֹנָיו בּוֹ; אִם יהוה לֹא יִשְׁמָר עִיר שָׁוְא שָׁקַד שׁוֹמֵר.

²It is vain for you that you rise early, and sit up late, you that eat the bread of toil; so He gives unto His beloved in sleep.

שָׁוְא לָכֶם מַשְׁכִּימֵי קוּם מְאַחֲרֵי שֶׁבֶת אֹכְלֵי לֶחֶם הָעֲצָבִים; כֵּן יִתֵּן לִידִידוֹ שֵׁנָא.

³Lo, children are a heritage of יהוה ; the fruit of the womb is a reward.

הִנֵּה נַחֲלַת יהוה בָּנִים: שָׂכָר פְּרִי הַבָּטֶן.

⁴As arrows in the hand of a mighty man, so are the children of one's youth.

כְּחִצִּים בְּיַד גִּבּוֹר כֵּן בְּנֵי הַנְּעוּרִים.

⁵Happy is the man that has his quiver full of them; they shall not be put to shame, when they speak with their enemies in the gate.

אַשְׁרֵי הַגֶּבֶר אֲשֶׁר מִלֵּא אֶת אַשְׁפָּתוֹ מֵהֶם: לֹא יֵבֹשׁוּ, כִּי יְדַבְּרוּ אֶת אוֹיְבִים בַּשָּׁעַר.

# תְּהִלָּה 128 Tehillah

¹Shir HaMa'alot. Happy is every one that fears יהוה , that walks in His ways.

שִׁיר הַמַּעֲלוֹת: אַשְׁרֵי כָּל יְרֵא יהוה הַהֹלֵךְ בִּדְרָכָיו.

²When you eat the labor of your hands, happy shall you be, and it shall be well with you.

יְגִיעַ כַּפֶּיךָ כִּי תֹאכֵל; אַשְׁרֶיךָ וְטוֹב לָךְ.

³Your wife shall be as a fruitful vine, in the innermost parts of your house; your children like olive plants, round about your table.

אֶשְׁתְּךָ כְּגֶפֶן פֹּרִיָּה בְּיַרְכְּתֵי בֵיתֶךָ: בָּנֶיךָ כִּשְׁתִלֵי זֵיתִים סָבִיב לְשֻׁלְחָנֶךָ.

⁴Behold, surely thus shall the man be blessed that fears יהוה .

⁴הִנֵּה כִי כֵן יְבֹרַךְ גָּבֶר יְרֵא יהוה .

⁵ יהוה bless you out of Tzion; and may you see the good of Yerushalayim all the days of your life;

⁵יְבָרֶכְךָ יהוה מִצִּיּוֹן: וּרְאֵה בְּטוּב יְרוּשָׁלָם כֹּל יְמֵי חַיֶּיךָ.

⁶And may you see your children's children. Shalom be upon Yisra'el!

⁶וּרְאֵה בָנִים לְבָנֶיךָ: שָׁלוֹם עַל יִשְׂרָאֵל.

# Tehillah 129 תְּהִלָּה

¹Shir HaMa'alot. "Much have they afflicted me from my youth up", let Yisra'el now say;

¹שִׁיר הַמַּעֲלוֹת: רַבַּת צְרָרוּנִי מִנְּעוּרַי יֹאמַר נָא יִשְׂרָאֵל.

²"Much have they afflicted me from my youth up; but they have not prevailed against me.

²רַבַּת צְרָרוּנִי מִנְּעוּרָי; גַּם לֹא יָכְלוּ לִי.

³The plowers plowed upon my back; they made long their furrows.

³עַל גַּבִּי חָרְשׁוּ חֹרְשִׁים; הֶאֱרִיכוּ למעונתם (לְמַעֲנִיתָם).

⁴ יהוה is a Tzadik; He has cut asunder the cords of the wicked."

⁴ יהוה צַדִּיק; קִצֵּץ עֲבוֹת רְשָׁעִים.

⁵Let them be ashamed and turned backward, all they that hate Tzion.

⁵יֵבֹשׁוּ וְיִסֹּגוּ אָחוֹר כֹּל שֹׂנְאֵי צִיּוֹן.

⁶Let them be as the grass upon the housetops, which withers before it springs up;

יִהְיוּ כַּחֲצִיר גַּגּוֹת שֶׁקַּדְמַת שָׁלַף יָבֵשׁ.

⁷Wherewith the reaper fills not his hand, nor he that binds sheaves his bosom.

שֶׁלֹּא מִלֵּא כַפּוֹ קוֹצֵר; וְחִצְנוֹ מְעַמֵּר.

⁸Neither do they that go by say, "The blessing of יהוה be upon you; we bless you in the Name of יהוה."

וְלֹא אָמְרוּ הָעֹבְרִים בִּרְכַּת יהוה אֲלֵיכֶם; בֵּרַכְנוּ אֶתְכֶם בְּשֵׁם יהוה .

# תְּהִלָּה 130 Tehillah

¹Shir HaMa'alot. Out of the depths have I called You, O יהוה .

שִׁיר הַמַּעֲלוֹת: מִמַּעֲמַקִּים קְרָאתִיךָ יהוה .

²Adonai, hearken unto my voice; let Your ears be attentive to the voice of my supplications.

אֲדֹנָי שִׁמְעָה בְקוֹלִי: תִּהְיֶינָה אָזְנֶיךָ קַשֻּׁבוֹת לְקוֹל תַּחֲנוּנָי.

³If You, Yah , should mark iniquities, O Adonai, who could stand?

אִם עֲוֹנוֹת תִּשְׁמָר יָהּ אֲדֹנָי מִי יַעֲמֹד.

⁴For with You there is forgiveness, that You may be feared.

כִּי עִמְּךָ הַסְּלִיחָה לְמַעַן תִּוָּרֵא.

⁵I wait for יהוה , my soul does wait, and in His D'var do I hope.

קִוִּיתִי יהוה קִוְּתָה נַפְשִׁי; וְלִדְבָרוֹ הוֹחָלְתִּי.

⁶My soul waits for Adonai, more than watchmen for the morning; yes, more than watchmen for the morning.

נַפְשִׁי לַאדֹנָי מִשֹּׁמְרִים לַבֹּקֶר שֹׁמְרִים לַבֹּקֶר.

499

[7]O Yisra'el, hope in יהוה ; for with יהוה there is compassion, and with Him is plenteous redemption.

יַחֵל יִשְׂרָאֵל אֶל יהוה: כִּי עִם יהוה הַחֶסֶד; וְהַרְבֵּה עִמּוֹ פְדוּת.

[8]And He will redeem Yisra'el from all his iniquities.

וְהוּא יִפְדֶּה אֶת יִשְׂרָאֵל מִכֹּל עֲוֹנֹתָיו.

# Tehillah 131 תְּהִלָּה

[1]Shir HaMa'alot; by David. יהוה , my heart is not haughty, nor my eyes lofty; neither do I exercise myself in things too great, or in things too wonderful for me.

שִׁיר הַמַּעֲלוֹת לְדָוִד: יהוה לֹא גָבַהּ לִבִּי וְלֹא רָמוּ עֵינַי; וְלֹא הִלַּכְתִּי בִגְדֹלוֹת וּבְנִפְלָאוֹת מִמֶּנִּי.

[2]Surely I have stilled and quieted my soul; like a weaned child with his mother; my soul is with me like a weaned child.

אִם לֹא שִׁוִּיתִי וְדוֹמַמְתִּי נַפְשִׁי: כְּגָמֻל עֲלֵי אִמּוֹ; כַּגָּמֻל עָלַי נַפְשִׁי.

[3]O Yisra'el, hope in יהוה from this time forth and forever.

יַחֵל יִשְׂרָאֵל אֶל יהוה מֵעַתָּה וְעַד עוֹלָם.

# Tehillah 132 תְּהִלָּה

[1]Shir HaMa'alot. יהוה , remember for David all his affliction;

שִׁיר הַמַּעֲלוֹת: זְכוֹר יהוה לְדָוִד אֶת כָּל עֻנּוֹתוֹ.

[2]How he swore unto יהוה , and vowed unto the Mighty One of Ya'akov:

אֲשֶׁר נִשְׁבַּע לַיהוה ; נָדַר לַאֲבִיר יַעֲקֹב.

³"Surely I will not come into the tent of my house, nor go up into the bed that is spread for me;

גאִם אָבֹא בְּאֹהֶל בֵּיתִי; אִם אֶעֱלֶה עַל עֶרֶשׂ יְצוּעָי.

⁴I will not give sleep to my eyes, nor slumber to my eyelids;

דאִם אֶתֵּן שְׁנַת לְעֵינָי; לְעַפְעַפַּי תְּנוּמָה.

⁵Until I find out a place for יהוה , a dwelling-place for the Mighty One of Ya'akov."

העַד אֶמְצָא מָקוֹם לַיהוה ; מִשְׁכָּנוֹת לַאֲבִיר יַעֲקֹב.

⁶Lo, we heard of it as being in Efrat; we found it in the field of the wood.

והִנֵּה שְׁמַעֲנוּהָ בְאֶפְרָתָה; מְצָאנוּהָ בִּשְׂדֵי יָעַר.

⁷Let us go into His Mishkan; let us worship at His footstool.

זנָבוֹאָה לְמִשְׁכְּנוֹתָיו; נִשְׁתַּחֲוֶה לַהֲדֹם רַגְלָיו.

⁸Arise, O יהוה , unto Your resting-place; You, and the Aron of Your strength.

חקוּמָה יהוה לִמְנוּחָתֶךָ: אַתָּה וַאֲרוֹן עֻזֶּךָ.

⁹Let Your Kohanim be clothed with righteousness; and let Your Khasidim shout for joy.

טכֹּהֲנֶיךָ יִלְבְּשׁוּ צֶדֶק; וַחֲסִידֶיךָ יְרַנֵּנוּ.

¹⁰For Your servant David's sake, turn not away the face of Your Mashi'akh.

יבַּעֲבוּר דָּוִד עַבְדֶּךָ אַל תָּשֵׁב פְּנֵי מְשִׁיחֶךָ.

¹¹ יהוה swore unto David in truth; He will not turn back from it: "Of the fruit of your body will I set upon your throne.

יאנִשְׁבַּע יהוה לְדָוִד אֱמֶת לֹא יָשׁוּב מִמֶּנָּה: מִפְּרִי בִטְנְךָ אָשִׁית לְכִסֵּא לָךְ.

<sup>12</sup>If your children keep My Brit and My testimony that I shall teach them, their children also forever shall sit upon your throne."

יב"אִם יִשְׁמְרוּ בָנֶיךָ בְּרִיתִי וְעֵדֹתִי זוֹ אֲלַמְּדֵם: גַּם בְּנֵיהֶם עֲדֵי עַד יֵשְׁבוּ לְכִסֵּא לָךְ.

<sup>13</sup>For יהוה has chosen Tzion; He has desired it for His habitation:

יג כִּי בָחַר יהוה בְּצִיּוֹן; אִוָּהּ לְמוֹשָׁב לוֹ.

<sup>14</sup>"This is My resting-place forever; here will I dwell; for I have desired it.

יד זֹאת מְנוּחָתִי עֲדֵי עַד: פֹּה אֵשֵׁב כִּי אִוִּתִיהָ.

<sup>15</sup>I will abundantly bless her provision; I will give her needy bread in plenty.

טו צֵידָהּ בָּרֵךְ אֲבָרֵךְ; אֶבְיוֹנֶיהָ אַשְׂבִּיעַ לָחֶם.

<sup>16</sup>Her Kohanim also will I clothe with Salvation; and her Khasidim shall shout aloud for joy.

טז וְכֹהֲנֶיהָ אַלְבִּישׁ יֶשַׁע; וַחֲסִידֶיהָ רַנֵּן יְרַנֵּנוּ.

<sup>17</sup>There will I make a horn to shoot up unto David, there have I ordered a lamp for My Mashi'akh.

יז שָׁם אַצְמִיחַ קֶרֶן לְדָוִד; עָרַכְתִּי נֵר לִמְשִׁיחִי.

<sup>18</sup>His enemies will I clothe with shame; but upon himself shall his crown shine."

יח אוֹיְבָיו אַלְבִּישׁ בֹּשֶׁת; וְעָלָיו יָצִיץ נִזְרוֹ.

# תְּהִלָּה 133 Tehillah

¹Shir HaMa'alot; by David. Behold, how good and how pleasant it is for brethren to dwell together in perfect unity!

שִׁיר הַמַּעֲלוֹת לְדָוִד: הִנֵּה מַה טוֹב וּמַה נָּעִים שֶׁבֶת אַחִים גַּם יָחַד.

²It is like the precious oil upon the head, coming down upon the beard; even the beard of Aharon, that comes down upon the collar of his garments;

כַּשֶּׁמֶן הַטּוֹב עַל הָרֹאשׁ יֹרֵד עַל הַזָּקָן זְקַן אַהֲרֹן: שֶׁיֹּרֵד עַל פִּי מִדּוֹתָיו.

³Like the dew of Khermon, that comes down upon the mountains of Tzion; for there יהוה commanded the blessing, even Khayim Ad HaOlam.

כְּטַל חֶרְמוֹן שֶׁיֹּרֵד עַל הַרְרֵי צִיּוֹן: כִּי שָׁם צִוָּה יהוה אֶת הַבְּרָכָה חַיִּים עַד הָעוֹלָם.

# תְּהִלָּה 134 Tehillah

¹Shir HaMa'alot. Behold! Bless יהוה , all you servants of יהוה , that stand in Beit יהוה in the night seasons.

שִׁיר הַמַּעֲלוֹת: הִנֵּה בָּרְכוּ אֶת יהוה כָּל עַבְדֵי יהוה הָעֹמְדִים בְּבֵית יהוה בַּלֵּילוֹת.

²Lift up your consecrated hands, and bless יהוה .

שְׂאוּ יְדֵכֶם קֹדֶשׁ; וּבָרְכוּ אֶת יהוה .

³ יהוה bless you out of Tzion; even He that made heaven and earth.

יְבָרֶכְךָ יהוה מִצִּיּוֹן: עֹשֵׂה שָׁמַיִם וָאָרֶץ.

# תְּהִלָּה 135 Tehillah

<sup>1</sup>Hallelu Yah! Praise the Name of יהוה ; give praise, O you servants of יהוה ,

אֲהַלְלוּ יָהּ : הַלְלוּ אֶת שֵׁם יהוה ; הַלְלוּ עַבְדֵי יהוה .

<sup>2</sup>You that stand in Beit יהוה , in the courts of Beit Eloheinu.

שֶׁעֹמְדִים בְּבֵית יהוה בְּחַצְרוֹת בֵּית אֱלֹהֵינוּ.

<sup>3</sup>Praise יהוה , for יהוה is good; sing praises unto His Name, for it is pleasant.

הַלְלוּ יָהּ כִּי טוֹב יהוה ; זַמְּרוּ לִשְׁמוֹ כִּי נָעִים.

<sup>4</sup>For יהוה has chosen Ya'akov unto Himself, and Yisra'el for His own treasure.

כִּי יַעֲקֹב בָּחַר לוֹ יָהּ ; יִשְׂרָאֵל לִסְגֻלָּתוֹ.

<sup>5</sup>For I know that יהוה is great, and that our Adonai is above all gods.

כִּי אֲנִי יָדַעְתִּי כִּי גָדוֹל יהוה ; וַאֲדֹנֵינוּ מִכָּל אֱלֹהִים.

<sup>6</sup>Whatsoever יהוה pleased, that has He done, in heaven and in earth, in the seas and in all deeps;

כֹּל אֲשֶׁר חָפֵץ יהוה עָשָׂה: בַּשָּׁמַיִם וּבָאָרֶץ בַּיַּמִּים וְכָל תְּהֹמוֹת.

<sup>7</sup>Who causes the vapors to ascend from the ends of the earth; He makes lightnings for the rain; He brings forth the wind out of His treasuries.

מַעֲלֶה נְשִׂאִים מִקְצֵה הָאָרֶץ: בְּרָקִים לַמָּטָר עָשָׂה; מוֹצֵא רוּחַ מֵאוֹצְרוֹתָיו.

<sup>8</sup>Who smote the first-born of Mitzrayim, both of man and beast.

שֶׁהִכָּה בְּכוֹרֵי מִצְרָיִם מֵאָדָם עַד בְּהֵמָה.

504

⁹He sent signs and wonders into the midst of you, O Mitzrayim, upon Paroh, and upon all his servants.

שָׁלַח אוֹתֹת וּמֹפְתִים בְּתוֹכֵכִי מִצְרָיִם: בְּפַרְעֹה וּבְכָל עֲבָדָיו.

¹⁰Who smote many nations, and slew mighty kings:

שֶׁהִכָּה גּוֹיִם רַבִּים; וְהָרַג מְלָכִים עֲצוּמִים.

¹¹Sikhon Melekh HaEmori, and Og Melekh Bashan, and all the kingdoms of Kena'an;

לְסִיחוֹן מֶלֶךְ הָאֱמֹרִי וּלְעוֹג מֶלֶךְ הַבָּשָׁן; וּלְכֹל מַמְלְכוֹת כְּנָעַן.

¹²And gave their land for a heritage, a heritage unto Yisra'el His people.

וְנָתַן אַרְצָם נַחֲלָה נַחֲלָה לְיִשְׂרָאֵל עַמּוֹ.

¹³O יהוה , Your Name endures forever; your memorial, O יהוה , throughout all generations.

יהוה שִׁמְךָ לְעוֹלָם; יהוה זִכְרְךָ לְדֹר וָדֹר.

¹⁴For יהוה will judge His people, and relent for His servants.

כִּי יָדִין יהוה עַמּוֹ; וְעַל עֲבָדָיו יִתְנֶחָם.

¹⁵The idols of the nations are silver and gold, the work of men's hands.

עֲצַבֵּי הַגּוֹיִם כֶּסֶף וְזָהָב; מַעֲשֵׂה יְדֵי אָדָם.

¹⁶They have mouths, but they speak not; eyes have they, but they see not;

פֶּה לָהֶם וְלֹא יְדַבֵּרוּ; עֵינַיִם לָהֶם וְלֹא יִרְאוּ.

¹⁷They have ears, but they hear not; neither is there any breath in their mouths.

אָזְנַיִם לָהֶם וְלֹא יַאֲזִינוּ; אַף אֵין יֶשׁ רוּחַ בְּפִיהֶם.

<sup>18</sup>They that make them shall be like unto them; yes, every one that trusts in them. | <sup>יח</sup>כְּמוֹהֶם יִהְיוּ עֹשֵׂיהֶם כֹּל אֲשֶׁר בֹּטֵחַ בָּהֶם.

<sup>19</sup>O Beit Yisra'el, bless יהוה ; O Beit Aharon, bless יהוה ; | <sup>יט</sup>בֵּית יִשְׂרָאֵל בָּרְכוּ אֶת יהוה ; בֵּית אַהֲרֹן בָּרְכוּ אֶת יהוה .

<sup>20</sup>O Beit Levi, bless יהוה ; you that fear יהוה , bless יהוה . | <sup>כ</sup>בֵּית הַלֵּוִי בָּרְכוּ אֶת יהוה ; יִרְאֵי יהוה בָּרְכוּ אֶת יהוה .

<sup>21</sup>Blessed is יהוה out of Tzion, who dwells in Yerushalayim. Hallelu Yah! | <sup>כא</sup>בָּרוּךְ יהוה מִצִּיּוֹן שֹׁכֵן יְרוּשָׁלָםִ: הַלְלוּ יָהּ !

# Tehillah 136 תְּהִלָּה

<sup>1</sup>O give thanks unto יהוה , for He is good, for His compassion endures forever. | <sup>א</sup>הוֹדוּ לַיהוה כִּי טוֹב: כִּי לְעוֹלָם חַסְדּוֹ.

<sup>2</sup>O give thanks unto the Elohim of gods, for His compassion endures forever. | <sup>ב</sup>הוֹדוּ לֵאלֹהֵי הָאֱלֹהִים: כִּי לְעוֹלָם חַסְדּוֹ.

<sup>3</sup>O give thanks unto the Adonai of lords, for His compassion endures forever. | <sup>ג</sup>הוֹדוּ לַאֲדֹנֵי הָאֲדֹנִים: כִּי לְעוֹלָם חַסְדּוֹ.

<sup>4</sup>To Him who alone does great wonders, for His compassion endures forever. | <sup>ד</sup>לְעֹשֵׂה נִפְלָאוֹת גְּדֹלוֹת לְבַדּוֹ: כִּי לְעוֹלָם חַסְדּוֹ.

⁵To Him that by understanding made the heavens, for His compassion endures forever.

הלְעֹשֵׂה הַשָּׁמַיִם בִּתְבוּנָה: כִּי לְעוֹלָם חַסְדּוֹ.

⁶To Him that spread forth the earth above the waters, for His compassion endures forever.

ולְרֹקַע הָאָרֶץ עַל הַמָּיִם: כִּי לְעוֹלָם חַסְדּוֹ.

⁷To Him that made great lights, for His compassion endures forever;

זלְעֹשֵׂה אוֹרִים גְּדֹלִים: כִּי לְעוֹלָם חַסְדּוֹ.

⁸The sun to rule by day, for His compassion endures forever;

חאֶת הַשֶּׁמֶשׁ לְמֶמְשֶׁלֶת בַּיּוֹם: כִּי לְעוֹלָם חַסְדּוֹ.

⁹The moon and stars to rule by night, for His compassion endures forever.

טאֶת הַיָּרֵחַ וְכוֹכָבִים לְמֶמְשְׁלוֹת בַּלָּיְלָה: כִּי לְעוֹלָם חַסְדּוֹ.

¹⁰To Him that smote Mitzrayim in their first-born, for His compassion endures forever;

ילְמַכֵּה מִצְרַיִם בִּבְכוֹרֵיהֶם: כִּי לְעוֹלָם חַסְדּוֹ.

¹¹And brought out Yisra'el from among them, for His compassion endures forever;

יאוַיּוֹצֵא יִשְׂרָאֵל מִתּוֹכָם: כִּי לְעוֹלָם חַסְדּוֹ.

¹²With a strong hand, and with an outstretched arm, for His compassion endures forever.

יבבְּיָד חֲזָקָה וּבִזְרוֹעַ נְטוּיָה: כִּי לְעוֹלָם חַסְדּוֹ.

¹³To Him who divided Yam Suf assunder, for His compassion endures forever;

יֹּלְגֹזֵר יַם סוּף לִגְזָרִים: כִּי לְעוֹלָם חַסְדּוֹ.

¹⁴And made Yisra'el to pass through the midst of it, for His compassion endures forever;

יֹּוְהֶעֱבִיר יִשְׂרָאֵל בְּתוֹכוֹ: כִּי לְעוֹלָם חַסְדּוֹ.

¹⁵But overthrew Paroh and his host in Yam Suf, for His compassion endures forever.

טֹוְנִעֵר פַּרְעֹה וְחֵילוֹ בְיַם סוּף: כִּי לְעוֹלָם חַסְדּוֹ.

¹⁶To Him that led His people through the wilderness, for His compassion endures forever.

טֹלְמוֹלִיךְ עַמּוֹ בַּמִּדְבָּר: כִּי לְעוֹלָם חַסְדּוֹ.

¹⁷To Him that smote great kings; for His compassion endures forever;

יֹלְמַכֵּה מְלָכִים גְּדֹלִים: כִּי לְעוֹלָם חַסְדּוֹ.

¹⁸And slew mighty kings, for His compassion endures forever.

יֹחוַיַּהֲרֹג מְלָכִים אַדִּירִים: כִּי לְעוֹלָם חַסְדּוֹ.

¹⁹Sikhon Melekh HaEmori, for His compassion endures forever;

יֹטלְסִיחוֹן מֶלֶךְ הָאֱמֹרִי: כִּי לְעוֹלָם חַסְדּוֹ.

²⁰And Og Melekh Bashan, for His compassion endures forever;

כֹוּלְעוֹג מֶלֶךְ הַבָּשָׁן: כִּי לְעוֹלָם חַסְדּוֹ.

²¹And gave their land for a heritage, for His compassion endures forever;

כֹאוְנָתַן אַרְצָם לְנַחֲלָה: כִּי לְעוֹלָם חַסְדּוֹ.

²²Even a heritage unto Yisra'el His servant, for His compassion endures forever.

כבנַחֲלָה לְיִשְׂרָאֵל עַבְדּוֹ: כִּי לְעוֹלָם חַסְדּוֹ.

²³Who remembered us in our low estate, for His compassion endures forever;

כגשֶׁבְּשִׁפְלֵנוּ זָכַר לָנוּ: כִּי לְעוֹלָם חַסְדּוֹ.

²⁴And has delivered us from our adversaries, for His compassion endures forever.

כדוַיִּפְרְקֵנוּ מִצָּרֵינוּ: כִּי לְעוֹלָם חַסְדּוֹ.

²⁵Who gives food to all bodies, for His compassion endures forever.

כהנֹתֵן לֶחֶם לְכָל בָּשָׂר: כִּי לְעוֹלָם חַסְדּוֹ.

²⁶O give thanks unto the Elohim of heaven, for His compassion endures forever.

כוהוֹדוּ לְאֵל הַשָּׁמָיִם: כִּי לְעוֹלָם חַסְדּוֹ.

# Tehillah 137 תְּהִלָּה

¹By the rivers of Bavel, there we sat down, yes, we wept, when we remembered Tzion.

אעַל נַהֲרוֹת בָּבֶל שָׁם יָשַׁבְנוּ גַּם בָּכִינוּ: בְּזָכְרֵנוּ אֶת צִיּוֹן.

²Upon the willows in the midst thereof we hanged up our Kinorot.

בעַל עֲרָבִים בְּתוֹכָהּ תָּלִינוּ כִּנֹּרוֹתֵינוּ.

509

³For there they that led us captive asked of us words of song, and our tormentors asked of us mirth: "Sing us one of the songs of Tzion."

ᵍכִּי שָׁם שְׁאֵלוּנוּ שׁוֹבֵינוּ דִּבְרֵי שִׁיר וְתוֹלָלֵינוּ שִׂמְחָה: שִׁירוּ לָנוּ מִשִּׁיר צִיּוֹן.

⁴How shall we sing a song of יהוה in a foreign land?

ᵍאֵיךְ נָשִׁיר אֶת שִׁיר יהוה: עַל אַדְמַת נֵכָר.

⁵If I forget you, O Yerushalayim, let my right hand forget her cunning.

ᵍאִם אֶשְׁכָּחֵךְ יְרוּשָׁלַם תִּשְׁכַּח יְמִינִי.

⁶Let my tongue cleave to the roof of my mouth, if I remember you not; if I set not Yerushalayim above my chiefest joy.

ᵍתִּדְבַּק לְשׁוֹנִי לְחִכִּי אִם לֹא אֶזְכְּרֵכִי: אִם לֹא אַעֲלֶה אֶת יְרוּשָׁלַם עַל רֹאשׁ שִׂמְחָתִי.

⁷Remember, O יהוה , against the children of Edom, the day of Yerushalayim; who said, "Raze it, raze it, even to the foundation thereof."

ᵍזְכֹר יהוה לִבְנֵי אֱדוֹם אֵת יוֹם יְרוּשָׁלַם: הָאֹמְרִים עָרוּ עָרוּ עַד הַיְסוֹד בָּהּ.

⁸O daughter of Bavel, that are to be destroyed; happy shall he be, that repays you as you have served us.

ᵍבַּת בָּבֶל הַשְּׁדוּדָה: אַשְׁרֵי שֶׁיְשַׁלֶּם לָךְ אֶת גְּמוּלֵךְ שֶׁגָּמַלְתְּ לָנוּ.

⁹Happy shall he be, that takes and dashes your little ones against the rock.

ᵍאַשְׁרֵי שֶׁיֹּאחֵז וְנִפֵּץ אֶת עֹלָלַיִךְ אֶל הַסָּלַע.

# תְּהִלָּה 138 Tehillah

אלְדָוִד: אוֹדְךָ בְּכָל לִבִּי; נֶגֶד אֱלֹהִים אֲזַמְּרֶךָּ.

[1]By David. I will give You thanks with my whole heart, in the presence of the mighty will I sing praises unto You.

באֶשְׁתַּחֲוֶה אֶל הֵיכַל קָדְשְׁךָ וְאוֹדֶה אֶת שְׁמֶךָ עַל חַסְדְּךָ וְעַל אֲמִתֶּךָ: כִּי הִגְדַּלְתָּ עַל כָּל שִׁמְךָ אִמְרָתֶךָ.

[2]I will bow down toward Your Heikhal Kadosh, and give thanks unto Your Name, for Your compassion and for Your truth; for You have magnified above all Your Name and Your Word.

גבְּיוֹם קָרָאתִי וַתַּעֲנֵנִי; תַּרְהִבֵנִי בְנַפְשִׁי עֹז.

[3]In the day that I called, You did answer me; You did encourage me in my soul with strength.

דיוֹדוּךָ יהוה כָּל מַלְכֵי אָרֶץ: כִּי שָׁמְעוּ אִמְרֵי פִיךָ.

[4]All the kings of the earth shall give You thanks, O יהוה , for they have heard the words of Your mouth.

הוְיָשִׁירוּ בְּדַרְכֵי יהוה : כִּי גָדוֹל כְּבוֹד יהוה .

[5]Yes, they shall sing of the ways of יהוה ; for great is the Kavod יהוה .

וכִּי רָם יהוה וְשָׁפָל יִרְאֶה; וְגָבֹהַּ מִמֶּרְחָק יְיֵדָע.

[6]For though יהוה is exalted, yet He regards the lowly, and the haughty He knows from afar.

<sup>7</sup>Though I walk in the midst of trouble, You quicken me; You stretch forth Your hand against the wrath of my enemies, and Your right hand does save me.

אִם־אֵלֵךְ בְּקֶרֶב צָרָה תְּחַיֵּנִי: עַל אַף אֹיְבַי תִּשְׁלַח יָדֶךָ; וְתוֹשִׁיעֵנִי יְמִינֶךָ.

<sup>8</sup> יהוה will accomplish that which concerns me; Your compassion, O יהוה, endures forever; forsake not the work of Your own hands.

ח יהוה יִגְמֹר בַּעֲדִי: יהוה חַסְדְּךָ לְעוֹלָם; מַעֲשֵׂי יָדֶיךָ אַל תֶּרֶף.

# Tehillah 139 תְּהִלָּה

<sup>1</sup>For the Leader. A Mizmor of David. O יהוה, You have searched me, and known me.

א לַמְנַצֵּחַ לְדָוִד מִזְמוֹר: יהוה חֲקַרְתַּנִי וַתֵּדָע.

<sup>2</sup>You know my sitting down and my rising up, You understand my thought afar off.

ב אַתָּה יָדַעְתָּ שִׁבְתִּי וְקוּמִי; בַּנְתָּה לְרֵעִי מֵרָחוֹק.

<sup>3</sup>You measure my going about and my lying down, and are acquainted with all my ways.

ג אָרְחִי וְרִבְעִי זֵרִיתָ; וְכָל דְּרָכַי הִסְכַּנְתָּה.

<sup>4</sup>For there is not a word in my tongue, but, lo, O יהוה, You know it altogether.

ד כִּי אֵין מִלָּה בִּלְשׁוֹנִי; הֵן יהוה יָדַעְתָּ כֻלָּהּ.

<sup>5</sup>You have hemmed me in behind and before, and laid Your hand upon me.

ה אָחוֹר וָקֶדֶם צַרְתָּנִי; וַתָּשֶׁת עָלַי כַּפֶּכָה.

⁶Such knowledge is too wonderful for me; too high, I cannot attain unto it.

פְּלָאִיה (פְּלִיאָה) דַעַת מִמֶּנִּי; נִשְׂגְּבָה לֹא אוּכַל לָהּ.

⁷Where shall I go from Your Ru'akh? Or where shall I flee from Your Presence?

אָנָה אֵלֵךְ מֵרוּחֶךָ; וְאָנָה מִפָּנֶיךָ אֶבְרָח.

⁸If I ascend up into heaven, You are there; if I make my bed in She'ol, behold, You are there.

אִם אֶסַּק שָׁמַיִם שָׁם אָתָּה; וְאַצִּיעָה שְּׁאוֹל הִנֶּךָ.

⁹If I take the wings of the morning, and dwell in the uttermost parts of the sea;

אֶשָּׂא כַנְפֵי שָׁחַר; אֶשְׁכְּנָה בְּאַחֲרִית יָם.

¹⁰Even there would Your hand lead me, and Your right hand would hold me.

גַּם שָׁם יָדְךָ תַנְחֵנִי; וְתֹאחֲזֵנִי יְמִינֶךָ.

¹¹And if I say, "Surely the darkness shall envelope me, and the light about me shall be night,"

וָאֹמַר אַךְ חֹשֶׁךְ יְשׁוּפֵנִי; וְלַיְלָה אוֹר בַּעֲדֵנִי.

¹²Even the darkness is not too dark for You, but the night shines as the day; the darkness is even as the light.

גַּם חֹשֶׁךְ לֹא יַחְשִׁיךְ מִמֶּךָ: וְלַיְלָה כַּיּוֹם יָאִיר כַּחֲשֵׁיכָה כָּאוֹרָה.

¹³For You have made my reins; You have knit me together in my mother's womb.

כִּי אַתָּה קָנִיתָ כִלְיֹתָי; תְּסֻכֵּנִי בְּבֶטֶן אִמִּי.

<sup>14</sup>I will give thanks unto You, for I am fearfully and wonderfully made; wonderful are Your works; and that my soul knows right well.

י״ד אוֹדְךָ עַל כִּי נוֹרָאוֹת נִפְלֵיתִי: נִפְלָאִים מַעֲשֶׂיךָ; וְנַפְשִׁי יֹדַעַת מְאֹד.

<sup>15</sup>My frame was not hidden from You, when I was made in secret, and curiously wrought in the lowest parts of the earth.

ט״ו לֹא נִכְחַד עָצְמִי מִמֶּךָּ: אֲשֶׁר עֻשֵּׂיתִי בַסֵּתֶר; רֻקַּמְתִּי בְּתַחְתִּיּוֹת אָרֶץ.

<sup>16</sup>Your eyes did see my unformed body, and in Your Sefer they were all written, even the days that were fashioned, when as yet there was none of them.

ט״ז גָּלְמִי רָאוּ עֵינֶיךָ וְעַל סִפְרְךָ כֻּלָּם יִכָּתֵבוּ: יָמִים יֻצָּרוּ; וְלֹא (וְלוֹ) אֶחָד בָּהֶם.

<sup>17</sup>How weighty also are Your thoughts unto me, O God! How great is the sum of them!

י״ז וְלִי מַה יָּקְרוּ רֵעֶיךָ אֵל; מֶה עָצְמוּ רָאשֵׁיהֶם.

<sup>18</sup>If I would count them, they are more in number than the sand; were I to come to the end of them, I would still be with You.

י״ח אֶסְפְּרֵם מֵחוֹל יִרְבּוּן; הֱקִיצֹתִי וְעוֹדִי עִמָּךְ.

<sup>19</sup>If You but would slay the wicked, O Elohim! Depart from me therefore, you men of blood!

י״ט אִם תִּקְטֹל אֱלוֹהַּ רָשָׁע; וְאַנְשֵׁי דָמִים סוּרוּ מֶנִּי.

<sup>20</sup>Who utter Your Name with wicked thought, they take it for falsehood, even Your enemies.

כאֲשֶׁר יִמְרוּךָ לִמְזִמָּה; נָשׂוּא לַשָּׁוְא עָרֶיךָ.

<sup>21</sup>Do not I oppose them, O יהוה, that oppose You? And do not I strive with those that rise up against You?

כאהֲלוֹא מְשַׂנְאֶיךָ יהוה אֶשְׂנָא; וּבִתְקוֹמְמֶיךָ אֶתְקוֹטָט.

<sup>22</sup>I oppose them with utmost opposition; I count them my enemies.

כבתַּכְלִית שִׂנְאָה שְׂנֵאתִים; לְאוֹיְבִים הָיוּ לִי.

<sup>23</sup>Search me, O Elohim, and know my heart, try me, and know my thoughts;

כגחָקְרֵנִי אֵל וְדַע לְבָבִי; בְּחָנֵנִי וְדַע שַׂרְעַפָּי.

<sup>24</sup>And see if there is any way in me that is grievous, and lead me in the Derekh Olam.

כדוּרְאֵה אִם דֶּרֶךְ עֹצֶב בִּי; וּנְחֵנִי בְּדֶרֶךְ עוֹלָם.

# Tehillah 140 תְּהִלָּה

<sup>1</sup>For the Leader. A Mizmor of David.

אלַמְנַצֵּחַ מִזְמוֹר לְדָוִד.

<sup>2</sup>Deliver me, O יהוה, from the evil man; preserve me from the violent men;

בחַלְּצֵנִי יהוה מֵאָדָם רָע; מֵאִישׁ חֲמָסִים תִּנְצְרֵנִי.

<sup>3</sup>Who devise evil things in their heart; every day do they stir up wars.

גאֲשֶׁר חָשְׁבוּ רָעוֹת בְּלֵב; כָּל יוֹם יָגוּרוּ מִלְחָמוֹת.

<sup>4</sup>They have sharpened their tongue like a serpent; vipers' venom is under their lips. Selah.

דשָׁנְנוּ לְשׁוֹנָם כְּמוֹ נָחָשׁ: חֲמַת עַכְשׁוּב תַּחַת שְׂפָתֵימוֹ סֶלָה.

⁵Keep me, O יהוה , from the hands of the wicked; preserve me from the violent man; who have purposed to make my steps slip.

שָׁמְרֵנִי יהוה מִידֵי רָשָׁע מֵאִישׁ חֲמָסִים תִּנְצְרֵנִי: אֲשֶׁר חָשְׁבוּ לִדְחוֹת פְּעָמָי.

⁶The proud have hidden a snare for me, and cords; they have spread a net by the wayside; they have set gins for me. Selah.

טָמְנוּ גֵאִים פַּח לִי וַחֲבָלִים פָּרְשׂוּ רֶשֶׁת לְיַד מַעְגָּל; מֹקְשִׁים שָׁתוּ לִי סֶלָה.

⁷I have said unto יהוה , "You are my God"; give ear, O יהוה , unto the voice of my supplications.

אָמַרְתִּי לַיהוה אֵלִי אָתָּה; הַאֲזִינָה יהוה קוֹל תַּחֲנוּנָי.

⁸O יהוה Adonai, the strength of my Salvation, who has screened my head in the day of battle,

יהוה אֲדֹנָי עֹז יְשׁוּעָתִי; סַכֹּתָה לְרֹאשִׁי בְּיוֹם נָשֶׁק.

⁹Grant not, O יהוה , the desires of the wicked; further not his evil device, so that they exalt themselves. Selah.

אַל תִּתֵּן יהוה מַאֲוַיֵּי רָשָׁע; זְמָמוֹ אַל תָּפֵק יָרוּמוּ סֶלָה.

¹⁰As for the head of those that encompass me, let the mischief of their own lips cover them.

רֹאשׁ מְסִבָּי עֲמַל שְׂפָתֵימוֹ יכסומו (יְכַסֵּימוֹ).

¹¹Let burning coals fall upon them; let them be cast into the fire, into deep pits, that they rise not up again.

יִמּוֹטוּ (יָמוּטוּ) עֲלֵיהֶם גֶּחָלִים: בָּאֵשׁ יַפִּלֵם; בְּמַהֲמֹרוֹת בַּל יָקוּמוּ.

<sup>12</sup>A slanderer shall not be established in the earth; the violent and evil man shall be hunted with thrust upon thrust.

יָּבֹּ‏אִישׁ לָשׁוֹן בַּל יִכּוֹן בָּאָרֶץ: אִישׁ חָמָס רָע יְצוּדֶנּוּ לְמַדְחֵפֹת.

<sup>13</sup>I know that יהוה will maintain the cause of the poor, and the right of the needy.

יַּגֹ‏ידעת (יָדַעְתִּי) כִּי יַעֲשֶׂה יהוה דִּין עָנִי: מִשְׁפַּט אֶבְיֹנִים.

<sup>14</sup>Surely the Tzadikim shall give thanks unto Your Name; the upright shall dwell in Your presence.

יֹּ‏דאַךְ צַדִּיקִים יוֹדוּ לִשְׁמֶךָ; יֵשְׁבוּ יְשָׁרִים אֶת פָּנֶיךָ.

# Tehillah 141 תְּהִלָּה

<sup>1</sup>A Mizmor of David. יהוה , יהוה I have called You; make haste unto me; give ear unto my voice, when I call unto You.

אָּ‏מִזְמוֹר לְדָוִד: יהוה קְרָאתִיךָ חוּשָׁה לִּי; הַאֲזִינָה קוֹלִי בְּקָרְאִי לָךְ.

<sup>2</sup>Let my tefilah be set forth as incense before You, the lifting up of my hands as the evening Minkhah.

בֹּ‏תִּכּוֹן תְּפִלָּתִי קְטֹרֶת לְפָנֶיךָ; מַשְׂאַת כַּפַּי מִנְחַת עָרֶב.

<sup>3</sup>Set a guard, O יהוה , to my mouth; keep watch at the door of my lips.

גֹּ‏שִׁיתָה יהוה שָׁמְרָה לְפִי; נִצְּרָה עַל דַּל שְׂפָתָי.

<sup>4</sup>Incline not my heart to any evil thing, to be occupied in deeds of wickedness with men that work iniquity; and let me not eat of their dainties.

דֹּ‏אַל תַּט לִבִּי לְדָבָר רָע לְהִתְעוֹלֵל עֲלִלוֹת בְּרֶשַׁע אֶת אִישִׁים פֹּעֲלֵי אָוֶן; וּבַל אֶלְחַם בְּמַנְעַמֵּיהֶם.

⁵Let a Tzadik smite me in kindness, and correct me; oil so choice let not my head refuse; for still is my tefilah because of their wickedness.

יֶהֶלְמֵנִי צַדִּיק חֶסֶד וְיוֹכִיחֵנִי שֶׁמֶן רֹאשׁ אַל יָנִי רֹאשִׁי: כִּי עוֹד וּתְפִלָּתִי בְּרָעוֹתֵיהֶם.

⁶Their judges are thrown down by the sides of the rock; and they shall hear my words, that they are sweet.

נִשְׁמְטוּ בִידֵי סֶלַע שֹׁפְטֵיהֶם; וְשָׁמְעוּ אֲמָרַי כִּי נָעֵמוּ.

⁷As when one cleaves and breaks up the earth, our bones are scattered at the mouth of She'ol.

כְּמוֹ פֹלֵחַ וּבֹקֵעַ בָּאָרֶץ נִפְזְרוּ עֲצָמֵינוּ לְפִי שְׁאוֹל.

⁸For my eyes are unto You, O יהוה Adonai; in You have I taken refuge, O pour not out my soul.

כִּי אֵלֶיךָ יהוה אֲדֹנָי עֵינָי; בְּכָה חָסִיתִי אַל תְּעַר נַפְשִׁי.

⁹Keep me from the snare which they have laid for me, and from the gins of the workers of iniquity.

שָׁמְרֵנִי מִידֵי פַח יָקְשׁוּ לִי; וּמֹקְשׁוֹת פֹּעֲלֵי אָוֶן.

¹⁰Let the wicked fall into their own nets, while I withal escape.

יִפְּלוּ בְמַכְמֹרָיו רְשָׁעִים; יַחַד אָנֹכִי עַד אֶעֱבוֹר.

# תְהִלָּה Tehillah 142

¹A Maskil of David, when he was in the cave; a Tefilah.

מַשְׂכִּיל לְדָוִד; בִּהְיוֹתוֹ בַמְּעָרָה תְפִלָּה.

²With my voice I cry unto יהוה ; with my voice I make supplication unto יהוה .

ג קוֹלִי אֶל יהוה אֶזְעָק; קוֹלִי אֶל יהוה אֶתְחַנָּן.

³I pour out my complaint before Him, I declare before Him my trouble;

ד אֶשְׁפֹּךְ לְפָנָיו שִׂיחִי; צָרָתִי לְפָנָיו אַגִּיד.

⁴When my spirit faints within me; You know my path; in the way wherein I walk have they hidden a snare for me.

ה בְּהִתְעַטֵּף עָלַי רוּחִי וְאַתָּה יָדַעְתָּ נְתִיבָתִי: בְּאֹרַח זוּ אֲהַלֵּךְ טָמְנוּ פַח לִי.

⁵Look on my right hand, and see, for there is no man that knows me; I have no way to flee; no man cares for my soul.

ה הַבֵּיט יָמִין וּרְאֵה וְאֵין לִי מַכִּיר: אָבַד מָנוֹס מִמֶּנִּי; אֵין דּוֹרֵשׁ לְנַפְשִׁי.

⁶I have cried unto You, O יהוה ; I have said, "You are my refuge, my portion in the land of the living."

ו זָעַקְתִּי אֵלֶיךָ יהוה : אָמַרְתִּי אַתָּה מַחְסִי; חֶלְקִי בְּאֶרֶץ הַחַיִּים.

⁷Attend unto my cry; for I am brought very low; deliver me from my persecutors; for they are too strong for me.

ז הַקְשִׁיבָה אֶל רִנָּתִי כִּי דַלּוֹתִי מְאֹד: הַצִּילֵנִי מֵרֹדְפַי כִּי אָמְצוּ מִמֶּנִּי.

⁸Bring my soul out of prison, that I may give thanks unto Your Name; the Tzadikim shall crown themselves because of me; for You will deal bountifully with me.

ח הוֹצִיאָה מִמַּסְגֵּר נַפְשִׁי לְהוֹדוֹת אֶת שְׁמֶךָ: בִּי יַכְתִּרוּ צַדִּיקִים כִּי תִגְמֹל עָלָי.

# Tehillah 143 תְּהִלָּה

[1] A Mizmor of David. O יהוה , hear my tefilah, give ear to my supplications; in Your faithfulness answer me, and in Your tzedaka.

אמִזְמוֹר לְדָוִד: יהוה שְׁמַע תְּפִלָּתִי הַאֲזִינָה אֶל תַּחֲנוּנַי; בֶּאֱמֻנָתְךָ עֲנֵנִי בְּצִדְקָתֶךָ.

[2] And enter not into judgment with Your servant; for in Your sight shall no man living be justified.

בוְאַל תָּבוֹא בְמִשְׁפָּט אֶת עַבְדֶּךָ: כִּי לֹא יִצְדַּק לְפָנֶיךָ כָל חָי.

[3] For the enemy has persecuted my soul; he has crushed my life down to the ground; he has made me to dwell in darkness, as those that have been long dead.

גכִּי רָדַף אוֹיֵב נַפְשִׁי דִּכָּא לָאָרֶץ חַיָּתִי; הוֹשִׁבַנִי בְמַחֲשַׁכִּים כְּמֵתֵי עוֹלָם.

[4] And my spirit faints within me; my heart within me is appalled.

דוַתִּתְעַטֵּף עָלַי רוּחִי; בְּתוֹכִי יִשְׁתּוֹמֵם לִבִּי.

[5] I remember the days of old; I meditate on all Your doing; I muse on the work of Your hands.

הזָכַרְתִּי יָמִים מִקֶּדֶם הָגִיתִי בְכָל פָּעֳלֶךָ; בְּמַעֲשֵׂה יָדֶיךָ אֲשׂוֹחֵחַ.

[6] I spread forth my hands unto You; my soul [thirsts] after You, as a weary land. Selah.

ופֵּרַשְׂתִּי יָדַי אֵלֶיךָ; נַפְשִׁי כְּאֶרֶץ עֲיֵפָה לְךָ סֶלָה.

[7] Answer me speedily, O יהוה , my spirit fails; hide not Your face from me; lest I become like them that go down into the pit.

זמַהֵר עֲנֵנִי יהוה כָּלְתָה רוּחִי: אַל תַּסְתֵּר פָּנֶיךָ מִמֶּנִּי; וְנִמְשַׁלְתִּי עִם יֹרְדֵי בוֹר.

<sup>8</sup>Cause me to hear Your compassion in the morning, for in You do I trust; cause me to know the way wherein I should walk, for unto You have I lifted up my soul.

הַשְׁמִיעֵנִי בַבֹּקֶר חַסְדְּךָ כִּי בְךָ בָטָחְתִּי: הוֹדִיעֵנִי דֶּרֶךְ זוּ אֵלֵךְ כִּי אֵלֶיךָ נָשָׂאתִי נַפְשִׁי.

<sup>9</sup>Deliver me from my enemies, O יהוה ; with You have I hidden myself.

הַצִּילֵנִי מֵאֹיְבַי יהוה אֵלֶיךָ כִסִּתִי.

<sup>10</sup>Teach me to do Your will, for You are my Elohim; let Your good Ru'akh lead me in an even land.

לַמְּדֵנִי לַעֲשׂוֹת רְצוֹנֶךָ כִּי אַתָּה אֱלוֹהָי: רוּחֲךָ טוֹבָה; תַּנְחֵנִי בְּאֶרֶץ מִישׁוֹר.

<sup>11</sup>For Your Name's sake, O יהוה , quicken me; in Your tzedaka bring my soul out of trouble.

לְמַעַן שִׁמְךָ יהוה תְּחַיֵּנִי; בְּצִדְקָתְךָ תוֹצִיא מִצָּרָה נַפְשִׁי.

<sup>12</sup>And in Your compassion cut off my enemies, and destroy all them that harass my soul; for I am Your servant.

וּבְחַסְדְּךָ תַּצְמִית אֹיְבָי: וְהַאֲבַדְתָּ כָּל צֹרְרֵי נַפְשִׁי כִּי אֲנִי עַבְדֶּךָ.

# תְּהִלָּה Tehillah 144

<sup>1</sup>By David. Blessed is יהוה צוּרִי my Rock, who trains my hands for war, and my fingers for battle;

לְדָוִד: בָּרוּךְ יהוה צוּרִי הַמְלַמֵּד יָדַי לַקְרָב; אֶצְבְּעוֹתַי לַמִּלְחָמָה.

521

²My compassion, and my fortress, my high tower, and my deliverer; my Magen, and He in whom I take refuge; who subdues my people under me.

חַסְדִּי וּמְצוּדָתִי מִשְׂגַּבִּי וּמְפַלְטִי לִי: מָגִנִּי וּבוֹ חָסִיתִי; הָרוֹדֵד עַמִּי תַחְתָּי.

³ יהוה , what is man, that You take knowledge of him? Or the son of man, that You make account of him?

יהוה מָה אָדָם וַתֵּדָעֵהוּ: בֶּן אֱנוֹשׁ וַתְּחַשְּׁבֵהוּ.

⁴Man is like unto a breath; his days are as a shadow that passes away.

אָדָם לַהֶבֶל דָּמָה; יָמָיו כְּצֵל עוֹבֵר.

⁵O יהוה , bend Your heavens, and come down; touch the mountains, that they may smoke.

יהוה הַט שָׁמֶיךָ וְתֵרֵד; גַּע בֶּהָרִים וְיֶעֱשָׁנוּ.

⁶Cast forth lightning, and scatter them; send out Your arrows, and discomfit them.

בְּרוֹק בָּרָק וּתְפִיצֵם; שְׁלַח חִצֶּיךָ וּתְהֻמֵּם.

⁷Stretch forth Your hands from on high; rescue me, and deliver me out of many waters, out of the hand of strangers;

שְׁלַח יָדֶיךָ מִמָּרוֹם: פְּצֵנִי וְהַצִּילֵנִי מִמַּיִם רַבִּים; מִיַּד בְּנֵי נֵכָר.

⁸Whose mouth speaks falsehood, and their right hand is a right hand of lying.

אֲשֶׁר פִּיהֶם דִּבֶּר שָׁוְא; וִימִינָם יְמִין שָׁקֶר.

⁹O Elohim, I will sing a new song unto You, upon a Nevel of ten strings will I sing unto You;

טאֱלֹהִים שִׁיר חָדָשׁ אָשִׁירָה לָּךְ; בְּנֵבֶל עָשׂוֹר אֲזַמְּרָה לָּךְ.

¹⁰Who gives Salvation unto kings, who rescues David Your servant from the hurtful sword.

יהַנּוֹתֵן תְּשׁוּעָה לַמְּלָכִים: הַפּוֹצֶה אֶת דָּוִד עַבְדּוֹ מֵחֶרֶב רָעָה.

¹¹Rescue me, and deliver me out of the hand of strangers, whose mouth speaks falsehood, and their right hand is a right hand of lying.

יאפְּצֵנִי וְהַצִּילֵנִי מִיַּד בְּנֵי נֵכָר; אֲשֶׁר פִּיהֶם דִּבֶּר שָׁוְא; וִימִינָם יְמִין שָׁקֶר.

¹²We whose sons are as plants grown up in their youth; whose daughters are as corner-pillars carved after the fashion of a palace;

יבאֲשֶׁר בָּנֵינוּ כִּנְטִעִים מְגֻדָּלִים בִּנְעוּרֵיהֶם: בְּנוֹתֵינוּ כְזָוִיֹּת מְחֻטָּבוֹת תַּבְנִית הֵיכָל.

¹³Whose garners are full, affording all manner of store; whose sheep increase by thousands and ten thousands in our fields;

יגמְזָוֵינוּ מְלֵאִים מְפִיקִים מִזַּן אֶל זַן: צֹאונֵנוּ מַאֲלִיפוֹת מְרֻבָּבוֹת בְּחוּצוֹתֵינוּ.

¹⁴Whose oxen are well laden; with no breach, and no going forth, and no outcry in our broad places;

ידאַלּוּפֵינוּ מְסֻבָּלִים: אֵין פֶּרֶץ וְאֵין יוֹצֵאת; וְאֵין צְוָחָה בִּרְחֹבֹתֵינוּ.

¹⁵Happy is the people that is in such a state. Yes, happy is the people whose Elohim is יהוה.

טואַשְׁרֵי הָעָם שֶׁכָּכָה לּוֹ: אַשְׁרֵי הָעָם שֶׁיהוה אֱלֹהָיו.

# תְּהִלָּה 145 Tehillah

¹A Tehillah of David. I will extol You, my Elohim, O Melekh; and I will bless Your Name forever and ever.

אתְּהִלָּה לְדָוִד: אֲרוֹמִמְךָ אֱלוֹהַי הַמֶּלֶךְ; וַאֲבָרְכָה שִׁמְךָ לְעוֹלָם וָעֶד.

²Every day will I bless You; and I will praise Your Name forever and ever.

בבְּכָל יוֹם אֲבָרְכֶךָּ; וַאֲהַלְלָה שִׁמְךָ לְעוֹלָם וָעֶד.

³Great is יהוה , and highly to be praised; and His greatness is unsearchable.

גגָּדוֹל יהוה וּמְהֻלָּל מְאֹד; וְלִגְדֻלָּתוֹ אֵין חֵקֶר.

⁴One generation shall laud Your works to another, and shall declare Your mighty acts.

דדּוֹר לְדוֹר יְשַׁבַּח מַעֲשֶׂיךָ; וּגְבוּרֹתֶיךָ יַגִּידוּ.

⁵The glorious splendor of Your majesty, and Your wondrous works, will I rehearse.

ההֲדַר כְּבוֹד הוֹדֶךָ וְדִבְרֵי נִפְלְאֹתֶיךָ אָשִׂיחָה.

⁶And men shall speak of the might of Your tremendous acts; and I will tell of Your greatness.

ווֶעֱזוּז נוֹרְאֹתֶיךָ יֹאמֵרוּ; (וּגְדֻלָּתְךָ) אֲסַפְּרֶנָּה.

⁷They shall utter the fame of Your great goodness, and shall sing of Your tzedaka.

זזֵכֶר רַב טוּבְךָ יַבִּיעוּ; וְצִדְקָתְךָ יְרַנֵּנוּ.

⁸ יהוה is gracious, and full of mercy; slow to anger, and of great compassion.

חחַנּוּן וְרַחוּם יהוה ; אֶרֶךְ אַפַּיִם וּגְדָל חָסֶד.

<sup>9</sup> יהוה is good to all; and His tender mercies are over all His works.

טוֹב יהוה לַכֹּל; וְרַחֲמָיו עַל כָּל מַעֲשָׂיו.

<sup>10</sup>All Your works shall praise You, O יהוה ; and Your Khasidim shall bless You.

יוֹדוּךָ יהוה כָּל מַעֲשֶׂיךָ; וַחֲסִידֶיךָ יְבָרְכוּכָה.

<sup>11</sup>They shall speak of the Kavod of Your Malkhut, and talk of Your might;

כְּבוֹד מַלְכוּתְךָ יֹאמֵרוּ; וּגְבוּרָתְךָ יְדַבֵּרוּ.

<sup>12</sup>To make known to the sons of men His mighty acts, and the glory of the majesty of His kingdom.

לְהוֹדִיעַ לִבְנֵי הָאָדָם גְּבוּרֹתָיו; וּכְבוֹד הֲדַר מַלְכוּתוֹ.

<sup>13</sup>Your Malkhut is a kingdom for all ages, and Your dominion endures throughout all generations.

מַלְכוּתְךָ מַלְכוּת כָּל עֹלָמִים; וּמֶמְשַׁלְתְּךָ בְּכָל דּוֹר וָדֹר.

<sup>14</sup> יהוה upholds all that fall, and raises up all those that are bowed down.

סוֹמֵךְ יהוה לְכָל הַנֹּפְלִים; וְזוֹקֵף לְכָל הַכְּפוּפִים.

<sup>15</sup>The eyes of all wait for You, and You give them their bread in its time.

עֵינֵי כֹל אֵלֶיךָ יְשַׂבֵּרוּ; וְאַתָּה נוֹתֵן לָהֶם אֶת אָכְלָם בְּעִתּוֹ.

<sup>16</sup>O open Your hand, and satisfy every living thing with favor.

פּוֹתֵחַ אֶת יָדֶךָ; וּמַשְׂבִּיעַ לְכָל חַי רָצוֹן.

<sup>17</sup> יהוה is righteous in all His ways, and gracious in all His works.

צַדִּיק יהוה בְּכָל דְּרָכָיו; וְחָסִיד בְּכָל מַעֲשָׂיו.

<sup>18</sup>יהוה is nigh unto all them that call upon Him, to all that call upon Him in truth.

יח<sup></sup>קָרוֹב יהוה לְכָל קֹרְאָיו לְכֹל אֲשֶׁר יִקְרָאֻהוּ בֶאֱמֶת.

<sup>19</sup>He will fulfill the desire of them that fear Him; He also will hear their cry, and will save them.

יט<sup></sup>רְצוֹן יְרֵאָיו יַעֲשֶׂה; וְאֶת שַׁוְעָתָם יִשְׁמַע וְיוֹשִׁיעֵם.

<sup>20</sup>יהוה preserves all them that love Him; but all the wicked will He destroy.

כ<sup></sup>שׁוֹמֵר יהוה אֶת כָּל אֹהֲבָיו; וְאֵת כָּל הָרְשָׁעִים יַשְׁמִיד.

<sup>21</sup>My mouth shall speak the Tehillah of יהוה; and let all flesh bless His consecrated Name forever and ever.

כא<sup></sup>תְּהִלַּת יהוה יְדַבֶּר פִּי; וִיבָרֵךְ כָּל בָּשָׂר שֵׁם קָדְשׁוֹ לְעוֹלָם וָעֶד.

# Tehillah 146 תְּהִלָּה

<sup>1</sup>Hallelu Yah! Praise יהוה, O my soul.

א<sup></sup>הַלְלוּ יָהּ : הַלְלִי נַפְשִׁי אֶת יהוה.

<sup>2</sup>I will praise יהוה while I live; I will sing unto my Elohim while I have my being.

ב<sup></sup>אֲהַלְלָה יהוה בְּחַיָּי; אֲזַמְּרָה לֵאלֹהַי בְּעוֹדִי.

<sup>3</sup>Put not your trust in princes, nor in the son of man, in whom there is no help.

ג<sup></sup>אַל תִּבְטְחוּ בִנְדִיבִים בְּבֶן אָדָם שֶׁאֵין לוֹ תְשׁוּעָה.

<sup>4</sup>His breath goes forth, he returns to his dust; in that very day his thoughts perish.

ד<sup></sup>תֵּצֵא רוּחוֹ יָשֻׁב לְאַדְמָתוֹ; בַּיּוֹם הַהוּא אָבְדוּ עֶשְׁתֹּנֹתָיו.

⁵Happy is he whose help is the Elohim of Ya'akov, whose hope is in יהוה his Elohim,

הַאַשְׁרֵי שֶׁאֵל יַעֲקֹב בְּעֶזְרוֹ: שִׂבְרוֹ עַל יהוה אֱלֹהָיו.

⁶Who made heaven and earth, the sea, and all that in them is; who keeps truth forever;

יֹעֹשֶׂה שָׁמַיִם וָאָרֶץ אֶת הַיָּם וְאֶת כָּל אֲשֶׁר בָּם; הַשֹּׁמֵר אֱמֶת לְעוֹלָם.

⁷Who executes justice for the oppressed; who gives bread to the hungry. יהוה looses the prisoners;

יֹעֹשֶׂה מִשְׁפָּט לָעֲשׁוּקִים נֹתֵן לֶחֶם לָרְעֵבִים; יהוה מַתִּיר אֲסוּרִים.

⁸ יהוה opens the eyes of the blind; יהוה raises up them that are bowed down; יהוה loves the Tzadikim;

ח יהוה פֹּקֵחַ עִוְרִים יהוה זֹקֵף כְּפוּפִים; יהוה אֹהֵב צַדִּיקִים.

⁹ יהוה preserves the strangers; He upholds the fatherless and the widow; but the way of the wicked He makes crooked.

ט יהוה שֹׁמֵר אֶת גֵּרִים יָתוֹם וְאַלְמָנָה יְעוֹדֵד; וְדֶרֶךְ רְשָׁעִים יְעַוֵּת.

¹⁰ יהוה will reign forever, your Elohim, O Tzion, unto all generations. Hallelu Yah!

יֹיִמְלֹךְ יהוה לְעוֹלָם אֱלֹהַיִךְ צִיּוֹן לְדֹר וָדֹר: הַלְלוּ יה !

# תְּהִלָּה Tehillah 147

¹Hallelu Yah; for it is good to sing praises unto our Elohim; for it is pleasant, and praise is comely.

אהַלְלוּ יה : כִּי טוֹב זַמְּרָה אֱלֹהֵינוּ כִּי נָעִים נָאוָה תְהִלָּה.

<sup>2</sup> יהוה    does build up
Yerushalayim, He gathers
together the dispersed of
Yisra'el;

²בּוֹנֵה יְרוּשָׁלַם יהוה ; נִדְחֵי
יִשְׂרָאֵל יְכַנֵּס.

<sup>3</sup>Who heals the broken in
heart, and binds up their
wounds.

³הָרֹפֵא לִשְׁבוּרֵי לֵב; וּמְחַבֵּשׁ
לְעַצְּבוֹתָם.

<sup>4</sup>He counts the number of
the stars; He gives them all
their names.

⁴מוֹנֶה מִסְפָּר    לַכּוֹכָבִים;
לְכֻלָּם שֵׁמוֹת יִקְרָא.

<sup>5</sup>Great is our Adonai, and
mighty in power; His
understanding is infinite.

⁵גָּדוֹל אֲדוֹנֵינוּ וְרַב כֹּחַ;
לִתְבוּנָתוֹ אֵין מִסְפָּר.

<sup>6</sup> יהוה    upholds the humble;
He brings the wicked down
to the ground.

⁶מְעוֹדֵד עֲנָוִים יהוה ; מַשְׁפִּיל
רְשָׁעִים עֲדֵי אָרֶץ.

<sup>7</sup>Sing unto    יהוה    with
thanksgiving, sing praises
upon the Kinor unto our
Elohim;

⁷עֱנוּ לַיהוה בְּתוֹדָה; זַמְּרוּ
לֵאלֹהֵינוּ בְכִנּוֹר.

<sup>8</sup>Who covers the heaven
with clouds, who prepares
rain for the earth, who
makes the mountains to
spring with grass.

⁸הַמְכַסֶּה שָׁמַיִם בְּעָבִים
הַמֵּכִין לָאָרֶץ מָטָר; הַמַּצְמִיחַ
הָרִים חָצִיר.

<sup>9</sup>He gives to the beast his
food, and to the young
ravens which cry.

⁹נוֹתֵן לִבְהֵמָה לַחְמָהּ; לִבְנֵי
עֹרֵב אֲשֶׁר יִקְרָאוּ.

<sup>10</sup>He delights not in the
strength of the horse; He
takes no pleasure in the legs
of a man.

¹⁰לֹא בִגְבוּרַת הַסּוּס יֶחְפָּץ;
לֹא בְשׁוֹקֵי הָאִישׁ יִרְצֶה.

[11] יהוה takes pleasure in them that fear Him, in those that wait for His compassion.

יארוֹצֶה יהוה אֶת יְרֵאָיו אֶת הַמְיַחֲלִים לְחַסְדּוֹ.

[12]Glorify יהוה , O Yerushalayim; praise your Elohim, O Tzion.

יבשַׁבְּחִי יְרוּשָׁלַם אֶת יהוה ; הַלְלִי אֱלֹהַיִךְ צִיּוֹן.

[13]For He has made strong the bars of your gates; He has blessed your children within you.

יגכִּי חִזַּק בְּרִיחֵי שְׁעָרָיִךְ; בֵּרַךְ בָּנַיִךְ בְּקִרְבֵּךְ.

[14]He makes your borders shalom; He gives you in plenty the fat of wheat.

ידהַשָּׂם גְּבוּלֵךְ שָׁלוֹם; חֵלֶב חִטִּים יַשְׂבִּיעֵךְ.

[15]He sends out His word upon earth; His D'var runs very swiftly.

טוהַשֹּׁלֵחַ אִמְרָתוֹ אָרֶץ; עַד מְהֵרָה יָרוּץ דְּבָרוֹ.

[16]He gives snow like wool; He scatters the white frost like ashes.

טזהַנֹּתֵן שֶׁלֶג כַּצָּמֶר; כְּפוֹר כָּאֵפֶר יְפַזֵּר.

[17]He casts forth His ice like crumbs; who can stand before His cold?

יזמַשְׁלִיךְ קַרְחוֹ כְפִתִּים; לִפְנֵי קָרָתוֹ מִי יַעֲמֹד.

[18]He sends forth His D'var, and melts them; He causes His wind to blow, and the waters flow.

יחיִשְׁלַח דְּבָרוֹ וְיַמְסֵם; יַשֵּׁב רוּחוֹ יִזְּלוּ מָיִם.

[19]He declares His D'var unto Ya'akov, His statutes and His ordinances unto Yisra'el.

יטמַגִּיד דְּבָרוֹ לְיַעֲקֹב; חֻקָּיו וּמִשְׁפָּטָיו לְיִשְׂרָאֵל.

²⁰He has not dealt so with any nation; and as for His ordinances, they have not known them. Hallelu Yah!

כ‎לֹא עָשָׂה כֵן לְכָל גּוֹי וּמִשְׁפָּטִים בַּל יְדָעוּם: הַלְלוּ יָהּ !

# תְּהִלָּה 148 Tehillah

¹Hallelu Yah!  Praise you, יהוה , from the heavens; praise Him in the heights.

א‎הַלְלוּ יָהּ : הַלְלוּ אֶת יהוה מִן הַשָּׁמַיִם; הַלְלוּהוּ בַּמְרוֹמִים.

²Praise Him, all His Malakhim; praise Him, all His armies.

ב‎הַלְלוּהוּ כָל מַלְאָכָיו; הַלְלוּהוּ כָּל צְבָאָו.

³Praise Him, sun and moon; praise Him, all you stars of light.

ג‎הַלְלוּהוּ שֶׁמֶשׁ וְיָרֵחַ; הַלְלוּהוּ כָּל כּוֹכְבֵי אוֹר.

⁴Praise Him, you heaven of heavens, and you waters that are above the heavens.

ד‎הַלְלוּהוּ שְׁמֵי הַשָּׁמָיִם; וְהַמַּיִם אֲשֶׁר מֵעַל הַשָּׁמָיִם.

⁵Let them praise the Name of יהוה ; for He commanded, and they were created.

ה‎יְהַלְלוּ אֶת שֵׁם יהוה : כִּי הוּא צִוָּה וְנִבְרָאוּ.

⁶He has also established them forever and ever; He has made a decree which shall not be transgressed.

ו‎וַיַּעֲמִידֵם לָעַד לְעוֹלָם; חָק נָתַן וְלֹא יַעֲבוֹר.

⁷Praise יהוה from the earth, you sea-monsters, and all deeps;

ז‎הַלְלוּ אֶת יהוה מִן הָאָרֶץ תַּנִּינִים וְכָל תְּהֹמוֹת.

[8]Fire and hail, snow and vapor, stormy wind, fulfilling His D'var; אֵשׁ וּבָרָד שֶׁלֶג וְקִיטוֹר; רוּחַ סְעָרָה עֹשָׂה דְבָרוֹ.

[9]Mountains and all hills, fruitful trees and all cedars; הֶהָרִים וְכָל גְּבָעוֹת; עֵץ פְּרִי וְכָל אֲרָזִים.

[10]Beasts and all cattle, creeping things and winged fowl; הַחַיָּה וְכָל בְּהֵמָה; רֶמֶשׂ וְצִפּוֹר כָּנָף.

[11]Kings of the earth and all peoples, princes and all judges of the earth; מַלְכֵי אֶרֶץ וְכָל לְאֻמִּים; שָׂרִים וְכָל שֹׁפְטֵי אָרֶץ.

[12]Both young men and maidens, old men and children; בַּחוּרִים וְגַם בְּתוּלוֹת; זְקֵנִים עִם נְעָרִים.

[13]Let them praise the Name of יהוה , for His Name alone is exalted; His splendor is above the earth and heaven. יְהַלְלוּ אֶת שֵׁם יהוה כִּי נִשְׂגָּב שְׁמוֹ לְבַדּוֹ: הוֹדוֹ עַל אֶרֶץ וְשָׁמָיִם.

[14]And He has lifted up a horn for His people, a Tehillah for all His Khasidim, even for the children of Yisra'el, a people near unto Him. Hallelu Yah! וַיָּרֶם קֶרֶן לְעַמּוֹ תְּהִלָּה לְכָל חֲסִידָיו לִבְנֵי יִשְׂרָאֵל עַם קְרֹבוֹ: הַלְלוּ יה !

## Tehillah 149 תְּהִלָּה

[1]Hallelu Yah! Sing unto יהוה a new song, and His praise in the congregation of the Khasidim. הַלְלוּ יה : שִׁירוּ לַיהוה שִׁיר חָדָשׁ; תְּהִלָּתוֹ בִּקְהַל חֲסִידִים.

²Let Yisra'el rejoice in his Maker; let B'nei Tzion be joyful in their Melekh.

יִשְׂמַח יִשְׂרָאֵל בְּעֹשָׂיו; בְּנֵי צִיּוֹן יָגִילוּ בְמַלְכָּם.

³Let them praise His Name in the dance; let them sing praises unto Him with the Tof and Kinor.

יְהַלְלוּ שְׁמוֹ בְמָחוֹל; בְּתֹף וְכִנּוֹר יְזַמְּרוּ לוֹ.

⁴For יהוה takes pleasure in His people; He adorns the humble with Yeshua[h].

כִּי רוֹצֶה יהוה בְּעַמּוֹ; יְפָאֵר עֲנָוִים בִּישׁוּעָה.

⁵Let the Khasidim exult in glory; let them sing for joy upon their beds.

יַעְלְזוּ חֲסִידִים בְּכָבוֹד; יְרַנְּנוּ עַל מִשְׁכְּבוֹתָם.

⁶Let the high praises of Elohim be in their mouth, and a two-edged sword in their hand;

רוֹמְמוֹת אֵל בִּגְרוֹנָם; וְחֶרֶב פִּיפִיּוֹת בְּיָדָם.

⁷To execute vengeance upon the nations, and chastisements upon the peoples;

לַעֲשׂוֹת נְקָמָה בַּגּוֹיִם; תּוֹכֵחוֹת בַּלְאֻמִּים.

⁸To bind their kings with chains, and their nobles with fetters of iron;

לֶאְסֹר מַלְכֵיהֶם בְּזִקִּים; וְנִכְבְּדֵיהֶם בְּכַבְלֵי בַרְזֶל.

⁹To execute upon them the judgment written; He is the splendor of all His Khasidim. Hallelu Yah!

לַעֲשׂוֹת בָּהֶם מִשְׁפָּט כָּתוּב הָדָר הוּא לְכָל חֲסִידָיו: הַלְלוּ יָהּ !

# Tehillah 150 תְּהִלָּה

[1]Hallelu Yah! Praise Elohim in His Kodesh; praise Him in the firmament of His power.

אהַלְלוּ יָהּ : הַלְלוּ אֵל בְּקׇדְשׁוֹ; הַלְלוּהוּ בִּרְקִיעַ עֻזּוֹ.

[2]Praise Him for His mighty acts; praise Him according to His abundant greatness.

בהַלְלוּהוּ בִגְבוּרֺתָיו; הַלְלוּהוּ כְּרֹב גֻּדְלוֹ.

[3]Praise Him with the blast of the Shofar; praise Him with the Nevel and Kinor.

גהַלְלוּהוּ בְּתֵקַע שׁוֹפָר; הַלְלוּהוּ בְּנֵבֶל וְכִנּוֹר.

[4]Praise Him with the Tof, and dance; praise Him with stringed instruments and the pipe.

דהַלְלוּהוּ בְּתֹף וּמָחוֹל; הַלְלוּהוּ בְּמִנִּים וְעֻגָב.

[5]Praise Him with the loud-sounding cymbals; praise Him with the clanging cymbals.

ההַלְלוּהוּ בְּצִלְצְלֵי שָׁמַע; הַלְלוּהוּ בְּצִלְצְלֵי תְרוּעָה.

[6]Let all of the Neshamah praise יהוה. Hallelu Yah!

וכֹּל הַנְּשָׁמָה תְּהַלֵּל יָהּ : הַלְלוּ יָהּ !

# Nighttime Prayers
## Shemah! The Greatest of Commandments

| | |
|---|---|
| Shema, Yisra'el: Eloheinu, יהוה Ekḥad. | שְׁמַע יִשְׂרָאֵל יהוה אֱלֹהֵינוּ יהוה<br>יהוה אֶחָד. |
| Barukḥ Shem K'vod, Malkḥuto, L'Olam Va'ed. | בָּרוּךְ שֵׁם כְּבוֹד מַלְכוּתוֹ<br>לְעֹלָם וָעֶד. |
| V'ahavta, et יהוה Eloheikḥa, b'kḥol l'vavekḥa uv'kḥol nafshekḥa, uv'kḥol me'odeikḥa. | וְאָהַבְתָּ אֵת יהוה אֱלֹהֶיךָ<br>בְּכָל לְבָבְךָ וּבְכָל נַפְשְׁךָ<br>וּבְכָל מְאֹדֶךָ. |
| V'hayu had'varim ha'eleh, asher anokḥi metzav'kḥa hayom, al levavekḥa. | וְהָיוּ הַדְּבָרִים הָאֵלֶּה אֲשֶׁר<br>אָנֹכִי מְצַוְּךָ הַיּוֹם עַל לְבָבֶךָ. |
| V'shinantam l'vaneikḥa, v'dibarta bam, b'shivtekḥa b'veiteikḥa uvlekḥtekḥa vaderekḥ, uvshokḥbekḥa uvkumeikḥa. | וְשִׁנַּנְתָּם לְבָנֶיךָ וְדִבַּרְתָּ בָּם<br>בְּשִׁבְתְּךָ בְּבֵיתֶךָ וּבְלֶכְתְּךָ<br>בַדֶּרֶךְ וּבְשָׁכְבְּךָ וּבְקוּמֶךָ. |
| Ukshartam l'oht, al yadeikḥa; v'hayu l'totafot bein eineikḥa. | וּקְשַׁרְתָּם לְאוֹת עַל יָדֶךָ<br>וְהָיוּ לְטֹטָפֹת בֵּין עֵינֶיךָ. |
| Ukḥtavtam al mezuzot beiteikḥa uvish'areikḥa. | וּכְתַבְתָּם עַל מְזֻזוֹת בֵּיתֶךָ<br>וּבִשְׁעָרֶיךָ. |
| V'ahavta lere'akḥa kamokḥa. | וְאָהַבְתָּ לְרֵעֲךָ כָּמוֹךָ. |

Shema, O Yisra'el, יהוה is our Elohim, יהוה is Ekhad. Blessed is the name of His Glorious Kingdom forever and ever. And you shall love יהוה your Elohim with all your heart, and with all

your soul, and with all your might. And these words, which I command you this day, shall be upon your heart; and you shall impress them upon your children, and shall talk of them when you sit in your house, and when you walk by the way, and when you lie down, and when you rise up. And you shall bind them for a sign upon your hand, and they shall be for frontlets between your eyes. And you shall write them upon the door-posts of your house, and upon your gates. And you shall love your neighbor as yourself.

# Tehillah 4 תְּהִלָּה

B'kori, aneini Elohei Tzidki, batzar hirkhavtah li; khoneini ush'mah tefilati.

בְּקָרְאִי עֲנֵנִי אֱלֹהֵי צִדְקִי בַּצָּר הִרְחַבְתָּ לִּי; חָנֵּנִי וּשְׁמַע תְּפִלָּתִי.

B'nei ish, ad meh kh'vodi likhlimah? Te'ehavun rik; tevak'shu khazav. Selah.

בְּנֵי אִישׁ עַד מֶה כְבוֹדִי לִכְלִמָּה תֶּאֱהָבוּן רִיק; תְּבַקְשׁוּ כָזָב סֶלָה.

Ude'u ki hiflah יהוה khasid lo; יהוה yishmah b'kori eilav.

וּדְעוּ כִּי הִפְלָה יהוה חָסִיד לוֹ; יהוה יִשְׁמַע בְּקָרְאִי אֵלָיו.

Rigzu, v'al tekheta'u; imru vilvavkhem, al miskavkhem, v'domu. Selah.

רִגְזוּ וְאַל תֶּחֱטָאוּ: אִמְרוּ בִלְבַבְכֶם עַל מִשְׁכַּבְכֶם; וְדֹמּוּ סֶלָה.

Zivkhu zivkhei tzedek; uvit'khu el יהוה.

זִבְחוּ זִבְחֵי צֶדֶק; וּבִטְחוּ אֶל יהוה.

Rabim omrim, mi yare'einu tov? Nesah aleinu or paneikha, יהוה.

רַבִּים אֹמְרִים מִי יַרְאֵנוּ טוֹב: נְסָה עָלֵינוּ אוֹר פָּנֶיךָ יהוה.

Natatah simkḥa v'libi; ⁷נָתַתָּה שִׂמְחָה בְלִבִּי; מֵעֵת
me'et d'ganam v'tirosham
rabu.
דְגָנָם וְתִירוֹשָׁם רָבּוּ.

B'shalom yakḥdav ⁹בְּשָׁלוֹם יַחְדָּו אֶשְׁכְּבָה
eshk'vah v'ishan: ki atah
יהוה l'vadad; lavetakḥ
toshiveini.
וְאִישָׁן: כִּי אַתָּה יהוה לְבָדָד;
לָבֶטַח תּוֹשִׁיבֵנִי.

²Answer me when I call, O Elohim of my righteousness, You who did set me free when I was in distress; be gracious unto me, and hear my prayer. ³O you sons of men, how long shall my glory be put to shame, in that you love vanity, and seek after falsehood? Selah. ⁴But know that יהוה has consecrated the Khasid as His own; יהוה will hear when I call unto Him. ⁵Tremble, and sin not; commune with your own heart upon your bed, and be still. Selah. ⁶Offer righteous sacrifices, and put your trust in יהוה . Many⁷ there are that say, "Oh that we could see some good!" יְהוה , lift up the light of Your countenance upon us. ⁸You have put gladness in my heart, more than when their grain and their wine increase. ⁹In perfect shalom will I lay me down and sleep; for You alone, יְהוה , make me dwell in safety.

# PARASHOT

| TORAH PARASHOT (Torah Portions) | HAFTARAH (Nevi'im Portions) | BRIT KHADASHAH (Renewed Covenant) |
|---|---|---|
| B'reshit (In The Beginning) B'reshit (Genesis) 1:1-6:8 | Yesha-Yahu (Isaiah) 42:5-43:10 | Yokhanan (John) 1:1-18 |
| No'akh (No'akh) B'reshit 6:9-11:32 | Yesha-Yahu (Isaiah) 54:1-55:5 | Matai (Matthew) 24:36-44 Luka (Luke) 1:5-80 |
| Lekh L'kha (For Yourself, Go) B'reshit 12:1-17:27 | Yesha-Yahu (Isaiah) 40:27-41:16 | Matai (Matthew) 1:1-17 Romim (Romans) 3:19-5:6 |
| Va'Yera (And יהוה Appeared) B'reshit 18:1-22:24 | Melakhim Bet (2nd Kings) 4:1-37 | Luka (Luke) 2:1-38 Ya'akov (James) 2:14-24 |
| Khayei Sarah (Life of Sarah) B'reshit 23:1-25:18 | Melakhim Alef (1st Kings) 1:1-31 | Matai (Matthew) 2:1-23; 8:19-22 Luka (Luke) 9:57-62 |
| Toldot (Generations) B'reshit 25:19-28:9 | Malakhi (Malachi) 1:1-2:7 | Luka (Luke) 3:1-18 Romim (Romans) 9:6-16 |
| VaYetzei (And He Went Out) B'reshit 28:10-32:3 | Hoshe'ah (Hosea) 12:13-14:10 | Matai (Matthew) 3:13-4:11 Yokhanan (John) 1:43-51 |

| | | |
|---|---|---|
| VaYishlakh (And He Sent) B'reshit 32:4-36:43 | Ovad-Yah (Obadiah) 1:1-21 | Yokhanan (John) 1:19-2:12 Korinti'im Alef (1st Corinthians) 5:1-13 |
| VaYeshev (And He Dwelt) B'reshit 37:1-40:23 | Amos (Amos) 2:6-3:8 | Yokhanan (John) 2:13-4:42 Ma'asei HaShlikhim (Acts [of] The Apostles) 7:9-16 |
| MiKetz (At The End) B'reshit 41:1-44:17 | Melakhim Alef (1st Kings) 3:15-4:1 | Luka (Luke) 4:16-31 Ma'asei HaShlikhim (Acts [of] The Apostles) 7:37-50 |
| VaYigash (Then He Came Near) B'reshit 44:18-47:27 | Yekhezkel (Yekhezkel) 37:15-28 | Yokhanan (John) 4:16-31; 10:11-19 |
| VaYekhi (And He Lived) B'reshit 47:28-50:26 | Melakhim Alef (1st Kings) 2:1-12 | Luka (Luke) 4:31-5:11 Kefa Alef (1st Peter) 1:17-2:17 Ivrim (Hebrews) 11:21-22 |
| Shemot (The Names) Shemot (Exodus) 1:1-6:1 | Yesha-Yahu (Isaiah) 27:6-29:23 | Luka (Luke) 5:12-39 Yokhanan (John) 17:1-26 |
| Va'Eirah (And I Appeared) Shemot 6:2-9:35 | Yekhezkel (Yekhezkel) 28:25-29:21 | Matai (Matthew) 12:1-14 Romim (Romans) 9:14-17 Korinti'im Bet (2nd Corinthians) 6:14-7:1 |
| Bo (Come) Shemot 10:1-13:16 | Yirme-Yahu (Jeremiah) 46:13-28 | Yokhanan Markos ([John-] Mark) 3:7-19 Hitgalut (Revelation) 19:1-16 |

| B'Shalakh (When He Let Go) Shemot 13:17-17:16 | Shoftim (Judges) 4:4-5:31 | Matai (Matthew) 5:1-48 Hitgalut (Revelation) 15:1-8 |
|---|---|---|
| Yitro (Yitro) Shemot 18:1-20:22 | Yesha-Yahu (Isaiah) 6:1-7:14; 9:5-6 | Matai (Matthew) 6:1-8:1 Timoteus Alef (1st Timothy) 3:1-13 |
| Mishpatim (Mishpatim) Shemot 21:1-24:18 | Yirme-Yahu (Jeremiah) 31:30-34; 34:8-22 | Luka (Luke) 7:1-8:3 Ivrim (Hebrews) 9:15-22 |
| Terumah (An Offering) Shemot 25:1-27:19 | Melakhim Alef (1st Kings) 5:12-6:13 | Matai (Matthew) 13:1-53 Ivrim (Hebrews) 8:1-13 |
| Tetzaveh (You Shall Command) Shemot 27:20-30:10 | Yekhezkel (Yekhezkel) 43:10-27 | Yokhanan Markos ([John- ] Mark) 4:35-5:43 Filipim (Philippians) 4:10-20 |
| Ki Tissa (When You Take) Shemot 30:11-34:35 | Melakhim Alef (1st Kings) 18:1-39 | Matai (Matthew) 9:35-11:1 Korinti'im Bet (2nd Corinthians) 3:1-8 |
| Vayakhel (And He Assembled) Shemot 35:1-38:20 | Melakhim Alef (1st Kings) 7:40-50 | Yokhanan Markos ([John- ] Mark) 6:14-29 Ivrim (Hebrews) 9:1-14 |
| Pekudei (The Accounts) Shemot 38:21-40:38 | Melakhim Alef (1st Kings) 7:51-8:21 | Yokhanan (John) 6:1-71 Ma'asei HaShlikhim (Acts [of] The Apostles) 1:1-11 |

| | | |
|---|---|---|
| VaYikra (And הוה׳ Called) VaYikra (Leviticus) 1:1-5:26 | Yesha-Yahu (Isaiah) 43:21-44:23 | Yokhanan Markos ([John- ] Mark) 7:1-30 Romim (Romans) 8:1-13 |
| Tzav (Give an order) VaYikra 6:1-8:36 | Yirme-Yahu (Jeremiah) 7:21-8:3; 9:22-23 | Yokhanan Markos ([John- ] Mark) 7:31-8:38 Romim (Romans) 12:1-8 |
| Sh'mini (The Eighth) VaYikra 9:1-11:47 | Shmu'el Bet (2nd Samuel) 6:1-7:17 | Yokhanan Markos ([John- ] Mark) 7:1-23; 9:1-13 |
| Tazria (Woman Is Delivered) VaYikra 12:1-13:59 | Melakhim Bet (2nd Kings) 4:42-5:19 | Matai (Matthew) 8:1-4 Luka (Luke) 17:11-19 |
| Metzora (The Leper) VaYikra 14:1-15:33 | Melakhim Bet (2nd Kings) 7:3-20 | Yokhanan Markos ([John- ] Mark) 5:24-34 |

| | | |
|---|---|---|
| Akharei Mot (After The Death) VaYikra 16:1-18:30 | Yesha-Yahu (Isaiah) 52:13-53:1-1 2 **The Haftarah was changed by the Rabbinic leaders, as it reveals the coming one, Yeshua HaMashiakh. | Yokhanan (John) 7:1-53 Ivrim (Hebrews) 7:23-10:25 |

| K'doshim (K'doshim)<br>VaYikra 19:1-20:27 | Yekhezkel<br>(Yekhezkel)<br>22:1-19<br>Amos<br>(Amos)<br>9:7-15 | Yokhanan (John)<br>8:1-10:21<br>Ma'asei HaShlikhim<br>(Acts [of] The<br>Apostles) 15:1-21 |
| --- | --- | --- |
| Emor (Speak)<br>VaYikra 21:1-24:23 | Yekhezkel<br>(Yekhezkel)<br>44:15-31 | Luka (Luke)<br>11:1-12:59<br>Kolosim (Colossians)<br>2:11-23 |
| Behar (In Har Sinai)<br>VaYikra 25:1-26:2 | Yirme-Yahu<br>(Jeremiah)<br>32:6-27 | Luka (Luke) 4:16-21<br>Galatim (Galatians)<br>5:1-13 |
| B'khukotai (In My<br>Khukot)<br>VaYikra 26:3-27:34 | Yirme-Yahu<br>(Jeremiah)<br>16:19-17:14 | Luka (Luke)<br>14:1-15:32<br>Efisim (Ephesians)<br>2:11-19 |
| BaMidbar<br>(In The Wilderness)<br>BaMidbar (Numbers)<br>1:1-4:20 | Hoshe'ah<br>(Hosea)<br>2:1-22 | Hitgalut (Revelation)<br>7:1-17<br>Luka (Luke)<br>16:1-17:10 |
| Naso (Take)<br>BaMidbar 4:21-7:89 | Shoftim<br>(Judges)<br>13:2-25 | Yokhanan (John)<br>11:1-54<br>Ma'asei HaShlikhim<br>(Acts [of] The<br>Apostles) 21:17-32 |
| B'ha'alotkha (When<br>You Light)<br>BaMidbar 8:1-12:16 | Zekhar-Yah<br>(Zechariah)<br>2:14-4:7 | Luka (Luke)<br>17:11-18:14<br>Ivrim (Hebrews)<br>4:1-16 |
| Sh'lakh L'kha<br>(Send For Yourself)<br>BaMidbar 13:1-15:41 | Yehoshua<br>(Joshua)<br>2:1-24 | Yokhanan Markos<br>([John- ] Mark)<br>10:1-45<br>Ivrim (Hebrews)<br>3:6-19 |

| | | |
|---|---|---|
| Korakh (Korakh) BaMidbar 16:1-18:32 | Shmu'el Alef (1st Samuel) 11:14-12:22 | Luka (Luke) 18:35-19:28 Yehudah (Jude) 1-25 |
| Khukat (The Statute Of) BaMidbar 19:1-22:1 | Shoftim (Judges) 11:1-33 | Matai (Matthew) 21:1-17 Yokhanan (John) 3:9-21 |
| Balak (Balak) BaMidbar 22:2-25:9 | Mikhah (Micah) 5:6-6:8 | Yokhanan Markos ([John- ] Mark) 11:12-26 Kefa Bet (2nd Peter) 2:1-22 |
| Pin'khas (Pin'khas) BaMidbar 25:10-29:39 | Melakhim Alef (1st Kings) 18:46-19:21 | Yokhanan Markos ([John- ] Mark) 11:27-12:37 Ma'asei HaShlikhim (Acts [of] The Apostles) 2:1-21 |
| Matot (The Tribes) BaMidbar 30:1-32:42 | Yirme-Yahu (Jeremiah) 1:1-2:3 | Matai (Matthew) 5:33-37; 23:1-39 |
| Masei (Stages Of) BaMidbar 33:1-36:13 | Yirme-Yahu (Jeremiah) 2:4-4:2 | Matai (Matthew) 24:1-25:46 Ya'akov (James) 4:1-12 |
| D'varim (The Words) D'varim (Deuteronomy) 1:1-3:22 | Yesha-Yahu (Isaiah) 1:1-27 | Yokhanan (John) 15:1-11 Yokhanan Markos ([John- ] Mark) 14:1-16 |

| | | |
|---|---|---|
| Va'etkhanan (And I Sought Favor) D'varim 3:23-7:11 | Yesha-Yahu (Isaiah) 40:1-26 | Matai (Matthew) 4:1-11 Yokhanan Markos ([John- ] Mark) 12:28-34 Luka (Luke) 22:13-38 |
| Ekev (Because) D'varim 7:12-11:25 | Yesha-Yahu (Isaiah) 49:14-51:3 Yesha-Yahu (Isaiah) 52:1-15 | Luka (Luke) 4:1-13 Yokhanan (John) 13:31-15:27 |
| Re'eh (See) D'varim 11:26-16:17 | Yesha-Yahu (Isaiah) 44:11-45:5; 54:11-55:5 | Yokhanan Alef (1st John) 2:18-25; 4:1-6 Yokhanan (John) 16:1-17:26 |
| Shoftim (Shoftim) D'varim 16:18-21:9 | Yesha-Yahu (Isaiah) 9:1-6; 49:1-6; 51:12-52:12 | Matai (Matthew) 26:47-27:10 Ma'asei HaShlikhim (Acts [of] The Apostles) 7:35-60 |
| Ki Tetzeh (When You Go Forth) D'varim 21:10-25:19 | Yesha-Yahu (Isaiah) 40:1-11; 54:1-10 | Yokhanan Markos ([John- ] Mark) 1:1-15 Luka (Luke) 23:1-25 |
| Ki Tavo (When you come) D'varim 26:1-29:8 | Yesha-Yahu (Isaiah) 60:1-22 | Matai (Mathew) 13:1-23 Luka (Luke) 23:26-56 |
| Nitzavim (You Are Standing) D'varim 29:9-30:20 | Yesha-Yahu (Isaiah) 61:10-63:9 | Romim (Romans) 9:30-10:13 Luka (Luke) 24:1-12; 24:44-45 |

| | | |
|---|---|---|
| VaYelekh (And He Went) D'varim 31:1-30 | Yesha-Yahu (Isaiah) 55:6-56:8 Hoshea (Hosea) 14:2-10 | Matai (Matthew) 28:16-20 Luka (Luke) 24:13-43 Ivrim (Hebrews) 13:5-8 |
| Ha'azinu (Give Ear) D'varim 32:1- 52 | Yo'el (Joel) 2:15-27 Shmu'el Bet (2nd Samuel) 22:1-51 | Romim (Romans) 10:14-21 Yokhanan (John) 20:26-21:25 Matai (Matthew) 27:11-28:20 |
| **Pesakh** (Passover: Haggadah - The Telling) Seder and first day of unleavened bread begins evening of the 14th Shabbat Shabbaton (High Sabbath) through the evening of the 15th Shemot (Exodus) 12:21-51 D'varim (Deuteronomy) 16 (spec. v8) BaMidbar (Numbers) 28:16-25 | Yehoshua (Joshua) 3:5-7, 5:2-6:1, 6:27 Yesha-Yahu (Isaiah) 52:13-53:12 | Matai (Matthew) 26-28 (spec. 26:17-32) Yokhanan Markos ([John- ] Mark) 14-16 (spec. 14:12-25) Luka (Luke) 2:41-52; 22:1-24:53 Yokhanan (John) 13:1-21:25 |

| | | |
|---|---|---|
| **Khag Matzot** (Festival of Unleavened Bread) The night of the 15th commemorates the day HaIvrim (The Israelites) left Mitzrayim (Egypt) and is the 2nd night of unleavened bread. Shemot (Exodus) 33:12-34:25 VaYikra (Leviticus) 22:26-23:44 | Melakhim Bet (2nd Kings) 23:1-9, 21-25 | Yokhanan Markos ([John- ] Mark) 14:12-25 Yokhanan (John) 18:28-40 Korinti'im Alef (1st Corinthians) 5:6-8 |
| **Khag Matzot Shabbat** (Weekly Shabbat during Unleavened Bread) The Pesakh season helps us recall the renewing of our freedom in Yeshua (Salvation) Shemot (Exodus) 33:12-34:25 BaMidbar (Numbers) 28:17-25 | Yekhezkel (Yekhezkel) 36:37-37:14 | Yokhanan Markos ([John- ] Mark) 14:12-25 Yokhanan (John) 21:1-25 |
| **Bikkurim** (First Fruits) Wave Sheaf Offering The first day of the week following Pesakh and the day Yeshua HaMashiakh rose from the dead VaYikra(Leviticus) 23:9-16 | Yehoshua (Joshua) 5:1-12 | Korinti'im Alef (1st Corinthians) 15:1-26 |

| | | |
|---|---|---|
| **Pesakh Sheva** (Passover 7th Day) The Pesakh season helps us recall the renewing of our freedom in Yeshua (Salvation). Shemot (Exodus) 13:17-15:27 BaMidbar (Numbers) 28:17-25 D'varim (Deuteronomy)15:19-1 6:17 D'varim (Deuteronomy) 26:1-19 Shabbat Shabbaton (High Sabbath) | Yesha-Yahu (Isaiah) 10:32-12:6 | Yokhanan (John) 21:1-25 Korinti'im Alef (1st Corinthians) 10:1-16 |
| **Khag Shavu'ot** (Festival of Weeks) First day of the week, seven weeks after Bikkurim Shemot (Exodus) 19:1-20:26 VaYikra(Leviticus) 23:16-22 BaMidbar (Numbers) 28:26-31 D'varim (Deuteronomy)16:9-12 ; 26:1-19 Shabbat Shabbaton | | Ma'asei HaShlikhim (Acts [of] The Apostles) 2:1-47 |

| | | |
|---|---|---|
| **Yom Teru'ah** (Day of the Awakening Blast) B'reshit 21:1-22:24 VaYikra23:23-25 BaMidbar 29:1-6 Shabbat Shabbaton | Yesha-Yahu (Isaiah) 26:1-27:13 | Matai(Matthew) 24:26-51 Hitgalut (Revelation) 19:1-21 |
| **Yom HaKippurim** (Day of the Atonements) VaYikra 16:1-34 and 23:1-44 BaMidbar 29:7-11 Shabbat Shabbaton (High Sabbath) COMPLETE FAST | Yesha-Yahu (Isaiah) 53:8-12 Yonah (Jonah) 1:1-4:11 | Yokhanan Alef (1st John) 1:1-2:2 Ivrim (Hebrews) 7:1-10:39 |
| **Khag Sukkot 1** (Festival of Tabernacles) Sukkot 1st Day Shabbat Shabbaton (High Sabbath) VaYikra (Leviticus) 22:26-23:44 BaMidbar 29:12-16 | Zekhar-Yah (Zechariah) 14:16-21 Tehillim (Psalms) 122:1-9 Tehillim (Psalms) 123:1-4 Tehillim (Psalms) 124:1-8 | Matai (Matthew) 17:1-27 |

| | | |
|---|---|---|
| **Khag Sukkot Shabbat** (Festival of Tabernacles) Weekly Shabbat during Sukkot Shemot (Exodus) 33:12-34:26 BaMidbar (Numbers) 29:17-31 | Zekhar-Yah (Zechariah) 14:16-21 Tehillim (Psalms) 122:1-9 Tehillim (Psalms) 123:1-4 Tehillim (Psalms) 124:1-8 | Hitgalut (Revelation) 21:1-27 |
| **Simkhat Torah** (Rejoicing in the Torah) Sh'mini Atzeret (Eighth Festivity of Sukkot) Shabbat Shabbaton<br><br>V'zot HaBerakha (And this is the Blessing) D'varim 33:1-34:12 | Yehoshua (Joshua) 1:1-18 Yesha-Yahu (Isaiah) 25:7-9 Yesha-Yahu (Isaiah) 26:19 | Hitgalut (Revelation) 22:1-21 Yokhanan (John) 12:48-50 Matai (Matthew) 17:1-9 Yehudah (Jude) 1:8-9 |

**Review Requested:**
We'd like to know if you enjoyed the book. Please consider leaving a review on the platform from which you purchased the book.